Topics in Advanced Econometrics

Volume II

Phoebus J. Dhrymes

Topics in Advanced Econometrics
Volume II

Linear and Nonlinear
Simultaneous Equations

Springer-Verlag
New York Berlin Heidelberg London Paris
Tokyo Hong Kong Barcelona Budapest

Phoebus J. Dhrymes
Department of Economics
Columbia University
New York, NY 10027
USA

Library of Congress Cataloging-in-Publication Data
Dhrymes, Phoebus J.
    Topics in advanced econometrics.
    (v. 2: Linear and nonlinear simultaneous equations)
    Includes bibliographical references
and index.
    Contents: [1] Probability foundations—v. 2. Linear
and nonlinear simultaneous equations.
    1. Econometrics. 2. Probabilities. I. Title.
HB139.D49   1989   330′.01′5195   89-27330
ISBN 0-387-94156-8

Printed on acid-free paper.

Production managed by Natalie Johnson; manufacturing supervised by Genieve Shaw.
Photocomposed copy produced using the author's LaTeX files.
Printed and bound by Braun-Brumfield, Inc., Ann Arbor, MI.
Printed in the United States of America.

9 8 7 6 5 4 3 2 1

ISBN 0-387-94156-8 Springer-Verlag New York Berlin Heidelberg
ISBN 3-540-94156-8 Springer-Verlag Berlin Heidelberg New York

To Ingram Olkin and Henri Theil, who stimulated
my early interest in econometrics

Preface

This book is intended for second year graduate students and professionals who have an interest in linear and nonlinear simultaneous equations models. It basically traces the evolution of econometrics beyond the general linear model (GLM), beginning with the general linear structural econometric model (GLSEM) and ending with the generalized method of moments (GMM). Thus, it covers the identification problem (Chapter 3), maximum likelihood (ML) methods (Chapters 3 and 4), two and three stage least squares (2SLS, 3SLS) (Chapters 1 and 2), the general nonlinear model (GNLM) (Chapter 5), the general nonlinear simultaneous equations model (GNLSEM), the special case of GNLSEM with additive errors, nonlinear two and three stage least squares (NL2SLS, NL3SLS), the GMM for GNLSEM, and finally ends with a brief overview of causality and related issues, (Chapter 6). There is no discussion either of limited dependent variables, or of unit root related topics.

It also contains a number of significant innovations. In a departure from the custom of the literature, identification and consistency for nonlinear models is handled through the Kullback information apparatus, as well as the theory of minimum contrast (MC) estimators. In fact, nearly all estimation problems handled in this volume can be approached through the theory of MC estimators. The power of this approach is demonstrated in Chapter 5, where the entire set of identification requirements for the GLSEM, in an ML context, is obtained almost effortlessly, through the apparatus of Kullback information.

The limiting distribution of dynamic GLSEM is handled through various convergence theorems for dependent sequences and a martingale difference central limit theorem on a step by step basis, so that the reader may appreciate the complexity of the problems and the manner in which such problems are resolved.

A simplified (two step) FIML estimator is derived whose computational complexity is quite analogous to that of 3SLS; this enables the reader to see precisely why the two estimators need not be numerically identical even if 3SLS is iterated.

The method of generalized moments (GMM) estimator is presented as a variant of a 3SLS-like estimator in the context of the GLSEM with additive errors.

Because notation has been a problem in this subject, [1] I have maintained a consistent notation throughout the volume, so that one can read about FIML, LIML, 2SLS, 3SLS, and GMM in the same notation and *mutatis mutandis* with the same conventions and formulations. This facilitates the teaching of the subject, and reduces the unproductive time devoted to reconciliation of alternative notations and conventions.

The material in this volume can be used as the basis for a variety of one semester or quarter courses, depending on the level of preparation of the class. If students are conversant with a modicum of modern probability theory, the material may be covered for the most part in a semester course. If not, one has the option of concentrating on Chapters 1, 3, and 4 and those parts of Chapter 2 that do not delve too deeply into asymptotic theory. Alternatively, one might devote a number of lectures on the probability background and let *Topics in Advanced Econometrics: Probability Foundations* (Volume I) serve as a reference for various convergence and central limit theorems needed in the development of asymptotic theory. Thus, a semester course may be based on Chapter 1, parts of Chapter 2, and parts of Chapters 5 and 6. This basically leaves out the classic identification discussion and ML estimation, but covers nonlinear methods in the context of the general linear model as well as the GNLSEM with additive errors.

In my own teaching, I devote approximately two weeks to various convergence results from *Topics in Advanced Econometrics: Probability Foundations* (Volume I) and, by and large, let this as well as my other book *Mathematics for Econometrics* serve as reference material. Normally, Chapter 6 is never reached, and is covered in the follow-up course on Time Series, the discussion of GMM serving as a natural interface between these two strands of the literature.

I have developed the contents of this volume over several years, and nearly every part has been utilized, at one time or another, as class notes at Columbia University. I wish to record here my appreciation for the many suggestions I have received from successive generations of students and

---

[1] It would not be an exaggeration to say that in reading the literature on this subject, perhaps more than half the effort involved is devoted to deciphering the particular notation and conventions of the material being studied.

hope that their advice has made the presentation smoother and more easily comprehensible.

Finally, the general tenor of the presentation, as well as the selection of topics, invariably reflects in part the author's conceptual framework and the role envisioned for the subject in scientific pursuits. It has always been my view that good empirical econometrics has to be informed by economic theory and, equally so, by econometric theory. This requires practitioners to have a thorough grounding in the techniques employed for the purpose of empirical inference. I deplore the employment of complex or opaque procedures when this is clearly not required by the problem at hand. Equally important, when writing on theoretical issues it is highly desirable to be sufficiently well aware of first principles. This enables the investigator to bring to bear the appropriate tools in the analysis of the issues under discussion and reduces excessive reliance on broad and general theorems to solve relatively straightforward problems, a feature not uncommon in the literature of econometric theory. These concerns have led me, on one hand, to give perhaps too extensive a discussion of the underlying conceptual framework, notational conventions, and the motivation and rationalization of the assumptions made, and on the other, they have led me to pursue most proofs as explicitly as I could manage.

I hope I have succeeded in setting forth the richness of the literature on the subject as it was developed in the past fifty years or so, and that this volume will be equally useful to the advanced student, as well as the interested professional both in economics and in other disciplines as well.

Phoebus J. Dhrymes

Bronxville, NY
July 1993

Contents

Contents of Volume I

1

Extension of Classical Methods I

1.1 Introduction

Econometrics deals with the problems encountered in measuring or quantifying economic relationships. In contrast to the natural and biological sciences, the data used by economists in studying such relationships are not, typically, experimentally derived. Thus, economists deal primarily with nonexperimental data.

The chief tool for analyzing experimental data is the General Linear Model (GLM), represented by [1]

$$y_t = x_t.\beta + u_t, \ t = 1, 2, 3, \ldots T \tag{1.1}$$

where y_t is the **dependent** and the elements of the $1 \times (n+1)$ row vector $x_t.$ are the **independent or explanatory** variables. The $(n+1) \times 1$ column vector β consists of the unknown parameters whose estimation is the subject of inference theory, in the context of the GLM. Often the variables in $x_t.$ are called the **regressors** and the variable y_t is called the **regressand**.

In an experimental setting the regressors, the elements of $x_t.$, are under the control of the investigator. By varying them, in ways he exclusively determines, he can observe and record the response these variations elicit in the variable of interest, here denoted by y_t . The investigator may then

---

[1] If a matrix is represented by $X = (x_{ti})$, $t = 1, 2, 3, \ldots, T$, $i = 1, 2, 3, \ldots, G$, its tth **row** is written as $x_t.$ and its ith **column** is written as $x_{.i}$.

hypothesize a relationship as in Eq. (1.1), where u_t is a random variable with certain properties. This random variable may reflect either errors of measurement (of the response in the variable y_t) or the intrinsically nondeterministic manner in which variations in the elements of the vector $x_{t.}$ affect y_t. In some loose sense, "causality" in this type of model is unidirectional, running exclusively from x to y. This is the distinctive characteristic of the conceptual framework of the GLM, as contrasted to that of the simultaneous equations model. One completes the specification of the properties of the system in (1) by asserting that the error term, u_t, is independent of the vector $x_{t.}$. This last condition is an important one. In the context of the GLM, inference represents the attempt to disentangle the systematic effects produced by $x_{t.}$ acting on y_t, from the nonsystematic, random effects registered on y_t, through the error term, u_t, which, moreover, **is not observable**. Unless these two sets of forces acting on y_t are **independent**, there is no hope that by observing $x_{t.}$ **alone** we should be able to separate, reliably, the two components.

While there are many instances in economics where the phenomenon of interest fits the abstract mold of the GLM as given above, there are even more cases that require a broader framework. For example, in examining the relationship between wages and prices (with possibly other variables playing a role as well), prices may respond to (be affected by) wages, but wages are no less affected by prices. Similarly, the amount of labor offered in the market (the "supply" of labor) is affected by wages, but observed wages are no less affected by the amount of labor offered. Or, in examining the relation between prices and "money" in a suitable context, an increase in the "supply of money" will increase prices, but often an increase in prices may very well lead to an increase in "money" in some broad sense, either because the monetary authorities are accommodative to an external "shock" that leads to an increase in prices (as when import prices rise sharply) or because economic agents are very inventive in making more intensive use of a given stock of "money" (an increase in the "money multiplier").

Since one function of economists is to make some (intellectual) sense and impose some (intellectual) order on the actions of economic agents, as reflected in the voluminous economic data available to us, the multiplicity of interpretations that may be put on the situations described above requires the introduction of some disciplined conceptual framework. Only then can we begin to adequately study such relationships.

In all the examples cited, we note two distinctive features that set them apart from the situations described as appropriately analyzable or measurable in terms of the GLM.

In the wage-labor and wage-price examples we deal with the activities of private economic agents, while in the money-prices example we deal with the actions of both private and public agents (the monetary authorities) reacting, perhaps continuously, to each other's activities. Thus, in this context, without a proper conceptual framework it is not always clear what is "cause" and what is "effect" or in less controversial terms what is primary action and what is reaction. Clearly, in a GLM framework there is never any doubt as to what is primary action (it is emphatically the values assumed by the elements of $x_t.$) and what is reaction; it is, evidently, the values assumed by y_t within the limits set by the error term u_t.

The conceptual framework for resolving these issues is the general equilibrium approach, in varying degrees of refinement and detail. It asserts that a number of economic entities are mutually determined through "instantaneous" interaction with each other, as well as through interaction with other economic entities whose behavior is given exogenously. This interaction takes place within, and is conditioned by, the technological and legal institutional framework characteristic of the economic system.

Thus, since the problems often dealt with by economists are more complex than those encompassed by the framework of the GLM; since conscious experimentation for the purposes of research alone is typically not an available route of investigation; and since simplification to the level of GLM analysis will do serious violence to the integrity of the results obtained, one is forced to more complex (simultaneous equations, or other types of) inference procedures.

But, there is another important difference in the examples referred to earlier, relative to the GLM framework. This is particularly evident in the wage-labor example, and is, indeed, characteristic of every market analysis. Since the very beginning of the discipline, more or less, economists made a clear distinction between supply and demand, at least conceptually. But if we are not content to merely discuss these issues in a philosophical or metaphysical context and wish to understand them in operational terms we need to measure their determinants. Or, alternatively, if we are curious as to how important is price in determining the quantity demanded, or the quantity supplied, or a number of other associated issues, we are led to examine the workings of actual markets where quantities are bought and sold and prices are determined. On the basis of such data, which reflect the activities of numerous economic agents, we would hope to arrive at reliable measurements of the determinants of supply and demand. When we attempt to do so, however, we discover to our dismay that **the data we have on quantity do not wear a label to tell us whether they refer to supply or demand**. Indeed, under a regime of freedom in contractual exchange, to every transaction there is, in the archaic phraseology of another era, a willing (and able) seller as well as a willing (and able) buyer. Thus, a simple regression of quantity on price will yield very ambiguous results, since it is not clear whether we have estimated the supply function, the demand function, or a linear combination of the two. This is an instance of the **identification problem** which, of course, could never arise in an experimental context; in econometrics, on the other hand, it is one of the central problems.

To recapitulate, what distinguishes many econometric problems from those encompassed by the GLM framework are two fundamental features of the former: the existence of the identification problem and the simultaneous determination and mutual interaction of (some) of the variables entering the relationships investigated. The latter implies "**bicausality**" so that (some) variables on the right hand side of an equation are themselves partly "determined" by the left hand variable in another part of the system. Thus, what is "cause" in one subset (equation) may very well be an "effect" in another subset (equation), and vice versa. Both are direct consequences of the fact that economists deal mainly with nonexperimental data and generally exercise little direct control over the relationships they seek to measure.

1.2   A Brief Historical Review

As we have stressed in the previous section, an important foundation of contemporary econometrics is the general equilibrium system. As early as the late nineteenth century the French-Swiss economist Leon Walras created an elegant system of the interaction and simultaneous determination of the variables determined by an economic system. The identification problem was beginning to be understood in the 1920s and 1930s. For an account of this and earlier work in econometrics see Christ (1985). Still, econometrics as a serious discipline did not really materialize until the 1940s, although empirical studies of economic relationships using some form of the GLM had already appeared in the early part of the nineteenth century. Important contributions of this era, i.e., the post-1930 period include the work by Frisch (1933), (1934), which gave a formulation of the simultaneous equations problem as an errors in variables system; two papers by Haavelmo (1943), (1944), for which, incidentally, he was awarded the Nobel Memorial Prize in Economics in 1989, laid the foundations for the simultaneous equations model as we know it today; the papers by Mann and Wald (1943), and Wald (1950) provided an extensive treatment of the estimation of stochastic difference equations and made an important contribution to the understanding of the identification problem and the maximum likelihood estimator for the simultaneous equations system. The task, however, was left incomplete, in that no exogenous variables were included in the specification, and no attempt was made to investigate the problem of estimating just a subset of the system. [2] In Jan Tinbergen's work, Tinbergen (1939), we have, perhaps, the first commissioned macroeconometric research.

The impetus for the rapid development of econometrics is to be traced to

---

[2] It is also fair to say that relatively few economists of the day could digest the contributions made by these papers.

the Great Depression and the "need" to understand and possibly control subsequent manifestations of the same phenomenon. A fortuitous confluence of circumstance was the appearance at about the same time (1936) of *The General Theory of Employment Interest and Money* by J.M. Keynes. Keynes offered a simpler framework in which macroeconomic issues could be analyzed, and pointed out the pivotal role of fiscal policy in combating severe recessions. It was, therefore, thought that if the relationships of the Keynesian macrosystem were measured properly, they could form the basis of a policy of active involvement, on the part of the central authorities, in the workings of the economy so that "business cycles" would be smoothed, or otherwise managed out of existence. Thus, by the 1940s we had a conceptual framework in which to put the set of economic relationships we wished to investigate, and an awareness of the fact that the nonexperimental character of economic data required inference procedures beyond those inherent in the GLM, as well as a "social need" for the results flowing out of such research.

As happens so frequently in the development of economics, the pressing problems of the time led to intellectual advances in the discipline. The pioneering papers by Frisch (1933), Tinbergen (1939), and Haavelmo (1943), (1944), noted above, laid the foundations for the proper formulation of the problem of handling the measurement of economic relations in a simultaneous equations context; the paper by Mann and Wald (1943), noted above, provided the first major intellectual breakthrough in formulating and estimating such models. The final intellectual breakthrough [3] came in two papers by Anderson and Rubin (1949), (1950), who introduced exogenous variables in the GLSEM and provided an explicit solution to the problem of estimating the parameters of just a subset of the complete simultaneous equations system. This was quickly followed by the popularization and extension of these fundamental results in the now famous Cowles Foundation Monograph 14, Hood and Koopmans (eds.) (1953). On the empirical side, although at an earlier time Tinbergen (1939) had produced a statistical study of the business cycles in his League of Nations work, the first implementation of the newly discovered techniques was by L.R. Klein and H. Barger (1954), who produced a miniscule model of the U.S. economy. This was quickly followed by an appreciably larger model by L.R. Klein and A.S. Goldberger (1955).

The techniques invented by Mann and Wald, and Anderson and Rubin, however, did not find widespread use immediately, because of the almost impossible computational burden they entailed, given the technology of the time. It remained for the important contribution of Theil (1953), (1958), as later explicated by L. R. Klein (1955), and independently discovered

---

[3] The simultaneous equations approach became known, subsequently, as the General Linear Structural Econometric Model (GLSEM).

by Basmann (1957), to register an impact on the practice of empirical researchers. Their work provided an extension of least squares to simultaneous equations systems known as Two Stage Least Squares (2SLS). This method, in contrast to that suggested by Anderson and Rubin, had the advantage of being much easier to grasp, given the training of economists at the time; it also had the virtue of being, computationally, far simpler.

The development of the subject in subsequent years has been marked by many and varied important contributions by a great number of individuals, far too numerous to mention in a brief review such as this. The current ubiquitous penetration of econometrics in nearly every aspect of economic discourse, as well as in the daily activities of government and business, owes much to the developments evoked by the Brookings Model Project, as well as advances in computer technology, which permitted the creation of data banks and sophisticated computer software that allow for an almost effortless implementation of even the most intricate inferential procedure devised.

Although many of the examples mentioned above are of a macroeconomic nature, it should not be thought that applications of the GLSEM are only appropriate in a macro context. In fact, there are many applications in microeconomics such as in representing the investment, dividend and external finance activities of firms as a system of simultaneous equations; or in modelling the choice of housing tenure (to buy or rent) and expenditures on shelter services by households, or in the sample selectivity problem, in the supply and demand for labor, to mention but a few.

In concluding this brief historical account, we should not fail to note that simultaneous equations estimation (inference) theory is a unique development of inference theory that evolved explicitly in response to the requirements of economists, operating within their universe of discourse with nonexperimental data.

In this and subsequent chapters, we shall develop the theory of inference for the general linear structural econometric model (GLSEM) and provide a reasonably complete discussion of its extension to the case of nonlinear models. The theory of inference for the GLM was treated exhaustively elsewhere, see Dhrymes (1978), and indeed, may be found in many other sources.

1.3   The Nature of the GLSEM

As we have remarked earlier, the ultimate justification for the GLSEM is the general equilibrium framework provided by economic theory, although applications can be made at a narrower, sectoral or market level. The essential requirement is that the system modelled should determine simultaneously the value of at least two (endogenous) variables; these variables should exhibit interaction, i.e., they should affect (have an impact on) each other and, moreover, should be affected by other variables, which are not affected by them.

The first class of variables are called **endogenous**, and the second class **predetermined** variables.

The equations of the GLSEM are of two general forms, (i) stochastic, and (ii) nonstochastic. Stochastic equations specify some relationship among two or more variables **which is exact** only up to an **additive error term (random variable)**. Nonstochastic equations specify a relationship among two or more variables which is **exact**. Nonstochastic equations are referred to as **identities**. Stochastic equations are, generally, referred to as **behavioral equations**. Stochastic equations originate with, and purport to describe, the behavior of economic agents or reflect aspects of the technology and legal institutional framework that characterize the system being modelled. For example, at the micro level, a demand relationship purports to describe the quantity of a good or service demanded by economic agents in response to the (other) variables appearing therein. Similarly, a supply relationship purports to describe the behavior of producers or sellers of a given good or service and, thus, describes the quantity one would offer in response to the (other) variables appearing therein.

A production function is another instance of a stochastic equation and represents the output of a given good or service forthcoming in response to the specified inputs. The justification for writing it as a stochastic equation is that the specified inputs have a determinate outcome in terms of output, only within a multiplicative or an additive error term.

At the macro level, a tax function is an instance of a relationship that originates with the legal institutional framework. Here, the argument for writing it as a stochastic equation shifts to an aggregation basis. After all, given each individual's taxable income and the taxation laws, tax liability is a matter of simple arithmetic and the relationship is exact. Even with the best data sources, however, we cannot hope to have access to all individuals' taxable income. Hence we modify our approach and deal with aggregates. Since the tax code is rather complex we end up by writing (aggregate) tax liability functions as stochastic equations.

This instance illustrates the crucial interaction between the three major elements of empirical research. First, there is the model specification which, within wide limits, is provided by economic theory; then, there is the theory of estimation which enables us to make concrete inference, given the model specification and the empirical evidence at hand. Finally, of course, there is the empirical evidence (data). Unfortunately, however, in order to study, in some workable detail, the functioning of an economic system, one requires massive data sets and, as a general principle, the larger the data set available to study a given relationship, the sharper the results obtained. On the other hand, data do not always correspond to the theoretical constructs contained in the system, as specified. Then, either the model is altered somewhat so that it is compatible with the sort of data available, or the estimation technique is modified so as to take into account the fact that there are "errors in variables"; or, alternatively, the data are used as they are, and one appeals to misspecification theory in order to get bounds on the errors of estimation (inconsistency or bias) that this may entail. Of course, one might also obtain new and better data, but this is not always an option.

Identities, generally, serve to define new symbols, and thus may be eliminated at the cost of more ponderous notation. An example of such an identity is

$$wH = W,$$

where w is the wage rate, H is hours worked, and W is wage income. Evidently, wage income (W) is not strictly necessary and may be omitted from the list of variables entering the model–it being replaced by w and H; this, however, would create a more ponderous notation. On the other hand, some (apparent) identities convey important economic information or assumptions. For example, let q_t^S, q_t^D refer to quantity supplied and demanded, respectively, of a given good, or service at time t. The apparent identity

$$q_t^S = q_t^D = q_t$$

again serves to define a new symbol, q_t, which refers to the transaction quantity, i.e., the quantity observed in the market at time t; in this instance, however, the identity is not as innocuous or innocent as the identity of the previous example, for it asserts that the observable **transaction quantity** (the only possible observation since q^S and q^D cannot, generally, be observed directly) **lies both on the demand and the supply function.** As such, it is an **assertion of market clearing through price flexibility.** In many functioning econometric models, such identities are not stated explicitly, but must be inferred from the nature of the relevant relationships as embedded in the model.

Finally, in closing these introductory sections, we may ask: Why bother quantifying economic relationships, particularly those of a GLSEM? Perhaps an answer is not required, at an academic level, since disinterested intellectual curiosity is just as potent a motive as the potential for useful applications. There are, of course many potential applications. For example, in economic theory certain results are possible only under certain conditions. Thus, the perfect competition model of production requires nonincreasing returns to scale. Are sectors of the economy characterized by increasing returns to scale? Or, we may ask, is the production process in a given industry characterized by an elasticity of substitution between labor and capital of unity, less than unity, or more than unity? At a more applied, policy level, there are many issues whose discussion and resolution essentially turn on econometric findings. For example, upon exchange rate variation how quickly do domestic prices adjust? If a tax cut is implemented, by how much would one expect employment to rise (or unemployment to fall) within a year? By how much, if any, would the price level rise within the year? Or, if growth in monetary aggregates is restricted, by how much would prices fall or their rate of increase be abated? If an investment tax credit is implemented and is deemed to be a permanent measure (or as permanent as anything in economic policy making can be) by how much, if any, would investment rise?

To all these questions there is the simple approach of *ex post hoc ergo propter hoc*, still favored by many economists. Thus, having deductively convinced ourselves that these policies would have the desirable effect within the confines of a certain frame of reference, we simply implement these policies and observe the "response" of the variables of interest. Such a simplistic measurement practice either presumes that the "response" in question is instantaneous or that nothing else of consequence is transpiring that may have an impact on the behavior of the relevant variables. In fact, both presumptions are patently false and only through careful specification of the relevant relationships, in the context of a GLSEM, can these issues be resolved satisfactorily. This is not to say that the evidence we obtain by these techniques is always unambiguous and clear cut, but only that it is the most effective way of making use of the resources available in attempting to resolve the issue raised.

Moreover, the disciplined use of a theoretical framework and its empirical implementation through the GLSEM, or other suitable methods, in dealing with such issues, offers the possibility of finding just how, and where, empirical evidence is inconsistent with theoretical construct and, thus, carries the potential for the latter's revision. Conversely, if one is not too keen to take refuge in the "speciality" of each case; if, in empirical research, one always maintains a tightly reasoned and coherent framework, modifying it only when the evidence of inadequacy is very compelling, one is more likely to avoid the temptation of treating every twist of events as *sui generis* and ultimately being overwhelmed by a plethora of special cases, events, and circumstances.

Regarding the nature of empirical evidence in the *post hoc ergo propter hoc* tradition, an example can be drawn from public utility regulation, such as power, light, and telecommunications. It is still the practice in many jurisdictions to argue, say, that the price elasticity of demand for telephone services is zero. Since utilities are assured a certain rate of return on their capital, when costs rise sufficiently, utilities demand, and are usually granted, a rate (price) increase in consequence. If, upon implementation of the rate increase, and quite independently, a recession ensues, total revenues may well decrease, while if the rate increase is followed by a vigorous economic expansion, it may well be that total revenues will increase, in relative terms, to a greater extent than the rate increase itself. In the first instance, one would conclude that the price elasticity is less than minus one (in an algebraic sense), while in the second one would conclude that it is positive!

1.4   The GLSEM: Assumptions and Notation

As we discussed at length in the previous section, the GLSEM is motivated by the general equilibrium system of economic theory, and is represented by the system of equations

$$y_{t.}B^* = x_{t.}C + u_{t.}, \quad t = 1, 2, 3, \dots, T, \tag{1.2}$$

where $y_{t.}$ is $1 \times m$, $x_{t.}$ is $1 \times G$ and denote, respectively, the row vectors containing the **current endogenous** (or **jointly dependent**) and the **predetermined** variables of the model.

The equations comprising the system in Eq. (1.2) may be either **behavioral** (stochastic) equations or **identities** (nonstochastic). In the formal discussion of the GLSEM it is convenient to think of identities as having been **substituted out** so that Eq. (1.2) contains only **behavioral equations**; when this is so the vector of error terms $u_{t.}$ will not contain elements which are identically zero (corresponding to the identities) and we may assert that $\{u_{t.}' : t = 1, 2, 3, \dots T\}$ is a sequence of independent identically distributed (i.i.d.) random vectors with

$$E(u_{t.}') = 0, \quad \text{Cov}(u_{t.}') = \Sigma > 0, \tag{1.3}$$

the covariance matrix Σ being positive definite (nonsingular). There is also another bit of complexity occasioned by the **identification problem**. If no restrictions are placed on the matrices $B^*(m \times m)$ and $C(G \times m)$, which contain the unknown parameters of the problem, then multiplying the system in Eq. (1.2), on the right, by the arbitrary nonsingular matrix H, we have

$$y_{t.}B^*H = x_{t.}CH + u_{t.}H. \tag{1.4}$$

In Eq. (1.4) the parameter matrices B^*H, CH are similarly unrestricted, and the error vector,

$$H'u_{t.}' : t = 1, 2, 3, \dots T,$$

is one of i.i.d. random variables with

$$E(H'u_{t.}') = 0, \quad \text{Cov}(H'u_{t.}') = H'\Sigma H > 0. \tag{1.5}$$

If a set of observations $(y_{t.}, x_{t.})$, $t = 1, 2, 3, \dots T$, is **compatible with the model** of Eqs. (1.2) and (1.3) it is **also compatible** with the model in Eqs. (1.4) and (1.5), so that these two versions of the GLSEM are **observationally equivalent**. Thus, if literally everything depends on everything else, there is no assurance that, if we use the data to make inferences regarding (estimate) the parameters of Eq. (1.2), we shall, in fact, obtain what we asked for. Thus, in approaching a problem for empirical analysis the economist cannot begin from a state of complete ignorance. If he does, of course, there is no reason why his intervention is required! Nor is there any reason why anyone should be interested in what he has to say. He can be dispensed with, without cost.

It is only by asserting some restrictions on the relationships in Eq. (1.2) that the problem of inference can be solved. At the same time, however, the economist not only expresses a view as to the manner in which the economic phenomenon under investigation operates, but is also making a, potentially, falsifiable statement about the real world. It is precisely these aspects that make economic analysis interesting, for if everything can be rationalized and every proposition can be accepted *sui generis*, then we have neither understood anything nor do we have any assurances that today's "explanations" will be valid tomorrow.

It is worth noting that a controversy of precisely this type was widely discussed in the early 1960s with the contention, primarily by Liu (1960), that, indeed, we have no basis for any *a priori* restrictions and hence the GLSEM is, in principle, not estimable! This view was convincingly refuted, at the time, by F.M. Fisher (1961), who argued that even though we might admit philosophically that no element of B^* and C is zero, yet it is patently the case that many elements of B^* and C would be very small. Ignoring very small elements is rather innocuous, and the impairment of properties suffered as a consequence, are correspondingly small as well. Since in every discipline theoretical structures are only an idealization of reality, the argument advanced by Liu is no reason why the GLSEM is not to be deemed a useful tool of analysis. A potentially more serious problem is the case of errors (of observation) in the exogenous variables of the GLSEM, to be defined below.

Incidentally the same argument would proscribe the use of the GLM as well, simply by arguing that "everything" **ought to be considered as an explanatory variable in any GLM formulation**. Since we will never have enough data to estimate the parameters of such a model this approach amounts to stating that nothing is knowable empirically.

We shall not discuss these ideas here, since they belong, more properly, to the realm of metaeconometrics.

The ultimate justification of any scientific procedure, is the results it yields in terms of advancing our understanding of the phenomenon under investigation, enabling us to predict and/or control its evolution. Prediction and control in economics are far more complicated than in the physical sciences, since our analysis is **conditional** on the exogenous variables whose study is not always within the universe of discourse of economics; control is also hampered by the fact that the monetary and fiscal authorities are not always able to exert complete control over the variables that serve as their control instruments and moreover their objectives may be continuously shaped (feedback) by the behavior of the system (endogenous variables) they seek to control. On the other side, the behavior of economic agents may change discontinuously in response to certain types of policy measures, as well as changes in the way in which they perceive themselves.

Many of these arguments may well have merit, but in the following text we shall not discuss the extent of their validity or merit; our purpose in this volume is confined to the development and exposition of the theory of estimation for the standard GLSEM and certain extensions of it.

1.4.1 Assumptions and Conventions

Whether the basic issues raised above have been dealt with satisfactorily or not, we shall begin the formal discussion of the GLSEM on the assertion that we are able to impose sufficient *a priori* restrictions on B^* and C so as to make the model in Eq. (1.2) distinguishable from that in Eq. (1.4), i.e., to render the equations of Eq. (1.2) **identifiable**. A formal discussion of the identification problem is postponed to Chapter 3, at which time we shall deal with it extensively.

We begin by noting that the vector of predetermined variables is given by

$$x_{t\cdot} = (y_{t-1\cdot},\ y_{t-2\cdot},\ \ldots,\ y_{t-k\cdot},\ p_{t\cdot}) \tag{1.6}$$

where $p_{t\cdot}$ is an s-element row vector of **exogenous variables**.

The basic set of assumptions under which we shall operate in much of our discussion is:

(A.1) The matrix of exogenous variables

$$P = (p_{t\cdot})\ t = 1, 2, 3, \ldots T,\ T > s,$$

is of full rank and [4]

$$\operatorname*{plim}_{T \to \infty} \frac{1}{T} P'P = M_{pp}$$

exists and is nonsingular (positive definite).

(A.1a) It is also asserted, or is derived as a consequence of A.1 and the stability of the model, that the matrix of predetermined variables, $X = (x_{t\cdot})$, $t = 1, 2, 3, \ldots, T$, $T > G$, is of full rank and

$$\operatorname*{plim}_{T \to \infty} \frac{1}{T} X'X = M_{xx}$$

exists and is nonsingular (positive definite).

(A.2) The matrix B^* is nonsingular.

(A.3) Some elements of B^* and C are known *a priori* to be zero (exclusion restrictions), so that the equations of the system are identified.

---

[4] The notation $\operatorname{plim}_{T \to \infty} \frac{1}{T} P'P = M_{pp}$ is meant to be understood as follows: (a) as an ordinary limit if the exogenous variables are taken as **nonstochastic**, or (b) as a probability limit if the exogenous variables are asserted to be **stochastic**.

(A.4) If the system is dynamic, i.e., it contains lagged endogenous variables, it is stable; this means that the roots of its characteristic equation (of the associated homogeneous vector difference equation) are less than unity in absolute value.

(A.5) The structural errors, $\{u_{t\cdot} : t = 0, \pm1, \pm2, \pm3, \ldots\}$, are a sequence of i.i.d. random vectors with $E(u'_{t\cdot}) = 0, \mathrm{Cov}(u'_{t\cdot}) = \Sigma$, where Σ is positive definite (notation: $\Sigma > 0$).[5] Moreover, they are **independent of the exogenous variables**, i.e., the elements of P.

Definition 1 (Structural Form). The representation of an economic system by the equation set in Eq. (1.2) is said to be the **structural form** of the system, and the equations in Eq. (1.2) are said to be the **structural equations** of the system.

Definition 2 (Reduced Form). The transformation of the set of equations in Eq. (1.2), as in

$$y_{t\cdot} = x_{t\cdot}\Pi + v_{t\cdot}, \quad \Pi = CD, \quad v_{t\cdot} = u_{t\cdot}D, \quad D = B^{*-1}, \quad t = 1, 2, \ldots, T, \quad (1.7)$$

is said to be the **reduced form** of the system, and the equations in Eq. (1.7) are said to be the **reduced form equations of the system.**

Remark 1. In the context of a proper theoretical framework one may derive "the rules of behavior" of economic agents. When these are exhibited in a system of equations such as Eq. (1.2), we assert that this represents the structural form of the system. What makes the form "structural" is our assertion (presumably in close correspondence with the *modus operandi* of the real world phenomenon we study) that economic agents, by their collective action, and given the information in the predetermined variables $x_{t\cdot}$, assign values to the endogenous variables $y_{t\cdot}$; and, further, that within an additive stochastic component, these values satisfy the equations of Eq. (1.2). Thus, the structural representation shows explicitly the linkages amongst the endogenous variables, as well as their (collective) direct dependence on the predetermined variables. By contrast, the reduced form shows only how economic agents by their collective actions assign values to y_t given the information in $x_{t\cdot}$. The differences between the reduced and structural form is that the latter shows explicitly the direct effect of a (generally small) set of variables (both endogenous and predetermined) on a given endogenous variable, while the former shows both the direct and indirect effects (generally through other endogenous variables) of all predetermined variables on a given endogenous variable.

---

[5] In effect this means that any identities that the model may have contained have been removed by substitution.

Generally, the structural form is more revealing of the manner in which an economic system is operating. The reduced form is less revealing. Indeed, a reduced form as in Eq. (1.7), estimated without reference as to its origin, i.e., without taking into account that $\Pi = CD$ and that C, D^{-1} are restricted by (A.3), may be compatible with **infinitely many structural forms** so long as they encompassed $y_t.$ and involved as predetermined variables only $x_t.$.

For completeness we offer the definition below, although this matter was covered in an earlier section.

Definition 3 (Classification of Variables). The elements of the m-element row vector $y_t.$ are said to be the **endogenous** or **jointly dependent** variables of the model. Sometimes they are also called (somewhat redundantly) **current endogenous** variables. The elements of the G-element row vector $x_t.$ are said to be the **predetermined** variables of the system. As the notation in Eq. (1.6) suggests, the predetermined variables are either **lagged endogenous** or **exogenous**. The basic characteristic of **exogenous variables** is that they are independent of the structural error sequence

$$\{u_t. : t = 0, \pm 1, \ \pm 2, \ \pm 3, \ldots\}.$$

Remark 2. The distinction between **current endogenous** and **predetermined** variables originated in the early development of econometrics where, invariably, it was assumed that the error process was one of i.i.d. random vectors. If the error process is a sequence of **independent** random vectors then, of course, all **lagged dependent (explanatory) variables** are independent of the error terms in the structural equations of the model. This property is also shared by the **exogenous variables**; thus, in this context, it makes sense to group together these two sets of variables into the class of **predetermined variables**. However, the class of exogenous **and** lagged endogenous variables is, fundamentally, an irrelevant one, which we help perpetuate by repeating. From the point of view of econometric theory, what matters is whether a variable at "time" t is, or is not, independent of the error vector $u_t.$. When the errors obey (A.5), then lagged endogenous variables are independent of $u_t.$ and the distinction makes sense. When, however, the errors exhibit some degree of autocorrelation **this will not be so** for all lagged endogenous variables. For example, if

$$u_t. = e_t. + e_{t-1}.\theta,$$

and $\{e'_t. : t = 0, 1, 2, \ldots\}$ is a sequence of i.i.d. random vectors, then $y_{t-r}.$, $r > 2$ would be independent of $u_t.$ but $y_{t-1}.$ **will not**. If

$$u'_t. = Ru'_{t-1}. + e'_t.,$$

then no lagged endogenous variable is, in principle, independent of $u_t.$. We shall revisit this issue at the end of this volume, in Chapter 6.

In nearly all our discussions of the GLSEM we shall operate under the following two conventions:

Convention 1 (Normalization Rule). In the ith equation it is possible to, and we do, set the coefficient of the variable y_{ti} equal to unity.

Remark 3. Convention 1 implies that

$$B^* = I - B, \tag{1.8}$$

with

$$B = (b_{ij}), \quad i, j = 1, 2, \ldots, m, \quad b_{ii} = 0, \quad i = 1, 2, \ldots, m.$$

Convention 2 (Enforcement of Exclusion Restrictions). Giving effect to (A.3), the ith equation contains $m_i (\leq m)$ endogenous and $G_i (\leq G)$ predetermined variables in its right hand side (i.e. as explanatory variables).

Remark 4. By Convention 2 the ith equation may be written as

$$y_{\cdot i} = Y_i \beta_{\cdot i} + X_i \gamma_{\cdot i} + u_{\cdot i}, \ i = 1, 2, \ldots, m,$$

where $Y = (y_{t \cdot})$, $X = (x_{t \cdot})$, $t = 1, 2, 3, \ldots, T$, and Y_i is the submatrix of Y containing the T observations on the m_i current endogenous variables (other than y_{ti}) not excluded from it by (A.3). Similarly X_i is the submatrix of X containing the T observations on the G_i predetermined variables not excluded from the ith equation, and $u_{\cdot i}$ simply contains the ith column of U, corresponding to the T observations on the structural errors of the ith equation.

1.4.2 Notation

In examining the estimation and related inference problems in the context of the GLSEM, we shall have to deal with many complex issues. It is imperative, therefore, that at the outset we should devise a notation that is flexible enough to handle them with ease; in this fashion we would not have to shift notation and thereby compound the complexity of an already very complex situation. We recall that the T observations on the GLSEM can be written as

$$YB^* = XC + U. \tag{1.9}$$

Giving effect to Convention 1 we can write

$$B^* = I - B. \tag{1.10}$$

If by $b_{\cdot i}^*$ and $e_{\cdot i} - b_{\cdot i}$ we denote the ith column of B^* and $I - B$, respectively, we have the relation

$$b_{\cdot i}^* = e_{\cdot i} - b_{\cdot i}, \tag{1.11}$$

where $e_{\cdot i}$ is an m-element column vector, all of whose elements are zero save the ith, which is unity. It is a consequence of Convention 1 that $b_{ii} = 0$ for **all** i.

Giving effect to Convention 2, we can write the T observations relative to the ith structural equation as

$$y_{\cdot i} = Y_i\beta_{\cdot i} + X_i\gamma_{\cdot i} + u_{\cdot i} = Z_i\delta_{\cdot i} + u_{\cdot i}, \qquad (1.12)$$

where

$$Z_i = (Y_i,\ X_i), \quad \delta_{\cdot i} = (\beta'_{\cdot i},\ \gamma'_{\cdot i})'. \qquad (1.13)$$

We note that $\beta_{\cdot i}$, $\gamma_{\cdot i}$ are subvectors of the ith column of B and C, respectively, and that the collection of vectors

$$\{\delta_{\cdot i} : i = 1, 2, \ldots, m\} \qquad (1.14)$$

represents the totality of the structural parameters that interest us. Often, however, **we have to deal with the matrices** B^*, B, C **as such** and it would be very convenient to show, in a simple way, the relation between these matrices, or their columns, and the collection of structural parameters as exhibited in Eq. (1.12).

Definition 4 (Partial Selection and Exclusion Matrices). Let L_{1i}, L_{2i} be permutations of m_i of the columns of I_m, and G_i of the columns of I_G, respectively, such that

$$YL_{1i} = Y_i, \quad XL_{2i} = X_i, \quad i = 1, 2, \ldots, m. \qquad (1.15)$$

Moreover, let L_{1i}^* be a permutation of the columns of I_m resulting **when we have eliminated from the latter its** i^{th} **column as well as the columns in** L_{1i}, and let L_{2i}^* be a permutation of the columns of I_G when we have eliminated from the latter the columns appearing in L_{2i}. Thus,

$$YL_{1i}^* = Y_i^* \quad \text{and} \quad XL_{2i}^* = X_i^*,$$

represent the matrices of observations on the current endogenous (Y_i^*), and predetermined (X_i^*) variables **excluded from the right hand side** (RHS) of the ith equation. The matrices L_{1i}, L_{2i} are said to be the **partial selection** matrices, and the matrices L_{1i}^*, L_{2i}^* are said to be the **partial exclusion** matrices, relative to the ith structural equation.

Proposition 1. The following statements are true.

   i. $\operatorname{rank}(L_{1i}) = m_i$, $\operatorname{rank}(L_{2i}) = G_i$, $m_i^* = m - m_i$, $i = 1, 2, \ldots, m$;

  ii. $\operatorname{rank}(L_{1i}^*) = m_i^* - 1$, $\operatorname{rank}(L_{2i}^*) = G_i^*$, $G_i^* = G - G_i$;

 iii. $b_{\cdot i} = L_{1i}\beta_{\cdot i}$, $c_{\cdot i} = L_{2i}\gamma_{\cdot i}$, $i = 1, 2, \ldots, m$.

Proof: The validity of i and ii is obvious by construction.

As for iii, note that the ith structural equation of Eq. (1.9) yields

$$y_{\cdot i} = Yb_{\cdot i} + Xc_{\cdot i} + u_{\cdot i}. \tag{1.16}$$

Invoking the restrictions imposed by (A.3) yields Eq. (1.12). Using the definitions in Eq. (1.15), we may rewrite Eq. (1.12) as

$$y_{\cdot i} = YL_{1i}\beta_{\cdot i} + XL_{2i}\gamma_{\cdot i} + u_{\cdot i}. \tag{1.17}$$

Comparing with Eq. (1.16), we have the desired result.

q.e.d.

Occasionally, we shall have reason to deal with the submatrices

$$Y_{\cdot i}^{\circ} = (y_{\cdot i}, \ Y_i), \quad i = 1, 2, \ldots, m. \tag{1.18}$$

Definition 5 (Partially Augmented Selection Matrices). The matrix

$$L_{1i}^{\circ} = (e_{\cdot i}, \ L_{1i}) \tag{1.19}$$

is said to be the **partially augmented selection matrix**, relative to the ith structural equation and has the property

$$YL_{1i}^{\circ} = Y_i^{\circ}. \tag{1.20}$$

Proposition 2. Let L_{1i}° be the partially augmented selection matrix relative to the ith structural equation. Then the following statements are true.

i. $\operatorname{rank}(L_{1i}^{\circ}) = m_i + 1$.

ii. $b_{\cdot i}^{*} = L_{1i}^{\circ}\beta_{\cdot i}^{\circ}$, $\quad c_{\cdot i} = L_{2i}\gamma_{\cdot i}$.

where $b_{\cdot i}^{*}$ is the ith column of B^{*} and $\beta_{\cdot i}^{\circ} = \begin{pmatrix} b_{ii}^{*} \\ -\beta_{\cdot i} \end{pmatrix}$.

Proof: The first statement is true by construction. As for the second statement, giving effect to (A.3) and Convention 2, we may write the ith equation of Eq. (1.9), viz., $Yb_{\cdot i}^{*} = Xc_{\cdot i} + u_{\cdot i}$, as

$$Y_i^{\circ}\beta_{\cdot i}^{\circ} = X_i\gamma_{\cdot i} + u_{\cdot i}. \tag{1.21}$$

Using Eq. (1.20) we can rewrite Eq. (1.21) as

$$YL_{1i}^{\circ}\beta_{\cdot i}^{\circ} = XL_{2i}\gamma_{\cdot i} + u_{\cdot i}.$$

Comparing with the ith equation of Eq. (1.9) we conclude,

$$b^*_{\cdot i} = L^\circ_{1i} \beta^\circ_{\cdot i} = L^\circ_{1i} \begin{pmatrix} b^*_{ii} \\ -\beta_{\cdot i} \end{pmatrix}, \qquad c_{\cdot i} = L_{2i} \gamma_{\cdot i}. \qquad (1.22)$$

By Convention 1, $b^*_{ii} = 1$, although this is immaterial in the present context.

q.e.d.

Occasionally, we shall also have to deal with the matrix

$$A^* = \begin{pmatrix} B^* \\ -C \end{pmatrix}, \qquad (1.23)$$

and the vectors

$$\delta^\circ_{\cdot i} = \begin{pmatrix} b^*_{ii} \\ -\delta_{\cdot i} \end{pmatrix}, \qquad \delta_{\cdot i} = (\beta'_{\cdot i}, \; \gamma'_{\cdot i})'. \qquad (1.24)$$

We have

Definition 6 (Exclusion, Selection and Augmented Selection Matrices). The $(m + G) \times (m^*_i + G^*_i - 1)$ matrix,

$$L^*_i = \begin{bmatrix} L^*_{1i} & 0 \\ 0 & L^*_{2i} \end{bmatrix}, \; i = 1, 2, \ldots, m,$$

is said to be the **exclusion matrix**, relative to the ith structural equation. The $(m + G) \times (m_i + G_i)$ matrix,

$$L_i = \begin{bmatrix} L_{1i} & 0 \\ 0 & L_{2i} \end{bmatrix}, \; i = 1, 2, \ldots, m,$$

is said to be the **selection matrix** relative to the (RHS of the) i^{th} structural equation. The $(m + G) \times (m_i + G_i + 1)$ matrix,

$$L^\circ_i = \begin{bmatrix} L^\circ_{1i} & 0 \\ 0 & L_{2i} \end{bmatrix}, \; i = 1, 2, \ldots, m,$$

is said to be the **augmented selection matrix** relative [6] to the ith structural equation. An immediate consequence is

Proposition 3. The following statements are true, for $i = 1, 2, ..., m$.

i. $\text{rank}(L^*_i) = m^*_i + G^*_i - 1$, $\text{rank}(L_i) = m_i + G_i$, $\text{rank}(L^\circ_i) = m_i + G_i + 1$;

---

[6] Note that this refers to **inclusion in the** i^{th} **equation**, meaning inclusion **in either the left or the right hand sides.**

ii. $a_{\cdot i}^* = L_i^\circ \delta_{\cdot i}^\circ$, where $a_{\cdot i}^*$ is the ith column of A^*

Proof: The statement in i is true by construction; as for ii we note that, using Propositions 1 and 2,

$$L_i^\circ \delta_{\cdot i}^\circ = \begin{bmatrix} L_{1i}^\circ \beta_{\cdot i}^\circ \\ -L_{2i} \gamma_{\cdot i} \end{bmatrix} = \begin{bmatrix} b_{\cdot i}^* \\ -c_{\cdot i} \end{bmatrix} = a_{\cdot i}^*$$

q.e.d.

Note that, defining

$$\bar{L}_{1i}^\circ = (L_{1i}^\circ,\ 0),\ \ \bar{L}_{2i}^\circ = (0,\ L_{2i}), \tag{1.25}$$

such that

$$L_i^\circ = \begin{bmatrix} \bar{L}_{1i}^\circ \\ \bar{L}_{2i}^\circ \end{bmatrix}, \tag{1.26}$$

and

$$\bar{L}_{1i} = (L_{1i},\ 0),\ \ \ \bar{L}_{2i} = (0,\ L_{2i}), \tag{1.27}$$

such that

$$L_i = \begin{bmatrix} \bar{L}_{1i} \\ \bar{L}_{2i} \end{bmatrix}, \tag{1.28}$$

we have

Proposition 4. The following statements are true.

i. $\text{vec}(A^*) = L^\circ \delta^\circ$,   where $L^\circ = \text{diag}(L_1^\circ,\ L_2^\circ, \ldots, L_m^\circ)$;

ii. $\text{vec}(B^*) = \bar{L}_1^\circ \delta^\circ,\ \text{vec}(C) = -\bar{L}_2^\circ \delta^\circ$, where

$$\bar{L}_1^\circ = \text{diag}(\bar{L}_{11}^\circ,\ \bar{L}_{12}^\circ, \ldots, \bar{L}_{1m}^\circ),\ \ \ \bar{L}_2^\circ = \text{diag}(\bar{L}_{21}^\circ,\ \bar{L}_{22}^\circ, \ldots, \bar{L}_{2m}^\circ),$$

and $\delta^\circ = (\delta_{\cdot i}^{\circ\prime},\ \delta_{\cdot 2}^{\circ\prime}, \ldots, \delta_{\cdot m}^{\circ\prime})$.

Proof : The ith subvector of $L^\circ \delta^\circ$ is given by $L_i^\circ \delta_{\cdot i}^\circ$, and the validity of i follows immediately from Proposition 3. The ith subvector of $\bar{L}_1^\circ \delta^\circ$ is given by $\bar{L}_{1i}^\circ \delta_{\cdot i}^\circ = L_{1i}^\circ \beta_{\cdot i}^\circ$, while the ith subvector of $\bar{L}_2^\circ \delta^\circ$ is given by

$$\bar{L}_{2i}^\circ \delta_{\cdot i}^\circ = -L_{2i} \gamma_{\cdot i}.$$

Hence, the validity of ii follows by Propositions 1 and 2.

q.e.d.

Remark 5. In addition to the augmented selection matrices introduced in Definition 6, it is necessary to introduce the notion of an **augmented exclusion** matrix. The need for this dual notation arises as follows: If, as in the maximum likelihood procedures, [7] which we shall take up in Chapter 3, we begin with the system in Eq. (1.2), identification is obtained by placing valid restrictions on the parameters appearing in each equation. In that context we need not impose a normalization convention **until the very end of the estimation process**. Thus, in such a setup the notation is designed to tell us which variables may appear in which **equations**. This means either on the "left" or the "right" side of the equation! Hence, the need for the augmented selection matrices. In the 2SLS context, however, we begin by imposing a normalization convention before we even consider estimation! In this context, the notation should be designed to tell us which (endogenous and/or predetermined) variables appear in **right hand side of a given equation**. Or, alternatively, which variables are **excluded** from the **right hand side**! Thus, the matrices L_i and L_i^*, as we have defined them above, are quite useful in both contexts. The augmented selection matrix

$$L_i^\circ = \begin{bmatrix} L_{1i}^\circ & 0 \\ 0 & L_{2i} \end{bmatrix}$$

however, has no role to play in 2SLS notation since, in that context, we know that, in the ith equation, the variable y_i appears on the "left" side with a coefficient of unity! On the other hand we **know**, again by the normalization convention, that y_i is excluded from the right hand side. Thus, if we need to impose the condition that certain coefficients of jointly dependent **explanatory variables are zero**, we must define a **partially augmented exclusion matrix** by

$$L_{1i}^{*\circ} = (e_{\cdot i}, L_{1i}^*).$$

This gives rise to the **augmented exclusion matrix**

$$L_i^{*\circ} = \begin{bmatrix} L_{1i}^{*\circ} & 0 \\ 0 & L_{2i}^* \end{bmatrix}. \tag{1.29}$$

The matrix above is evidently of dimension $(m+G) \times (m_i^* + G_i^*)$ and of full column rank. This dual notation is, also, useful in preserving the condition that what we include plus what we exclude (in the right hand side of a structural equation) amounts to the totality of the variables in question. For example, (L_{1i}°, L_{1i}^*) is simply a permutation of (all) of the columns of the identity matrix of order m, and this is appropriate notation in a maximum likelihood context. However, (L_{1i}, L_{1i}^*) **is not a permutation**

---

[7] The identification problem was first posed in the context of maximum likelihood estimation; hence, the discussion of this problem and all attendant notation and conventions tend to implicitly refer to that context.

of all such columns, since it is missing the ith **column** of the identity matrix! Thus, it is not appropriate notation in the 2SLS and 3SLS context, where we need to employ L_{1i} and we have no use for L_{1i}°. The introduction of the augmented exclusion matrix, in Eq. (1.29), rectifies this problem, in that $(L_{1i}, L_{1i}^{*\circ})$ is an $m \times m$ matrix, which represents a permutation of the columns of an identity matrix of order m.

Finally, we note in passing that $\bar{L}_{1i}^\circ$ is $m \times (m_i + G_i + 1)$ and $\bar{L}_{2i}^\circ$ is $G \times (m_i + G_i + 1)$, while $\bar{L}_{1i}, \bar{L}_{2i}$ are, respectively, $m \times (m_i + G_i)$ and $G \times (m_i + G_i)$.

1.5   Inconsistency of OLS Estimators

We now examine the problem of estimating the parameters of a structural equation by (ordinary) least squares methods (OLS) and show that OLS estimators are inconsistent.

The ith structural equation is given by

$$y_{.i} = Z_i \delta_{.i} + u_{.i}, \tag{1.30}$$

where

$$Z_i = (Y_i, \; X_i), \quad \delta_{.i} = (\beta'_{.i}, \; \gamma'_{.i})'.$$

From (A.5) we infer that the vector $u_{.i}$, which contains the T "observations" on the structural error u_{ti}, obeys

$$E(u_{.i}) = 0, \quad \text{Cov}(u_{.i}) = \sigma_{ii} I_T.$$

The OLS estimator is given by

$$\tilde{\delta}_{.i} = (Z_i' Z_i)^{-1} Z_i' y_{.i}, \tag{1.31}$$

and its properties are easily established by substituting in Eq. (1.31) the expression for $y_{.i}$ in Eq. (1.30), to obtain

$$\tilde{\delta}_{.i} = \delta_{.i} + (Z_i' Z_i)^{-1} Z_i' u_{.i}. \tag{1.32}$$

It is evident that the expectation of $\tilde{\delta}_{.i}$, given X, is not necessarily $\delta_{.i}$; indeed, the expectation need not even exist, so that, generally, the OLS estimator is **biased**. To examine its consistency we need to determine the probability limits

$$\plim_{T \to \infty} \frac{Z_i' Z_i}{T}, \quad \plim_{T \to \infty} \frac{Z_i' u_{.i}}{T}.$$

We note

$$\frac{Z_i' Z_i}{T} = \frac{1}{T} \begin{bmatrix} Y_i' Y_i & Y_i' X_i \\ X_i' Y_i & X_i' X_i \end{bmatrix} \tag{1.33}$$

and observe that, in order to examine the probability limit of this matrix, it is more convenient to express Y_i through its reduced from representation, i.e., as a submatrix of

$$Y = X\Pi + V, \quad V = (v_t.), \quad t = 1, 2, 3 \ldots, T. \tag{1.34}$$

In Eq. (1.34) we have a compact matrix representation of the T observations on the reduced form system as exhibited in Eq. (1.7). Since we need to examine the limits

$$\operatorname*{plim}_{T \to \infty} \frac{1}{T} Y'Y, \quad \operatorname*{plim}_{T \to \infty} \frac{1}{T} Y'X.$$

we find, from the reduced form representation,

$$Y'Y = \Pi'X'X\Pi + \Pi'X'V + V'X\Pi + V'V$$

$$Y'X = \Pi'X'X + V'X.$$

Thus,

$$\operatorname*{p\,lim}_{T \to \infty} \frac{1}{T} X'V = \operatorname*{plim}_{T \to \infty} \frac{1}{T} \sum_{t=1}^{T} x_t'.v_t.. \tag{1.35}$$

In order to simplify our exposition at this early stage, we introduce

Convention 3. The matrix X contains only exogenous variables.

We shall, subsequently, remove this restriction. Now, conditionally on the sequence

$$\{x_t' : t = 1, 2, 3, \ldots, T\},$$

the right member of Eq. (1.35) contains, by assumption (A.5), a sequence of independent random variables with

$$E[\operatorname{vec}(x_t'.v_t.)] = 0, \quad \operatorname{Cov}[\operatorname{vec}(x_t'.v_t.)] = \Omega \otimes x_t'.x_t..$$

Hence,

$$\frac{1}{T} E(X'V) = 0, \quad \operatorname{Cov}\left[\frac{1}{T}\operatorname{vec}(X'V)\right] = \Omega \otimes \frac{X'X}{T^2},$$

and we conclude that

$$\frac{1}{T} X'V$$

converges in quadratic mean to the null (zero) matrix, and thus,

$$\operatorname*{plim}_{T \to \infty} \frac{1}{T} X'V = 0, \quad \operatorname*{plim}_{T \to \infty} \frac{1}{T} V'X = 0. \tag{1.36}$$

Finally, we examine

$$\plim_{T \to \infty} \frac{1}{T} V'V = \plim_{T \to \infty} \frac{1}{T} \sum_{t=1}^{T} v'_{t\cdot} v_{t\cdot}. \tag{1.37}$$

The vectors $\{v'_{t\cdot} : t \geq 1\}$ were defined in Eq. (1.7), so that the right member of Eq. (1.37) contains a sequence of i.i.d. random elements with

$$E(v'_{t\cdot} v_{t\cdot}) = D'\Sigma D = \Omega. \tag{1.38}$$

Remark 6. In the future we shall always refer to the covariance matrix of the reduced form errors by Ω, i.e. we shall employ the notation,

$$\mathrm{Cov}(v'_{t\cdot}) = E(v'_{t\cdot} v_{t\cdot}) = \Omega \ (= D'\Sigma D). \tag{1.39}$$

The preceding discussion has established that

$$\plim_{T \to \infty} \frac{1}{T} Y'Y = \Pi' M_{xx} \Pi + \Omega, \quad \plim_{T \to \infty} \frac{1}{T} Y'X = \Pi' M_{xx}. \tag{1.40}$$

Using the selection matrix notation of the previous section, we obtain

$$\plim_{T \to \infty} \frac{Y'_i Y_i}{T} = L'_{1i} \Pi' M_{xx} \Pi L_{1i} + L'_{1i} \Omega L_{1i} \tag{1.41}$$

$$\plim_{T \to \infty} \frac{Y'_i X_i}{T} = L'_{1i} \Pi' M_{xx} L_{2i}$$

$$\plim_{T \to \infty} \frac{X'_i X_i}{T} = L'_{2i} M_{xx} L_{2i},$$

so that

$$\plim_{T \to \infty} \frac{1}{T} Z'_i Z_i = \begin{bmatrix} \Pi'_i M_{xx} \Pi_i & \Pi'_i M_{xx} L_{2i} \\ L'_{2i} M_{xx} \Pi_i & L'_{2i} M_{xx} L_{2i} \end{bmatrix} + \begin{bmatrix} \Omega_{ii} & 0 \\ 0 & 0 \end{bmatrix}.$$

Evidently, the matrix Π_i, above, is the submatrix of Π corresponding to the reduced form representation of the current endogenous variables that appear as explanatory variables in the ith equation, i.e., in the representation

$$Y_i = X\Pi_i + V_i.$$

We obtain this result, through the operation

$$Y_i = Y L_{1i} = (X\Pi + V) L_{1i} = X\Pi_i + V_i, \tag{1.42}$$

so that

$$\Pi_i = \Pi L_{1i}, \quad V_i = V L_{1i},$$

and Ω_{ii} is the covariance matrix of the reduced form errors appearing in Eq. (1.42). Notice that, defining

$$S_i = (\Pi_i, \ L_{2i}), \tag{1.43}$$

the probability limit above becomes

$$\underset{T\to\infty}{\text{plim}} \frac{1}{T} Z_i' Z_i = S_i' M_{xx} S_i + \begin{bmatrix} \Omega_{ii} & 0 \\ 0 & 0 \end{bmatrix}. \tag{1.44}$$

In order to complete our discussion, we need to show that the right member of Eq. (1.44) is nonsingular, and that the probability limit of

$$\frac{1}{T} Z_i' u_{\cdot i}$$

vanishes. Since showing the validity of the first assertion involves an argument that is very crucial in subsequent developments as well, we digress to discuss these issues below, in Remarks 7, 8, and Proposition 5.

Remark 7. The matrix S_i will play a very important role in the development of the theory of two stage and three stage least squares (2SLS), (3SLS). It will be recalled that in the introductory sections of this chapter we alluded to the identification problem in econometrics and how this is dealt with, in the context of the GLSEM, by **exclusion restrictions**. It is this feature that is responsible for writing, as we did, the ith structural equation in Eq. (1.30). Earlier, we had also defined the partial selection matrix L_{2i}, and the partial exclusion matrix L_{2i}^*, so that, given a fixed numbering (ordering) of the predetermined variables, i.e. the columns of X, we obtain

$$X L_{2i} = X_i, \quad X L_{2i}^* = X_i^*$$

where, we remind the reader, X_i^* contains the predetermined variables excluded, by (A.3), from the ith structural equation. It is easy to see that

$$\text{rank}(L_{2i}) = G_i, \quad \text{rank}(L_{2i}^*) = G_i^*, \tag{1.45}$$

and, consequently, that

$$J_i = (L_{2i}, \ L_{2i}^*) \tag{1.46}$$

is a square matrix of rank G.

Remark 8. When we discuss the identification problem formally we shall show that, given Convention 1, the identifiability of the ith structural equation is equivalent to the statement that the rank of the submatrix of Π_i, corresponding to the variables X_i^*, i.e., those excluded from the ith structural equation by (A.3), is m_i. We now explore the implications of this fact.

Proposition 5. Let X_i^* be the matrix of observations on the predetermined variables, excluded by (A.3) from the ith structural equation. If the **latter is identified, so that the submatrix of Π_i corresponding to X_i^* is of rank** m_i, then the matrix S_i defined in Eq. (1.43) is of full rank, i.e.

$$\text{rank}(S_i) = m_i + G_i, \quad i = 1, 2, 3, \ldots, m. \tag{1.47}$$

Proof: Since the matrix J_i of Eq. (1.46) is nonsingular, we have

$$\text{rank}(S_i) = \text{rank}(J_i' S_i).$$

But,

$$J_i' S_i = \begin{pmatrix} L_{2i}' \\ L_{2i}^{*\prime} \end{pmatrix} (\Pi_i, \ L_{2i}) = \begin{bmatrix} \Pi_{1i} & I_{Gi} \\ \Pi_{2i} & 0 \end{bmatrix}.$$

Moreover, the identifiability of the ith structural equation implies

$$\text{rank}(\Pi_{2i}) = m_i \,^8$$

Let α, β be, respectively, arbitrary m_i and G_i element column vectors and note that

$$J_i' S_i \begin{bmatrix} \alpha \\ \beta \end{bmatrix} = \begin{bmatrix} \Pi_{1i}\alpha + \beta \\ \Pi_{2i}\alpha \end{bmatrix} = 0 \tag{1.48}$$

implies

$$\alpha = 0.$$

in view of the identifiability of the ith structural equation; but, this further implies that

$$\beta = 0,$$

Thus, we see that $\alpha = 0$, $\beta = 0$ are the only vectors satisfying Eq. (1.48), which implies that

$$\text{rank}(S_i) = m_i + G_i.$$

$$\text{q.e.d.}$$

Remark 9. In a later chapter we shall take up extensively the problem of identification. At that stage, we shall prove that the ith structural equation is identified if and only if

$$\text{rank}(\Pi_{2i}) = m_i.$$

The relevance of the condition in Eq. (1.47), as well as Proposition 5, in the context of the current discussion, is the following: in order to obtain

---

[8] This is the fact that is assumed true; its proof will be given in Chapter 3, where the identification problem will be discussed extensively.

the OLS estimator, it must be true that the matrix in Eq. (1.33) is invertible; moreover, from Eq. (1.44) we see that we must also require that the limit matrix is nonsingular; otherwise, the OLS estimator will fail to exist, asymptotically. The first matrix in the right member of Eq. (1.44), however, is nonsingular, by virtue of Proposition 5 and the assertion that the first equation is identified. This ensures that the OLS estimator of the parameters of a structural equation is well defined, both in finite samples and asymptotically. For 2SLS, it is further required that the sample equivalent of this matrix, viz.

$$\tilde{Z}_i' \tilde{Z}_i = \tilde{S}_i' X' X \tilde{S}_i,$$

be nonsingular in order to ensure that it (2SLS estimator) exists. For that, we must have that

$$\tilde{S}_i = (\tilde{\Pi}_i, \ L_{2i})$$

is of full rank. Proposition 5 states that if the ith structural equation is identified then S_i is of full rank. Thus, Proposition 5 ensures the existence of 2SLS estimators for the parameters of an identified equation, and establishes the role played by the identification requirements in 2SLS (and 3SLS) estimation methods.

Returning now to the discussion of the inconsistency of OLS, we have in Eq. (1.44), as an immediate consequence of Proposition 5 and (A.1a), that

$$S_i' M_{xx} S_i$$

is invertible and hence that

$$\operatorname*{plim}_{T \to \infty} \frac{1}{T} Z_i' Z_i$$

is invertible as well. Finally, we need to examine

$$\operatorname*{plim}_{T \to \infty} \frac{1}{T} Z_i' u_{\cdot i}.$$

Now

$$\frac{1}{T} Z_i' u_{\cdot i} = \frac{1}{T} L_i' \begin{pmatrix} Y' \\ X' \end{pmatrix} u_{\cdot i}$$

where L_i was defined in Definition 6. Consequently, we need only examine

$$\operatorname*{p\,lim}_{T \to \infty} \frac{1}{T} V' u_{\cdot i}, \quad \operatorname*{p\,lim}_{T \to \infty} \frac{1}{T} X' u_{\cdot i}.$$

The second probability limit is easily seen to vanish, by the same type of argument leading to Eq. (1.36). As for the first,

$$\frac{1}{T} V' u_{\cdot i} = \frac{1}{T} D' U' u_{\cdot i} = D' \frac{1}{T} U' u_{\cdot i} = D' \frac{1}{T} \sum_{t=1}^{T} u_{t \cdot}' u_{ti} \xrightarrow{P} D' \sigma_{\cdot i},$$

where $\sigma_{\cdot i}$ is the ith column of Σ, and the notation $a \xrightarrow{P} b$ means that a converges in probability to b. We have, thus, established

Theorem 1. Consider the GLSEM subject to assumptions (A.1) through (A.5) and Conventions 1 through 3. Then, the OLS estimator of the ith structural equation is inconsistent and its inconsistency is given by

$$\plim_{T \to \infty} (\tilde{\delta}_{\cdot i} - \delta_{\cdot i})_{OLS} = \left[S_i' M_{xx} S_i + \begin{pmatrix} \Omega_{ii} & 0 \\ 0 & 0 \end{pmatrix} \right]^{-1} \left[\begin{array}{c} D_i' \sigma_{\cdot i} \\ 0 \end{array} \right], \qquad (1.49)$$

where

$$D_i = DL_{1i}.$$

Remark 10. It is seen from Eq. (1.49) that the "reason" OLS is inconsistent as an estimator of the structural parameters $\delta_{\cdot i}$, is the term

$$D_i' \sigma_{\cdot i} \neq 0, \qquad (1.50)$$

which results from the fact that a subset of the explanatory (right hand) variables in the ith structural equation, viz. the Y_i, are correlated with the structural error term $u_{\cdot i}$. If, somehow, we could eliminate or overcome this dependence we could utilize least squares procedures to obtain (at least) consistent estimators. It is this observation that forms the basis of the two stage least squares (2SLS) as initially developed by H. Theil (1953), (1958) and R. Basmann (1957).

1.6   Two Stage Least Squares (2SLS)

1.6.1   The Original Derivation

Using the reduced form representation of Y_i, we can write the ith structural equation as

$$y_{\cdot i} = (X\Pi_i + V_i)\beta_{\cdot i} + X_i\gamma_{\cdot i} + u_{\cdot i}$$

$$= X\Pi_i\beta_{\cdot i} + X_i\gamma_{\cdot i} + u_{\cdot i} + V_i\beta_{\cdot i}, \quad \text{or}$$

$$y_{\cdot i} = X\Pi_i\beta_{\cdot i} + X_i\gamma_{\cdot i} + u_{\cdot i}^*. \qquad (1.51)$$

By writing it as in Eq. (1.51) we "overcome" the dependence problem referred to in Remark 10. We have, however, burdened the error term and, moreover, Eq. (1.51) requires us to know Π_i which, unfortunately, we do not. It was Theil's important contribution to the evolution of econometrics to suggest that Π_i be replaced by its OLS estimator, $\tilde{\Pi}_i$, so that Eq. (1.51) is rendered as

$$y_{\cdot i} = X\tilde{\Pi}_i\beta_{\cdot i} + X_i\gamma_{\cdot i} + \tilde{u}_{\cdot i}^*,$$

where
$$\tilde{u}^*_{\cdot i} = u_{\cdot i} + \tilde{V}_{\cdot i}\beta_{\cdot i}.$$

Alternatively, we reach the same formulation if we write

$$Y_i = \tilde{Y}_i + \tilde{V}_i, \quad \tilde{Y}_i = X\tilde{\Pi}_i, \quad \tilde{V}_i = Y_i - \tilde{Y}_i,$$

observe that $\tilde{Y}_i$ and $\tilde{V}_i$ are essentially **orthogonal**, and render the structural equation above as

$$y_{\cdot i} = \tilde{Y}_i\beta_{\cdot i} + X_i\gamma_{\cdot i} + \tilde{u}^*_{\cdot i}, \tag{1.52}$$

or

$$y_{\cdot i} = \tilde{Z}_i\delta_{\cdot i} + \tilde{u}^*_{\cdot i}, \quad \tilde{Z}_i = (\tilde{Y}_i, \ X_i). \tag{1.53}$$

The 2SLS estimator is obtained by applying OLS to the estimation of parameters in Eq. (1.53). Thus, the 2SLS estimator, as originally suggested by Theil, is

$$\tilde{\delta}_{\cdot i} = (\tilde{Z}'_i\tilde{Z}_i)^{-1}\tilde{Z}'_i y_{\cdot i}. \tag{1.54}$$

Remark 11. In the discussion above, the term **two stage** least squares is quite appropriate in that, conceptually, one may think of the first stage as obtaining, by least squares, $\tilde{Y}_i$, and of the second stage as obtaining, again by least squares, the structural estimator $\tilde{\delta}_{\cdot i}$. **Needless to say, computationally, the estimator is obtained in one step.** On the other hand, this formulation, while instructive and intuitively very appealing, is not very useful in suggesting extensions, or in facilitating its discussion relative to other estimators. Thus, we shall provide an alternative formulation.

1.6.2   An Alternative Formulation

Since, by (A1.a) and Convention 3, X is a matrix of full rank, $X'X$ **is positive definite**. Thus, there exists a **nonsingular matrix**, R, such that

$$X'X = RR'. \tag{1.55}$$

Consider now the transformation

$$R^{-1}X'y_{\cdot i} = R^{-1}X'Z_i\delta_{\cdot i} + R^{-1}X'u_{\cdot i}. \tag{1.56}$$

Remark 12. The formulation of the problem as above was introduced into the literature by Dhrymes (1969). The transformation in Eq. (1.53) may be rationalized and motivated as an attempt to render the problem as nearly similar to the GLM as possible. One of the distinguishing characteristics of the GLM

$$y = X\beta + u,$$

is that its explanatory variables, i.e., the columns of X, are uncorrelated with (or independent of) the errors, say u.

Explicitly, the consistency of the OLS estimator of β requires

$$\plim_{T \to \infty} \frac{1}{T} X'u = 0.$$

Note that, in Eq. (1.56), transforming only by the matrix of predetermined variables, X, would not accomplish the objective just noted, since

$$\plim_{T \to \infty} \frac{1}{T} Z_i' X X' u_{\cdot i} \neq 0,$$

owing to the fact that $\plim_{T \to \infty}(Z_i'X/T) = S_i' M_{xx}$, which is a well defined finite entity, while the term $X'u_{\cdot i}$ may become unbounded. On the other hand,

$$\plim_{T \to \infty} \frac{1}{T} (R^{-1}X'Z_i)' R^{-1} X' u_{\cdot i} = \plim_{T \to \infty} \frac{1}{T} Z_i' X \left(\frac{X'X}{T} \right)^{-1} \frac{X'u_{\cdot i}}{T} = 0$$

$$(1.57)$$

which, thus, accomplishes the desired objective. As we shall see later on, in Chapter 6, this is basically the motivation and procedure applied in the case of certain types of **nonlinear** simultaneous equations models. Returning now to Eq. (1.56), put

$$R^{-1}X'y_{\cdot i} = w_{\cdot i}, \ R^{-1}X'Z_i = Q_i, \ R^{-1}X'u_{\cdot i} = r_{\cdot i}, \qquad (1.58)$$

and, thus, write the transform of the ith structural equation as

$$w_{\cdot i} = Q_i \delta_{\cdot i} + r_{\cdot i}, \ i = 1, 2, \ldots, m. \qquad (1.59)$$

We shall prove the fundamental

Theorem 2. Consider the GLSEM under assumptions (A.1) through (A.5) and Conventions 1 through 3. Then, **the 2SLS estimator of the parameters of the ith structural equation is the OLS estimator of the parameters in Eq. (1.59) and it is a consistent estimator of $\delta_{\cdot i}$.**

Proof: First we note that

$$Q_i = R^{-1}X'Z_i = R'\tilde{S}_i, \ \ \tilde{S}_i = (\tilde{\Pi}_i, \ L_{2i}). \qquad (1.60)$$

Thus, the OLS estimator in the context of Eq. (1.59) is

$$\tilde{\delta}_{\cdot i} = (Q_i'Q_i)^{-1}Q_i'w_{\cdot i} = (\tilde{S}_i'RR'\tilde{S}_i)^{-1}\tilde{S}_i'X'y_{\cdot i}. \qquad (1.61)$$

Since

$$\tilde{Z}_i = (\tilde{Y}_i, \ X_i) = X\tilde{S}_i, \ \ RR' = X'X,$$

a comparison with Eq. (1.54) shows Eq. (1.61) to be exactly the 2SLS estimator, as claimed. Consistency is easily shown by noting

$$
\operatorname*{plim}_{T\to\infty}(\tilde{\delta}_{\cdot i} - \delta_{\cdot i})_{2SLS} = \operatorname*{plim}_{T\to\infty}\left(\tilde{S}_i' \frac{X'X}{T} \tilde{S}_i\right)^{-1} \operatorname*{plim}_{T\to\infty} \frac{1}{T} \tilde{S}_i' X' u_{\cdot i}.
$$

The matrix $\tilde{S}_i'(X'X/T)\tilde{S}_i \xrightarrow{P} S_i' M_{xx} S_i$, which is nonsingular by Proposition 5, and moreover $\tilde{S}_i'(X'u_{\cdot i}/T) \xrightarrow{P} S_i' \operatorname{plim}_{T\to\infty}(X'u_{\cdot i}/T) = 0$.

q.e.d.

Remark 13. Evidently, the procedure above is effective in extending the range of application of OLS to structural equations because the transformation renders the "explanatory" variables (asymptotically) uncorrelated with the structural error term, while the properties of the latter are not disturbed. But since the GLSEM contains many equations it would be convenient to deal with all of them simultaneously instead of one at a time.

Now applying the transformation in Eq. (1.56) to all structural equations, and setting

$$
w = (w_{\cdot 1}', w_{\cdot 2}', \ldots, w_{\cdot m}')', \quad Q = \operatorname{diag}(Q_1, Q_2, \ldots, Q_m) \quad (1.62)
$$
$$
\delta = (\delta_{\cdot 1}', \delta_{\cdot 2}', \ldots, \delta_{\cdot m}')', \quad r = (r_{\cdot 1}', r_{\cdot 2}', \ldots, r_{\cdot m}')' \quad (1.63)
$$

we can write the entire system in the compact form

$$
w = Q\delta + r, \quad (1.64)
$$

which displays, explicitly, the vector of unknown structural parameters contained in the system as a whole. As an immediate consequence of the definitions above we have

Corollary 1. Under the conditions of Theorem 1, the (systemwide) 2SLS estimator of the (vector of) unknown structural parameters of the GLSEM, as exhibited in Eq. (1.61), is given by

$$
\tilde{\delta} = (Q'Q)^{-1} Q' w \quad (1.65)
$$

and, moreover, $\operatorname{plim}_{T\to\infty} \tilde{\delta} = \delta$, i.e. $\tilde{\delta}$ of Eq. (1.65) is a consistent estimator of the true parameter vector δ .

Proof: The ith subvector of Eq. (1.65) is simply

$$
\tilde{\delta}_{\cdot i} = (Q_i' Q_i)^{-1} Q_i' w_{\cdot i},
$$

which is exactly the representation of the 2SLS estimator of the structural parameters contained in the ith structural equation.

q.e.d.

Remark 14. The GLSEM as transformed and exhibited in Eq. (1.64) is said to be in **canonical structural form** (CSF), and "looks" very much like a GLM, in the sense that

$$Q = (I \otimes R')\tilde{S}, \quad S = \text{diag}(S_1, \, S_2, \ldots, S_m), \qquad (1.66)$$

S is of full rank (why?) and

$$\plim_{T \to \infty} \frac{Q'Q}{T} = S'(I \otimes M_{xx})S \qquad (1.67)$$

$$\plim_{T \to \infty} \frac{Q'r}{T} = \plim_{T \to \infty} \tilde{S}' \frac{(I \otimes X')u}{T} = 0, \quad u = \text{vec}(U). \qquad (1.68)$$

Note further that, in the single equation or systemwide CSF representation, the 2SLS estimator is obtained by minimizing

$$(w_{\cdot i} - Q_i \delta_{\cdot i})'(w_{\cdot i} - Q_i \delta_{\cdot i}) = (y_{\cdot i} - Z_i \delta_{\cdot i})' X (X'X)^{-1} X'(y_{\cdot i} - Z_i \delta_{\cdot i})$$

and

$$(w - Q\delta)'(w - Q\delta) = (y - Z^*\delta)'[I \otimes X(X'X)^{-1}X'](y - Z^*\delta),$$

respectively. By analogy with the notion of *Mahalanobis distance*, [9] we may think of the 2SLS (and later 3SLS) estimator as a minimum distance like estimator.

The conditions in Eq. (1.68) ensure, at least, the consistency of the OLS estimator of δ, in the context of Eq. (1.64). But, is this OLS estimator efficient as well? Arguing by analogy with the standard GLM, our response would be that this would depend on the covariance structure of the error, here the vector r. Since, by construction,

$$r = (I \otimes R^{-1}X')u \qquad (1.69)$$

we see that, under Convention 3, we easily establish

$$E(r \mid X) = 0, \quad E(r) = 0,$$

$$\text{Cov}(r \mid X) = \Sigma \otimes I_G = \Phi. \qquad (1.70)$$

This is so since, if a conditional moment does not depend on a given variable then it is the unconditional moment as well, relative to that variable.

But Eq. (1.70) suggests that Aitken-like procedures will yield estimators with better properties.

---

[9] If ξ_i, $i = 1, 2$, are normal vectors with means, respectively μ_i and common covariance matrix Σ, the entity $(\mu_1 - \mu_2)'\Sigma^{-1}(\mu_1 - \mu_2)$ is said to be their **Mahalanobis** distance, after the Indian statistician P.C. Mahalanobis who first introduced this measure in classifying populations.

1.7 Three Stage Least Squares (3SLS)

Implementing the suggestion made in Remark 14, we note that the Aitken estimator is given by

$$\bar{\delta} = (Q'\Phi^{-1}Q)^{-1}Q'\Phi^{-1}w. \tag{1.71}$$

However, we rarely know the structural error covariance matrix Σ; hence, we rarely know Φ and, thus, the estimator in Eq. (1.71) is **not feasible**.

In practice, we deal with the **feasible** Aitken estimator obtained by substituting, in Eq. (1.71), the consistent estimator

$$\tilde{\Phi} = \tilde{\Sigma} \otimes I_G, \tag{1.72}$$

in lieu of the unknown matrix Φ. This yields

$$\hat{\delta} = (Q'\tilde{\Phi}^{-1}Q)^{-1}Q'\tilde{\Phi}^{-1}w. \tag{1.73}$$

We have

Definition 7. The estimator exhibited in Eq. (1.73) is said to be the three stage least squares (3SLS) estimator of the unknown vector of structural parameters, δ, of the GLSEM.

Remark 15. The term three stage least squares is intuitively explained as follows: in the first stage, we obtain by least squares the estimator of the reduced form

$$\tilde{\Pi} = (X'X)^{-1}X'Y. \tag{1.74}$$

In the second stage we obtain the 2SLS estimator of δ, say $\tilde{\delta}$, and, thus, the residuals

$$\tilde{u}_{\cdot i} = y_{\cdot i} - Z_i\tilde{\delta}_{\cdot i}, \quad i = 1, 2, \ldots, m, \tag{1.75}$$

from which we compute the consistent estimator of the elements of Σ through

$$\tilde{\sigma}_{ij} = \frac{1}{T}\tilde{u}'_{\cdot i}\tilde{u}_{\cdot j}, \quad i, j = 1, 2, \ldots, m. \tag{1.76}$$

Finally, in the third stage we obtain, by (generalized) least squares, the 3SLS estimator of δ.

Needless to say, computationally, the 3SLS estimator is not obtained in three steps but in one since, by substitution, we easily find

$$\tilde{\sigma}_{ij} = \frac{1}{T}y'_{\cdot i}[I - X\tilde{S}_i(\tilde{S}'_iX'X\tilde{S}_i)^{-1}Z'_i][I - Z_j(\tilde{S}'_jX'X\tilde{S}_j)^{-1}\tilde{S}'_jX']y_{\cdot j}$$

and

$$\tilde{S}'_iX'X\tilde{S}_i = \begin{bmatrix} Y'_iX(X'X)^{-1}X'Y_i & Y'_iX_i \\ X'_iY_i & X'_iX_i \end{bmatrix},$$

$$X\tilde{S}_i = [X(X'X)^{-1}X'Y_i, \; X_i],$$

so that all that is required for 3SLS (or 2SLS) is the computation of the squares and cross product matrices

$$Y'Y, \; Y'X, \; X'X,$$

and the inverse

$$(X'X)^{-1}.$$

Given the above, the 2SLS and 3SLS estimators are easily obtained by suitable manipulations of certain submatrices thereof.

We shall postpone the discussion of the asymptotic properties of the two procedures to a later chapter. Here we ask instead: Are there any circumstances under which the two procedures will, numerically, coincide? To answer this question, we shall elaborate somewhat on our earlier discussion of the identification problem.

We recall, from Proposition 5, that identification of the ith structural equation implies that

$$\text{rank}(S_i) = m_i + G_i. \tag{1.77}$$

This suggests

Definition 8. Consider the GLSEM under the conditions of Theorem 2. The ith structural equation is said to be **just identified** if Eq. (1.77) holds and, in addition, $G = G_i + m_i$.

It is said to be **overidentified** if Eq. (1.77) holds and, in addition,

$$G \geq G_i + m_i.$$

It is said to be **underidentified** if $G < m_i + G_i$.

Definition 9. A structural equation is said to be **identified** or **identifiable** if it is either **just-** or **overidentified** in the sense of Definition 8. Otherwise, it is said to be **underidentified** or **nonidentified** or **nonidentifiable**.

Remark 16. Since the matrices S_i , above, are of dimension $G \times (m_i + G_i)$, the S_i matrix corresponding to a **just identified** structural equation is square and, hence, nonsingular. Of lesser interest is the observation that to an overidentified structural equation there corresponds a rectangular matrix S_i , with more rows than columns. Evidently, to an **underidentified** equation there corresponds a rectangular matrix S_i which has fewer rows than columns. This means, of course, that the equation (its parameters) cannot be identified since the rank condition in Eq. (1.77) cannot be satisfied.

We are now able to prove a number of interesting results.

Theorem 3. Consider the GLSEM as in Theorem 2; then

   i. if all the equations of the system are just identified, or

   ii. if (it is known that) $\sigma_{ij} = 0$, $i \neq j$,

and this is enforced in the estimation phase, the 2SLS and 3SLS estimators of the system parameter vector **are numerically identical.**

Proof: If the assertion in i. is valid then the S_i, $i = 1, 2, \ldots, m$, are all nonsingular matrices. Hence, with probability one, the matrices Q_i are nonsingular. Thus

$$\hat{\delta}_{3SLS} = (Q'\tilde{\Phi}^{-1}Q)^{-1}Q'\tilde{\Phi}^{-1}w = Q^{-1}w,$$

$$\tilde{\delta}_{2SLS} = (Q'Q)^{-1}Q'w = Q^{-1}w$$

which establishes the validity of the first part.

As for the second, we note that under the conditions in ii.,

$$\tilde{\delta}_{3SLS} = \begin{bmatrix} \left(\frac{Q_1'Q_1}{\tilde{\sigma}_{11}}\right)^{-1} & 0 & \cdots & 0 \\ 0 & \left(\frac{Q_2'Q_2}{\tilde{\sigma}_{22}}\right)^{-1} & \cdots & 0 \\ \vdots & \vdots & \vdots & \vdots \\ 0 & 0 & \cdots & \left(\frac{Q_m'Q_m}{\tilde{\sigma}_{mm}}\right)^{-1} \end{bmatrix} \begin{bmatrix} \frac{Q_1'w_{\cdot 1}}{\tilde{\sigma}_{11}} \\ \frac{Q_2'w_{\cdot 2}}{\tilde{\sigma}_{22}} \\ \vdots \\ \frac{Q_m'w_{\cdot m}}{\tilde{\sigma}_{mm}} \end{bmatrix} = \begin{bmatrix} c_{\cdot 1} \\ c_{\cdot 2} \\ \vdots \\ c_{\cdot m} \end{bmatrix},$$

where $c_{\cdot i} = (Q_i'Q_i)^{-1}Q_i'w_{\cdot i}$, $i = 1, 2, \ldots, m$. Similarly,

$$\tilde{\delta}_{(2SLS)} = \begin{bmatrix} (Q_1'Q_1)^{-1}Q_1'w_{\cdot 1} \\ (Q_2'Q_2)^{-1}Q_2'w_{\cdot 2} \\ \vdots \\ (Q_m'Q_m)^{-1}Q_m'w_{\cdot m} \end{bmatrix},$$

which establishes the claim of the theorem.

q.e.d.

Remark 17. One may wonder why is it that the results above hold; i.e., intuitively, what is the difference between the two procedures and why do they coincide in these two instances? Well, any inferential procedure, of the type we are likely to deal with in this book, is essentially addressed to the problem of disentangling the impact exerted, on a given set of variables, by observable and unobservable factors. In the GLM we want to disentangle the influence of the regressors (the x's) from the influence exerted by "the error term." At our disposal we have observations only on the dependent variable, y, and the explanatory variables, the x's. Similarly, in the context of the GLSEM we wish to disentangle the influence of the y's and the x's, on any given endogenous variable, from that exerted by the structural error. We have at our disposal observations only on the y's and the x's. But in this task, the only information that matters, fundamentally, is that part that is independent of, or, minimally, uncorrelated with the error. Evidently, that part of our information which is correlated with the error cannot serve reliably in this fashion, since its impact cannot be separated from that of the latter, in the absence of observations on the error term! Now, in the GLSEM the only variables that meet the criterion of uncorrelatedness or independence of the structural errors are the **predetermined variables**. [10] There are exactly G such variables. If we have $m_i + G_i$ parameters to estimate in the ith structural equation, then we "need" at least that many "variables" (or linearly independent combinations of variables) which are, at least asymptotically, uncorrelated with the structural errors of the model. Hence, intuitively, if

$$G \geq m_i + G_i$$

the task of inference can be accomplished. On the other hand, if

$$G < m_i + G_i,$$

inference cannot be satisfactorily carried out, and the ith equation is said to be **underidentified**.

Now, if the equations of the system are **overidentified**, i.e. if $G > G_i + m_i$, for all i, 2SLS does not use all of the information available in estimating the parameters of the ith structural equation. On the other hand, 3SLS uses the information relevant from the jth equation $(j \neq i)$ in order to estimate the parameters of the ith equation. This information is relevant, since if

$$\sigma_{ij} \neq 0, \quad i \neq j$$

the ith and j^{th} equations are connected through the correlation of their error terms! Hence, we would expect 3SLS to be efficient relative to 2SLS – a fact we shall demonstrate formally at a later stage.

When, however, all equations are **just identified**, i.e. $G = G_i + m_i$, for all i, all information possibly available is brought to bear on the **estimation of the parameters in each and every equation**. Hence, nothing

---

[10] This is so in the standard case, where the structural errors are assumed to be i.i.d. random vectors. If the errors are autocorrelated, this would not be so. In fact, if it is only asserted that the structural errors are merely covariance stationary then the only variables that can be counted upon to meet this criterion are the **exogenous** variables, which are independent of the error sequence by assumption!

can be gained by utilizing the information contained in equations other than the ith in estimating the parameters of that equation – hence the result that 2SLS and 3SLS are equivalent. Similarly, when

$$\sigma_{ij} = 0, \quad i \neq j,$$

then even though not all possibly available information is brought to bear in estimating the parameters of the ith equation, still there is no vehicle by which information in the jth equation, $(j \neq i)$, can be brought to bear on the estimation of the parameters of the ith. Thus, when the uncorrelatedness condition

$$\sigma_{ij} = 0, \quad i \neq j$$

is enforced at the estimation stage, 2SLS and 3SLS are also equivalent.

A natural question to ask after this discussion is : What if only a subset of the equations are identified, or the covariance matrix is only block diagonal? What simplifications, if any, ensue?

We proceed to answer these questions in a series of small steps. First, we have the obvious but useful

Corollary 2. Consider the GLSEM under the conditions of Theorem 3. Then, for any **just identified equation** the 2SLS residuals from its canonical structural form (CSF) **are identically zero.** Moreover, the 2SLS residuals from the usual (standard) structural form (SF) are orthogonal to the matrix of predetermined variables.

Proof: From Theorem 3, a just identified structural equation yields

$$\tilde{\delta}_{\cdot i} = Q_i^{-1} w_{\cdot i}.$$

Hence,

$$\tilde{r}_{\cdot i} = w_{\cdot i} - Q_i \tilde{\delta}_{\cdot i} = w_i - Q_i Q_i^{-1} w_{\cdot i} = 0.$$

We further note that

$$0 = \tilde{r}_{\cdot i} = R^{-1} X'(y_{\cdot i} - Z_i \tilde{\delta}_{\cdot i}) = R^{-1} X' \tilde{u}_{\cdot i},$$

where $\tilde{u}_{\cdot i}$ are the 2SLS residuals from the standard SF. Since R is obviously nonsingular we conclude

$$X' \tilde{u}_{\cdot i} = 0.$$

q.e.d.

It would be interesting to inquire whether the same is true of 3SLS residuals. The answer, in general, is no, and is a simple implication of

Corollary 3. Consider the GLSEM under the conditions of Theorem 3, and partition it into two subsets, the first consisting, say, of the first $m_*(< m)$ structural equations, and the second consisting of the remaining $m^*(= m - m_*)$ structural equations. Partition the matrices

$$Q, \quad \tilde{\Sigma}, \quad \tilde{\Phi}^{-1}, \quad \Sigma,$$

and the vectors w, δ (and r), conformably. In particular, let

$$\Sigma = \begin{bmatrix} \Sigma_{11} & \Sigma_{12} \\ \Sigma_{21} & \Sigma_{22} \end{bmatrix}$$

such that Σ_{11}, Σ_{22} correspond to the two subsystems, respectively.
The following statements are true:

i. if $\Sigma_{12} = 0$, $\Sigma_{21} = 0$, **and this is enforced at the estimation phase**, we can obtain the 3SLS estimator of $\delta_{(1)}$, $\delta_{(2)}$, once the system has been put in canonical structural form (CSF), by treating the two subsystems as (two) distinct GLSEMs and obtaining the 3SLS estimator of $\delta_{(1)}$ solely in the context of the first subsystem, and the 3SLS estimator of $\delta_{(2)}$ solely in the context of the second subsystem.

ii. if, instead of $\Sigma_{12} = 0$, $\Sigma_{21} = 0$, Σ is a general positive definite matrix but **the equations of the first subsystem are just identified**, and those of the second **overidentified**, then upon expressing the (entire) system in CSF, the 3SLS estimator of $\delta_{(2)}$ can be obtained **without reference to the first subsystem**, i.e. by obtaining the 3SLS estimator of the parameters of the overidentified subsystem, treating it as a distinct GLSEM; the 3SLS estimator of $\delta_{(1)}$ can be obtained as the 2SLS estimator of the parameters of the **just identified subsystem** plus a correction factor involving the (3SLS) residuals from the overidentified subsystem.

Proof: Although the Corollary refers to two conceptually distinct situations, their proof is very similar, and hence we have stated them together.
    Now, putting the entire system in CSF we can express the 3SLS estimator of its parameters as

$$Q'_{(1)}\tilde{\Phi}^{11}Q_{(1)}\delta_{(1)} + Q'_{(1)}\tilde{\Phi}^{12}Q_{(2)}\delta_{(2)} = Q'_{(1)}\tilde{\Phi}^{11}w_{(1)} + Q'_{(1)}\tilde{\Phi}^{12}w_{(2)}$$

$$Q'_{(2)}\tilde{\Phi}^{21}Q_{(1)}\delta_{(1)} + Q'_{(2)}\tilde{\Phi}^{22}Q_{(2)}\delta_{(2)} = Q'_{(2)}\tilde{\Phi}^{21}w_{(1)} + Q'_{(2)}\tilde{\Phi}^{22}w_{(2)}, \quad (1.78)$$

in the obvious partition notation, so that, for example, the first subsystem of m^* equations is

$$w_{(1)} = Q_{(1)}\delta_{(1)} + r_{(1)} \quad (1.79)$$

while the second subsystem of $m^*(= m - m^*)$ structural equations is given by

$$w_{(2)} = Q_{(2)}\delta_{(2)} + r_{(2)}.\qquad(1.80)$$

It is relatively simple to express Eq. (1.78), in partially solved form, as

$$\tilde{\delta}_{(1)} = (Q'_{(1)}\tilde{\Phi}^{11}Q_{(1)})^{-1}[Q'_{(1)}\tilde{\Phi}^{11}w_{(1)} + Q'_{(1)}\tilde{\Phi}^{12}(w_{(2)} - Q_{(2)}\tilde{\delta}_{(2)})]$$

$$\tilde{\delta}_{(2)} = (Q'_{(2)}\tilde{\Phi}^{22}Q_{(2)})^{-1}[Q'_{(2)}\tilde{\Phi}^{22}w_2 + Q'_{(2)}\tilde{\Phi}^{21}(w_1 - Q_{(1)}\tilde{\delta}_{(1)})],\quad(1.81)$$

which gives the 3SLS estimator of the parameters of one subsystem as a function of the 3SLS residuals from the other subsystem.

To prove part i, we note that if the conditions $\Sigma_{12} = 0$, $\Sigma_{21} = 0$ are enforced at the estimation phase

$$\tilde{\Phi}^{12} = \tilde{\Sigma}^{12} \otimes I = 0, \quad \tilde{\Phi}^{21} = \tilde{\Sigma}^{21} \otimes I = 0, \quad \tilde{\Phi}^{11} = \tilde{\Sigma}_{11}^{-1} \otimes I = \tilde{\Phi}_{11}^{-1}, \quad \tilde{\Phi}^{22} = \tilde{\Phi}_{22}^{-1}.$$

Thus, Eq. (1.81) reduces to

$$\tilde{\delta}_{(1)} = (Q'_{(1)}\tilde{\Phi}_{11}^{-1}Q_{(1)})^{-1}Q'_{(1)}\tilde{\Phi}_{11}^{-1}w_{(1)}$$

$$\tilde{\delta}_{(2)} = (Q'_{(2)}\tilde{\Phi}_{22}^{-1}Q_{(2)})^{-1}Q'_{(2)}\tilde{\Phi}_{22}^{-1}w_{(2)}.\qquad(1.82)$$

But Eq. (1.82) represents the 3SLS estimator of $\delta_{(1)}$ based solely on Eq. (1.79) and the 3SLS estimator of $\delta_{(2)}$ based solely on Eq. (1.80).

To prove part ii, we note that under its conditions, since the equations in Eq. (1.79) are **just identified**, the matrix $Q_{(1)}$ is **square and invertible**. Using this fact, we easily reduce Eq. (1.81) to

$$\tilde{\delta}_{(1)} = Q_{(1)}^{-1}w_{(1)} - Q_{(1)}^{-1}\tilde{\Phi}_{12}\tilde{\Phi}_{22}^{-1}(w_{(2)} - Q_{(2)}\tilde{\delta}_{(2)})$$

$$\tilde{\delta}_{(2)} = (Q_{(2)}\tilde{\Phi}_{22}^{-1}Q_{(2)})^{-1}Q'_{(2)}\tilde{\Phi}_{22}^{-1}w_{(2)},\qquad(1.83)$$

which shows that the 3SLS estimator of $\delta_{(2)}$ can be obtained as the 3SLS estimator of $\delta_{(2)}$ relying solely on the **overidentified subsystem**, i.e., relying solely on Eq. (1.80).

Moreover, the 3SLS estimator of $\delta_{(1)}$ is expressed as the 2SLS estimator $(Q_{(1)}^{-1}w_{(1)})$ plus a correction factor involving the 3SLS residuals **from the overidentified** system.

q.e.d.

Remark 18. Earlier, we asked whether the 3SLS residuals of a just identified equation in CSF are null, as is the case with 2SLS residuals; or, alternatively, whether they are orthogonal to the matrix of predetermined variables X. The answer is emphatically no, as is evident from the first equation of Eq. (1.83), unless the entire GLSEM is just identified. Thus, from Eq. (1.83) we obtain

$$w_{(1)} - Q_{(1)}\tilde{\delta}_{(1)} = \tilde{\Phi}_{12}\tilde{\Phi}_{22}^{-1}(w_{(2)} - Q_{(2)}\tilde{\delta}_{(2)}) \tag{1.84}$$

which shows such residuals to be a linear transformation of the (3SLS) residuals from the remaining (overidentified) equations, and as such, generally, nonnull. Of course, **if the second system is just identified as well**, then the second equation of Eq. (1.83) implies

$$\tilde{\delta}_{(2)} = Q_{(2)}^{-1}w_{(2)}, \quad w_{(2)} - Q_{(2)}\tilde{\delta}_{(2)} = 0$$

and we are reduced to the case where **all the equations of the GLSEM are just identified**. We have already demonstrated that, when this is so, the 2SLS and 3SLS estimators are identical.

1.8   Restricted 2SLS and 3SLS Estimators

Often, the situation arises that the economic theory underlying the phenomenon studied requires that the **vector** δ obey certain restrictions; moreover, it would not be unusual that such restrictions apply to parameters belonging to more than one equation. Implementing this procedure entails estimating the parameter vector δ, subject to such restrictions or, otherwise, using restricted least squares theory to test their validity. Indeed, we may also use the inference theory connected with restricted estimators to test the validity of some of the overidentifying restrictions routinely imposed on the GLSEM. We shall return to this topic at the end of this chapter.

We now investigate the following problem. Consider the GLSEM in CSF, i.e.,

$$w = Q\delta + r, \tag{1.85}$$

and let H be $n \times K$, $K = \sum_{i=1}^{m}(m_i + G_i)$ such that

$$\text{rank}(H) = n, \tag{1.86}$$

and its elements are known; let h be $n \times 1$ with known elements, and let it be desired to estimate the parameters of Eq. (1.85) subject to

$$H\delta = h. \tag{1.87}$$

Remark 19. The rank condition in Eq. (1.86) does not constitute a restriction on the generality of the results we are about to obtain. For example, if H^* is $(n + \tau) \times K$ of rank n and h^* is $(n + \tau) \times 1$ and we impose the restrictions $H^*\delta = h^*$ then, **to the extent that these restrictions form a consistent system of equations**, they can be reduced to

$$\begin{pmatrix} H \\ 0 \end{pmatrix} \delta = \begin{pmatrix} h \\ 0 \end{pmatrix},$$

which is simply Eq. (1.87) in conjunction with Eq. (1.86).

Now the 2SLS restricted estimator can be defined as the one that solves the problem

$$\min_{\delta} \frac{1}{T}(w - Q\delta)'(w - Q\delta)$$

subject to

$$H\delta = h.$$

The first order conditions to this problem are found by setting to zero the derivatives of

$$\Lambda = (1/T)(w - Q\delta)'(w - Q\delta) + 2\lambda'(h - H\delta) \tag{1.88}$$

with respect to δ and the vector of Lagrange multipliers λ. These conditions imply

$$\tilde{\delta}_{2SLSR} = \tilde{\delta}_{2SLS} + (Q'Q/T)^{-1}H'[H(Q'Q/T)^{-1}H']^{-1}(h - H\tilde{\delta}_{2SLS})$$

$$\tilde{\lambda} = [H(Q'Q/T)^{-1}H']^{-1}(h - H\tilde{\delta}_{2SLS}) \tag{1.89}$$

where $\tilde{\delta}_{2SLSR}$, $\tilde{\delta}_{2SLS}$ denote, respectively, the restricted and unrestricted 2SLS estimators of δ.

The restricted 3SLS estimator can easily be obtained by noting that 3SLS may be thought to be derived by minimizing with respect to δ

$$\frac{1}{T}(w - Q\delta)'\Phi^{-1}(w - Q\delta)$$

given a prior consistent estimator of Φ. Thus, the restricted 3SLS estimator can be obtained by solving the first order conditions of a Lagrangian problem similar to that in Eq. (1.88). The derivatives with respect to δ and λ of

$$\Lambda = (1/T)(w - Q\delta)'\tilde{\Phi}^{-1}(w - Q\delta) + 2\lambda'(h - H\delta) \tag{1.90}$$

imply

$$\frac{\partial\Lambda}{\partial\delta} = -(2/T)(w - Q\delta)'\tilde{\Phi}^{-1}Q - 2\lambda'H = 0,$$

$$\frac{\partial\Lambda}{\partial\delta} = 2(h - H\delta)' = 0.$$

Solving for δ and λ we find

$$\tilde{\delta}_{3SLSR} = \tilde{\delta}_{3SLS} + (Q'\tilde{\Phi}^{-1}Q/T)^{-1}H'[H(Q'\tilde{\Phi}^{-1}Q/T)^{-1}H']^{-1}(h - H\tilde{\delta}_{3SLS})$$

$$\tilde{\lambda} = [H(Q'\hat{\Phi}^{-1}Q/T)^{-1}H']^{-1}[h - H\tilde{\delta}_{3SLS}]. \tag{1.91}$$

The first equation in Eq. (1.91) gives the estimator that **minimizes**, with respect to δ,

$$\frac{1}{T}(w - Q\delta)'\tilde{\Phi}^{-1}(w - Q\delta),$$

subject to $H\delta = h$. Formally, the GLSEM in canonical structural form (CSF) can be thought of, as a system of GLMs; thus, the mechanics of operating with restricted estimators are identical with those in the context of the standard GLM. The latter problem is treated extensively elsewhere, see Dhrymes (1978). [11]

Remark 20. The perceptive reader will have noticed, from the previous section, that the 2SLS estimator **is not essentially** a systemwide estimator. It was presented as such only for simplicity and economy of exposition, and for ease of comparison with the 3SLS estimator which is **essentially a systemwide estimator.** What is meant by that is that 3SLS "naturally" obtains an estimator for all the parameters of the system (i.e., the elements of the vector δ) simultaneously. The 2SLS estimator, on the other hand, is "naturally" a single equation procedure, i.e., it obtains estimators of the subvectors, $\delta_{\cdot i}$, of δ one at a time–i.e., it estimates the parameters of the structural equations, one equation at a time. To the extent that the restrictions imposed by H "cut across" equations, i.e., the rows of H act on parameters appearing in more than one structural equation, the "single equation" character of 2SLS is destroyed. One may ask, then, why use the restricted estimator in Eq. (1.89) instead of that in Eq. (1.91). There may be many possible responses to that, but we need not discuss the merits or disadvantages of the two procedures. We simply treat the matter as a conceptual problem, and one to which we have provided a solution. It is neither desirable nor necessary, at this juncture, to enter upon a discourse on the possible applications of either procedure; we leave this to the judgement of the user, given the properties (as well as the vulnerabilities) of the two sets of estimators.

---

[11] The difference here is that we have divided the minimand by T, while in the GLM context we did not do so. It is necessary, in the GLSEM context, since the justification for this estimation procedure is essentially asymptotic. If we fail to divide by T, sample information embodied in $Q'Q$, or $Q'\tilde{\Phi}^{-1}Q$, which grows with T, will ultimately overwhelm or render irrelevant the "information" in the constraint $H\delta = h$, which does not. This is evident from the second equation of Eq. (1.91) which shows that if we fail to divide by T, the Lagrangian multiplier displayed therein would be ill defined, in the limit.

1.9   Tests of Prior Restrictions

1.9.1   Generalities

In previous sections, we derived the basic 2SLS and 3SLS estimators for the standard GLSEM. In the next chapter we shall derive their limiting distribution, and when we do so we shall have the means of carrying out various inferential procedures on the parameters of the GLSEM. We further note that in our derivations we have made use of *a priori* information, to the extent that some variables have been excluded from some equations. The perceptive reader would have noted, by now, that the estimation procedure we have employed does not allow us to **test the validity of the prior restrictions we have placed on our specification of the structural equations**; thus, we must assert that the specification imposed by the prior restrictions is correct but, we have no means of deciding *a posteriori* whether we were justified in imposing such restrictions. An "identifiability" test was given by Anderson and Rubin in the context of maximum likelihood estimation, and a test analogous to that was proposed by Basmann (1961) in the context of 2SLS, but it is fair to say that both have had relatively little impact on empirical applications. Sometime ago, Hausman (1978) proposed a test based on the difference between a consistent and an efficient estimator of the same parameter. The test statistic has, under the null, a certain chi squared limiting distribution; under the alternative, it has a noncentral chi square limiting distribution, with a certain **noncentrality parameter**. In our context, this procedure involves comparing the 2SLS and 3SLS estimators of the same parametric set. In Hausman's initial motivation, this procedure was asserted to be capable of testing the condition that

$$\operatorname*{plim}_{T\to\infty} \frac{X'U}{T} = 0,$$

without any reference as to the specific circumstances that may invalidate it. Thus, it was viewed as a **general misspecification test** that could test as a basis for testing the validity of all assumptions underlying the GLSEM. It was argued that, under the standard assumptions, the test statistic ought to assume certain values with a certain probability; if the test statistic fell in the rejection region, this would mean that the evidence of the sample did not support one of the implications of the set of assumptions underlying the GLSEM. Consequently, one or more of those assumptions should be rejected, or at least questioned very seriously. The test result, however, is quite incapable of informing us as to what condition has failed and thus the "reason" why the asymptotic orthogonality above is violated. Consequently, it is of little utility.

As is quite evident from the formulation above and was, in fact, developed in the subsequent literature, the framework in which this test is placed is too loose to yield powerful results. To appreciate this fact, we note that the statistic proposed is of the form

$$\psi_H = T \left(\hat{\delta}_{(2SLS)} - \hat{\delta}_{(3SLS)} \right)' (C_{2SLS} - C_{3SLS})_g \left(\hat{\delta}_{(2SLS)} - \hat{\delta}_{(3SLS)} \right) \sim \chi_d^2,$$

where $d = \text{rank}[(C_{2SLS} - C_{3SLS})_g]$, and the notation A_g indicates the **generalized inverse**. [12] It is clear that there are many circumstances under which the statistic ψ_H may not be asymptotically chi squared, such as, for example: the error process is one of (independent) but not identically distributed random vectors; some of the prior restrictions are invalid; some of the exogenous variables are not independent of the error process, and so on. Since no specific alternative is stated and the test is not designed with some specific consequence in mind, it is not clear how we can interpret the results of such tests.

In order to remedy these deficiencies we shall give an alternative procedure that specifically addresses the question of whether the prior restrictions imposed on the structure are valid, given that the validity of all other assumptions is not disputed. We shall do so by creating the basis for a much more direct approach, which operates in the following context: we assume the standard GLSEM, and we treat the enumeration of the dependent and predetermined variables in the context of the entire model as being correct, i.e. we treat them as **maintained hypotheses**. What is open to question, i.e. what may be treated as **testable hypotheses**, are the exclusion restrictions in each equation.

1.9.2   A Restricted Least Squares Interpretation of 2SLS and 3SLS

We begin our discussion by postulating the conditions of the GLSEM as given in Section 1.4.1, together with Convention 1; instead of Convention 2, however, we do not implement the restrictions in assumption (A.3) prior to estimation, but rather estimate parameters subject to that restriction. Thus, in the framework of the CSF, the 2SLS procedure is derived in the context of the following problem:

$$\min_{a_{\cdot i}} S_{T1}(a_{\cdot i}) = \frac{1}{T}(w_{\cdot i} - Q a_{\cdot i})'(w_{\cdot i} - Q a_{\cdot i}) \tag{1.92}$$

---

[12] If A is an $m \times n$ matrix then its generalized inverse, or g-inverse, is a unique $n \times m$ matrix, say A_g, such that

   i. $AA_gA = A$,

   ii. $A_gAA_g = A_g$,

   iii. AA_g and A_gA are symmetric matrices.

For further discussion see Dhrymes (1984), Ch. 3.

subject to

$$2L_i^{*\circ'} a_{\cdot i} = 0$$

where

$$L_i^{*\circ} = \begin{bmatrix} L_{1i}^{*\circ} & 0 \\ 0 & L_{2i}^* \end{bmatrix}, \quad L_{1i}^{*\circ} = (e_{\cdot i}, L_{1i}^*)$$

$$Q = R^{-1} X' Z, \quad A = (B', C')', \tag{1.93}$$

$a_{\cdot i}$ is the ith column of A, and L_{1i}^* is as defined in Remark 5; thus, note that $L_{1i}^{*\circ}$ is of full rank and dimension $m \times m - m_i$.[13] The matrix L_{2i}^* is as given in Definition 4 and is a permutation of $G_i^* = G - G_i$ columns of the matrix I_G. Notice, further, that in Eq. (1.93) we have defined Q in a slightly different manner than we did in previous sections; precisely, earlier we had defined $Q_i = R^{-1} X' Z_i$ and $Q = \text{diag}(Q_1, Q_2, \ldots, Q_m)$. In this contex (of LM-derived 2SLS and 3SLS derived estimators) it is much more convenient to define $Q = R^{-1} X' Z$ so that the Q_i of previous sections are simply the **submatrices of Q corresponding to the ith equation of the system**. For the notation to be totally consistent we **should have defined in the earlier sections $Q^* = \text{diag}(Q_1, Q_2, \ldots, Q_m)$**. We did not do so in the interest of notational simplicity. The likelihood of confusion is eliminated if the reader remembers that the definition $Q = R^{-1} X' Z$ occurs **only in the discussion of LM-derived 2SLS and 3SLS estimators and topics ancillary to that**.

Remark 21. We recall from Proposition 3 that the matrix L_i^* is of dimension $(m + G) \times (m_i^* + G_i^* - 1)$ and

$$\text{rank}(L_i^*) = m_i^* + G_i^* - 1.$$

It follows immediately that $L_i^{*\circ}$ is of dimension $(m + G) \times (m_i^* + G_i^*)$ and rank $m_i^* + G_i^*$, so that the matrix of restrictions in the constrained problem above is of full column rank. Letting $\lambda_{\cdot i}$ denote the vector of Lagrange multipliers, the first order conditions yield the set of equations

$$\begin{bmatrix} \frac{Q'Q}{T} & L_i^{*\circ} \\ L_i^{*\circ'} & 0 \end{bmatrix} \begin{bmatrix} a_{\cdot i} \\ \lambda_{\cdot i} \end{bmatrix} = \begin{bmatrix} \frac{Q' w_{\cdot i}}{T} \\ 0 \end{bmatrix}. \tag{1.94}$$

We observe that the matrix to be inverted in Eq. (1.94), for obtaining the estimators of the parameters and the Lagrange multipliers, is not of the

---

[13] This notation is necessary since, in this context, the normalization convention is imposed *ab initio*. Hence, we need notation to indicate the current endogenous variables that are excluded **from the right hand side** of the ith equation. In the maximum likelihood context, where no normalization convention is imposed until the very end, we need notation to indicate exclusion of current endogenous variables **from the ith equation**. Hence the dual notation.

standard partitioned form in that both diagonal blocks $(Q'Q/T)$ and 0 are singular. Due to a result in Dhrymes (1984),[14] the matrix above will be nonsingular if

$$\frac{Q'Q}{T} + L_i^{*\circ} L_i^{*\circ'}$$

is nonsingular. Since the matrix in question is sample dependent we shall deal with a suitable probability limit which depends only on the underlying structure. It is easy to demonstrate that

$$\operatorname*{plim}_{T\to\infty} \frac{Q'Q}{T} = (\Pi,\ I)' M_{xx}(\Pi,\ I) = K \tag{1.95}$$

where K is a matrix of dimension $(m + G) \times (m + G)$ and rank G. To show that the estimators defined by the solution to Eq. (1.94) exist, we need to show the validity of

Proposition 6. The matrix

$$K + L_i^{*\circ} L_i^{*\circ'}$$

is of full rank (nonsingular) if and only if the ith equation is identified.

Proof: Suppose the matrix above is of full rank, then

$$L_i'(K + L_i^{*\circ} L_i^{*\circ'})L_i$$

is also nonsingular. But this matrix is precisely

$$S_i' M_{xx} S_i$$

the nonsingularity of which [15] implies the identifiability of the ith structural equation.

---

[14] Specifically, see Proposition A.1, p.142.

[15] As we shall learn when we take up the discussion of maximum likelihood methods, the proper criterion for the identification of the ith equation is that the matrix $L_i^{\circ'} K L_i^{\circ}$ is of rank $m_i + G_i$. Its dimension, however, is $m_i + G_i + 1$, which affords us one degree of freedom. It is this feature that requires us to impose some normalization convention. Thus, in the context of the discussion of this section, where the **normalization convention is part of the initial specification**, we skip this slight complication and concentrate, instead, on the rank condition, as we have stated it above. The reader would do well to bear in mind, however, that, in the absence of an initial normalizing convention, the proper condition for the identifiability of the ith structural equation is that the $(m_i + G_i + 1) \times (m_i + G_i + 1)$ matrix

$$L_i^{\circ'} K L_i^{\circ} = \begin{bmatrix} (e_{\cdot i}', 0)K(e_{\cdot i}', 0)' & (e_{\cdot i}', 0)K L_i \\ L_i' K(e_{\cdot i}', 0)' & L_i' K L_i \end{bmatrix}$$

is of rank $m_i + G_i$. If the conventional normalization can be imposed on the ith equation, then we can state that the equation in question is identified if and only if $L_i' K L_i = S_i' M_{xx} S_i$, is of full rank, i.e., it is **nonsingular**.

Next suppose the ith equation is identified; we show that the matrix $K + L_i^{*\circ} L_i^{*\circ'}$ is nonsingular. Consider the matrix

$$H_i^\circ = (L_i, L_i^{*\circ}),\qquad (1.96)$$

and note that it is a nonsingular matrix of order $m + G$. If $K + L_i^{*\circ} L_i^{*\circ'}$ is singular, its column null space contains at least one nonnull $m + G$-element column vector, say h. We may thus write

$$h = H_i^\circ e,\quad e = (e_{(1)}', e_{(2)}')',\qquad (1.97)$$

where $e_{(1)}$ and $e_{(2)}$ are, respectively, $m_i + G_i$- and $m - m_i + G_i^*$-element column vectors. Thus, we have

$$0 = h'(K + L_i^{*\circ} L_i^{*\circ'})h = e' H_i^{\circ'}(K + L_i^{*\circ} L_i^{*\circ'})H_i^\circ e = e' H_i^{\circ'} K H_i^\circ e + e_{(2)}' e_{(2)}.\qquad (1.98)$$

Since the first quadratic form in the rightmost member is positive semidefinite, we must have that $e_{(2)} = 0$. This in turn implies that the first quadratic form obeys $e_{(1)}' L_i' K L_i e_{(1)} = 0$, or that $L_i' K L_i$ is singular, unless $e_{(1)} = 0$. The former, however, is ruled out by the identification of the equation in question. Thus Eq. (1.98) can hold only for $h = 0$ and we conclude that $K + L_i^{*\circ} L_i^{*\circ'}$ is nonsingular.

q.e.d.

Thus, Eq. (1.94) may be solved uniquely, to obtain

$$\hat{a}_{\cdot i} = \tilde{E}_{2i}\left(\frac{Q' w_{\cdot i}}{T}\right),\quad \hat{\lambda}_{\cdot i} = \left(L_i^{*\circ'} \tilde{V}_{2i} L_i^{*\circ}\right)^{-1} L_i^{*\circ'} \tilde{V}_{2i}\left(\frac{Q' w_{\cdot i}}{T}\right),\quad (1.99)$$

where

$$\tilde{V}_{2i} = \left(\tilde{K} + L_i^{*\circ} L_i^{*\circ'}\right)^{-1},\quad \tilde{K} = \frac{Q'Q}{T}$$

$$\tilde{E}_{2i} = [\tilde{V}_{2i} - \tilde{V}_{2i} L_i^{*\circ}(L_i^{*\circ'} \tilde{V}_{2i} L_i^{*\circ})^{-1} L_i^{*\circ'} \tilde{V}_{2i}].\qquad (1.100)$$

Making the appropriate substitutions in Eq. (1.99) and noting that

$$\tilde{V}_{2i}\frac{Q' w_{\cdot i}}{T} = a_{\cdot i} - \tilde{V}_{2i} L_i^{*\circ} L_i^{*\circ'} a_{\cdot i} + \tilde{V}_{2i}(\tilde{\Pi}, I)'\frac{X' u_{\cdot i}}{T},$$

we establish that

$$\hat{a}_{\cdot i} - a_{\cdot i} = -\tilde{V}_{2i} L_i^{*\circ}(L_i^{*\circ'} \tilde{V}_{2i} L_i^{*\circ})^{-1} L_i^{*\circ'} a_{\cdot i}\qquad (1.101)$$

$$+ [\tilde{V}_{2i} - \tilde{V}_{2i} L_i^{*\circ}(L_i^{*\circ'} \tilde{V}_{2i} L_i^{*\circ})^{-1} L_i^{*\circ'} \tilde{V}_{2i}](\tilde{\Pi}, I)'\frac{X' u_{\cdot i}}{T}$$

$$\hat{\lambda}_{\cdot i} = -[I - (L_i^{*\circ'} \tilde{V}_{2i} L_i^{*\circ})^{-1}] L_i^{*\circ'} a_{\cdot i}\qquad (1.102)$$

$$+ (L_i^{*\circ'} \tilde{V}_{2i} L_i^{*\circ})^{-1} L_i^{*\circ'} \tilde{V}_{2i}(\tilde{\Pi}, I)'\frac{X' u_{\cdot i}}{T},$$

since

$$Z'X(X'X)^{-1} = (\tilde{\Pi}, \, I)'.$$

Although it is intuitively clear that the estimator in Eq. (1.101) **is the 2SLS estimator**, a formal demonstration of this fact is in order. To do so, we first observe that

$$L_i'(\hat{a}_{\cdot i} - a_{\cdot i}) = \hat{\delta}_{\cdot i} - \delta_{\cdot i},$$

and moreover, according to the standard specification, $L_i^{*\circ'} a_{\cdot i} = 0$. Next, note that

$$[\tilde{V}_{2i} - \tilde{V}_{2i} L_i^{*\circ} (L_i^{*\circ'} \tilde{V}_{2i} L_i^{*\circ})^{-1} L_i^{*\circ'} \tilde{V}_{2i}] L_i^{*\circ} = 0,$$

and in addition,

$$H_i^\circ H_i^{\circ'} = L_i L_i' + L_i^{*\circ} L_i^{*\circ'} = I.$$

This is so since the matrix H_i° of Eq. (1.96) is orthogonal; thus, we conclude

$$L_i'(\hat{a}_{\cdot i} - a_{\cdot i}) = L_i'[\tilde{V}_{2i} - \tilde{V}_{2i} L_i^{*\circ} (L_i^{*\circ'} \tilde{V}_{2i} L_i^{*\circ})^{-1} L_i^{*\circ'} \tilde{V}_{2i}] L_i L_i'(\tilde{\Pi}, \, I)' \frac{X' u_{\cdot i}}{T}.$$

To complete the demonstration we need only show that

$$L_i' \left[\tilde{V}_{2i} - \tilde{V}_{2i} L_i^{*\circ} (L_i^{*\circ'} \tilde{V}_{2i} L_i^{*\circ})^{-1} L_i^{*\circ'} \tilde{V}_{2i} \right] L_i = (\tilde{S}_i' \tilde{M}_{xx} \tilde{S}_i)^{-1}, \qquad (1.103)$$

where

$$\tilde{M}_{xx} = \frac{X'X}{T}.$$

We note, however, that the matrix (in square brackets) in the left member of Eq. (1.103) is the inverse of the $(1,1)$ block of $\tilde{J}^{-1}$, where

$$\tilde{J} = H_i^{\circ'} \tilde{V}_{2i} H_i^\circ = \begin{bmatrix} L_i' \tilde{V}_{2i} L_i & L_i' \tilde{V}_{2i} L_i^{*\circ} \\ L_i^{*\circ'} \tilde{V}_{2i} L_i & L_i^{*\circ'} \tilde{V}_{2i} L_i^{*\circ} \end{bmatrix}, \qquad (1.104)$$

$$\tilde{J}^{-1} = \left(H_i^{\circ'} \tilde{V}_{2i} H_i^\circ \right)^{-1} = H_i^{\circ'} \tilde{V}_{2i}^{-1} H_i^\circ = \begin{bmatrix} L_i' \tilde{K} L_i & L_i' \tilde{K} L_i^{*\circ} \\ L_i^{*\circ'} \tilde{K} L_i & L_i^{*\circ'} \tilde{K} L_i^{*\circ} + I \end{bmatrix}.$$

It follows, immediately, from Eq. (1.104) that

$$(L_i' \tilde{K} L_i)^{-1} = L_i' \left[\tilde{V}_{2i} - \tilde{V}_{2i} L_i^{*\circ} (L_i^{*\circ'} \tilde{V}_{2i} L_i^{*\circ})^{-1} L_i^{*\circ'} \tilde{V}_{2i} \right] L_i, \qquad (1.105)$$

$$L_i' \tilde{K} L_i = \tilde{S}_i' \tilde{M}_{xx} \tilde{S}_i, \quad \tilde{K} = (\tilde{\Pi}, I)' \tilde{M}_{xx} (\tilde{\Pi}, I), \quad (\tilde{\Pi}, I) L_i = \tilde{S}_i$$

which completes the formal demonstration that the restricted least squares version of the 2SLS estimator is, indeed, what was claimed to be.

We close this section, by giving the generalization of this procedure to the systemwide 2SLS and 3SLS estimators. For the systemwide 2SLS estimator, we formulate the problem as

$$\min_a S_{T2}(a) = \frac{1}{T}[w - (I \otimes Q)a]'[w - (I \otimes Q)a] \qquad (1.106)$$

subject to

$$2L^{*\circ'}a = 0, \quad \text{where} \quad a = \text{vec}\begin{pmatrix} B \\ C \end{pmatrix},$$

and, evidently, $L^{*\circ} = \text{diag}(L_1^{*\circ}, L_2^{*\circ}, \ldots, L_m^{*\circ})$.

For the 3SLS estimator, given a prior (consistent) estimate of the covariance matrix, say, $\tilde{\Phi} = (\tilde{\Sigma} \otimes I)$, the problem may be posed as

$$\min_a S_{T3}(a) = \frac{1}{T}[w - (I \otimes Q)a]'\tilde{\Phi}^{-1}[w - (I \otimes Q)a] \qquad (1.107)$$

subject to

$$2L^{*\circ'}a = 0.$$

The solution to this problem renders the 3SLS as a **restricted** GLS, or a **restricted** feasible Aitken estimator of the structural parameters of the system.

We now show that the formal aspects of these problems are identical to those encountered when we considered a single equation; thus, the objective function of the formulation in Eq. (1.105) is

$$\Lambda_2 = \frac{1}{T}[w - (I \otimes Q)a]'[w - (I \otimes Q)a] + 2\lambda'L^{*\circ'}a$$

and the equations to be solved for the estimators and the Lagrange multipliers (first order conditions) are

$$\begin{bmatrix} A_{11} & L^{*\circ} \\ L^{*\circ'} & 0 \end{bmatrix}\begin{bmatrix} a \\ \lambda \end{bmatrix} = \begin{bmatrix} \frac{1}{T}(I \otimes Q)'w \\ 0 \end{bmatrix}$$

where $A_{11} = (1/T)(I \otimes Q)'(I \otimes Q)$ and $\lambda = (\lambda'_{\cdot 1}, \ldots, \lambda'_{\cdot m})'$ denotes the multipliers corresponding to the restrictions on the parameters (appearing in the right hand side) of the m structural equations. The solution, then, gives the systemwide 2SLS estimator – including those parameters set to zero by prior information.

For the 3SLS case, i.e. the formulation given in Eq. (1.107), the objective function is

$$\Lambda_3 = \frac{1}{T}[w - (I \otimes Q)a]'\tilde{\Phi}^{-1}[w - (I \otimes Q)a] + 2\lambda'L^{*\circ'}a$$

and the first order conditions are

$$\begin{bmatrix} A_{11} & L^{*\circ} \\ L^{*\circ'} & 0 \end{bmatrix}\begin{bmatrix} a \\ \lambda \end{bmatrix} = \begin{bmatrix} \frac{1}{T}(I \otimes Q)'\tilde{\Phi}^{-1}w \\ 0 \end{bmatrix}$$

where $A_{11} = (1/T)(I \otimes Q)'\tilde{\Phi}^{-1}(I \otimes Q)$ and $\lambda = (\lambda'_{\cdot 1}, \ldots, \lambda'_{\cdot m})'$ denotes the multipliers corresponding to the restrictions on the parameters (appearing in the right hand side) of the m structural equations. The solution to that system gives the 3SLS estimator – including all the parameters set to zero by prior information.

It is quite apparent that the two procedures are formally identical with that employed in the case of a single equation. Thus, in the interest of brevity we shall give the relevant representations only for the 3SLS. Solving the matrix equation above yields,

$$\hat{a} = \tilde{E}_3 \left(\frac{(\tilde{\Sigma}^{-1} \otimes Q)' w}{T} \right),$$

$$\hat{\lambda} = \left(L^{*\circ'} \tilde{V}_3 L^{*\circ} \right)^{-1} L^{*\circ'} \tilde{V}_3 \left[\frac{(\tilde{\Sigma}^{-1} \otimes Q)' w}{T} \right], \tag{1.108}$$

where

$$\tilde{V}_3 = \left[(\tilde{\Sigma}^{-1} \otimes \tilde{K}) + L^{*\circ} L^{*\circ'} \right]^{-1}, \quad \tilde{K} = \frac{Q'Q}{T}$$

$$\tilde{E}_3 = [\tilde{V}_3 - \tilde{V}_3 L^{*\circ} (L^{*\circ'} \tilde{V}_3 L^{*\circ})^{-1} L^{*\circ'} \tilde{V}_3]. \tag{1.109}$$

Making the appropriate substitutions in Eq. (1.108) we establish that

$$\hat{a} - a = -\tilde{V}_3 L^{*\circ} (L^{*\circ'} \tilde{V}_3 L^{*\circ})^{-1} L^{*\circ'} a \tag{1.110}$$

$$+ [\tilde{V}_3 - \tilde{V}_3 L^{*\circ} (L^{*\circ'} \tilde{V}_3 L^{*\circ})^{-1} L^{*\circ'} \tilde{V}_3][\tilde{\Sigma}^{-1} \otimes (\tilde{\Pi}, I)'] \frac{(I \otimes X)' u}{T}$$

$$\hat{\lambda} = -[I - (L^{*\circ'} \tilde{V}_3 L^{*\circ})^{-1}] L^{*\circ'} a \tag{1.111}$$

$$+ (L^{*\circ'} \tilde{V}_3 L^{*\circ})^{-1} L^{*\circ'} \tilde{V}_3 [\tilde{\Sigma}^{-1} \otimes (\tilde{\Pi}, I)'] \frac{(I \otimes X)' u}{T}.$$

Remark 22. The procedure outlined above enables us to carry out specification tests utilizing efficient estimators, without having to compute inefficient consistent estimators for comparison. Thus, if we choose a subset of the prior restrictions for testing, we can test for their validity using the limiting distribution of certain subsets of Lagrange multipliers; we do not need, as in the case of Hausman's test, to obtain the 2SLS estimators and base our test on the difference between them. The precise nature of the tests and their characteristics will be taken up in Chapter 2, after we have derived the limiting distribution of the underlying 2SLS and 3SLS estimators.

Remark 23. In this chapter we have given **three independent** derivations of the 2SLS and 3SLS estimators. First, the original derivation as given by Theil for 2SLS, and as given by Theil and Zellner (1962) for 3SLS; second, we have given a derivation based on the canonical structural form (CSF) first given in Dhrymes (1969). Both these procedures impose the prior restrictions **before estimation**, and obtain parameter estimates given these restrictions. The third procedure again operates with the CSF, but imposes the prior restrictions, **other than normalization**, by means of Lagrange multipliers and **obtains simultaneously** estimates of all the parameters as well as the Lagrange multipliers (treated as additional parameters). This procedure **is to be distinguished from** restricted 2SLS and 3SLS, where the *a priori* restrictions, including normalization conventions, are imposed **before estimation** and **only additional restrictions**, (beyond the *a priori* restrictions) are imposed by means of Lagrange multipliers.

Each of the three derivations has its own attractions; the first is evidently of historical significance; the second facilitates the understanding of simultaneous equations inference in this context since, in CSF, 2SLS and 3SLS can be rendered as OLS and GLS problems, respectively. Finally, the third derivation makes it particularly simple to test the validity of prior restrictions.

Questions and Problems

1. In connection with the discussion surrounding Eqs. (1.41) and (1.42) verify that

$$\Pi L_{1i} = \Pi_i, \ L_{2i}' M_{xx} L_{2i} = M_{x_i x_i}, \ L_{1i}' \Omega L_{1i} = \Omega_{ii}$$

   where

$$M_{x_i x_i} = \operatorname*{plim}_{T \to \infty} \frac{X_i' X_i}{T}.$$

2. In connection with the discussion surrounding Eq. (1.48) show that

$$J_i' S_i = \begin{bmatrix} \Pi_{1i} & I_{Gi} \\ \Pi_{2i} & 0 \end{bmatrix}.$$

   Hint: $X \Pi_i = X_i \Pi_{1i} + X_i^* \Pi_{2i} = X J_i J_i' \Pi_i$.

3. In the discussion of the inconsistency of the OLS estimator of the parameters of a structural equation, show that if

$$S_i' M_{xx} S_i$$

   is invertible, so is

$$S_i' M_{xx} S_i + \begin{bmatrix} \Omega_{ii} & 0 \\ 0 & 0 \end{bmatrix}.$$

   Hint: Ω_{ii} is positive definite.

4. In the discussion following Eq. (1.52) show that if

$$Y_i = \tilde{Y}_i + \tilde{V}_i$$

where $\tilde{V}_i$ is the matrix of OLS residuals, then $\tilde{V}_i' \tilde{Y}_i = 0$

Hint: $\tilde{V}_i = [I - X(X'X)^{-1}X']Y_i$.

5. In connection with Eq. (1.63) show that Q is of full rank.

Hint: All equations of the GLSEM are assumed to be identified.

6. In connection with the proof of part ii. of Corollary 3, verify the reduction of Eq. (1.81) to Eq. (1.83), when the first system is just identified.

Hint: Use the partitioned inverse form for Σ^{-1}, viz.

$$\Sigma^{22} = (\Sigma_{22} - \Sigma_{21}\Sigma_{11}^{-1}\Sigma_{12})^{-1}, \quad \Sigma^{12} = -\Sigma_{11}^{-1}\Sigma_{12}\Sigma^{22},$$

$$\Sigma^{21} = -\Sigma_{22}^{-1}\Sigma_{21}\Sigma^{11}, \quad \Sigma^{11} = (\Sigma_{11} - \Sigma_{12}\Sigma_{22}^{-1}\Sigma_{21})^{-1}.$$

7. Justify the estimators in Eq. (1.89) by explicitly deriving the first order conditions.

8. Derive the first order conditions represented by Eq. (1.94). Also show that the matrix H_i° of Eq. (1.96) is orthogonal.

9. In connection with the estimators in Eq. (1.101), verify their derivation, using the following result for symmetric matrices [16]

$$\begin{bmatrix} A_{11} & A_{12} \\ A_{21} & A_{22} \end{bmatrix}^{-1} = \begin{bmatrix} \frac{Q'Q}{T} & L_i^{*\circ} \\ L_i^{*\circ'} & 0 \end{bmatrix}^{-1} = \begin{bmatrix} B_{11} & B_{12} \\ B_{21} & B_{22} \end{bmatrix};$$

$$B_{11} = \tilde{V}_{2i} - \tilde{V}_{2i}L_i^{*\circ}V_{22}L_i^{*\circ'}\tilde{V}_{2i}, \quad B_{12} = -\tilde{V}_{2i}L_i^{*\circ}V_{22}';$$

$$B_{21} = -V_{22}L_i^{*\circ'}\tilde{V}_{2i}, \quad B_{22} = V_{22} - V_{22}L_i^{*\circ'}\tilde{V}_{2i}L_i^{*\circ};$$

$$\tilde{V}_{2i} = (A_{11} + A_{12}A_{21})^{-1}, \quad V_{22} = (A_{22} - A_{21}\tilde{V}_{2i}A_{12} - A_{21}\tilde{V}_{2i}A_{12}A_{22})^{-1}.$$

Note: The condition that $I - L_i^{*\circ'}\tilde{V}_{2i}L_i^{*\circ}$ be nonsingular in the reference above may be dispensed with, i.e. the proof can be carried out in the absence of this condition.

10. In Proposition 6, verify that $L_i'(K + L_i^{*\circ}L_i^{*\circ'})L_i = S_i'M_{xx}S_i$.

Hint: $S_i = (\Pi_i, I)$.

11. In the proof of Proposition 6, verify that the condition $L_i'KL_i$ is singular implies that the ith equation is not identified.

---

[16] Dhrymes (1984), Corollary A.1, p. 143.

Appendix to Chapter 1

Preliminaries to Hausman's Test

In the last sections of the preceding chapter we had discussed how the validity of the prior restrictions may be tested, and we had mentioned a test proposed by Hausman (1978). In view of the fact that there is a substantial body of empirical research that relies, at least partially, on that test it is useful that the practicing econometrician have a working knowledge of it, its attractive features, as well as its limitations. On the other hand, the test *per se* is only of peripheral and minor interest in the context of our discussion, and for this reason its discussion is carried out in the appendix.

An important element in the derivation of the Hausman test and its distribution is to show that the difference between the two estimators compared, i.e. the consistent and the efficient estimator, is **asymptotically independent** of the efficient estimator. This feature, actually, has a much broader aspect and is a salient property of **minimum variance estimators**. We begin the analysis of this subject by exploring the characterization of the minimum variance estimator and certain other pertinent aspects of this topic. [17]

Proposition A1. Let $(\Omega, \mathcal{A}, P)$ be a probability space and $P_\Theta = \{P_\theta : \theta \in \Theta\}$ be a collection of probability measures (defined on $\mathcal{A}$), where

---

[17] The ensuing discussion is a modification and extension of the treatment of this subject in Rao (1972).

$\Theta \subset R^k$, i.e., we are dealing with a k-dimensional parameter space. Let U_g be a class of estimators, $\tilde{\theta}_1$, such that

$$E(\tilde{\theta}_1) = g(\theta).$$

Let U_0 be the class of estimators, say $\tilde{\theta}_2$, such that $E(\tilde{\theta}_2) = 0$. Suppose, further, that

$$\text{Cov}(\tilde{\theta}_1 \mid \theta = \theta_0) = C_{11} > 0, \quad \text{Cov}(\tilde{\theta}_2 \mid \theta = \theta_0) = C_{22} > 0.$$

A necessary and sufficient condition that an estimator, $\tilde{\theta}_1$, be a minimum variance estimator for $g(\theta)$, at the point $\theta = \theta_0$, is that

$$\text{Cov}(\tilde{\theta}_1, \tilde{\theta}_2 \mid \theta = \theta_0) = C_{12} = 0.$$

Proof: (Necessity) Let $\tilde{\theta}_1$ be the minimum variance estimator at the point θ_0 and let $\tilde{\theta}_2 \in U_0$. Let

$$A = C_{12}C_{22}^{-1}, \quad t \in R \text{ (i.e. } t \text{ is a scalar)},$$

and consider

$$\text{Cov}(\tilde{\theta}_1 + tA\tilde{\theta}_2 \mid \theta = \theta_0) = C_{11} + (t^2 + 2t)C_{12}C_{22}^{-1}C_{21}.$$

If $C_{12} \neq 0$, we obtain a contradiction by taking $t = -1$. Hence, necessity is proved.

(Sufficiency) Let $\tilde{\theta}_1, \tilde{\theta}_3 \in U_g$, and suppose $\tilde{\theta}_1$ is the minimum variance estimator. Then, $\tilde{\theta} = \tilde{\theta}_1 - \tilde{\theta}_3 \in U_0$. By the previous discussion, $\text{Cov}(\tilde{\theta}_1, \tilde{\theta} \mid \theta = \theta_0) = 0$, which implies $C_{13} = C_{11}$. Consequently,

$$0 \leq \text{Cov}(\tilde{\theta}_1 - \tilde{\theta}_3 \mid \theta = \theta_0) = C_{11} - C_{13} - C_{31} + C_{33} = C_{33} - C_{11},$$

which proves sufficiency.

$$\text{q.e.d.}$$

Definition A1. In the context of Proposition A1, let

$$X_i : \Omega \longrightarrow R^n, \quad i = 1, 2, \ldots, T,$$

be a sequence of (n-element) random vectors. A statistic, $\tilde{\theta}$, is said to be **sufficient** for θ , if and only if for every set $A \in \mathcal{A}$ there exist $\mathcal{A}$-measurable functions, h_θ and r such that

$$P_\theta(A) = h_\theta(A)r(A),$$

and r does not contain θ .

A statistic $\tilde{\theta}_1$ is said to be **complete** if and only if for every $\mathcal{A}$-measurable function, g,

$$\int_\Omega g(\tilde{\theta}_1) d P_\theta = 0$$

implies $g(\tilde{\theta}_1) = 0$, a.c. (almost certainly, or with probability one), for every $P_\theta \in P_\Theta$.

Remark A1. The characterization of a sufficient statistic may also be rendered in the more familiar form, $\tilde{\theta}(X_1, X_2, \ldots, X_T)$ is sufficient for θ if and only if the joint density of the observations, say f, obeys

$$f(X_1, X_2, \ldots, X_T) = p(\tilde{\theta}; \theta) r(X_1, X_2, \ldots, X_T),$$

where p is (proportional to) the density of $\tilde{\theta}$ and r **does not depend on** θ.

We now prove the important

Proposition A2 (Rao-Blackwell Theorem). In the context of Definition A1, let $\tilde{\theta}$ be a sufficient statistic for the parameter $\theta \in \Theta$, and let $\tilde{\theta}_1$ be any other estimator. The following statements are true.

  i. If $\tilde{\theta}_1$ is **unbiased for** $h(\theta)$ then

$$E[s(\tilde{\theta})] = h(\theta),$$

   where $s(\tilde{\theta}) = E(\tilde{\theta}_1 \mid \tilde{\theta})$, i.e., it is the conditional expectation of $\tilde{\theta}_1$ **given** $\tilde{\theta}$.

 ii. For any measurable function, h, $\tilde{\theta}_1$ is an inefficient estimator of $h(\theta)$, in the mean square error (MSE) sense, i.e.,

$$E[\tilde{\theta}_1 - h(\theta)][\tilde{\theta}_1 - h(\theta)]' \geq E[s(\tilde{\theta}) - h(\theta)][s(\tilde{\theta}) - h(\theta)]'.$$

iii. If W is **any convex loss function**

$$E[W(\tilde{\theta}_1, \theta)] \geq E[W(s(\tilde{\theta}), \theta)].$$

Proof: We note that, by the property of conditional expectations,

$$E[s(\tilde{\theta})] = E_{\tilde{\theta}}[E(\tilde{\theta}_1 \mid \tilde{\theta})] = E(\tilde{\theta}_1) = h(\theta),$$

which proves part i of the proposition.

To prove part ii, introduce the notation,

$$h_1^* = \tilde{\theta}_1 - h(\theta), \quad h_2^* = \tilde{\theta}_1 - s(\tilde{\theta}), \quad h^* = s(\tilde{\theta}) - h(\theta),$$

and note that

$$h_1^* h_1^{*'} = [h_2^* + h^*][h_2^* + h^*]' = h_2^* h_2^{*'} + h^* h^{*'} + h_2^* h^{*'} + h^* h_2^{*'}.$$

Taking expectations conditional on $\tilde{\theta}$, the last two members of the right-most member above vanish, so that taking expectations again, with respect to $\tilde{\theta}$, we obtain

$$\text{MSE}(\tilde{\theta}_1) - \text{MSE}[s(\tilde{\theta})] = E(h_2^* h_2^{*'}) \geq 0,$$

which proves part i.

As for part iii, we note that by the convexity of W, see for example Proposition 14, in Dhrymes (1989, p. 107),

$$E[W(\tilde{\theta}_1, \theta) \mid \tilde{\theta}] \geq W[E(\tilde{\theta}_1 \mid \tilde{\theta})] = W[s(\tilde{\theta}), \theta].$$

Consequently, taking expectations again with respect to $\tilde{\theta}$, we find $E[W(\tilde{\theta}_1, \theta)] \geq E[W(s(\tilde{\theta}), \theta)]$.

q.e.d.

The result above is used to construct an efficient estimator within the class of unbiased estimators, when an unbiased estimator and a sufficient statistic exist for the parameter in question. Thus, suppose $\tilde{\theta}_i$, $i = 1, 2$ are, respectively, an **unbiased** estimator and a **sufficient statistic**, not necessarily unbiased, for a given parameter θ. Clearly, the conditional expectation $E(\tilde{\theta}_1 \mid \tilde{\theta}_2) = g(\tilde{\theta}_2)$ is a sufficient statistic for θ. Moreover,

$$E[E(\tilde{\theta}_1 \mid \tilde{\theta}_2)] = \theta,$$

since $\tilde{\theta}_1$ is an unbiased estimator. By the Rao-Blackwell theorem,

$$\text{Cov}(\tilde{\theta}_1) - \text{Cov}[\text{g}(\tilde{\theta}_2)] \geq 0.$$

In fact, if a **complete sufficient statistic** is available for a given parameter, and if an unbiased estimator for the parameter in question exists, we can find a **unique minimum variance estimator**.

Remark A2. The test suggested by Hausman, essentially, employs the insights gained from Propositions A1 and A2 in order to test for misspecification in the case of the GLSEM and, indeed, other circumstances as well. What is meant by misspecification is, generally, the condition that the explanatory variables in the GLM (the variables in the matrix X), or the predetermined variables in the GLSEM, are not uncorrelated with the error sequence. Its great advantage is that a test of this kind is almost always available, and in a great variety of circumstances. Its disadvantage and severe limitation is that since the alternative is not clearly stated the intepretation of the results of such tests is highly problematic.

Examples

To illustrate the procedure and the problems involved, consider the GLM $y = X\beta + u$, under the standard assumptions; suppose we wish to test the hypothesis $\text{Cov}(u) = \Sigma$, where Σ is an appropriate covariance matrix for which a consistent estimator, say $\tilde{\Sigma}$, is available. Let $\tilde{\beta}_i$, $i = 1, 2$, be the OLS and GLS (feasible Aitken) estimators of β. Note that both estimators are consistent and if the null is correct (i.e., if, indeed, $\text{Cov}(u) = \Sigma$,) the GLS estimator is **asymptotically** efficient relative to the OLS estimator. From the discussion above we are led to consider

$$\sqrt{T}(\tilde{\beta}_1 - \tilde{\beta}_2).$$

When we deal with limiting distributions in Chapter 2, the development therein will imply that

$$\sqrt{T}(\tilde{\beta}_1 - \tilde{\beta}_2) \sim N(0, C_{OLS} - C_{GLS}),$$

where

$$C_{OLS} = \plim_{T \to \infty} \left(\frac{X'X}{T}\right)^{-1} \left(\frac{X'\Sigma X}{T}\right) \left(\frac{X'X}{T}\right)^{-1},$$

$$C_{GLS} = \plim_{T \to \infty} \left(\frac{X'\Sigma^{-1}X}{T}\right)^{-1}.$$

Thus, the difference $\sqrt{T}(\tilde{\beta}_1 - \tilde{\beta}_2)$, may be taken to be, asymptotically, an unbiased estimator of zero. Again, from Chapter 2, we may establish that the limiting distribution of

$$\sqrt{T}\begin{pmatrix} \tilde{\beta}_1 - \tilde{\beta}_2 \\ \tilde{\beta}_2 \end{pmatrix} \sim N(0, G),$$

where

$$G = \begin{bmatrix} C_{OLS} - C_{GLS} & 0 \\ 0 & C_{GLS} \end{bmatrix}.$$

This shows that, asymptotically, $\tilde{\beta}_1 - \tilde{\beta}_2$ is (uncorrelated) independent of $\tilde{\beta}_2$. By Proposition A1, [18] we conclude that $\tilde{\beta}_2$ is the minimum variance estimator. It follows, then, that the specification test statistic suggested by Hausman is given, asymptotically, by

$$T(\tilde{\beta}_1 - \tilde{\beta}_2)'(C_{OLS} - C_{GLS})_g(\tilde{\beta}_1 - \tilde{\beta}_2) \sim \chi^2_{\text{rank}(C_{OLS} - C_{GLS})}.$$

---

[18] Strictly speaking, in order to invoke Proposition A1 we must show that $\tilde{\beta}_2$ is, asymptotically, uncorrelated with **every** unbiased estimator of zero. On the other hand, we could show by more direct means that $\tilde{\beta}_2$ satisfies the Cramer-Rao bound.

It is not entirely clear just what rejection (or acceptance) would mean in this context. It could mean, for example, that the covariance matrix is not of the particular form specified; in such a case rejection would have nothing to do with the issue of whether $(X'u/T) \xrightarrow{P} 0$.

Perhaps another example will give a sharper illustration of the ambiguities entailed by such tests. Consider again the **standard** GLM above, and suppose it is desired to examine the restriction $R\beta = r$, where R and r are appropriate and known matrix and vector, respectively. Let

$$\tilde{\beta}_1 = C_1 y, \quad \tilde{\beta}_2 = \tilde{\beta}_1 + (X'X)^{-1} R'C(r - R\tilde{\beta}_1), \quad C = [R(X'X)^{-1}R]^{-1},$$

i.e., $\tilde{\beta}_2$ is the **restricted least squares** estimator. If the error sequence obeys the standard conditions then

$$(\tilde{\beta}_1 - \tilde{\beta}_2) \sim N(0, \sigma^2 (X'X)^{-1} R'CR(X'X)^{-1}).$$

As in the standard Hausman context, when $R\beta = r$ is true, we have an efficient estimator, viz. $\tilde{\beta}_2$. The OLS estimator, $\hat{\beta}_1$, is inefficient when the parameter constraint holds but, is nonetheless consistent whether the condition $R\beta = r$ is or is not valid. Moreover, the restricted estimator will be **inconsistent** if the condition above fails to hold. From the distribution above we can now construct the Hausman statistic. Before we do, however, let us simplify the notation somewhat. Put

$$H = (X'X)^{-1} R'CR(X'X)^{-1}, \quad \tilde{\beta} = (\tilde{\beta}_1 - \tilde{\beta}_2),$$

and note that

$$\tilde{\beta} = (X'X)^{-1} R'C(R\beta - r) + HX'u.$$

Thus under the null, $R\beta = r$,

$$\text{Cov}(\tilde{\beta}) = \sigma^2 H,$$

and, again under the null, $R\beta = r$, the misspecification test statistic is

$$\mu = \frac{\tilde{\beta}' H_g \tilde{\beta}}{\sigma^2},$$

where H_g is the generalized inverse of H. After some manipulation we may write the equation above as

$$\mu = \frac{u' XHX'u}{\sigma^2}.$$

Since, for finite samples, σ^2 is not known, we may divide μ by $u'Nu/\sigma^2$, where $N = I - X(X'X)^{-1}X'$, thereby obtaining the statistic

$$\mu^* = \frac{u' XHX'u}{u'Nu}.$$

It may be verified that the numerator and denominator quadratic forms are mutually independent, and distributed as chi squared with degrees of freedom $k = \text{rank}(R)$ and $T-n-1$, respectively. This holds when the error sequence is assumed to be normal and there are $n+1$ explanatory variables (including the constant term). One may further verify that the statistic above is simply **proportional to the likelihood ratio test statistic for testing the hypothesis that** $R\beta = r$, **as against the alternative that** $R\beta \neq r$. Thus, in the Hausman context, if the specification test leads to rejection it is just not clear what it is that is being rejected! In the standard framework, and since nothing else is in doubt, **by assumption**, rejection would simply mean, by Eq. (1.124), that the restrictions $R\beta = r$ are not valid. The point could, perhaps, be made most clearly when $R = (0, 0, \ldots, 1)$, $r = 0$, so that what we have is the simple test that the coefficient of the last variable is zero. Thus, when we carry out this simple, standard test and the outcome is rejection, does this also carry an implication that something else is wrong with the remaining specification? Conversely, if it is accepted, are we thereby assured that the remainder of the specification is necessarily correct, within the level of significance?

Remark A3. The preceding discussion highlights some of the problems with many nonspecific tests that have gained considerable popularity in recent times. When, in the classical context, we test a hypothesis on the presence of a variable in a model, i.e. test for the significance of the coefficient of the variable in question, the test has a precise interpretation and operating characteristics, under the specified conditions. This is so because, in that context, one operates under a certain set of conditions, called by econometricians the **maintained hypotheses**, whose validity is **not** questioned during the test. The only thing that is in doubt is whether the coefficient of the particular variable is or is not zero. That the model in question contains, at most, the explanatory variables enumerated is not in doubt. Hence, the test outcome has (or may have) a precise and sharp interpretation. The test outcome merely serves to assure us that the presence of the variable in question is or is not supported by the evidence, as the case may be. It does not imply anything beyond this simple fact, and the structure of the test reflects the precision and limited nature of the question being asked of the data. On the other hand, this does not necessarily mean that, in some fundamental or broader sense, the outcome of the test is valid or true. **It is true, if the maintained hypotheses do, in fact, hold**. But, it conveys no information as to whether, in fact, the maintained hypotheses are or are not valid. If one wishes to test the validity of (some of) the maintained hypotheses one is free to propose a certain range of alternatives and design a test appropriate to the circumstances.

Given the simplicity of the test formulation, in the particular example above, it is quite clear what it is that may lead to rejection. In more complex situations the intepretation may not be as simple. Thus, in the case of the

GLSEM, the misspecification test statistic suggested by Hausman, takes the form,

$$\phi_{3H} = T(\delta_{2SLS} - \delta_{3SLS})'(C_{2SLS} - C_{3SLS})_g(\delta_{2SLS} - \delta_{3SLS}),$$

which is asymptotically distributed as chi square with s degrees of freedom, where $s = \text{rank}(C_{2SLS} - C_{3SLS})$. Here, acceptance or rejection do not have a clear cut intepretation. For example, if some of the overidentifying restrictions are invalid, we have a violation that may lead to rejection. This test, however, is not properly crafted to detect this problem. It may detect it but, perhaps, not as effectively as other tests designed with this possibility in mind.

The preceding is, of course, a very verbose way of saying that the power characteristics of the Hausman test are rather weak and generally indeterminate since the parameteric structure of the alternative is not clearly delineated.

2

Extension of Classical Methods II

2.1 Limiting Distributions

2.1.1 *Preliminaries*

Our purpose in this section is to derive the limiting distribution of the 2SLS and 3SLS estimators obtained in Chapter 1. In that chapter we derived several types of estimators, viz., the standard 2SLS and 3SLS, the restricted 2SLS and 3SLS, unrestricted reduced form (OLS) estimators; we have also presented an alternative derivation of 2SLS and 3SLS, obtained by minimizing the objective function(s) when the prior restrictions are imposed by the device of Lagrange multipliers. This is in contrast to the standard derivation where such restrictions are imposed directly, by substitution. We shall now show that all these procedures involve, basically, the same fundamental problem, viz., the determination of the limiting behavior of the entity

$$\xi_T^{*'} = \frac{(I \otimes X')u}{\sqrt{T}}. \tag{2.1}$$

From the proof of Theorem 3, in Chapter 1, and the definition of the CSF in Eq. (1.64), we find

$$\sqrt{T}(\tilde{\delta} - \delta)_{2SLS} = \left(\frac{Q'Q}{T}\right)^{-1} \frac{Q'r}{\sqrt{T}}$$

$$\sqrt{T}(\tilde{\delta} - \delta)_{3SLS} = \left(\frac{Q'\tilde{\Phi}^{-1}Q}{T}\right)^{-1} \frac{Q'\tilde{\Phi}^{-1}r}{\sqrt{T}}.$$

Bearing in mind the definitions

$$Q = (I \otimes R')\tilde{S}, \quad r = (I \otimes R^{-1})(I \otimes X')u, \quad u = \text{vec}(U),$$

we have

$$\sqrt{T}(\tilde{\delta} - \delta)_{2SLS} = \left[\tilde{S}'\left(I \otimes \frac{X'X}{T}\right)\tilde{S}\right]^{-1}\tilde{S}'\left[\frac{(I \otimes X')u}{\sqrt{T}}\right] \tag{2.2}$$

$$\sqrt{T}(\tilde{\delta} - \delta)_{3SLS} = \left[\tilde{S}'\left(\tilde{\Sigma}^{-1} \otimes \frac{X'X}{T}\right)\tilde{S}\right]^{-1}\tilde{S}'(\tilde{\Sigma}^{-1} \otimes I)\left[\frac{(I \otimes X')u}{\sqrt{T}}\right].$$

From Proposition 28, Corollary 6 in Ch. 4 of Dhrymes (1989), and the discussion of the previous chapter, we conclude that the limiting distribution of the estimators is given by the equivalencies

$$\sqrt{T}(\tilde{\delta} - \delta)_{2SLS} \sim A_2 \frac{(I \otimes X')u}{\sqrt{T}}, \quad \sqrt{T}(\tilde{\delta} - \delta)_{3SLS} \sim A_3 \frac{(I \otimes X')u}{\sqrt{T}}, \tag{2.3}$$

where

$$A_3 = \underset{T \to \infty}{\text{plim}}\left[\tilde{S}'\left(\tilde{\Sigma}^{-1} \otimes \frac{X'X}{T}\right)\tilde{S}\right]^{-1}\tilde{S}'(\tilde{\Sigma}^{-1} \otimes I)$$

$$= [S'(\Sigma^{-1} \otimes M_{xx})S]^{-1}S'\Phi^{-1}$$

$$A_2 = \underset{T \to \infty}{\text{plim}}\left[\tilde{S}'\left(I \otimes \frac{X'X}{T}\right)\tilde{S}\right]^{-1}\tilde{S}' = [S'(I \otimes M_{xx})S]^{-1}S'$$

$$M_{xx} = \underset{T \to \infty}{\text{plim}}\frac{X'X}{T} = \bar{R}\bar{R}'. \tag{2.4}$$

Similarly, from Eqs. (1.89) and (1.91) (of Chapter 1) we find

$$\sqrt{T}\begin{pmatrix}\tilde{\delta} - \delta \\ \tilde{\lambda}\end{pmatrix}_{2SLSR} = \begin{pmatrix}\tilde{A}_{11} \\ \tilde{A}_{21}\end{pmatrix}\tilde{S}'\frac{(I \otimes X')u}{\sqrt{T}}$$

$$\sqrt{T}\begin{pmatrix}\tilde{\delta} - \delta \\ \tilde{\lambda}\end{pmatrix}_{3SLSR} = \begin{pmatrix}\tilde{E}_{11} \\ \tilde{E}_{21}\end{pmatrix}\tilde{S}'\tilde{\Phi}^{-1}\frac{(I \otimes X')u}{\sqrt{T}}, \tag{2.5}$$

where

$$\tilde{A}_{11} = \tilde{C}_2^0 - \tilde{C}_2^0 H'(H\tilde{C}_2^0 H')^{-1}H\tilde{C}_2^0$$

$$\tilde{A}_{21} = -(H\tilde{C}_2^0 H')^{-1}H\tilde{C}_2^0$$

$$\tilde{C}_2^0 = \left(\frac{Q'Q}{T}\right)^{-1}$$

$$\tilde{E}_{11} = \tilde{C}_3 - \tilde{C}_3 H'(H\tilde{C}_3 H')^{-1}H\tilde{C}_3$$

$$\tilde{E}_{21} = -(H\tilde{C}_3 H')^{-1} H\tilde{C}_3$$

$$\tilde{C}_3 = \left(\frac{Q'\tilde{\Phi}^{-1}Q}{T}\right)^{-1},$$

and H is the matrix of restrictions. Moreover, we easily establish that

$$A_{11} = \plim_{T\to\infty} \tilde{A}_{11} = C_2^0 - C_2^0 H'(HC_2^0 H')^{-1}HC_2^0$$

$$A_{21} = \plim_{T\to\infty} \tilde{A}_{21} = -(HC_2^0 H')^{-1}HC_2^0$$

$$C_2^0 = \plim_{T\to\infty} C_2^0 = (S^{*'}S^*)^{-1}$$

$$E_{11} = \plim_{T\to\infty} \tilde{E}_{11} = C_3 - C_3 H'(HC_3 H')^{-1}HC_3$$

$$E_{21} = \plim_{T\to\infty} \tilde{E}_{21} = -(HC_3 H')^{-1}HC_3$$

$$C_3 = \plim_{T\to\infty} \tilde{C}_3 = (S^{*'}\Phi^{-1}S^*)^{-1}$$

$$S^* = (I \otimes \bar{R}')S. \tag{2.6}$$

Finally, since the imposition of the prior restrictions by means of the method of Lagrange multipliers is just another case of restricted least squares or restricted generalized least squares we conclude that, in each case we have handled this far, the problem of the limiting distribution of the estimators in question is reduced to the problem of the limiting distribution of the entity in Eq. (2.1).

In the discussion below we shall obtain the limiting distribution of the estimators we have derived at three stages of complexity: first, in the case where the GLSEM is static, i.e, it **does not contain** lagged dependent variables **and** the structural errors are **jointly normal**; second, in the case where the GLSEM is static but **the structural errors are not necessarily jointly normal**; third, in the case where the GLSEM **does contain lagged dependent variables, i.e. it is dynamic**; in this case no simplification is entailed by whether or not the structural errors are jointly normal. Thus, we shall not consider this special (normal) case, dealing instead with a **dynamic model whose structural errors are not necessarily normal**.

2.1.2 Limiting Distributions for Static GLSEM

Jointly Normal Errors

We examine the simplest case of a static model with jointly normal errors. In many ways this is a rather simple problem, since the most difficult aspect of this derivation was bypassed in the transition to Eq. (2.3). Still operating within the framework of assumptions (A.1) through (A.5) and bearing in mind that the matrix X consists only of its **exogenous** component P, we add the further requirement that, for all t,

$$u'_{t.} \sim N(0, \Sigma).$$

Since the matrix of structural errors is given by $U = (u_{t.})$, $t = 1, 2, \ldots, T$, we have that

$$\text{vec}(U) = u$$

implies that

$$\text{Cov}(u) = \Sigma \otimes I_T = \Phi.$$

Consequently, for every T

$$\xi_T^* \sim N\left(0, \Sigma \otimes \frac{X'X}{T}\right),$$

and letting $T \to \infty$ we obtain [1]

$$\xi_T^* \xrightarrow{\text{d}} \xi \sim N(0, \Sigma \otimes M_{xx}).$$

Since the 2SLS and 3SLS estimators are, asymptotically, simple linear transformations of the random vector ξ we conclude

$$\sqrt{T}(\tilde{\delta} - \delta)_{2SLS} \sim N(0, C_2)$$
$$\sqrt{T}(\tilde{\delta} - \delta)_{3SLS} \sim N(0, C_3), \tag{2.7}$$

where,

$$C_2 = A_2(\Sigma \otimes M_{xx})A'_2, \qquad C_3 = A_3(\Sigma \otimes M_{xx})A'_3. \tag{2.8}$$

Nonnormal Errors

In this section we shall derive the limiting distribution of the estimators, **dispensing with the normality assumption**, but still maintaining that X contains **only its exogenous component**. The complication introduced is that we no longer know what is the distribution of ξ_T^* and, thus, we need to invoke an appropriate central limit theorem (CLT). Unfortunately, in order to do so in a responsible way, and without excessive "hand waving", we need to introduce more structure into our discussion. The structure required is treated extensively [2] in Dhrymes (1989). The basic

---

[1] The notation $\xi_T^{*'} \xrightarrow{\text{d}} \xi$, below, is to be read "the random vector $\xi_T^{*'}$ converges in distribution to the random vector ξ"; the notation $\xi \sim N(0, \Theta)$ is to be read in the usual fashion, i.e. "the random vector ξ has the multivariate normal distribution with mean zero and covariance matrix Θ".

[2] Indeed, the volume *Topics in Advanced Econometrics: Probability Foundations*, New York: Springer-Verlag, 1989, was written explicitly for the purpose of providing a readily accessible reference to the underlying mea sure and probability theory required for most problems likely to arise in classical econometrics. The volume presupposes prior training in analysis and a modicum of mathematical maturity. Otherwise, it attempts to be reasonably self-contained.

random elements of the problem are the random vectors $\{u'_{t.} : t \geq 1\}$; the context also includes the **exogenous** sequence $\{x'_{t.} : t \geq 1\}$ and the parameter space, which consists of the admissible values of the triplet (B^*, C, Σ). Thus, let (Ω, $\mathcal{A}$, $\mathcal{P}$) be a (sufficiently large) probability space [3] such that the sequence $\{u'_{t.} : t \geq 1\}$ may be defined on it and such that it also contains the collection of "events" corresponding to the sequence $\{\xi^*_T : T \geq 1\}$, i.e. ξ^*_T is $\mathcal{A}$-measurable, for every T. Let

$$\mathcal{A}_t = \sigma(u'_{s.}, s \leq t), \tag{2.9}$$

i.e. $\mathcal{A}_t$ is the σ-algebra **generated** by the first t random vectors. It is clear that $\mathcal{A}_{t-1} \subset \mathcal{A}_t \subset \mathcal{A}$, and that $\xi'_{t.}$ is $\mathcal{A}_t$-measurable. Moreover, if $\mathcal{A}_{tT}$ is the σ-algebra corresponding to $\frac{u'_{t.}}{\sqrt{T}}$, then ξ'_{tT} is $\mathcal{A}_{tT}$-measurable and $\mathcal{A}_{t-1,T} \subset \mathcal{A}_{tT}$. In this probabilistic framework we need to apply a CLT on the triangular array $\xi^*_T = \sum_{t=1}^{T} \xi_{tT}$ as $T \to \infty$. To better understand the structure of the problem confronting us, and using the results in Ch. 4, Sec. 2, of Dhrymes (1984), we can write

$$\xi^{*'}_T = \frac{(I \otimes X')u}{\sqrt{T}} = \frac{1}{\sqrt{T}} \mathrm{vec}(X'U) = \frac{1}{\sqrt{T}} \sum_{t=1}^{T} \mathrm{vec}(x'_{t.} u_{t.})$$

$$= \frac{1}{\sqrt{T}} \sum_{t=1}^{T} (I \otimes x'_{t.}) u'_{t.} = \sum_{t=1}^{T} \xi'_{tT}. \tag{2.10}$$

$$\xi_{tT.} = \frac{1}{\sqrt{T}} \xi_{t.,} \quad \xi'_{t.} = (I \otimes x'_{t.}) u'_{t.}. \tag{2.11}$$

and we see that, in view of assumption (A.5) in Chapter 1, we require a CLT for independent, **not identically** distributed random variables. This is so since the summands in Eq. (2.10) obey

$$E(\xi'_{t.}) = 0, \qquad \Psi_t = \mathrm{Cov}(\xi'_{tT.}) = \frac{1}{T}(\Sigma \otimes x'_{t.} x_{t.}),$$

and, moreover,

$$\sum_{t=1}^{T} \Psi_t \longrightarrow \Sigma \otimes M_{xx}. \tag{2.12}$$

We further note from Proposition 34, Ch. 4 in Dhrymes (1989), that for a sequence of random vectors, $\{X_n : n \geq 1\}$,

$$X_n \xrightarrow{\mathrm{d}} X,$$

---

[3] In (Ω, $\mathcal{A}$, $\mathcal{P}$), Ω is said to be the sample space, which remains a primitive concept, $\mathcal{A}$ is a σ-algebra of its subsets and $\mathcal{P}$ is a probability measure defined on $\mathcal{A}$.

if and only if **for any** conformable real vector λ

$$\lambda' X_n \overset{d}{\to} \lambda' X.$$

To apply this setup to our context, let

$$\zeta_T = \xi_T^* \lambda = \sum_{t=1}^{T} \zeta_{tT}, \qquad \zeta_{tT} = \xi_{tT}.\lambda, \tag{2.13}$$

and note that the random variables ζ_{tT} constitute, for each T, a sequence of independent, not identically distributed, square integrable (i.e. having finite second moments), $\mathcal{A}_{tT}$-measurable, random variables obeying

$$E(\zeta_{tT}) = 0, \qquad \text{Var}(\zeta_{tT}) = \lambda' \left(\Sigma \otimes \frac{x'_{t.}x_{t.}}{T} \right) \lambda = \sigma_{tT}^2,$$

where

$$\sum_{t=1}^{T} \sigma_{tT}^2 = \lambda' \left(\Sigma \otimes \frac{X'X}{T} \right) \lambda \longrightarrow \lambda'(\Sigma \otimes M_{xx})\lambda \geq 0. \tag{2.14}$$

It follows, then, from Proposition 45, Ch. 4, in Dhrymes (1989), that to prove that ζ_T converges in distribution, it will suffice to show that the sequence above obeys a **Lindeberg condition**.

Lemma 1. Given the context provided in the informal discussion above, the sequence $\{\zeta_{tT} : t \leq T, \ T \geq 1\}$ obeys a Lindeberg condition, i.e. if we define

$$\mathcal{L}_T = \sum_{t=1}^{T} \int_{|\zeta_{tT}| > \frac{1}{r}} |\zeta_{tT}|^2 \ d\mathcal{P}, \tag{2.15}$$

then,

$$\lim_{T \to \infty} \mathcal{L}_T = 0. \tag{2.16}$$

Proof: Note that

$$|\zeta_{tT}|^2 \leq \frac{1}{T} |\lambda|^2 \| I \otimes x'_{t.} \|^2 |u'_{t.}|^2,$$

where the notation $\| A \|$ indicates the norm of a matrix, defined as the square root of $\text{tr}(AA')$. Note that

$$\| I_m \otimes x'_{t.} \|^2 = \text{tr}(I_m \otimes x'_{t.}x_{t.}) = m(x_{t.}x'_{t.}),$$

define

$$A_{tT1} = \left\{ \omega : |\zeta_{tT}| > \frac{1}{r} \right\}$$

$$A_{tT2} = \left\{ \omega : |u'_{t.}| > \frac{\sqrt{T}}{r |\lambda| [m(x_{t.}x'_{t.})]^{(1/2)}} \right\} \tag{2.17}$$

and observe that $A_{tT1} \subset A_{tT2}$, owing to the fact that

$$\frac{1}{r} < |\zeta_{tT}| \leq \frac{1}{\sqrt{T}} |\lambda| [m(x_t.x'_t.)]^{(1/2)} |u'_t.|.$$

Consequently, the integral in Eq. (2.15) may be evaluated as

$$\int_{|\zeta_{tT}|>\frac{1}{r}} |\zeta_{tT}|^2 d\mathcal{P} \leq |\lambda|^2 \frac{m(x_t.x'_t.)}{T} \int_{|u'_t.|>\frac{1}{r|\lambda| (mx_t.x'_t./T)^{(1/2)}}} |u'_t.|^2 d\mathcal{P}.$$

Even though we have simplified considerably the representation of the integral of the Lindeberg condition, we are still not able show that it vanishes asymptotically. Further simplifications are required. We note, however, that we have not used the assumption in (A.5), i.e. the i.i.d. assumption regarding the basic structural errors, nor have we used assumption (A.1) or (A.1a), viz. that the limit of $(X'X/T)$ is well behaved. [4] The fact that the structural errors are i.i.d. means that we can remove the subscript t from the integrand; the fact that $(X'X/T) \longrightarrow M_{xx}$ has implications that are derived in the appendix to this chapter. In particular, it implies that if we put

$$\alpha_T^2 = \frac{\max_{t\leq T} x_t.x'_t.}{T}, \quad \text{then} \quad \alpha_T \to 0,$$

in the same mode of convergence as the matrix above.

Now, define

$$A_T = \left\{ \omega : |u'_t.| > \frac{1}{r|\lambda| m^{(1/2)}\alpha_T} \right\},$$

and note that $A_{tT2} \subset A_T$. It follows, therefore, that

$$\mathcal{L}_T \leq |\lambda|^2 \, \mathrm{m} \, \mathrm{tr}\left(\frac{X'X}{T}\right) \int_{A_T} |u'_1.|^2 d\mathcal{P}. \tag{2.18}$$

The conclusion follows immediately, if we note that as $T \longrightarrow \infty$ the integral above converges to zero, owing to the finiteness of the second moments

---

[4] It would appear that, in order to prove the consistency and asymptotic normality of the 2SLS and 3SLS estimators, the minimum set of conditions we can place on the exogenous variables is that $d_T^2 \longrightarrow \infty$ and

$$\lim_{T\to\infty} \sup_{t\leq T} \frac{x_t.x'_t.}{d_T^2} = 0, \quad \text{where} \quad d_T^2 = \mathrm{tr}X'X.$$

In such a case we would not have dealt, for example, with $\sqrt{T}(\tilde{\delta} - \delta)_{2SLS}$, but rather with $d_T(\tilde{\delta} - \delta)_{2SLS}$, and ξ_T^* would not have been divided by $\sqrt{T}$, but rather by d_T. It has been traditional in this literature, however, to assume that the second moments of explanatory variables are well defined both in finite samples and in the limit and this fact accounts for the normalization by $\sqrt{T}$.

of the structural errors and the fact that for every λ and m, the trace [in the right member of Eq. (2.18)] converges to $m \, \mathrm{tr} M_{xx} < \infty$.

q.e.d.

Corollary 1. Under the conditions of Lemma 1,

$$\xi_T^{*'} \xrightarrow{d} \xi^*, \quad \xi^* \sim N(0, \Sigma \otimes M).$$

Proof: By Proposition 45, Ch. 4, in Dhrymes (1989),

$$\zeta_T \xrightarrow{d} \zeta, \quad \zeta \sim N(0, \lambda'(\Sigma \otimes M_{xx})\lambda).$$

Since $\zeta_T = \xi_T^* \lambda$, it further follows by Proposition 34, in the same chapter above, that

$$\xi_T^* \xrightarrow{d} \xi^*, \quad \xi^* \sim N(0, \Sigma \otimes M_{xx}).$$

q.e.d.

A Digression

If the reader is comfortable with the integrations performed above, it is quite unnecessary to read this section. Its purpose is to show the relationship between the Lebesgue integrals, above, in the context of taking expectations, with respect to a probability measure, and the Riemann or Riemann-Stieltjes integrals performed with respect to densities or cumulative distribution functions.

In the context of the discussion in the preceding sections, we looked at random variables (r.v.) as real valued measurable functions, say X, such that

$$X : \Omega \to R,$$

and their expectation was defined by

$$E(X) = \int_\Omega X(\omega) \, d\mathcal{P}(\omega) \text{ or } \int_\Omega X(\omega) \, \mathcal{P}(d\omega).$$

Roughly speaking, what we do in such integrals is to look at the range of the function, i.e. the values assumed by the function and, choosing a partition thereof, i.e. choosing a set of disjoint intervals covering the range, **we find their inverse images**. These are sets in the **domain** of the function that give rise to values assumed by the function in the chosen (range) intervals. We then take a representative value in each interval, multiply by the **measure of its inverse image** and sum. We do this for all possible partitions. The value of the integral is defined to be the unique value of this sum, if it exists, as the number of intervals in the partition tend to infinity, over all possible partition schemes.

The expected value of a r.v. above, was represented as a Lebesgue integral; the reader, however, is more apt to be familiar with expectation as

$$E(X) = \int_{-\infty}^{\infty} \xi \, dF(\xi), \quad \text{or} \quad \int_{-\infty}^{\infty} \xi f(\xi) \, d\xi,$$

which we shall consider a single class, the class of Riemann-Stieltjes integrals. In the first representation the random variable is not assumed to have a density function, only a cumulative distribution function (cdf), F, and the integral is taken to be the Riemann-Stieltjes integral; in the second representation, F is assumed to be differentiable with density function f, so that "$dF = f \, dx$", and the integral is taken to be the ordinary Riemann integral of elementary calculus. Since we have given two basic representations of the same entity, $E(X)$, the Lebesgue and Riemann-Stieltjes versions of the integral "ought" to give us the same value. Without taking up the fine subtleties of the two procedures we give below the relationship between them in the case where both integrals make sense. [5]

Given a r.v., say X, defined on the probability space $(\Omega, \mathcal{A}, \mathcal{P})$, with values in the Borel space $(R, \mathcal{B})$, it (the r.v.) induces a probability measure, say P_X [6] on the Borel space, such that for every $B \in \mathcal{B}$,

$$P_X(B) = \mathcal{P}(A),$$

where $A = X^{-1}(B)$, i.e. A is the **inverse image** of B under X. Since $X(\Omega) = R$, and X induces the probability measure P_X on the Borel space $(R, \mathcal{B})$, if we make the change in variable,

$$\xi = X(\omega),$$

we find

$$\int_{\Omega} X(\omega) \, d\mathcal{P} = \int_{R} \xi \, dP_X.$$

To round out our discussion, we need only show the connection between the probability distribution (measure), P_X, and the cdf, say F_X. Again, without going into the mathematical details of the matter, define for the special sets $B = (-\infty, x]$, for $x \in R$, the **point function**,

$$F_X(x) = P_X(B).$$

---

[5] Since mathematicians do not go out of their way to invent redundancies, the reader would surmise that sometimes the Riemann and/or Riemann-Stieltjes integral fail to exist, where in some fundamental sense they "ought to exist". In fact, this was the motivation for the Lebesgue integral which coincides with the Riemann-Stieltjes integral, when both exist and, moreover, it is defined in situations where the latter is not.

[6] This probability measure is also termed the **probability distribution** of the r.v., and is to be distinguished from the cdf of the r.v. The connection between the two will be shown below.

Since the class of sets $\{B : B = (-\infty, \; x], \;\; x \in R\}$ can be shown to generate the (Borel) σ-algebra $\mathcal{B}$, we can write

$$\int_R \xi \, dP_X = \int_{-\infty}^{\infty} \xi \, dF_X(\xi).$$

Moreover, if the original probability measure, $\mathcal{P}$, has a **density**, i.e. if it is **absolutely continuous** with respect to a σ-finite measure, say μ, then by the Radon-Nikodym theorem, Proposition 26, Ch.1 in Dhrymes (1989), there exists a nonnegative measurable function, say ϕ, such that for every set $A \in \mathcal{A}$,

$$\mathcal{P}(A) = \int_A \phi \, d\mu.$$

To relate this to our previous discussion, we note that the change in variable, $\xi = X(\omega)$, together with the relation $A = X^{-1}(B)$, implies, for the special sets $B = (-\infty, \; x]$, $x \in R$,

$$\mathcal{P}(A) = P_X(B) = \int_{-\infty}^{x} f_X(\xi) \, d\xi = F_X(x),$$

where $f_X(\xi) = \phi[X^{-1}(\xi)]$. Consequently, in the case of absolutely continuous measures, we have the relation,

$$\int_{\Omega} X \, d\mathcal{P} = \int_{-\infty}^{\infty} \xi f_X(\xi) \, d\xi,$$

where f_X is the density function of the r.v. X; thus, the expectation of the latter is rendered in the familiar form, which is shown to be equivalent to the form required in the context of the probability space $(\Omega, \; \mathcal{A}, \; \mathcal{P})$.

2.1.3 Limiting Distributions for Dynamic GLSEM

Generalities

If the GLSEM we are dealing with is **dynamic**, i.e. if it contains lagged dependent variables, then whether the structural errors are jointly normal or not, we face a very serious complication. To appreciate the nature of the difficulty refer to Eqs. (2.10) and (2.11) of the preceding discussion. If the elements of x_t. are **all exogenous** then the summands of Eq. (2.10), i.e. the vectors $\xi'_t. = (u'_t. \otimes x'_t.)$ constitute a sequence of **independent, but not identically distributed random elements**. If, on the other hand,

$$x_t. = (p_t., y_{t-1}., y_{t-2}., \ldots, y_{t-k}.)$$

so that the model is **dynamic**, then the vectors $\xi_t.$, above, constitute a sequence of **dependent random elements**. Consequently, in order to handle the limiting distribution problem in this case we need to invoke a CLT for dependent random variables and, moreover, we need to obtain the final form of the model. The latter is the task to which we now turn.

Lag Operators

The discussion here will, in many respects, duplicate the material presented in Ch. 5, Sec. 2, of Dhrymes (1984) under the title "Vector Difference Equations with Constant Coefficients". The reader desiring greater detail is referred to that source. In the current discussion this brief review is intended, mainly, to establish notation. We recall that a **lag operator**, denoted here by L is defined by the property

$$Lx_t = x_{t-1}. \tag{2.19}$$

Powers of the operator denote repeated application of the operator above, i.e.

$$L^2 x_t = Lx_{t-1} = x_{t-2}, \quad \text{and generally} \quad L^k x_t = x_{t-k}. \tag{2.20}$$

The identity operator, I, and the zero operator, $\mathbf{O}$, are defined, respectively, by the operations below, for all functions x_t,

$$I x_t = x_t, \quad \mathbf{O} x_t = 0. \tag{2.21}$$

Generally these last two operators will not be written out explicitly, unless the context requires it for clarity. Finally note that by convention we define the zeroth power of L to be the **identity** operator, i.e.

$$L^0 = I, \quad \text{or, alternatively,} \quad L^0 x_t = x_t. \tag{2.22}$$

The lag operator is, in addition, linear in the sense that

$$(a_n L^n + a_m L^m) x_t = a_n x_{t-n} + a_m x_{t-m}$$

and obeys the law of exponents, i.e.

$$L^k L^s x_t = L^k x_{t-s} = x_{t-s-k} = L^{k+s} x_t, \quad \text{or} \quad L^k L^s = L^{k+s}.$$

Thus, polynomials in the operator L, with real or complex coefficients, for example $a_0 I + a_1 L + a_2 L^2$, have a perfectly straightforward meaning. In fact, it may be shown that the algebra of polynomials of degree $n \geq 0$ in the lag operator L over the field of real or complex numbers (i.e. with real or complex coefficients) is isomorphic to the algebra of polynomials in the real or complex indeterminate, say t. What this means is that if an operation is desired to be performed on polynomials in the lag operator, we may first replace L and its powers by the real indeterminate, say t, perform the desired operation and then replace t and its powers by the operator L and its powers. The resulting entity is the product of the (originally desired) operation involving the two polynomials in the lag operator. A few examples may help clarify matters.

Example 1. Consider the polynomials

$$A_i(L) = \sum_{j=1}^{n_i} a_{ji} L^j, \quad i = 1, 2, \ldots, m.$$

Evidently,

$$A_i(L)x_t = \sum_{j=1}^{n_i} a_{ji} x_{t-j}.$$

The sum of any two polynomials, say $A_s(L) + A_k(L)$, on the assertion that $n_s \le n_k$, is given by

$$A_{sk}(L) = \sum_{j=1}^{n_s} (a_{js} + a_{jk})L^j + \sum_{j=n_s+1}^{n_k} a_{jk} L^j.$$

To illustrate multiplication, let $n_1 = 2$, $n_2 = 3$; then

$$A_1(L)A_2(L) = (a_{01} + a_{02})I + (a_{01}a_{12} + a_{02}a_{11})L + \cdots + a_{21}a_{32}L^5.$$

Example 2. Suppose

$$A(L) = I - \lambda L.$$

What meaning is to be ascribed to the entity $(I - \lambda L)^{-1}$, by which we wish to denote the **operator inverse** to $A(L) = (I - \lambda L)$, i.e. the operator obeying

$$A(L)(I - \lambda L)^{-1} = I.$$

By the discussion just above we may write, formally,

$$(I - \lambda L)^{-1} = \sum_{j=0}^{\infty} \lambda^j L^j,$$

and the question remains as to how we are to interpret the right member above, and whether there are any restrictions on the circumstances that guarantee the validity of this interpretation. To explore the issues that underlie this question put

$$y_t = (I - \lambda L)^{-1} x_t, \tag{2.23}$$

and apply the operator $(I - \lambda L)$ to both sides to obtain

$$y_t = \lambda y_{t-1} + x_t, \tag{2.24}$$

which is simply a first order difference equation with forcing function x_t. Now suppose the x-sequence obeys

$$\begin{aligned} x_t &= 0 \quad \text{for } t < 0 \\ &= \bar{x} \quad \text{for } t \ge 0. \end{aligned}$$

In Eq. (2.24), solving the difference equation with this particular forcing function yields

$$y_t = \lambda^t y_0 + \bar{x} \sum_{j=0}^{t-1} \lambda^j$$

where y_0 indicates the "initial" condition, i.e. the value assumed by the process, y, at "time zero"; in this particular case it so happens that $y_0 = \bar{x}$, but this need not be the case at all times. Now, if $|\lambda| < 1$ the role of initial conditions declines in significance as we move away from "time zero". On the other hand if $|\lambda| \geq 1$ then the significance of initial conditions either remains undisturbed or is actually magnified as we move away from "time zero". An extreme illustration of the consequences of such parametric specification is afforded by the following x-sequence:

$$\begin{aligned} x_t &= 0 \quad \text{for } t < 0 \\ &= \bar{x} \quad \text{for } t = 0 \\ &= 0 \quad \text{for } t > 0, \end{aligned}$$

which yields the solution,

$$y_t = \lambda^t y_0.$$

If $|\lambda| \geq 1$, we see that even though the x-process departed from its null state only momentarily, it has induced on the y-process a permanent change in behavior; in fact if $|\lambda| > 1$ the temporary departure in the x-process has changed the y-process from a null state to one that exhibits its logarithm as a pure time trend, when λ is real! In this volume, we **rule out** such situations and we shall therefore insist, that $|\lambda| < 1$, which means that when we consider the characteristic polynomial $(1 - \lambda z) = 0$ (with complex z), we shall consider admissible only parametric specifications of λ that permit convergence for z on the unit circle, i.e. for $|z| = 1$; specifically, we require $|\lambda| < 1$. With this interpretation we can now write

$$(I - \lambda L)^{-1} = \sum_{j=0}^{\infty} \lambda^j L^j$$

and the meaning of $(I - \lambda L)^{-1} x_t$ is quite unambiguous.

Before we leave this topic it should be pointed out that the operator framework we have just established is quite well suited to producing formal solutions for difference equations. For example, let $y_t.$ and $x_t.$ be m- and n-element vectors respectively and suppose they obey

$$y_t. = y_{t-1}.A' + x_t.B'.$$

A formal solution is given, immediately, as

$$y_t'. = (I - AL)^{-1} Bx_t'. \tag{2.25}$$

provided the matrix A is stable, i.e. it has roots less than unity in absolute value. If so, then we have the explicit representation

$$(I - AL)^{-1} = \sum_{j=0}^{\infty} A^j L^j, \quad A^j = P\Lambda^j P^{-1}$$

where P is the matrix[7] of characteristic vectors and Λ is the (diagonal) matrix of the characteristic roots of the matrix A. The particular solution of Eq. (2.26) may then be represented operationally as

$$y'_{t.} = \sum_{j=0}^{\infty} P\Lambda^j P^{-1} B x'_{t-j.}.$$

The Final Form of a Dynamic GLSEM

When the model is dynamic, the vector $x_{t.}$ is the vector of **predetermined** variables and, as such, it contains both **lagged dependent** and **exogenous** variables, i.e. we may write, in a slight departure from our earlier custom, $x_{t.} = (p_{t.}, y_{t-1.}, y_{t-2.}, \ldots, y_{t-k.})$. This implies that the maximal lag contained in the **structural** model is k and that the exogenous variables of the model are contained in the s-element vector, $p_{t.}$. To ensure maximal compatibility of notation, relative to the static case, partition the matrix C, in the structural representation $y_{t.} B^* = x_{t.} C + u_{t.}$, as

$$C' = \left(C'_0, C'_1, \ldots, C'_k \right)$$

so that we may write the structural model as

$$y_{t.} B^* = p_{t.} C_0 + y_{t-1.} C_1 + y_{t-2.} C_2 + \cdots + y_{t-k.} C_k + u_{t.}. \tag{2.26}$$

Using the operator notation developed above, and writing the system in **column vector form**, we find

$$B^{*'} y'_{t.} = \sum_{j=1}^{k} C'_j L^j y'_{t.} + C'_0 p'_{t.} + u'_{t.}.$$

Multiplying through by the transpose of $B^{*-1} = D$, i.e. **obtaining the reduced form**, we have

$$\Pi(L) y'_{t.} = \Pi'_0 p'_{t.} + v'_{t.}.$$

$$\Pi(L) = \left(I - \sum_{j=1}^{k} \Pi'_j L^j \right)$$

$$\Pi'_j = D' C'_j, \; j = 0, 1, 2, \ldots, k, \quad v_{t.} = u_{t.} D. \tag{2.27}$$

---

[7] The matrix P will be nonsingular if A has distinct roots, which is assumed for the purposes of this discussion.

Assuming stability, and abstracting from initial conditions, the final form of the model may be found by inverting the operator $\Pi(L)$, which is simply a matrix **whose typical element is a polynomial of degree at most k in the lag operator L**. In view of the isomorphism alluded to above, we may find the inverse of the operator $\Pi(L)$, constructively, i.e. by obtaining the *adjoint* of the matrix $\Pi(L)$ and dividing each element by the determinant $b(L) = |\Pi(L)|$. Doing so yields,

$$y'_{t.} = \frac{H(L)}{b(L)} p'_{t.} + \frac{G(L)}{b(L)} u'_{t.}, \tag{2.28}$$

where

$$
\begin{aligned}
A(L) &= \text{adjoint of } \Pi(L) \\
b(L) &= |\Pi(L)| \\
H(L) &= A(L)\Pi'_0, \quad G(L) = A(L)D'. \tag{2.29}
\end{aligned}
$$

It only remains to give meaning to the operator $(I/b(L))$. But this is rather simple in terms of our discussion in Example 2. First, consider the polynomial equation

$$b^*(z) = z^n + b_1 z^{n-1} + b_2 z^{n-2} + \cdots + b_n = 0, \quad n = mk. \tag{2.30}$$

in the complex indeterminate, z. The order of the polynomial is $n = mk$, which is verified by noting that each element of $\Pi(L)$ is a polynomial of degree at most k, and the determinant consists of the sum of all possible products formed by taking one term from each row (or column). Since $\Pi(L)$ is an $m \times m$ matrix the conclusion follows immediately. Now, let $z_i, \ i = 1, 2, \ldots, n$ be the roots of the equation above. By the fundamental theorem of algebra we can write

$$b^*(z) = \prod_{j=1}^n (z - z_j).$$

The characteristic function [8] of the difference equation describing the dynamic GLSEM, however, is given not by Eq. (2.30) but by

$$b(z) = 1 + b_1 z + b_2 z^2 + \ldots + b_n z^n. \tag{2.31}$$

It is a further remarkable result from algebra that the roots of Eq. (2.31) are simply the inverse of the roots of Eq. (2.30), i.e. that the roots of the equation above are given by

$$\lambda_j = \frac{1}{z_j}, \quad j = 1, 2, \ldots, n.$$

---

[8] When one states that an equation or a system is **stable** one generally means that the roots of the characteristic function or the characteristic equation of the system are less than unity in absolute value.

We may therefore write

$$b(z) = \prod_{j=1}^{n}(1 - \lambda_j z),$$

and, using the isomorphism alluded to above, conclude that

$$b(L) = \prod_{j=1}^{n}(I - \lambda_j L), \quad \text{and therefore} \quad \frac{I}{b(L)} = \prod_{j=1}^{n}(I - \lambda_j L)^{-1}.$$

The meaning of the last representation, however, had been made quite clear in Example 2. Thus, provided the model is **stable**, there is no ambiguity as to the meaning of the representation of the solution given in Eq. (2.28), which is also known as the **final form of the GLSEM**, without initial conditions. Putting, now, in the obvious notation,

$$y_{t\cdot} = \bar{y}_{t\cdot} + v_{t\cdot}^*, \quad t \geq 1 \tag{2.32}$$

we have that the first component, $\bar{y}$, **depends only on the exogenous variables and their lags**, and as such is clearly independent of the error component $v_{t\cdot}^*$. We also note that the matrix X, may be represented as

$$X = (P, \ \bar{Y}_{-1}, \ \bar{Y}_{-2}, \dots, \bar{Y}_{-k}) + (0, V_*), \tag{2.33}$$

where

$$V_* = (V_{-1}^*, V_{-2}^*, \dots, V_{-k}^*). \tag{2.34}$$

We note, for future reference, that

$$v_{t\cdot}^{*'} = \frac{G(L)}{b(L)} u_{t\cdot}' = \sum_{\tau=0}^{\infty} G_\tau u_{t-\tau\cdot}', \quad \sum_{\tau=0}^{\infty} G_\tau = \frac{G(I)}{b(I)}. \tag{2.35}$$

The entity $G(I)/b(I)$ is well defined and finite, since unity is not one of the roots of the characteristic equation of the system. It is, further, simple to demonstrate that

$$\text{Cov}(v_{t\cdot}^{*'}) = \sum_{\tau=0}^{\infty} G_\tau \Sigma G_\tau' = H(0), \tag{2.36}$$

$$\text{Cov}(v_{t-i\cdot}^{*'}, v_{t-j\cdot}^{*'}) = \sum_{\tau=0}^{\infty} G_{\tau+(i-j)} \Sigma G_\tau' = H(i-j), \quad i \geq j,$$

and, moreover, that $H(i-j) = H'(j-i)$. Thus, we may write,

$$E\left(\frac{V_*'V_*}{T}\right) = H = \begin{bmatrix} H(0) & H'(1) & \dots & H'(k-1) \\ H(1) & H(0) & \dots & H'(k-2) \\ \vdots & \vdots & & \vdots \\ H(k-2) & H(k-3) & \dots & H'(1) \\ H(k-1) & H(k-2) & \dots & H(0) \end{bmatrix} \tag{2.37}$$

In the dynamic case, we must also derive the limit of $X'X/T$, which is a somewhat laborious exercise. First we note that, by the preceding discussion,

$$X = \bar{X} + (0, V_*), \quad \bar{X} = (P, \bar{Y}_{-1}, \bar{Y}_{-2}, \ldots, \bar{Y}_{-k})$$

and, thus, we would expect that

$$\operatorname*{plim}_{T \to \infty} \frac{X'X}{T} = \operatorname*{plim}_{T \to \infty} \frac{\bar{X}'\bar{X}}{T} + H^*,$$

where

$$H^* = \begin{bmatrix} 0 & 0 \\ 0 & H \end{bmatrix}. \tag{2.38}$$

This is so since

$$\frac{X'X}{T} = \frac{\bar{X}'\bar{X}}{T} + \frac{(0, V_*)'(0, V_*)}{T} + \frac{(0, V_*)'\bar{X}}{T} + \frac{\bar{X}(0, V_*)}{T}$$

and, for every $i \geq 0$, we would expect

$$\frac{\bar{X}'V_{-i}^*}{T} \xrightarrow{\text{P}} 0, \quad \frac{V_*'V_*}{T} \xrightarrow{\text{P}} H. \tag{2.39}$$

The proof of these conjecture is quite cumbersome and is, thus, relegated to the appendix of this chapter.

Limiting Distributions for the Dynamic Model

In this section we provide the details of establishing the limiting distribution when the model is dynamic. Returning to the context of Eqs. (2.10) and (2.11), of this chapter, we need to find the limiting distribution of

$$\xi_T^{*'} = \frac{1}{\sqrt{T}} \sum_{t=1}^{T} \operatorname{vec}(x_{t\cdot}'u_{t\cdot}) = \frac{1}{\sqrt{T}} \sum_{t=1}^{T} \xi_{t\cdot}', \quad \xi_{t\cdot}' = (I \otimes x_{t\cdot}')u_{t\cdot}'.$$

An alternative notation for $\xi_{t\cdot}'$ is

$$\xi_{t\cdot}' = (u_{t\cdot}' \otimes x_{t\cdot}').$$

The important difference between the nature of the problem in the static and dynamic cases is that in the former, the individual summands, i.e. the vectors $\xi_{t\cdot}$ constitute a sequence of **independent**, though not identically distributed, random vectors, while in the latter (dynamic) case they form a sequence of **dependent** vectors. To see this note that from the representation implicit in Eqs. (2.32) and (2.33) we have

$$x_{t\cdot} = \bar{x}_{t\cdot} + (0, v_{t-1\cdot}^*, v_{t-2\cdot}^*, \ldots, v_{t-k\cdot}^*) = \bar{x}_{t\cdot} + w_{t\cdot}^*. \tag{2.40}$$

so that, for example, $\xi_t.$ and $\xi_{t+1}.$ have $v^*_{t-1}., v^*_{t-2}., \ldots, v^*_{t-k+1}.$ in common; thus, they cannot be independent, in fact they are not even uncorrelated! To examine the issues arising in the dynamic context we introduce the probability space, the family of nested sub σ-algebras defined in connection with Eq. (2.5), and we also stipulate that $\mathcal{A}_{-j} = (\emptyset, \Omega)$ for $j = 0, 1, \ldots, k$, i.e. we take initial conditions as given and nonstochastic. Moreover, as we had done in the earlier discussion we convert the problem to one involving the **scalar** random variables

$$\zeta_T = \xi^*_T \lambda = \sum_{t=1}^{T} \zeta_{tT}, \quad \zeta_{tT} = \frac{1}{\sqrt{T}} (u_t. \otimes x_t.) \lambda,$$

where λ is an arbitrary conformable real vector. We note first that ζ_{tT} is $\mathcal{A}_{tT}$-measurable and that the stochastic sequence $\{(\zeta_{tT}, \mathcal{A}_{tT}) : t \leq T\}$ is, for each $T \geq 1$ a **martingale difference**, owing to the fact that $E(\zeta_{tT}) = 0$. Moreover, it may be shown to obey a Lindeberg condition. Thus, we have

Lemma 2. In the context of the dynamic GLSEM subject to assumptions (A.1) through (A.5), of Chapter 1, and the preceding discussion, the martingale difference $\{(\zeta_{tT}, \mathcal{A}_{tT}) : t \leq T\}$ obeys a Lindeberg condition, i.e. if we put, for arbitrary integer r,

$$\mathcal{L}_T = \sum_{t=1}^{T} \int_{|\zeta_{tT}| > \frac{1}{r}} |\zeta_{tT}|^2 \, dP(\omega \mid \mathcal{A}_{t-1,T}), \quad \text{then} \quad \plim_{T \to \infty} \mathcal{L}_T = 0. \quad (2.41)$$

Proof: We note that

$$|\zeta_{tT}|^2 \leq \frac{1}{T} |\lambda|^2 \| (I \otimes x'_t.) \|^2 |u'_t.|^2,$$

and we also define, for arbitrary integer, r,

$$A_{tT1} = \left\{ \omega : |\zeta_{tT}| > \frac{1}{r} \right\} \quad A_{tT2} = \left\{ \omega : |u'_t.| > \frac{\sqrt{T}}{c_0 q_t} \right\},$$

where

$$c_0 = rm^{(1/2)} |\lambda|, \quad q_t = (x_t. x'_t.)^{(1/2)}.$$

Since $X'X/T$ converges, defining

$$\alpha_T^2 = \frac{\max_{t \leq T} x_t. x'_t.}{T},$$

we note, by the results in the appendix to this chapter, that $\alpha_T \to 0$. Moreover, putting

$$A_{tT3} = \left\{ \omega : |u'_t.| > \frac{1}{c_0 \alpha_T} \right\} = \left\{ \omega : |u'_1.| > \frac{1}{c_0 \alpha_T} \right\} = A_T,$$

we observe that $A_{tT1} \subset A_{tT2} \subset A_{tT3}$. Consequently, we may write the integral of the Lindeberg condition as

$$
\begin{aligned}
L_{tT} &= \int_{|\zeta_{tT}| > \frac{1}{r}} | \zeta_{tT} |^2 \, d\mathcal{P}(\omega \mid A_{t-1,T}) \\[2mm]
&\leq \frac{1}{T} | \lambda |^2 \, m(x_t . x'_t.) \int_{A_{tT1}} | u'_t. |^2 \, d\mathcal{P} \\[2mm]
&\leq \frac{1}{T} | \lambda |^2 \, m(x_t . x'_t.) \int_{A_{tT2}} | u'_t. |^2 \, d\mathcal{P} \\[2mm]
&\leq \frac{1}{T} | \lambda |^2 \, m(x_t . x'_t.) \int_{A_{tT3}} | u'_1. |^2 \, d\mathcal{P}.
\end{aligned}
\tag{2.42}
$$

In the preceding the first inequality is the result of the application of the triangle inequality, and of taking outside the integrand entities which are $A_{t-1,T}$-measurable; the second and third inequalities simply follow because of set inclusions, i.e. $A_{tT1} \subset A_{tT2} \subset A_{tT3}$ and the fact that the vectors $u_t.$, $t \geq 1$ are **identically** distributed. Thus, we may deduce from Eq. (2.42)

$$
\mathcal{L}_T \leq (m \mid \lambda \mid^2) \mathrm{tr} \left(\frac{X'X}{T} \right) \int_{A_T} | u_1. |^2 \, d\mathcal{P}.
\tag{2.43}
$$

Since

$$
\plim_{T \to \infty} \mathrm{tr} \left(\frac{X'X}{T} \right) = \mathrm{tr} M_{xx} < \infty, \quad \text{we conclude}
$$

$$
\plim_{T \to \infty} \int_{|u'_1.| > \frac{1}{c_0 \alpha T}} | u'_1. |^2 \, d\mathcal{P} = 0,
$$

(the last equality is valid because $(1/\alpha_T) \overset{\mathrm{P}}{\to} \infty$,) and the lemma is proved.

$$\text{q.e.d.}$$

We are now in a position to prove

Lemma 3. Under the conditions of Lemma 2,

$$
\xi^{*'}_T \overset{\mathrm{d}}{\to} \xi^{*'}, \quad \xi^{*'} \sim N(0, \Sigma \otimes M_{xx}).
$$

Proof: From Proposition 21, Ch. 5 of Dhrymes (1989), we may show that

$\zeta_T \xrightarrow{d} \zeta$ by showing that

$$\sum_{t=1}^{T} E(\zeta_{tT}^2 \mid \mathcal{A}_{t-1,T}) \xrightarrow{P} \sigma^2 \geq 0. \tag{2.44}$$

Since

$$E(\zeta_{tT}^2 \mid \mathcal{A}_{t-1,T}) = \lambda' \left(\Sigma \otimes \frac{x_{t\cdot}' x_{t\cdot}}{T} \right) \lambda$$

it follows that

$$\sum_{t=1}^{T} E(\zeta_{tT}^2 \mid \mathcal{A}_{t-1,T}) = \lambda' \left(\Sigma \otimes \frac{X'X}{T} \right) \lambda \xrightarrow{P} \lambda'(\Sigma \otimes M_{xx})\lambda \geq 0,$$

which demonstrates that for every conformable real vector, λ,

$$\zeta_T \xrightarrow{d} \zeta, \quad \text{and} \quad \zeta \sim N[0, \lambda'(\Sigma \otimes M_{xx})\lambda].$$

It follows, therefore, from Proposition 34, Ch. 4 of the reference above, that

$$\xi_T^{*'} \xrightarrow{d} \xi^{*'}, \quad \text{and} \quad \xi^{*'} \sim N(0, \Sigma \otimes M_{xx}).$$

q.e.d.

We may therefore summarize our discussion in the important

Theorem 1. Consider the GLSEM, of Chapter 1, subject to the assumptions (A.1) through (A.5). Whether the model is static or dynamic all estimators considered this far, i.e. the 2SLS, 3SLS, restricted 2SLS and restricted 3SLS etimators are, asymptotically, of the generic form

$$\sqrt{T}\left(\tilde{\delta} - \delta\right) \sim A\,\xi_T^{*'},$$

where

$$\xi_T^{*'} \xrightarrow{d} \xi^{*'}, \quad \xi^{*'} \sim N(0, \Sigma \otimes M_{xx}),$$

and A is a fixed nonstochastic matrix specific to the particular estimator.

Proof: Lemmata 2 and 3.

Now that we have completed the technical task of establishing the limiting distribution of the 2SLS, 3SLS and all other estimators derived from them, we may summarize the properties of such estimators, beyond their consistency and asymptotic normality.

Theorem 2. Consider the GLSEM, as in Theorem 1. Then the following statements are true:

i. 3SLS are efficient relative to 2SLS estimators, unless

    a. $\sigma_{ij} = 0$, for $i \neq j$, or

    b. all equations of the system are just identified;

ii. restricted 3SLS estimators are efficient relative to unrestricted 3SLS estimators;

iii. restricted 2SLS estimators are not necessarily efficient relative to unrestricted 2SLS estimators.

Proof: Using the results of Eqs. (2.6), (2.7) and (2.8), putting $M_{xx} = \bar{R}\bar{R}'$ and $S^* = (I \otimes \bar{R}')S$, etc., we can write the covariance matrices of the limiting distribution of the 2SLS and 3SLS estimators, respectively, as

$$C_2 = (S^{*'}S^*)^{-1}S^{*'}\Phi S^*(S^{*'}S^*)^{-1}, \quad C_3 = (S^{*'}\Phi^{-1}S^*)^{-1}.$$

The efficiency of 3SLS relative to 2SLS is quite evident. It may be established by exactly the same argument one uses to establish the efficiency of the Aitken vis-à-vis the OLS estimator when, in the standard GLM, the covariance matrix is not scalar.

To establish part i.a we note that when $\sigma_{ij} = 0$, $i \neq j$, the ith diagonal block of C_2 is $\sigma_{ii}(S_i^{*'}S_i^*)^{-1}$, which is exactly the ith diagonal block of C_3.

As for part i.b we note that when all equations of the system are just identified, S^* **is a nonsingular matrix**, so that we have

$$C_2 = S^{*-1}S^{*'-1}S^{*'}\Phi S^* S^{*-1}S^{*'-1} = S^{*-1}\Phi S^{*'-1} = C_3.$$

To prove parts ii and iii we first begin by noting that Theorem 1 implies that restricted 2SLS and 3SLS estimators are asymptotically normally distributed with respective covariance matrices

$$C_{2R} = (I - (S^{*'}S^*)^{-1}H'P_2H)C_2(I - H'P_2H(S^{*'}S^*)^{-1}),$$
$$C_{3R} = (I - (S^{*'}\Phi^{-1}S^*)^{-1}H'P_3H)C_3(I - H'P_3H(S^{*'}\Phi^{-1}S^*)^{-1}),$$

where H is the matrix of restrictions, which is of full row rank, say r_*, and

$$P_2 = \left(H(S^{*'}S^*)^{-1}H'\right)^{-1}, \quad P_3 = \left(H(S^{*'}\Phi^{-1}S^*)^{-1}H'\right)^{-1}.$$

A simple computation shows that

$$C_3 - C_{3R} = C_3 H' P_3 H C_3 \geq 0,$$

which completes the proof of part ii.

As for part iii we have that

$$C_2 - C_{2R} = C_2 - [I - (S^{*'} S^*)^{-1} H' P_2 H] C_2 [I - H' P_2 H (S^{*'} S^*)^{-1}].$$

In order to evaluate it, we note that $(S^{*'} S^*)^{-1} H' P_2 H$ is a nonsymmetric matrix of dimension equal to the number of parameters to be estimated, viz. $k = \sum_{i=1}^m (G_i + m_i)$. As for its rank, we note that the nonzero roots of

$$| \lambda I - (S^{*'} S^*)^{-1} H' P_2 H | = 0,$$

are exactly those of

$$| \lambda I - P_2 H (S^{*'} S^*)^{-1} H' | = 0,$$

which, evidently, consist of r_* unities, where r_* is the rank of H. Let E be the matrix of characteristic vectors, which is assumed to be nonsingular, and note that we have the representation,

$$(S^{*'} S^*)^{-1} H' P_2 H = E \begin{bmatrix} 0 & 0 \\ 0 & I_{r_*} \end{bmatrix} E^{-1}.$$

It follows, therefore, that

$$E^{-1} (C_2 - C_{2R}) E'^{-1} = E^{-1} C_2 E'^{-1} - \begin{bmatrix} I_{k-r_*} & 0 \\ 0 & 0 \end{bmatrix} E^{-1} C_2 E'^{-1} \begin{bmatrix} I_{k-r_*} & 0 \\ 0 & 0 \end{bmatrix}.$$

Partitioning,

$$E^{-1} C_2 E'^{-1} = \begin{bmatrix} C^*_{2(11)} & C^*_{2(12)} \\ C^*_{2(21)} & C^*_{2(22)} \end{bmatrix},$$

conformably with that of the matrix of characteristic roots, we can rewrite the difference as

$$E^{-1} (C_2 - C_{2R}) E'^{-1} = \begin{bmatrix} 0 & C^*_{2(12)} \\ C^*_{2(21)} & C^*_{2(22)} \end{bmatrix}.$$

It is evident that unless $C^*_{2(12)} = 0$, the difference of the two covariance matrices above is indefinite.

q.e.d.

The result in part iii of Theorem 2 confirms the observation made at the time we considered restricted 2SLS, viz. that having **restrictions across equations** destroys the fundamental character of 2SLS as a single equation procedure; as we see now it gains us nothing, in the sense that we cannot prove that the restricted estimator is efficient relative to the unrestricted 2SLS estimator. Thus, its usefulness is questionable. The reader is invited to ask (and answer) the question: what about the case where restrictions do not apply across equations?

2.2   Forecasting from the GLSEM

2.2.1   Generalities

Forecasting from an econometric model, involves the following steps: (a) estimation of the model's parameters; (b) selection of the period over which to forecast, i.e. selection of the forecasting horizon; (c) specification of the values of the exogenous variables over the forecasting horizon.

Put in these terms, forecasting is, generally, a conditional activity; thus, if we are given certain conditions expected to prevail in the future, or more precisely if we are given the requisite future values of the exogenous variables contained in the model, we may produce an estimate of the values to be assumed by the dependent variables of the model, over the forecasting horizon, on the assertion that the structural integrity of the model is preserved.

Although, intellectually, this is a very neat distinction between what is being given and what is to be forecast, in practice we really do not know the future values to be assumed by the exogenous variables. Thus, often the basis on which forecasts are executed is in error; this means that what we forecast is not the conditional mean of the dependent variables given the values of the exogenous variables, but rather the "conditional" mean given a "noisy" set of exogenous variables. Hence, generally, the forecast error bands we shall deduce in the ensuing discussion would be an incorrect assessment of the uncertainty surrounding each forecast, and frequently an underestimate, even if it is granted that the model is perfectly specified.

Having pointed this out, it is not clear what one should do about it since it is, generally, the case that the exogenous variables cannot be "predicted" on a systematic basis that allows for the computation of credible measures of uncertainty, such as (estimates of the mean and) the variance of the values assigned to the exogenous variables over the forecasting horizon. Our discussion will be conducted on the assertion that such values are known with certainty and would leave it to the user of such procedures to assign appropriate uncertainty measures to them.

The first question that arises, operationally, is whether we should forecast from the structural form,

$$YB^* = XC + U, \qquad (2.45)$$

or from the reduced form. [9]

---

[9] There is also the subsidiary question of whether we should use the **restricted** or the **unrestricted reduced form**. We shall presently introduce these terms systematically into our discussion.

2.2.2   Forecasting from the URF

Forecasting from the (unrestricted) reduced form (URF), i.e. using estimates of Π that **ignore the fact that** $\Pi = CD$, is a subject that more
properly belongs in the study of the GLM. Thus, if we have a sample,
$Z = (Y, X)$, we may estimate the URF as

$$\tilde{\Pi} = (X'X)^{-1}X'Y.$$

Suppose, now, that it is desired to forecast the dependent variables[10] τ
periods into the future, i.e. it is desired to forecast the dependent variables
$\{y_{T+j\cdot} : j = 1, 2, \ldots, \tau\}$. Before we proceed with the operational aspects
of forecasting, we note that it is **not possible to forecast from the
structural form**. This is easily seen, in the framework established above,
if we write, say, the ith equation as

$$y_{T+j,i} = y_{T+j\cdot}L_{1i}\beta_{\cdot i} + x_{T+j\cdot}L_{2i}\gamma_{\cdot i} + u_{T+j,i},$$

for $j = 1, 2, \ldots, \tau$. Even if we have consistent estimates of the structural
parameters $\beta_{\cdot i}$, $\gamma_{\cdot i}$, and ignore the structural error, we see that in order
to forecast the conditional mean of $y_{T+j,i}$ we require knowledge, at least,
of those jointly dependent variables that appear in the right hand member
of that equation. Generally, such information is not available!

Thus, it would appear that in order to forecast one dependent variable
for some period outside the sample, we require knowledge of (nearly) all
other dependent variables. Needless to say, this is an impossible situation
and we conclude that **we can forecast only from the reduced form**,
which exhibits the jointly dependent variables as explicit functions of the
predetermined or exogenous variables, as well as (transforms) of the structural errors.

When feasible, the forecasting task is further complicated, depending on
whether the model is dynamic or static, (i.e. whether it does or does not
contain **lagged dependent variables**), so that $x_{t\cdot} = (y_{t-1\cdot}, \ldots, y_{t-k\cdot}, p_{t\cdot})$,
or is given by $x_{t\cdot} = p_{t\cdot}$.

Static Models

We deal first with the static case; in this context $x_{T+j\cdot} = p_{T+j\cdot}$, $j = 1, 2, \ldots, m$, and the forecast is

$$\hat{y}_{T+j\cdot} = p_{T+j\cdot}\hat{\Pi}, \quad j = 1, 2, \ldots, \tau. \tag{2.46}$$

---

[10] This is a slightly inaccurate verbal rendition of the more precise concept of
"forecasting the conditional mean of the dependent variables, given knowledge of
the exogenous variables over the forecasting horizon". As the reader well appreci-
ates, this is a rather ponderous phrase and, more often than not, we shall employ
the nontechnical mode of rendering this as "forecasting the dependent variables
of the model".

The **forecast error** is given by

$$e_{T+j\cdot}=y_{T+j\cdot}-\hat{y}_{T+j\cdot}=v_{T+j\cdot}-p_{T+j\cdot}\left(\tilde{\Pi}-\Pi\right)=v_{T+j\cdot}-[(I\otimes p_{T+j\cdot})(\hat{\pi}-\pi)]',$$
$$(2.47)$$

where $\pi=\mathrm{vec}(\Pi)$; it is fairly straightforward to see that

$$E(e'_{T+j\cdot})=0,\qquad\mathrm{Cov}(e'_{T+j\cdot})=\Omega+(I\otimes p_{T+j\cdot})\,\mathrm{Cov}(\hat{\pi})\,(I\otimes p_{T+j\cdot})'.$$

Alternatively, we may deal with the forecast itself and, thus, define

$$E(\hat{y}_{T+j\cdot})=p_{T+j\cdot}E(\tilde{\Pi}),\quad\mathrm{Cov}(\hat{y}'_{T+j\cdot})=(I\otimes p_{T+j\cdot})\,\mathrm{Cov}(\hat{\pi})\,(I\otimes p_{T+j\cdot})'.$$
$$(2.48)$$

Remark 1. It is apparent from the definitions above that it makes very little substantive difference whether we deal with the forecast or the forecast error. We also observe from Eq. (2.46) that the forecast, $\hat{y}_{T+j\cdot}$, is an **unbiased estimator** of the conditional mean of the dependent variables given the exogenous variables, **if and only if** $E(e'_{T+j\cdot})=0$, provided the expectation $E(\hat{\Pi})=\Pi$ exists. In addition, the covariance matrices of the two constructs, $\hat{y}_{T+j\cdot}$ and $e_{T+j\cdot}$, differ only by the reduced form covariance matrix Ω, which does not depend on the particular method of forecast.

If we have two **unbiased** competing forecasts (of the same entity), based on the same model, let

$$\Sigma_{ji}=\mathrm{Cov}(e^{(i)}_{T+j\cdot}),\quad i=1,2,\qquad\qquad(2.49)$$

be their respective forecast error covariance matrix for the jth period beyond the sample. In order to rank such forecasts we introduce

Definition 1. Let $e^{(i)}_{T+j\cdot}$, $i=1,2$, be the forecast error, in the context of the preceding discussion corresponding, respectively, to the estimator $\hat{\Pi}^{(i)}$. If both are unbiased forecasts, we say that the first is **efficient relative** to the second forecast if and only if $\Sigma_{j2}-\Sigma_{j1}\geq0$.

Obtaining an explicit expression for the covariances in Eq. (2.49), we find

$$\Sigma_{ji}=\Omega+(I_m\otimes p_{T+j\cdot})\mathrm{Cov}(\hat{\pi}^{(i)})(I_m\otimes p'_{T+j\cdot}).\qquad(2.50)$$

Consequently,

$$\Sigma_{j2}-\Sigma_{j1}=(I_m\otimes p_{T+j\cdot})\left[\mathrm{Cov}(\hat{\pi}^{(2)})-\mathrm{Cov}(\hat{\pi}^{(1)})\right](I_m\otimes p'_{T+j\cdot}).\quad(2.51)$$

Several things are apparent from Eq. (2.51). First, since the conditioning variables, the $p's$, are essentially arbitrary, we conclude that **efficiency in estimation is equivalent to forecast efficiency**, since in Eq. (2.51)

$$\Sigma_{j2}-\Sigma_{j1}\geq0,\quad\text{if and only if}\quad\mathrm{Cov}(\hat{\pi}^{(2)})-\mathrm{Cov}(\hat{\pi}^{(1)})\geq0.$$

Second, **the ranking of two forecasts cannot depend on the particular period** j, i.e. if one forecasting procedure is efficient relative to another for the first period of the forecasting horizon, then this ranking will persist for all periods j, beyond the end of the sample. Thus, the subscript j may be dropped from the covariance matrices and we are able to state, unambiguously, that

$$\Sigma_2 - \Sigma_1 \geq 0, \quad \text{if and only if} \quad \mathrm{Cov}(\hat{\pi}^{(2)}) - \mathrm{Cov}(\hat{\pi}^{(1)}) \geq 0.$$

The results above are direct consequences of the fact that the forecast is a simple **linear transformation** of the estimate of the reduced form parameter matrix, Π.

A confidence interval about any (scalar) forecast can be constructed on the basis of the distribution of the underlying parameter estimator; similarly, a confidence ellipsoid can be constructed about any **vector** forecast, given the same information.

Example 3. Suppose it is given that

$$\hat{\pi} \sim N(\pi, \Psi),$$

and that Ψ is known. The forecast $\hat{y}'_{T+j\cdot} = (I \otimes p_{T+j\cdot})\hat{\pi}$ obeys

$$\hat{y}'_{T+j\cdot} \sim N[(I \otimes p_{T+j\cdot})\pi, \ (I \otimes p_{T+j\cdot})\Psi(I \otimes p_{T+j\cdot})'].$$

Consequently, there exists a constant k_α, such that the ellipsoid (with center $\hat{y}_{T+j\cdot}$)

$$(\bar{y}_{T+j\cdot} - \hat{y}_{T+j\cdot})\left[(I \otimes p_{T+j\cdot})\Psi(I \otimes p_{T+j\cdot})'\right]_g (\bar{y}_{T+j\cdot} - \hat{y}_{T+j\cdot})' \leq k_\alpha$$

contains the conditional expectation of the dependent given the predetermined variables, ($\bar{y}_{T+j\cdot}$), with probability $1-\alpha$. In the preceding we have used the generalized inverse of the covariance matrix of the forecast in order to cover the eventuality that singularities may be present.

Example 4. Suppose everything is as in Example 3, except that now we only have the **limiting distributional assertion**

$$\sqrt{T}(\hat{\pi} - \pi) \sim N(0, \Psi)$$

and Ψ is not known, although a consistent estimator, $\hat{\Psi}$, is available. In such a case the properties noted above are not available in **finite** samples; on the other hand, all such claims remain valid **asymptotically**. In particular, we note that, asymptotically,

$$T(\hat{y}_{T+j\cdot} - \bar{y}_{T+j\cdot})\left[(I \otimes p_{T+j\cdot})\hat{\Psi}(I \otimes p_{T+j\cdot})'\right]_g (\hat{y}_{T+j\cdot} - \bar{y}_{T+j\cdot})' \sim \chi_r,$$

where r is the minimum of the number of elements in $\bar{y}$ and the rank of the (covariance) matrix of the forecast. The distributional statement above is to be understood, strictly speaking, in a limiting sense, i.e. on the assertion that the sample size increases indefinitely – for $T \to \infty$. Evidently, this is not quite sensible since we cannot let $T \to \infty$ **and** forecast beyond T. Thus, the statement above is best understood as an approximation that becomes increasing valid as the sample size increases! Let k_α be the $1 - \alpha$ percentile of the relevant distribution, and interpret the relation

$$T(\bar{y}_{T+j\cdot} - \hat{y}_{T+j\cdot})\left[(I \otimes p_{T+j\cdot})\Psi(I \otimes p_{T+j\cdot})'\right]_g (\bar{y}_{T+j\cdot} - \hat{y}_{T+j\cdot})' \leq k_\alpha, \quad (2.52)$$

as an ellipsoid with center at $\hat{y}'_{T+j\cdot}$. Given the assertions above, we may interpret the relationship in Eq. (2.52) as an ellipsoid with center at $\hat{y}'_{T+j\cdot}$ which, **for sufficiently large** T, **will cover the "true" conditional mean,** $\bar{y}_{T+j\cdot}$, **with probability, approximately,** $1 - \alpha$.

Dynamic Models

In dealing with dynamic models in a previous section we had employed lag operators and we had obtained a formal solution of the underlying difference equation involved, by inverting an appropriate polynomial operator. This particular approach is not useful in the present context since in making forecasts from a dynamic model **it is very important that we take into account initial conditions**. The formal solution obtained earlier does away with initial conditions and, thus, may be interpreted as a long run solution. If we are to predict or forecast $y_{T+1\cdot}$ given information up to time T it would be foolhardy to ignore the information conveyed by $y_{T-i\cdot}$, for $i = 1, 2, \ldots, k$. Thus, an alternative approach is indicated. Given the model

$$y_{t\cdot} = y_{t-1\cdot}\Pi_1 + y_{t-2\cdot}\Pi_2 + \ldots + y_{t-k\cdot}\Pi_k + p_{t\cdot}\Pi_0 + v_{t\cdot}, \quad (2.53)$$

$$= x_{t\cdot}\Pi + v_{t\cdot}, \quad \Pi = (\Pi_1', \pi_2', \ldots, \Pi_k', \Pi_0')', \quad (2.54)$$

and observations for $t = 1, 2, \ldots, T$, we obtain the estimators of the parameter matrices, $\hat{\Pi}_i$, $i = 0, 1, 2, \ldots, k$, by some appropriate method, and we forecast

$$\hat{y}_{T+\tau\cdot} = \hat{y}_{T+\tau-1\cdot}\hat{\Pi}_1 + \hat{y}_{T+\tau-2\cdot}\hat{\Pi}_2 + \cdots + \hat{y}_{T+\tau-k\cdot}\hat{\Pi}_k + p_{T+\tau\cdot}^*, \quad (2.55)$$

where, for ease of notation we have put $p_{T+\tau\cdot}^* = p_{T+\tau\cdot}\hat{\Pi}_0$. Write this as

$$\hat{y}'_{T+\tau\cdot} = \hat{A}_1^{(\tau)}y'_{T\cdot} + \hat{A}_2^{(\tau)}y'_{T-1\cdot} + \cdots + \hat{A}_k^{(\tau)}y'_{T-k+1\cdot}$$

$$+ \hat{B}_1^{(\tau)}p_{T+1\cdot}^{*'} + \hat{B}_2^{(\tau)}p_{T+2\cdot}^{*'} + \ldots + \hat{B}_\tau^{(\tau)}p_{T+\tau\cdot}^{*'}.$$

$$\hat{A}_1^{(1)} = \hat{\Pi}_1', \quad \hat{A}_2^{(1)} = \hat{\Pi}_2', \ldots, \hat{A}_k^{(1)} = \hat{\Pi}_k'. \quad (2.56)$$

We shall now attempt to determine the matrices $A_i^{(j)}$ and $B_s^{(j)}$ for $i = 1, 2, \ldots, k$, $s = 1, 2, \ldots, \tau$ and $j = 1, 2, \ldots \tau$, by establishing a recursive relation. Thus,

$$
\hat{y}'_{T+j\cdot} = \hat{A}_1^{(1)} \left[\sum_{i=1}^{k} \hat{A}_i^{(j-1)} y'_{T-i+1\cdot} \right] + \hat{A}_2^{(1)} \left[\sum_{i=1}^{k} \hat{A}_i^{(j-2)} y'_{T-i+1\cdot} \right] + \cdots
$$

$$
+ \hat{A}_k^{(1)} \left[\sum_{i=1}^{k} \hat{A}_i^{(j-k)} y'_{T-i+1\cdot} \right] + \hat{A}_1^{(1)} \left[\sum_{s=1}^{j-1} \hat{B}_s^{(j-1)} p_{T+s\cdot}^{*'} \right]
$$

$$
+ \hat{A}_2^{(1)} \left[\sum_{s=1}^{j-1} \hat{B}_s^{(j-2)} p_{T+s\cdot}^{*'} \right] + \cdots
$$

$$
+ \hat{A}_k^{(1)} \left[\sum_{s=1}^{j-k} \hat{B}_s^{(j-k)} p_{T+s\cdot}^{*'} \right] + p_{T+j\cdot}^{*'}. \tag{2.57}
$$

Collecting terms we find

$$
\hat{A}_i^{(j)} = \sum_{s=1}^{k} \hat{A}_s^{(1)} \hat{A}_i^{(j-s)} \quad \hat{B}_r^{(j)} = \sum_{s=1}^{k} \hat{A}_s^{(1)} \hat{B}_r^{(j-s)}, \quad B_r^{(j)} = A_1^{(j-r)}, \tag{2.58}
$$

where $i = 1, 2, \ldots, k$, $r = 1, 2, \ldots, j$ and $j = 1, 2, \ldots, \tau$. In order to make the formal definitions of Eq. (2.57) operational, we need to impose certain "initial conditions", beyond those imposed in Eq. (2.56). These conditions may be summarized in Eq. (2.59) below.

$$
\begin{aligned}
A_i^{(-s)} &= 0, \ s > 0, \\
A_i^{(0)} &= I, \ i = 1, 2, \ldots, k \\
B_i^{(j)} &= I, \ i = j, \ \text{or} \ j = 0, \\
B_i^{(j)} &= 0, \ j < i, \ \text{as well as for } j < 0. \tag{2.59}
\end{aligned}
$$

Remark 2. It should be stressed again that the avoidance of the formal solution of Eq. (2.26), in generating the forecast of Eq. (2.54) or (2.55) is not a matter of whim. The form in Eq. (2.26), while analytically very useful, would be totally inappropriate for generating forecasts. First, its use, as it stands, would oblige us to generate a forecast in the form

$$
\hat{y}'_{T+\tau\cdot} = \sum_{j=0}^{T+\tau} \hat{H}_j p'_{T+\tau-j\cdot}, \tag{2.60}
$$

where the matrices H_j are defined implicitly in the expansion of the operator $H(L)/b(L)$ in Eq. (2.28), i.e.

$$\frac{H(L)}{b(L)} = \sum_{j=0}^{\infty} H_j L^j .$$

Second, even if initial conditions were to be taken into account, by considering the general solution to the homogeneous part of the vector difference equation, this approach would still be undesirable in that it would require additional computational burdens entailed by the extraction of the characteristic roots, and their associated characteristic vectors, i.e. it would entail the solution of the equation (where $z = e^{i\theta}$ is the complex indeterminate)

$$\left| I - \sum_{j=1}^{k} \Pi'_j z^j \right| = 0, \tag{2.61}$$

before obtaining the estimators of the matrices H_j.

Having now completed the discussion of how to obtain forecasts from a dynamic model, [11] we next take up the issue of how to determine the degree of uncertainty surrounding such forecasts. We note that, when dealing with dynamic models, the simple linear properties of static models vanish and the resulting nonlinearities make the distributional issues a great deal more complicated. In the static case of the discussion immediately preceding, we had noted that the forecast was simply a linear transformation of the estimated parameters. Hence, its distribution was easily derived; this is, decidedly, not the case in the current context.

Distributional Aspects of Forecasts from Dynamic Models

Solving the model in Eq. (2.26) or (2.53), and the "initial conditions", $y_{T\cdot}, y_{T-1\cdot}, \ldots, y_{T-k+1\cdot}$, as given, we obtain

$$y'_{T+\tau\cdot} = A_1^{(\tau)} y'_{T\cdot} + A_2^{(\tau)} y'_{T-1\cdot} + \cdots + A_k^{(\tau)} y'_{T-k+1\cdot}$$

$$+ B_1^{(\tau)} \Pi'_0 p'_{T+1\cdot} + B_2^{(\tau)} \Pi'_0 p'_{T+2\cdot} + \cdots + B_\tau^{(\tau)} \Pi'_0 p'_{T+\tau\cdot}$$

$$+ B_1^{(\tau)} v'_{T+1\cdot} + B_2^{(\tau)} v'_{T+2\cdot} + \cdots + B_\tau^{(\tau)} v'_{T+\tau\cdot}. \tag{2.62}$$

Consequently,

$$\bar{y}_{T+\tau\cdot} = E\left(y_{T+\tau\cdot} \mid y_{T\cdot}, y_{T-1\cdot}, \ldots, y_{T-k+1\cdot}, p_{T+1\cdot}, \ldots, p_{T+\tau\cdot} \right)$$

---

[11] In the language of engineering such a model would be termed a vector autoregressive model with "forcing function(s)" $p_{t\cdot}$ and $v_{t\cdot}$, or perhaps more appropriately a **stochastic vector autoregressive model** with "forcing function" $p_{t\cdot}$.

$$= A_1^{(\tau)} y_T' + A_2^{(\tau)} y_{T-1}' + \ldots + A_k^{(\tau)} y_{T-k+1}'. \tag{2.63}$$

$$+ B_1^{(\tau)} \Pi_0' p_{T+1}' + B_2^{(\tau)} \Pi_0' p_{T+2}' + \ldots + B_\tau^{(\tau)} \Pi_0' p_{T+\tau}',$$

and from Eqs. (2.56), (2.57), (2.62), and (2.63), we obtain

$$\hat{y}_{T+\tau} - \bar{y}_{T+\tau} = \sum_{s=1}^{k} y_{T-s+1} \left(\hat{A}_s^{(\tau)} - A_s^{(\tau)} \right)' \tag{2.64}$$

$$+ \sum_{j=1}^{\tau} p_{T+j} \left(\hat{A}_1^{(\tau-j)} \hat{\Pi}_0' - A_1^{(\tau-j)} \Pi_0' \right)'$$

Although Eq. (2.64) might appear hopeless, in fact, it can serve as the basis for some asymptotic theory regarding forecasts with dynamic models. It may be shown that the entities $(\hat{A}_s^{(\tau)} - A_s^{(\tau)})'$ involve terms of the form, [12] say, $\hat{\Pi}_i^m \hat{\Pi}_j^n - \Pi_i^m \Pi_j^n$, and sums of terms of this form. We see, however, that by adding and subtracting $\Pi_i^m \hat{\Pi}_j^n$

$$\hat{\Pi}_i^m \hat{\Pi}_j^n - \Pi_i^m \Pi_j^n = (\hat{\Pi}_i^m - \Pi_i^m)\hat{\Pi}_j^n + \Pi_i^m (\hat{\Pi}_j^n - \Pi_j^n).$$

Hence, the only remaining problem is a suitable representation for entities of the form $(\hat{\Pi}_j^n - \Pi_j^n)$. But it is a rather simple operation to show that

$$(\hat{\Pi}_j^n - \Pi_j^n) = \sum_{i=1}^{n} \Pi_j^{i-1} (\hat{\Pi}_j - \Pi_j)\hat{\Pi}_j^{n-i}. \tag{2.65}$$

Thus, we conclude that there exist matrices, say $(A_{ji}^{(\tau)} \otimes B_{ji}^{(\tau)})$, such that

$$\text{vec}\left((\hat{A}_i^{(\tau)} - A_i^{(\tau)})' \right) = \sum_{j=1}^{k} (A_{ji}^{(\tau)} \otimes B_{ji}^{(\tau)})(\hat{\pi}_j - \pi_j), \tag{2.66}$$

where $(\hat{\pi}_j - \pi_j) = \text{vec}(\hat{\Pi}_j - \Pi_j)$. The remaining term obeys

$$\hat{\Pi}_0 \hat{A}_1^{(\tau-j)'} - \Pi_0 A_1^{(\tau-j)'} = (\hat{\Pi}_0 - \Pi_0)\hat{A}_1^{(\tau-j)'} + \Pi_0 \left(\hat{A}_1^{(\tau-j)} - A_1^{(\tau-j)} \right)'.$$

---

[12] When a model with lags of order k is considered, i.e. when we are dealing with a kth order vector difference equation, we need to deal with products of at most k terms. In such a case it may be shown that

$$\hat{\Pi}_1^{s_1} \hat{\Pi}_2^{s_2} \cdots \hat{\Pi}_k^{s_k} - \Pi_1^{s_1} \Pi_2^{s_2} \cdots \Pi_k^{s_k} = \sum_{r=1}^{k} \left[\left(\prod_{i=1}^{r-1} \Pi_i^{s_i} \right) (\hat{\Pi}_r^{s_r} - \Pi_r^{s_r}) \left(\prod_{i=r+1}^{k} \hat{\Pi}_i^{s_i} \right) \right].$$

Thus, the ensuing discussion is fully relevant and exhaustive.

Thus,

$$\text{vec}\left(\left(\hat{A}_1^{(\tau-j)}\hat{\Pi}_0' - A_1^{(\tau-j)}\Pi_0'\right)'\right) = \Pi_0^* \sum_{s=1}^{k}\left(\left(A_{s1}^{(\tau-j)} \otimes B_{s1}^{(\tau-j)}\right)(\hat{\pi}_s - \pi_s)\right)$$

$$+(\hat{A}_1^{(\tau-j)} \otimes I)(\hat{\pi}_0 - \pi_0),$$

$$\Pi_0^* = (I \otimes \Pi_0). \tag{2.67}$$

Substituting in Eq. (2.64) we obtain

$$\text{vec}(\hat{y}_{T+\tau\cdot} - \bar{y}_{T+\tau\cdot}) = \sum_{j=1}^{k}(F_{j1} + F_{j2})(\hat{\pi}_j - \pi_j) \tag{2.68}$$

$$+\left[\sum_{i=1}^{\tau}(A_1^{(\tau-i)} \otimes p_{T+i\cdot})\right](\hat{\pi}_0 - \pi_0)$$

$$F_{j1} = \sum_{s=1}^{k}\left(\left(I \otimes y_{T-s+1\cdot}\right)(A_{js}^{(\tau)} \otimes B_{js}^{(\tau)})\right)$$

$$F_{j2} = \sum_{i=1}^{\tau}\left(\left(I \otimes p_{T+i\cdot}\Pi_0\right)(A_{j1}^{(\tau-i)} \otimes B_{j1}^{(\tau-i)})\right)$$

for $j = 1, 2, \ldots, k$; moreover, defining

$$S_{(j)}^{(\tau)} = \sum_{s=1}^{k}(I \otimes y_{T-s+1\cdot})(A_{js}^{(\tau)} \otimes B_{js}^{(\tau)})$$

$$+\sum_{i=1}^{\tau}(I \otimes p_{T+i\cdot}\Pi_0)(A_{j1}^{(\tau-i)} \otimes B_{j1}^{(\tau-i)})$$

$$S_{(0)}^{(\tau)} = \sum_{i=1}^{\tau}(\hat{A}_1^{(\tau-i)} \otimes p_{T+i\cdot})$$

$$S^{(\tau)} = (S_{(1)}^{(\tau)}, S_{(2)}^{(\tau)}, \ldots, S_{(k)}^{(\tau)}, S_{(0)}^{(\tau)})$$

$$\Pi = (\Pi_1', \Pi_2', \ldots, \Pi_k', \Pi_0')', \tag{2.69}$$

we can represent the vector of forecasts as

$$S^{(\tau)}\begin{bmatrix} \hat{\pi}_1 - \pi_1 \\ \hat{\pi}_2 - \pi_2 \\ \vdots \\ \hat{\pi}_k - \pi_k \\ \hat{\pi}_0 - \pi_0 \end{bmatrix} = \text{vec}(\hat{y}_{T+\tau\cdot} - \bar{y}_{T+\tau\cdot}). \tag{2.70}$$

Comparing the vector in the left member of Eq. (2.70) with $\text{vec}(\hat{\Pi} - \Pi)$ we note that while the two have the same number, [13] and exactly the same type, of elements their arrangement is different. But his means that there exists a permutation matrix, say $I'_{(n,n)}$, such that

$$I'_{(n,n)} \begin{bmatrix} \hat{\pi}_1 - \pi_1 \\ \hat{\pi}_2 - \pi_2 \\ \vdots \\ \hat{\pi}_k - \pi_k \\ \hat{\pi}_0 - \pi_0 \end{bmatrix} = \text{vec}(\hat{\Pi} - \Pi) = (\hat{\pi} - \pi), \quad n = m(mk + s),$$

where Π is as defined in Eq. (2.69). It follows, therefore, that

$$\text{vec}(\hat{y}_{T+\tau\cdot} - \bar{y}_{T+\tau\cdot}) = S^{(\tau)} I_{(n,n)} (\hat{\pi} - \pi). \tag{2.71}$$

Thus, if it is known that $\sqrt{T}(\hat{\pi} - \pi)$ has a limiting distribution of the form, say,

$$\sqrt{T}(\hat{\pi} - \pi) \sim N(0, \ \Psi),$$

then, if the sample is sufficiently large, we would be able to argue that

$$T(\hat{y}_{T+\tau\cdot} - \bar{y}_{T+\tau\cdot})(S^{(\tau)} I_{(n,n)} \Psi I'_{(n,n)} S^{(\tau)'})_g (\hat{y}_{T+\tau\cdot} - \bar{y}_{T+\tau\cdot})' \sim \chi_r^2, \tag{2.72}$$

where,

$$r = \text{rank}\left[(S^{(\tau)} I_{(n,n)} \Psi I'_{(n,n)} S^{(\tau)'})_g\right],$$

and $(S^{(\tau)} I_{(n,n)} \Psi I'_{(n,n)} S^{(\tau)'})_g$ is the generalized inverse. We summarize the development immediately above in

Theorem 3. Consider the GLSEM of Theorem 1 and suppose it is given that the limiting distribution of the URF obeys

$$\sqrt{T}(\hat{\pi} - \pi) \sim N(0, \ \Psi).$$

Then,

i. if the model is static,

$$T(\hat{y}_{T+\tau\cdot} - \bar{y}_{T+\tau\cdot}) \left((I \otimes p_{T+j\cdot})\hat{\Psi}(I \otimes p_{T+j\cdot})'\right)_g (\hat{y}_{T+\tau\cdot} - \bar{y}_{T+\tau\cdot})' \sim \chi_r^2;$$

ii. if the model is dynamic,

$$T(\hat{y}_{T+\tau\cdot} - \bar{y}_{T+\tau\cdot})(S^{(\tau)} I_{(n,n)} \hat{\Psi} I'_{(n,n)} S^{(\tau)'})_g (\hat{y}_{T+\tau\cdot} - \bar{y}_{T+\tau\cdot})' \sim \chi_r^2,$$

where r is the rank of the generalized inverse, and $\hat{\Psi}$ is a consistent estimator of Ψ.

Proof: See the discussion in the last two (sub)sections.

---

[13] We remind the reader that by assumption (A.1), of Chapter 1, the number of **exogenous** variables, i.e. the number of elements in $p_{t\cdot}$, is s; thus the vectors in question have $n = m(mk + s)$ elements.

2.2.3   Forecasting from the RRF

In this section we take up the question of whether a gain in the efficiency of forecasts would accrue when we use the **restricted reduced form (RRF)**, i.e. when we use estimates of Π, that take account of the fact that $\Pi = CD$. Given the preceding discussion, the question may be rephrased as: Is the restricted reduced form efficient, relative to the unrestricted reduced form? In terms of the intuitive perception of the problem, one would expect that since in the RRF we take into account the a priori restrictions on the structural parameters, therefore, the resulting estimators would be relatively efficient. It will turn out that this view is basically correct, although not literally as stated.

Properties of the RRF

Since the RRF is derived from the relationship

$$\Pi = CD, \quad D = (I - B)^{-1},$$

we must look to the properties of the estimators of the matrices C and B for determining the properties of Π. Let their estimators be, respectively, $\hat{C}$, $\hat{D}$, $\hat{\Pi}$ and consider

$$
\begin{aligned}
\hat{\Pi} - \Pi &= \hat{C}\hat{D} - CD = \hat{C}\hat{D} - \hat{C}D + \hat{C}D - CD \\
&= \hat{C}\hat{D}(D^{-1} - \hat{D}^{-1})D + (\hat{C} - C)D,
\end{aligned}
$$

which may be rewritten more constructively as

$$\hat{C}\hat{D} - CD = \hat{\Pi} - \Pi = (\hat{C}\hat{D}, \quad I)\begin{bmatrix} \hat{B} - B \\ \hat{C} - C \end{bmatrix} D. \tag{2.73}$$

If we put $A = (B', \ C')'$, we note that $\mathrm{vec}(A) = L\delta$, where δ is the vector of structural parameters in the entire system not specified a priori (to be zero or one). Using the results in Ch. 4 of Dhrymes (1984), we may write

$$
\begin{aligned}
\sqrt{T}\left(\mathrm{vec}(\hat{\Pi} - \Pi)\right) &= \sqrt{T}(\hat{\pi} - \pi) = \sqrt{T}\left(D' \otimes (\hat{\Pi}, \ I)\right)\mathrm{vec}(A - \hat{A}) \\
&= \sqrt{T}\left(D' \otimes (\hat{\Pi}, \ I)\right)L[\sqrt{T}(\hat{\delta} - \delta)] \\
&= (D' \otimes I)\hat{S}[\sqrt{T}(\hat{\delta} - \delta)], \tag{2.74}
\end{aligned}
$$

where $S = [I \otimes (\Pi, I)]L$ is as defined in Chapter 1. Combining the discussion above with that of the previous two (sub) sections we conclude that whether the GLSEM is static or dynamic the difference between "a τ period ahead forecast" and the (relevant) conditional mean is given by

$$\sqrt{T}\mathrm{vec}(\hat{y}_{T+\tau\cdot} - \bar{y}_{T+\tau\cdot})_{(i)} = F_{(i)}\sqrt{T}(\hat{\pi} - \pi)_{(i)},$$

where $i = 1$ stands for the URF, $i = 2$ stands for the RRF, **induced by the 2SLS estimator of the structural parameters** and $i = 3$ stands for the RRF **induced by the 3SLS estimator of the structural parameters.** Thus we have, for the URF and the static model,

$$\sqrt{T}\text{vec}(\hat{y}_{T+\tau\cdot} - \bar{y}_{T+\tau\cdot})_{(1)} = (I \otimes p_{T+\tau\cdot})(\hat{\pi} - \pi)_{URF} \quad \text{and}$$

$$= S^{(\tau)}\sqrt{T}(\hat{\pi} - \pi)_{URF}, \tag{2.75}$$

for the dynamic model. For the 2SLS induced restricted reduced form, we find for the static model

$$\sqrt{T}(\hat{\pi} - \pi)_{RRF(2SLS)} = (D' \otimes I)\hat{S}\sqrt{T}(\hat{\delta} - \delta)_{2SLS},$$
$$\sqrt{T}\text{vec}(\hat{y}_{T+\tau\cdot} - \bar{y}_{T+\tau\cdot})_{(2)} = (I \otimes p_{T+\tau\cdot})\sqrt{T}(\hat{\pi} - \pi)_{RRF(2SLS)} \quad \text{and}$$

$$= S^{(\tau)}\sqrt{T}(\hat{\pi} - \pi)_{RRF(2SLS)}. \tag{2.76}$$

for the dynamic model. Finally, for 3SLS induced restricted reduced forms, we find for the static model

$$\sqrt{T}(\hat{\pi} - \pi)_{RRF(3SLS)} = (D' \otimes I)\hat{S}\sqrt{T}(\hat{\delta} - \delta)_{3SLS}$$
$$\sqrt{T}\text{vec}(\hat{y}_{T+\tau\cdot} - \bar{y}_{T+\tau\cdot})_{(3)} = (I \otimes p_{T+\tau\cdot})\sqrt{T}(\hat{\pi} - \pi)_{RRF(3SLS)} \quad \text{and}$$

$$= S^{(\tau)}\sqrt{T}(\hat{\pi} - \pi)_{RRF(3SLS)}, \tag{2.77}$$

for the dynamic model.

Remark 3. As we had found in the discussion of URF the (suitably normalized) deviation of the forecast from the conditional mean of the dependent variables is, asymptotically, i.e. for large samples, a linear transformation of the deviation of the reduced form estimate from the underlying parameter. This holds true whether we deal with static or dynamic models. Thus, whether one type of forecast is "efficient" relative to another depends crucially on a similar comparison of the limiting distributions of the underlying reduced form estimators.

Up to this point we have considered three types of estimators for the reduced form: first, the unrestricted reduced form, obtained through the regression of the jointly dependent on the predetermined variables; second, the 2SLS induced restricted reduced form, in which the estimator of the matrix Π is derived from the 2SLS estimators of the underlying structural matrices, B, C; and, finally, the 3SLS induced reduced form which derives an estimator of the reduced form matrix Π through the 3SLS estimator of the underlying structural parameter matrices, B, C.[14] It follows from the

---

[14] In subsequent chapters we shall examine other structural estimators such as

preceding discussion that before we can deal with the relative efficiencies of various forecasting procedures we must first prove a result regarding the **relative efficiencies of the various estimators of the reduced form**. The properties of the reduced form estimators considered are given in the theorems below.

Theorem 4. Under the conditions of Theorem 1, the following statements are true:

i. asymptotically,

$$\sqrt{T}(\hat{\pi} - \pi)_{URF} \sim N(0,\ G_{(1)}), \quad G_{(1)} = (D \otimes \bar{R}^{-1})'\Phi(D \otimes \bar{R}^{-1})$$

and $\Phi = \Sigma \otimes I_G$;

ii. asymptotically,

$$\sqrt{T}(\hat{\pi} - \pi)_{RRF(2SLS)} \sim N(0,\ G_{(2)}), \quad J = S^*(S^{*'}S^*)^{-1}S^{*'},$$

where
$$G_{(2)} = (D \otimes \bar{R}^{-1})'J\Phi J(D \otimes \bar{R}^{-1}), \quad S^* = (I \otimes \bar{R}')S;$$

iii. asymptotically,

$$\sqrt{T}(\hat{\pi} - \pi)_{RRF(3SLS)} \sim N(0,\ G_{(3)}),$$

$$G_{(3)} = (D \otimes \bar{R}^{-1})'S^*(S^{*'}\Phi^{-1}S^*)^{-1}S^{*'}(D \otimes \bar{R}^{-1}).$$

Proof: The proof of i is straightforward; since $\hat{\Pi} = (X'X)^{-1}X'Y$ we find, upon substitution

$$\hat{\Pi} - \Pi = (X'X)^{-1}X'UD, \quad \text{or}$$

$$\sqrt{T}(\hat{\pi} - \pi)_{URF} = (D \otimes I)'\left[I \otimes \left(\frac{X'X}{T}\right)^{-1}\right]\frac{1}{\sqrt{T}}(I \otimes X')\,u.$$

Noting that $M_{xx} = \bar{R}\bar{R}'$, the conclusion is immediate.

As for parts ii and iii, we have that

$$(\hat{\pi} - \pi)_{RRF} = (D \otimes I)'\hat{S}(\hat{\delta} - \delta);$$

Full Information Maximum Likelihood (FIML), Limited Information Maximum Likelihood (LIML), and Indirect Least Squares (ILS) estimators. We shall show, in due course, that the first two are equivalent to the 3SLS and 2SLS estimators, respectively, in the sense that their limiting distributions are identical. ILS is an estimator that reverses the process and, thus, derives the structural parameter estimators from those of the **unrestricted** reduced form.

thus, for the 2SLS estimator we conclude

$$\sqrt{T}(\hat{\pi} - \pi)_{RRF(2SLS)} \sim N\left(0, \ (D \otimes I)'SC_2S'(D \otimes I)\right), \qquad (2.78)$$

while for the 3SLS estimator we find

$$\sqrt{T}(\hat{\pi} - \pi)_{RRF(3SLS)} \sim N\left(0, \ (D \otimes I)'SC_3S'(D \otimes I)\right). \qquad (2.79)$$

From Eqs. (2.4), (2.6) and (2.8) we determine

$$C_2 = (S^{*'}S^*)^{-1}S^{*'}\Phi S^*(S^{*'}S^*)^{-1}, \quad C_3 = (S^{*'}\Phi^{-1}S^*)^{-1}$$

and $(D \otimes I)'S = (D \otimes \bar{R}^{-1})'S^*$, which concludes the proof of the theorem.

q.e.d.

While the discussion above has established the limiting distribution of the various reduced form estimators, the following theorem establishes their relative efficiencies.

Theorem 5. Under the conditions of Theorem 3, the following statements are true:

   i. $G_{(1)} - G_{(3)} \geq 0$;

  ii. $G_{(2)} - G_{(3)} \geq 0$;

 iii. $G_{(1)} - G_{(2)} \geq 0$, if and only if $\Phi_{21}^* = 0$; otherwise it is indefinite;

 iv. $\Phi_{21}^* = 0$, if at least one of the following three conditions holds, otherwise $\Phi_{21}^* \neq 0$;

    1. $\sigma_{ij} = 0$, for all $i \neq j$;

    2. all equations are just identified;

    3. $\sigma_{ij} \neq 0$, for some pair say (i_0, j_0), implies that the corresponding equations are just identified.

Proof: Put

$$G_{(1)} - G_{(3)} = (D \otimes \bar{R}^{-1})'[\Phi - S^*(S^{*'}\Phi^{-1}S^*)^{-1}S^*](D \otimes \bar{R}^{-1});$$

the matrix in the left member is positive semidefinite if and only if

$$\Phi - S^*(S^{*'}\Phi^{-1}S^*)^{-1}S^{*'} \geq 0.$$

Consider the characteristic equation

$$\mid \lambda\Phi - S^*(S^{*'}\Phi^{-1}S^*)^{-1}S^{*'} \mid = 0,$$

and note that it has exactly the same characteristic roots as

$$| \lambda I - S^*(S^{*'}\Phi^{-1}S^*)^{-1}S^{*'}\Phi^{-1} | = 0,$$

whose nonzero characteristic roots are exactly those of

$$| \mu I - (S^{*'}\Phi^{-1}S^*)^{-1}S^{*'}\Phi^{-1}S^* | = | \mu I - I_k | = 0, \quad k = \sum_{i=1}^{m}(m_i + G_i).$$

Using the results in Ch. 2 of Dhrymes (1984), we conclude that there exists a nonsingular matrix P such that

$$\Phi = PP', \quad S^*(S^{*'}\Phi^{-1}S^*)^{-1}S^{*'} = P \begin{bmatrix} I_k & 0 \\ 0 & 0 \end{bmatrix} P,$$

so that

$$\Phi - S^*(S^{*'}\Phi^{-1}S^*)^{-1}S^{*'} = P \begin{bmatrix} 0 & 0 \\ 0 & I_{mG-k} \end{bmatrix} P' \geq 0.$$

To prove part ii we note that

$$G_{(2)} - G_{(3)} = (D \otimes \bar{R}^{-1})'S^*[C_2 - C_3]S^{*'}(D \otimes \bar{R}^{-1}),$$

which is evidently positive semidefinite due to the fact that 3SLS is efficient relative to 2SLS, i.e. that $C_2 - C_3 \geq 0$.

As for part iii we have that

$$G_{(1)} - G_{(2)} = (D \otimes \bar{R}^{-1})'[\Phi - J\Phi J](D \otimes \bar{R}^{-1}), \quad \text{where} \quad J = S^*(S^{*'}S^*)^{-1}S^{*'}.$$

In view of the fact that $(D \otimes \bar{R}^{-1})$ is **nonsingular**, the matrix in the left member above is positive semidefinite, negative semidefinite or indefinite according to whether the matrix in square brackets (in the right member above) does or does not share these properties. Since J is a symmetric idempotent matrix, it obeys $k = \text{rank}(J) = \sum_{i=1}^{m}(m_i + G_i) \leq mG$. Thus, there exists an **orthogonal** matrix E, such that

$$J = E \begin{bmatrix} I_k & 0 \\ 0 & 0 \end{bmatrix} E'.$$

Consequently, we can write

$$E'[\Phi - J\Phi J]E = \Phi^* - \begin{bmatrix} I_k & 0 \\ 0 & 0 \end{bmatrix} \Phi^* \begin{bmatrix} I_k & 0 \\ 0 & 0 \end{bmatrix} = \begin{bmatrix} 0 & \Phi_{12}^* \\ \Phi_{21}^* & \Phi_{22}^* \end{bmatrix},$$

where $\Phi^* = E'\Phi E$. Since, by assumption, Φ is nonsingular, it follows that Φ_{22}^* is also nonsingular. Thus, $G_{(1)} - G_{(2)} \geq 0$, if and only if $\Phi_{21}^* = 0$. The sufficiency part of this statement is obvious, so let us demonstrate its necessity. Thus, suppose $G_{(1)} - G_{(2)} \geq 0$ and $\Phi_{21}^* \neq 0$; we derive a contradiction. Since the latter holds there exists at least one vector, say $\alpha \neq 0$, such that $\Phi_{21}^* \alpha \neq 0$. Consider, then

$$\phi(\alpha, \beta) = 2\alpha' \Phi_{12}^* \beta + \beta' \Phi_{22}^* \beta$$

$$= 3\alpha' \Phi_{12}^* \Phi_{22}^{*-1} \Phi_{21}^* \alpha > 0, \quad \text{for} \quad \beta = \Phi_{22}^{*-1} \Phi_{21}^* \alpha,$$

$$= -\alpha' \Phi_{12}^* \Phi_{22}^{*-1} \Phi_{21}^* \alpha < 0, \quad \text{for} \quad \beta = -\Phi_{22}^{*-1} \Phi_{21}^* \alpha.$$

Thus, the matrix $G_{(1)} - G_{(2)}$ is **indefinite** unless special circumstances hold, which brings us to the consideration of part iv.

To prove part iv we note that $J = \text{diag}(J_1, J_2, \ldots, J_m)$, where $J_i = S_i^* (S_i^{*'} S_i^*)^{-1} S_i^{*'}$, for $i = 1, 2, \ldots, m$ and each is symmetric idempotent of rank $m_i + G_i$. Let E_i be their respective matrices of characteristic vectors and partition $E_i = (E_{i1}, E_{i2})$, such that E_{i1} corresponds to the unit (characteristic) roots and E_{i2} corresponds to the zero roots. Define

$$E_{(1)} = \text{diag}(E_{11}, E_{21}, \ldots, E_{m1}), \quad E_{(2)} = \text{diag}(E_{12}, E_{22}, \ldots, E_{m2})$$

and note that $E = (E_{(1)}, E_{(2)})$. Consequently,

$$\Phi_{12}^* = \left(\sigma_{ij} E_{i1}' E_{j2}\right), \quad \Phi_{21}^* = \left(\sigma_{ji} E_{j2}' E_{i1}\right), \tag{2.80}$$

and we see that $\Phi_{12}^* = 0$ if $\sigma_{ij} = 0$, or if $E_{i1}' E_{j2} = 0$, for all i and j. It is interesting to note that if all equations of the system are **just identified**, the condition $E_{i1}' E_{j2} = 0$ obviously does hold, [15]; conversely, if $E_{i1}' E_{j2} = 0$, for all i and j **then all equations in the system are just identified**. To see this let ν_s denote the **dimension of the column null space**, i.e, the nullity of E_{s1}'. By the condition above we have

$$E_{11}' E_{s2} = 0, \quad \text{for all} \quad s.$$

Since E_{12} is a **basis** for the column null space of E_{11}', there exists a unique matrix, say C_{s2}, such that $E_{s2} = E_{12} C_{s2}$, and moreover, we must have $\nu_s \leq \nu_1$. Repeating this argument with E_{21}, E_{31}, etc., we conclude that

$$\nu_1 \geq \nu_s, \nu_2 \geq \nu_s, \ldots, \nu_m \geq \nu_s, \quad \text{for} \quad s = 1, 2, \ldots, m.$$

But this implies that $\nu_s = \nu_1$, for all s. Similarly, from the condition $E_{12}' E_{s1} = 0$, for all s, we conclude that $E_{s1} = E_{11} C_{s1}$ and, moreover, that the dimension of the column null space of E_{12} is equal to that of the column null space of E_{s2}, for all s. This means that the matrices, C_{s1}

---

[15] A particularly simple way of justifying this claim is to note that, in the case where all equations are just identified, $J_s = I_G$, for all $s = 1, 2, \ldots, m$; thus, $\Phi - J\Phi J = 0$!

are square and **nonsingular** and have the same dimension for all s; the same is true of the matrices C_{s2}. Using the results above we find

$$J_s E_{s1} = E_{s1}, \quad \text{or} \quad J_s E_{11} C_{s1} = E_{11} C_{s1}, \quad \text{or} \quad J_s E_{11} = E_{11}, \qquad (2.81)$$

which implies that E_{11} is the matrix of characteristic vectors corresponding to the unit roots of J_s, for all s. By a similar argument we establish that $J_s E_{12} = 0$, for all s. We have now established that $E_s = E_1 C_s$, where $C_s = \text{diag}(C_{s1}, C_{s2})$; since we must also have $E_s' E_s = E_s E_s' = I_G$, we conclude that the block components of C_s must each be **orthogonal matrices**. Consequently, since

$$J_s = E_s \begin{bmatrix} I_{k_s} & 0 \\ 0 & 0 \end{bmatrix} E_s' = E_1 C_s \begin{bmatrix} I_{k_s} & 0 \\ 0 & 0 \end{bmatrix} C_s' E_1' = E_{11} C_{s1} C_{s1}' E_{11}' = E_{11} E_{11}',$$

we conclude that $J_s = J_1$, for all s. Moreover,

$$S_i^{*'} J_i = S_i^{*'}, \quad \text{or} \quad S_i^{*'} J_1 = S_i^{*'}, \quad i = 1, 2, \dots m. \qquad (2.82)$$

Since all predetermined variables of the system appear in at least one equation, the part of Eq. (2.82) above that reads

$$L_{2i}' \bar{R} J_1 = L_{2i}' \bar{R}, \quad \text{implies} \quad \bar{R} J_1 = \bar{R}, \quad \text{or} \quad J_1 = I.$$

In turn, this result leads to the conclusion that S_i is a square invertible matrix, for every i, or that **every equation of the system is just identified**.

Finally, as to part iv.3 we note that if whenever $\sigma_{ij} \neq 0$, we have that the ith and j^{th} equations are just identified, then from the discussion above $E_{i1}' E_{j2} = 0$, so that $\Phi_{21}^* = 0$.

$$\text{q.e.d.}$$

Remark 4. The results of Theorem 5 appear to be partly counterintuitive, particularly those in parts iii and iv. One would be tempted to think that if "more information is used", as in the case of RRF(2SLS), one would gain some efficiency over the case where "less information is used", as in the case of URF. A little reflection, however, would show that the conclusions of this theorem do not violate this intuition. The trouble is that we are not necessarily, or unambiguously, using "more information" in the case of RRF(2SLS) vis-à-vis the case of URF. We remind the reader that, in this context, there are two types of information; one is sample information, the other is "a priori" information. In URF we are using **all sample information** in estimating every element of the parameter matrix Π, **but none of the prior information**, i.e. we do not use the fact that $\Pi = CD$ and, thus, we do not use any of the prior restrictions placed on the elements of these structural matrices. By contrast, RRF(2SLS) uses **all prior**

information, i.e. uses the fact that $\Pi = CD$, and respects all prior restrictions on the structural matrices, but does not necessarily use all sample information. [16] Since the two procedures leave out, or fail to use, a different subset of the information available, it is not surprising that our formal discussion finds that it is not possible to place an unambiguous ranking on the relative efficiency of URF and RRF(2SLS) estimators.

It is now almost anticlimactic to discuss the limiting distribution and ranking for various forecasting procedures.

Theorem 6. Under the conditions of Theorem 5, for $\tau \geq 1$, and on the assertion that the sample size, T, is sufficiently large, the following statements are true: [17]

For static models:

i.1 $\sqrt{T}\mathrm{vec}\left((\hat{y}_{T+\tau\cdot} - \bar{y}_{T+\tau\cdot})_{URF}\right) \sim N\left(0, \ (I \otimes p_{T+\tau\cdot})G_{(1)}(I \otimes p_{T+\tau\cdot})'\right) ;$

i.2 $\sqrt{T}\mathrm{vec}\left((\hat{y}_{T+\tau\cdot} - \bar{y}_{T+\tau\cdot})_{RRF(2SLS)}\right) \sim N\left(0, \ G_{(2)}^*\right) ,$
where $G_{(2)}^* = (I \otimes p_{T+\tau\cdot})G_{(2)}(I \otimes p_{T+\tau\cdot})' ;$

i.3 $\sqrt{T}\mathrm{vec}\left((\hat{y}_{T+\tau\cdot} - \bar{y}_{T+\tau\cdot})_{RRF(3SLS)}\right) \sim N\left(0, \ G_{(3)}^*\right) ,$
where $G_{(3)}^* = (I \otimes p_{T+\tau\cdot})G_{(3)}(I \otimes p_{T+\tau\cdot})' .$

For dynamic models:

ii.1 $\sqrt{T}\mathrm{vec}\left((\hat{y}_{T+\tau\cdot} - \bar{y}_{T+\tau\cdot})_{URF}\right) \sim N\left(0, \ S^{(\tau)}G_{(1)}S^{(\tau)'}\right) ;$

ii.2 $\sqrt{T}\mathrm{vec}\left((\hat{y}_{T+\tau\cdot} - \bar{y}_{T+\tau\cdot})_{RRF(2SLS)}\right) \sim N\left(0, \ S^{(\tau)}G_{(2)}S^{(\tau)'}\right) ;$

---

[16] In this context, it is the failure of 2SLS to use all sample information that renders it inefficient relative to the 3SLS estimation procedure.

[17] The statement of this theorem contains certain logical incongruities, viz. when we contemplate the distribution of the normalized deviations of the left members we simultaneously want to take the "initial conditions", i.e. the $y_{T\cdot}, \ y_{T-1\cdot}, \ldots, y_{T-k+1\cdot}$, as **given**, but we also wish to utilize the limiting distribution of the underlying structural parameters, which, of course, depends on these very initial conditions! Thus, if one wished to be exceedingly puristic one should not have stated these results as a "theorem". On the other hand, in rare occasions such as now, we may use the statement of a theorem in order to summarize prominently the results of a certain discussion. Thus, Theorem 6 is to be viewed in this light, and should be thought of as a framework for a good working approximation in empirical applications, and **not** as a rigorous derivation of the distribution of forecasts from a dynamic GLSEM. This is quite reasonable since, normally, one would expect that the number of lags, k, would be quite small relative to the number of observations, T.

ii.3 $\sqrt{T}\text{vec}\left((\hat{y}_{T+\tau\cdot} - \bar{y}_{T+\tau\cdot})_{RRF(3SLS)}\right) \sim N\left(0,\ S^{(\tau)}G_{(3)}S^{(\tau)'}\right).$

Proof: The results follow immediately from Eqs. (2.75), (2.76), (2.77), and Theorem 4.

$$\text{q.e.d.}$$

Remark 5. In view our discussion thus far, it would be rather pedantic to set forth another theorem regarding the ranking of the various forecasting procedures in terms of relative efficiencies. It is quite apparent from Theorem 6, that these rankings follow exactly the results of Theorem 5. Thus, further discussion of this aspect is quite unnecessary.

Remark 6. If we wish to consider the behavior of the forecast error, i.e. if we examine $y_{T+\tau\cdot} - \hat{y}_{T+\tau\cdot}$ instead of $\hat{y}_{T+\tau\cdot} - \bar{y}_{T+\tau\cdot}$, then in the case of **static models** we ought to modify the results of Theorem 6 only to the extent of adding Ω to the covariance matrix of the relevant limiting distribution. This is so since $y_{T+\tau\cdot} = \bar{y}_{T+\tau\cdot} + v_{T+\tau\cdot}$.

In the case of **dynamic models**, however, the correction is more substantial, since from Eqs. (2.65) and (2.66)

$$y'_{T+\tau\cdot} = \bar{y}'_{T+\tau\cdot} + \sum_{i=1}^{\tau} B_i^{(\tau)} v'_{T+i\cdot} = \bar{y}'_{T+\tau\cdot} + \sum_{i=1}^{\tau} A_1^{(\tau-i)} v'_{T+i\cdot},$$

and the forecast error contains the additional term $\sum_{i=1}^{\tau} A_1^{(\tau-i)} v'_{T+i\cdot}$, whose covariance matrix is

$$\Omega^{(\tau)} = \sum_{i=1}^{\tau} A_1^{(\tau-i)} \Omega A_1^{(\tau-i)'}.$$

Thus, the correction to be made to the relevant limiting distribution in dynamic cases is $\Omega^{(\tau)}$. Two features of this situation are to be pointed out. First, for given lag structure, $\Omega^{(\tau)}$ is **an increasing function of** τ . This can be seen most readily with the change in index, $j = \tau - i$, so that $\Omega^{(\tau)} = \sum_{j=0}^{\tau-1} A_1^{(j)} \Omega A_1^{(j)'}$. Second, no matter how well the conditional mean is forecast, the variance of the forecast error is bound to increase the farther away we move from the sample. This is largely a consequence of the fact that, even if the exogenous sequence is **constant over the forecasting horizon**, the other uncertainty component obeys $\Omega^{(\tau_2)} > \Omega^{(\tau_1)}$, whenever $\tau_2 > \tau_1$. This is a **reflection of the fact that the farther away we move from the end of the sample, the less reliable become the "initial conditions" we employ in the forecast**; hence, the uncertainty attached to the forecast error increases!

2.3   The Vector Autoregressive Model (VAR)

The VAR model origininated with Mann and Wald (1943) (MW), who investigated the estimation and limiting distribution of parameter estimators in the context of a system of stochastic inear difference equations. In fact, MW dealt with a simultaneous equations model containing **no exogenous** variables, i.e its only predetermined variables (beyond the constant term) were **lagged endogenous**. In its contemporary version it has an early antecedent in the paper by Wabha (1969), which deals with a general (vector) distributed lag, a special case of which is what econometricians of the time would have called a (vector) rational distributed lag model. A reduced version of the latter yields a variant of the VAR with exogenous variables. However, the VAR had relatively little impact on the empirical literature until it was popularized by Sims (1980), and was embraced by macroeconomists who held that the prior restrictions imposed in the context of the GLSEM were too numerous, of uncertain validity, and at any rate the existence of **genuinely exogenous** variables was extremely doubtful. In its estimation mode, Sims' version of the VAR is basically the reduced form of a GLSEM **without exogenous variables**, much in the style of the earlier MW version. To see what is involved consider again the dynamic model of the previous sections

$$y_{t\cdot}B^* = y_{t-1\cdot}C_1 + y_{t-2\cdot}C_2 + \cdots + y_{t-k\cdot}C_k + u_{t\cdot}, \quad t = 1, 2, \ldots, T. \quad (2.83)$$

If, as is customary in this literature, **no prior restrictions** are placed on the coefficient matrices B^*, C_i, $i = 1, 2, \ldots k$, nor on the covariance matrix, Σ, of the error process, the model is overly parametrized. This is merely another way of stating that the parameters of the model **cannot be identified**. Thus, certain identifying restrictions are required. The approach in the VAR context is to assert that $u'_{t\cdot} : t \geq 1$ is i.i.d., with mean zero and **covariance matrix** I_m. This does not quite dispose of the identification problem, since multiplication on the right by an **orthogonal** matrix leaves all conditions undisturbed. Thus, to fully identify the model we need also impose the condition that the parameter matrices B^* and C_i, $i = 1, 2, \ldots, k$, **do not have common factors**. Now, we have identification in the sense that we cannot confuse the model in Eq. (2.83) with what is obtained through postmultiplication by a nonsingular or orthogonal matrix, say H.[18] Occasionally, the model above is referred to as the

---

[18] It is interesting that what began as an attempt to get away from *a priori* restrictions on the structural parameters, i.e. the elements of the matrices B^* and C_i, $i = 1, 2, 3, \ldots, k$, turned out to impose very stringent restrictions indeed on the **covariance matrix** of the structural errors. This is particularly striking since there is hardly any theoretical underpinning, or even serious discussion, regarding the nature of the error process. It is important to recognize that in moving from the GLSEM to its simpler variant, the VAR model, we do not eliminate the need

structural VAR model.

It is, however, difficult, if not impossible, to estimate the model as postulated above; in empirical work one employs its **reduced form**,

$$y_{t\cdot} \; = \; y_{t-1\cdot}\Pi_1 + y_{t-2\cdot}\Pi_2 + \cdots + y_{t-k\cdot}\Pi_k + v_{t\cdot},$$

$$\Pi_i \; = \; C_i B^{*-1}, \; i = 1, 2, \ldots, k, \; v_{t\cdot} \; = \; u_{t\cdot}B^{*-1}, \tag{2.84}$$

often termed the **reduced form VAR**. Since the economic structural hypotheses are contained in the parameters (elements) of the matrices B^*, $C_i, i = 1, 2, \ldots, k$, we need to find a way to obtain information on them from estimates of the Π_i, and the covariance matrix of the reduced form errors, $\Omega = B^{*'-1}B^{*-1}$. But, even if this product is known (or estimated) **it is not possible, without further restrictions, to effect the desired decomposition uniquely**. For example, if A is a positive definite matrix and is decomposed by P so that $A = P'P$, **it is also decomposed by** QP, where Q is an **orthogonal matrix**. Thus, in order to **recover uniquely** B^* from $B^{*'-1}B^{*-1}$ we must put *a priori* restrictions on B^*. Evidently, the number of restrictions required is the number of orthogonality conditions plus the m **normalizing** conditions setting $\sigma_{ii} = 1$, i.e. $m(m + 1)/2$ conditions in all. Since B^* contains m^2 elements and the number of restrictions required in order to obtain a unique decomposition is $m(m + 1)/2$, B^* is left with **only** $m(m - 1)/2$ free elements.

Remark 7. Note that for just identification in the standard GLSEM we require m^2 restrictions, m per equation; in that context, however, we identify both the structural parameters and the covariance parameters, i.e. the elements of the covariance matrix, Σ, of the (structural) error process. In the VAR context, on the other hand, we assume *ab initio* $m(m + 1)/2$ restrictions by setting $\Sigma = I$; these include, implicitly, m normalizing conditions. Thus, the number of non-normalizing restrictions is $m(m - 1)/2$. In addition, we impose $m^2 - m(m - 1)/2$ restrictions in order to uniquely recover an estimator of B^* from that of the **reduced form covariance matrix**, or m^2 restrictions in all. In this light, it is seen that the structural VAR model places exactly the same number of prior restrictions on the model as is required for **just identification** in the context of the GLSEM, but it prescribes these restrictions without recourse to the (relevant) economic theory. As we shall see later, in Chapter 4, there may well be several just identified structural models that are compatible with a given reduced form.

---

for prior restrictions, we merely trade one set of prior restrictions for another. Which of the two approaches is to be preferred, therefore, cannot be based wholly on the simplicity of the VAR specification, but only on whether it enables us to understand the workings of the system under study more completely or more reliably.

2.4   Instrumental Variables (IV)

The term instrumental variable (IV) has a well defined meaning only in an appropriate context; more precisely, a variable w_t may be an instrumental variable in one context, but not necessarily in another. We shall give below a definition in the context of the GLSEM, and the reader may extrapolate to its meaning in other contexts.

Definition 2. A set of variables, $w_{t\cdot}$, $t = 1, 2, \ldots, T$, is said to be a **set of instrumental variables**, relative to the GLSEM of Eq. (1.12), in Chapter 1, if and only if, for every $i = 1, 2, \ldots, m$, there exists a submatrix, W_i, of the matrix $W = (w_{t\cdot})$, satisfying the conditions

   i. $[W_i'(Y_i, X_i)]/T \xrightarrow{\text{P}} F_i$, and F_i is **nonsingular**;

   ii. $W_i' u_{\cdot i}/T \xrightarrow{\text{P}} 0$.

Example 6. The use of instrumental variables is suggested by the method of moments; the latter uses a postulated functional relation and the fact that sample moments, under certain conditions, are consistent estimators of the respective population moments. This easily allows for estimation of the parameters of the underlying functional relation. For example, suppose that we have the simple supply demand model

$$
\begin{aligned}
q_t^S &= a + b p_{t-1} + u_{t1} \\
q_t^D &= \alpha + \beta p_t + u_{t2} \\
q_t^D &= q_t^S, \quad \text{competitive equilibrium.}
\end{aligned}
\tag{2.85}
$$

If we have observations on market transactions, the implication is that we observe the **equilibrium transaction quantities**. Thus, the model to be fitted to the data (q_t, p_t), $t = 1, 2, \ldots, T$ is

$$
\begin{aligned}
q_t &= a + b p_{t-1} + u_{t1} \\
p_t &= \alpha_* + \beta_* q_t + u_{t2}^*, \quad \alpha_* = -\frac{1}{\beta}, \quad \beta_* = -\frac{1}{\beta}, \quad u_{t2}^* = -\frac{1}{\beta} u_{t2}.
\end{aligned}
$$

Suppose that u_{t1} and u_{t2} are **mutually independent**, so that the system above is **simply recursive**, and consider the relationship of the sample moments to the parameters of the problem. Thus,

$$
\begin{aligned}
s_{qp_{-1}} &= b s_{p_{-1}p_{-1}} + s_{p_{-1}1}, \quad s_{qq} = b^2 s_{p_{-1}p_{-1}} + s_{11}, \\
s_{pp_{-1}} &= \beta_* s_{qp_{-1}} + s_{p_{-1}2}, \quad s_{pp} = \beta_*^2 s_{qq} + s_{22}^*,
\end{aligned}
\tag{2.86}
$$

where the notation s_{xy} denotes the sample covariance between x and y. Since by the conditions of the problem $s_{p_{-1}2}$ and $s_{p_{-1}1}$, the sample covariances between p_{-1} and u_2, u_1, respectively, converge to zero in probability, we may eliminate them from Eq. (2.86) to obtain

$$s_{qp_{-1}} = bs_{p_{-1}p_{-1}}, \quad s_{qq} = b^2 s_{p_{-1}p_{-1}} + s_{11},$$
$$s_{pp_{-1}} = \beta_* s_{qp_{-1}}, \quad s_{pp} = \beta_*^2 s_{qq} + s_{22}^*, \tag{2.87}$$

which can be solved for consistent estimators of the unknown parameters β_*, b, σ_{11} and σ_{22}. From the relations $\bar{p} - \hat{\beta}_* \bar{q} = \hat{\alpha}_*$ and $\bar{q} - \hat{b}\bar{p}_{-1} = \hat{a}$, we also obtain estimators for α_*, a and, if desired, for α and β as well, thus completing the solution of the problem.

Remark 8. Instrumental variables were very much *en vogue* in the econometric literature of the 1950s, partly as a reaction to earlier work, in the 1940s, that showed that least squares procedures, applied to structural equations, or to errors in variables models yield **inconsistent estimators**. The perceptive reader would have noticed, from the definition, that the conditions defining instrumental variables are precisely the conditions needed to render the resulting estimators **consistent**. In fact, the pairing of the "consistency" and "instrumental variables" concepts in the 1950s was so strong amongst econometricians, that in the period following the early dissemination of Theil's results on 2SLS (1953) it was Klein's (1955) demonstration that the estimator in question was an "instrumental variables" estimator that clinched the argument for its consistency. The class of instrumental variables estimators is useful mainly as an alternative designation of the class of **consistent estimators** of a given parameter(s). It is not, otherwise, particularly useful. Thus, in the definition above, no one can give *a priori*, even in a stated context, a definitive enumeration or description of the elements of the matrix W beyond that contained in Definition 2! On the other hand, if we confine our attention to a relatively small class of instruments it may be possible to find an optimal IV estimator.

2.4.1   2SLS and 3SLS as IV Estimators

It is now relatively simple to show that the basic 2SLS and 3SLS estimators have a representation as IV estimators. Thus, consider again the ith structural equation in CSF, i.e.

$$w_{\cdot i} = Q_i \delta_{\cdot i} + r_{\cdot i}, \quad i = 1, 2, \ldots, m. \tag{2.88}$$

Given Definition 2, the matrix $R^{-1}X'(Y, X)$ is a matrix of instrumental variables relative to the GLSEM in Eq. (2.88). This is so since Q_i is one of its submatrices and, for every i, we have $(Q_i'Q_i/T) \xrightarrow{P} S_i' M_{xx} S_i > 0$, while $(Q_i' r_{\cdot i}/T) \xrightarrow{P} 0$. Next, if we consider the collection of all structrural equations, viz.

$$w = Q\delta + r, \quad Q = \text{diag}(Q_1, Q_2, \ldots, Q_m), \tag{2.89}$$

we note that for some initial consistent estimator of Σ, the matrix $\tilde{\Phi}^{-1}Q$ is a matrix of instrumental variables since

$$\frac{Q'\tilde{\Phi}^{-1}Q}{T} \xrightarrow{\mathrm{P}} S^{*'}\Phi^{-1}S^* > 0, \quad \text{and} \quad \frac{Q'\tilde{\Phi}^{-1}r}{T} \xrightarrow{\mathrm{P}} 0. \tag{2.90}$$

Definition 3. Let $y_{\cdot i} = Z_i \delta_{\cdot i} + u_{\cdot i}$ be one of the structural equations of a GLSEM, as in Eq. (1.12) of Chapter 1. Let W be a matrix of instrumental variables and let W_i be a submatrix of W, of the same dimension as Z_i. The solution, $\tilde{\delta}_{\cdot i(IV)}$, of

$$W_i' y_{\cdot i} = W_i' Z_i \delta_{\cdot i} \tag{2.91}$$

is said to be the **instrumental variables (IV) estimator** of the parameter $\delta_{\cdot i}$.

An immediate consequence of Definitions 2 and 3 is

Theorem 7. Consider the GLSEM in CSF form, as in Eqs. (2.88) and (2.89); the 2SLS and 3SLS estimators of the parameter vector δ are IV estimators.

Proof: We note that Q and $\tilde{\Phi}^{-1}Q$ are both instrumental matrices relative to the model in Eq. (2.89). The 2SLS and 3SLS estimators are, respectively, the solutions of $Q'Q\delta = Q'w$, and $Q'\tilde{\Phi}^{-1}Q\delta = Q'\tilde{\Phi}^{-1}w$, and as such are, by Definition 3, IV estimators.

q.e.d.

Remark 9. Occasionally the meaning of the terms 2SLS or 3SLS is stretched beyond all reasonable bounds. A case in point is the following; suppose one has the model

$$y_t = x_{t\cdot}\beta + u_t, \tag{2.92}$$

where $x_{t\cdot}$ is an $n+1$-element vector of "explanatory" variables. Suppose, further, that one thinks of the variables $x_{t,n-1}$ and x_{tn} as being, together with y_t, **jointly dependent** variables in a vaguely defined simultaneous equations system. A procedure, often referred to in the literature as 2SLS, consists of (a) regressing $x_{t,n-1}$ and x_{tn} on a set of ad hoc "exogenous" variables, say $p_{t\cdot}$, sometimes also called "instruments", obtaining, $\hat{x}_{t,n-1} = p_{t\cdot}\hat{b}_{\cdot n-1}$, $\hat{x}_{tn} = p_{t\cdot}\hat{b}_{\cdot n}$ and (b) regressing y_t on $\hat{x}_{t\cdot} = (x_{t0}, x_{t1}, \ldots, x_{t,n-2}, \hat{x}_{t,n-1}, \hat{x}_{tn})$ to obtain the "2SLS" estimator of β, say $\hat{\beta}$. To the extent that $p_{t\cdot}$ contains the variables x_{ti}, for $i = 0, 1, 2, \ldots, n-2$, the estimator described above is a two stage least squares procedure, in the sense that we are doing least squares twice; it is, however, best thought of as simply an IV estimator with instrumental matrix $\hat{X} = (x_{\cdot 0}, x_{\cdot 1}, \ldots, x_{\cdot n-2}, \tilde{x}_{\cdot n-1}, \tilde{x}_{\cdot n})$, since it is the solution of $\hat{X}'X\beta = \hat{X}'y$, in the usual notation.

While this procedure has certain aspects in common with 2SLS, it represents a gross misuse of terminology to call what it yields a "2SLS estimator". That term should be reserved for the case where all of the predetermined variables **in the complete system** are being employed, since there are evidently differences in the relative efficiencies of such estimators, depending on the choice of instruments. It should more properly termed an IV procedure, or at best **a 2SLS-like procedure with an ill defined underlying model**. If the variables x_{ti}, for $i = 0, 1, 2, \ldots, n-2$, are not included among the elements of $p_{t\cdot}$, the properties of the resulting "2SLS" estimator are hard to pin down, since some orthogonality properties will be lost. The logic of the procedure, however, would strongly argue for their inclusion.

We shall now examine this estimator more closely. Thus, in the context of the model in Eq. (2.88), the limiting distribution of the 2SLS estimator of $\delta_{\cdot i}$ minus the true parameter, is normal with mean zero and covariance matrix $\sigma_{ii}^2 (S_i' M S_i)^{-1}$.

To employ the alternative "2SLS" procedure, we need to choose the "instruments", say $X L_{0i}$. Since we have argued earlier that the logic of the procedure requires that all predetermined variables appearing in the ith equation should be employed as "instruments", the columns of L_{0i} **should** contain those of L_{2i}, and perhaps certain others. The exclusion matrix is given by L_{2i}^*, which we may write as $L_{2i}^* = (L_{3i}, L_{3i}^*)$. If we wish to allow for additional predetermined variables from the model to be employed as instruments, let them be selected by L_{3i} so that the instruments for i^{th} equation are given by

$$X_{0i} = X L_{0i}, \qquad L_{0i} = (L_{2i}, L_{3i}). \tag{2.93}$$

We suppose there are n "instruments" and $n \leq G$, where G is the number of predetermined variables.

Remark 10. One might wonder why we have not allowed for variables outside the model to appear as "instruments". A little reflection will convince us that if a variable does not appear in the reduced form, its coefficient would converge to zero in probability when **the model is correctly specified**. For that reason we refrained from considering this eventuality. We should remark, however, that if not all appropriate variables had been included in the complete model specification, the inclusion of "irrelevant" variables would not necessarily result in their ("irrelevant" variables') coefficients vanishing in probability, **if such variables are correlated with excluded relevant variables**.

Consider now the equation

$$y_{\cdot i} = Z_i \delta_{\cdot i} + u_{\cdot i}, \qquad Z_i = (Y_i, \ X_i).$$

Replacing Y_i by

$$\tilde{Y}_i = X_{0i} \tilde{\Pi}_{0i}, \qquad \tilde{\Pi}_{0i} = (X_{0i}' X_{0i})^{-1} X_{0i}' Y_i, \tag{2.94}$$

we obtain the estimator

$$\tilde{\delta}_{\cdot i} = (\tilde{Z}_i' \tilde{Z}_i)^{-1} \tilde{Z}_i' y_{\cdot i}, \tag{2.95}$$

which, after some manipulation, yields the result that

$$\sqrt{T}(\tilde{\delta}_{\cdot i} - \delta_{\cdot i}) \overset{d}{\to} \zeta^* \sim N(0, \sigma_{ii} C_{0i}), \tag{2.96}$$

$$C_{0i} = \begin{bmatrix} \bar{\Pi}_{0i}' L_{0i}' M_{xx} L_{0i} \bar{\Pi}_{0i} & \Pi_i' M_{xx} L_{2i} \\ L_{2i}' M_{xx} \Pi_i & L_{2i}' M_{xx} L_{2i} \end{bmatrix}^{-1},$$

where $\bar{\Pi}_{0i} = \text{p}\lim_{T \to \infty} \tilde{\Pi}_{0i}$.

From previous results we have that

$$\sqrt{T}(\hat{\delta}_{\cdot i} - \delta_{\cdot i})_{2SLS} \sim N(0, \sigma_{ii} C_{2i}), \quad C_{2i} = (S_i' M S_i)^{-1}, \quad S_i = (\Pi_i, \ L_{2i}).$$

We may now prove

Theorem 8. The "2SLS" estimator of Eq. (2.100) is inefficient relative to the 2SLS estimator unless $L_{0i} = I_G$, i.e. all predetermined variables of the model are employed as "instruments".

Proof: We note that

$$\tilde{\Pi}_{0i} = (L_{0i}' X' X L_{0i})^{-1} L_{0i}' X'[X\Pi_i + V_i] \overset{P}{\to} \bar{\Pi}_{0i}$$
$$\bar{\Pi}_{0i} = \Pi_{0i} + (L_{0i}' M_{xx} L_{0i})^{-1} L_{0i}' M_{xx} L_{3i}^* \Pi_{3i}^*, \tag{2.97}$$

where L_{3i}^* is the complement of L_{0i} in I_G, i.e. it consists of the columns of I_G **not contained** in L_{0i}, and Π_{3i}^* is the matrix of coefficients of the variables XL_{3i}^*, i.e. the predetermined variables not utilized as "instruments", in the reduced form representation of Y_i. Note, further, that

$$\Pi_i = (L_{0i}, \ L_{3i}^*)(L_{0i}, \ L_{3i}^*)' \Pi_i = L_{0i} \Pi_{0i} + L_{3i}^* \Pi_{3i}^*. \tag{2.98}$$

Consequently,

$$C_{2i}^{-1} - C_{0i}^{-1} = \begin{bmatrix} F & 0 \\ 0 & 0 \end{bmatrix}, \quad F = \Pi_i M_{xx} \Pi_i - \bar{\Pi}_{0i} L_{0i}' M_{xx} L_{0i} \bar{\Pi}_{0i}. \tag{2.99}$$

After some manipulation we find

$$F = \Pi_{3i}^{*'}[J_{22} - J_{21} J_{11}^{-1} J_{12}]\Pi_{3i}^* \geq 0,$$

where J is the **nonsingular matrix**

$$J = (L_{0i}, L_{3i}^*)' M_{xx}(L_{0i}, L_{3i}^*), \quad \text{and hence } C_{2i}^{-1} - C_{0i}^{-1} \geq 0.$$

Consequently, by Proposition 65 in Dhrymes (1984),

$$C_{0i} - C_{2i} \geq 0,$$

unless (if and only if) $G = n$.

q.e.d.

2.4.2   2SLS and 3SLS as Optimal IV Estimators

In exploring this topic it is more convenient to employ the original notation, viz.,

$$y_{\cdot i} = Z_i \delta_{\cdot i} + u_{\cdot i}, \quad Z_i = (Y_i, X_i), \quad i = 1, 2, \ldots, m. \tag{2.100}$$

Let W be the matrix of potential instruments and W_i the submatrix of W appropriate for the ith equation of Eq. (2.100). The IV estimator, in that context, is given by

$$\tilde{\delta}_{\cdot i(IV)} = (W_i' Z_i)^{-1} W_i' y_{\cdot i} = \delta_{\cdot i} + (W_i' Z_i)^{-1} W_i' u_{\cdot i}. \tag{2.101}$$

Under the standard assumptions, fully explored earlier in this chapter, it may be shown that

$$\sqrt{T}(\tilde{\delta}_{\cdot i} - \delta_{\cdot i})_{IV} \xrightarrow{\mathrm{d}} N(0, C_{i(IV)}), \tag{2.102}$$

where

$$C_{i(IV)} = \plim_{T \to \infty} \left(\frac{W_i' Z_i}{T} \right)^{-1} \left(\frac{W_i' W_i}{T} \right) \left(\frac{Z_i' W_i}{T} \right)^{-1}. \tag{2.103}$$

Nothing further can be said about the efficiency aspects of such estimators, unless the class of instruments is defined more precisely. For example, it was shown in Dhrymes (1974, pp. 300ff), that the (asymptotic) **generalized variance** [19] of the IV estimator is minimized if and only if the coefficient of vector correlation [20] between the variables in Z_i and the instruments employed, is **maximized**. Moreover, it was shown that if the class of admissible instruments is given by

$$\mathcal{C} = \{W : W = X\tilde{A}\}, \tag{2.104}$$

such that $\plim_{T \to \infty} \tilde{A}$ is a nonrandom matrix, then 2SLS is optimal within that class. Optimality was defined by the condition that its generalized variance be (asymptotically) no larger than the generalized variance of any other IV estimator generated by using instruments within that class. In

---

[19] If x is a random vector with mean μ and covariance matrix Σ, the generalized variance of the vector is defined to be $|\Sigma|$, i.e. it is the **determinant of its covariance matrix**.

[20] The coefficient of vector correlation between two vectors x and y, of dimension n, m and covariance matrices, Σ_{11}, Σ_{22}, respectively, and "cross-covariance" matrix Σ_{12}, where $m \leq n$, is given by

$$r_{c(y, x)} = (-1)^{n+m} \frac{\begin{vmatrix} 0 & \Sigma_{21} \\ \Sigma_{12} & \Sigma_{11} \end{vmatrix}}{|\Sigma_{22}| \, |\Sigma_{11}|}.$$

addition, it was hinted therein that optimality could, also, be defined in terms of the usual definition of efficiency, viz., that the difference of the relevant (asymptotic) covariance matrices be positive semidefinite.

In this section, we shall show that the single equation 2SLS estimator is efficient, in the latter sense, on an equation by equation basis; however, it is not necessarily efficient on a systemwide basis. We shall further show that the 3SLS estimator is an optimal IV estimator, on a systemwide basis, again in terms of the latter criterion.

Thus, suppose $W_i = X\tilde{A}_i$ and, consequently,

$$C_{i(IV)}(A_i) = \sigma_{ii} \left(A_i' M_{xx} S_i\right)^{-1} A_i' M_{xx} A_i \left(S_i' M_{xx} A_i\right)^{-1}. \qquad (2.105)$$

For the particular choice $\tilde{A}_i = \tilde{S}_i$, we find

$$W_i = X\tilde{S}_i = \tilde{Z}_i, \quad C_{i(IV)}(S_i) = \sigma_{ii} \left(S_i' M_{xx} S_i\right)^{-1},$$

which verifies, again, that the single equation 2SLS is an IV estimator. We shall now show that if A_i is **any nonrandom** matrix then

$$C_{i(IV)}(A_i) - C_{i(IV)}(S_i) \geq 0.$$

Let

$$E = \left[C_{i(IV)}(S_i)\right]^{-1} - \left[C_{i(IV)}(A_i)\right]^{-1} \qquad (2.106)$$

$$= S_i' M_{xx} \left[M_{xx}^{-1} - A_i \left(A_i' M_{xx} A_i\right)^{-1} A_i'\right] M_{xx} S_i,$$

and consider the characteristic roots of $A_i \left(A_i' M_{xx} A_i\right)^{-1} A_i'$ in the metric of M_{xx}^{-1}, i.e. consider

$$\mid \lambda M_{xx}^{-1} - A_i \left(A_i' M_{xx} A_i\right)^{-1} A_i' \mid = 0. \qquad (2.107)$$

But, Eq. (2.107) has exactly the same roots as

$$\mid \lambda I - A_i \left(A_i' M_{xx} A_i\right)^{-1} A_i' M_{xx} \mid = 0,$$

which has exactly the same **nonzero roots** as

$$\mid \mu I - \left(A_i' M_{xx} A_i\right)^{-1} A_i' M_{xx} A_i \mid = 0.$$

The latter, evidently, has $m_i + G_i$ unit roots. Consequently, by Proposition 63 in Dhrymes (1984), there exists a nonsingular matrix, say H, such that

$$M_{xx}^{-1} = H H', \quad A_i \left(A_i' M_{xx} A_i\right)^{-1} A_i' = H \begin{bmatrix} I_{m_i+G_i} & 0 \\ 0 & 0 \end{bmatrix} H'. \qquad (2.108)$$

Thus, from Eq. (2.108), we find

$$E = S_i' M_{xx} H \begin{bmatrix} 0 & 0 \\ 0 & I_{G-G_i-m_i} \end{bmatrix} H' M_{xx} S_i \geq 0.$$

It follows, therefore, from Proposition 65, Dhrymes (1984), that

$$C_{i(IV)}(A_i) - C_{i(IV)}(S_i) \geq 0,$$

i.e. that the 2SLS single equation estimator, on an equation by equation basis, is an optimal IV estimator, in the sense that the covariance matrix of its limiting distribution is no larger than the covariance matrix of the limiting distribution of any other IV estimator, utilizing instruments in $\mathcal{C}$. The natural question to ask next, is whether, for the system as a whole, 2SLS is the optimal IV estimator. To address this issue, write the entire system by simply stacking the equations of Eq. (2.100), to obtain

$$y = Z^* \delta + u, \quad Z^* = \text{diag}(Z_1, Z_2, \ldots, Z_m). \tag{2.109}$$

Remaining within the instrumental class $\mathcal{C}$ means that the matrix of instrumental variables is of the form

$$W^* = (I \otimes X)\, \tilde{A}, \quad \tilde{A} = \text{diag}(\tilde{A}_1, \tilde{A}_2, \ldots, \tilde{A}_m).$$

Hence, the systemwide IV estimator is given by [21]

$$\tilde{\delta}_{LIV} = \left(W^{*'} Z^*\right)^{-1} W^{*'} y = \delta + \left(W^{*'} Z^*\right)^{-1} W^{*'} u, \tag{2.110}$$

and, by the discussion of earlier sections,

$$\sqrt{T} \left(\tilde{\delta} - \delta\right)_{LIV} \xrightarrow{d} N(0, C_{LIV}) \tag{2.111}$$

$$C_{LIV} = [A' (I \otimes M_{xx}) A]^{-1} A' (\Sigma \otimes M_{xx}) A [S' (I \otimes M_{xx}) A]^{-1}.$$

We note that, in this notation, the 2SLS (systemwide) estimator has a normal limiting distribution with covariance matrix

$$C_{2SLS} = [S'(I \otimes M_{xx})S]^{-1} [S'(\Sigma \otimes M_{xx})S] [S'(I \otimes M_{xx})S]^{-1}. \tag{2.112}$$

The difference of the, respective, inverses of the (systemwide) 2SLS and LIV estimators is given by

$$E = S'(I \otimes M_{xx})(J_1 - J_2)(I \otimes M_{xx})S \tag{2.113}$$

$$J_1 = S[S'(\Sigma \otimes M_{xx})S]^{-1} S', \quad J_2 = A[A'(\Sigma \otimes M_{xx})A]^{-1} A'$$

---

[21] The subscript LIV means Limited Information Instrumental Variable; the terminology may be justified in view of the fact that this estimator, while taking into account all prior restrictions, does not utilize the covariance structure of the model. This is to be distinguished from the Limited Information Iterative Instrumental Variable estimator LIIV to be discussed at a later stage.

and E is positive semidefinite, negative semidefinite or indefinite if and only if $J_1 - J_2$ has the corresponding property.

We shall now show that the matrix difference, $J_1 - J_2$, is **indefinite**. Consider the characteristic roots of J_1 in the metric of $(\Sigma \otimes M_{xx})^{-1}$. By an argument parallel to that employed above, we may show that the characteristic roots in question consist of $k = \sum_{i=1}^{m}(m_i + G_i)$ **unit roots** and $d = mG - k$ **zero roots**. Thus, by Proposition 63, Dhrymes (1984), there exists a nonsingular matrix, say H, such that

$$HH' = (\Sigma \otimes M_{xx})^{-1} \qquad (2.114)$$

$$H \begin{bmatrix} I_k & 0 \\ 0 & 0 \end{bmatrix} H' = S[S'(\Sigma \otimes M_{xx})S]^{-1} S' = J_1$$

Employing **exactly** the same argument with respect to the matrix J_2, we conclude that there exists a nonsingular matrix, say H^*, such that

$$H^* H^{*'} = (\Sigma \otimes M_{xx})^{-1} \qquad (2.115)$$

$$H^* \begin{bmatrix} I_k & 0 \\ 0 & 0 \end{bmatrix} H^{*'} = A[A'(\Sigma \otimes M_{xx})A]^{-1} A' = J_2.$$

Comparing the first equations in Eqs. (2.114) and (2.115), it is apparent that $H^* = HF$, where F is an **orthogonal** matrix. Thus, Eq. (2.113) may be rewritten as

$$E = S'(I \otimes M_{xx})H \left[\begin{pmatrix} I_k & 0 \\ 0 & 0 \end{pmatrix} - F \begin{pmatrix} I_k & 0 \\ 0 & 0 \end{pmatrix} F' \right] H'(I \otimes M_{xx})S, \quad (2.116)$$

and, consequently, E is positive semidefinite, negative semidefinite or indefinite, if and only if the matrix in square brackets has the corresponding property. The matrix in square brackets, however, is indefinite. To establish this, partition $F = (F_1, F_2)$, so that F_1 contains the first k columns and F_2 contains the remaining $d = mG - k$ columns. Since F is orthogonal, it follows that $F_1'F_2 = 0$. Let $f_{\cdot s}$, for $s \in (1, 2, \ldots, k)$ be one of the columns of F_1. Then

$$f_{\cdot s}' \left[\begin{pmatrix} I_k & 0 \\ 0 & 0 \end{pmatrix} - F \begin{pmatrix} I_k & 0 \\ 0 & 0 \end{pmatrix} F' \right] f_{\cdot s} = f_{\cdot s(k)}' f_{\cdot s(k)} - 1 \leq 0, \qquad (2.117)$$

where $f_{\cdot s(k)}$ consists of the first k elements of $f_{\cdot s}$. The right member of the equation, above, must be **strictly negative** for at least one $s \in (1, 2, \ldots, k)$, unless $E = 0$. To see this partition $F_1 = (F_{11}', F_{21}')'$, where F_{11} is $k \times k$, and note that $f_{\cdot s(k)}' f_{\cdot s(k)} - 1 = 0$, for $s = 1, 2, 3, \ldots, k$ **means that** $F_{21} = 0$. In turn this implies, from Eq. (2.116), that $E = 0$.

Moreover, the fact that F is **orthogonal** implies [22] that $E = 0$, for any choice of A; evidently, this is a contradiction, and we conclude that the right member of Eq. (2.117) is **strictly** negative, for at least one of the columns of F_1. Next, let $f_{\cdot s}$ be an arbitrary vector in F_2 and note that

$$f'_{\cdot s} \left[\begin{pmatrix} I_k & 0 \\ 0 & 0 \end{pmatrix} - F \begin{pmatrix} I_k & 0 \\ 0 & 0 \end{pmatrix} F' \right] f_{\cdot s} = f'_{\cdot s(k)} f_{\cdot s(k)} \geq 0. \qquad (2.118)$$

The right member of Eq. (2.118) must be **strictly positive** for at least one $s \in (k+1, k+2, \ldots, mG)$, for otherwise $F_{12} = 0$. When this is so, by the argument given in the footnote below, we must conclude that $E = 0$, for arbitrary choice of A, which is a contradiction. Thus, for least one s we must have $f'_{\cdot s(k)} f_{\cdot s(k)} > 0$, Hence, we have shown that E which completes the demonstration that E is an indefinite matrix and, consequently, that $C_{LIV} - C_{2SLS}$ is an indefinite matrix.

The optimality of the 3SLS estimator is rather simple to establish. Again, in the current notation, the 3SLS estimator is given by

$$\tilde{\delta}_{3SLS} = \left[\tilde{Z}^{*\prime} (\tilde{\Sigma}^{-1} \otimes I) \tilde{Z}^* \right]^{-1} \tilde{Z}^{*\prime} (\tilde{\Sigma}^{-1} \otimes I) y. \qquad (2.119)$$

Since we wish to deal with a full information instrumental variable (FIV) estimator, we should slightly rewrite the class of potential instruments as

$$\mathcal{C} = \{W : W = (I \otimes X)(\tilde{\Sigma}^{-1} \otimes I)\tilde{A}\}, \tilde{A} = \mathrm{diag}(\tilde{A}_1, \tilde{A}_2, \ldots, \tilde{A}_m),$$

such that $\mathrm{plim}_{T\to\infty} \tilde{\Sigma}^{-1} = \Sigma^{-1}$, $\mathrm{plim}_{T\to\infty} \tilde{A} = A$ are well defined non-stochastic matrices. Again, it is easy to verify that 3SLS is a FIV estimator, by noting that the choice $W = (\tilde{\Sigma}^{-1} \otimes X)\tilde{S}$ yields precisely the 3SLS estimator. Similarly, by standard arguments, we conclude that

$$\sqrt{T} \left(\tilde{\delta} - \delta \right)_{FIV} \xrightarrow{d} N(0, C_{FIV}), \quad \text{where}$$

$$C_{FIV} = [A'(\Sigma^{-1} \otimes M_{xx})S]^{-1} [A'(\Sigma^{-1} \otimes M_{xx})A] [S'(\Sigma^{-1} \otimes M_{xx})A]^{-1}. \qquad (2.120)$$

---

[22] Suppose

$$F = \begin{bmatrix} F_{11} & 0 \\ F_{21} & F_{22} \end{bmatrix};$$

then, from

$$I = \begin{bmatrix} F'_{11} & F'_{21} \\ 0 & F'_{22} \end{bmatrix} \begin{bmatrix} F_{11} & 0 \\ F_{21} & F_{22} \end{bmatrix} = \begin{bmatrix} F'_{11}F_{11} + F'_{21}F_{21} & F'_{21}F_{22} \\ F'_{22}F_{21} & F'_{22}F_{22} \end{bmatrix},$$

we conclude that F_{22} is a $d \times d$ **orthogonal matrix**. Consequently, the condition $F'_{22}F_{21} = 0$ implies $F_{21} = 0$, which, in turn, means that F_{11} is **also an orthogonal matrix**. Therefore, when $F_{21} = 0$, or, for that matter, when $F_{12} = 0$, the matrix E is null. Hence, if $A \neq S$, $F_{12} \neq 0$ **and** $F_{21} \neq 0$.

To show the optimality of 3SLS we proceed, *mutatis mutandis*, in the same manner as we did in the case of single equation 2SLS. Thus, define the matrix

$$E = C_{3SLS}^{-1} - C_{FIV}^{-1} = S'(\Sigma^{-1} \otimes M_{xx}) \left[(\Sigma \otimes M_{xx}^{-1}) - J \right] (\Sigma^{-1} \otimes M_{xx}),$$
(2.121)

where $J = A \left[A'(\Sigma^{-1} \otimes M_{xx})A \right]^{-1} A'$, and consider the latter's characteristic roots in the metric of $(\Sigma \otimes M_{xx}^{-1})$, i.e. the roots (solutions) of

$$\left| \lambda(\Sigma \otimes M_{xx}^{-1}) - A \left[A'(\Sigma^{-1} \otimes M_{xx})A \right]^{-1} A' \right| = 0.$$
(2.122)

But, Eq. (2.122) has exactly the same roots as

$$\left| \lambda I - A \left[A'(\Sigma^{-1} \otimes M_{xx})A \right]^{-1} A'(\Sigma^{-1} \otimes M_{xx}) \right| = 0,$$

which has exactly the same **nonzero roots** as

$$\left| \mu I - \left[A'[\Sigma^{-1} \otimes M_{xx})A \right]^{-1} A'(\Sigma^{-1} \otimes M_{xx})A \right| = 0.$$

The latter, evidently, has k unit roots. Consequently, by Proposition 63 in Dhrymes (1984), there exists a nonsingular matrix, say H, such that

$$A \left[A'(\Sigma^{-1} \otimes M_{xx})A \right]^{-1} A' = H \begin{bmatrix} I_k & 0 \\ 0 & 0 \end{bmatrix} H',$$

$$(\Sigma \otimes M_{xx}^{-1}) = HH'.$$

Thus, from Eq. (2.123), we find

$$E = S'(\Sigma^{-1} \otimes M_{xx})H \begin{bmatrix} 0 & 0 \\ 0 & I_d \end{bmatrix} H'(\Sigma^{-1} \otimes M_{xx})S \geq 0,$$

thus showing that the 3SLS estimator is efficient relative to any FIV estimator generated by employing instruments in $\mathcal{C}$. We summarize the results of the discussion above in

Theorem 9. Consider the GLSEM of Chapter 1, subject to conditions (A.1) through (A.5) and as exhibited in Eq. (2.100), above. Then, the following statements are true:

i. Given the class of instruments $\mathcal{C} = \{W : W = X\tilde{A}\}$, such that $\text{plim}_{T\to\infty} \tilde{A} = A$ is a well defined nonstochastic matrix,

i.1 the single equation 2SLS is an **optimal IV estimator**, in the sense that $C_{i(IV)} - C_{i(2SLS)} \geq 0$, where $C_{i(IV)}$ is the covariance matrix of the limiting distribution of any IV estimator obtained by utilizing instruments within the class $\mathcal{C}$, and $C_{i(2SLS)}$ is the covariance matrix of the limiting distribution of the 2SLS estimator;

i.2 the systemwide 2SLS estimator is not necessarily efficient relative to any systemwide IV estimator utilizing instruments in the class $\mathcal{C}$, in the sense that the difference of the covariance matrices in their respective limiting distributions is indefinite.

ii. Given the class of instruments $\mathcal{C} = \{W : W = (\tilde{\Sigma}^{-1} \otimes X)\tilde{A}\}$, such that $\text{plim}_{T \to \infty} \tilde{\Sigma}^{-1} = \Sigma^{-1}$, $\text{plim}_{T \to \infty} \tilde{A} = A$ are well defined nonstochastic matrices, the 3SLS estimator is an optimal FIV estimator, in the sense that the $C_{FIV} - C_{3SLS} \geq 0$, where the two matrices are, respectively, the covariance matrices of the limiting distributions of the FIV and 3SLS estimators.

2.5   IV and Insufficient Sample Size

2.5.1   The Nature of the Problem

The 2SLS (and 3SLS) procedure creates "excessive" data demands, even though the parameters to be estimated in each structural equation may be quite small. The problem lies with the necessity of estimating the reduced form, which is an integral (conceptual) part of the two procedures. Thus, when we are dealing with a sizable model, the fact that the latter may contain quite a large number of predetermined variables may render it impossible to estimate its reduced form. This occurs because the matrix X, which is $T \times G$ may be such that $T - G$, is **quite small or even negative**! When this is so, of course, the reduced form may be estimated very poorly, or may not be obtainable at all. The first will eventuate when $T - G \geq 0$, but small, and the second when $T - G < 0$, thus violating condition (A.1a) of Chapter 1.

When the problem was first encountered, applied econometricians responded by a number of ingenious, if futile, alternatives. One such alternative was the use of the generalized inverse. More precisely, for the case $T - G < 0$, it was proposed that since the entity

$$\hat{\Pi} = (X'X)^{-1}X'Y$$

does not exist (because the inverse $(X'X)^{-1}$ does not exist), it should be substituted by

$$\tilde{\Pi} = (X'X)_g X'Y = X_g Y,$$

where $(X'X)_g$ the **generalized inverse** of $X'X$.

As is made clear in Ch. 3 of Dhrymes (1984), this approach obtains a (unique) solution at the cost of imposing certain restrictions on the parameter estimates. Such restrictions have no economic content or motivation and merely require that of all matrices Π satisfying the condition, $X'X\Pi = X'Y$, the one chosen, $\tilde{\Pi}$, should have **minimal norm**!

Another proposal was to use the **principal components** of the variables in X, for estimating the reduced form. Without going into the details of the definition and derivation of principal components, let us say, for the purposes of this discussion, that the process of obtaining principal components entails the extraction of the characteristic roots of $X'X$ and their associated characteristic vectors; subsequently, one is to choose a number of these characteristic vectors, say k_*, which must be "much less" than T (typically only a small fraction of T), corresponding to the k_* largest characteristic roots. Let these characteristic vectors be denoted by E_k. The principal components, for the purposes of this discussion, may be defined by $W_{k_*} = X E_{k_*}$. One then estimates $\tilde{\Gamma}^{(k_*)} = (W'_{k_*} W_{k_*})^{-1} W'_{k_*} Y$, and for the explanatory dependent variables appearing in the structural equations, say Y_i, one substitutes $\tilde{Y}_i = W_{k_*} \tilde{\Gamma}^{(k_*)}_i$. Thereafter one follows the standard 2SLS procedure. [23] Of course, these procedures can be shown to be consistent, only by showing that as the sample increases in size the need for them disappears, so that we ultimately revert to the standard 2SLS technique. [24] Needless to say, the same may be said of taking $k_* = T$. This choice implies that $\tilde{Y} = W_T \tilde{\Gamma}^{(T)} = Y$, so that the principal components procedure with $T = k_*$ is simply an elaborate process for applying Ordinary Least Squares (OLS) in order to estimate the parameters of a structural equation(s). The fact that, as the sample size increases, we move toward the standard 2SLS procedure cannot possibly be used to defend the use of thisprocedure in any instance where $T < G$!

2.5.2 Iterated Instrumental Variables (IIV)

The resolution of the problem encountered in the previous section is contained in the observation that while collectively the number of predetermined variables in a model may be quite large, the number of parameters to be estimated in each structural equation is, typically, rather small.

The method of IIV proceeds as follows: let X be the matrix of predetermined variables in the system as a whole, and let it be desired to estimate the parameters of the ith structural equation. It is assumed that it is always possible to choose instrumental variables (columns of X) for every equation. To this effect, choose $X_{0i} = X L_{0i} = X(L_{4i}, L_{2i})$, where L_{4i} is of dimension $G \times m_i$ and corresponds to the choice of instruments in lieu of the dependent variables in Y_i and L_{2i} corresponds to choosing as instruments the predetermined variables in X_i. Thus, in this scheme, **we always**

---

[23] Since there are as many well defined characteristic vectors as the rank of the matrix $X'X$, it follows that the recommended procedure fails to utilize some of the information contained in the X matrix. Thus, it would appear that we wish to advance matters **simply by ignoring some of the relevant information!**

[24] This is the justification given, e.g., in Dhrymes (1970), which is fairly representative of the prevailing view at the time.

choose as instruments the predetermined variables appearing in the structural equation dealt with. Given the choice of instruments, we proceed in three steps: (a) we obtain the initial IV estimators

$$\tilde{\delta}^{(0)}_{\cdot i} = (X'_{0i} Z_i)^{-1} X'_{0i} y_{\cdot i}, \quad i = 1, 2, \dots, m; \tag{2.123}$$

(b) subsequently, we estimate the **restricted reduced form**

$$\tilde{\Pi}^{(0)} = \tilde{C}^{(0)} \tilde{D}^{(0)}, \quad \tilde{Y}^{(0)} = X \tilde{\Pi}^{(0)}, \quad \tilde{Z}^{(0)}_i = (\tilde{Y}^{(0)}_i, X_i); \tag{2.124}$$

(c) we obtain the IIV estimator as

$$\tilde{\delta}^{(1)}_{\cdot i} = (\tilde{Z}^{(0)'}_i Z_i)^{-1} \tilde{Z}^{(0)'}_i y_{\cdot i}, \quad i = 1, 2, \dots, m. \tag{2.125}$$

Although this estimator may be further iterated, i.e, we may now recompute the (restricted) reduced form, obtaining the new estimator, $\tilde{\Pi}^{(1)}$, thus obtaining the second iterate $\tilde{\delta}^{(2)}_{\cdot i}$, and so on until convergence. As it turns out, nothing will be gained (asymptotically) by iteration to convergence since the first iterate, i.e. the estimator in Eq. (2.125), has **exactly the same asymptotic properties as the converging iterate**.

This is a single equation estimator and hence does not take advantage of relevant information that may be contained in other equations. Thus, it is more appropriately termed the **limited information iterated instrumental variables** (LIIV) estimator.

Evidently, we can define an "efficient" estimator by analogy to 3SLS. In particular, we may repeat (a), (b) and (c) of the LIIV estimator, but at stage (c) we also obtain estimators of the covariance matrix parameters

$$\tilde{\sigma}_{ij} = \frac{1}{T} \left(y_{\cdot i} - Z_i \tilde{\delta}_{\cdot i} \right)' \left(y_{\cdot j} - Z_j \tilde{\delta}_{\cdot j} \right), \tag{2.126}$$

and the instrumental matrix

$$(\tilde{\Sigma}^{-1} \otimes I)\tilde{Z}^*, \quad \text{where} \quad \tilde{Z}^* = \text{diag}(\tilde{Z}_1, \tilde{Z}_2, \dots, \tilde{Z}_m);$$

finally, (d) we obtain the "efficient" estimator as

$$\tilde{\delta} = \left(\tilde{Z}^{*'} (\tilde{\Sigma}^{-1} \otimes I) Z^* \right)^{-1} \tilde{Z}^{*'} y, \tag{2.127}$$

where we have written the entire system not in CSF but as

$$y = Z^* \delta + u, \quad Z^* = \text{diag}(Z_1, Z_2, \dots, Z_m). \tag{2.128}$$

Again by analogy with 3SLS we term this the **full information iterated instrumental variables** (FIIV) estimator. We shall justify this terminology below where we shall show that FIIV is efficient relative to the LIIV estimator. We now establish the salient properties of such estimators.

Theorem 10. Consider the GLSEM of Chapter 1, subject to conditions (A.1) through (A.5) and as exhibited in Eq. (2.128), above. Then, the following statements are true:

i. the LIIV estimator, as discussed above, is consistent;

ii. the LIIV estimator is asymptotically equivalent to the 2SLS estimator, in the sense that their limiting distributions are identical;

iii. the FIIV estimator, as described above, is consistent;

iv. the FIIV estimator is asymptotically equivalent to the 3SLS estimator, in the sense that their limiting distributions are equivalent;

v. the FIIV estimator is efficient relative to the LIIV estimator.

Proof: In proving parts i and ii we shall employ the systemwide form the LIIV estimator. From the description of the estimator above, the instrumental matrix is $\tilde{Z}^*$. Thus, the systemwide LIIV estimator is given by $\tilde{\delta} = \left(\tilde{Z}^{*\prime} Z^*\right)^{-1} \tilde{Z}^{*\prime} y$. Since $\tilde{Z}_i = X(\tilde{\Pi}_i, L_{2i}) = X\tilde{S}_i$, we see that the LIIV estimator above may also be rendered as

$$\sqrt{T}(\tilde{\delta} - \delta)_{LIIV} = \left[\tilde{S}'\left(I \otimes \frac{X'X}{T}\right)\tilde{S}\right]^{-1} \tilde{S}'\frac{1}{\sqrt{T}}(I \otimes X')u, \qquad (2.129)$$

which shows (a) that the LIIV estimator is consistent, and, comparing with Eqs. (2.3) and (2.4), (b) that its limiting distribution is identical with that of the 2SLS estimator.

To prove iii and iv we note that, since $\tilde{Z}^* = (I \otimes X)\tilde{S}$, the FIIV estimator may be rendered as

$$\sqrt{T}(\tilde{\delta} - \delta)_{FIIV} = \left[\tilde{S}'\left(\tilde{\Sigma}^{-1} \otimes \frac{X'X}{T}\right)\tilde{S}\right]^{-1} \tilde{S}'(\tilde{\Sigma}^{-1} \otimes I)\frac{1}{\sqrt{T}}(I \otimes X')u. \qquad (2.130)$$

Moreover, since $\tilde{\Pi} \xrightarrow{P} \Pi$, and $\tilde{\Sigma} \xrightarrow{P} \Sigma$, we see that the FIIV estimator is consistent and, comparing with Eqs. (2.7) and (2.8), that its limiting distribution is identical with that of the 3SLS estimator.

As for part v, this follows from parts ii and iv and Theorem 3.

q.e.d.

Corollary 2. Neither the LIIV nor the FIIV estimators are improved, in their asymptotic properties, by iteration.

Proof: From the representation in Eqs. (2.129) and (2.130) it is clear that only the consistency property of $\tilde{\Pi}$ and/or $\tilde{\Sigma}$ enters into the argument for the consistency or asymptotic normality of the LIIV and FIIV estimators. Hence, how Π and Σ are initially estimated is immaterial.

q.e.d.

Remark 11. The corollary should not convey the impression that how we choose the initial instruments is immaterial; only that this is so in the limit, i.e. when the sample increases indefinitely. Nonetheless, it is a good practice, in finite samples, to choose one's initial instruments with some care and to iterate the procedure at least once, so as to overcome any adverse effects of an inept initial instrument selection.

2.6 k-class and Double k-class Estimators

This topic is touched upon only as a historical footnote, and not because any salient implication of these constructs has led to important discoveries. [25]

We recall that one of the many possible representations of the 2SLS estimator is its representation as the solution of

$$
\begin{bmatrix} Y_i'Y_i - \hat{V}_i'\hat{V}_i & Y_i'X_i \\ X_i'Y_i & X_i'X_i \end{bmatrix} \begin{bmatrix} \beta_{\cdot i} \\ \gamma_{\cdot i} \end{bmatrix} = \begin{bmatrix} Y_i' - \hat{V}_i' \\ X_i' \end{bmatrix} y_{\cdot i}.
$$

The k-class estimator, of the parameters of a structural equation, is defined as

$$
\begin{bmatrix} \tilde{\beta}_{\cdot i} \\ \tilde{\gamma}_{\cdot i} \end{bmatrix}_{(k)} = \begin{bmatrix} Y_i'Y_i - k\hat{V}_i'\hat{V}_i & Y_i'X_i \\ X_i'Y_i & X_i'X_i \end{bmatrix}^{-1} \begin{bmatrix} Y_i' - k\hat{V}_i' \\ X_i' \end{bmatrix} y_{\cdot i}, \tag{2.131}
$$

while the double k-class estimator is given by

$$
\begin{bmatrix} \tilde{\beta}_{\cdot i} \\ \tilde{\gamma}_{\cdot i} \end{bmatrix}_{(k_1,k_2)} = \begin{bmatrix} Y_i'Y_i - k_1\hat{V}_i'\hat{V}_i & Y_i'X_i \\ X_i'Y_i & X_i'X_i \end{bmatrix}^{-1} \begin{bmatrix} Y_i' - k_2\hat{V}_i' \\ X_i' \end{bmatrix} y_{\cdot i}. \tag{2.132}
$$

In order that the consistency property be retained it is necessary that the parameters k, k_1, k_2 converge to unity with T.

These estimators were obtained in the hope that when the small sample theory of 2SLS and 3SLS estimation was ultimately established, manipulation of the parameters k, or k_1, k_2 would yield desirable properties in small samples. Unfortunately, the general theory of small sample distributions proved to be elusive and virtually unobtainable for practical purposes, and such estimators were never able to fulfill their potential.

---

[25] The k class of estimators was introduced in Theil (1958), the double k-class by Nagar (1962); in this connection we should also mention the work of Zellner (1986), and Zellner, Bauwens and van Dijk (1988). The last two references have a Bayesian orientation and are, perhaps, more appropriately referred to in the context of the discussion of indirect least squares (ILS) estimation in Chapter 4.

2.7 Distribution of LM Derived Estimators

We recall from Chapter 1, particularly in connection with the discussion surrounding Eqs. (1.101) and (1.108), that the 2SLS and 3SLS estimators obtained by the method of Lagrange multipliers, as **restricted least squares** and **restricted generalized least squares**, respectively, obey the following:

For **single equation 2SLS**,

$$\sqrt{T}\begin{pmatrix} \hat{a}_{\cdot i} - a_{\cdot i} \\ \hat{\lambda}_{\cdot i} \end{pmatrix}_{2SLS} = \begin{bmatrix} \tilde{E}_{2i} L_i L_i'(\tilde{\Pi},\ I)' \\ \tilde{J}_{22(2i)}^{-1} L_i^{*\circ'} \tilde{V}_{2i}(\tilde{\Pi},\ I)' \end{bmatrix} \frac{X'u_{\cdot i}}{\sqrt{T}}, \qquad (2.133)$$

where

$$H_i^\circ = (L_i,\ L_i^{*\circ}), \quad \tilde{J}_{(2i)} = H_i^{\circ'} \tilde{V}_{2i} H_i^\circ, \quad \tilde{V}_{2i}^{-1} = \tilde{K} + L_i^{*\circ} L_i^{*\circ'} \quad (2.134)$$

$$\tilde{E}_{2i} = \tilde{V}_{2i} - \tilde{V}_{2i} L_i^{*\circ} \tilde{J}_{22(2i)}^{-1} L_i^{*\circ} \tilde{V}_{2i}, \quad \tilde{J}_{22(2i)} = L_i^{*\circ'} \tilde{V}_{2i} L_i^{*\circ}, \quad \tilde{K} = \frac{Q'Q}{T}.$$

For **systemwide 2SLS**,

$$\sqrt{T}\begin{pmatrix} \hat{a} - a \\ \hat{\lambda} \end{pmatrix}_{2SLS} = \begin{bmatrix} \tilde{E}_2 LL' \left(I \otimes (\tilde{\Pi},\ I)' \right) \\ \tilde{J}_{22(2)}^{-1} L^{*\circ'} \tilde{V}_2 \left(I \otimes (\tilde{\Pi},\ I)' \right) \end{bmatrix} \frac{(I \otimes X)'u}{\sqrt{T}}, \quad (2.135)$$

and the ancillary definitions of Eq. (2.134) remain, *mutatis mutandis*, the same, i.e.

$$\tilde{V}_2^{-1} = (I \otimes \tilde{K}) + L^{*\circ} L^{*\circ'}, \quad H^\circ = (L,\ L^{*\circ}), \quad \text{etc.}$$

For **3SLS**,

$$\sqrt{T}\begin{pmatrix} \hat{a} - a \\ \hat{\lambda} \end{pmatrix}_{3SLS} = \begin{bmatrix} \tilde{E}_3 LL' \left(\tilde{\Sigma}^{-1} \otimes (\tilde{\Pi},\ I)' \right) \\ \tilde{J}_{22(3)}^{-1} L^{*\circ'} \tilde{V}_3 \left(\tilde{\Sigma}^{-1} \otimes (\tilde{\Pi},\ I)' \right) \end{bmatrix} \frac{(I \otimes X)'u}{\sqrt{T}}, $$
$$(2.136)$$

where $\tilde{\Sigma}$ is a prior, consistent estimator and, in this case,

$$\tilde{V}_3^{-1} = (\tilde{\Sigma}^{-1} \otimes \tilde{K}) + L^{*\circ} L^{*\circ'},$$

all other subsidiary definitions remaining as before. It is, thus, quite evident that the limiting distribution problem, in this context, is exactly the same as the one solved at the beginning of this chapter. We conclude therefore that, asymptotically,

$$\sqrt{T}\left(\frac{\hat{a}_{\cdot i} - a_{\cdot i}}{\hat{\lambda}_{\cdot i}}\right)_{2SLS} \sim N(0, \Psi_{2i}),$$

$$\sqrt{T}\left(\frac{\hat{a} - a}{\hat{\lambda}}\right)_{2SLS} \sim N(0, \Psi_2)$$

$$\sqrt{T}\left(\frac{\hat{a} - a}{\hat{\lambda}}\right)_{3SLS} \sim N(0, \Psi_3), \qquad (2.137)$$

where

$$\Psi_2 = \begin{bmatrix} A_{11(2)} & 0 \\ 0 & A_{22(2)} \end{bmatrix}, \quad \Psi_3 = \begin{bmatrix} A_{11(3)} & 0 \\ 0 & A_{22(3)} \end{bmatrix}, \qquad (2.138)$$

and, in the case of systemwide 2SLS,

$$A_{11(2)} = E_2 L[L'(\Sigma \otimes K)L]L'E_2, \quad \mathcal{K}_2 = I \otimes K, \quad V_2^{-1} = \mathcal{K}_2 + L^{*\circ}L^{*\circ'},$$

$$A_{22(2)} = J_{22(2)}^{-1} - I, \quad E_2 L = V_2 L - V_2 L^{*\circ} J_{22(2)}^{-1} J_{21(2)}, \qquad (2.139)$$

while for 3SLS, we have

$$A_{11(3)} = E_3 L(L'\mathcal{K}_3 L)L'E_3, \quad \mathcal{K}_3 = \Sigma^{-1} \otimes K, \quad A_{22(3)} = J_{22(3)}^{-1} - I,$$

$$E_3 L = V_3 L - V_3 L^{*\circ} J_{22(3)}^{-1} J_{21(3)}, \quad V_3^{-1} = \mathcal{K}_3 + L^{*\circ}L^{*\circ'}. \qquad (2.140)$$

In the preceding, E, V_i, J_{ij}, K, etc., are simply the probability limits of the corresponding tilded entities. As for the single equation 2SLS representation, the covariance matrix Ψ_{2i} is the ith diagonal block of Ψ_2, i.e.

$$\Psi_{2i} = \begin{bmatrix} A_{11(2)}^i & 0 \\ 0 & A_{22(2)}^i \end{bmatrix}, \quad A_{11(2)}^i = \sigma_{ii} E_{2i} L_i (L_i' K L_i) L_i' E_{2i}, \qquad (2.141)$$

$$A_{22(2)}^i = \sigma_{ii}(J_{22(2i)}^{-1} - I), \quad J_{22(2i)} = L_i^{*\circ'} V_{2i} L_i^{*\circ}, \quad V_{2i}^{-1} = K + L_i^{*\circ} L_i^{*\circ'}.$$

In the 3SLS context,

$$\Psi_3 = \begin{bmatrix} A_{11(3)} & 0 \\ 0 & A_{22(3)} \end{bmatrix}, \quad A_{11(3)} = E_3 LL'(\Sigma^{-1} \otimes K)LL'E_3,$$

$$E_3 L = V_3\left(L - L^{*\circ}[L^{*\circ'}V_3 L^{*\circ}]^{-1}L^{*\circ'}V_3 L\right),$$

$$A_{22(3)} = J_{22(3)}^{-1} - I \quad J_{22(3)} = L^{*\circ'}V_3 L^{*\circ}. \qquad (2.142)$$

2.8   Properties of Specification Tests

2.8.1   Single Equation 2SLS

Here, we examine the properties of the various tests of prior restrictions, touched upon briefly at the end of Chapter 1. For maximal clarity of presentation, we shall begin our discussion of the properties of identification and specification tests with the case of single equation 2SLS. In the next section, we shall also examine the conformity variants of these tests and, thereafter, we shall extend our discussion to systemwide 2SLS, as well as 3SLS. The precise meaning of these terms is made clear below.

Definition 4. In the context of the GLSEM of Theorem 2, a test for the validity **of all prior restrictions**, is said to be an **identification test**. A test for the validity of a **subset of such restrictions, whose rejection does not call into question the identifiability of the system, or the equation in question**, is said to be [26] a **misspecification** test.

Given the manner in which we have formulated the estimation problem, by enforcing the prior restrictions through the method of Lagrange multipliers, we have at least two distinct ways of operating. First, we can carry out such tests by testing the associated Lagrange multipliers. Such tests are termed **Lagrange multiplier tests (LMT)**. Second, we can refrain from imposing a subset of such prior restrictions, and then test the "extra" coefficients estimated, to determine whether they are significantly different from zero. Such tests are termed **conformity tests (CT)**. Of course, there is also the additional procedure of **likelihood ratio tests (LRT)**, when the distribution of the structural errors is known, and we employ the maximum likelihood principle in estimating the relevant parameters. This procedure is, generally, not available in the context of 2SLS and 3SLS, since these estimators are obtained in a distribution free context. These concepts are formalized below.

---

[26] The terms "identification" and "misspecification" are introduced only in deference to the literature. As we shall see at a later stage, a distinction between the two is rather illusory. In the early development of this topic, however, Anderson and Rubin (1949), (1950), as well as Koopmans and Hood (1953), have introduced tests based on the rank of certain submatrices of the reduced form, which were termed identification tests; it was implicit in their discussion, and was later explicitly claimed by Kadane (1974), that these tests were equivalent to a test on the validity of **all prior restrictions**. At the same time Anderson and Rubin alluded to a test for the validity of only a subset of the (over) identifying restrictions. A rejection outcome, in the context of such a test, does not invalidate or call into question the identifiability of the equation, or system, under consideration. Thus, such tests may be termed misspecification tests, in the tradition of the early work by Theil on misspecification analysis.

Definition 5. Let $\theta \in R^k$ be a k-dimensional parameter of interest. A test of the hypothesis $H_0 : f(\theta) = 0$, where f is an s-dimensional vector function, $s \leq k$, as against the alternative that there are no restrictions, may be carried out in three basic fashions:

i. if the distribution function of the underlying data is known, one may apply the likelihood ratio principle, and the resulting test is said to be the **likelihood ratio test**;

ii. if a suitable function is to be extremized in order that estimators be obtained, then

   1. we may impose the restriction by the method of Lagrange multipliers; in this case we obtain an s-dimensional vector of Lagrange multipliers and, in addition, an estimator, say, $\tilde{\theta}_{(1)}$ that obeys the condition $f(\tilde{\theta}_{(1)}) = 0$. A test of the hypothesis above, based on the mean of the (limiting) distribution of the associated Lagrange multiplier estimators, is said to be a **Lagrange multiplier test**;

   2. we may estimate the parameter without reference to the restriction, thus obtaining the estimator $\tilde{\theta}_{(2)}$, (which does not necessarily obey the condition $f(\tilde{\theta}_{(2)}) = 0$). We may, then, seek to determine whether this **unrestricted** estimator **conforms to the restriction**. Precisely, this entails testing the hypothesis that the mean of the distribution of $f(\tilde{\theta}_{(2)})$ is zero. Such a test is said to be a **conformity test**.

LM Identification and Specification Tests

From Eqs. (2.133), and (1.102) (from Chapter 1), we can write the expression for the Lagrange multiplier (LM) estimator, more fully, as

$$\hat{\lambda}_{\cdot i} = (\tilde{J}_{22(2i)}^{-1} - I)L_i^{*o'}a_{\cdot i} + \tilde{J}_{22(2i)}^{-1}L_i^{*o'}\tilde{\sigma}_{ii}^{1/2}\tilde{V}_{2i}\tilde{D}'\frac{\bar{R}^{-1}X'u_{\cdot i}}{T\tilde{\sigma}_{ii}^{1/2}},$$

$$\tilde{D} = \bar{R}'(\tilde{\Pi}, I), \quad \bar{R}\bar{R}' = M_{xx}, \quad \tilde{K} = \tilde{D}'\tilde{D}. \tag{2.143}$$

It follows immediately, from Eq. (2.143), that under the null hypothesis, $L_i^{*o'}a_{\cdot i} = 0$, the LM identification test statistic obeys

$$\phi_{2i} = T\hat{\lambda}_{\cdot i}'\frac{(\tilde{J}_{22(2i)}^{-1} - I)_g}{\tilde{\sigma}_{ii}}\hat{\lambda}_{\cdot i} \xrightarrow{d} \chi_{d_i}^2, \tag{2.144}$$

where $d_i = G - G_i - m_i$. To see why this is so, note that putting

$$J_{2i} = H_i^{o'}V_{2i}H_i^o = \begin{bmatrix} L_i'V_{2i}L_i & L_i'V_{2i}L_i^{*o} \\ L_i^{*o'}V_{2i}L_i & L_i^{*o'}V_{2i}L_i^{*o} \end{bmatrix}, \tag{2.145}$$

$$J_{2i}^{-1} = H_i^{\circ'} V_{2i}^{-1} H_i^{\circ} = \begin{bmatrix} L_i'KL_i & L_i'KL_i^{*\circ} \\ L_i^{*\circ'}KL_i & L_i^{*\circ'}KL_i^{*\circ} + I \end{bmatrix}, \qquad (2.146)$$

we conclude

$$J_{22(2i)}^{-1} = I + L_i^{*\circ'}KL_i^{*\circ} - L_i^{*\circ'}KL_i \left(L_i'KL_i\right)^{-1} L_i'KL_i^{*\circ}. \qquad (2.147)$$

It is interesting that we can prove the following

Lemma 4. The matrix $J_{22(2i)}^{-1}$ has m unit roots, and d_i roots greater than unity. The matrix $J_{22(2i)}^{-1} - I$ is of rank d_i.

Proof: We consider the characteristic equation $\left|\nu I - J_{22(2i)}\right| = 0$; this has the same nonzero roots as

$$\left|\nu V_{2i}^{-1} - L_i^{*\circ}L_i^{*\circ'}\right| = 0. \qquad (2.148)$$

Since $L_i^{*\circ}L_i^{*\circ'}$ is of rank $m_i^* + G_i^*$, Eq. (2.148 has $m_i + G_i$ zero roots. For $\nu = 1$, the equation above becomes $|K| = 0$; since K is a matrix of dimension $m + G$ and rank G, it is evident that Eq. (2.148), and hence $J_{22(2i)}$, has m unit roots. But Eq. (2.148) may be rewritten as $\left|(1-\nu)V_{2i}^{-1} - K\right| = 0$. Since $K \geq 0$, its roots are nonnegative; consequently, any $\nu's$ satisfying the equation above obey $\nu_j \in [0,1]$. Thus, Eq. (2.148) has $d_i = G - m_i - G_i$ roots in the interval $(0,1)$; hence, the roots of $J_{22(2i)}$ are given by

$$\begin{aligned} \nu_j &< 1, \quad j = 1, 2, \ldots, m, \\ &= 1, \quad j = m+1, m+2, \ldots, m + d_i. \end{aligned} \qquad (2.149)$$

Now, if ν_i is a root of $J_{22(2i)}$ then $1/\nu_i$ is a root of $J_{22(2i)}^{-1}$. Hence, $J_{22(2i)}^{-1}$ has m unit roots, and d_i roots greater than unity. Moreover, letting N be the diagonal matrix containing its characteristic roots, we have $J_{22(2i)}^{-1} = PNP'$. If P_1 is the matrix containing the charcteristic vectors corresponding to the roots that are **greater than unity**, we obtain

$$J_{22(2i)}^{-1} - I = P \begin{bmatrix} N_1 & 0 \\ 0 & I \end{bmatrix} P' - PP' = P_1 \Lambda P_1', \qquad (2.150)$$

where $\Lambda = N_1 - I > 0$, and N_1 is the diagonal matrix containing the characteristic roots exceeding unity. Thus, the rank of $J_{22(2i)}^{-1} - I$ is d_i.

q.e.d.

In view of Lemma 4, the generalized inverse [27] of $J_{22(2i)}^{-1} - I$ has m zero roots and d_i positive roots. It further follows from Eq. (2.150) that the

---

[27] For a definition of the generalized inverse see footnote 12, of Chapter 1.

representation of its g-inverse is given by $P_1\Lambda^{-1}P_1$. Consequently, we may rewrite the identification test statistic as $\phi_{2i} = (\tilde{\sigma}_{ii}/T)\hat{\lambda}'_{\cdot i}\tilde{P}_1\tilde{\Lambda}^{-1}\tilde{P}'_1\hat{\lambda}_{\cdot i}$, where we have used the representation $(\tilde{J}^{-1}_{22(2i)} - I)_g = \tilde{P}_1\tilde{\Lambda}^{-1}\tilde{P}'_1$. By the preceding discussion,

$$\frac{\sqrt{T}}{\sqrt{\tilde{\sigma}_{ii}}}\tilde{\Lambda}^{-1/2}\tilde{P}'_1\hat{\lambda}_{\cdot i} \xrightarrow{\mathrm{d}} N(0,\ I_{d_i}),$$

which justifies the claim in Eq. (2.144).

An interesting characteristic of statistical tests is their power, or power function. This determines the ability of the test procedure to discriminate against false hypotheses, i.e. it determines the probability of rejection, when the null is false. In our case, when the null is false we see, from Eq. (2.143), that the limiting distribution is not well defined, in that its mean becomes the limit of $\sqrt{T}(J^{-1}_{22(2i)} - I)L^{*\circ'}_i a_{\cdot i}$, which is not well defined. Thus, it has become customary, in this context, to deal with so called **local alternatives**, i.e. if

$H_0 : L^{*\circ'}_i a_{\cdot i} = 0 ,$

the (local) alternative is

$H_1 : (1/\sqrt{T})L^{*\circ'}_i a_{\cdot i} \neq 0 .$

Hence, under this local alternative we have

$$\sqrt{T}\hat{\lambda}_{\cdot i} = (\tilde{J}^{-1}_{22(2i)} - I)L^{*\circ'}_i a_{\cdot i} + \tilde{J}^{-1}_{22(2i)}L^{*\circ'}_i \tilde{V}_{2i}\tilde{\sigma}^{1/2}_{ii}\tilde{D}'\frac{\bar{R}^{-1}X'u_{\cdot i}}{\sqrt{T\tilde{\sigma}_{ii}}}. \qquad (2.151)$$

Since, asymptotically,

$$\frac{\bar{R}^{-1}X'u_{\cdot i}}{\sqrt{T\tilde{\sigma}_{ii}}} = \zeta_T \xrightarrow{\mathrm{d}} N(0, I), \qquad (2.152)$$

it follows that, under the local alternative

$$\sqrt{T}\hat{\lambda}_{\cdot i} \sim N\left(\mu,\ \sigma_{ii}(J^{-1}_{22(2i)} - I)\right),$$

and the identification test statistic obeys

$$\phi_{2i} = T\hat{\lambda}'_{\cdot i}\frac{(\tilde{J}^{-1}_{22(2i)} - I)_g}{\tilde{\sigma}_{ii}}\hat{\lambda}_{\cdot i} \xrightarrow{\mathrm{d}} \chi^2_{d_i}(\theta_{2(i)}), \qquad (2.153)$$

where

$$\theta_{2i} = \frac{1}{2\sigma_{ii}}\mu'(J^{-1}_{22(2i)} - I)_g\mu, \quad \mu = (J^{-1}_{22(2i)} - I)L^{*\circ'}_i a_{\cdot i}. \qquad (2.154)$$

is the noncentrality parameter. [28]

Generally, for a given departure from the null hypothesis, the larger the noncentrality parameter the more powerful the test, i.e. the higher is the probability of rejection.

Remark 12. It is somewhat counterintuitive to discover, in Lemma 6, that the covariance matrix of the LM vector is singular, since, generally, we are not aware of any linear dependency or any other restrictions on these entities. A little reflection, however, will convince us that at least m restrictions must be placed on the parameters, potentially appearing in each structural equation. This is so, since there are only G information sources independent of the structural error process. These are the predetermined (or exogenous as the case may be) variables of the system; on the other hand, we have, by convention, placed $G_i^* + m_i^*$ restrictions on the potential explanatory variables of the ith structural equation; unless $G_i^* + m_i^* \geq m$, the **order condition for identification** is not satisfied. Thus, it is a (minimum) requirement of estimability, or identifiability, that in each equation at least m restrictions be placed on the potential explanatory variables. But, this means that if the equation is identified, at least m of the LM must not be binding. In effect this would seem to imply that, if a model can be estimated then *ipso facto* it must be identified, and we cannot possibly test (it) for identification.

Remark 13. In carrying out specification tests, it is commonly thought that if, say, the sth restriction is not binding, i.e. if, in fact, it is true, the Lagrange multiplier associated with it would be, in the limit, null; hence, that a test of this hypothesis would merely involve a test that the mean of the (limiting distribution of the) corresponding Lagrange multiplier is zero. Unfortunately, this conception of the problem is overly simplistic; in fact, specification tests are somewhat more complicated than merely testing that the mean of a group of Lagrange multipliers as estimated above is null, although it would appear so by inspection of the relevant test statistic. To see this, consider again the expression of the Lagrange multiplier estimators given in Eq. (2.143). Thus,

$$\hat{\lambda}_{\cdot i} = (\tilde{J}_{22(2i)}^{-1} - I)L_i^{*\circ'} a_{\cdot i} + \tilde{J}_{22(2i)}^{-1} L_i^{*\circ'} \tilde{V}_{2i} \tilde{\sigma}_{ii}^{1/2} \tilde{D}' \frac{\bar{R}^{-1} X' u_{\cdot i}}{T \sqrt{\tilde{\sigma}_{ii}}}.$$

Suppose we specify that, in fact,

$$F_s' L_i^{*\circ'} a_{\cdot i} = 0,$$

but

$$F_s^{*'} L_i^{*\circ'} a_{\cdot i} \neq 0, \tag{2.155}$$

---

[28] For a discussion of the **noncentral chi square distribution** see Dhrymes (1978), appendix of Chapter 2, or Johnson and Kotz (1970), Ch. 28.

where F_s is a permutation of s of the columns of $I_{G_i^* + m_i^*}$, corresponding to the subset of prior restrictions we are currently asserting to be true; F_s^* is the complement of F_s, i.e. it consists of (a permutation of) the remaining columns of the identity matrix. Does it follow that the limiting distribution of $F_s' \hat{\lambda}_{.i}$ is normal with mean zero and covariance matrix

$$\sigma_{ii} F_s' (J_{22}^{-1} - I) F_s ?$$

The answer is generally, no, since premultiplying the equation exhibiting the LM vector above by F_s', and imposing the condition $F_s' L_i^{*\circ'} a_{.i} = 0$, transforms the first term of the right member of that equation into

$$F_s' (\tilde{J}_{22(2i)}^{-1} - I) F_s^* F_s^{*'} L_i^{*\circ'} a_{.i}.$$

Since F_s^* is the complement of F_s, the fact that $F_s' L_i^{*\circ'} a_{.i} = 0$ does not imply that the expression above is necessarily zero. Thus, the limiting distribution in question may not have mean zero; indeed, it may not even be well defined.

The preceding indicates that there is an obstacle in designing specification tests. Our next task is to remove it. Suppose that, for $s \leq G - G_i - m_i$, [29] there exists an $s \times s$ submatrix of $J_{22(2i)}^{-1} - I$, such that $F_s' (J_{22(2i)}^{-1} - I) F_s > 0$; consider, then,

$$F_s' \hat{\lambda}_{.i} = F_s' (\tilde{J}_{22(2i)}^{-1} - I)(F_s F_s' + F_s^* F_s^{*'}) L_i^{*\circ'} a_{.i} + F_s' \tilde{J}_{22(2i)}^{-1} L_i^{*\circ'} \tilde{V}_{2i} \frac{Q' r_{.i}}{T}$$

$$= \{[F_s' (\tilde{J}_{22(2i)}^{-1} - I) F_s] F_s' + [F_s' (\tilde{J}_{22(2i)}^{-1} - I) F_s^*] F_s^{*'} \} L_i^{*\circ'} a_{.i}$$

$$+ F_s' \tilde{J}_{22(2i)}^{-1} L_i^{*\circ'} \tilde{V}_{2i} \frac{Q' r_{.i}}{T}.$$

As we have pointed out above, even if $F_s' L_i^{*\circ'} a_{.i} = 0$, the mean of the limiting distribution of $\sqrt{T} F_s' \hat{\lambda}_{.i}$, need not be zero. However, if we take as a maintained hypothesis that

$$F_s^{*'} L_i^{*\circ'} a_{.i} = 0,$$

the mean of the limiting distribution is zero if and only if

$$F_s' L_i^{*\circ'} a_{.i} = 0.$$

---

[29] The fact that the rank of $J_{22(2i)}^{-1} - I$ is $G - G_i - m_i$, guarantees that there exists at least one nonsingular submatrix of order $s \leq G - G_i - m_i$. The number of such nonsingular submatrices of order $s = G - G_i - m_i$ determines the number of choices we have for selecting the m *a priori* restrictions taken to be "most true", or taken to be maintained hypotheses, not subject to test.

To implement this insight, take $s = G - G_i - m_i$, the maximum possible, and specify that the minimal number of prior restrictions hold; for example, the investigator may choose the m prior restrictions he considers "most true", or most valid. Since, from a mathematical point of view, it does not matter just which m of the restrictions one considers "most true", let these be given by

$$F_s^{*'} L_i^{*o'} a_{\cdot i} = 0. \tag{2.156}$$

With Eq. (2.156) as a **maintained hypothesis**, we may write

$$\tilde{\Psi}_{2(s,i)} F_s' \hat{\lambda}_{\cdot i} = F_s' L_i^{*o'} a_{\cdot i} + \tilde{\Psi}_{2(s,i)} F_s' \tilde{J}_{22(2i)}^{-1} L_i^{*o'} \tilde{V}_{2i} \tilde{\sigma}_{ii}^{1/2} \tilde{D}' \frac{\bar{R}^{-1} X' u_{\cdot i}}{T \sqrt{\tilde{\sigma}_{ii}}}$$

$$\tilde{\Psi}_{2(s,i)} = [F_s' (\tilde{J}_{22(2i)}^{-1} - I) F_s]^{-1}. \tag{2.157}$$

This is the desired representation, since it discloses precisely the transform of the Lagrange multipliers needed to test a particular restriction, or a particular set of restrictions. Set the left member of (of the first set of) Eq. (2.157) equal to ξ_T and note that, under the null hypothesis,

$$F_s' L_i^{*o'} a_{\cdot i} = 0, \tag{2.158}$$

we may conclude

$$\sqrt{T} \xi_T \sim N(0, \sigma_{ii} \Psi_{2(s,i)}). \tag{2.159}$$

The distribution in Eq. (2.159) is the basis for carrying out all specification tests.

Let us now consider the (specification) test of the hypothesis

$H_0 : F_{s_i}' L_i^{*o'} a_{\cdot i} = 0$,

as against the (local) alternative

$H_1 : (1/\sqrt{T}) F_{s_i}' L_i^{*o'} a_{\cdot i} \neq 0$,

where $s_i \leq G - G_i + m_i$, it being understood that $F_{s_i}^{*'} L_i^{*o'} a_{\cdot i} = 0$ is a **maintained hypothesis**. The test statistic is, evidently,

$$\phi_{2(s_i,i)} = T \hat{\lambda}_{\cdot i}' F_s \left(\frac{\tilde{\Psi}_{2(s_i,i)}}{\tilde{\sigma}_{ii}} \right) F_s' \hat{\lambda}_{\cdot i},$$

which may also be written in the more revealing form,

$$\phi_{2(s_i,i)} = \zeta_T' \tilde{D} \tilde{V}_{2i} L_i^{*o} \tilde{J}_{22(2i)}^{-1} F_{s_i} \tilde{\Psi}_{2(s_i,i)} F_{s_i}' \tilde{J}_{22(2i)}^{-1} L_i^{*o'} \tilde{V}_{2i} \tilde{D}' \zeta_T. \tag{2.160}$$

Under H_0, it is simple to show that

$$\phi_{2(s_i,i)} \xrightarrow{d} \chi_{s_i}^2;$$

under H_1, it may be shown that

$$\phi_{2(s_i,i)} \xrightarrow{d} \chi^2_{s_i}(\theta_{2(s_i,i)}),$$

where

$$\theta_{2(s_i,i)} = \frac{1}{2\sigma_{ii}}\mu F'_{s_i}(J^{-1}_{22(2i)} - I)F_{s_i}\mu, \quad \mu = F'_{s_i}L^{*o'}_i a_{\cdot i}.$$

Relation to Conformity Tests

In this section, we examine the relation of the misspecification test (test for overidentifying restrictions) developed above, and its natural counterpart in the form of a **conformity test**. [30]

Operating, again, in the single equation context, consider the ith structural equation

$$w_{\cdot i} = Qa_{\cdot i} + r_{\cdot i},$$

which would, normally, be estimated subject to the prior restrictions

$$L^{*o'}_i a_{\cdot i} = 0.$$

Let it be desired to test a subset of s such restrictions for validity. Let the subset in question be denoted by

$$L^{*(2)'}_i a_{\cdot i} = 0, \tag{2.161}$$

so that we may write $L^{*o}_i = (L^{*(1)}_i, \ L^{*(2)}_i)$. The selection matrix now becomes

$$L^{(1)}_i = (L_i, \ L^{*(2)}_i), \tag{2.162}$$

where L_i and L^*_i are the selection and exclusion matrices of previous sections, respectively. Enforcing the maintained hypothesis, i.e. imposing the restrictions

$$L^{*(1)'}_i a_{\cdot i} = 0, \tag{2.163}$$

we denote by $\tilde{\delta}_{\cdot i(u)}$ the 2SLS estimator resulting from the imposition of the restrictions in Eq. (2.163) **only**. Ironically, we term this the unrestricted estimator and denote the corresponding parameter vector by

$$\delta_{\cdot i(u)} = \begin{bmatrix} \delta_{\cdot i} \\ \delta^{(2)}_{\cdot i(u)} \end{bmatrix}, \tag{2.164}$$

---

[30] Such tests are often called, in the literature, "Wald tests". I personally prefer the term "conformity test", in that the test seeks to determine whether a set of **unrestricted** estimators conform to the requirements of a given set of restrictions. Whenever we test for significance of a single parameter, we carry out a conformity test. There is no reason why, when we operate in a slightly more complicated context, we should attach characterizations that are noninformative as to the nature of the test.

where $\delta_{\cdot i} = (\beta'_{\cdot i},\ \gamma'_{\cdot i})'$ has exactly the same meaning as in previous sections. Thus, $\delta^{(2)}_{\cdot i(u)}$ represents the "extra" parameters being estimated in order to test the validity of a subset of the overidentifying restrictions. By the previous discussion, we easily conclude that the marginal limiting distribution of the excess parameters is given by

$$\sqrt{T}\left(\tilde{\delta}^{(2)}_{\cdot i(u)} - \delta^{(2)}_{\cdot i(u)}\right) \sim N(0, \sigma_{ii}\Psi^*_{2(s,i)}), \tag{2.165}$$

where

$$\Psi^*_{2(s,i)} = \left[L^{*(2)'}_i KL^{*(2)}_i - L^{*(2)'}_i KL_i(L'_i KL_i)^{-1}L'_i KL^{*(2)}_i\right]^{-1}. \tag{2.166}$$

Thus, the conformity test for the validity of the particular subset of s overidentifying restrictions is given by

$$\phi^*_{2(s,i)} = T\,\tilde{\delta}^{(2)'}_{\cdot i(u)}\left(\frac{\tilde{\Psi}^{*-1}_{2(s,i)}}{\tilde{\sigma}_{ii}}\right)\tilde{\delta}^{(2)}_{\cdot i(u)}.$$

The question now arises as to the relation of this test to that discussed earlier. More precisely, in connection with Eq. (2.161) let F_s be such that

$$L^{*\circ}_i F_s = L^{*(2)}_i, \tag{2.167}$$

i.e. it is the matrix that selects the s prior restrictions subject to test. From Eqs. (2.157) and (2.159), we conclude that the LM test statistic (for the validity of the subset of restrictions $F'_s L^{*\circ'}_i a_{\cdot i} = 0$) is

$$\phi_{2(s,i)} = T\,\hat{\lambda}'_{\cdot i}F'_s\left(\frac{\tilde{\Psi}_{2(s,i)}}{\tilde{\sigma}_{ii}}\right)F'_s\hat{\lambda}_{\cdot i}, \tag{2.168}$$

which may also be rendered as

$$\phi_{2(s,i)} = \zeta'_T \tilde{D}\tilde{V}_{2i}L^{*\circ}_i \tilde{J}^{-1}_{22(2i)} F_s \tilde{\Psi}_{2(s,i)} F'_s \tilde{J}^{-1}_{22(2i)} L^{*\circ'}_i \tilde{V}_{2i}\tilde{D}'\zeta_T.$$

Under the null, it obeys $\phi_{2(s,i)} \xrightarrow{d} \chi^2_s$. Finally, we note that under the local alternative, $(1/\sqrt{T})F'_s L^{*\circ'}_i a_{\cdot i} \neq 0$, the noncentrality parameter is the same for both tests, and is given by

$$\theta_{2(s,i)} = \frac{1}{2}\,a'_{\cdot i}L^{*\circ}_i F_s\left(\frac{\Psi^{-1}_{2(s,i)}}{\sigma_{ii}}\right)F'_s L^{*\circ'}_i a_{\cdot i}, \tag{2.169}$$

owing to the fact that $\Psi^*_{2(s,i)} = \Psi_{2(s,i)}$. Thus, the two tests are, asymptotically, equivalent. We shall now show that the two tests are numerically equivalent as well, i.e. that $\phi_{2(s,i)} = \phi^*_{2(s,i)}$. To this effect, consider

$$\sqrt{T}\left(\tilde{\delta}^{(2)}_{\cdot i(u)} - \delta^{(2)}_{\cdot i(u)}\right) = \tilde{\Psi}^*_{2(s,i)}\tilde{N}'\tilde{\sigma}^{1/2}_{ii}\tilde{D}'\frac{\bar{R}^{-1}X'u_{\cdot i}}{\sqrt{T}\tilde{\sigma}_{ii}}. \tag{2.170}$$

where, in this context,

$$\tilde{N} = L_i^{*(2)} - L_i(L_i'\tilde{K}L_i)^{-1}L_i'\tilde{K}L_i^{*(2)}.$$

Let $\zeta_T = (\bar{R}^{-1}X'u_{\cdot i}/\sqrt{T}\tilde{\sigma}_{ii})$, and note that

$$\phi_{2(s,i)} = \zeta_T'\tilde{D}\tilde{V}_{2i}L_i^{*\circ}\tilde{J}_{22}^{-1}F_s\tilde{\Psi}_{2(s,i)}F_s'\tilde{J}_{22(2i)}^{-1}L_i^{*\circ'}\tilde{V}_{2i}\tilde{D}'\zeta_T$$

$$\phi_{2(s,i)}^* = \zeta_T'\tilde{D}\tilde{N}\tilde{\Psi}_{2(s,i)}^*\tilde{N}'\tilde{D}'\zeta_T. \tag{2.171}$$

Using the fact that $L_i^{*\circ}L_i^{*\circ'} = I - L_iL_i'$, we obtain

$$L_i^{*\circ'}\tilde{V}_{2i}F_s = L_i^{*(2)} + L_i^{*\circ}L_i^{*'\circ}\tilde{N}.$$

Moreover, since $L_i'\tilde{K}\tilde{N} = 0$, we conclude that

$$\tilde{V}_{2i}L_i^{*\circ}\tilde{J}_{22(2i)}F_s = \tilde{N}. \tag{2.172}$$

It is also quite evident that $\tilde{\Psi}_{2(s,i)} = \tilde{\Psi}_{2(s,i)}^*$, so that, **provided that the same estimator, $\tilde{\sigma}_{ii}$, is used in both test statistics,**

$$\phi_{2(s,i)} = \phi_{2(s,i)}^*.$$

We have therefore proved

Theorem 11. In the context of Theorem 2, the conformity and LM test statistics, respectively $\phi_{2(s,i)}^*$ and $\phi_{2(s,i)}$ in Eq. (2.171), for testing the validity of **any subset of** $s \leq G - G_i - m_i$ prior restrictions, i.e. for testing

$$H_0 : F_s'L_i^{*\circ'}a_{\cdot i} = 0,$$

as against the local alternatives

$$H_1 : (1/\sqrt{T})F_s'L_i^{*\circ'}a_{\cdot i} \neq 0,$$

are asymptotically equivalent. Moreover, they are also numerically equivalent **provided the same estimator is used for the covariance matrix of the structural errors.**

Proof: See the preceding discussion.

2.8.2 Systemwide 2SLS and 3SLS

"Identification" Tests

In the interest of brevity we shall discuss only the case of 3SLS. [31] From Eq. (1.110), of Chapter 1, we may write a fuller representation of the LM

---

[31] Since 2SLS is inherently a single equation procedure, this omission is of little consequence. In fact, the only novel feature in a systemwide context, is the

estimators as

$$\hat{\lambda} = (\tilde{J}_{22(3)}^{-1} - I)L^{*\circ'}a + \frac{1}{\sqrt{T}}\tilde{J}_{22(3)}^{-1}L^{*\circ'}\tilde{V}_3\tilde{D}'_*\zeta_T, \qquad (2.173)$$

where, now

$$\tilde{V}_3^{-1} = \tilde{K}_3 + L^{*\circ}L^{*\circ'}, \quad \tilde{K}_3 = \tilde{\Sigma}^{-1} \otimes \tilde{K}, \quad \tilde{K} = \frac{Q'Q}{T},$$

$$\tilde{D}_* = \tilde{\Sigma}^{-1/2} \otimes \tilde{D}, \quad \zeta_T = \frac{(\tilde{\Sigma}^{-1/2} \otimes \bar{R}^{-1}X')u}{\sqrt{T}}. \qquad (2.174)$$

Under the null, i.e. when $L^{*\circ'}a = 0$, it is simple to conclude, in view of the discussion in the initial sections of this chapter, that

$$\sqrt{T}\hat{\lambda} \xrightarrow{d} N(0, J_{22(3)}^{-1} - I). \qquad (2.175)$$

Hence, the identification test statistic obeys

$$\phi_3 = T\hat{\lambda}'(J_{22(3)}^{-1} - I)_g\hat{\lambda} \xrightarrow{d} \chi_d^2, \quad d = mG - k. \qquad (2.176)$$

It is easily determined that, under the local alternative $H_1 : (1/\sqrt{T})L^{*\circ'}a \neq 0$,

$$\phi_3 \xrightarrow{d} \chi_d^2(\theta_3), \qquad (2.177)$$

where the **noncentrality parameter** is given by

$$\theta_3 = \frac{1}{2}a'L^{*\circ}(J_{22(3)}^{-1} - I)(J_{22(3)}^{-1} - I)_g(J_{22(3)}^{-1} - I)L^{*\circ'}a$$

$$= \frac{1}{2}a'L^{*\circ}(J_{22(3)}^{-1} - I)L^{*\circ'}a. \qquad (2.178)$$

Misspecification Tests

Following exactly the argument leading to Eq. (2.157), let F_{s_i} be a permutation of $s_i \leq G - G_i - m_i$ columns of the matrix $I_{m_i^* + G_i^*}$, and let

$$F_s = \text{diag}(F_{s_1}, F_{s_2}, \ldots, F_{s_m}), \quad F_s^* = \text{diag}(F_{s_1}^*, F_{s_2}^*, \ldots, F_{s_m}^*), \quad (2.179)$$

such that $F_{s_i}^*$ is the complement of F_{s_i}, i.e. it is a permutation of the remaining columns of $I_{m_i^* + G_i^*}$. It is an immediate consequence of the definition that

$$(F_s, F_s^*)'(F_s, F_s^*) = I, \quad (F_s, F_s^*)(F_s, F_s^*)' = I. \qquad (2.180)$$

---

treatment of tests involving restrictions from several equations. In such a case, the covariance of the limiting distribution must involve not only (submatrices of) the covariance matrix for a given equation(s), but their cross covariance matrices as well. Beyond this, the situation is exactly the same as that studied in the previous section.

Taking $s_i = G - G_i - m_i$, i.e. the maximum possible, or, conversely, selecting the m^2 prior restrictions considered "most valid", [32] we consider the following representation of the LM estimator

$$\tilde{\Psi}_{3(s)} F_s' \hat{\lambda} = F_s' L^{*\circ\prime} a + \tilde{\Psi}_{3(s)} [F_s(\tilde{J}_{22(3)}^{-1} - I)F_{s*}] F_{s*}' L^{*\circ\prime} a$$

$$+ \frac{1}{\sqrt{T}} \tilde{\Psi}_{3(s)} F_s' \tilde{J}_{22}^{-1} L^{*\circ\prime} \tilde{V}_3 \tilde{D}_*' \zeta_T,$$

$$\tilde{\Psi}_{3(s)} = [F_s'(\tilde{J}_{22(3)}^{-1} - I)F_s]^{-1}. \qquad (2.181)$$

Under the null hypothesis, we conclude that

$$\sqrt{T}(\tilde{\Psi}_{3(s)} F_s' \hat{\lambda}) \xrightarrow{d} N(0, \Psi_{3(s)}), \qquad (2.182)$$

which is the basis for all misspecification tests. The **specification test statistic** is given by

$$\phi_{3(s)} = \zeta_T' \tilde{D}_* \tilde{V}_3 L^{*\circ} \tilde{J}_{22(3)}^{-1} F_s \tilde{\Psi}_{3(s)} F_s' \tilde{J}_{22}^{-1} L^{*\circ\prime} \tilde{V}_3 \tilde{D}_*' \zeta_T,$$

$$= T\hat{\lambda}' F_s \tilde{\Psi}_{3(s)} F_s' \hat{\lambda} \xrightarrow{d} \chi_d^2. \qquad (2.183)$$

The preceding is to be interpreted as follows: having chosen the m^2 maintained restrictions as those given by $F_s^{*\prime} L^{*\circ\prime} a = 0$, we consider all remaining restrictions as testable, and Eq. (2.183) represents the relevant test statistic. If only a subset of the overidentifying restrictions is open to test (smaller than the maximal possible), then define F_s so that it chooses precisely these restrictions, and define F_{s*} so that it chooses all remaining prior restrictions. When this is so, the degrees of freedom parameter in Eq. (2.176) is not d but rather, rank(F_s). In either case, under the local alternative,

$$\frac{1}{\sqrt{T}} F_s' L^{*\circ\prime} a \neq 0,$$

the test statistic obeys

$$\phi_{3(s)} \xrightarrow{d} \chi_{\text{rank}(F_s)}^2(\theta_{3(s)}), \qquad (2.184)$$

where the noncentrality parameter is given by

$$\theta_{3(s)} = \frac{1}{2} a' L^{*\circ} F_s \Psi_{3(s)}^{-1} F_s' L^{*\circ\prime} a = \frac{1}{2} a' L^{*\circ} F_s F_s'(J_{22(3)}^{-1} - I)F_s F_s' L^{*\circ\prime} a. \qquad (2.185)$$

---

[32] In view of the fact that $(J_{22(3)}^{-1} - I)$ is of rank $mG - k$, with $k = \sum_{i=1}^m (m_i + G_i)$, identification of the system implies that there exists at least one nonsingular submatrix of order $mG - k$. The number of such nonsingular submatrices determines the number of possible selections of the m^2 "most valid" prior restrictions. Note, further, that when s_i is selected to be the maximum possible, it is equal to the the degree of overidentification of the ith equation, i.e. $s_i = d_i$, and $s = d$ where, evidently, $s = \sum_{i=1}^m s_i$, and $d = \sum_{i=1}^m d_i$.

Relation to Conformity Tests

To create maximal correspondence to the notation employed in earlier sections, let $L^{*(2)'}a = F_s'L^{*\circ'}a$ be the set of prior restrictions we are opening up for test. **All other prior restrictions are assumed to hold,** i.e. they are treated as maintained hypotheses. It follows that, if we put $L^{*\circ} = (L^{*(1)}, L^{*(2)})$ then the **exclusion matrix** is given by $L^{*(1)}$, while the **inclusion matrix** is given by $(L, L^{*(2)})$. Writing the CSF of the system as

$$w = (I \otimes Q)(L, L^{*(2)}) \begin{pmatrix} \delta \\ \delta^{(2)}_{(u)} \end{pmatrix} + r, \quad \delta = L'a, \quad \delta^{(2)}_{(u)} = L^{*(2)'}a,$$

we obtain, by the partitioned inverse representation of 3SLS,

$$\hat{\delta}^{(2)}_{(u)} = \delta^{(2)}_{(u)} + \frac{1}{\sqrt{T}} \tilde{\Psi}^*_{3(s)} \tilde{N}' \tilde{D}'_* \zeta_T \tag{2.186}$$

where

$$\tilde{\Psi}^*_{3(s)} = \left[L^{*(2)'} \tilde{K}_* L^{*(2)} - L^{*(2)'} \tilde{K}_3 L (L' \tilde{K}_3 L)^{-1} L' \tilde{K}_3 L^{*(2)} \right]^{-1}$$

$$\tilde{N} = L^{*(2)} - L(L' \tilde{K}_3 L)^{-1} L' \tilde{K}_3 L^{*(2)}, \tag{2.187}$$

and $\mathcal{D}_*$, ζ_T are as defined above. In view of the fact that $L^{*(2)} = L^{*\circ} F_s$, we may write the representation in Eq. (2.186) as

$$\sqrt{T} F_s' L^{*\circ'} (\hat{a} - a)_{3SLS} = \tilde{\Psi}^*_{3(s)} \tilde{N}' \tilde{D}'_* \zeta_T. \tag{2.188}$$

It follows immediately, from the discussion of the early sections of this chapter, that

$$\sqrt{T} F_s' L^{*\circ'} (\hat{a} - a)_{3SLS} \overset{d}{\to} N(0, \Psi^*_{3(s)}). \tag{2.189}$$

We note that

$$\Psi^{*-1}_{3(s)} = F_s'[L^{*\circ'} K_3 L^{*\circ} - L^{*\circ'} K_3 L (L' K_3 L)^{-1} L' K_3 L^{*\circ}] F_s,$$

and from the preceding and the analog of Eq. (2.147) in the case of 3SLS, we conclude

$$\Psi^{*-1}_{3(s)} = F_s'(J_{22}^{-1} - I) F_s = \Psi^{-1}_{3(s)}. \tag{2.190}$$

Thus, in the context of the maintained hypothesis, $F_{s*}'L^{*\circ'}a = 0$, the 3SLS-based conformity test statistic of the null

$$H_0 : L^{*(2)'}a = F_s'L^{*\circ'}a = 0,$$

as against the local alternative

$$H_1 : (1/\sqrt{T}) F_s'L^{*\circ'}a \neq 0,$$

is given by

$$\phi_{3(s)}^* = \zeta_T' \tilde{\mathcal{D}}_* \tilde{N} \tilde{\Psi}_{3(s)}^* \tilde{\Psi}_{3(s)}^{*-1} \tilde{\Psi}_{3(s)}^* \tilde{N}' \tilde{\mathcal{D}}_*' \zeta_T. \tag{2.191}$$

Under the null, $F_s' L^{*\circ'} a = 0$, the statistic above obeys,

$$\phi_{3(s)}^* \xrightarrow{\text{d}} \chi^2_{\text{rank}(F_s)}, \tag{2.192}$$

while, under the local alternative, it obeys

$$\phi_{3(s)}^* \xrightarrow{\text{d}} \chi^2_{\text{rank}(F_s)}(\theta_{3(s)}^*), \quad \theta_{3(s)}^* = \frac{1}{2} a' L^{*\circ} F_s F_s' (J_{22}^{-1} - I) F_s F_s' L^{*\circ'} a. \tag{2.193}$$

A comparison with Eqs. (2.184) and (2.185) shows that the two tests based on 3SLS estimators, the LMT and the CT for misspecification, are asymptotically equivalent, in the sense that they have the same limiting distribution under the null, and under the local alternative they, also, have the **same noncentrality parameter**. The question now arises as to whether they are numerically identical. Inspection of the basic representation of the two tests, shows that the only potential difference between the two might arise in obtaining the estimator of the structural error covariance matrix, $\tilde{\Sigma}$. If we denote the "natural" [33] estimator in the case of the LMT by $\tilde{\Sigma}_{LMT}$, and in the case of the CT by $\tilde{\Sigma}_{CT}$, we obtain

$$\tilde{\Sigma}_{LMT} - \tilde{\Sigma}_{CT} \geq 0,$$

which, in finite samples, will create a systematic difference between the statistics [34] $\phi_{3(s)}$ and $\phi_{3(s)}^*$. On the other hand, if a **common prior estimator**, say $\tilde{\Sigma}$, is used in **both procedures**, the two statistics, for the LMT as well as the CT, are **numerically identical.** This is easily demonstrated, as in the single equation 2SLS, by showing that, with a common prior estimator $\tilde{\Sigma}$,

$$\tilde{N} = \tilde{V}_{11} L^{*\circ} \tilde{J}_{22}^{-1} F_s.$$

The preceding discussion has established

Theorem 12. In the context of Theorem 2, the conformity and LM test statistics, of Eqs. (2.191) and (2.183), respectively, for testing the validity of any subset of s prior restrictions, such that $s = \sum_{i=1}^m s_i$ and $s_i \leq G - G_i - m_i$, i.e. for testing

$$H_0 : F_s' L^{*\circ'} a = L^{*(2)'} a = 0,$$

---

[33] Perhaps one should term this the "estimator that is obtained without much thought".

[34] In the literature, it is shown that the LMT statistic is not less than the CT statistic. See, for example, Engel (1983).

as against the local alternative

$$H_1 : (1/\sqrt{T})F_s'L^{*\circ'}a \neq 0,$$

are asymptotically equivalent. Moreover, they are also **numerically equivalent** provided that, in both test statistics, the **same estimator** is used for the covariance matrix of the structural errors.

Proof: See the preceding discussion.

2.8.3 Relation to Hausman's Test

In this section, we obtain a representation of the test statistic from Hausman (1978), and compare its properties with those of the test obtained in the previous section(s). In the interest of brevity, we concentrate on the comparison with 3SLS-based tests. Although Hausman has given several other variants of his test, we shall examine only the original proposal. It may be noted, however, that all such tests are motivated by the desire to test a hypothesis structure, the null of which holds, if all assumptions made are in fact true, and fails to hold when any one of a number of assumptions is, in fact, not true. For maximal comparability with the exposition of previous sections, we examine the hypothesis

$$H_0 : L^{*\circ'}a = 0,$$

as against the local alternative

$$H_1 : (1/\sqrt{T})L^{*\circ'}a \neq 0,$$

i.e. we test for the validity of all prior restrictions in the system, or, in the context of our discussion, we carry an "identification" test for the system as a whole. The statistic of the Hausman test is given by

$$\phi_{3H} = T\left(\hat{a}_{2SLS} - \hat{a}_{3SLS}\right)' L\left(C_{2SLS} - C_{3SLS}\right)_g L'\left(\hat{a}_{2SLS} - \hat{a}_{3SLS}\right). \tag{2.194}$$

We shall compare the noncentrality and degrees of freedom parameters of this statistic with those of the statistic ϕ_3, in Eq. (2.176). Evidently, the same procedure is applicable to a single equation but, in such a case, the derivation of the test statistic and the relevant noncentrality parameter parameter is much too tedious to be pursued here. From Eqs. (2.136) and (2.137) we find, after some manipulation,

$$\hat{a}_{2SLS} = \tilde{E}_2\tilde{K}_2LL'a + \tilde{E}_2\tilde{K}_2L^{*\circ}L^{*\circ'}a + \tilde{E}LL'\tilde{D}'\frac{(I \otimes \bar{R}^{-1}X')u}{T},$$

$$\hat{a}_{3SLS} = \tilde{E}_3\tilde{K}_3LL'a + \tilde{E}_3\tilde{K}_3L^{*\circ}L^{*\circ'}a + \tilde{E}_3LL'\tilde{D}_*'\frac{1}{\sqrt{T}}\zeta_T, \tag{2.195}$$

where $\tilde{\mathcal{K}}_i, \tilde{V}_i, E_i, i = 2, 3,$ etc., are the entities whose probability limits were defined in Eqs. (2.139) and (2.140). Noting that, in either 2SLS or (*mutatis mutandis*) 3SLS, $L'\tilde{E}\tilde{\mathcal{K}}L = I$, and letting

$$\tilde{H}_{23} = \left[\left(\tilde{J}_{12(3)} \tilde{J}_{22(3)}^{-1} \right) - \left(\tilde{J}_{12(2)} \tilde{J}_{22(2)}^{-1} \right) \right], \qquad (2.196)$$

we may conclude that Hausman's test statistic in Eq. (2.194) has, under the appropriate local alternative, the noncentrality parameter

$$\theta_{3H} = \frac{1}{2} a' L^{*\circ} \bar{H}'_{23} \left(C_{2SLS} - C_{3SLS} \right)_g \bar{H}_{23} L^{*\circ'} a, \qquad (2.197)$$

where $\bar{H}_{23}$ is the probability limit of $\tilde{H}_{23}$. The degrees of freedom parameter is given by the rank of the generalized inverse, above. This is, also, the rank of the matrix $C_{2SLS} - C_{3SLS}$. Since

$$C_{2SLS} - C_{3SLS} = C_{2SLS} \left(C_{3SLS}^{-1} - C_{2SLS}^{-1} \right) C_{3SLS}, \qquad (2.198)$$

the rank in question is simply the rank of $C_{3SLS}^{-1} - C_{2SLS}^{-1}$. Putting $\Phi = \Sigma \otimes I_G$, we note, from Theorem 2, that

$$C_{2SLS} = (S^{*'} S^*)^{-1} S^{*'} \Phi S^* (S^{*'} S^*)^{-1}, \quad C_{3SLS} = (S^{*'} \Phi^{-1} S^*)^{-1}. \quad (2.199)$$

Consider, now

$$S^{*'} \Phi^{-1} = S^{*'} S^* (S^{*'} \Phi S^*)^{-1} S^{*'} + C_*, \qquad (2.200)$$

$$S^{*'} = S^{*'} S^* (S^{*'} \Phi S^*)^{-1} S^{*'} \Phi + C_* \Phi, \qquad (2.201)$$

$$C_* \Phi S^* = 0, \qquad (2.202)$$

and postmultiply Eq. (2.200) by the transpose of Eq. (2.201), to obtain

$$C_{3SLS}^{-1} - C_{2SLS}^{-1} = C_* \Phi C_*'. \qquad (2.203)$$

It is apparent that the rank we wish to determine is the rank of C_*. We shall now show that

$$\text{rank}(C_*) \leq \min \left[\text{rank}(S^*), \text{rank} \left(\Phi^{-1} - S^* (S^{*'} \Phi S^*)^{-1} S^{*'} \right) \right]. \quad (2.204)$$

By Proposition 63 in Dhrymes (1984), there exists a nonsingular matrix, say P, such that

$$\Phi^{-1} = PP', \quad S^* (S^{*'} \Phi S^*)^{-1} S^{*'} = P\Lambda P',$$

where Λ is a diagonal matrix containing the characteristic roots of

$$S^* (S^{*'} \Phi S^*)^{-1} S^{*'}$$

in the metric of Φ^{-1}. These, however, are also the characteristic roots of

$$\left| \lambda I - S^* (S^{*'} \Phi S^*)^{-1} S^{*'} \Phi \right| = 0.$$

In addition, the nonzero roots of the equation above are exactly those of

$$\left| \lambda I - (S^{*'} \Phi S^*)^{-1} S^{*'} \Phi S^* \right| = 0.$$

The latter, however, has exactly $k = \sum_{i=1}^{m} (m_i + G_i)$, unit roots. Hence,

$$\Phi^{-1} - S^* (S^{*'} \Phi S^*)^{-1} S^{*'} = P \begin{bmatrix} I_d & 0 \\ 0 & 0 \end{bmatrix} P', \quad d = mG - k, \qquad (2.205)$$

and we conclude that

$$\text{rank}(C_{2SLS} - C_{3SLS}) \leq \min(k, \, d), \quad \phi_{3H} \sim \chi_s^2, \quad s \leq \min(k, d). \quad (2.206)$$

The "identification" test suggested by the LM derivation of 2SLS and 3SLS estimators has, for 3SLS-based tests, the characteristics

$$\phi_3 = T \tilde{\lambda}' \left(\tilde{J}_{22(3)}^{-1} - I \right)_g \tilde{\lambda},$$

$$\phi_3 \xrightarrow{\text{d}} \chi_d^2, \quad \text{with noncentrality parameter}$$

$$\theta_3 = \frac{1}{2} a' L^{*\circ} (J_{22(3)}^{-1} - I) L^{*\circ'} a. \qquad (2.207)$$

The results of the preceding discussion may be summarized in

Theorem 13. In the context of Theorem 2, the following statements are true.

   i. The test statistic for Hausman's test has the characteristics

$$\phi_{3H} = T \left(\hat{a}_{2SLS} - \hat{a}_{3SLS} \right)' L \left(C_{2SLS} - C_{3SLS} \right)_g L' \left(\hat{a}_{2SLS} - \hat{a}_{3SLS} \right),$$

$$\phi_{3H} \xrightarrow{\text{d}} \chi_s^2, \quad s \leq \min(k, \, d), \quad \text{with noncentrality parameter}$$

$$\theta_{3H} = \frac{1}{2} a' L^{*\circ} \bar{H}_{23}' \left(C_{2SLS} - C_{3SLS} \right)_g \bar{H}_{23} L^{*\circ'} a.$$

   ii. The "identification" test statistic obtained in this chapter [35] has the characteristics

$$\phi_3 = T \tilde{\lambda}' \left(\tilde{J}_{22(3)}^{-1} - I \right)_g \tilde{\lambda},$$

$$\phi_3 \xrightarrow{\text{d}} \chi_d^2, \quad \text{with noncentrality parameter}$$

$$\theta_3 = \frac{1}{2} a' L^{*\circ} (J_{22(3)}^{-1} - I) L^{*\circ'} a.$$

---

[35] The statistic given in this discussion is based on 3SLS estimators, but the same result holds, *mutatis mutandis*, for systemwide, as well as single equation 2SLS estimators.

Proof: See the preceding discussion.

Questions and Problems

1. Verify Eq. (2.10) and, in particular, verify that

$$\text{vec}(X'U) = \sum_{t=1}^{T}(I \otimes x'_{t.})u'_{t.} = \sum_{t=1}^{T}(u'_{t.} \otimes x'_{t.}).$$

2. Obtain the inverse of the matrix $A(L) = (a_{ij}(L))$, where $a_{ij}(L)$ is a polynomial of degree, at most m, in the lag operator L. If

$$[A(L)]^{-1} = B(L) = (b_{ij}(L)),$$

what is the nature of the operators $b_{ij}(L)$?

3. Show that restricted 2SLS is efficient relative to the unrestricted 2SLS estimator, when the restrictions do not apply across equations. (Hint: Consider the difference $C_{2i} - C_{2Ri}$, where the matrices are, respectively, the covariance matrices of the limiting distribution of the unrestricted and restricted 2SLS estimators of the parameters of the ith structural equation.)

4. In Eq. (2.58) verify that $B_r^{(j)} = A_1^{(j-r)}$.

5. Verify Eqs. (2.65) and (2.66).

6. Verify the expression in footnote 15.

7. Verify Eq. (2.74).

8. Verify the Eqs. (2.81) through (2.82).

9. Verify Eqs. (2.97), (2.98) and (2.99).

10. Verify Eqs. (2.111) and (2.116).

11. In Eqs. (2.98), and (2.99)

    i. verify that $\bar{\Pi}'_{0i}L_{0i}M_{xx}L_{2i} = \Pi'_i M_{xx}L_{2i}$;

    ii. verify that $F \geq 0$.

    Hint: (a) Notice that $\left(I - M_{xx}L_{0i}(L'_{0i}M_{xx}L_{0i})^{-1}L'_{0i}\right)M_{xx}L_{2i} = 0$;
(b) Notice that $\Pi_i = L_{0i}\Pi_{0i} + L^*_{3i}\Pi^*_{3i}$.

12. Give a complete proof that the matrix

$$\begin{bmatrix} I_k & 0 \\ 0 & 0 \end{bmatrix} - F \begin{bmatrix} I_k & 0 \\ 0 & 0 \end{bmatrix} F',$$

of Eq. (2.116), is indefinite, where F is an orthogonal matrix.

13. In Eqs. (2.133), (2.135), and (2.136), justify the presence of the terms LL', or $L_i L_i'$, as the case may be, between $\tilde{E}$ and the term following.
   Hint: $\tilde{E} L^{*\circ} = 0$.

14. In Eq. (2.170), verify that for $\delta^{(2)}_{\cdot i(u)} = 0$,

$$\sqrt{T} \tilde{\delta}^{(2)}_{\cdot i(u)} = \tilde{\Psi}^*_{2(s,i)} \tilde{N}' \tilde{\sigma}_{11}^{1/2} \tilde{D}' \frac{\bar{R}^{-1} X' u_{\cdot i}}{\sqrt{T}}.$$

   Hint: Consider the system

$$\begin{bmatrix} L_i' \tilde{K} L_i & L_i' \tilde{K} L_i^{*(2)} \\ L_i^{*(2)'} \tilde{K} L_i & L_i^{*(2)'} \tilde{K} L_i^{*(2)} \end{bmatrix}^{-1} \frac{1}{T} \begin{pmatrix} L_i' Q' w_{\cdot i} \\ L_i^{*(2)'} Q' w_{\cdot i} \end{pmatrix} = \begin{pmatrix} \hat{\delta}_{\cdot i} \\ \hat{\delta}_{\cdot i(u)} \end{pmatrix}.$$

15. In Eq. (2.172) show, step by step, that

$$\tilde{N} = \tilde{V}_{2i} L_i^{*\circ} \tilde{J}_{22(2i)}^{-1} F_s.$$

   Hint: $J_{22}^{-1} = J^{22} - J^{21}(J^{11})^{-1} J^{12}$.

16. In Eqs. (2.197) and (2.207), verify the derivation of the noncentrality parameter.

17. In connection with the proof of Lemma A2, in the appendix, show that

$$\frac{I}{(I - \lambda_1 L)(I - \lambda_2 L)} = \sum_{k=0}^{\infty} \gamma_k L^k, \quad \lambda_1 > \lambda_2 \geq 0, \quad |\gamma_k| \leq c_0 \lambda_1^k,$$

for a suitable constant c_0.

   Hint: $(\sum_{j=0}^{\infty} \lambda_1^j L^j)(\sum_{s=0}^{\infty} \lambda_2^s L^s) = \sum_{k=0}^{\infty} \gamma_k L^k$, with $\gamma_k = \sum_{s=0}^{k} \lambda_2^s \lambda_1^{k-s}$.

Appendix to Chapter 2

Convergence of Second Moment Matrices

Many arguments in the preceding chapter require the use of certain implications of the assertion that second moment matrices converge. Here we present the relevant results so as not to disrupt the orderly development of the discussion of econometric issues in the text.

Consider the $T \times G$ matrix X, which may be either **nonstochastic or stochastic**; we need to show that if it obeys

$$\frac{X'X}{T} \to M_{xx} > 0 \quad \text{then} \quad \max_{t \leq T} \frac{x_t . x_t'}{T} \to 0,$$

in the same mode of convergence, whether it is in the form of an ordinary limit (OL), or convergence in probability (P), or convergence a.c. (i.e. with probability one).

Lemma A1. Consider the sequence $\{x_t. : t \geq 1\}$, which may be either

   i. one of nonstochastic vectors lying in a space $\mathcal{X} \subseteq R^n$;

  ii. or one of random vectors defined on the probability space $(\Omega, \mathcal{A}, \mathrm{P})$.

If

$$\frac{X'X}{T} \xrightarrow{\text{OL, P, or a.c.}} M_{xx},$$

i.e. either as an ordinary limit, or as convergence in probability, or as convergence a.c., where M_{xx} is a well defined nonstochastic, positive (semi) definite matrix, the following statements are true:

   i. $\text{tr}(X'X/T) \overset{\text{OL, P, or a.c.}}{\longrightarrow} \text{tr} M_{xx}$;

   ii. $\text{tr}(X'X) \overset{\text{OL, P, or a.c.}}{\longrightarrow} +\infty$;

   iii. $(\max_{t \leq T} x_t . x'_t . / T) \overset{\text{OL, P, or a.c.}}{\longrightarrow} 0$.

Proof: The proof of i is obvious; in fact, since the trace can serve as a norm for positive (semi) definite matrices, i implies convergence in norm; but if the norm converges, all elements converge, so that i implies the premise, and that is true for all three modes of convergence.

The proof of ii is equally obvious, since $\text{tr}(X'X) = T \text{tr}(X'X/T)$.

To prove iii note that, putting $D_T = \sum_{t=1}^{T} x_t . x'_t .$, we have

$$\frac{D_T}{T} - \frac{D_{T-1}}{T-1} \frac{T-1}{T} = \frac{x_T . x'_T .}{T} \overset{\text{OL P or a.c.}}{\longrightarrow} 0. \qquad (2.A.1)$$

We first examine convergence as an ordinary limit; thus, suppose the condition above holds but

$$\lim_{T \to \infty} \frac{\max_{t \leq T} x_t . x'_t .}{T} = c > 0;$$

then there exists a (sub)sequence $\{T_i : i \geq 1\}$, such that

$$\frac{\max_{t \leq T_i} x_t . x'_t .}{T_i} \geq c - \frac{1}{q} > 0$$

for an arbitrary integer q ; this implies the existence of a further subsequence

$$\frac{x_{t_i} . x'_{t_i} .}{t_i} \geq c - \frac{1}{q} > 0$$

and, consequently (for that subsequence), that

$$\lim_{i \to \infty} \frac{x_{t_i} . x'_{t_i} .}{t_i} = c > 0,$$

which is a contradiction. Thus,

$$\lim_{T \to \infty} \frac{\max_{t \leq T} x_t . x'_t .}{T} = 0,$$

which proves iii for nonstochastic sequences. For stochastic sequences, define the sets, for arbitrary integer r,

$$A_{t,r} = \left\{ \omega : x_t.x_t'. > \frac{t}{r} \right\} = \left\{ \omega : \frac{x_t.x_t'.}{T} > \frac{t}{Tr}, \ t \leq T \right\},$$

$$A_{tT} = \left\{ \omega : \frac{x_t.x_t'.}{T} > \frac{1}{r}, \ t \leq T \right\}.$$

and note that $A_{tT} \subset A_{t,r}$. From Eq. (2.A.1), it follows that if the convergence therein is convergence in probability,

$$\lim_{T \to \infty} \mathcal{P}(A_{t,r}) = 0;$$

if the convergence therein is convergence a.c., and $A_r^* = \limsup_{t \to \infty} A_{t,r}$,

$$\mathcal{P}(A_r^*) = 0.$$

Next, consider the sets

$$B_{T,r} = \left\{ \omega : \frac{\max_{t \leq T} x_t.x_t'.}{T} > \frac{1}{r} \right\};$$

we shall complete the proof of iii by showing that if in Eq. (2.A.1) we have convergence in probability, or convergence a.c. then for arbitrary r

$$\lim_{T \to \infty} \mathcal{P}(B_{T,r}) = 0, \quad \mathcal{P}(B_r^*) = 0, \quad \text{respectively,}$$

where $B_r^* = \limsup_{T \to \infty} B_{T,r}$. Suppose in Eq. (2.A.1) we have convergence in probability, and

$$\lim_{T \to \infty} \mathcal{P}(B_{T,r}) = \phi > 0;$$

then there exists a subsequence $\{T_i : i \geq 1\}$, for which

$$\mathcal{P}(B_{T_i,r}) \geq \phi - \frac{1}{q} > 0,$$

for arbitrary integer, q. Moreover, there exists a corresponding subsequence $\{A_{t_i,r} : i \geq 1\}$, defined by the operation

$$\frac{x_{t_i}.x_{t_i}'.}{T_i} = \max_{t \leq T_i} \frac{x_t.x_t'.}{T_i},$$

such that $A_{t_i,r} \supseteq B_{T_i,r}$, and for which

$$\lim_{i \to \infty} \mathcal{P}(A_{t_i,r}) \geq \lim_{i \to \infty} \mathcal{P}(B_{T_i,r}) \geq \phi > 0.$$

This is a contradiction; consequently, $\lim_{T\to\infty} \mathcal{P}(B_{T,r}) = 0$, as required.

Next, suppose we have convergence a.c., i.e. $\mathcal{P}(A_r^*) = 0$, and $\mathcal{P}(B_r^*) = \phi > 0$. This means that the "event" $\omega \in B_{T,r}$, i.o., occurs with positive probability. Consequently, there exists a subsequence, say $\{T_i : i \geq 1\}$, for which $\mathcal{P}(B_{T_i,r}) \geq \phi - (1/q) > 0$, q being an arbitrary integer and, moreover, $\lim_{i\to\infty} B_{T_i,r} = B_r^*$. Let

$$\frac{\max_{t\leq T_i} x_{t\cdot}.x_{t\cdot}'}{T_i} = \frac{x_{t_i\cdot}.x_{t_i\cdot}'}{T_i}.$$

Since $B_{T_i,r} \subseteq A_{t_i,r}$, implies $\mathcal{P}(A_{t_i,r}) \geq \mathcal{P}(B_{T_i,r}) \geq \phi - (1/q) > 0$, it follows that

$$\lim_{i\to\infty} \mathcal{P}(A_{t_i,r}) \geq \phi > 0,$$

which is a contradiction; consequently, $\mathcal{P}(B_r^*) = 0$, as required.

q.e.d.

Corollary A1. Under the conditions of Lemma A1

$$\frac{\max_{t\leq T} x_{t\cdot}'.x_{t\cdot}}{T} \xrightarrow{\text{OL P or a.c.}} 0,$$

according as $(X'X/T) \xrightarrow{\text{OL P or a.c.}} M_{xx}$, respectively.

Proof: We note that $\|x_{t\cdot}'.x_{t\cdot}\| = x_{t\cdot}.x_{t\cdot}'$. Thus the corollary follows from iii of the lemma.

q.e.d.

Convergence for Dependent Sequences

Preliminaries and Miscellaneous

We begin by discussing the question of how to deal with convergence issues involving random vectors and matrices, because most textbook discussions of such issues focus on (scalar) random variables. When dealing with relatively simple problems it is often rather an easy matter to obtain the covariance matrix of an estimator and show that it vanishes as $T \longrightarrow \infty$. This approach, in effect, is quite attractive when dealing with the standard general linear model. As problems become more complex, however, these procedures do not work as well, and it behooves us to have a standard way for approaching such problems. This issue is dealt with, for example, in Ch. 4 of Dhrymes (1989) where there is some discussion of the theory of random elements. The latter are simply transformations from the sample space, Ω, to a general metric space, say (Ψ, ρ), where ρ is the metric in question. Thus, a random element, say X, is simply the transformation

$$X : \Omega \longrightarrow \Psi,$$

while a random variable, say ξ, is the transformation

$$\xi : \Omega \longrightarrow R,$$

where R is the set of real numbers. In most of econometrics we deal with vectors and matrices of real numbers, although we sometimes have occasion to use sample paths, or realizations of certain stochastic processes, which are random functions of "time".

In the context of the former it is difficult to deal with issues of convergence on an element by element basis, even though this has the advantage of allowing us to continue operating in the realm of (scalar) random variables. Instead, it would be desirable to find a way of dealing with them as a single entity. This is afforded us by the theory of random elements. Note that an m-element random vector, say X, is a transformation,

$$X : \Omega \longrightarrow R^m$$

where $(R^m, \| \cdot \|)$ is the m-dimensional normed Euclidean space. Given the usual norm, i.e. if $x \in R^m$, then $\| x \| = (x_1^2 + x_2^2 + \cdots + x_m^2)^{\frac{1}{2}}$, we can define a metric by $\rho(x, y) = \| x - y \|$. The same approach may be applied to random matrices, since if A is a matrix of dimension $m \times n$ we may think of it as an element in the space R^{mn} by simply dealing with $a = \text{vec}(A)$. Thus, we may define a norm for a matrix, in view of the preceding, by the operation [36]

$$\| A \|^2 = \text{vec}(A)' \text{vec}(A) = \text{tr}(A'A) = \text{tr}(AA') = \sum_{i,j} a_{ij}^2.$$

This leads us immediately to the conclusion that if we wish to show that a sequence of random elements, say $X = \{X_n : n \geq 0\}$, converges to X_0,

---

[36] There are, of course, other possibilities. For example, if A is $m \times n$ its norm may be defined as the **square root of the largest characteristic root** of $A'A$ or AA'. This rests on the fact that if A_i, $i = 1, 2$, are (symmetric) **positive (semi) definite** matrices, it may be shown that

$$\lambda_{\max}(A_1 + A_2) \leq \lambda_{\max}(A_1) + \lambda_{\max}(A_2).$$

Since the norm is a function, say $\| \cdot \|$, defined on the elements of a space, say x, such that (a) $\|x\| \geq 0$, and $\|x\| = 0$ if and only if $x = 0$; (b) for any scalar α, $\|\alpha x\| = |\alpha| \|x\|$; (c) $\|x + y\| \leq \|x\| + \|y\|$, the relation above means that the **largest characteristic root of a positive semidefinite (symmetric)** matrix can serve as a norm for that class of matrices. In terms of the earlier definition, if A is positive semidefinite, its roots are nonnegative and the charactersitic roots of $A'A$ are the squares of the characteristic roots of A. We shall have occasion to use this norm at a later point in our discussion.

in probability, a.c., or in mean of order p, i.e. L^p convergence, it will be sufficient to show, respectively,

$$\| X_n - X_0 \| \overset{\text{P}}{\to} 0, \quad \| X_n - X_0 \| \overset{\text{a.c.}}{\to} 0, \quad E\left(\| X_n - X_0 \|^p\right) \longrightarrow 0.$$

Note that since $\| X \|$ is, for every random element, X, a random variable, the usual implications hold, i.e. convergence a.c., and at least L^2 convergence, imply convergence in probability.

Finally, we note that the mean of a random element is said to exist whenever $E(\| X \|) < \infty$, and the variance of a random element is defined by

$$\text{Var}(X) = E \| X - E(X) \|^2, \quad \text{provided} \;\; X - E(X)$$

is a random element. This need not be so in arbitrary metric spaces, but this is always so in the context of Euclidean m-space, where a random element is a random vector, and its expectation is an m-dimensional vector of constants.

Returning now to the discussion at hand we need to show that for every $i = 1, 2, \ldots, k$, $(\bar{X}'V^*_{-i}/T) \overset{\text{P}}{\to} 0$. Since the expectation of this entity is zero, and we are required to show that

$$\left\| \frac{\bar{X}'V^*_{-i}}{T} \right\| \overset{\text{P}}{\to} 0,$$

it will be sufficient to show that

$$E\left(\left\| \frac{\bar{X}'V^*_{-i}}{T} \right\|^2 \right) \longrightarrow 0.$$

This is so, since if we put

$$\alpha_T = \frac{\bar{X}'V_*}{T}, \quad \text{we have that} \;\; \sigma_T^2 = \text{Var}(\alpha_T) = E\left\| \frac{\bar{X}'V_*}{T} \right\|^2.$$

Hence, if $\sigma_T^2 \longrightarrow 0$ we conclude that, for any integer, r, however large,

$$\text{Probability}\left(\| \alpha_T \| > \frac{1}{r} \right) \longrightarrow 0,$$

which shows convergence in probability. Actually, this is a rather circuitous route, since in fact we show convergence in quadratic mean, and then use the fact that the latter implies convergence in probability. A direct approach would involve utilizing Proposition 15 in Ch. 5 of Dhrymes (1989), but the verification of the three conditions therein is actually more difficult than the approach followed here.

Convergence of Second Moments of Final Form Errors

We begin with

Lemma A2. Given assumptions (A.1) through (A.5), of Chapter 1, and in the context of the discussion of the final form of the dynamic model, for each $i = 0, 1, 2, \ldots, k$

$$\frac{\bar{X}' V_{-i}^*}{T} \xrightarrow{P} 0.$$

Proof: For notational ease we deal with the case $i = 0$; other cases are absolutely identical. Using the results in Ch. 4, of Dhrymes (1984), we can vectorize the entity above to

$$\psi_T = \frac{1}{T} \mathrm{vec}(\bar{X}' V^*) = \frac{1}{T} \sum_{t=1}^{T} (I \otimes \bar{x}'_{t.}) v_{t.}^* = \frac{1}{T} \sum_{t=1}^{T} (v_{t.}^{*'} \otimes \bar{x}'_{t.}).$$

Since $E(\psi_T) = 0$, by the preceding discussion it will be sufficient to show that

$$\lim_{T \to \infty} E \parallel \psi_T \parallel^2 = 0.$$

To further simplify the notation, put $z_{.t} = (v_{t.}^{*'} \otimes \bar{x}'_{t.})$, and note that

$$
\begin{aligned}
J_T &= E \parallel \psi_T \parallel^2 = \frac{1}{T^2} \sum_{t=1}^{T} \sum_{t'=1}^{T} E(z'_{.t} z_{.t'}) \\
&= \frac{1}{T^2} \sum_{t=1}^{T} \sum_{t'=1}^{T} E(v_{t.}^* v_{t.'}^{*'}) (\bar{x}_{t.} \bar{x}'_{t.'}) = \sum_{t=1}^{T} \sum_{t'=1}^{T} \mathrm{tr}(H(t-t'))(\bar{x}_{t.} \bar{x}'_{t.'}) \\
&= \frac{1}{T} \left[\mathrm{tr} H(0) \frac{\mathrm{tr} \bar{X}' \bar{X}}{T} + 2 \sum_{\tau=1}^{T-1} H(\tau) \left(\frac{1}{T} \sum_{t=1}^{T-\tau} \bar{x}_{t.} \bar{x}'_{t+\tau.} \right) \right] \\
&\leq \frac{1}{T} \left[K \frac{\mathrm{tr}(\bar{X}' \bar{X})}{T} \left(\sum_{\tau=0}^{T-1} \lambda_{\max}^{\tau} \right) \right] \longrightarrow 0, \quad \text{with } T.
\end{aligned}
$$

The expression after the first inequality follows from (a) replacing

$$\left\| \frac{1}{T} \sum_{t=1}^{T-\tau} \bar{x}_{t.} \bar{x}'_{t+\tau.} \right\| \qquad \text{by} \qquad \frac{\mathrm{tr}(\bar{X}' \bar{X})}{T},$$

which is perfectly accurate, neglecting large end point effects, and (b) using the bound $| \mathrm{tr} H(\tau) | \leq K_1 \lambda_{\max}^{\tau}$, which is justified as follows: first, we note that $H(\tau) = H(-\tau)'$ and, moreover that $H(\tau) = \sum_{j=0}^{\infty} G_{\tau+j} \Sigma G'_j$, where G_j is the coefficient of L^j, in the expansion of $\Pi(L)^{-1}$. Letting λ_i, $i = 1, 2, 3, \ldots, n$, be the roots of Eq. (2.31), in Chapter 2, we have

$$\lambda_{\max} = \max_{i \leq n} | \lambda_i | < 1,$$

since the system is assumed to be stable. Consequently,

$$\sum_{\tau=0}^{\infty} \lambda_{\max}^{\tau} = \frac{1}{1 - \lambda_{\max}} < \infty.$$

q.e.d.

Remark A1. We note, with interest, that Proposition 32 Ch. 5, in Dhrymes (1989) shows that for (zero mean) covariance stationary sequences, $\{\xi_j : j \geq 1\}$, the entity $(\sum_{j=1}^{n} \xi_j / n)$, converges in mean square to zero if and only if

$$\lim_{n \to \infty} \frac{1}{n} \sum_{j=0}^{n} R(j) = 0, \quad \text{where} \quad R(j) = E(\xi_{t+j} \xi_t).$$

Moreover, in the proof of Lemma A2, convergence (to zero) of the entity $(\sum_{j=0}^{T-1} | \operatorname{tr} H(j) | / T)$ has played a crucial role; finally note that in the vector context $H(j)$ is, roughly, the analog of $R(j)$!

Just to anticipate our discussion, we also note from Proposition 34, Ch. 5 of the same reference above, that for **normal** stationary sequences the entity

$$\frac{1}{n} \sum_{j=1}^{n} \xi_j \xi_{j+\tau} \xrightarrow{\mathrm{L}^2} R(\tau),$$

if and only if

$$\lim_{n \to \infty} \frac{1}{n} \sum_{j=0}^{n-1} (R(j))^2 = 0.$$

Finally, we should point out that, roughly speaking, in the case of random vectors $\| H(j) \|^2$ corresponds to $(R(j))^2$!

We turn our attention now to the requirement that we show that

$$\frac{V_*' V_*}{T} \xrightarrow{\mathrm{P}} H.$$

Since the typical block element of the matrix above is given by

$$\frac{V_{-i+s}^{*'} V_{-i}^{*}}{T}$$

it will suffice to show that, for $0 \leq s \leq k$,

$$\frac{V_{-i+s}^{*'} V_{-i}^{*}}{T} \xrightarrow{\mathrm{P}} H(s).$$

We shall follow exactly the approach of Lemma A2, and show, in fact, convergence in quadratic mean which, as noted earlier, implies convergence in probability. We formalize our discussion in

Lemma A3. Given assumptions (A.1) through (A.5), and the preceding discussion, and explicitly assuming that the structural errors are jointly normal [37] then

$$\frac{1}{T} V_*' V_* \xrightarrow{P} H.$$

Proof: Since the typical block element is given by $(V_{-i+s}^{*'} V_{-i}^*/T)$, it will suffice to show that it converges in quadratic mean to $H(s) = E(V_{-i+s}^{*'} V_{-i}^*/T)$. Let $h_s = \text{vec}(H(s))$, $z_{.t} = (v_{t-i.}^{*'} \otimes v_{t-i+s.}^*) - h_s$, and note that we are required to show

$$J_T \longrightarrow 0, \quad \text{where} \quad J_T = E \left\| \frac{1}{T} \sum_{t=1}^{T} z_{.t} \right\|^2.$$

We have

$$T^2 J_T = \sum_{t=1}^{T} \sum_{t'=1}^{T} E(z_{.t}' z_{.t'})$$

$$= \sum_{t=1}^{T} \sum_{t'=1}^{T} \left[E\left((v_{t-i.}^* . v_{t'-i.}^{*'})(v_{t-i+s.}^* . v_{t'-i+s.}^{*'}) \right) - E\left((v_{t-i.}^* \otimes v_{t-i+s.}^*) h_s \right) \right]$$

$$- \sum_{t=1}^{T} \sum_{t'=1}^{T} \left[E\left(h_s'(v_{t'-i.}^{*'} . v_{t'-i+s.}^{*'}) \right) + h_s' h_s \right]$$

$$= \sum_{t=1}^{T} \sum_{t'=1}^{T} \left[E\left((v_{t-i.}^* . v_{t'-i.}^{*'})(v_{t-i+s.}^* . v_{t'-i+s.}^{*'}) \right) - h_s' h_s \right]$$

$$= \sum_{t=1}^{T} \sum_{t'=1}^{T} (J_{tt'} - h_s' h_s).$$

We now come to the laborious part of evaluating $J_{tt'}$. [38] In that evaluation

---

[37] The normality assumption is invoked here only so that the reader will have relatively easy access to the underlying basic result for scalar sequences, in part ii, Proposition 34, Ch. 5 of Dhrymes (1989). The proof of Lemma A3 is, in fact, an adaptation of the proof of that proposition. The reader should further note that normality is not used for any other purpose in the remainder of this discussion.

[38] It is only at this stage that the normality assumption plays a role in simplifying the derivation. If the assumption had not been made then, in addition to the three termsin Eq. (2.A.2) below, one would have had to deal with the cumulants of the distribution in question. This means there would be, in Eq. (2.A.2), additional terms involving the cumulants. Thus, there is no material difference between assuming normality, and assuming that the sums of the cumulants converge to zero, since no other use of the normality assumption is being made.

we have to compute the expectation

$$E\left((v^*_{t-i\cdot}v^{*'}_{t'-i\cdot})(v^*_{t-i+s\cdot}v^{*'}_{t'-i+s\cdot})\right) = \sum_{j_1=1}^{m}\sum_{j_2=1}^{m} E\left(\zeta_{tj_1}\zeta_{t'j_2}\right),$$

where $\zeta_{tj_1} = (v^*_{t-i,j_1}v^*_{t'-i,j_1})$ and $\zeta_{t'j_2} = (v^*_{t-i+s,j_2}v^*_{t'-i+s,j_2})$. In the right member, above, the expectation yields three components

$$E(v^*_{t-i,j_1}v^*_{t'-i,j_1})\,E(v^*_{t-i+s,j_2}v^*_{t'-i+s,j_2}) = h^{(t-t')}_{j_1,j_1}h^{(t-t')}_{j_2,j_2}$$

$$E(v^*_{t-i,j_1}v^*_{t-i+s,j_2})\,E(v^*_{t'-i+s,j_1}v^*_{t'-i+s,j_2}) = h^{(-s)}_{j_1,j_2}h^{(-s)}_{j_1,j_2}$$

$$E(v^*_{t-i,j_1}v^*_{t'-i+s,j_2})\,E(v^*_{t'-i,j_1}v^*_{t-i+s,j_2}) = h^{(t-t'-s)}_{j_1,j_2}h^{(t'-t-s)}_{j_1,j_2}. \qquad (2.A.2)$$

Since $H(s) = H(-s)'$, $H(t'-t-s) = H(t-t'+s)'$, we conclude that

$$J_{tt'} = (\mathrm{tr}H(t-t'))^2 + h'_s h_s + \mathrm{tr}\left(H(t-t'-s)H(t-t'+s)\right);$$

moreover, since $(\mathrm{tr}H(t-t'))^2 \le \| H(t-t') \|^2$, we obtain

$$J_T = \frac{1}{T^2}\sum_{t=1}^{T}\sum_{t'=1}^{T}\left[(\mathrm{tr}H(t-t'))^2 + n\mathrm{tr}(H(t-t'-s)H(t-t'+s))\right]$$

$$\le \frac{1}{T^2}\sum_{t=1}^{T}\sum_{t'=1}^{T}\left(\| H(t-t') \|^2 + \| H(t-t'+s) \|^2\right)$$

$$+\frac{1}{T^2}\sum_{t=1}^{T}\sum_{t'=1}^{T}\left(\| H(t-t'-s) \|^2\right).$$

Since the terms following the inequality above converge to zero with T, the proof is complete.

q.e.d.

Remark A2. In the proof above we have made use of a number of results which were assumed to be known or, at least, easily grasped in the context of the discussion. Should this not be the case, here is a brief demonstration.

We have asserted that for any square matrix, A,

$$(\mathrm{tr}(A))^2 \le \| A \|^2 .$$

The proof of this is trivial if one notes that

$$\mathrm{tr}(A) = \mathrm{vec}(A)'\mathrm{vec}(I_m), \qquad \| A \|^2 = \mathrm{vec}(A)'\mathrm{vec}(A).$$

We have, also, made use of the fact that

$$| \mathrm{tr}(AB) | \le \| A \|^2 + \| B \|^2 .$$

To establish the validity of this claim, let $a = \text{vec}(A)$ and $b = \text{vec}(B)$, and note that by the Cauchy inequality we have

$$| \text{tr}(A'B) | = | a'b | \leq \| A \| \, \| B \| \leq \| A \|^2 + \| B \|^2 .$$

This is so since for nonnegative c, d we have $(c - d)^2 \geq 0$; consequently, we obtain $c^2 + d^2 \geq 2cd \geq cd$, which establishes the inequality above. But this is precisely what is required to justify the inequality in the expression for the entity J_T, or more specifically, it justifies the inequality

$$| \text{tr} \, (H(t - t' - s)H(t - t' + s)) | \leq \| H(t - t' - s) \|^2 + \| H(t - t' + s) \|^2 .$$

Finally, we have asserted that, for any [39] $0 \leq s \leq k$,

$$\frac{1}{T^2} \sum_{t=1}^{T} \sum_{t'=1}^{T} \| H(t - t' + s) \|^2 \longrightarrow 0, \quad \text{with } T.$$

Let us write the components of J_T, defined near the end of the proof of Lemma A3, as J_{T1}, J_{T2}, and J_{T3}. The second component corresponds to the term $\| H(t - t' + s) \|^2$, and it will be sufficient to show that this converges to zero with T. We have

$$J_{T2} = \frac{1}{T^2} \sum_{t=1}^{T} \sum_{t'=1}^{T} \| H(t - t' + s) \|^2 = \frac{1}{T^2} \sum_{t=1}^{T-s} \sum_{t'=1}^{t+s} \| H(t - t' + s) \|^2$$

$$+ \frac{1}{T^2} \sum_{t=1}^{T-s-1} \sum_{t'=t+s+1}^{T} \| H(t' - t - s) \|^2$$

$$= \frac{1}{T^2} \sum_{t=1}^{T-s} \sum_{j=0}^{t-1+s} \| H(j) \|^2 + \frac{1}{T^2} \sum_{t=1}^{T-s-1} \sum_{j=1}^{T-t-s} \| H(j) \|^2$$

$$\leq \frac{K}{T^2} \sum_{t=1}^{T-s} \sum_{j=0}^{t-1+s} \lambda_{\max}^{2j} + \frac{K}{T^2} \sum_{t=1}^{T-s-1} \sum_{j=1}^{T-t-s} \lambda_{\max}^{2j}$$

$$= \frac{K}{T^2} \sum_{t=1}^{T-s} \left(\frac{1 - \lambda_{\max}^{2(t+s)}}{1 - \lambda_{\max}^2} \right) + \frac{K}{T^2} \sum_{t=1}^{T-s-1} \left(\frac{\lambda_{\max}^2 - \lambda_{\max}^{2(T-s-t+1)}}{1 - \lambda_{\max}^2} \right)$$

$$= \frac{K}{T^2(1 - \lambda_{\max}^2)} \left[(T - s)(1 + \lambda_{\max}^2) - \lambda_{\max}^2 - \frac{\lambda_{\max}^{2(s+1)}}{1 - \lambda_{\max}^2} \right]$$

---

[39] Even though, for the sake of definiteness, we require s to be nonnegative, whether it is or is not does not matter at all. This is so since the terms following the inequality, at the end of the proof, are **symmetric** in s, and we are trying to show that such terms converge to zero with T.

$$+ \frac{K}{T^2(1 - \lambda_{\max}^2)} \left[-\frac{\lambda_{\max}^4}{1 - \lambda_{\max}^2} + \frac{\lambda_{\max}^{2(T+1)}}{1 - \lambda_{\max}^2} + \frac{\lambda_{\max}^{2(T-s+1)}}{1 - \lambda_{\max}^2} \right],$$

which, evidently, converges to zero with T, as claimed in the proof of Lemma A3.

3
Maximum Likelihood Methods I

3.1 Introduction

In dealing with the problem of estimating the parameters of a **structural system of equations** we had not, in previous chapters, explicitly stated the form of the density of the random terms appearing in the system. Indeed, the estimation aspects of classical least squares techniques and their generalization to systems of equations are **distribution free**, so that no explicit assumption need be made with respect to the distribution of the error terms beyond the assertion that they have mean zero and finite variance. Furthermore, the **identification problem** was treated rather indirectly, typically as a condition for the invertibility of certain matrices or for the existence of a solution to a certain set of equations; thus, the deeper significance of the problem may have escaped the reader.

In this chapter we shall introduce, explicitly and at the outset, assumptions regarding the density function of the structural errors and in the context of this fully specified model we shall discuss the identification problem and the derivation of parameter estimators using **maximum likelihood methods**.

3.2   The Identification Problem

3.2.1   Generalities

The nature of the identification problem is best introduced by means of an example. Suppose $\{X_t : t = 1, 2, 3, \ldots, T\}$ is a random sample characterized by the univariate density function $N(\mu, \sigma^2)$. Suppose further that it is known that $\mu = \mu_1 + \mu_2$. Does the sample convey any information on the two components, μ_1, μ_2? Or, put differently, can the sample distinguish between two different parametric configurations? For example, let ν be any real number and put

$$\mu_1^* = \mu_1 + \nu, \ \mu_2^* = \mu_2 - \nu.$$

Can the sample differentiate between the component sets (μ_1, μ_2) and (μ_1^*, μ_2^*)? Although the answer is no, and intuitively quite obvious, let us probe into the elemental aspects of inference for the "reasons" why we cannot distinguish between the two parametric configurations above. Confining ourselves to maximum likelihood procedures we observe that the sample data convey information regarding the underlying parameters through the **likelihood function**; the latter, we remind the reader, is simply the joint density function of the observations. The "reason" why the likelihood function conveys such information is that, depending on the **underlying parameters**, some sample observations are more "likely" than others. Thus, in the example above, if $\mu = 1,000$ and $\sigma^2 = 1/4$ positive observations are more likely to occur than negative ones. The converse will be true if $\mu = -1,000$ and $\sigma^2 = 1/4$.

More precisely, given the observations in the sample, the likelihood function may be viewed as a function of the unknown parameters; thus, any inference procedure relying on this density function must, of necessity, determine estimators which are definitely affected by the manner in which the parameters enter the likelihood function as well as by the sample observations. A look at the question as originally posed shows the likelihood function to be

$$(2\pi)^{-T/2}(\sigma^2)^{-T/2}\exp\left\{-\frac{1}{2\sigma^2}\sum_{t=1}^{T}(x_t - \mu_1 - \mu_2)^2\right\}.$$

If μ_1, μ_2 are replaced by μ_1^*, μ_2^* the likelihood function is not altered— as indeed is the case if μ_1, μ_2 are replaced by their sum, μ. Thus, it is completely immaterial, in terms of the likelihood function, that μ is made up of two components μ_1 and μ_2. All that matters is their sum and it is on this quantity that the likelihood function provides some information, through the sample mean $\bar{x}$, which is known to have certain desirable properties as an estimator of μ.

The import of the preceding informal discussion is the following: inferential procedures are based on the premise that sample observations tell us something about the parameters characterizing the population whence such observations originate. The link between observations and parametric configurations comes through the likelihood function. An obvious corollary is that **if two parametric configurations lead to the same likelihood function there is no hope of distinguishing between them on the basis of sample information alone, no matter how large the sample is**. This is the essence of the identification problem which is seen to be the label we put on a situation in which we may ask the data (sample information) to tell us something that they cannot possibly reveal.

3.2.2 *The Simple Supply-Demand Model*

The simple supply-demand competitive equilibrium model consists of three equations

$$
\begin{aligned}
q_t^D &= \alpha + \beta p_t + u_{t1} \\
q_t^S &= a + b p_t + u_{t2} \\
q_t^S &= q_t^D,
\end{aligned}
\tag{3.1}
$$

being, respectively, the demand and supply functions, and the equilibrium condition. Observations generated by this system consist of the pairs, say $\{(q_t, p_t) : t = 1, 2, \ldots, T\}$, since the system determines only the transaction quantity q and the price p at which the transaction has taken place. Thus, making use of the third equation we can write, equivalently,

$$
\begin{aligned}
q_t &= \alpha + \beta p_t + u_{t1} \\
q_t &= a + b p_t + u_{t2}.
\end{aligned}
\tag{3.2}
$$

Now, as we pointed out earlier, this system determines the transaction price and quantity, which may be written, from the reduced form, as

$$
\begin{aligned}
q_t &= \frac{(\beta - b)a + (a - \alpha)b}{\beta - b} + \frac{\beta u_{t2} - b u_{t1}}{\beta - b} \\
p_t &= \frac{a - \alpha}{\beta - b} + \frac{u_{t2} - u_{t1}}{\beta - b}.
\end{aligned}
\tag{3.3}
$$

It is clear that, under the standard assumptions regarding the error terms, we have

$$
\begin{aligned}
E(q_t) &= \pi_{01} = \frac{(\beta - b)a + (a - \alpha)b}{\beta - b} \\
E(p_t) &= \pi_{02} = \frac{a - \alpha}{\beta - b}.
\end{aligned}
$$

Thus, the observations (q_t, p_t) would constitute a random scatter of points around (π_{01}, π_{02}).

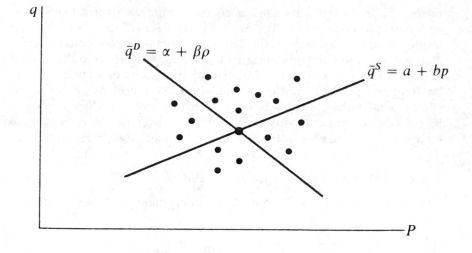

In the diagram above, we have plotted the supply and demand curves, suppressing their random components; the plot in $(q,\ p)$ space reveals a cluster around the "equilibrium" point $(\pi_{01},\ \pi_{02})$. It is intuitively clear that the available sample information could not possibly allow us to differentiate between the true supply and demand functions, and families of other curves that also happen to intersect at the point $\pi_{0.} = (\pi_{01},\ \pi_{02})$.

To show a bit more formally the issues involved, let us introduce compact notation and explicit assumptions regarding the error processes. Putting

$$y_{t.} = (q_t, p_t),\quad B = \begin{bmatrix} 1 & 1 \\ -\beta & -b \end{bmatrix},\quad \pi_{0.} = (\pi_{01}, \pi_{02}),\quad v_{t.} = (v_{t1}, v_{t2})$$

where

$$v_{t1} = \frac{\beta u_{t2} - b u_{t1}}{\beta - b},\qquad v_{t2} = \frac{u_{t2} - u_{t1}}{\beta - b},$$

and asserting

$$(u_{t1},\ u_{t2})' \sim N(0,\ \Sigma), \tag{3.4}$$

we have that

$$v'_{t.} \sim N(0,\ \Omega),\quad \Omega = B'^{-1}\Sigma B^{-1}.$$

If the observations for $t = 1, 2, \ldots, T$ are mutually independent, the log likelihood function (LF) may be written as

$$L(\pi_{0.},\ \Omega; y) = -T\ln(2\pi) - \frac{T}{2}\ln|\Omega| - \frac{1}{2}\sum_{t=1}^{T}(y_{t.} - \pi_{0.})\Omega^{-1}(y_{t.} - \pi_{0.})'.$$

Letting $\gamma' = (\alpha,\ a)$ we see, immediately, that $\pi_{0.} = \gamma'B^{-1}$. If F is a nonsingular matrix, define

$$\gamma^{*'} = \gamma'F,\qquad B^* = BF,\qquad \Sigma^* = F'\Sigma F,$$

and observe that the parameters entering the likelihood function, i.e. Ω and π_0. (which are defined on the basis of the quantities γ, B, Σ), are not affected by the transformation above. One easily verifies that

$$\gamma^{*'}B^{*-1} = \gamma'FF^{-1}B^{-1} = \gamma'B^{-1} = \pi_0.$$
$$B^{*'-1}\Sigma^*B^{*-1} = B^{'-1}F^{'-1}F'\Sigma FF^{-1}B^{-1} = B^{'-1}\Sigma B^{-1} = \Omega.$$

Thus, the likelihood function cannot distinguish between the parametric configurations (γ, B, Σ) and $(\gamma^*, B^*, \Sigma^*)$ which are connected by a (suitable) nonsingular linear transformation.

3.2.3 Identification by Exclusion Restrictions

Consider the usual general linear structural econometric model (GLSEM)

$$y_t.B^* = x_t.C + u_t., \quad t = 1, 2, 3, \ldots, T \tag{3.5}$$

where we have written B^* for the earlier notation $I - B$; here we shall not initially impose normalization constraints, as we did when we discussed 2SLS or 3SLS. Indeed, it is a property of certain maximum likelihood methods that normalizations can be imposed at the end of the estimation process! Thus, we have greater flexibility — a matter that will become quite apparent at a later stage. At any rate we need not, at this stage, put $B^* = I - B$ as was the case in Chapter 1.

Let

$$u_t'. \sim N(0, \Sigma), \quad \Sigma > 0, \tag{3.6}$$

and suppose $\{u_t'. : t = 1, 2, 3, \ldots, T\}$ is a sequence of i.i.d. random vectors. The reduced form of the system is

$$y_t. = x_t.\Pi + v_t., \quad t = 1, 2, 3, \ldots, T, \quad \Pi = CD, \quad D = B^{*-1}, \quad v_t. = u_t.D.$$

It follows that $v_t'. \sim N(0, \Omega)$, $\Omega = D'\Sigma D$. The (LF) of the observations is easily obtained from the reduced form as

$$L(A^*, \Sigma; Y, X) = -\frac{Tm}{2}\ln(2\pi) - \frac{T}{2}\ln|\Omega| - \frac{1}{2}\text{tr}(Y - X\Pi)\Omega^{-1}(Y - X\Pi)', \tag{3.7}$$

where

$$Y = (y_{ti}), \quad X = (x_{tj}), \quad t = 1, 2, 3, \ldots, T, \quad i = 1, 2, \ldots, m, \quad j = 1, 2, \ldots, G.$$

We shall show in the next section that the likelihood function is exactly the same whether it is derived from the reduced or structural form. For the moment, we shall take this fact as given. We now formalize the concept of identification, following the early discussion in Hood and Koopmans (1953).

Definition 1. Suppose Eqs. (3.5) and (3.6) describe an economic system. The triplet $(B^*,\ C,\ \Sigma)$ is called a **structure** if all constituent elements (of the three matrices) are known.

Remark 1. If the condition in Eq. (3.6) is not imposed, let $f(\cdot)$ be the joint density of the elements of the matrix $U = (u_{ti})$, $t = 1, 2, \ldots, T$, $i = 1, 2, \ldots, m$. We shall define $(B^*,\ C,\ f(\cdot))$ to be a structure if the elements of B^*, C and the parameters of the density $f(\cdot)$ are completely known. Since much of our discussion will be confined to the case where the structural errors have a zero mean multivariate normal distribution, it is sufficient to deal, initially, with the covariance matrix alone.

Definition 2. In connection with Eqs. (3.5) and (3.6) a **model** is the set of structures satisfying all (known) a priori restrictions on the elements of $(B^*,\ C,\ \Sigma)$.

Example 1. Consider Eq. (3.2) in conjunction with Eq. (3.4). If nothing is known about Σ then a model is the set of 7-tuplets

$$(\alpha,\ \beta,\ a,\ b,\ \sigma_{11},\ \sigma_{12},\ \sigma_{22})$$

such that Σ is a positive definite matrix. A structure is a particular 7-tuplet obtained by assigning numerical values to its elements. Now suppose it is known that $\sigma_{12} = 0$. Then a model is the set of admissible 7-tuplets, i.e., 7-tuplets of the form $(\alpha,\ \beta,\ a,\ b,\ \sigma_{11},\ 0,\ \sigma_{22})$ and a structure is a particular 7-tuplet obtained by assigning (admissible) numerical values to its (unspecified) elements.

Similarly suppose that in addition to $\sigma_{12} = 0$ it is known that $a = 0$. Then a model is the set of 7-tuplets of the form $(\alpha,\ \beta,\ 0,\ b,\ \sigma_{11},\ 0,\ \sigma_{22})$ and a structure is a particular 7-tuplet obtained by assigning numerical values to its (unspecified) elements such that (in both cases) σ_{11}, σ_{22} are positive.

Central to the identification problem is the concept of observationally equivalent structures, which we define below.

Definition 3. Two structures, S_1, S_2, are said to be **observationally equivalent** if and only if they lead to the same likelihood function.

Example 2. Let S_1 be $(B_1^*, C_1,\ \Sigma_1)$ and S_2 be $(B_2^*,\ C_2,\ \Sigma_2)$. From Eq. (3.7) we see that under S_1 the likelihood function is defined solely by the parameters $\Omega_1 = D_1' \Sigma_1 D_1$, $\Pi_1 = C_1 D_1$, $D_1 = B_1^{*-1}$. Under S_2, it is determined by the parameters $\Omega_2 = D_2' \Sigma_2 D_2$, $\Pi_2 = C_2 D_2$, $D_2 = B_2^{*-1}$. We immediately have

Theorem 1. Two structures $(B_1^*,\ C_1,\ \Sigma_1)$, $(B_2^*,\ C_2,\ \Sigma_2)$ are said to be **observationally equivalent** if and only if there exists a (nonsingular) matrix F such that

$$B_2^* = B_1^* F, \qquad C_2 = C_1 F, \qquad \Sigma_2 = F' \Sigma_1 F.$$

Proof: Since the likelihood function is determined solely by the parameters Ω, Π it will be sufficient to establish the conditions under which $\Pi_1 = \Pi_2$, and $\Omega_1 = \Omega_2$. But by definition $\Pi = C B^{*-1}$; consequently,

$$C_1 B_1^{*-1} = \Pi_1 = \Pi_2 = C_2 B_2^{*-1}$$

if and only if

$$C_2 = C_1 F, \qquad B_2^* = B_1^* F \tag{3.8}$$

for some nonsingular matrix F. Moreover,

$$B_1^{*'-1} \Sigma_1 B_1^{*-1} = \Omega_1 = \Omega_2 = B_2^{*'-1} \Sigma_2 B_2^{*-1}$$

if and only if the second condition in Eq. (3.8) holds and, in addition,

$$\Sigma_2 = F' \Sigma_1 F. \tag{3.9}$$

Thus, two structures are observationally equivalent if and only if the conditions Eqs. (3.8) and (3.9) hold.

q.e.d.

It is convenient now to introduce

Definition 4. Let (B_1^*, C_1, Σ_1) be a structure; consider the transformation

$$B_2^* = B_1^* F, \; C_2 = C_1 F, \; \Sigma_2 = F' \Sigma_1 F.$$

The transformation (matrix) F and the resulting structure (B_2^*, C_2, Σ_2) are said to be **admissible** if and only if (B_2^*, C_2, Σ_2) satisfies all (known) a priori restrictions, and F is nonsingular.

Remark 2. The concepts of model, structure and admissible transformation are connected as follows: Referring to Eqs. (3.5) and (3.6) let (B^*, C, Σ) be a structure; let $\mathcal{Q}$ be the set of all admissible transformations. A model $\mathcal{M}$ is the set of structures

$$\mathcal{M} = \{(B^* F, CF, F' \Sigma F) : F \in \mathcal{Q}.\}$$

We recall that when we examined 2SLS and 3SLS estimation it was necessary to impose a convention, *ab initio*, that in each equation exactly one dependent variable had a coefficient of unity. Here we have not imposed such a convention, since normalization rules of the type just mentioned may be imposed far more flexibly in this context. By the same token, however, the reader will note that if we multiply any equation of the system by an arbitrary nonnull constant, say $c \neq 0$, nothing we know about the equation will change since, typically, we only know that certain structural coefficients are zero. Hence, at this stage, we have no way of distinguishing an equation from a (scalar) multiple thereof. This leads us to

Definition 5. Let S be a structure and let F be an admissible transformation; the transformation is said to be **trivial** with respect to the ith equation if and only if the ith column of F is of the form $ce_{\cdot i}$ where $c \neq 0$ and $e_{\cdot i}$ is a (column) vector all of whose elements are zero save the ith which is unity.

Definition 6. Consider the system in Eqs. (3.5) and (3.6). The ith equation is said to be **identified** if and only if all (observationally) equivalent structures are connected by admissible transformations, F, which are **trivial** with respect to the ith equation. The entire system is said to be identified if and only if every equation is identified, i.e. if all admissible transformations, F, are diagonal.

Example 3. Return to the supply-demand model and write it a bit more generally as

$$\beta_1 q_t^D + \beta_2 p_t = \alpha_0 + u_{t1}$$

$$b_1 q_t^S + b_2 p_t = a_0 + u_{t2}$$

$$q_t^D = q_t^S.$$

As before, we can use the equilibrium condition to simplify the system, thus obtaining

$$\beta_1 q_t + \beta_2 p_t = \alpha_0 + u_{t1}$$

$$b_1 q_t + b_2 p_t = a_0 + u_{t2}.$$

If nothing further is known about the parameters, the matrices B^*, C, Σ of the definitions above are

$$B^* = \begin{bmatrix} \beta_1 & b_1 \\ \beta_2 & b_2 \end{bmatrix}, \qquad C = (\alpha_0, \, a_0), \qquad \Sigma = \begin{bmatrix} \sigma_{11} & \sigma_{12} \\ \sigma_{21} & \sigma_{22} \end{bmatrix},$$

with the stipulation that B^* be nonsingular and Σ positive definite. If F is any (conformable) nonsingular matrix, it is clear that

$$B^* F, \qquad (\alpha_0, \, a_0)F, \qquad F'\Sigma F$$

will also satisfy all a priori restrictions and, thus, that it is observationally equivalent to the earlier specification. Now suppose that in the first equation we discover that another variable, say x_{t1}, is relevant. Revising, we can now write

$$\beta_1 q_t + \beta_2 p_t = \alpha_0 + \alpha_1 x_{t1} + u_{t1}$$
$$b_1 q_t + b_2 p_t = a_0 + u_{t2}.$$

The matrices can now be written as

$$B^* = \begin{bmatrix} \beta_1 & b_1 \\ \beta_2 & b_2 \end{bmatrix}, \quad C = \begin{bmatrix} \alpha_0 & a_0 \\ \alpha_1 & 0 \end{bmatrix}, \quad \Sigma = \begin{bmatrix} \sigma_{11} & \sigma_{12} \\ \sigma_{21} & \sigma_{22} \end{bmatrix},$$

with the stipulation that B^* be nonsingular, Σ positive definite, and $\alpha_1 \neq 0$. It is clear now that all equivalent structures are no longer connected by an unrestricted nonsingular matrix, F. Thus, let

$$F = \begin{bmatrix} f_{11} & f_{12} \\ f_{21} & f_{22} \end{bmatrix}$$

be the matrix connecting equivalent structures. We ought to have

$$CF = \begin{bmatrix} \alpha_0 f_{11} + a_0 f_{21} & \alpha_0 f_{12} + a_0 f_{22} \\ \alpha_1 f_{11} & \alpha_1 f_{12} \end{bmatrix}$$

with $\alpha_1 f_{12} = 0$, since all equivalent structures will have to satisfy a priori restrictions. Hence the matrix F is of the form

$$F = \begin{bmatrix} f_{11} & 0 \\ f_{21} & f_{22} \end{bmatrix}$$

which, by Definitions 5 and 6, shows that the second equation is identified, while by Definition 6 it shows that the system is not identified in the sense that the latter contains at least one equation (here the first) which is not identified.

Example 4. Suppose it is further discovered, in the system above, that a variable, x_{t2}, is relevant for the second equation. The system now becomes

$$\beta_1 q_t + \beta_2 p_t = \alpha_0 + \alpha_1 x_{t1} + u_{t1}$$
$$b_1 q_t + b_2 p_t = a_0 + a_2 x_{t2} + u_{t2}.$$

The C matrix is now given by

$$C = \begin{bmatrix} \alpha_0 & a_0 \\ \alpha_1 & 0 \\ 0 & a_2 \end{bmatrix},$$

with the stipulation $\alpha_1 \neq 0$, $a_2 \neq 0$.

As before, observationally equivalent structures have to obey a priori restrictions, i.e.

$$CF = \begin{bmatrix} \alpha_0 f_{11} + a_0 f_{21} & \alpha_0 f_{12} + a_0 f_{22} \\ \alpha_1 f_{11} & \alpha_1 f_{12} \\ a_2 f_{21} & a_2 f_{22} \end{bmatrix},$$

such that

$$a_2 f_{21} = 0, \qquad \alpha_1 f_{12} = 0.$$

But these conditions immediately imply that

$$f_{21} = f_{12} = 0,$$

which shows that all matrices F connecting observationally equivalent structures have to be **diagonal**. Hence, that the system is identified.

Remark 3. It should be apparent from the preceding example that an assertion that a model (or an equation) is identified implies certain restrictions on the rank of certain matrices. Thus, in Example 3 if the rank of the second row of C is not one, i.e. if $\alpha_1 = 0$, identification is lost. Similarly in Example 4, identification of the system is lost if $\alpha_1 = a_2 = 0$ — whether we know this fact or not. Thus the reader ought to be clearly aware that identification is not gained by simply asserting that certain variables are present in certain equations. The variables in question must, in fact, belong there in the sense that, say, $\alpha_1 \neq 0$, $a_2 \neq 0$, in Example 4.

We shall now take up the characterization of identifiability conditions in terms of the rank of certain (sub) matrices defining a given structure.

Theorem 2. Consider the system

$$y_{t\cdot} B^* = x_{t\cdot} C + u_{t\cdot}, \qquad t = 1, 2, 3, \dots, T$$

together with $u'_{t\cdot} \sim N(0, \Sigma)$, Σ being positive definite. As usual B^* is asserted to be nonsingular. Consider, for definiteness, the first equation and suppose that a priori restrictions on its parameters are such that

$$b^*_{\cdot 1} = \begin{bmatrix} \beta^\circ_{\cdot 1} \\ 0 \end{bmatrix}, \qquad c_{\cdot 1} = \begin{bmatrix} \gamma_{\cdot 1} \\ 0 \end{bmatrix}$$

where $b^*_{\cdot 1}$, $c_{\cdot 1}$ are, respectively, the first column of B^*, C and $\beta^\circ_{\cdot 1}$ has $m_1 + 1$ elements, while $\gamma_{\cdot 1}$ has G_1 elements. Partition

$$B^* = \begin{bmatrix} \beta^\circ_{\cdot 1} & B^*_{12} \\ 0 & B^*_{22} \end{bmatrix}, \qquad C = \begin{bmatrix} \gamma_{\cdot 1} & C_{12} \\ 0 & C_{22} \end{bmatrix}.$$

Then, the first equation is identified if and only if

$$\operatorname{rank} \begin{bmatrix} B^*_{22} \\ C_{22} \end{bmatrix} = m - 1.$$

Proof: Consider the set of admissible structures; all such structures are of the form (where f_{11} is a scalar, F_{21} is $(m-1) \times 1$, etc.)

$$\begin{bmatrix} \beta^\circ_{\cdot 1} & B^*_{12} \\ 0 & B^*_{22} \\ \gamma_{\cdot 1} & C_{12} \\ 0 & C_{22} \end{bmatrix} \begin{bmatrix} f_{11} & F_{12} \\ F_{21} & F_{22} \end{bmatrix} = \begin{bmatrix} \beta^\circ_{\cdot 1} f_{11} + B^*_{12} F_{21} & \beta^\circ_{\cdot 1} F_{12} + B^*_{12} F_{22} \\ B^*_{22} F_{21} & B^*_{22} F_{22} \\ \gamma_{\cdot 1} f_{11} + C_{12} F_{21} & \gamma_{\cdot 1} F_{12} + C_{12} F_{22} \\ C_{22} F_{21} & C_{22} F_{22} \end{bmatrix},$$

for some admissible matrix F. Because F is admissible we must have

$$\begin{bmatrix} B_{22}^* \\ C_{22} \end{bmatrix} F_{21} = 0. \tag{3.10}$$

Now, by definition, the first equation is identified if and only if all admissible structures involve a matrix F such that

$$F_{21} = 0. \tag{3.11}$$

Suppose that

$$\text{rank} \begin{bmatrix} B_{22}^* \\ C_{22} \end{bmatrix} = m - 1.$$

Then, Eq. (3.10) implies Eq. (3.11) (since the matrix in Eq. (3.10) has $m - 1$ columns) and the first equation is identified; this is so, since the transformation F is trivial with respect to the first equation. Conversely, suppose the first equation is identified and

$$\text{rank} \begin{bmatrix} B_{22}^* \\ C_{22} \end{bmatrix} < m - 1.$$

We shall show that this involves a contradiction, thus completing the proof. Since the matrix above is of rank less than $m - 1$ there exists a nonnull vector, say F_{21}, such that

$$\begin{bmatrix} B_{22}^* \\ C_{22} \end{bmatrix} F_{21} = 0.$$

Let $f_{11} \neq 0$ be a scalar and consider the matrix

$$F = \begin{bmatrix} f_{11} & 0 \\ F_{21} & I \end{bmatrix}. \tag{3.12}$$

The matrix in Eq. (3.12) is admissible since it is nonsingular and it respects all a priori restrictions. Precisely,

$$\begin{bmatrix} \beta_{\cdot 1}^\circ & B_{12}^* \\ 0 & B_{22}^* \\ \gamma_{\cdot 1} & C_{12} \\ 0 & C_{22} \end{bmatrix} \begin{bmatrix} f_{11} & 0 \\ F_{21} & I \end{bmatrix} = \begin{bmatrix} \beta_{\cdot 1}^\circ f_{11} + B_{12}^* F_{21} & B_{12}^* \\ B_{22}^* F_{21} & B_{22}^* \\ \gamma_{\cdot 1} f_{11} + C_{12} F_{21} & C_{12} \\ C_{22} F_{21} & C_{22} \end{bmatrix}.$$

By construction,

$$\begin{bmatrix} B_{22}^* \\ C_{22} \end{bmatrix} F_{21} = 0$$

and the parameters of all other equations remain undisturbed. Thus, all a priori restrictions are respected. On the other hand, the transformation is not trivial with respect to the first equation since $F_{21} \neq 0$. Hence the first equation is not identified, which is a contradiction, thus establishing the condition

$$\text{rank} \begin{bmatrix} B_{22}^* \\ C_{22} \end{bmatrix} = m - 1.$$

q.e.d.

Remark 4. The condition of Theorem 2 is referred to as **the rank condition for identifiability**. Noting that the matrix $(B_{22}^{*\prime}, C_{22}')'$ has $(m - m_1 - 1) + (G - G_1)$ rows we conclude, in view of the rank condition, that we must have as a **necessary** condition

$$m - m_1 - 1 + G - G_1 \geq m - 1,$$

or, equivalently,

$$G \geq m_1 + G_1,$$

which is the condition we encountered earlier, in the context of 2SLS and 3SLS estimation, and which is termed the **order condition**.

Example 5. Consider the model of Example 4 and note that,

$$a_2 = (B_{22}^{*\prime}, C_{22}')',$$

since in this case B_{22}^* has no elements. Thus, identification of the first equation requires that

$$\text{rank}(a_2) = 1.$$

In other words, it must be the case that $a_2 \neq 0$. Thus, the reader should be disabused of the notion that just because we write x_{t2} as a predetermined variable in the second equation, we thereby ensure identification. **In some sense the variables enumerated must really be there.** Otherwise we are merely fulfilling the necessary (order) condition, while the necessary and sufficient (rank) condition may be violated. Similarly, if we consider the identifiability of the second equation we need to form the matrix of coefficients of the jointly dependent variables excluded therefrom (B_{22}^* of Theorem 2). Here, this matrix has no elements since the second equation contains both dependent variables. We also need to consider the matrix of the coefficients of the predetermined variables excluded from the second equation (C_{22} of Theorem 2). This matrix is simply α_1. Thus, the matrix corresponding to $(B_{22}^{*\prime}, C_{22}')'$ of Theorem 2 is the scalar α_1. Consequently, to ensure identifiability of the second equation we must have

$$\text{rank}(\alpha_1) = m - 1 = 1,$$

which means

$$\alpha_1 \neq 0.$$

Example 6. The preceding example does not, perhaps, have enough dimensions to illustrate sufficiently the nature of the rank and order conditions just derived. Thus, consider the model

$$b_{11}y_{t1} + b_{21}y_{t2} \qquad = c_{11}x_{t1} + c_{21}x_{t2} \qquad\qquad + u_{t1}$$
$$b_{12}y_{t1} \qquad + b_{32}y_{t3} = c_{12}x_{t1} \qquad\qquad + c_{32}x_{t3} + u_{t2}$$
$$b_{23}y_{t2} + b_{33}y_{t3} = c_{13}x_{t1} + c_{33}x_{t3} + c_{43}x_{t4} + u_{t3},$$

or more compactly

$$y_{t\cdot} \begin{bmatrix} b_{11} & b_{12} & 0 \\ b_{21} & 0 & b_{23} \\ 0 & b_{32} & b_{33} \end{bmatrix} = x_{t\cdot} \begin{bmatrix} c_{11} & c_{12} & c_{13} \\ c_{21} & 0 & 0 \\ 0 & c_{32} & c_{33} \\ 0 & 0 & c_{43} \end{bmatrix} + u_{t\cdot\cdot}$$

In this context, for the first equation, we have

$$B_{22}^* = (b_{32},\, b_{33}), \qquad C_{22} = \begin{bmatrix} c_{32} & c_{33} \\ 0 & c_{43} \end{bmatrix}.$$

Consequently, the rank condition is

$$\text{rank} \begin{bmatrix} b_{32} & b_{33} \\ c_{32} & c_{33} \\ 0 & c_{43} \end{bmatrix} = m - 1 = 3 - 1 = 2.$$

The condition, thus, rules out the case $b_{32} = c_{32} = 0$, which entails loss of identification for the first equation. **Thus, not only is it necessary for us not to know that b_{32}, c_{32} are null, but it is necessary that it be true that b_{32} and c_{32} are not null.** For the second equation we have

$$B_{22}^* = (b_{21},\, b_{23}), \qquad C_{22} = \begin{bmatrix} c_{21} & 0 \\ 0 & c_{43} \end{bmatrix}.$$

Again

$$\text{rank} \begin{bmatrix} b_{21} & b_{23} \\ c_{21} & 0 \\ 0 & c_{43} \end{bmatrix} = 2$$

rules out $b_{23} = 0$, $c_{43} = 0$; or $b_{21} = 0$, $c_{21} = 0$. Any of these circumstances reduce the rank of the matrix to at most one and, thus, produce nonidentification for the second equation.

For the third equation we have

$$B_{22}^* = (b_{11},\, b_{12}), \qquad C_{22} = (c_{21},\, 0).$$

Again

$$\text{rank} = \begin{bmatrix} b_{11} & b_{12} \\ c_{21} & 0 \end{bmatrix} = 2$$

rules out $b_{12} = 0$; or $c_{21} = 0$; or $b_{11} = c_{21} = 0$. Either of these conditions will render the third equation nonidentified.

Remark 5. Identification of structural parameters by exclusion restrictions means, intuitively, that the equations of the system must be sufficiently different from each other (by containing sufficiently different sets of variables) so that they cannot be mistaken for linear combinations of other equations in the system. It is this eventuality that is **ruled out in substance by the rank condition and in form by the order condition**.

3.2.4 Identification by Linear Restrictions

The preceding discussion can be extended to more general types of restrictions; the reader ought not to remain with the impression that only exclusion restrictions are capable of inducing identification. In the following we shall discuss the conditions under which identification can be obtained by **linear restrictions** on the parameters appearing in a given equation(s).

Definition 7. Consider the system in Eqs. (3.5) and (3.6) and let $A^* = (B^{*'}, -C')'$; moreover, let Φ_i, $h_{\cdot i}$ be an $n_i \times m + G$ matrix and an $(m + G)$-element column vector, respectively, both with known elements. Suppose

$$\Phi_i a^*_{\cdot i} = h_{\cdot i}.$$

If the relation above represents a valid set of restrictions on the structural parameters of the ith equation, then, Φ_i is said to be the matrix of linear restrictions. If $h_{\cdot i} = 0$ the restrictions are said to be (linear) homogeneous; if $h_{\cdot i} \neq 0$, the restrictions are said to be (linear) inhomogeneous.

Example 7. Suppose one restriction states that, in the first equation, the coefficients of the first and third predetermined variables add up to three, and another that the coefficients of the second and fourth endogenous variables in the first equation are the same. This may be represented as the inhomogeneous linear restriction

$$\Phi_1 a^*_{\cdot 1} = h_{\cdot 1}, \quad \Phi_1 = \begin{bmatrix} 0 & 0 & 0 & 0 & \cdots & 1 & 0 & 1 & \cdots \\ 0 & 1 & 0 & -1 & \cdots & 0 & 0 & 0 & \cdots \end{bmatrix}, \quad h_{\cdot 1} = (3, 0)'.$$

where $a^*_{\cdot 1}$ is the first column of A^*.

In general, each homogeneous linear restriction on the elements of (a column of) the matrix A^* can be written in the form of a row vector, say ϕ', all of whose elements are known, and the condition $\phi' a^*_{\cdot 1} = 0$.

In this framework, how can we characterize identification of a given equation of the system? The answer is given by

Theorem 3. Put $A^* = (B^{*'}, -C')'$ and consider the system in Theorem

2. Let Φ_i be the matrix of (homogeneous) linear a priori restrictions on the first equation. The latter is identified if and only if

$$\text{rank}(\Phi_i A^*) = m - 1.$$

To facilitate the proof of this theorem we first give two auxiliary lemmata.

Lemma 1. Let Q be $m \times n$, $m \geq n$, of rank $r \leq n$. Let $\nu(Q)$ be the (column) null space of Q, the elements of which are defined by

$$\nu(Q) = \{x : Qx = 0\}.$$

Let k be the dimension of the null space. Then

$$r + k = n.$$

Proof: See Proposition 5 in Dhrymes (1984).

For notational simplicity we deal below with the first equation; the argument is identical for any equation, say the ith.

Lemma 2. Consider the system in Theorem 2, and A^* as in Theorem 3; the first equation of the system is identified if and only if **any** vector p satisfying $\Phi_1 A^* p = 0$, is of the form $p = ce_{.1}$, where $e_{.1}$ is a column vector all of whose elements are zero, save the first which is unity, and Φ_1 is the matrix of (linear homogeneous) restrictions on the parameters of the first equation of the system in Theorem 2.

Proof: Suppose the first equation is identified, and there exists a vector $p \neq ce_{.1}$ such that

$$\Phi_1 A^* p = 0. \tag{3.13}$$

We shall show that this leads to a contradiction. We first note that since $A^* e_{.1} = a^*_{.1}$ we have

$$\Phi_1 A^* e_{.1} = 0.$$

Let p be a vector satisfying Eq. (3.13) and such that $p \neq ce_{.1}$. Hence, we may write $p = (p_{11}, F'_{21})'$, with $F_{21} \neq 0$. Choose $c \neq 0$, and such that in defining

$$f_{.1} = p + ce_{.1} = (f_{11}, F'_{21})'$$

we have that $f_{11} \neq 0$, $F_{21} \neq 0$. Consider now the matrix

$$F = \begin{bmatrix} f_{11} & 0 \\ F_{21} & I \end{bmatrix}.$$

By construction, $f_{11} \neq 0$, $F_{21} \neq 0$. Moreover, we can show that F is **admissible**, since it leaves all equations undisturbed, except for the first, and for the latter it implies, $A^*f_{.1} = A^*p + cA^*e_{.1}$. In turn, this means that $\Phi_1 A^* f_{.1} = 0$, which shows admissibility. Thus, we have an admissible transformation (matrix) F , whose first column is not of the form $ce_{.1}$. This shows that the first equation is not identified, which is a contradiction. Hence, the only vectors p satisfying Eq. (3.13) are of the form

$$p = ce_{.1}. \tag{3.14}$$

Conversely, suppose that the only vectors p satisfying Eq. (3.13) are of the form of Eq. (3.14); we shall show that the first equation is identified. Let F be any admissible matrix and let $f_{.1}$ be its first column. Thus, the parameters of the first equation, for any equivalent (admissible) structure, are given by $A^*f_{.1}$. Since F is admissible, all a priori restrictions are satisfied. In particular, we have $\Phi_1 A^* f_{.1} = 0$. But, by supposition, the only vectors, say p , satisying Eq. (3.13) are of the form in Eq. (3.14). Thus, the first column of **any** admissible matrix, say $f_{.1}$, must be of the form $f_{.1} = ce_{.1}$ and consequently, **any** admissible matrix F must of the form

$$F = \begin{bmatrix} f_{11} & F_{12} \\ 0 & F_{22} \end{bmatrix},$$

which shows that the first equation is identified.

q.e.d.

We may now proceed to the

Proof of Theorem 3: We first show that the rank condition is sufficient. Thus, let Φ_i be the matrix of (homogeneous) linear restrictions on the parameters of the ith equation and suppose that $\operatorname{rank}(\Phi_i A^*) = m - 1$. By Lemma 1 the dimension of the (column) null space of $\Phi_i A^*$ is one; consequently, all solutions, p , to

$$\Phi_i A^* p = 0 \quad \text{are of the form} \quad p = ce_{.i}. \tag{3.15}$$

It follows, by Lemma 2, that the ith equation is identified.

Conversely, suppose that the ith equation is identified. By Lemma 2, all solutions to Eq. (3.15) are of the form $p = ce_{.i}$. Hence, the dimension of the (column) null space of $\Phi_i A^*$ is one; it follows, by Lemma 1, that the rank of the matrix is $m - 1$.

q.e.d.

The case of inhomogeneous linear restrictions is handled in essentially the same fashion.

Remark 6. The perceptive reader would have noted that in Chs. 1 and 2 we had, in fact, made use of the analog of the matrix Φ_i . This was the exclusion matrix L_i^* and the augmented exclusion matrix $L^{*\circ}$, of Definitions 4, 5, 6 and Remark 5, of Chapter 1. In particular, recall that in the LM derivation of 2SLS (and 3SLS) we minimized a certain function, subject to $L_{\cdot i}^* a_{\cdot i} = 0$. In that context, normalization had been imposed *ab initio*. To use the same device in the present context, where normalization has not been imposed, we need to employ the augmented exclusion matrix, in the form of **an inhomogeneous linear restriction** $L_i^{*\circ'} a_{\cdot i}^* = h_{\cdot i}$, where $h_{\cdot i}$ is an $m_i^* + G_i^*$ -element vector all of whose elements are zero, save the first which is unity.

Remark 7. Notice further that the imposition of the normaliztion convention changes slightly the characterization of identification. In general the normalization convention, employed throughout Chapter 1, may be expressed in this framework by stating that the (matrices of linear) restrictions take the form

$$\Phi_i a_{\cdot i}^* = h_{\cdot i}, \qquad i = 1, 2, \ldots, m, \tag{3.16}$$

where the **first** row of Φ_i is $e_{\cdot i}'$, i.e. an m -element row vector all of whose elements are zero, save the ith , which is unity, and the other rows reflect the usual set of (a priori) identifying exclusion restrictions, and/or possibly other types of restrictions.

If A^* is any admissible matrix of structural coefficients, then all admissible coefficient matrices, say $A^\#$, are connected to it by an admissible transformation, representable by an admissible matrix, say F . Under F , the parameters of the ith equation become $a_{\cdot i}^\# = A^* f_{\cdot i}$, where $f_{\cdot i}$ is the ith column of F . Since the latter is an admissible matrix, we must have

$$\Phi a_{\cdot i}^\# = \Phi_i A^* f_{\cdot i} = h_{\cdot i}. \tag{3.17}$$

If the ith equation is identified, then we must have for all admissible matrices, F , that their i^{th} columns obey $f_{\cdot i} = c e_{\cdot i}$. Hence, we must have

$$h_{\cdot i} = \Phi_i A^* f_{\cdot i} = c \Phi_i a_{\cdot i}^* = c h_{\cdot i}, \tag{3.18}$$

which, in view of the preceding discussion, implies $c = 1$.

Thus, we are led to the following specialization of Definition 6,

Definition 8. In the context of Definition 6, suppose the ith equation is subject to the **inhomogeneous linear restriction**

$$\Phi_i a_{\cdot i}^* = h_{\cdot i}, \quad i = 1, 2, \ldots, m,$$

where Φ_i is an $n_i \times m+G$ matrix of restrictions. The ith equation is identified if and only if all observationally equivalent structures are connected by admissible transformations whose matrix representation, F, has for its ith column $e_{.i}$. The **system is identified** if and only if all equations are identified.

It is immediate from the preceding discussion, that the imposition of the normalization convention, as in the 2SLS and 3SLS context, means that for **identified systems the only admissible transformation matrices are simply the identity matrices**. Thus, no ambiguity remains in the intepretation of parameters.

We should, further, remark that it is possible to obtain identification by restrictions on the covariance matrix of the structural errors. This is particularly easy to see in a maximum likelihood context. The presence of such restrictions effectively limits the class of admissible transformation matrices. It is, then, a question of whether the known restrictions on the covariance matrix, and those on the structural coefficients, constitute a set sufficiently strong to limit the class of admissible transformation matrices to the class of **identity matrices**. We shall consider this topic, briefly, at a later section.

We now prove the variant of Theorem 3, applicable to the case of inhomogeneous restrictions.

Theorem 4. In the context of Theorem 3, suppose the parameters of the ith structural equation are subject to the inhomogenous linear restriction $\Phi_i a_{.i}^* = h_{.i}$, $i = 1, 2, \ldots, m$. The ith structural equation is identified if and only if

$$\text{rank}(\Phi_i A^*) = m.$$

Proof: Suppose $\text{rank}(\Phi_i A^*) = m$, we show that the ith equation is identified. Let F be **any admissible** matrix and $f_{.i}$ be its ith column. Due to the admissibility of F, we obtain $\Phi_i A^* e_{.i} = h_{.i}$, $\Phi_i A^* f_{.i} = h_{.i}$, which implies $\Phi_i A^* (e_{.i} - f_{.i}) = 0$. In view of the rank condition, this implies that for any admissible transformation matrix, its ith column obeys $e_{.i} = f_{.i}$; thus, by Definition 8, we conclude that the equation in question is identifiable.

Conversely, suppose that the ith equation is identifiable and $\text{rank}(\Phi_i A^*) < m$. We show this leads to a contradiction. By the rank condition above, there exists a nonnull vector, say $q \neq c e_{.i}$, $c \neq 0$, such that $\Phi_i A^* q = 0$. Consider now the matrix F which is the identity matrix of order m, except that its ith column is given by $f_{.i} = q + e_{.i} \neq e_{.i}$. This matrix is admissible since all equations other than the ith remain undisturbed and for the latter we have $\Phi_i A^* f_{.i} = \Phi_i A^* (q + e_{.i}) = h_{.i}$, which shows that the restrictions on the ith equation are obeyed as well. This implies that the equation is not identified, which is a contradiction.

q.e.d.

Corollary 1. In the context of Theorem 4, the system as a whole is identified by the exclusion and normalization conditions $L^{*\circ'} \text{vec}(A^*) = \text{vec}(H)$, if and only if $\text{rank}[L^{*\circ'}(I_m \otimes A^*] = m^2$, where H is a matrix whose i^{th} column is $h_{\cdot i}$, or as an alternative description, it is a matrix whose first row consists of unities, and every other element is null, and $L^{*\circ} = \text{diag}(L_1^{*\circ}, L_2^{*\circ}, \ldots, L_m^{*\circ})$, is the augmented exclusion matrix for the system as a whole.

Proof: The ith component of the restrictions is given by $L_i^{*\circ'} a_{\cdot i}^* = h_{\cdot i}$, and the conclusion follows immediately from Theorem 4.

q.e.d.

Remark 8. An interesting by product of the preceding discussion is that it yields an answer to the question: **what is the minimum number of restrictions that must be imposed on the** i^{th} **equation for identification?** For simplicity, consider the case where we are dealing only with exclusion restrictions and normalization. We may, thus, put $\Phi_i = L_i^{*\circ'}$ and the restrictions may be stated as $L_i^{*\circ'} a_{\cdot i}^* = h_{\cdot i}$, where by Convention 2, the row dimension of $L_i^{*\circ'}$ is given by $n_i = m_i^* + G_i^* = m + G - m_i - G_i$. This is precisely the number of restrictions, including normalization, imposed on the ith equation. By Theorem 4, we must have $n_i \geq m$, so that m **is the minimum number of restrictions that must be imposed, for identification, on the** i^{th} **equation.** It then follows from Corollary 1 that the minimum number of restrictions that must be placed, for identification, on the system as a whole is m^2.

3.2.5 Identification and the Reduced Form

An alternative way in which the identification problem may be posed is the following: If the matrix of reduced form coefficients, Π, is given, can we determine the elements of (some of the columns of) B^* and C, or are there infinitely many such matrices from which Π may have arisen? Indeed, a method of estimation called indirect least squares was inspired by exactly this sort of consideration. We shall examine this method at a later stage, but for the moment let us press on with an informal inquiry into the identification implications of the question just posed.

Since the reduced form is given by $\Pi = CB^{*-1}$, we may also write $\Pi B^* = C$. Concentrating on the first equation, we may write

$$\begin{bmatrix} \Pi_{11}^\circ & \Pi_{12} \\ \Pi_{21}^\circ & \Pi_{22} \end{bmatrix} \begin{bmatrix} \beta_{\cdot 1}^\circ & B_{12}^* \\ 0 & B_{22}^* \end{bmatrix} = \begin{bmatrix} \gamma_{\cdot 1} & C_{12} \\ 0 & C_{22} \end{bmatrix}, \tag{3.19}$$

where Π_{11}° is $G_1 \times (m_1 + 1)$, Π_{12} is $G_1 \times (m_1^* - 1)$, Π_{21}° is $G_1^* \times (m_1 + 1)$, Π_{22} is $G_1^* \times (m_1^* - 1)$, and G_1^*, m_1^* are the complements of G_1 and m_1, respectively, i.e. $G_1^* = G - G_1$ and $m_1^* = m - m_1$. The relations of relevance (to the first equation) are

$$\Pi_{11}^\circ \beta_{\cdot 1}^\circ = \gamma_{\cdot 1}, \quad \Pi_{21}^\circ \beta_{\cdot 1}^\circ = 0, \tag{3.20}$$

and the question is: Given Π_{11}° and Π_{21}° can we determine $\beta_{\cdot 1}^\circ$ and $\gamma_{\cdot 1}$?

Clearly, the system in Eq. (3.20) is decomposable; thus, if from the second subset we can determine $\beta_{\cdot 1}^\circ$, $\gamma_{\cdot 1}$ is easily determined from the first subset. If no such determination can be made from the second subset then, evidently, we cannot determine $\gamma_{\cdot 1}$ either. We recall, from the discussion of the identification problem in a structural context, that identifiability is required only to within a multiplicative constant;[1] thus, if $\beta_{\cdot 1}^\circ$ can be determined to within a multiplicative constant from the second subset, the same will be true of $\gamma_{\cdot 1}$. For this to be the case, it must be true that the dimension of the column null space of Π_{21}° is unity which, by Lemma 1, implies the condition that the rank of that matrix must be m_1. We formalize this discussion below and we state the theorem in general terms, i.e. in terms of the ith equation.

Theorem 5. In the context of the model in Eqs. (3.5) and (3.6), the following statements are true:

i. **absent any normalization**, the ith equation is identified if and only if

$$\text{rank}(L_{2i}^{*'}\Pi L_{1i}^\circ) = \text{rank}(\Pi_{2i}^\circ) = m_i, \quad i = 1, 2, \ldots, m;$$

ii. **given the usual normalization convention**, (i.e. assuming that it is possible to, and we do, set the coefficient of y_{ti} in the ith equation equal to unity) the ith equation is identified if and only if

$$\text{rank}(L_{2i}^{*'}\Pi L_{1i}) = \text{rank}(\Pi_{2i}) = m_i, \quad i = 1, 2, \ldots, m.$$

Proof: We remind the reader that a complete discussion of selection and exclusion matrices may be found in Definitions 4, 5 and 6, of Chapter 1. Moreover,

$$(y_{\cdot i}, Y_i) = Y_i^\circ = Y L_{1i}^\circ, \ Y_i = Y L_{1i}, \ X_i^* = X L_{2i}^*, \ \Pi L_{1i}^\circ = \Pi_i^\circ, \ \Pi L_{1i} = \Pi_i.$$

The last two entities represent the matrix of coefficients in the reduced form representation of Y_i° and Y_i, respectively. It is natural to define,

$$\Pi_{2i}^\circ = L_{2i}^{*'}\Pi L_{1i}^\circ, \quad \Pi_{2i} = L_{2i}^{*'}\Pi L_{1i}.$$

---

[1] This is true **absent any normalization convention**. When a normalization convention is imposed, **no ambiguity remains**, i.e. the parameters in question are uniquely determined.

The first of these denotes the matrix of coefficients of the predetermined variables excluded from the ith equation, i.e. the variables in X_i^*, as they appear in the reduced form representation of the variables in Y_i°; the second denotes the matrix of coefficients of the predetermined variables excluded from the ith equation, i.e. the variables in X_i^*, as they appear in the reduced form representation of the variables in Y_i.

To prove i suppose (B^*, C, Σ), $(\bar{B}^*, \bar{C}, \bar{\Sigma})$ are two observationally equivalent structures. Since the matrix of reduced form coefficients is invariant we must have the relations

$$\Pi_i^\circ \beta_{\cdot i}^\circ = c_{\cdot i}, \qquad \Pi_i^\circ \bar{\beta}_{\cdot i}^\circ = \bar{c}_{\cdot i}.$$

Premultiplying each by $(L_{2i}, L_{2i}^*)'$, we find

$$\Pi_{1i}^\circ \beta_{\cdot i}^\circ = \gamma_{\cdot i}, \qquad \Pi_{1i}^\circ \bar{\beta}_{\cdot i}^\circ = \bar{\gamma}_{\cdot i}$$
$$\Pi_{2i}^\circ \beta_{\cdot i}^\circ = 0, \qquad \Pi_{2i}^\circ \bar{\beta}_{\cdot i}^\circ = 0,$$

in the obvious notation. Now, suppose $\mathrm{rank}(\Pi_{2i}^\circ) = m_i$. By Lemma 1, its column null space is of dimension one and, consequently, all solutions to the equation $\Pi_{21}^\circ p = 0$, are of the form $p = c\beta_{\cdot i}^\circ$, where $\beta_{\cdot i}^\circ$ is some basic solution. Hence, the equation system above implies that if

$$(B^*, C, \Sigma), \qquad (\bar{B}^*, \bar{C}, \bar{\Sigma})$$

are **any two observationally equivalent structures**, the ith columns of the two sets of coefficient matrices are scalar multiples of each other. Hence, the ith equation is identified. Conversely, suppose the ith erquation is identified. Then, from the equation system above we conclude that $\bar{\beta}_{\cdot i}^\circ = c\beta_{\cdot i}^\circ$ and $\bar{\gamma}_{\cdot i} = c\gamma_{\cdot i}$. Thus, by Lemma 1, we conclude that $\mathrm{rank}(\Pi_{2i}^\circ) = m_i$, which concludes the proof of part i.

As for part ii, proceeding in exactly the same fashion and noting that under normalization $\beta_{\cdot i}^\circ = (1, -\beta_{\cdot i}')'$, we have, for two observationally equivalent structures, the relations

$$\begin{bmatrix} \Pi_{1i} & I \\ \Pi_{2i} & 0 \end{bmatrix} \begin{bmatrix} \beta_{\cdot i} \\ \gamma_{\cdot i} \end{bmatrix} = \pi_{\cdot i}, \qquad \begin{bmatrix} \Pi_{1i} & I \\ \Pi_{2i} & 0 \end{bmatrix} \begin{bmatrix} \bar{\beta}_{\cdot i} \\ \bar{\gamma}_{\cdot i} \end{bmatrix} = \pi_{\cdot i}. \qquad (3.21)$$

Now, suppose $\mathrm{rank}(\Pi_{2i}) = m_i$; then, clearly the matrix of the system(s) in Eq. (3.21) is of rank $m_i + G_i$, due to the fact that the identity matrix is of order G_i. Hence, the matrix of the system(s) is nonsingular and, consequently, $\beta_{\cdot i} = \bar{\beta}_{\cdot i}$, $\gamma_{\cdot i} = \bar{\gamma}_{\cdot i}$. This implies that all observationally equivalent structures are connected by transformations, whose matrix representations have for their i^{th} column, $e_{\cdot i}$. But, by Definition 8, this means that the ith equation is identified.

Conversely, suppose that the ith equation is identified; by Definition 8, we must then have, in the two systems above, $\beta_{\cdot i} = \bar{\beta}_{\cdot i}$, $\gamma_{\cdot i} = \bar{\gamma}_{\cdot i}$. But this implies that the matrix of the system is nonsingular and it is easy to see [2] that this implies that $\mathrm{rank}(\Pi_{2i}) = m_i$.

q.e.d.

Corollary 2. Let

$$S_i = (\Pi_i, L_{2i}), \qquad E_i = (L_{2i}, \ L_{2i}^*)'S_i, \ \ i = 1, 2, \ldots, m.$$

The following statements are true:

i. $\mathrm{rank}(S_i) = \mathrm{rank}(E_i)$;

ii. $\mathrm{rank}(E_i) = m_i + G_i$, if and only if $\mathrm{rank}(L_{2i}^{*'}\Pi_i) = m_i$, $\quad i = 1, 2, \ldots, m$.

Proof: We first note that

$$E_i = \begin{bmatrix} \Pi_{1i} & I \\ \Pi_{2i} & 0 \end{bmatrix},$$

and, thus, it is the matrix of the system(s) in the proof of part ii of Theorem 5, above. The proof of part i of the corollary is quite evident from the definition of E_i and the fact that $(L_{2i}, \ L_{2i}^*)$ is simply a permutation of the columns of an identity matrix of order G .

As for part ii, note that for $\alpha = (\alpha_{\cdot 1}', \ \alpha_{\cdot 2}')'$, we have

$$E_i\alpha = \begin{bmatrix} \Pi_{1i} & I \\ \Pi_{2i} & 0 \end{bmatrix} \begin{bmatrix} \alpha_{\cdot 1} \\ \alpha_{\cdot 2} \end{bmatrix} = \begin{bmatrix} \Pi_{11}\alpha_{\cdot 1} + \alpha_{\cdot 2} \\ \Pi_{21}\alpha_{\cdot 1} \end{bmatrix}.$$

Consequently, if $\mathrm{rank}(E_i) = m_i + G_i$, then the equation $E_i\alpha = 0$ is satisfied only for $\alpha = 0$; therefore, the equation $\Pi_{2i}\alpha_{\cdot 1} = 0$ is satisfied only for $\alpha_{\cdot 1} = 0$. This implies that $\mathrm{rank}(\Pi_{2i}) = m_i$.

Conversely, suppose $\mathrm{rank}(\Pi_{2i}) = m_i$; then in the condition $E_i\alpha = 0$, we must have $\alpha_{\cdot 1} = 0$. But this immediately implies that $\alpha_{\cdot 2} = 0$ and, hence, that $E_i\alpha = 0$ **is satisfied only with** $\alpha = 0$. But this means that $\mathrm{rank}(E_i) = m_i + G_i$.

q.e.d.

Remark 9. The conditions we have derived in Theorem 5, and especially the condition $\mathrm{rank}(\Pi_{2i}^\circ) = m_i$, is, by far, the most popular characterization of identification in the literature. In many ways this is most unfortunate since the reader is given no indication as to how such condition could possibly be connected with what one would normally understand by the concept of identification. The latter, in turn, is typically put in the following setting:

---

[2] For clarity see the corollary at the end of this proof.

in describing the working of an economic entity by means of a simultaneous equations system, one begins with the proposition that "everything depends on everything else", i.e. one begins in a state of near complete ignorance. One then "obtains" identification by placing restrictions on the elements of the coefficient matrices, B^* and C. These restrictions reflect the economist's substantive knowledge of the entity under study. What "makes" one equation different, or distinguishable, from another is that it is subjected to a different set of restrictions than are other equations. The condition we have obtained earlier, viz.

$$\text{rank} \begin{bmatrix} B_{22}^* \\ C_{22} \end{bmatrix} = m - 1,$$

makes this aspect quite clear, in contrast to the conditions obtained in Theorem 5.

We observe that, referring to the first equation, the matrix above is $(G + m - m_1 - G_1 - 1) \times (m - 1)$. We also note that B_{22}^*, C_{22} are the matrices of coefficients, in the remainder of the system, of the dependent and predetermined variables, respectively, excluded from the first equation. The condition requires that the rank of the matrix be $m - 1$, which is the maximum possible. This, of course, implies the **order condition**

$$G + m - m_1 - G_1 - 1 \geq m - 1.$$

Notice that this means that in each equation we must impose a minimum of m restrictions, including the normalization condition, a fact we had already noted in Remark 8, above. This is just another way of saying that we cannot "include too many" variables or, alternatively, we must place a "sufficient" number of restrictions in each equation. The rank condition, however, states that given the restrictions on the equation we cannot place the "wrong kind" or "too many" restrictions on the remaining equations, in the sense that "too many" of the variables excluded from the first equation are also excluded from them as well, lest they be disturbingly similar to the first. This is the essential meaning of the rank condition. The economist, presumably, has considerable intuition, at the structural level, as to what variables may or may not be included in any given equation. He has, however, relatively little information as to his intuition's implications for the reduced form.

We have now obtained two characterizations of identification, one in terms of the structural, and another in terms of the reduced form. The reader should note that since identification is (separately) equivalent to these two conditions they, in turn, should be equivalent to each other.

For pedagogical reasons, however, we offer an independent proof of equivalence. To reduce excessive discussion for a minor point we confine our attention to the case where no normalization convention has been imposed.

Theorem 6. Consider the system in Eqs. (3.5) and (3.6) and the problem of the identification of the ith equation by exclusion restrictions. The two characterizations

$$\text{rank}\begin{bmatrix} B_{22}^* \\ C_{22} \end{bmatrix} = m - 1, \qquad \text{rank}(\Pi_{21}^\circ) = m_1$$

are equivalent.

Proof: In view of Eqs. (3.19) and (3.20), we can write (for the specific case $i = 1$),

$$\begin{bmatrix} 0 & I \\ \Pi_{21}^\circ & \Pi_{22} \end{bmatrix} \begin{bmatrix} \beta_{\cdot 1}^\circ & B_{12}^* \\ 0 & B_{22}^* \end{bmatrix} = \begin{bmatrix} 0 & B_{22}^* \\ \Pi_{21}^\circ \beta_{\cdot 1}^\circ & C_{22} \end{bmatrix} = \begin{bmatrix} 0 & B_{22}^* \\ 0 & C_{22} \end{bmatrix}. \qquad (3.22)$$

For notational convenience, put

$$A_1 = \begin{bmatrix} 0 & I \\ \Pi_{21}^\circ & \Pi_{22} \end{bmatrix}, \qquad A_2 = \begin{bmatrix} 0 & B_{22}^* \\ 0 & C_{22} \end{bmatrix}, \qquad A_3 = \begin{bmatrix} B_{22}^* \\ C_{22} \end{bmatrix},$$

and note that, in view of Eq. (3.22) and the nonsingularity of B^*, we must have

$$\text{rank}(A_1) = \text{rank}\begin{bmatrix} 0 & B_{22}^* \\ \Pi_{21}^\circ \beta_{\cdot 1}^\circ & C_{22} \end{bmatrix} = \text{rank}(A_2) = \text{rank}(A_3). \qquad (3.23)$$

Moreover, note that A_1 is $(m_1^* + G_1^*) \times m$, and by Eq. (3.23), **its column null space is of the same dimension as that of** A_2. Thus, we have the characterization

$$\nu(A_1) = \{\alpha : A_1\alpha = 0\} = \{\alpha : \alpha = (\bar{\alpha}_{\cdot 1}', 0)', \ \Pi_{21}^\circ \bar{\alpha}_{\cdot 1} = 0\},$$

i.e. the null space of A_1 consists of vectors of the form $\phi^* = (\phi', 0)'$, such that $\phi \in \nu(\Pi_{21}^\circ)$. Now suppose

$$\text{rank}\begin{bmatrix} B_{22}^* \\ C_{22} \end{bmatrix} = m - 1; \qquad (3.24)$$

we need to show that

$$\text{rank}(\Pi_{21}^\circ) = m_1. \qquad (3.25)$$

From Eq. (3.24) we conclude that the dimension of the column null space of A_1 is one; this implies that the **dimension of the column null space of** Π_{21}° **is also one** and, thus, Eq. (3.25) holds.

Conversely, suppose that Eq. (3.25) holds; we will show that Eq. (3.24) is true. Since Eq. (3.25) holds, the dimension of the column null space of the matrix is unity and, by the previous argument, the same is true of A_1. Thus, [3]

$$\text{rank}(A_1) = m - 1.$$

---

[3] This assumes implicitly, as does the entire discussion of Theorem 6, that the **order condition for identification is satisfied**, i.e. that $m_1^* + G_1^* \geq m - 1$.

The conclusion, then, follows immediately from Eq. (3.23).

q.e.d.

3.2.6 Covariance and Cross Equation Restrictions

In previous sections, we considered the identification problem in the classical context. The major concern, therein, was to obtain conditions under which identification of the structural parameters of a given equation, may be established by imposing restrictions on that equation alone, leaving the covariance structure of the error process completely unconstrained. It is interesting to note that many situations arise in which it is natural to impose covariance restrictions; this is the case, for example, in panel data based models, where it is not unreasonable to argue that the error process consists of two components, one relating to the particular individual in the sample, and other pertaining to the time of the observation. In this framework, it is typically asserted that the two components are **independent**. This amounts to a set of covariance restrictions.

In a somewhat different context, when dealing with "rational expectations" models, we encounter **cross equation** restrictions. This arises because, in such models, "expected" quantities are represented as the conditional expectation of the relevant variables, as obtained from the (solution of the) model. Consequently, the representation of an "expected" quantity may well (and typically does) involve parameters from other equations, thus creating cross equation restrictions.

Let us examine first how covariance restrictions may aid in the identification process. Consider again the simple supply-demand model

$$q_t^D = \alpha + \beta p_t + u_{t1}^*, \quad q_t^S = a + b p_t + u_{t2}^*, \quad q_t^D = q_t^S.$$

Making use of the third equation above, and properly normalizing the system, we obtain

$$q_t = \alpha + \beta p_t + u_{t1}^*, \quad p_t = -\frac{a}{b} + \frac{1}{b} q_t - \frac{1}{b} u_{t2}^*.$$

As is evident from the preceding discussion, neither of the two equations above are identified. If it is given that $a = 0$, the second (price) equation is identified but the first (quantity) is not. This is so because the quantity equation cannot be distinguished from a linear combination of the quantity and price equations since, in the standard context, there are no covariance restrictions. Even though, typically, we leave the covariance matrix of the structural errors unrestricted, here we are interested in the question: would restrictions on the latter bring about identification of the first equation? To provide a framework for this discussion, we observe that, in nearly all estimation procedures explored this far, we have made use only of first and second moments. Since we have two variables, we can compute from our sample five moments, viz. the two means $\bar{p}$, $\bar{q}$, and the three second moments s_{qq}, s_{pp}, and s_{pq}, i.e. the sample variance of quantity and price, respectively, and their sample covariance. The model, on the other hand, contains six parameters, viz. b, α, β, σ_{11}, σ_{22}, and σ_{12}, in the obvious notation. Thus, if it is true that $\sigma_{12} = 0$ there is at least the possibility that the model will become completely identified. To this end, we employ the method of moments, in which we use the structure above to write the sample moments of the observables as a function of the uknown parameters. Before we do so, we write the model in the more convenient form,

$$q_t = \alpha + \beta p_t + u_{t1}, \quad p_t = b' q_t + u_{t2},$$

where $u_{t1} = u_{t1}^*$, $b' = (1/b)$, and $u_{t2} = -b' u_{t2}^*$. Although it is somewhat inaccurate, we shall continue to denote the variances of u_{ti}, by σ_{ii}, respectively, $i = 1, 2$. It is still true that $\text{Cov}(u_{t1}, u_{t2}) = 0$.

Omitting terms whose probability limit is **null** as, for example, $\bar{u}_1$, $\bar{u}_2$, the first and second moments of the observables are given by

$$\bar{q} = \alpha + \beta \bar{p}, \quad \bar{p} = b' \bar{q} \tag{3.26}$$

$$s_{qq} = \beta s_{pq} + s_{q1}, \quad s_{qp} = \beta s_{pp} + s_{p1} \tag{3.27}$$

$$s_{pp} = b' s_{pq} + s_{p2}, \quad s_{pq} = b' s_{qq} + s_{q2}, \tag{3.28}$$

where s_{qi} is the sample covariance between q and u_{ti} and s_{pi} is the sample covariance between p and u_{ti}, respectively, $i = 1, 2$. From the second equation of Eq. (3.26) we find $\hat{b}' = (\bar{p}/\bar{q})$. After further manipulation we obtain,

$$\hat{\beta} = \frac{s_{qp} - (\bar{p}/\bar{q}) s_{qq}}{s_{pp} - (\bar{p}/\bar{q}) s_{pq}}, \quad \hat{\alpha} = \bar{q} - \hat{\beta} \bar{p}, \quad \hat{b} = \frac{\bar{q}}{\bar{p}}. \tag{3.29}$$

It is possible to obtain estimators of the variances by substituting the estimators above in Eqs. (3.27) and (3.29); the estimators of the variances, thus obtained, could not be guaranteed to be positive, however. To ensure that, it is preferable to estimate the variances in the standard fashion,

$$\hat{\sigma}_{11} = \frac{1}{T} \sum_{t=1}^{T} (q_t - \hat{\alpha} - \hat{\beta} p_t)^2, \quad \hat{\sigma}_{22} = \frac{1}{T} \sum_{t=1}^{T} (p_t - \hat{b}' q_t)^2. \tag{3.30}$$

Since the sample moments may be easily shown to converge, in probability, to the corresponding parameters, the parameter estimators obtained above will also converge, in probability, to the corresponding parameters. Hence, we have shown how covariance restrictions may aid in identifying the parameters of a model.

Recursive Systems

A case where covariance restrictions play an important role in the identification and estimation of structural parameters, is the recursive model. We have

Definition 9. Consider the standard GLSEM

$$YB^* = XC + U.$$

If the matrix B^* is upper triangular, i.e. $b_{ij}^* = 0$ for $i > j$, and moreover, if Σ is diagonal, the GLSEM is said to be simply recursive.
 Let B^* be a **block** matrix, i.e.

$$B^* = \begin{bmatrix} B_{11}^* & B_{12}^* & \cdots & B_{1n}^* \\ B_{21}^* & B_{22}^* & \cdots & B_{2n}^* \\ \vdots & \vdots & \vdots & \vdots \\ B_{n1}^* & B_{n2}^* & \cdots & B_{nn}^* \end{bmatrix}, \tag{3.31}$$

where each block, B_{ij}^*, is an $s_i \times s_j$ matrix. Partition Σ conformably, i.e. let

$$\Sigma = \begin{bmatrix} \Sigma_{11} & \Sigma_{12} & \cdots & \Sigma_{1n} \\ \Sigma_{21} & \Sigma_{22} & \cdots & \Sigma_{2n} \\ \vdots & \vdots & \vdots & \vdots \\ \Sigma_{n1} & \Sigma_{n2} & \cdots & \Sigma_{nn} \end{bmatrix}, \tag{3.32}$$

where Σ_{ij} is a matrix of dimension $s_i \times s_j$. If $B_{ij}^* = 0$, for $i > j$, **and** $\Sigma_{ij} = 0$, for $i \neq j$, i.e. if B^* is upper block triangular and Σ is block diagonal, the GLSEM is said to be a block recursive system.
 Consider, now, the second equation of a simply recursive system, impose the normalization convention and suppose no other prior restrictions are available. The second equation reads

$$y_{t2} = \beta_{12} y_{t1} + x_t.c_{\cdot 2} + u_{t2}. \tag{3.33}$$

If we apply to this equation, mechanically, the criteria of Theorem 2, particularly the necessary (order) condition of Remark 4, we shall find that $m_2 = 1$, $G_2 = G$. Since, evidently, $m_2 + G_2 > G$, the necessary condition for identification fails, and hence, we should be obliged to conclude that this equation is not identifiable. This, however, would be a gross error and highlights the significance of Remark 2, of Chapter 1. It was stated, therein, that the division between current endogenous and predetermined variables is an artificial one, from the point of view of econometric theory. What is important, in an estimation context, is whether an "explanatory " variable is or is not correlated with (or independent of) the structural error of the equation in which it occurs. To explore this insight let us consider the correlation structure between the vector $y_{t\cdot}$, and the structural error, $u_{t\cdot}$. From the reduced form we find

$$y_{t\cdot} = x_{t\cdot}\Pi + u_{t\cdot}D, \quad D = B^{*-1}. \tag{3.34}$$

Consequently,

$$\text{Cov}(y_{t\cdot}, u_{t\cdot}) = D'\Sigma. \tag{3.35}$$

Since, in the case of a **simply recursive system**, D is **upper triangular** and Σ is **diagonal**, it follows that

$$D'\Sigma = \begin{bmatrix} \sigma_{11}d_{11} & 0 & 0 & \cdots & 0 \\ \sigma_{11}d_{12} & \sigma_{22}d_{22} & 0 & \cdots & 0 \\ \sigma_{11}d_{13} & \sigma_{22}d_{23} & \sigma_{33}d_{33} & \cdots & 0 \\ \vdots & \vdots & \vdots & \cdots & \vdots \\ \sigma_{11}d_{1m} & \sigma_{22}d_{2m} & \sigma_{33}d_{3m} & \cdots & \sigma_{mm}d_{mm} \end{bmatrix}. \tag{3.36}$$

Thus, y_{t1} is not correlated with (or is independent of) u_{ti}, for $i > 1$; in general, Eq. (3.36) shows that y_{ti} is not correlated with (or is independent of) u_{tj}, for $j > i$. It follows, therefore, that, in the ith equation of the system, the y_{tj}, for $j < i$, can be treated as "predetermined" variables. Consequently, **even though no (zero) restrictions are placed on the elements of the matrix** C, all parameters of the ith equation are **identified**. On the other hand, if we apply, mechanically, the results of Theorem 2, we should find that, since $G_i = G$, the necessary (order) condition for identification is violated. The point to be noted, however, is that for this equation the number of "predetermined" variables is (at most) $G + i - 1$, and the number of parameters to be estimated is also (at most) $G + i - 1$. Thus, this equation is certainly identified.

Similarly, in the case of **block recursive systems**, we have

$$D'\Sigma = \begin{bmatrix} D'_{11}\Sigma_{11} & 0 & 0 & \cdots & 0 \\ D'_{12}\Sigma_{11} & D'_{22}\Sigma_{22} & 0 & \cdots & 0 \\ D'_{13}\Sigma_{11} & D'_{23}\Sigma_{22} & D'_{33}\Sigma_{33} & \cdots & 0 \\ \vdots & \vdots & \vdots & \cdots & \vdots \\ D'_{1n}\Sigma_{11} & D'_{2n}\Sigma_{22} & D'_{3n}\Sigma_{33} & \cdots & D'_{nn}\Sigma_{nn} \end{bmatrix}. \tag{3.37}$$

To examine identification issues, more precisely in this context, partition conformably the vectors, $y_{t\cdot}$ and $u_{t\cdot}$,

$$y_{t\cdot} = (y_{t\cdot}^1, y_{t\cdot}^2, \ldots, y_{t\cdot}^n), \quad u_{t\cdot} = (u_{t\cdot}^1, u_{t\cdot}^2, \ldots, u_{t\cdot}^n),$$

where $y_{t\cdot}^i$ and $u_{t\cdot}^i$ are s_i-element row (sub)vectors. The ith subsystem implied by Eq. (3.31) may be written as

$$y_{t\cdot}^i B_{ii}^* = -\sum_{j=1}^{i-1} y_{t\cdot}^j B_{ji}^* + x_{t\cdot}C_{(i)} + u_{t\cdot}^i,$$

where $C = (C_{(1)}, C_{(2)}, \ldots, C_{(n)})$, and each $C_{(i)}$ is a $G \times s_i$ matrix corresponding to the ith subsystem.

The implication of Eq. (3.32) is that, in the subsystem above, the "dependent (explanatory) variables" $y_{t\cdot}^j$, $j < i$, are uncorrelated with (or independent of) $u_{t\cdot}^i$ and hence, in the ith subsystem, may be treated as predetermined variables. Consequently, in deciding on the identifiability of parameters in this (i^{th}) subsystem, only the subset of y's having coefficients in the matrix B_{ii}^* are the "current endogenous" variables.

In both, the simply recursive and block recursive cases, it is rather simple to see how restrictions on the covariance matrix of the system contribute to the identification of parameters. They do so by creating what may be called **equation specific** predetermined variables; precisely, they do so by drawing a sharp distinction between variables that are jointly dependent in an economic sense, i.e. in the sense they are simultaneously determined by the operation of the economic system, and variables that are correlated with (or jointly dependent on) the structural errors. This is close to the concept of weak exogeneity which we shall briefly examine in Chapter 6.

Panel Data Based Models

Panel **data sets** consist of observations over a number of individuals, say N, over several time periods, say T. The typical simultaneous equations model may be of the form

$$y_{ti\cdot}B^* = x_{ti\cdot}C + u_{ti\cdot}, \quad i = 1, 2, \ldots, N, \quad t = 1, 2, \ldots, T. \tag{3.38}$$

In this particular example the (structural) matrices B^* and C do not vary over individuals or time. Some partial variations may be allowed in the form of **fixed effects**. In this discussion, we ignore this aspect and concentrate on the error process specification.

What is indicated by Eq. (3.38) is that (over time) we have T observations on the same number of individuals, N. The vectors $u_{ti\cdot}$ and $y_{ti\cdot}$ each contain m elements, and their j^{th} element pertains to the jth equation; each equation describes certain aspects of the behavior of the individual in question, at time t. If the specification of $u_{ti\cdot}$ is left completely general then for, the entire set of observations, we should be dealing with a covariance matrix of order mTN, containing an impossibly large number of parameters. This alone would have the effect of preventing the identification of parameters in the model. If we look at the typical element of the error vector, i.e. u_{tij} we note that it has three points of reference. It is the disturbance adhering to the jth **equation of the** i^{th} **individual at time** t. It is typically assumed, in such models, that the three effects act **independently and linearly**. Thus, one tends to write $u_{tij} = g_j(\eta_i + \epsilon_t) + \psi_{tij}$, $g = (g_1, g_2, \ldots, g_m)'$, where $\{\eta_i : i = 1, 2, 3, \ldots, N\}$ is a sequence of i.i.d. random variables, with mean zero and variance σ_η^2, $\{\epsilon_t : t = 1, 2, 3, \ldots, T\}$ is, similarly, a zero mean sequence of i.i.d. random variables with variance σ_ϵ^2 and $\{\psi_{ti\cdot} : t = 1, 2, 3, \ldots, T, \; i = 1, 2, \ldots N\}$ is, also, a sequence of zero mean i.i.d. random vectors with covariance matrix Σ. Moreover, the three components are mutually independent. If we write down the observations on this model, lexicographically, ordering first the equations from one to m, in a row, then for **fixed time** ordering individuals from one to N and finally, ordering "time" from one to T, we shall obtain the matrix of error terms, say U, as

$$U = (U'_{(1)}, U'_{(2)}, \ldots, U'_{(T)})', \tag{3.39}$$

where

$$U_{(t)} = (u_{ti\cdot}), \quad i = 1, 2, \ldots, N, \tag{3.40}$$

$u_{ti\cdot}$ being the ith **row of** $U_{(t)}$. From the preceding discussion it follows immediately that

$$
\begin{aligned}
E(u'_{ti\cdot} u_{ti\cdot}) &= (\sigma_\eta^2 + \sigma_\epsilon^2) g g' + \Sigma, \quad \text{for all } i \text{ and } T \\
E(u'_{ti\cdot} u_{ts\cdot}) &= \sigma_\epsilon^2 g g', \quad \text{for all } t \text{ and } s \neq i \\
E(u'_{ti\cdot} u_{t'i\cdot}) &= \sigma_\eta^2 g g', \quad \text{for all } i \text{ and } t \neq t' \\
E(u'_{ti\cdot} u_{t's\cdot}) &= 0, \quad \text{for } t \neq t' \text{ and } s \neq i.
\end{aligned}
\tag{3.41}
$$

In fact, examining the results above, we note that the equation-relevant parameters, g_j, appear **always in conjunction with** σ_η^2 or σ_ϵ^2, or both. For this reason, these parameters cannot be separately identified, which compels us to normalize one of them, for example to take, say $\sigma_\eta^2 = 1$.

The reader desiring more detailed exposition of such matters is referred to Hsiao (1983), (1985).

3.2.7 A More General Framework

In the previous section, we had examined the identification problem in the classical context, in which the chief concern is to obtain conditions under which the parameters of a given equation may be identified by linear restrictions, and we had extended it slightly, by showing how covariance restrictions may help identify structural parameters. This framework does not easily address issues involving, for example, nonlinear restrictions on parameters, or cross equation restrictions that may result from the rational expectations hypothesis, inherent nonlinearities in the parametric structure, general linear restrictions on variances and covariances (see Problem 3), identification of some parameters in a given equation, but not of others, and so on. For these, and other, reasons it may be convenient to create a somewhat broader context. First, note that the basic definition of identifiability, Definition 6, above, leads to the characterization: **all (admissible) observationally equivalent structures are connected by trivial transformations**. Moreover, if normalization is also imposed, the characterization may be amended to read, **all (admissible) observationally**

equivalent structures are connected by identity transformations. In a context in which we either deal with normal distributions, or in the estimation procedures we only employ (functions of) first and second moments of the observables, the characterization above implies that if the reduced form matrix, Π is given, [4] it should be possible to derive, uniquely, the structural parameters of the system. [5] Thus, we have an equivalent characterization of identifiability, viz. that **given Π, the (structural) parameters of a given equation, or of the entire system, are uniquely determined therefrom**.

Consider now the set of observations on the dependent variables, $y_t.$, $t = 1, 2, 3, \ldots, T$ and let $\mathcal{P}$ denote their cumulative distribution function, (cdf). In a broader context, we would wish the structure, say S, to specify completely this cdf, so that given the vector of observations $y = \text{vec}(Y)$, where $Y = (y_{ti})$, the entity $\mathcal{P}(y \mid S)$ can be computed numerically. In the broadest possible context, we may wish S to specify the type of cdf, in addition to whatever parameters may be involved. For our purposes, it will suffice to assume a specific cdf or, if possible, leave it completely unspecified, and confine our attention to whatever parameters may be involved in the first and second moments of the observables, and the structural errors. In such a case, the structure will be indexed by a vector $\theta \in \Theta$ with $\Theta \subseteq R^n$. [6] As in the classical context, there may very well be restrictions, linear or otherwise, placed on the parameter vector θ and, again as in the classical context, structures that obey all prior restrictions are said to be **admissible.** This leads to

Definition 10. In the context above, two admissible structures, $S_1 = S(\theta_1)$, and $S_2 = S(\theta_2)$, are said to be **observationally equivalent** if and only if

$$\mathcal{P}(y \mid S_1) = \mathcal{P}(y \mid S_2),$$

for all observations y.

Since the context is very general, it is conceivable that there may exist more

---

[4] This means, **strictly**, that the true parameter matrix itself, **not its estimate**, is given.

[5] In fact, it is precisely this approach that had been followed in Theorem 5 of the preceding discussion, so that this is not a particularly novel aspect of the framework in the context of which identification is discussed.

[6] The subset Θ, of n-dimensional Euclidean space, R^n, indicates the range of admissible parameters. For example, if one of the elements of θ stands for the variance of one of the structural errors we would expect its range to be $(0, \infty)$. Other parameters may well have a much more restricted range. The point is that numerical values outside the set Θ are simply **not admissible**.

To anticipate a later requirement, we note now that if $\theta^\circ \in \Theta$, an ϵ-neighborhood of θ° is the collection of all points $\theta \in \Theta$, whose distance from θ° is less than $\epsilon > 0$. This entity is usually denoted by $N(\theta^\circ; \epsilon)$.

than one isolated vectors, say θ°, θ^{*}, both in Θ, such that the two admissible structures, say $S^{\circ} = S(\theta^{\circ})$, and $S^{*} = S(\theta^{*})$, are observationally equivalent. This leads to

Definition 11. Let $S^{\circ} = S(\theta^{\circ})$ be an admissible structure; it is said to be **globally identified**, if and only if there does not exist any other (admissible) structure, $S = S(\theta)$, $\theta \in \Theta$, such that $\mathcal{P}(y \mid S) = \mathcal{P}(y \mid S^{\circ})$. If $N(\theta^{\circ}; \epsilon) \subset \Theta$ is an ϵ-neighborhood of θ°, $\epsilon > 0$, the structure S° is said to be **locally identified** if and only if there is no other $\theta \in N$, such that $\mathcal{P}(y \mid S) = \mathcal{P}(y \mid S^{\circ})$.

Remark 10. What is being said in the definition is basically this: given the admissible parameter set Θ, a structure $S^{\circ} = S(\theta^{\circ})$, with $\theta^{\circ} \in \Theta$, is globally identified, if it is admissible and if all observationally equivalent structures, $S(\theta)$, obey $\theta = \theta^{\circ}$. It is locally identified in the ϵ-neighborhood, $N(\theta^{\circ}; \epsilon)$, $\epsilon > 0$, if and only if all admissible observationally equivalent structures, $S(\theta)$, with $\theta \in N$, obey $\theta = \theta^{\circ}$.

Just as a simple exercise, in order to amplify the meaning of these definitions, consider the case of the standard GLSEM, where the parameter matrices are given by $B^{*}(\theta)$, $C(\theta)$, and nothing is known a priori regarding the structural errors' covariance matrix. Moreover, either if normality is assumed, or if we take into account, at most, second moments then the system is identified **globally**, if the structure $(B^{*}(\theta), C(\theta))$ is admissible, and knowledge of Π **uniquely determines** θ, given all prior restrictions. It is said to be identified **locally**, in an ϵ-neighborhood of θ° say N, if the structure is admissible and for $\theta \in N$, knowledge of Π uniquely determines θ, given all prior prior restrictions. The concept of **local identifiction** is not particularly useful since, as we shall see in Chapter 5, in the general nonlinear context desirable properties of estimators are obtained **only** on the assertion that an appropriate function has been extremized. The concept of **local identification** is useful when dealing with **local maxima or minima** but not when dealing with global extrema, as is required in nonlinear problems.

A Mathematical Digression

In the context created above, the mathematical tools needed for identification concern the issue of existence of unique solutions for systems of linear (or nonlinear) equations and certain other implications of the result in Lemma 1. The issue of unique solutions for linear equations is discussed in Chapter 3 of Dhrymes (1984). In this connection we have

Definition 12. Let A be a real matrix of dimension $n \times m$, and b a real n-element (column) vector. The system of linear equations

$$Ax = b,$$

is said to be **consistent** if it has at least one solution. Otherwise, it is said to be **not consistent**.

What does it mean for the system above to be not consistent? To be precise let us suppose that $n \geq m$, and that the rank of A is $r \leq m$. By Proposition 9, in Dhrymes (1984), there exists a nonsingular matrix, say H, that reduces A to an **upper echelon** matrix, i.e.

$$HA = \begin{pmatrix} A_1 \\ 0 \end{pmatrix}, \quad \text{and} \quad \text{rank}(A_1) = r, \tag{3.42}$$

where A_1 is $r \times m$. Thus, the system of equations is reduced to

$$HAx = \begin{pmatrix} A_1 \\ 0 \end{pmatrix} x = \begin{pmatrix} b_1 \\ b_2 \end{pmatrix}. \tag{3.43}$$

If the system above is consistent, we must have $b_2 = 0$. This is so since if, for example $r = m$, A_1 is nonsingular and the solution is unique, i.e. $x = A_1^{-1} b_1$. If $r < m$, we have infinitely many solutions. Hence, if $b_2 = 0$, the system is consistent. If $b_2 \neq 0$, evidently, the system is not consistent, since the last $m - r$ equations read $0 = b_2$, but $b_2 \neq 0$. We can put this result in canonical form by noting that since $b_2 \neq 0$, there exists a vector, say ϕ^* such that $\phi^{*'} b_2 = 1$. The preceding discussion may be summarized in

Lemma 3. Let A be an $n \times m$ matrix and b an n-element column vector, both with real elements. The system of linear equations

$$Ax = b,$$

is **not consistent** if and only if there exists a vector, say ϕ [7] such that $\phi' A = 0$ **and** $\phi' b = 1$.

As we have seen, in the discussion immediately preceding, a consistent system of equations always has **at least one solution**, even if $m \neq n$. The question is: when does it have a unique solution? From Corollaries 20 and 21 in Dhrymes (1984), we find that a unique solution exists if and only if

$$A_g A = I, \tag{3.44}$$

i.e. when the **generalized inverse of** A is a left inverse. This occurs when rank$(A) = m$, in which case the generalized inverse is given by

$$A_g = (A'A)^{-1} A'. \tag{3.45}$$

Hence, we may state the following useful result.

---

[7] In terms of the preceding discussion, take $\phi' = \phi^{*'} H$.

Lemma 4. Consider the system of linear equations of Lemma 3, and suppose $n \geq m$ and rank$(A) = m$. Then, either the system has a **unique solution**, or the system is **not consistent**.

The next two results, below, play a useful role in establishing the identification of (linear) parametric functions.

Lemma 5. Let A be a real matrix of dimension $n \times m$, $n \geq m$, rank $r \leq m$, and define

$$\nu(A) = \{x : Ax = 0\}, \quad \rho(A) = \left\{ y : y' = \sum_{i=1}^{n} c_i a_i \right\}, \qquad (3.46)$$

respectively, the (column) null space, and the row space of the matrix A. The following statements are true:

- i. $\nu(A)$ and $\rho(A)$ are subspaces of R^m, of dimension $m - r$ and r, respectively;

- ii. $\nu(A)$ is **orthogonal** to $\rho(A)$, denoted by $\nu(A) \perp \rho(A)$, i.e. for any $x \in \nu(A)$ and $y \in \rho(A)$, we have $x'y = 0$;

- iii. $\nu(A)$ is the **orthogonal complement of** $\rho(A)$ in R^m, denoted by $R^m = \nu(A) \oplus \rho(A)$, i.e. for every $y \in R^m$ there exists a unique representation

$$y = y_1 + y_2, \quad \text{where} \quad y_1 \in \rho(A), \ y_2 \in \nu(A).$$

Proof: In the proof of i, the fact that the two entities in question are subspaces of R^m is self evident; thus, we concentrate on the proof of dimensions. By a series of row operations, represented by the nonsingular matrix H, we can reduce A to upper echelon form, i.e.

$$HA = \begin{pmatrix} A_1 \\ 0 \end{pmatrix},$$

where A_1 is an $r \times m$ matrix of rank r. Since H is nonsingular, $Ax = 0$ if and only if $HAx = 0$; the latter, however, is valid if and only if $A_1 x = 0$. The dimensions of the two subspaces follow immediately from Lemma 1.

As for the proof of ii and iii, we note that the rows of A span an r-dimensional subspace of R^m, whose elements are of the form $y' = \sum_{i=1}^{m} c_i a_i$, a_i being the ith row of A. Moreover, we note from the definition that $x \in \nu(A)$, if and only if $a_i x = 0$, for all $i = 1, 2, 3, \ldots, m$; this proves ii. By the properties of vector spaces, there exists an **orthogonal basis** for $\rho(A)$, say $\alpha^{(r)} = \{\alpha_{.1}, \alpha_{.2}, \ldots, \alpha_{.r}\}$. Since $\nu(A)$ is **orthogonal to** $\rho(A)$, there exists an orthogonal basis for the former, say $\alpha^{(m-r)} = \{\alpha_{.r+1}, \alpha_{.r+2}, \ldots, \alpha_{.m}\}$, such that the vectors in $\alpha^{(m-r)}$ are **orthogonal** to those in $\alpha^{(r)}$. But then $(\alpha^{(r)}, \alpha^{(m-r)})$ is an orthogonal basis for R^m, and each vector, $y \in R^m$, has a unique representation in this basis as, say, $y = \sum_{i=1}^{r} d_i \alpha_{.i} + \sum_{i=r+1}^{m} d_i \alpha_{.i} = y_1 + y_2$, where, evidently, $y_1 \in \rho(A)$, $y_2 \in \nu(A)$.

q.e.d.

Corollary 3. Let A, B be real matrices of dimension $n \times m$, $q \times m$, respectively, and suppose $\nu(A) \subseteq \nu(B)$. Then, $\rho(B) \subseteq \rho(A)$, i.e. there exists a (unique) matrix H such that $B = HA$.

Proof: It will suffice to show that the dimension of $\rho(B)$ is equal to or less than the dimension of $\rho(A)$, and that if $y \in \rho(B)$ then $y \in \rho(A)$. Since $\nu(A) \subseteq \nu(B)$, let $m - r$ be the dimension of $\nu(A)$; by Lemma 5, the dimension of $\rho(A)$ is r. Consequently, the dimension of $\nu(B)$ is $m - s$, where $s \leq r$, and thus, the dimension of $\rho(B)$ is $s \leq r$. Next, let $y \in \rho(B)$. Since it is also true that $y \in R^m$, we have the representations

$$y = y_1^B + 0, \quad y = y_1^A + y_2^A, \tag{3.47}$$

where $y_1^A \in \rho(A)$ and $y_2^A \in \nu(A)$. If $y_2^A = 0$, the proof is complete; thus, suppose not. Since $\nu(A) \subseteq \nu(B)$ we have that $y_2^A \in \nu(B)$. Since $y_1^A \in R^m$ we have the representation

$$y_1^A = z_1^B + z_2^B, \quad z_1^B \in \rho(B), \quad z_2^B \in \nu(B).$$

If $z_2^B = 0$ then $y_1^A \in \rho(B)$ and we have, in Eq. (3.47), two distinct representations of y in terms of $\rho(B)$ and its orthogonal complement $\nu(B)$, which is a contradiction. Thus, suppose that $z_2(B) \neq 0$; substituting, in the second representation in Eq. (3.47), we find

$$y = z_1^B + z_2^B + y_2^A = z_1^B + z_2^{*B}.$$

Since $z_2^{*B} \neq 0$ (why?), comparison with the first representation in Eq. (3.47) shows two distinct decompositions of the vector y, in terms $\rho(B)$ and its orthogonal complement. This is a contradiction, and implies that $y_2^A = 0$.

q.e.d.

The discussion above does not provide all the tools required to deal with the question of identification for models that are nonlinear in parameters and/or are subject to nonlinear parametric restrictions. For example, if in the standard GLSEM we have $B^*(\theta)$, $C(\theta)$ and the system is subject to the nonlinear restrictions $\Psi(\theta) = \psi$, global identifiability requires that given Π we can find a unique θ satisfying the equations

$$L^{*\circ'} a^* = h, \quad [I \otimes (\Pi, I)] a^* = 0, \quad \phi(\theta) = a^*, \quad \Psi(\theta) = \psi,$$

$$A^* = (B^{*'}, -C')', \quad \phi(\theta) = \text{vec}[A^*(\theta)], \tag{3.48}$$

or, more compactly

$$
\begin{pmatrix} L^{*\circ'} a^* \\ [I \otimes (\Pi, I)] a^* \\ \phi(\theta) \\ \Psi(\theta) \end{pmatrix} = \begin{pmatrix} h \\ 0 \\ a^* \\ \psi \end{pmatrix},
\tag{3.49}
$$

where $h = \text{vec}(H)$, as defined in Corollary 1, $a^* = \text{vec}(A^*)$, and ψ is a constant, independent of θ. The first two sets in Eq. (3.49) is what is required to identify the unrestricted elements of A^*, i.e. ignoring the fact that they depend on θ. The third set indicates the manner in which these parameters depend on θ. The fourth set exhibits the nonlinear restrictions that may have been placed on θ.

It is actually difficult to imagine that *bona fide* constraints are to be placed on the fundamental parameters, θ, although this could well be so in some special cases. In the absence of any *bona fide* restrictions on the underlying parameters,[8] the condition $\Psi(\theta) = \psi$ is best understood as defining the admissible parameter space, i.e. the set $\Theta \subseteq R^n$, of previous discussions. For the most part, however, we shall ignore the fourth set.

What we have in Eq. (3.49) is a transformation from the set of admissible parameters $\Theta \subseteq R^n$ to the reduced form and structural parameters Π and a^*; given Π, the first two sets enable us to determine uniquely the (unrestricted) structural parameters a^*, i.e. unrestricted in that we do not take into account their dependence on θ. The third set ought to be used to determine θ, given a^*. Nothing in the preceding discussion has prepared us for this nonlinear relationship; in particular, we do not know what is required for identification of the underlying parameter θ given information on the (larger) set, a^*. The fourth set we ignore. To reiterate: the first two sets in Eq. (3.49) enable us to determine a^* from Π, and we have dealt with these requirements earlier. The third set should enable us to determine θ given a^*. This is the task to which we now turn.

Lemma 6. Let

$$g : R^s \longrightarrow R^q,$$

and consider the equations

$$g(x, z) = 0,
\tag{3.50}$$

---

[8] In many instances it is true that some fundamental parameters ought to obey certain inequality constraints, such as, for example, a marginal propensity to consume parameter ought to lie in the open interval from zero to one. In actual practice, however, such constraints are not imposed on the estimation procedure, possibly because it is mathematically awkward to do so. Rather, one estimates the model and, if the estimate lies in the admissible space there is no problem; if not, one may think of ways in which one may obtain estimates that are admissible, including the possible imposition of the constraints on the estimating procedure.

where $x \in R^s$ and $z \in R^q$, $q \geq s$. Suppose, further, that

  i. the functions g_i, $i = 1, 2, \ldots, q$, have continuous first order derivatives;

  ii. in an ϵ-neighborhood of x°, $N(x^\circ; \epsilon)$, the Jacobian matrix

$$J(x, z^\circ) = \frac{\partial g}{\partial x}(x, z^\circ), \qquad (3.51)$$

is of rank s, for all $x \in N(x^\circ; \epsilon)$.

Then, x° is uniquely determined, in the sense that if $g(x, z^\circ) = g(x^\circ, z^\circ)$ then $x = x^\circ$.

Proof: Suppose not; then there is an ϵ-neighborhood, $N(x^\circ; \epsilon)$, and $x \in N$ such that $x \neq x^\circ$ and $g(x, z^\circ) = g(x^\circ, z^\circ)$. By the mean value theorem of calculus we have,

$$g(x, z^\circ) = g(x^\circ, z^\circ) + \frac{\partial g}{\partial x}(x^*, z^\circ)(x - x^\circ), \ \mid x^* - x^\circ \mid \leq \mid x - x^\circ \mid,$$

or more conveniently,

$$g(x, z^\circ) - g(x^\circ, z^\circ) = J(x^*, z^\circ)(x - x^\circ). \qquad (3.52)$$

But Eq. (3.52) implies

$$J(x^*, z^\circ)(x - x^\circ) = 0, \quad \text{and} \quad x - x^\circ \neq 0,$$

which, in turn, implies that rank$[J(x^*, z^\circ)] < s$, thus creating a contradiction.

q.e.d.

Remark 11. With a view to further applications of Lemma 6, we note the following. First, we do not need to **assume** that $J(x, z^\circ)$ is of rank s in $N(x^\circ; \epsilon)$. It is sufficient to assume that $J(x^\circ, z^\circ)$ is of rank s. By **the continuity of its elements**, $J(x, z^\circ)$ would be of rank s in some ϵ-neighborhood of x°. Second, the argument, in the proof above, does not give us a unique representation of the difference,

$$x - x^\circ = [J(x^*, z^\circ)]^{-1} [g(x, z^\circ) - g(x^\circ, z^\circ)],$$

unless J is a **square matrix, which in general it will not be.** Third, if an x° exists, such that $g(x^\circ, z^\circ) = g(x, z^\circ)$, the preceding shows that x° is **uniquely determined** by z°. Fourth, it resolves the remaining issue in the identification problem noted above, viz. it gives the necessary and sufficient condition for identifying the parameter θ given a^*. Thus, if the true vector of structural parameters is given by $a^{*\circ} = \phi(\theta^\circ)$ and we seek to establish whether knowledge of $a^{*\circ}$ determines uniquely the true parameter vector θ°, put

$$x = \theta, \quad z^\circ = a^{*\circ}, \quad a^* = \phi(\theta), \quad g(\theta, a^{*\circ}) = \phi(\theta) - a^{*\circ},$$

and note that for θ in a neighborhood of θ°

$$g(\theta, a^{*\circ}) - g(\theta^\circ, a^{*\circ}) = J(\theta^*, a^{*\circ})(\theta - \theta^\circ).$$

If J is of rank n, the dimension of the vector θ, in a neighborhood of θ°, the left member of the equation above is null if and only if $\theta = \theta^\circ$. Thus, locally, θ is uniquely determined by a^*. This supplies the required tool to deal with nonlinear identification problems. It has the disadvantage that it is local in nature. As we shall see in Chapter 5, when we take up general nonlinear issues more fully, there are better ways of attacking this problem. What we have provided above is rooted in the simultaneous equations literature and, though incomplete, it certainly deserves to be pointed out.

Classical Identification in the New Framework

In the framework created above, the structural parameters of an equation, say the ith, are identified (assuming no restrictions on covariances) if and only if, given Π and (all) the prior restrictions, the structural parameters can be uniquely determined. Note that $\Pi B^* = C$ or $(\Pi, I)A^* = 0$; the restrictions on the ith equation, including normalization, are given by

$$L_i^{*\circ'} a_{\cdot i}^* = h_{\cdot i}, \tag{3.53}$$

where $h_{\cdot i}$ is an $m_i^* + G_i^*$-element column vector with zeros everywhere, except for the first element, which is unity. Thus, the structural parameters of the ith equation satisfy the following system of equations

$$\begin{bmatrix} L_{1i}^{*\circ'} & 0 \\ 0 & L_{2i}^{*'} \\ \Pi & I \end{bmatrix} a_{\cdot i}^* = \Phi_i a_{\cdot i}^* = h_{\cdot i}, \tag{3.54}$$

where Φ_i is of order $(G + m_i^* + G_i^*) \times (m + G)$. Notice that such systems as those in Eq. (3.54), above, are necessarily consistent (Why?). The elements of $a_{\cdot i}^*$ are identified, in the new framework, if and only if

$$\operatorname{rank}(\Phi_i) = m + G. \tag{3.55}$$

A necessary condition is

$$G + m_i^* + G_i^* \geq m + G, \quad \text{or} \quad G \geq m_i + G_i,$$

which, of course, agrees with the order condition we had established earlier in Remark 4. We now show that this criterion for identification is equivalent to that given above in the classical framework.

Theorem 7. Consider the system in Eqs. (3.5) and (3.6) and the problem of the identification of the ith equation by exclusion restrictions (and normalization). The three characterizations

$$\text{rank} \begin{bmatrix} B_{22}^* \\ C_{22} \end{bmatrix} = m - 1, \quad \text{rank}(\Pi_{2i}^\circ) = m_i, \quad \text{rank}(\Phi_i) = m + G$$

are equivalent, where Φ_i is as defined in Eq. (3.54).

Proof: Define

$$J_i = \begin{bmatrix} L_{1i} & L_{1i}^{*\circ} & 0 & 0 \\ 0 & 0 & L_{2i} & L_{2i}^* \end{bmatrix}, \tag{3.56}$$

and note that it is a **nonsingular** matrix of order $m + G$. Hence,

$$\text{rank}(\Phi_i J_i) = \text{rank}(\Phi_i). \tag{3.57}$$

On the other hand,

$$\Phi_i J_i = \begin{bmatrix} 0 & I_{m_i^*} & 0 & 0 \\ 0 & 0 & 0 & I_{G_i^*} \\ \Pi_i & \Pi_i^{*\circ} & L_{2i} & L_{2i}^* \end{bmatrix}; \tag{3.58}$$

by means of right multiplication by a nonsingular matrix, say Ψ, we may interchange the positions of the third and second column blocks to obtain,

$$\Phi_i J_i \Psi = \begin{bmatrix} 0 & 0 & I_{m_i^*} & 0 \\ 0 & 0 & 0 & I_{G_i^*} \\ \Pi_i & L_{2i} & \Pi_i^{*\circ} & L_{2i}^* \end{bmatrix} = \Phi_i^*. \tag{3.59}$$

Combining the first and second column blocks of Φ_i^*, and noting that $S_i = (\Pi_i, L_{2i})$, we may write

$$\Phi_i^* = \begin{bmatrix} 0 & I_{m_i^*} & 0 \\ 0 & 0 & I_{G_i^*} \\ S_i & \Pi_i^{*\circ} & L_{2i}^* \end{bmatrix}. \tag{3.60}$$

Evidently, (a) $\text{rank}(\Phi_i^*) = \text{rank}(\Phi_i)$, (b) the three column blocks are linearly independent (relative to each other) and (c) the rank of the last two column blocks is $m_i^* + G_i^*$. It follows immediately that $\text{rank}(\Phi_i^*) = m + G$, if and only if $\text{rank}(S_i) = m_i + G_i$. By Corollary 3, $\text{rank}(S_i) = m_i + G_i$, if and only if $\text{rank}(\Pi_{2i}) = m_i$; by Theorem 5, $\text{rank}(\Pi_{2i}) = m_i$ if and only if the ith equation is identified, and by Theorem 6, this is equivalent to the rank condition on the **structural parameters**, thus completing the demonstration of the equivalence of the three criteria for identification.

q.e.d.

Remark 12. What we have gained by the new framework [9] is greater flexibility in discussing issues of identification. In the classical context, by imposing **first** the prior restrictions and **then** examining issues of identification we make ourselves prisoners of the particular restrictions imposed. This is so since, generally, an approach that works well in a specific context may not work well in another. For example, cross equation restrictions are not easily handled in the classical context, but can be handled rather routinely in this context. Moreover, in this new framework, we can also routinely tackle identification issues involving the entire system, rather than just one equation at a time. In the standard model, identification of the ith equation requires that the system below have unique solution.

$$(\Pi,\ I)a^*_{\cdot i} = 0, \quad L^{*\circ'}_i a^*_{\cdot i} = h_{\cdot i}, \quad i = 1, 2, 3, \ldots, m.$$

Putting $L^{*\circ} = \mathrm{diag}(L^{*\circ}_1, L^{*\circ}_2, \ldots, L^{*\circ}_m)$, we can write the requirements for

---

[9] Actually, even though this framework is new in our discussion, and indeed in many contemporary discussions of the identification problem, it is not new at all. It is the formulation given to the problem by Abraham Wald (1950) who, in a terse **seven page** paper set forth the fundamental ideas for the resolution of the identification problem. To paraphrase him, and express his ideas in our notation, he observed that, in the standard context, the likelihood function (or the second moments of the observables) fundamentally depend on the reduced form coefficient matrix Π, and the reduced form covariance matrix, Ω. Consequently, identification is attained when, given these two matrices, and whatever prior restrictions may be available on the structural matrices B^*, C, and the structural error covariance matrix Σ, a certain system of equations has a unique solution, in terms of the elements of the last three matrices. The system in question consists of two parts; first, that which has to do with restrictions, normalizations and conditions on the structural coefficients, and second, that which has to do with the restrictions, and conditions, that are known to hold relative to the structural error covariance matrix. Precisely, the system is

$$\begin{pmatrix} I \otimes (\Pi,\ I) & 0 \\ L^{*\circ'} & 0 \\ \Psi_1 & 0 \\ (I \otimes B^{*'}\Omega)F & -I \\ 0 & \Psi_2 \end{pmatrix} \begin{pmatrix} a^* \\ \sigma \end{pmatrix} = \begin{pmatrix} 0 \\ h \\ \psi_1 \\ 0 \\ \psi_2 \end{pmatrix},$$

where F is a (row) selection matrix such that $Fa^* = b^*$, $b^* = \mathrm{vec}(B^*)$, $\sigma = \mathrm{vec}(\Sigma)$, $h = \mathrm{vec}(H)$ where, as implicitly defined in Corollary 1, H is a matrix whose first row consists of unities and all other elements are null; the pairs (Ψ_1, ψ_1), (Ψ_2, ψ_2), pertain to any additional restrictions (beyond zero and normalization) on the elements of A^*, and restrictions that may be placed on the elements of Σ, respectively. The last two types of restrictions are generally omitted from most discussions. Since we are dealing with a **nonlinear system of equations**, the condition for a unique (local) solution in an ϵ-neighborhood of a point, say a^0, σ^0, is that the Jacobian matrix be of full column rank at that point.

the identification of the entire system, in a slightly rearranged form, as

$$\begin{pmatrix} I \otimes (\Pi,\, I) \\ L^{*\circ\prime} \end{pmatrix} a^* = \begin{pmatrix} 0 \\ h \end{pmatrix}, \tag{3.61}$$

where h is an appropriate column of zeros and ones, resulting from the exclusion and normalization restrictions. In this case, of course, since we are dealing with the system as a whole, the identification condition is that the matrix in the left member above be of rank $m(m+G)$. Imposition of additional restrictions that cut across equations presents no problem at all. Suppose these restrictions are of the form $\Psi a^* = \psi$. The requirement of identification still remains as stated earlier, viz. that in the system

$$\Phi a^* = \begin{pmatrix} 0 \\ h \\ \psi \end{pmatrix}, \quad \text{where} \quad \Phi = \begin{pmatrix} I \otimes (\Pi,\, I) \\ L^{*\circ\prime} \\ \Psi \end{pmatrix}, \tag{3.62}$$

the matrix Φ be of rank $m(m+G)$. Notice, interpreting the following in a reasonable fashion, that a system which is identified by exclusion restrictions alone **will continue to be identified, even if additional restrictions are imposed.** On the other hand, a system **could very well be not identified by exclusion restrictions alone, but may become identified if additional (valid) restrictions are imposed, say cross equation restrictions**.

Identification of Parametric Functions

In this section we take up the question of the identification of parametric functions of the form, say Pa^*, or on an equation by equation basis, $P_i a^*_{\cdot i}$. We begin with

Definition 13. In the context of the GLSEM of Eqs. (3.5) and (3.6) a set of parametric functions, Pa^*, is said to be **identified** if, given Π and all prior restrictions on the structural parameters, its value is uniquely determined.

In the general context of Eq. (3.62), Definition 13 states that, given Π, and a^* satisfying Eq. (3.62), Pa^* is uniquely determined. It is important to realize that **identification of a^* is not required in order to obtain identification of Pa^***, i.e. **a unique solution to Eq. (3.62) is not necessary for the identification of the parametric functions, Pa**. The criterion for the identification of parametric functions is given by

Theorem 8. In the context of Definition 13 and a GLSEM satisfying Eq. (3.62), the parametric function Pa^*, where P is $n \times m(m+G)$, $n < m(m+G)$, is identified if and only if P lies **in the row space of** Φ, i.e. if there exists a matrix, say Γ such that $P = \Gamma\Phi$.

Proof: Suppose P is in the row space of Φ; given **any** a^* satisfying

$$\Phi a^* = (0, h^{'}, \psi^{'})^{'}, \tag{3.63}$$

we have

$$Pa^* = \Gamma\Phi a^* = \Gamma(0, h^{'}, \psi^{'})^{'}; \tag{3.64}$$

this does not depend on which solution, a^*, is chosen; thus Pa^* is **uniquely determined**.

Conversely, suppose that for every solution a^* of Eq. (3.63), Pa^* is uniquely determined; we show that $P = \Gamma\Phi$, for some matrix Γ. Now, if the system in Eq. (3.63) has unique solution, the proof is complete since Φ is of full rank; thus, suppose $\text{rank}(\Phi) < m(m+G)$ and let a be in the column null space of Φ, i.e. $\Phi a = 0$. If a^* is any solution of Eq. (3.63), and a is in the column null space of Φ, $a + a^*$ is also a solution of Eq. (3.63). Since Pa^* is uniquely determined for any solution to Eq. (3.63), it follows that

$$P(a + a^*) = Pa^*, \quad \text{or} \quad Pa = 0, \quad whenever \quad \Phi a = 0.$$

This implies that the **column null space of** Φ is contained in the column null space of P. But, by Lemma 5 above, the column null space of a matrix is simply the orthogonal complement of its row space. [10] Moreover, by Corollary 3 $\rho(P) \subseteq \rho(\Phi)$, i.e. the row space of Φ contains the row space of P, which implies that there exists a matrix, say Γ, such that $P = \Gamma\Phi$.

q.e.d.

3.2.8 Parametric Nonlinearities and Identification

In this section we examine the question of identification when the system is nonlinear in parameters, i.e.

$$YB^*(\theta) = XC(\theta) + U, \quad \text{or} \quad ZA^* = U, \ Z = (Y, Z). \tag{3.65}$$

The usual exclusion restrictions and normalizations of Conventions 1 and 2 continue to hold, and in addition, we have

$$\phi(\theta) = a^*[= \text{vec}(A^*)], \tag{3.66}$$

---

[10] We recall that, if A is $n \times m$, its column null space is the collection

$$\nu(A) = \{x : Ax = 0\},$$

and as such it is a subspace of m-dimensional Euclidean space. Note also that if $x \in \nu(A)$ then **it is orthogonal to all the rows of** A. Since the row space of A consists of all linear combinations of its rows, it follows that the row space of A, say $\rho(A)$, and its column null space, say $\nu(A)$, are orthogonal complements.

which sets forth the dependence of the structural coefficients on the underlying parameter vector θ. It is assumed that ϕ is continuously differentiable. Note, further, that $a^{*\circ} = \phi(\theta^\circ)$, where θ is the "true" parameter. Identification requirements for this system are given in

Theorem 9. Consider the general simultaneous equations model of Eq. (3.65), and suppose that Conventions 1 and 2 are in effect. In the usual notation, with $z^\circ = (\text{vec}(\Pi^\circ)', a^{*\circ'})'$ define

$$g(\theta, z^\circ) = \begin{bmatrix} L^{*\circ'} a^{*\circ} \\ [I \otimes (\Pi^\circ, I)]a^{*\circ} \\ \phi(\theta) \end{bmatrix} - \begin{bmatrix} h \\ 0 \\ a^{*\circ} \end{bmatrix} = 0. \qquad (3.67)$$

The underlying parameter vector θ is **locally identified**, if (and only if) **given** $\Pi = \Pi^\circ$, and $a^* = a^{*\circ}$

$$J(\theta^\circ, z^\circ) = \frac{\partial \phi}{\partial \theta}(\theta^\circ, z^\circ)$$

is a matrix of rank n (which is the dimension of the vector θ).

Proof: Since nothing is assumed regarding the covariance structure of the problem, local identification is equivalent to being able to determine uniquely, in some appropriate neighborhood, the parameter θ given z°, or given Π° and all relevant prior restrictions on the parameters a^*. Since the relevant restrictions are given in Eq. (3.67), the question is whether the latter determines θ uniquely, given the reduced form matrix Π°. Evidently, the system above is a consistent set of equations so that at least one solution exists. Let this be denoted by θ°. Using the arguments of Lemma 6, we have, for $\theta \in N(\theta^\circ; \epsilon)$, and $\epsilon > 0$,

$$\phi(\theta, z^\circ) - \phi(\theta^\circ, \Pi^\circ) = J(\theta^*, z^\circ)(\theta - \theta^\circ).$$

Since the functions in ϕ are continuously differentiable, it follows that the matrix $J(\theta^*, \Pi^\circ)$ is of rank n, in $N(\theta^\circ; \epsilon)$ where $|\theta^* - \theta^\circ| \leq |\theta - \theta^\circ|$. Thus, $\phi(\theta, z^\circ) - \phi(\theta^\circ, \Pi^\circ) = 0$ if and only if $\theta = \theta^\circ$, completing the proof of sufficiency.

Conversely, suppose the system is locally identified, i.e. if for any $\theta \in N(\theta^\circ; \epsilon)$, $\phi(\theta, z^\circ) - \phi(\theta^\circ, z^\circ) = 0$ if and only if $\theta = \theta^\circ$. This is equivalent to stating that, for $\theta^* \in N$, $J(\theta^*, z^\circ)(\theta - \theta^\circ = 0$, if and only if $\theta = \theta^\circ$.

q.e.d.

In closing this section, we note that identification issues resulting from the imposition of covariance restrictions may easily be placed in the context of Theorem 9. See Problem 3, at the end of this chapter.

3.3 ML Estimation of the RF

3.3.1 General Discussion and ILS

Although the method known as "Indirect Least Squares" (ILS) will be formally discussed in the next chapter, it is useful to examine, now, the basic idea that motivates it, in order to better understand the complexities and the tradeoffs involved in simultaneous equations estimation. By juxtaposing ILS and FIML [11] estimation, we would be better able to understand the attraction of ILS, in the early years of modern econometrics (the 1950s), as a method of estimating structural parameters, and perhaps gain some insight into other related methods, such as **minimum distance** estimators. The latter involve estimation of the structural parameters by solving the problem

$$\min_{B^*,C} \text{tr}[\hat{\Pi} - CB^{*-1}]'W[\hat{\Pi} - CB^{*-1}]$$

where W is an appropriate positive definite "weight" matrix, $\hat{\Pi}$ is the OLS estimate of the unrestricted reduced form, and all prior restrictions are imposed; i.e. the minimization takes place only relative to the elements of the structural matrices on which no restrictions have been placed.

We recall that the model we deal with is $y_t.B^* = x_t.C + u_t.$, $t = 1, 2, 3, \ldots, T$, the reduced form (RF) of which is

$$y_t. = x_t.\Pi + v_t., \quad \Pi = CD, \quad D = B^{*-1}, \quad t = 1, 2, 3, \ldots, T, \quad (3.68)$$

where $\text{Cov}(v_t') = D'\Sigma D$, and we assert that the structural errors, $u_t.$, are i.i.d. random vectors obeying

$$u_t' \sim N(0, \Sigma), \quad \Sigma > 0. \quad (3.69)$$

In estimating the parameters of the model, we can proceed in one of two basic ways: we can treat each equation (or perhaps a block of equations) in isolation, as we did when discussing two stage least squares (2SLS) techniques, or we can estimate all the unknown structural parameters simultaneously as we did in the case of three stage least squares (3SLS).

The two approaches are referred to, respectively, in the context of maximum likelihood techniques, as **limited information maximum likelihood** (LIML) and **full information maximum likelihood** (FIML).

Before considering the derivation of the FIML estimator, we shall give a brief account of the maximum likelihood estimator for the reduced form parameters. This will elucidate the nature of likelihood functions in the case of multiple equations systems and set forth, in a rather simple context, the notation and techniques to be employed in the more complex

---

[11] This acronym means full information maximum likelihood and its meaning will become transparent as the discussion unfolds.

settings involved when we deal with FIML and particularly LIML estimation. Thus, our first task is to obtain the likelihood function with respect to the reduced form. Since the vectors $v_{t.}$ are the basic random variables of the reduced form, we must look to them in formulating the appropriate likelihood function.

In view of Eq. (3.69) the joint distribution (likelihood function) of such vectors is given by

$$p(v_{1.}, v_{2.}, \ldots, v_{T.}) = \prod_{t=1}^{T}[(2\pi)^{-m/2} \mid \Omega \mid^{-1/2} \exp(-1/2)v_{t.}\Omega^{-1}v_{t.}']. \quad (3.70)$$

Unfortunately, however, the form given in Eq. (3.70) is not a very useful one. First, it does not include all the parameters of interest; in particular, it does not contain the matrix Π. Second, it **does not contain any observable quantities**. It is clear, then, that it cannot possibly be used to make any inference about, i.e. estimate, the reduced form parameters of interest. Yet this difficulty is easily removed by the simple transformation

$$v_{t.} = y_{t.} - x_{t.}\Pi \quad (3.71)$$

so that we no longer deal with the $v_{t.}$ but rather the $y_{t.}$. This transformation corrects the two deficiencies of the likelihood function as exhibited in Eq. (3.70). First, it introduces the reduced form parameter matrix Π and, second, in the place of the unobservable $v_{t.}$ it introduces the observable quantities $y_{t.}$ and $x_{t.}$.

Since Eq. (3.70) is the joint density of the $v_{t.}$, and the Jacobian of the transformation in Eq. (3.71) is unity, the joint density of the $y_{t.}$ is given by

$$p(\Pi, \Omega) = (2\pi)^{-mT/2} \mid \Omega \mid^{-T/2} \exp\left\{-\frac{1}{2}\sum_{t=1}^{T}(y_{t.} - x_{t.}\Pi)\Omega^{-1}(y_{t.} - x_{t.}\Pi)'\right\}.$$
$$(3.72)$$

In view of the relations in Eq. (3.68), we see that the joint density of the current endogenous variables, conditioned on the predetermined ones, embodies all the information conveyed by the sample on the structure's entire set of parameters. It is important that this fact be clearly understood, as well as the fact that Eq. (3.72) is the basic likelihood function, whether one deals with problems of ILS, RF, FIML or LIML estimation.

Let us explain why this is so. First, we note that as a matter of notation we can write

$$\sum_{t=1}^{T}(y_{t.} - x_{t.}\Pi)\Omega^{-1}(y_{t.} - x_{t.}\Pi)' = \operatorname{tr}(Y - X\Pi)\Omega^{-1}(Y - X\Pi)', \quad (3.73)$$

and, using Eq. (3.68), we see that

$$(Y - X\Pi)\Omega^{-1}(Y - X\Pi)' = (Y - X\Pi)B^*\Sigma^{-1}B^{*'}(Y - X\Pi)'$$

$$= (YB^* - XC)\Sigma^{-1}(YB^* - XC)'.$$

Moreover, $|\Omega|^{-1} = |B^{*'}B^*||\Sigma|^{-1}$. Thus, as a **matter of notational change only**, we can rewrite Eq. (3.72) as

$$p(B^*, C, \Sigma) = (2\pi)^{-mT/2}|\Sigma|^{-T/2}|B^{*'}B^*|^{T/2} \tag{3.74}$$

$$\times \exp\left\{-\frac{1}{2}\sum_{t=1}^{T}(y_{t.}B^* - x_{t.}C)\Sigma^{-1}(y_{t.}B^* - x_{t.}C)'\right\}.$$

We can easily verify that Eq. (3.74) is the likelihood function we shall obtain, when we operate **directly** with the joint density of the structural disturbances, and then effect the transformation

$$u_{t.} = y_{t.}B^* - x_{t.}C, \tag{3.75}$$

whose Jacobian is $|B^{*'}B^*|^{1/2}$. Two features of the likelihood function should be noted. First, notice that in Eq. (3.74) the structural parameters enter in a highly nonlinear fashion through the Jacobian term $|B^{*'}B^*|^{1/2}$. Second, observe that the parameters of the reduced form enter the likelihood function, as expressed in Eq. (3.72), in a rather simple manner. These observations contain the essential elements of the two procedures we consider in this section, viz. ILS and FIML. In ILS, we seek to estimate the structural parameters, i.e. the (uknown) elements of B^* and C by first estimating, without restrictions, the elements of the matrix Π; we then use these estimators in seeking to make inferences concerning the structural parameters of interest. Under this scheme, we operate with the likelihood function as exhibited in Eq. (3.72) and treat the elements of Π as free parameters. That is, we neglect the relations conveyed by Eq. (3.68), and the fact that *a priori* restrictions on B^* and C will, in general, imply some restrictions on $\Pi = CB^{*-1}$.

In FIML, by constrast, we make use of all *a priori* restrictions, we operate with the likelihood function as exhibited in Eq. (3.74), and we seek to estimate the unknown structural parameters by directly maximizing that function.

Clearly, under some circumstances the two procedures are equivalent, but this will not always be so; indeed, typically, it will not be. On the other hand, it is important to realize that ILS uses exactly the same likelihood function as FIML, but deals instead with a **reparametrized** problem, i.e. it deals with the estimation of Π, and attempts to recover from it information about the structural parameters. In the ILS framework, we have to estimate the Gm elements of Π, and infer therefrom estimators for B^*

and C, given the *a priori* restrictions. The original problem, and the FIML framework, involves the direct estimation of the unknown structural parameters; according to our convention, there are $G_i + m_i$ unknown structural parameters in the "right hand side" of the ith equation. If the necessary conditions for identifiability are satisfied for all equations, the number of unknown structural parameters in the system obeys

$$\sum_{i=1}^{m}(G_i + m_i) \leq Gm. \tag{3.76}$$

Thus, in the reparametrized problem dealt with by ILS, we are called upon to estimate a number of parameters that are a well-defined function of a smaller number of structural parameters. One does this because the new parametric representation makes the logarithm of the likelihood function **quadratic** in Π, and it is rather simple to maximize quadratic functions. The price paid for this is that we estimate a larger set of parameters than we need to and, if just identifiability conditions do not hold, it is not possible to recover (uniquely) from reduced form estimators information concerning the structural parameters. [12] In the FIML scheme of estimation, we estimate the unknown structural parameters directly, but then we have to contend with a likelihood function which, in its logarithmic form, contains the **highly nonlinear term** $\ln \mid B^{*'} B^* \mid$.

To conclude this preliminary exposition, ILS estimation of structural parameters purchases simplicity at the cost of proliferating the number of parameters estimated; ILS cannot produce unique structural estimators unless the equations of the system are just identified.

On the other hand, FIML estimation economizes on the number of parameters to be estimated, at the cost of dealing with a more complex form of the likelihood function.

3.3.2   Estimation of the Reduced Form

We now return to the problem of estimating the (unrestricted) reduced form matrix Π. In view of Eq. (3.68) and Eq. (3.73), we may write the logarithm of the likelihood function as

$$L(\Pi, \Omega) = -\frac{mT}{2}\ln(2\pi) - \frac{T}{2}\ln \mid \Omega \mid -\frac{1}{2}\mathrm{tr}\Omega^{-1}(Y - X\Pi)'(Y - X\Pi). \tag{3.77}$$

Differentiating with respect to π_{rs}, $r = 1, 2, \ldots, G$, $s = 1, 2, \ldots, m$, we obtain the first order conditions, see Dhrymes (1984) Section 4.3,

$$\frac{\partial L}{\partial \Pi} = X'X\Pi\Omega^{-1} - X'Y\Omega^{-1} = 0.$$

---

[12] This may be done by solving $\hat{\Pi}B^* = C$, for the unknown elements of B^* and C, given the prior restrictions and normalizations. Except for the case of **just identification** unique ILS estimators are not available.

Since Ω is nonsingular, we conclude

$$\hat{\Pi} = (X'X)^{-1}X'Y. \tag{3.78}$$

That $\hat{\Pi}$, of Eq. (3.78), represents a maximum is ensured by the fact that L is a concave function of Π. We also note that $\hat{\Pi}$ of Eq. (3.78) is exactly the OLS estimator. This is, of course, not surprising, for it is apparent from the LF and Proposition 89 in Dhrymes (1984), that maximization of Eq. (3.77) is equivalent to **minimization** of

$$\psi = \sum_{t=1}^{T}(y_{t\cdot} - x_{t\cdot}\Pi)\Omega^{-1}(y_{t\cdot} - x_{t\cdot}\Pi)' = \text{tr}(Y - X\Pi)\Omega^{-1}(Y - X\Pi)'$$

$$= (y - X^*\pi)'\Phi^{-1}(y - X^*\pi), \tag{3.79}$$

where,

$$y = \text{vec}(Y) = \left(y'_{\cdot 1}, y'_{\cdot 2}, \dots, y'_{\cdot m}\right)', \quad X^* = I_m \otimes X,$$

$$\pi = \text{vec}(\Pi) = \left(\pi'_{\cdot 1}, \pi'_{\cdot 2}, \dots, \pi'_{\cdot m}\right)', \quad \Phi^{-1} = \Omega^{-1} \otimes I_T, \tag{3.80}$$

$y_{\cdot i}$ and $\pi_{\cdot j}$ being, respectively, the ith and j^{th} columns of Y and Π. But minimization of Eq. (3.79) with respect to the elements of π yields their **Aitken estimator** and thus the Aitken estimator of Π. As shown in Ch. 3 of Dhrymes (1978), when all equations of a system contain the same "explanatory" varia bles, Aitken and OLS estimators **coincide**. Since, as we see from Eq. (3.78), the maximum likelihood estimator of Π does not depend on Ω, it follows quite easily that an estimator of the latter can be obtained by maximizing the **concentrated** likelihood function

$$L(\Omega) = -\frac{mT}{2}\ln(2\pi) + \frac{T}{2}\ln |\Omega^{-1}| - \frac{T}{2}\text{tr}\Omega^{-1}W \tag{3.81}$$

where

$$(w_{ij}) = W = \frac{1}{T}(Y - X\hat{\Pi})'(Y - X\hat{\Pi}) = \frac{1}{T}Y'[I - X(X'X)^{-1}X']Y. \tag{3.82}$$

We observe

$$\text{tr}\,\Omega^{-1}W = \sum_{i=1}^{m}\sum_{j=1}^{m}\omega^{ij}w_{ji}. \tag{3.83}$$

Now, since there is a unique relation between the elements of Ω and Ω^{-1}, it is immaterial whether we maximize with respect to the elements of $\Omega = (\omega_{ij})$ or those of $\Omega^{-1} = (\omega^{ij})$. Evidently, in the case of Eq. (3.81) it is much simpler to maximize with respect to the elements of Ω^{-1}, i.e. the ω^{ij}. The first order conditions for this operation are

$$\frac{\partial L}{\partial \Omega^{-1}} = \frac{T}{2}\Omega - \frac{T}{2}W = 0,$$

a result that follows easily from Propositions 98 and 102 in Dhrymes (1984), and the fact that W is symmetric. Thus, the ML estimator of Ω is

$$\hat{\Omega} = S = \frac{1}{T} Y' N Y, \qquad N = I - X(X'X)^{-1} X'. \qquad (3.84)$$

To derive the covariance matrix of the reduced form estimator it is more convenient to revert to the notation of Eq. (3.79) and write the reduced form as

$$y = X^* \pi + v, \qquad v = (v'_{.1}, v'_{.2}, \dots, v'_{.m})', \qquad (3.85)$$

the $v_{.i}$ being the ith column of V, $i = 1, 2, \dots, m$. Evidently, the OLS (and Aitken) estimator of π is

$$\hat{\pi} = (X^{*'} X^*)^{-1} X^{*'} y = \pi + (X^{*'} X^*)^{-1} X^{*'} v. \qquad (3.86)$$

Since $\text{Cov}(v) = \Omega \otimes I_T = \Phi$, it follows immediately that

$$\hat{\pi} \sim N\left(\pi, \ \Omega \otimes (X'X)^{-1}\right). \qquad (3.87)$$

Furthermore, the marginal distribution of the ith subvector of π (and hence the marginal distribution of the parameters in the ith equation of the reduced form) is given by $\hat{\pi}_{.i} \sim N\left(\pi_{.i}, \omega_{ii}(X'X)^{-1}\right)$. It is clear from the preceding that the (unrestricted) reduced form of a GLSEM is simply a set of general linear models, with the requirement that all equations contain the same right hand variables.

3.4 FIML Estimation

We now turn to the problem of estimating the structural parameters of the system by maximizing directly the likelihood function as exhibited in Eq. (3.74) or, equivalently, its logarithm as exhibited in Eq. (3.77).

As a matter of notation, we have

$$\psi = \sum_{t=1}^{T} (y_{t.} B^* - x_{t.} C) \Sigma^{-1} (y_{t.} B^* - x_{t.} C)' = \text{tr}(Z A^* \Sigma^{-1} A^{*'} Z')$$

$$= T \text{tr} \, \Sigma^{-1} A^{*'} M A^*, \qquad (3.88)$$

where $M = (1/T) Z'Z$, $A^* = (B^{*'}, -C')'$, $Z = (Y, \ X)$ it being understood that, apart from normalization, all a priori restrictions on the elements of B^* and C have now been imposed so that these matrices contain some elements that are known to be zero. Thus, we may write the LF, more conveniently, as

$$L(B^*, C, \Sigma; Y, X) = -\frac{mT}{2} \ln(2\pi) - \frac{T}{2} \ln |\Sigma| + \frac{T}{2} \ln |B^{*'} B^*|$$

$$- \frac{T}{2} \text{tr} \, \Sigma^{-1} A^{*'} M A^*. \qquad (3.89)$$

To maximize L with respect to the unknown elements of B^*, C and with respect to Σ, we proceed stepwise; we first obtain an estimator for Σ in terms of the unknown parameters of A. Inserting this maximizing value of Σ in Eq. (3.89), we obtain the "concentrated" likelihood function, which is now solely [13] a function of A^*. The final step consists in maximizing the "concentrated" likelihood function with respect to A^*.

Let us now see what this procedure involves. Proceeding exactly as we did just prior to Eq. (3.84) above, we find that maximizing Eq. (3.89) with respect to σ^{ij}, $i,j = 1, 2, \ldots, m$ yields

$$\hat{\Sigma} = A^{*'} M A^*. \tag{3.90}$$

Inserting Eq. (3.90) in Eq. (3.89) we find the "concentrated" likelihood function

$$L(B^*, C; Y, X) = -\frac{mT}{2}[\ln(2\pi) + 1] + \frac{T}{2}\ln \mid B^{*'} B^* \mid -\frac{T}{2}\ln \mid A^{*'} M A^* \mid \tag{3.91}$$

which is now to be maximized with respect to the unknown elements of B^* and C. It is apparent from Eq. (3.91) that the unknown parameters enter the likelihood function in a highly nonlinear fashion. This precludes our finding an explicit expression for the estimators of B^* and C; the equations of the first order conditions can be solved only by iterative methods. Many algorithms are available for the solution of such sets of equations. Their major drawback is that, unless the LF is **strictly concave**, they do not guarantee that upon convergence we have found the solution corresponding to the *maximum maximorum*, but only to a **local maximum**. Strictly speaking this **is not** what the ML procedure seeks to attain.

Now, assuming that such estimators can be obtained, what are their probabilistic properties?

Although in Chapter 5 we shall examinine the ML estimator in a general nonlinear context, it will suffice for the present to appeal to the general theory of maximum likelihood in a simpler context, and assert that maximum likelihood estimators are consistent and asymptotically efficient, in the minimum variance bound (MVB) sense. Moreover, their asymptotic distribution is normal. If we put

$$\delta = (\delta'_{.1}, \delta'_{.2}, \ldots, \delta'_{.m})', \quad \delta'_{.i} = (\beta'_{.i}, \gamma'_{.i}), \tag{3.92}$$

---

[13] We remind the reader that, in this context, one does not suppose any *a priori* knowledge concerning the covariance matrix $\Sigma = (\sigma_{ij})$, so that all that is asserted about Σ is that it is a positive definite symmetric matrix. On the other hand, if prior information is available, in the form of zero covariance restrictions, there is no reason why it could not be incorporated. In this case, maximization will take place **only with respect to the uknown or unrestricted elements of** Σ.

where $\beta_{.i}$ and $\gamma_{.i}$ represent the (unknown) structural coefficients of the ith equation (after the standard normalization has been imposed), it will be shown, at the end of this chapter that asymptotically,

$$\sqrt{T}(\hat{\delta} - \delta^0) \sim N(0, \Psi), \tag{3.93}$$

where

$$\Psi = - \left[\operatorname*{plim}_{T\to\infty} \frac{1}{T} \frac{\partial^2 L}{\partial\delta\partial\delta}(\delta^0)\right]^{-1}, \tag{3.94}$$

L is the concentrated LF of Eq. (3.91), $\hat{\delta}$ is the FIML estimator of δ, and δ^0 is the true parameter vector.

3.5 Simplified FIML Estimators

Although the discussion in the previous section has dealt with the problem in complete generality, it is clear that the FIML estimator is rather difficult to obtain in practice. Write the concentrated likelihood function of Eq. (3.91) in the equivalent, but more useful form,

$$L(B^*, C; Y, X) = -\frac{mT}{2}[\ln(2\pi) + 1] - \frac{T}{2}\ln|W| \tag{3.95}$$

$$+ \frac{T}{2}\ln|B^{*'}WB^*| - \frac{T}{2}\ln|\Sigma|$$

where, of course,

$$W = \frac{1}{T}Y'NY, \quad N = I - X(X'X)^{-1}X', \quad \Sigma = A^{*'}MA^*. \tag{3.96}$$

Putting

$$P = B^{*'}WB^* \tag{3.97}$$

we see that, after the standard normalization and all a priori restrictions have been imposed, the typical elements of P and Σ, respectively, p_{ij} and s_{ij} are given by

$$p_{ij} = \frac{1}{T}(y_{.i} - Y_i\beta_{.i})'N(y_{.j} - Y_j\beta_{.j}) \tag{3.98}$$

$$s_{ij} = \frac{1}{T}(y_{.i} - Z_i\delta_{.i})'(y_{.j} - Z_j\delta_{.j}), \quad i, j = 1, 2, \ldots, m.$$

To explore the problem of simplification for the FIML estimator it is convenient to reintroduce the selection matrices we employed earlier. Thus, recall that L_{1i}° is an $m \times (m_i + 1)$ selection matrix such that

$$b_{.i}^* = L_{1i}^\circ\beta_{.i}^\circ, \quad YL_{1i}^\circ = (y_{.i}, \ Y_i) = Y_i^\circ, \tag{3.99}$$

$$\operatorname{rank}(L_{1i}^\circ) = m_i + 1, \quad i = 1, 2, 3, \ldots, m,$$

where $b_{\cdot i}^*$ is the ith column of B^* and

$$\beta_{\cdot i}^\circ = (1 - \beta_{\cdot i}')', \quad i = 1, 2, 3, \ldots, m. \tag{3.100}$$

Similarly, recall that L_{2i} is a $G \times G_i$ selection matrix such that

$$X L_{2i} = X_i, \quad \text{rank}(L_{2i}) = G_i, \quad c_{\cdot i} = L_{2i}\gamma_{\cdot i}, \quad i = 1, 2, 3, \ldots, m.$$

If we put

$$\delta_{\cdot i}^\circ = (\beta_{\cdot i}^{\circ\prime}, -\gamma_{\cdot i}')', \ i = 1, 2, \ldots, m \tag{3.101}$$

we easily verify that the ith column of A^* may be written as

$$a_{\cdot i}^* = (b_{\cdot i}^{*\prime} - c_{\cdot i}')' = L_i^\circ \delta_{\cdot i}^\circ, \quad \delta_{\cdot i}^\circ = (1 - \delta_{\cdot i}')', \tag{3.102}$$

the last equation in Eq. (3.102) reflecting the standard normalization. We further note that, if we put

$$\overline{L}_{1i}^\circ = [L_{1i}^\circ, 0], \quad \overline{L}_{2i}^\circ = [0, \ L_{2i}] \tag{3.103}$$

where $\overline{L}_{1i}^\circ$ is $m \times (m_i + G_i + 1)$, L_{2i}° is $G \times (m_i + G_i + 1)$ we have

$$L_i^\circ = \begin{bmatrix} \overline{L}_{1i}^\circ \\ \overline{L}_{2i}^\circ \end{bmatrix}, \quad L^\circ = \text{diag}(L_1^\circ, L_2^\circ, \ldots, L_m^\circ).$$

Finally, if we wish the L_{ij} to refer **only** to parameters not under normalization, i.e. to parameters corresponding to "right hand" variables, it is easily seen that we should deal with L_{1i} and L_{2i} defined by

$$YL_{1i} = Y_i, \quad XL_{2i} = X_i, \quad b_{\cdot i} = L_{1i}\beta_{\cdot i}, \quad c_{\cdot i} = L_{2i}\gamma_{\cdot i}$$
$$B^* = I - B, \quad B = (b_{\cdot 1}, b_{\cdot 2}, \ldots, b_{\cdot m}), \quad L = \text{diag}(L_1, L_2, \ldots, L_m),$$
$$\overline{L}_{1i} = (L_{1i}, 0) \quad \overline{L}_{2i} = (0, \ L_{2i}) \quad L_i = \begin{bmatrix} \overline{L}_{1i} \\ \overline{L}_{2i} \end{bmatrix},$$

such that $\overline{L}_{1i}$ is $m \times (m_i + G_i)$, $\overline{L}_{2i}$ is $G \times (m_i + G_i)$ and so on.

Generally, the superscripted notation, say L_{1i}° or L_i° , differs from the nonsuperscripted notation, say L_{1i} or L_i , in that the latter **is simply the former, without its first column**, which corresponds to the coefficient being normalized in the ith equation; hence, L_{1i} , L_i have exactly the same number of rows as L_{1i}° , L_i° , respectively, but have **one less column** due to the fact that the variable whose coefficient is normalized to be unity, is now a "left hand" and not a "right hand" variable. With the aid of this notation we can easily write

$$\text{vec}(A^*) = L^\circ \delta^\circ, \quad B^* = I^* A^*, \quad I^* = (I_m, 0_{m \times G}), \quad \text{vec}(B^*) = (I \otimes I^*)L^\circ \delta^\circ, \tag{3.104}$$

where

$$\delta^{\circ'} = (\delta^{\circ'}_{\cdot 1}, \delta^{\circ'}_{\cdot 2}, \delta^{\circ'}_{\cdot 3}, \dots, \delta^{\circ'}_{\cdot m})'. \tag{3.105}$$

This will enable us to give a convenient representation to the first order conditions of FIML. Specifically, we have

$$\frac{\partial L}{\partial \delta} = -\frac{T}{2} \left[\frac{\partial \ln |A'MA|}{\partial \delta} - \frac{\partial \ln |B^{*'}WB^{*}|}{\partial \delta} \right] = 0, \tag{3.106}$$

where

$$\delta' = (\delta'_{\cdot 1}, \delta'_{\cdot 2}, \dots, \delta'_{\cdot m})', \tag{3.107}$$

i.e. it is δ°, after the removal of all normalized coefficients and a sign change.

Using Proposition 104, Corollaries 36 and 37 in Dhrymes (1984), we note that if, in $F = G'HG$, H is symmetric, the elements of the matrix G are functions of a vector, say α, and F is nonsigular,

$$\frac{\partial \ln |F|}{\partial \alpha} = 2\mathrm{vec}(G)'(F^{-1} \otimes H)\frac{\partial \mathrm{vec}(G)}{\partial \alpha}. \tag{3.108}$$

With Eqs. (3.108) and (3.104) in mind, we conclude

$$\frac{\partial \ln |A'MA|}{\partial \delta} = 2\mathrm{vec}(A)'(\Sigma^{-1} \otimes M)L^{\circ}\frac{\partial \delta^{\circ}}{\partial \delta}$$

$$\frac{\partial \ln |B^{*'}WB^{*}|}{\partial \delta} = 2\mathrm{vec}(B^{*})'(P^{-1} \otimes W)(I \otimes I^{*})L^{\circ}\frac{\partial \delta^{\circ}}{\partial \delta}. \tag{3.109}$$

It is easy to see that

$$\frac{\partial \delta^{\circ}_{\cdot i}}{\partial \delta_{\cdot j}} = 0, \qquad i \neq j$$

$$= \begin{bmatrix} 0 \\ -I_{mi+Gi} \end{bmatrix}, \quad i = j \tag{3.110}$$

and, consequently,

$$L^{\circ}\frac{\partial \delta^{\circ}}{\partial \delta} = -L. \tag{3.111}$$

Writing Eq. (3.109) in the more customary column form, making use of Eq. (3.98), and giving effect to the standard normalization, we can rewrite Eq. (3.106) as

$$\sum_{j=1}^{m} s^{ij} Z'_i(y_{\cdot j} - Z_j\delta_{\cdot j}) - \sum_{j=1}^{m} p^{ij} \bar{Z}'_i N(y_{\cdot j} - \bar{Z}_j\delta_{\cdot j}) = 0, \ i = 1, 2, 3, \dots, m$$

$$\tag{3.112}$$

where $Z_i = (Y_i, \; X_i)$, $\bar{Z}_i = (Y, \; 0)$ or, more compactly, as

$$[Z^{*'}(\Sigma^{-1} \otimes I_T)Z^* - \bar{Z}^{*'}(P^{-1} \otimes I_T)\bar{Z}^*]\delta = [Z^{*'}(\Sigma^{-1} \otimes N) - \bar{Z}^{*'}(P^{-1} \otimes N)]y \tag{3.113}$$

where

$$Z^* = \text{diag}(Z_1, Z_2, \ldots, Z_m), \qquad \bar{Z}^* = \text{diag}(\bar{Z}_1, \; \bar{Z}_2, \ldots, \bar{Z}_m) \tag{3.114}$$

Remark 13. The expression in Eq. (3.113) obscures the complexity of the problem since the unknown parameter, δ, enters the matrices P and Σ and this is not made clear by the notation. On the other hand, and more importantly, it suggests a two step procedure similar in spirit to the 3SLS estimator. If an initial consistent estimator of δ is available, say $\tilde{\delta}$, we can use it to estimate the elements of Σ and P, thus obtaining, say, $\tilde{\Sigma}, \tilde{P}$. The substitution of these consistent estimators therein renders the relations of Eq. (3.113) linear in δ. If the matrix of the system is nonsingular, then we may obtain the two step simplified FIML estimator.

An alternative simplified estimator can be obtained by a version of the so-called method of scoring. The latter, first suggested by Fisher (1950), and Rao (1950), applies to all ML problems and is, thus, not confined to FIML in this context, nor does it take into account the specific features of the GLSEM whose parameters we seek to estimate. If, in this discussion, we denote by $L_T(\theta)$, the log likelihood function, divided by T, and by θ the parameter set of interest, we observe that the ML estimator of θ, say $\hat{\theta}$, satisfies (normally)

$$\frac{\partial L_T}{\partial \theta}(\hat{\theta}) = 0.$$

If θ^0 is the true parameter point, we can write, by the mean value theorem,

$$\frac{\partial L_T}{\partial \theta}(\hat{\theta}) = \frac{\partial L_T}{\partial \theta}(\theta^0) + \frac{\partial^2 L}{\partial \theta \partial \theta}(\bar{\theta})(\hat{\theta} - \theta^0); \tag{3.115}$$

$\bar{\theta}$ is a point lying between θ and θ^0, i.e. $|\bar{\theta} - \theta^0| \leq |\hat{\theta} - \theta^0|$. Strictly speaking, the method of scoring proceeds as above, **after** replacing the Hessian in Eq. (3.115) by its expected value, although we shall not do so in this exposition.

We can arrive at the estimator by beginning from an initial point, say $\theta_{(0)}$, and ask what correction to $\theta_{(0)}$ will make the right member of Eq. (3.115) zero, i.e. we set [14]

$$0 = \frac{\partial L_T}{\partial \theta}(\theta_{(0)}) + \frac{\partial^2 L_T}{\partial \theta \partial \theta}(\theta_{(0)})(\theta - \theta_{(0)}).$$

---

[14] Incidentally, in the discriminant analysis literature the elements of $\partial L/\partial \theta$ are said to be the efficient scores; hence, the term **method of scoring**.

Solving for θ we find, say,

$$\theta_{(1)} = \theta_{(0)} - \left[\frac{\partial^2 L_T}{\partial\theta\partial\theta}(\theta_{(0)})\right]^{-1} \frac{\partial L_T}{\partial\theta}(\theta_{(0)});$$

repeating we have, generally,

$$\theta_{(k)} = \theta_{(k-1)} - \left[\frac{\partial^2 L_T}{\partial\theta\partial\theta}(\theta_{(k-1)})\right]^{-1} \frac{\partial L_T}{\partial\theta}(\theta_{(k-1)}) \qquad (3.116)$$

provided the matrix

$$\frac{\partial^2 L_T}{\partial\theta\partial\theta}(\cdot)$$

remains nonsingular.

Upon convergence, i.e. when $\theta_{(n)} \approx \theta_{(n-1)}$, within the convergence criterion, we have found a vector which, for all intents and purposes, is a solution of

$$\frac{\partial L_T}{\partial\theta} = 0.$$

This is so since if in Eq. (3.116) $\theta_{(n)} \approx \theta_{(n-1)}$ then,

$$\left[\frac{\partial^2 L_T}{\partial\theta\partial\theta}(\theta_{(n-1)})\right]^{-1} \frac{\partial L_T}{\partial\theta}(\theta_{(n-1)}) = 0 \qquad (3.117)$$

which, due to the nonsigularity of the matrix above, implies

$$\frac{\partial L_T}{\partial\theta}(\theta_{(n-1)}) = 0,$$

so that $\theta_{(n-1)}$ is a solution to the normal equations of ML.

Remark 14. The method of scoring is the prototype of many iterative methods for solving nonlinear systems of equations, now available in standard computer software packages. Often, at what initial point we begin the iteration will determine whether the procedure converges and, if it does, the point to which it converges. But even if convergence is obtained, showing the consistency of the resulting estimator may be difficult or doubtful, unless one shows that one has converged to the *maximum maximorum* of the LF. Thus, if the LF is not known to be strictly concave, it is **very important to begin the iteration with an initial consistent estimator**. Since at each step consistency is maintained, if we converge we know that we have found a consistent root of the normal equations of ML.

3.6   Properties of Simplified Estimators

3.6.1   Consistency

We shall discuss in detail the first simplified estimator given in the preceding section. Evidently, similar conclusions will hold with respect to the modified method of scoring estimator as well.

We recall that the simplified FIML estimator is obtained by solving for δ in Eq. (3.113), after substitution of $\tilde{\Sigma}$ and $\tilde{P}$, for Σ and P, respectively. This yields the estimator

$$\hat{\delta} = C_T^{-1} \frac{1}{T} [Z^{*'} (\tilde{\Sigma}^{-1} \otimes I_T) - \bar{Z}^{*'} (\tilde{P}^{-1} \otimes N)] y \qquad (3.118)$$

where

$$C_T = \frac{1}{T} [Z^{*'} (\tilde{\Sigma}^{-1} \otimes I_T) Z^* - \bar{Z}^{*'} (\tilde{P}^{-1} \otimes N) \bar{Z}^*]. \qquad (3.119)$$

We shall first prove the consistency of this estimator subject to the requirement that the unknown parameters appearing in Σ and P have been consistently estimated.

Lemma 7. If $\tilde{\Sigma}$ and $\tilde{P}$ are obtained by the use of a prior consistent estimator of δ then the estimator given by Eq. (3.118) is consistent, under the standard assumptions for the GLSEM.

Proof: We note that, since

$$y = Z^* \delta + u, \qquad u = \text{vec}(U)$$

substituting in Eq. (3.118) yields

$$\hat{\delta} - \delta = C_T^{-1} \zeta_T, \qquad \zeta_T = \frac{1}{T} \left[Z^{*'} (\tilde{\Sigma}^{-1} \otimes I_T) - \bar{Z}^{*'} (\tilde{P}^{-1} \otimes N) \right] u. \qquad (3.120)$$

This is so, since

$$\bar{Z}^{*'} (\tilde{P}^{-1} \otimes N) Z^* = \bar{Z}^{*'} (\tilde{P}^{-1} \otimes N) \bar{Z}^*.$$

Next, we note that

$$Z^* = (I \otimes Z) L, \qquad \bar{Z}^* = (I \otimes \bar{Z}) L, \qquad Z = (Y, X), \qquad \bar{Z} = (Y, 0)$$

and, consequently, that adding and substracting $L'(\tilde{\Sigma}^{-1} \otimes \bar{Z}' N \bar{Z}) L$ (in the bracketed expression of Eq. (3.119)), yields

$$C_T = \frac{1}{T} \left[L'(\tilde{\Sigma}^{-1} \otimes \bar{Z}' \bar{Z}) L \right] + \frac{1}{T} L' \left[(\tilde{\Sigma}^{-1} - \tilde{P}^{-1}) \otimes \bar{Z}' N \bar{Z} \right] L = C_{T1} + C_{T2}. \qquad (3.121)$$

Moreover, adding and subtracting $\bar{Z}^{*'}(\tilde{\Sigma}^{-1} \otimes N)$ (in the bracketed expression of Eq. (3.120)), yields,

$$\zeta_T = \frac{1}{T} L'(\tilde{\Sigma}^{-1} \otimes \tilde{Z}') u + \frac{1}{T} L' \left[(\tilde{\Sigma}^{-1} - \tilde{P}^{-1}) \otimes (N\bar{Z})' \right] u = \zeta_{T1} + \zeta_{T2}.$$
(3.122)

Given the consistency of the initial estimator of δ, we easily establish

$$\tilde{P} \overset{\text{P}}{\to} B^{*'} \Omega B^* = \Sigma, \qquad \tilde{\Sigma} \overset{\text{P}}{\to} \Sigma. \qquad (3.123)$$

Consequently,

$$C_{T2} \overset{\text{P}}{\to} 0, \quad M_{xx} = \plim_{T \to \infty} (X'X/T), \quad C_{T1} \overset{\text{P}}{\to} L'[\Sigma^{-1} \otimes (\Pi, I)' M_{xx}(\Pi, I)] L,$$
(3.124)

where the latter may be shown to be nonsingular.

Thus, to complete the proof of the Lemma we need only show that

$$\frac{1}{T} \left[(\tilde{\Sigma}^{-1} - \tilde{P}^{-1}) \otimes (N\bar{Z})' \right] u \overset{\text{P}}{\to} 0, \quad \frac{1}{T} (\tilde{\Sigma}^{-1} \otimes \tilde{Z}') u \overset{\text{P}}{\to} 0.$$

But this is simple to establish since $(\tilde{\Sigma}^{-1} - \tilde{P}^{-1}) \overset{\text{P}}{\to} 0$, while $(N\bar{Z}' u/T)$ converges to a fixed finite entity, and

$$\frac{1}{T}(\tilde{\Sigma}^{-1} \otimes \tilde{Z}') u = \frac{1}{T}(\tilde{\Sigma}^{-1} \otimes \tilde{\Pi}')(I \otimes X') u \overset{\text{P}}{\to} 0,$$

in view of the conistency of $\tilde{\Sigma}$, $\tilde{\Pi}$ and the fact that $(X'U/T) \overset{\text{P}}{\to} 0$.

q.e.d.

Corollary 4. The matrix C_T^{-1}, has the same probability limit as the covariance matrix of the limiting distribution of the 3SLS estimator, where C_T is the matrix to be inverted in order to obtain the simplified FIML estimator.

Proof: We have shown in the proof of the Lemma that $\plim_{T \to \infty} C_T = L'[\Sigma^{-1} \otimes (\Pi, I)' M_{xx}(\Pi, I)] L$. But the (i, j) block element of the matrix is

$$\sigma^{ij} L_i'(\Pi, I)' M_{xx}(\Pi, I) L_j = \sigma^{ij} S_i' M_{xx} S_j.$$

The right hand member of the equation above, however, is simply the (i, j) block element of $S'(\Sigma^{-1} \otimes M_{xx}) S$, the inverse of which is, according to Eqs. (2.2) and (2.8) of Chapter 2, the covariance matrix of the limiting distirbution of the 3SLS estimator.

q.e.d.

Corollary 5. The 3SLS estimator of the parameter δ can be expressed in the form

$$(\tilde{\delta} - \delta^0)_{3SLS} = C_{T1}^{-1}\zeta_{T1}.$$

Proof: From Eq. (3.118) we have that

$$C_{T1} = \frac{1}{T}L'(\tilde{\Sigma}^{-1} \otimes \tilde{Z}'\tilde{Z})L = \tilde{S}'\left(\tilde{\Sigma}^{-1} \otimes \frac{X'X}{T}\right)\tilde{S}$$

$$\zeta_{T1} = \frac{1}{T}L'(\tilde{\Sigma}^{-1} \otimes \tilde{Z}')u = \tilde{S}'(\tilde{\Sigma}^{-1} \otimes I_T)\frac{(I \otimes X')u}{T}.$$

It follows, immediately, from Eq. (1.2) of Chapter 1 that $(\tilde{\delta} - \delta^0)_{3SLS} = C_{T1}^{-1}\zeta_{T1}$, where δ^0 is the true parameter vector.

q.e.d.

Remark 15. It may be thought that Corollary 5 has also established that the simplified FIML and 3SLS estimators are equivalent, in the sense that they have the same limiting distribution. While, in fact, they do have the same limiting distribution this cannot be established solely on the basis of Corollary 5. What we must show is that $\sqrt{T}(C_{T1}^{-1}\zeta_{T1} - C_T^{-1}\zeta_T)$ converges in distribution (or in probability) to the degenerate random variable, i.e. it converges to zero.

Lemma 8. The simplified FIML and 3SLS estimators have the same limiting distribution.

Proof: Denoting the simplified FIML estimator by SFIML, we have to show that

$$\sqrt{T}[(\tilde{\delta} - \delta^0)_{SFIML} - (\tilde{\delta} - \delta^0)_{3SLS}] \xrightarrow{\text{P or d}} 0.$$

Noting that

$$\sqrt{T}(C_T^{-1}\zeta_T - C_{T1}^{-1}\zeta_{T1}) = C_T^{-1}\sqrt{T}(\zeta_T - \zeta_{T1}) + (C_T^{-1} - C_{T1}^{-1})\sqrt{T}\zeta_{T1}, \quad (3.125)$$

and in view of Lemma 7, we need only show that $\sqrt{T}\zeta_{T2} \xrightarrow{\text{d}} 0$ and that $\sqrt{T}\zeta_{T1}$, is an a.c. finite random vector, i.e. as $T \longrightarrow \infty$ its limiting distribution is well defined and the probability of assuming unbounded values is zero. Considering the second term first, we recall that we have established, in Lemma 7, that $(C_T - C_{T1}) \xrightarrow{\text{P}} 0$; moreover,

$$\sqrt{T}\zeta_{t1} = \tilde{S}'(\tilde{\Sigma}^{-1} \otimes I_T)\frac{(I \otimes X')u}{\sqrt{T}},$$

and in Chapter 2 we have established, under a variety of circumstances, that

$$\sqrt{T}\zeta_{t1} \sim N(0, S'(\Sigma^{-1} \otimes M_{xx})S).$$

By Corollary 6 in Ch. 4 of Dhrymes (1989), we have $(C_T^{-1} - C_{T1}^{-1})\sqrt{T}\zeta_{T1} \xrightarrow{d}$ 0 . We now consider the first term, $C_T^{-1}\sqrt{T}\zeta_{T2}$; since C_T^{-1} is well behaved in the limit, we concentrate on $\sqrt{T}\zeta_{T2}$, which in view of Proposition 86, Corollary 22, of Dhrymes (1984), may be rewritten as

$$\sqrt{T}\zeta_{T2} = \frac{1}{\sqrt{T}}L'\text{vec}[\bar{Z}'NU(\tilde{\Sigma}^{-1} - \tilde{P}^{-1})]. \tag{3.126}$$

Moreover,

$$\tilde{\Sigma}^{-1} - \tilde{P}^{-1} = \tilde{\Sigma}^{-1}\tilde{B}^{*'}(W - \tilde{B}^{*'-1}\tilde{\Sigma}\tilde{B}^{*-1})\tilde{B}^*\tilde{P}^{-1}$$
$$T\tilde{B}^{*'-1}\tilde{\Sigma}\tilde{B}^{*-1} = \tilde{B}^{*'-1}\tilde{A}'Z'Z\tilde{A}\tilde{B}^{*-1} = (Y - X\tilde{\Pi})'(Y - X\tilde{\Pi})$$
$$= [V - X(\tilde{\Pi} - \Pi)]'[V - X(\tilde{\Pi} - \Pi)],$$

where $\tilde{\Pi} = \tilde{C}\tilde{B}^{*-1}$ is the restricted reduced form estimator implied by the initial consistent estimator of δ . Consequently, Eq. (3.126) may be written as

$$T^{\frac{1}{2}}\zeta_{T2} = L'\left(I \otimes \frac{\bar{Z}'NU}{T}\right)\left(\tilde{P}^{-1}\tilde{B}^{*'} \otimes \tilde{\Sigma}^{-1}\tilde{B}^{*'}\right)$$
$$\times \frac{1}{T^{\frac{1}{2}}}\left[Y'NY - (Y - X\tilde{\Pi})'(Y - X\tilde{\Pi})\right]. \tag{3.127}$$

Since the first component of the right member of Eq. (3.127) is easily seen to converge to zero, in probability, we need only examine the last term, and noting that $Y'NY = V'NV$ we obtain

$$E_T = \frac{1}{T^{\frac{1}{2}}}[Y'NY - (Y - X\tilde{\Pi})'(Y - X\tilde{\Pi})] = \frac{1}{T^{\frac{1}{2}}}[(\tilde{\Pi} - \Pi)'X'X(\tilde{\Pi} - \Pi)]$$
$$- \frac{1}{T^{\frac{1}{2}}}\left[(\tilde{\Pi} - \Pi)'X'V + V'X(\tilde{\Pi} - \Pi) + V'X(X'X)^{-1}X'V\right].$$

In view of the fact that, as we have established in Chapter 2,

$$\sqrt{T}(\tilde{\pi} - \pi)_{RRF} \text{ and } \frac{X'V}{\sqrt{T}} = (D' \otimes I_G)\frac{(I \otimes X)'u}{\sqrt{T}},$$

have a well defined limiting distribution, we conclude that

$$(\tilde{\Pi} - \Pi)'X'X(\tilde{\Pi} - \Pi) \xrightarrow{d} \zeta'M_{xx}\zeta,$$

where ζ is a random matrix, of dimension $G \times m$, whose elements have a jointly normal distribution. Thus, the first term in the right member in the representation of E_T converges in distribution to zero. The second and third terms involve entities of the form

$$\sqrt{T}(\tilde{\Pi} - \Pi)'\frac{X'V}{T},$$

which, evidently, converge to zero in distribution. The fourth, and final term, is of the form

$$\frac{V'X}{T}\left(\frac{X'X}{T}\right)^{-1}\frac{X'V}{\sqrt{T}},$$

which, also, converges to zero in distribution. Hence, we conclude that the entity $\sqrt{T}\zeta_{T2}$, in Eq. (3.127), converges in distribution to zero.

q.e.d.

Remark 16. Since the limiting distribution of the initial estimator of δ plays no role in the proof above, it follows that, asymptotically, it is irrelevant how the initial estimator is obtained. All that matters is that it be consistent and that the limiting distribution of the induced reduced form estimator be defined. For this purpose it is sufficient that the initial estimator itself have a well defined limiting distribution. Another important aspect that emerges from the preceding argument is that no asymptotic gain results from the iteration of the process; iteration, in this context, means that, given the modified FIML estimator, we recompute the elements of Σ^{-1} and P^{-1} to obtain a second modified FIML estimator and so on. Of course this discussion is not meant to convey the impression that how we obtain the initial estimator and whether we iterate or not are totally irrelevant aspects. Evidently, in a small sample context it would, indeed, matter how "good" the initial estimator is; in many instances it would be strongly indicated that the procedure be iterated a few times so as to minimize the impact of an inept initial choice.

Finally, we note that while it may be of little consequence how the initial consistent estimator is obtained, **in the ML context it matters whether we do or do not know a priori the covariance matrix of the structural errors**. This is in contrast to the 3SLS estimator where this knowledge, or lack of it, is of no consequence. We shall take up this matter in Chapter 6, where we shall examine nonlinear ML estimation more systematically.

3.7 Limiting Distribution of FIML

We now turn to the derivation of the limiting distribution of the FIML estimator. Reverting to the concentrated likelihood function in Eq. (3.97) we note that the FIML estimator is found as a root (solution) of

$$\frac{\partial L}{\partial \delta} = 0.$$

Suppose this solution can be found by an iterative process beginning with an initial consistent estimator of δ. Then, the converging iterate, say $\hat{\delta}$, is the FIML estimator, since it is a consistent root of the equation above, i.e. it is a consistent estimator and satisfies

$$\frac{\partial L}{\partial \delta}(\hat{\delta}) = 0. \tag{3.128}$$

To find its limiting distribution we proceed as follows: by the mean value theorem, write

$$\frac{\partial L}{\partial \delta}(\hat{\delta}) = \frac{\partial L}{\partial \delta}(\delta^0) + \frac{\partial^2 L}{\partial \delta \partial \delta}(\delta*)(\hat{\delta} - \delta^0), \tag{3.129}$$

where δ^* obeys $\mid \delta^* - \delta^0 \mid < \mid \hat{\delta} - \delta^0 \mid$, and δ^0 is the true parameter vector. Because of Eq. (3.129), we can write Eq. (3.128) as

$$\sqrt{T}(\hat{\delta} - \delta^0) = - \left[\frac{1}{T} \frac{\partial^2 L}{\partial \delta \partial \delta}(\delta^*) \right]^{-1} \frac{1}{\sqrt{T}} \frac{\partial L}{\partial \delta}(\delta^0). \tag{3.130}$$

Two things may be noted about Eq. (3.130); first, δ^* converges, at least in probability, to δ^0, in view of equation Eq. (3.129) and the fact that $\hat{\delta}$ is the FIML estimator of δ and hence consistent; second, if we can show that

$$\plim_{T \to \infty} \frac{1}{T} \frac{\partial^2 L}{\partial \delta \partial \delta}(\delta^*)$$

converges to a well defined matrix, then the limiting distribution of

$\sqrt{T}(\hat{\delta} - \delta^0)$ can be obtained from the limiting distribution of $\dfrac{1}{\sqrt{T}} \dfrac{\partial L}{\partial \delta}(\delta^0)$.

Now, using equation Eqs. (3.109) and (3.111) we find

$$\frac{\partial L}{\partial \delta} = T[\text{vec}(A)'(\tilde{\Sigma}^{-1} \otimes M)L - \text{vec}(B^*)'(\tilde{P}^{-1} \otimes \bar{W})L_1].$$

Writing this in the customary column form, bearing in mind the definition of $\tilde{\Sigma}$ and $\tilde{P}$, noting that these quantities are to be evaluated at the true parameter vector and employing Proposition 86, Corollary 22, Dhrymes (1984), we can write

$$\frac{1}{\sqrt{T}} \left[\frac{\partial L}{\partial \delta}(\delta^0) \right]' = \sqrt{T} \left\{ L' \text{vec}(MA^*(A^{*'}MA^*)^{-1}] - \bar{L}_1' \text{vec}[WB^*(B^{*'}WB^*)^{-1}] \right\}.$$

Moreover

$$\bar{L}_1' \text{vec}[WB^*(B^{*'}WB^*)^{-1}] = \bar{L}_1' \text{vec}(B^{*'-1}) = L' \text{vec}(\bar{B}^{*'-1}),$$

where $\bar{B}^{*'-1} = I^{*'}B^{*'-1}$, $I^* = (I_m, \ 0_{m \times G})$ and thus, we have the simplification,

$$\frac{1}{\sqrt{T}} \left[\frac{\partial L}{\partial \delta}(\delta^0) \right]' = L' \sqrt{T} \text{vec}[MA^*(A^{*'}MA^*)^{-1} - \bar{B}^{*'-1}.] \tag{3.131}$$

But since Eq. (3.131) is to be evaluated at the true parameter vector we note, first, $A^{*'} M A^* = (U'U/T)$, so that

$$
\begin{aligned}
E &= M A^* (A^{*'} M A^*)^{-1} - \bar{B}^{*'-1} = \left(M A^* - \bar{B}^{*'-1}\frac{U'U}{T} \right) \left(\frac{U'U}{T} \right)^{-1} \\
&= \frac{1}{T}(Z' - \bar{B}^{*'-1}U')U \left(\frac{U'U}{T} \right)^{-1} \\
&= (\Pi, I)'\frac{X'U}{T} \left(\frac{U'U}{T} \right)^{-1}.
\end{aligned}
\tag{3.132}
$$

This is so since $M A^* = (Z'U/T)$ and

$$
Z' - \bar{B}^{*'-1}U' = \begin{pmatrix} Y' \\ X' \end{pmatrix} - \begin{pmatrix} \bar{B}^{*'-1}A^{*'}Z' \\ 0 \end{pmatrix} = \begin{pmatrix} Y' \\ X' \end{pmatrix} - \begin{pmatrix} Y' - \Pi'X' \\ 0 \end{pmatrix}.
$$

Therefore, we have the representation

$$
\frac{1}{\sqrt{T}} \left[\frac{\partial L}{\partial \delta}(\delta^0) \right]' = L'(\tilde{\Sigma}^{-1} \otimes (\tilde{\Pi}, I)')\frac{(I \otimes X)'u}{\sqrt{T}} = S'(\tilde{\Sigma}^{-1} \otimes I_G)\frac{(I \otimes X)'u}{\sqrt{T}},
\tag{3.133}
$$

which we have shown under a variety of circumstances, in Chapter 2, to have the limiting distribution

$$
\frac{1}{\sqrt{T}} \left[\frac{\partial L}{\partial \delta}(\delta^0) \right]' \sim N \left(0, S'(\Sigma^{-1} \otimes M_{xx})S \right).
\tag{3.134}
$$

Thus, to complete the derivation of the limiting distribution of the FIML estimator we need only obtain the limit of $\frac{\partial^2 L}{\partial \delta \partial \delta} = \frac{\partial}{\partial \delta}(\frac{\partial L}{\partial \delta})'$; from Eq. (3.133), we have

$$
\frac{1}{T} \frac{\partial^2 L}{\partial \delta \partial \delta} = \frac{\partial}{\partial \delta}\{L'\mathrm{vec}[M A^* (A^{*'} M A^*)^{-1}] - \bar{L}_1'\mathrm{vec}[W B^*(B^{*'} W B^*)^{-1}]\}.
$$

We note that the two terms in the right member of the equation above are, roughly speaking, of the same form; thus, it would be not be necessary to duplicate the differentiation process in its entirety. We shall provide, in the case of the second term, only the detail necessary to supplement the discussion of the derivative of the first term. Because the parameters of interest, viz. A^* and B^*, appear in two different locations, the following two alternative representations are required, in order to facilitate differentiation:

$$
\mathrm{vec}\left[M A^* (A^{*'} M A^*)^{-1} \right] = \left[(A^{*'} M A^*)^{-1} \otimes M \right] \mathrm{vec}(A^*), \text{ or}
$$

$$
= (I_m \otimes M A^*) \mathrm{vec}(A^{*'} M A^*)^{-1}
$$

$$
\mathrm{vec}(A^{*'} M A^*) = \left(I_m \otimes A^{*'} M \right) \mathrm{vec}(A^*), \text{ or}
$$

$$
= \left(A^{*'} M \otimes I_m \right) \mathrm{vec}(A^{*'}),
\tag{3.135}
$$

for the first term and

$$\mathrm{vec}\left[WB^*(B^{*'}WB^*)^{-1}\right] = \left[(B^{*'}WB^*)^{-1} \otimes W\right]\mathrm{vec}(B^*), \text{ or}$$

$$= (I_m \otimes WB^*)\,\mathrm{vec}(B^{*'}WB^*)^{-1}$$

$$\mathrm{vec}(B^{*'}WB^*) = \left(I_m \otimes B^{*'}W\right)\mathrm{vec}(B^*), \text{ or}$$

$$= \left(B^{*'}W \otimes I_m\right)\mathrm{vec}(B^{*'}), \qquad (3.136)$$

for the second.

From Ch. 4 in Dhrymes (1984), we find

$$\frac{\partial\mathrm{vec}(A^{*'}MA^*)^{-1}}{\partial\delta} = \frac{\partial\mathrm{vec}(A^{*'}MA^*)^{-1}}{\partial\mathrm{vec}(A^{*'}MA^*)}\frac{\partial\mathrm{vec}(A^{*'}MA^*)}{\partial\mathrm{vec}(A^*)}\frac{\partial\mathrm{vec}(A^*)}{\partial\delta},$$

$$\frac{\partial\mathrm{vec}(A^{*'}MA^*)^{-1}}{\partial\mathrm{vec}(A^{*'}MA^*)} = -(A^{*'}MA^*)^{-1} \otimes (A^{*'}MA^*)^{-1}, \qquad (3.137)$$

$$\frac{\partial\mathrm{vec}(A^{*'}MA^*)}{\partial\mathrm{vec}(A^*)} = (I \otimes A^{*'}M) + (A^{*'}M \otimes I)\frac{\partial\mathrm{vec}(A^{*'})}{\partial\mathrm{vec}(A^*)}.$$

Since

$$\frac{\partial\mathrm{vec}(A^{*'})}{\partial\mathrm{vec}(A^*)} \neq \frac{\partial\mathrm{vec}(A^*)}{\partial\mathrm{vec}(A^*)},$$

we are faced with considerable complications, and the orderly development of our discussion requires a brief digression.

Lemma 9. Given any matrix, say F, of dimesnion $m \times n$, there exists a permutation matrix, say $I_{(m,n)}$, of dimension $mn \times mn$, such that $\mathrm{vec}(F) = I_{(m,n)}\mathrm{vec}(F')$.

Proof: We note that $\mathrm{vec}(F)$ and $\mathrm{vec}(F')$ contain **exactly the same elements** which, however, **are arranged differently in the two displays**. The first subvector of $\mathrm{vec}(F)$ contains the first **column** of F, while the first subvector of $\mathrm{vec}(F')$ contains the **first row of F transposed**, and similarly for the other rows and columns of F. In particular, the first **element is the same for both vector displays**; however, the second element of $\mathrm{vec}(F)$ is the $(m+1)^{st}$ of $\mathrm{vec}(F')$, the third element of the former is the $(2m+1)^{st}$ element of the latter and so on. Thus, if we arrange *seriatim* the first, $(m+1)^{st}$, $(2m+1)^{st}$, $\ldots$, $((n-1)m+1)^{st}$; the second, $(m+2)^{nd}$, $(2m+2)^{nd}$, $\ldots$, $((n-1)m+2)^{nd}$; $\ldots$; the mth, $2m^{th}$, $3m^{th}$, $\ldots$, nm^{th} elements of $\mathrm{vec}(F')$ we shall simply obtain the display corresponding to $\mathrm{vec}(F)$. Now, if we perform a similar rearrangement on the **rows** of the identity matrix of order mn, we shall obtain the permutation matrix $I_{(m,n)}$, which has the representation, [15]

$$I_{(m,n)} = (I_m \otimes e_{.1}, I_m \otimes e_{.2}, I_m \otimes e_{.3}, \ldots, I_m \otimes e_{.n})',$$

where the $e_{.i}$ **are** n**-element column vectors, all of whose elements are zero, save the** i^{th}**, which is unity.**

q.e.d.

Corollary 5. $I'_{(m,n)} = I_{(n,m)}$.

Proof: Applying Lemma 9 to the matrix F', whose dimension is $n \times m$, we find

$$\text{vec}(F') = I_{(n,m)}\text{vec}(F),$$

or, using again the results of the lemma above,

$$\text{vec}(F) = I_{(m,n)}I_{(n,m)}\text{vec}(F).$$

We note that the permutation matrices $I_{(m,n)}$ or $I_{(n,m)}$ **depend only on the dimension(s) of the matrices,** F, F'**, and not on their particular elements**; thus, since $\text{vec}(F)$ is essentially arbitrary in the relation above, we conclude $I_{(m,n)}I_{(n,m)} = I_{nm}$, or $I_{(n,m)} = I_{(m,n)}^{-1}$. Since permutation matrices are **orthogonal**, we have $I_{(m,n)}^{-1} = I'_{(m,n)}$. But this implies, $I'_{(m,n)} = I_{(n,m)}$.

q.e.d.

Another useful result is

Lemma 10. Given arbitrary matrices, say, F, H, of dimension(s) $m \times n$ and $r \times s$, respectively, there exist permutation matrices, $I_{(m,r)}$ and $I_{(s,n)}$ such that $H \otimes F = I_{(m,r)}(F \otimes H)I_{(s,n)}$.

Proof: Let X be an arbitrary conformable matrix and consider the entity FXH'; by the preceding discussion,

$$\begin{aligned}(H \otimes F)\text{vec}(X) &= \text{vec}(FXH') = I_{(m,r)}\text{vec}(HX'F') \\ &= I_{(m,r)}(F \otimes H)\text{vec}(X') = I_{(m,r)}(F \otimes H)I_{(s,n)}\text{vec}(X).\end{aligned}$$

---

[15] Note that a **permutation** matrix is, by definition, an identity matrix a number of whose columns or rows have been interchanged. Note, further, that the order of the indices, m, n is significant. Thus, the matrix $I_{(n,m)}$ is given by

$$I_{(n,m)} = (I_n \otimes e_{.1}, I_n \otimes e_{.2}, I_n \otimes e_{.3}, \ldots, I_n \otimes e_{.m})',$$

where the $e_{.i}$ are m**-element column vectors, all of whose elements are zero, save the** i^{th}**, which is unity.**

Since, given its dimension, the matrix X is arbitrary, we conclude,

$$(H \otimes F) = I_{(m,r)}(F \otimes H)I_{(s,n)}.$$

q.e.d.

Returning now to our primary discussion, and noting that

$$\text{vec}(A^{*'}) = I_{(m,\ m+G)}\text{vec}(A^*),$$

we can write

$$(A^{*'}M \otimes I)\frac{\partial \text{vec}(A^{*'})}{\partial \text{vec}(A^*)} = I_{(m,m)}I'_{(m,m)}(A^{*'}M \otimes I)I_{(m,m+G)}, \text{ or}$$

$$= I_{(m,m)}(I \otimes A^{*'}M). \quad (3.138)$$

Thus, we obtain

$$\frac{\partial \text{vec}(A^{*'}MA^*)}{\partial \text{vec}(A^*)} = [I + I_{(m,m)}](I \otimes A^{*'}M).$$

In Eq. (3.136), we need only obtain the derivative of $\text{vec}(B^{*'}WB^*)$ with respect to $\text{vec}(B^*)$ and the derivative of the latter with respect to δ, since everything else therein is completely analogous to the corresponding part of Eq. (3.135); such derivatives have been fully derived in Eqs. (3.137) and (3.138). Thus, we note

$$\frac{\partial \text{vec}(B^{*'}WB^*)}{\partial \text{vec}(B^*)} = (I_m \otimes B^{*'}W) + (B^{*'}W \otimes I_m)\frac{\partial \text{vec}(B^{*'})}{\partial \text{vec}(B^*)}$$

$$\frac{\partial \text{vec}(B^*)}{\partial \delta} = -(I \otimes I^*)L. \quad (3.139)$$

Since

$$(B^{*'}W \otimes I_m)\frac{\partial \text{vec}(B^{*'})}{\partial \text{vec}(B^*)} = I_{(m,m)}I'_{(m,m)}(B^{*'}W \otimes I)I_{(m,m)}$$

$$= I_{(m,m)}(I_m \otimes B^{*'}W), \quad (3.140)$$

we can write

$$\frac{\partial \text{vec}(B^{*'}WB^*)}{\partial \text{vec}(B^*)} = [I + I_{(m,m)}](I_m \otimes B^{*'}W).$$

Combining the results above, we may write the Hessian of the LF as

$$\frac{1}{T}\frac{\partial^2 L}{\partial \delta \partial \delta} = \frac{1}{T}\frac{\partial}{\partial \delta}\left(\frac{\partial L}{\partial \delta}\right)' = L'E_{T1}L - L'(I \otimes I^*)'E_{T2}(I \otimes I^*)L, \quad (3.141)$$

where

$$E_{T1} = -\left[(A^{*'}MA^*)^{-1} \otimes M\right] + (I_m \otimes MA^*)$$

$$\times \left[(A^{*'}MA^*)^{-1} \otimes (A^{*'}MA^*)^{-1}\right](I + I_{(m,m)})(I_m \otimes A^{*'}M)$$

$$E_{T2} = -\left[(B^{*'}WB^*)^{-1} \otimes W\right] + (I_m \otimes WB^*) \qquad (3.142)$$

$$\times \left[(B^{*'}WB^*)^{-1} \otimes (B^{*'}WB^*)^{-1}\right](I + I_{(m,m)})(I_m \otimes B^{*'}W).$$

To establish the desired limit, we note that (evaluating at the true parameter point δ^0) we obtain

$$(A^{*'}MA^*) = \frac{A^{*'}Z'ZA^*}{T} \xrightarrow{\text{P}} \Sigma, \quad MA^* = \frac{Z'U}{T} \xrightarrow{\text{P}} I^{*'}B^{*'-1}\Sigma,$$

$$(B^{*'}WB^*) \xrightarrow{\text{P}} \Sigma, \quad WB^* = V'NVB^* \xrightarrow{\text{P}} B^{*'-1}\Sigma. \qquad (3.143)$$

It follows from the derivation above that

$$L'E_{T1}L \xrightarrow{\text{P}} -L'\left(\Sigma^{-1} \otimes M_{zz}\right)L + L'(I_m \otimes B^{*'-1}\Sigma I^{*'}) \qquad (3.144)$$

$$\times (\Sigma^{-1} \otimes \Sigma^{-1})(I + I_{(m,m)})(I_m \otimes I^*\Sigma B^{*-1})L$$

$$= -L'\left(\Sigma^{-1} \otimes M_{zz}\right)L + 2L'\left(\Sigma^{-1} \otimes \Omega^*\right)L, \quad \text{where}$$

$$\Omega^* = I^{*'}\Omega I^*, \quad M = \frac{Z'Z}{T} \xrightarrow{\text{P}} M_{zz}, \quad \bar{B}^{*'-1} = I^{*'}B^{*'-1}.$$

Similarly, one may establish

$$J_T = L'(I \otimes I^*)'E_{T2}(I \otimes I^*)L$$

$$\xrightarrow{\text{P}} -L'\left(\Sigma^{-1} \otimes I^{*'}\Omega I^*\right)L + 2L'\left(I_m \otimes I^{*'}B^{*'-1}\Sigma\right)(\Sigma^{-1} \otimes \Sigma^{-1})$$

$$\times \left(I_m \otimes \Sigma B^{*-1}I^*\right)L$$

$$= -L'\left(\Sigma^{-1} \otimes \Omega^*\right)L + 2L'(\Sigma^{-1} \otimes \Omega^*)L. \qquad (3.145)$$

Consequently, the limit of the Hessian of the log likelihood function is given by

$$\frac{1}{T}\frac{\partial^2 L}{\partial\delta\partial\delta}(\delta^0) \xrightarrow{\text{P}} -L'(\Sigma^{-1} \otimes M_{zz})L + L'(\Sigma^{-1} \otimes \Omega)L$$

$$= -L' \left[(\Sigma^{-1} \otimes M_{zz}) - \left(\Sigma^{-1} \otimes \begin{bmatrix} \Omega & 0 \\ 0 & 0 \end{bmatrix} \right) \right] L$$

$$= -L' \left(\Sigma^{-1} \otimes \begin{bmatrix} \Omega + \Pi' M_{xx} \Pi - \Omega & \Pi' M_{xx} \\ M_{xx} \Pi & M_{xx} \end{bmatrix} \right) L$$

$$= -L' \left[\Sigma^{-1} \otimes (\Pi, I)' M_{xx}(\Pi, I) \right] L$$

$$= -S'(\Sigma^{-1} \otimes M_{xx})S. \tag{3.146}$$

To recapitulate our findings: first, the FIML estimator, assumed to be found as the converging iterate of a process beginning with an initial consistent estimator, is consistent, i.e, $\hat{\delta} \xrightarrow{P} \delta^0$; second, we have shown that it obeys

$$\sqrt{T}(\hat{\delta} - \delta^0) = - \left[\frac{1}{T} \frac{\partial^2 L}{\partial \delta \partial \delta}(\delta^*) \right]^{-1} \frac{1}{\sqrt{T}} \frac{\partial L}{\partial \delta}(\delta^0),$$

where $| \delta^* - \delta^0 | \leq | \hat{\delta} - \delta^0) |$; third, that

$$\frac{1}{T} \frac{\partial^2 L}{\partial \delta \partial \delta}(\delta*) \xrightarrow{P} -S'(\Sigma^{-1} \otimes M_{xx})S;$$

fourth, that

$$\frac{1}{\sqrt{T}} \frac{\partial L}{\partial \delta}(\delta^0) \sim N \left(0, S'(\Sigma^{-1} \otimes M_{xx})S \right).$$

The informal discussion of this section has, therefore, proved

Theorem 10. Consider the GLSEM

$$y_{t.}B^* = x_{t.}C + u_{t.}, \ t = 1, 2, 3, \ldots, T,$$

under the standard assumptions and suppose, further, that the error process

$$\{u'_{t.} : t = 1, 2, 3, \ldots\},$$

is one of the i.i.d. random variable such that

$$u'_{t.} \sim N(0, \ \Sigma)$$

and Σ is positive definite.

Let $L(\delta; Y, X)$ be the concentrated log likelihood function. Then

i. the FIML estimator of δ, $\hat{\delta}$, may be found by (converging) iteration, beginning with an initial consistent estimator; it obeys

$$\frac{\partial L}{\partial \delta}(\hat{\delta}) = 0,$$

and, subject to the standard normalization, has the limiting distribution

$$\sqrt{T}(\hat{\delta} - \delta^0) \sim N\left(0, \; (S'(\Sigma^{-1} \otimes M_{xx})S)^{-1}\right);$$

ii. the simplified FIML estimator, obtained as the solution of Eq. (3.113), with the elements of $\tilde{\Sigma}^{-1}$ and $\tilde{P}^{-1}$ computed on the basis of an initial consistent estimator of δ, has the limiting distribution

$$\sqrt{T}(\hat{\delta} - \delta^0) \sim N\left(0, \; (S'(\Sigma^{-1} \otimes M_{xx})S)^{-1}\right),$$

and hence is asymptotically equivalent to the FIML estimator;

iii. no asymptotic gain is obtained by iterating the process yielding the simplified FIML estimator;

iv. the estimators under i and ii are asymptotically equivalent to the 3SLS estimator.

Remark 17. Note that the FIML, simplified FIML, and 3SLS estimators essentially solve Eq. (3.113). The FIML estimator takes account of the fact that δ enters in $\tilde{\Sigma}$ and $\tilde{P}$, and obtains a solution by iterating to convergence.

The simplified FIML estimator evaluates $\tilde{\Sigma}$ and $\tilde{P}$ at an initial consistent estimator of δ, **and then solves the resulting linear system for the desired estimator.**

The 3SLS procedure replaces $\tilde{P}$ by $\tilde{\Sigma}$ and otherwise proceeds as the simplified FIML estimator.

Questions and Problems

1. Consider the system

$$
\begin{aligned}
y_{t1} &= \beta_{21}y_{t2} + \gamma_{01} + \gamma_{11}x_{t1} + \gamma_{21}x_{t2} + \quad\quad + u_{t1} \\
y_{t2} &= \quad\quad\quad\; + \gamma_{02} + \gamma_{12}x_{t1} + \quad\quad\quad + \gamma_{32}x_{t3} + u_{t2}.
\end{aligned}
$$

a. Determine the matrices corresponding to B_{22}^*, C_{22} of the discussion in section 3.2.5.

b. Determine the reduced form of the system and the matrix Π_{21} of the discussion of section 3.2.5.

c. Determine whether the system is identified. Justify your answer.

2. In the solution exhibited in Eq. (3.29), verify the expression for $\hat{\beta}$.

Hint: Note that, from the reduced form, (s_{p1}/b') has the same probability limit as s_{q1}.

3. Consider the standard GLSEM of Eqs. (3.5) and (3.6) and subject to the restrictions and normalizations implied by Conventions 1 and 2. Suppose we now impose, **additionally**, the covariance restrictions,

$$\Psi\sigma = h_2, \quad \text{where} \quad \sigma = \text{vec}(\Sigma).$$

Show that the conditions for identification of the system's parameters, in this context, can be obtained from Theorem 9.

Hint: Use Theorem 1 and Definition 6, to show that identification, in this context, is equivalent to: given the reduced form matrix Π and the covariance matrix of the reduced form errors Ω, plus whatever restrictions and normalizations may be applicable, we may obtain a unique solution for the uknown parameters in the structural and covariance matrices, i.e. we may find a unique solution in terms of a^* and σ to the system of equations

$$[I\otimes(\Pi, I)]a^* = 0, \quad L^{*\circ'}a^* = h, \quad \Psi_1 a^* = \psi_1, \quad \Psi_2\sigma = \psi_2, \quad (I\otimes B^{*'}\Omega)b^* = \sigma,$$

where $b^* = \text{vec}(B^*)$.

4. Verify that Eq. (3.78) represents the maximum of Eq. (3.77) with respect to Π, for given Ω.

5. Verify that the representations in Eqs. (3.112) and (3.113) are equivalent.

Hint: Obtain the ith subvector in Eq. (3.113).

6. Verify, in connection with equations Eqs. (3.113) and (3.114), that

$$\bar{Z}^{*'}(\tilde{P}^{-1}\otimes N)Z^* = \bar{Z}^{*'}(\tilde{P}^{-1}\otimes N)\bar{Z}^*$$

Hint: $XN = 0, \ NX = 0$.

7. Verify that

$$(\Pi, I)L_i = S_i.$$

Hint: $\bar{L}_i = \begin{bmatrix} \bar{L}_{1i} \\ \bar{L}_{2i} \end{bmatrix}, \ \bar{L}_{1i} = (L_{1i}, \ 0), \ \bar{L}_{2i} = (0, \ L_{2i})$.]

8. Verify the operations involved in the transition from Eq. (3.126) to Eq. (3.127).

Hint: $\tilde{\Sigma}^{-1} - \tilde{P}^{-1} = \tilde{\Sigma}^{-1}(\tilde{P}-\tilde{\Sigma})\tilde{P}^{-1}$, $\text{vec}(A_1 A_2 A_3) = (A_3' \otimes A_1)\text{vec}(A_2)$.

9. Verify the relations in Eq. (3.135).

10. Verify that

$$WB^{*-1} \xrightarrow{P} B^{*'}\Sigma^{-1}, \quad \text{and} \quad MA^* \xrightarrow{P} \begin{bmatrix} B^{*'-1}\Sigma \\ 0 \end{bmatrix}.$$

11. Verify the relations in Eqs. (3.142) and (3.143).

12. Verify the relations in Eqs. (3.146) and (3.147).

13. Verify the respresentation in footnote 16.

14. Verify, in Lemma 9, that the matrix $I_{(m,n)}$ does not depend on the specific elements of the matrix F.

4

LIML Estimation Methods

4.1 The "Concentrated" Likelihood Function

4.1.1 A Subset of $m*$ Structural Equations

As we pointed out in the previous chapter, LIML is an estimation procedure that uses a priori information pertaining **only** to the equation (or equations) whose parameters we are interested in estimating. A priori restrictions on the parameters of the remaining equations are completely ignored.

Because LIML is a relatively complex procedure, let us give an outline of the estimation strategy before actually deriving the LIML estimator. Thus, suppose we are interested in estimating the parameters of a subset of $m * (\le m)$ equations. Or, alternatively, suppose that, because of the cumbersome nature of the system we must solve in order to obtain FIML estimators, we wish to break up the system into small subsystems, thus reducing the computational complexity involved, and estimate the parameters of each subsystem separately. Obviously, in doing so we cannot, of course, ignore the remainder of the system. On the other hand, we cannot handle all equations symmetrically, as we do with FIML, for then no computational economy arises. The strategy is to concentrate on the parameters of the subsystem of interest without being forced to ignore a great deal of information in the process. How can this be done? We could eliminate the parameters of the remainder of the system by partially maximizing the likelihood function with respect to such parameters. Of course, proceeding in this fashion we shall ignore all *a priori* restrictions applicable to them.

This last remark is essential. First, by ignoring such *a priori* rerstrictions we greatly simplify the process of maximization, and second, this feature constitutes the essential distinction between FIML and LIML.

Having expressed the likelihood function in "concentrated" form, i.e. in a form involving **only** the parameters of the subsystem of interest, we proceed to obtain maximum likelihood estimators in much the same way as in FIML. We maximize the "concentrated" likelihood function with respect to the unknown parameters it contains, taking the *a priori* restrictions on the subsystem in question fully into account.

Suppose that we are interested in the parameters of the first $m*(\leq m)$ equations. Partition the covariance matrix of the error terms of the system

$$\Sigma = \begin{bmatrix} \Sigma_{11} & \Sigma_{12} \\ \Sigma_{21} & \Sigma_{22} \end{bmatrix}, \tag{4.1}$$

where Σ_{11} is the covariance matrix of the error terms appearing in the first m^* equations, Σ_{22} is the covariance matrix corresponding to the error terms appearing the remaining $(m - m^*)$ equations, and Σ_{12}, Σ_{21} are the appropriate "cross covariance" matrices.

Next, we wish to transform the system in such a way that

i. the two subsystems are mutually independent;

ii. we do not disturb the parameters of the subsystem of interest.

If condition i is satisfied, the information "lost" by not explicitly taking it into account is "minimized" since the second subsystem is unrelated (stochastically) to the first. If ii is also satisfied, it is possible to obtain estimators for the parameters of interest directly.

Of course, we should point out that a price is still being paid for this simplification. The price is that the maximizing values of the parameters of the second (ignored) subsystem do not necessarily satisfy the *a priori* restrictions on them. Thus, when used to obtain the concentrated likelihood function, these values entail LIML estimators that will generally be different from what they would have been if all *a priori* restrictions were respected in the estimation scheme. If the latter holds, we are, of course, reduced to FIML estimation.

Let us, now, see whether a transformation that accomplishes i and ii actually exists. Recall that $A^* = (B^*, -C')'$ and partition $A^* = (\alpha_0, A_0)$, so that α_0 contains the parameters of the first m^* equations of interest, i.e. it consists of the first m^* columns of A^*. If H is the (conformably partitioned) transforming matrix, and if it is to accomplish our objectives under conditions i and ii above, we must have

$$H = \begin{bmatrix} H_{11} & H_{12} \\ H_{21} & H_{22} \end{bmatrix}, \quad H'\Sigma H = \begin{bmatrix} \Sigma_{11} & 0 \\ 0 & P \end{bmatrix}, \quad A^*H = (\alpha_0, A_0^*). \tag{4.2}$$

To make the requirements on H perfectly transparent, we note that the sample on the structural model can be written as $ZA^* = U$, $Z = (Y, X)$. Transforming by H on the right, [1] we find,

$$ZA^*H = UH, \tag{4.3}$$

and from the set of requirements in Eq. (4.2) we infer that the transforming matrix, H, must (at least) be of the form,

$$H = \begin{bmatrix} I & H_{12} \\ 0 & H_{22} \end{bmatrix}. \tag{4.4}$$

The covariance matrix of the transformed system is,

$$H'\Sigma H = \begin{bmatrix} \Sigma_{11} & \Sigma_{11}H_{12} + \Sigma_{12}H_{22} \\ H'_{12}\Sigma_{11} + H'_{22}\Sigma_{21} & \Sigma_{22}^* \end{bmatrix}, \tag{4.5}$$

where $\Sigma_{22}^* = H'_{12}\Sigma_{11}H_{12} + H'_{22}\Sigma_{21}H_{12} + H'_{12}\Sigma_{12}H_{22} + H'_{22}\Sigma_{22}H_{22}$.

By the requirements of Eq. (4.2), and the representation in Eq. (4.5), we see that H_{12} must be chosen so that

$$\Sigma_{11}H_{12} + \Sigma_{12}H_{22} = 0. \tag{4.6}$$

But this means

$$H_{12} = -\Sigma_{11}^{-1}\Sigma_{12}H_{22}. \tag{4.7}$$

Finally, substituting Eq. (4.7) in the lower right hand block of Eq. (4.5), we find

$$\Sigma_{22}^* = H'_{22}(\Sigma_{22} - \Sigma_{21}\Sigma_{11}^{-1}\Sigma_{12})H_{22}.$$

Since Σ is positive definite, so is $\Sigma_{22} - \Sigma_{21}\Sigma_{11}^{-1}\Sigma_{12}$. Thus, there exists a matrix, say H_{22}^{-1}, such that

$$H_{22}'^{-1}H_{22}^{-1} = \Sigma_{22} - \Sigma_{21}\Sigma_{11}^{-1}\Sigma_{12}. \tag{4.8}$$

In particular, we may choose H_{22} so that the second equation in Eq. (4.2) is satisfied with $P = I$, simply by choosing H_{22} so as to satisfy Eq. (4.8). We further note that, with this choice of H, the transformed coefficient matrix becomes

$$A^*H = (\alpha_0, \ A_0^*), \quad \text{where} \quad A_0^* = (A_0 - \alpha_0\Sigma_{11}^{-1}\Sigma_{12})H_{22}. \tag{4.9}$$

Thus, we have established that there exists a matrix H satisfying conditions i and ii above, and it is of the form

$$H = \begin{bmatrix} I & -\Sigma_{11}^{-1}\Sigma_{12}H_{22} \\ 0 & H_{22} \end{bmatrix}, \tag{4.10}$$

---

[1] As an exercise, the reader might ask himself : Why transform on the right and not, for example, on the left? Hint: Recall that we are dealing with observations on the vectors $z_t. A^* = u_t$.

where H_{22} is chosen so that

$$H'_{22}(\Sigma_{22} - \Sigma_{21}\Sigma_{11}^{-1}\Sigma_{12})H_{22} = I. \tag{4.11}$$

Now, what is the LF of the transformed system? Since $\{u_{t\cdot} : t = 1, 2, \ldots, T\}$ is an i.i.d. sequence of zero mean normal vectors with covariance matrix, $\Sigma > 0$, we conclude that the vectors $H'u'_{t\cdot}$ have the same properties, except that

$$\text{Cov}(H'u'_{t\cdot}) = H'E(u'_{t\cdot}u_{t\cdot})H = H'\Sigma H. \tag{4.12}$$

The joint density of these vectors is

$$p(u_{1\cdot}H, \ldots, u_{t\cdot}H) = (2\pi)^{-mT/2} \mid H'\Sigma H \mid^{-T/2} \tag{4.13}$$

$$\times \exp\left[-\frac{1}{2}\sum_{t=1}^{T}(u_{t\cdot}H)(H^{-1}\Sigma^{-1}H'^{-1})(u_{t\cdot}H)'\right].$$

Consider the transformation

$$u_{t\cdot}H = y_{t\cdot}B^*H - x_{t\cdot}CH \tag{4.14}$$

and note that the Jacobian is given by

$$J = \mid H'B^{*'}B^*H \mid^{1/2}. \tag{4.15}$$

Hence the LF of the current endogenous variables is

$$L(A^*, H, \Sigma; Y, X) = -\frac{mT}{2}\ln(2\pi) - \frac{T}{2}\ln \mid H'\Sigma H \mid \tag{4.16}$$

$$+\frac{T}{2}\ln \mid H'B^*B^{*'}H \mid -\frac{1}{2}\sum_{t=1}^{T}(z_{t\cdot}A^*H)(H'\Sigma H)^{-1}(z_{t\cdot}A^*H)',$$

where $z_{t\cdot} = (y_{t\cdot}, x_{t\cdot})$. Using the notation in Eqs. (4.3) and (4.4), we can rewrite the last term of the right hand member of Eq. (4.16) as

$$\sum_{t=1}^{T}(z_{t\cdot}A^*H)(H'\Sigma H)^{-1}(z_{t\cdot}A^*H)' = \text{tr}(ZA^*H)(H'\Sigma H)^{-1}(ZA^*H)'.$$

$$\tag{4.17}$$

Our next step is to use the properties of the transforming matrix H so as to derive a notation that separates, as far as possible, the parameters of interest from those in which we have no interest. Thus, partition

$$A^*H = \begin{bmatrix} B^*H \\ -CH \end{bmatrix} = \begin{bmatrix} B_I & B_{II} \\ C_I & C_{II} \end{bmatrix} = (\alpha_0, A_0^*). \tag{4.18}$$

The obvious meaning is that

$$B^{**} = B^*H = (B_I, B_{II}), \quad \alpha_0 = \begin{bmatrix} B_I \\ C_I \end{bmatrix}, \quad -CH = (C_I, C_{II}), \tag{4.19}$$

and $A_0^* = (B_{II}', \ C_{II}')'$. We have, therefore,

$$\mathrm{tr}(ZA^*H)(H'\Sigma H)^{-1}(ZA^*H)' = T\mathrm{tr}\begin{bmatrix} \Sigma_{11}^{-1} & 0 \\ 0 & I \end{bmatrix}\begin{bmatrix} \alpha_0' \\ A_0^{*'} \end{bmatrix} M \begin{bmatrix} \alpha_0' \\ A_0^{*'} \end{bmatrix}'$$

$$= T\mathrm{tr}(\Sigma_{11}^{-1}\alpha_0' M\alpha_0) + T\mathrm{tr}(A_0^{*'} M A_0^*), \tag{4.20}$$

where $M = (Z'Z/T)$. We may, therefore, write the LF as

$$L(\alpha_0, \ \Sigma_{11}, \ A_0^*; \ Y, \ X) = c - \frac{T}{2}\ln | \Sigma_{11} | + \frac{T}{2}\ln | B^{**'} B^{**} |$$

$$- \frac{T}{2}\mathrm{tr}(\Sigma_{11}^{-1}\alpha_0' M\alpha_0) - \frac{T}{2}\mathrm{tr}(A_0^{*'} M A_0^*), \tag{4.21}$$

where $c = -(mT/2)\ln(2\pi)$. We observe that the transformation has simplified matters considerably, in that the parameters of interest, $(\alpha_0, \ \Sigma_{11})$, are almost completely segregated from those in which we have no interest, namely, A_0^*. A substantial nonlinearity still remains, however, in that the Jacobian term contains a submatrix of α_0, viz. B_I, and a submatrix of A_0^*, viz. B_{II}. Our next step is to eliminate the nuisance parameters in A_0^* by partially maximizing Eq. (4.21) with respect to them, and substituting therein their maximizing values. We stress again that in maximizing with respect to A_0^*, **we neglect all** *a priori* **restrictions** on its elements and thus, we are left to deal with a smaller, and perhaps simpler, system of equations in obtaining an estimator for α_0.

The first order conditions for partial maximization with respect to A_0^* are

$$\frac{\partial L}{\partial \mathrm{vec}(A_0^*)} = \frac{T}{2}\left(\frac{\partial \ln | B^{**'} B^{**} |}{\partial \mathrm{vec}(B_{II})}, \ 0\right) - \frac{T}{2}\frac{\partial \mathrm{tr}A_0^{*'} M A_0^*}{\partial \mathrm{vec}(A_0^*)} = 0, \tag{4.22}$$

where we have made use of the notation of Eq. (4.19), i.e. $B^{**} = (B_I, \ B_{II})$. From Proposition 104, Corollaries 36 and 37, Dhrymes (1984), we obtain

$$\frac{\partial \ln | B^{**'} B^{**} |}{\partial \mathrm{vec}(B_{II})} = 2\mathrm{vec}(B^{**})'[(B^{**'} B^{**})^{-1} \otimes I]\frac{\partial \mathrm{vec}(B^{**})}{\partial \mathrm{vec}(B_{II})}$$

$$= 2\mathrm{vec}[B^{**}(B^{**'} B^{**})^{-1}]'\begin{bmatrix} 0 \\ I_{m-m^*} \end{bmatrix}$$

$$= 2\mathrm{vec}(B^{**'-1})'\begin{bmatrix} 0 \\ I_{m-m^*} \end{bmatrix}. \tag{4.23}$$

If we put

$$B^{**'-1} = (J_1, \ J_2) \tag{4.24}$$

we obtain

$$\frac{\partial \ln | B^{**'} B^{**} |}{\partial \mathrm{vec}(B_{II})} = 2\mathrm{vec}(J_2)',$$

or,

$$\frac{\partial \ln | B^{**'} B^{**} |}{\partial B_{II}} = 2J_2. \tag{4.25}$$

Moreover, since

$$\frac{\partial \text{tr}(A_0^{*'} M A_0^*)}{\partial \text{vec}(A_0^*)} = 2\text{vec}(A_0^*)'(I \otimes M)$$

we have

$$\frac{\partial \text{tr}(A_0^{*'} M A_0^*)}{\partial (A_0^*)} = 2M A_0^*. \tag{4.26}$$

Thus, writing the first order conditions of Eq. (4.22) in matrix, rather than vector, form yields

$$\begin{bmatrix} J_2 \\ 0 \end{bmatrix} - M A_0^* = 0. \tag{4.27}$$

We further observe that, since

$$I = B^{**'} B^{**'-1} = B^{**'} J = \begin{bmatrix} B_I' J_1 & B_I' J_2 \\ B_{II}' J_1 & B_{II}' J_2 \end{bmatrix}, \tag{4.28}$$

we must have

$$B_I' J_1 = I, \quad B_{II}' J_2 = I, \quad B_I' J_2 = 0, \quad B_{II}' J_1 = 0. \tag{4.29}$$

Let us partition M by

$$M = \frac{1}{T} \begin{bmatrix} Y'Y & Y'X \\ X'Y & X'X \end{bmatrix} = \begin{bmatrix} \tilde{M}_{yy} & \tilde{M}_{yx} \\ \tilde{M}_{xy} & \tilde{M}_{xx} \end{bmatrix} \tag{4.30}$$

and note that

$$M A_0^* = \begin{bmatrix} \tilde{M}_{yy} B_{II} + \tilde{M}_{yx} C_{II} \\ \tilde{M}_{xy} B_{II} + \tilde{M}_{xx} C_{II} \end{bmatrix}. \tag{4.31}$$

Hence, Eq. (4.27) merely states that

$$J_2 = \tilde{M}_{yy} B_{II} + \tilde{M}_{yx} C_{II}, \quad 0 = \tilde{M}_{xy} B_{II} + \tilde{M}_{xx} C_{II}. \tag{4.32}$$

Eliminating C_{II} from Eq. (4.32), we find [2]

$$J_2 = W B_{II}, \quad W = \tilde{M}_{yy} - \tilde{M}_{yx} \tilde{M}_{xx}^{-1} \tilde{M}_{xy}. \tag{4.33}$$

It will be extremely difficult, if not impossible, to find an explicit expression for the elements of A_0^* in terms of the elements of α_0. Fortunately, this is not necessary; what we need, in order to obtain the "concentrated" likelihood function, are the maximizing values of $\text{tr}(A_0^{*'} M A_0^*)$ and

---

[2] Notice, incidentally, that W is the second moment matrix of residuals of the OLS estimated reduced form of the (entire) system.

$\ln \mid B^{**'} B^{**} \mid$. But from Eqs. (4.19) and (4.27) we have

$$A_0^{*'} M A_0^* = (B_{II}', \ C_{II}') \begin{bmatrix} J_2 \\ 0 \end{bmatrix} = B_{II}' J_2. \tag{4.34}$$

Furthermore, in view of Eq. (4.29), $B_{II}' J_2 = I_{m-m^*}$, so that

$$\text{tr}(A_0^{*'} M A_0^*) = \text{tr}(I_{m-m*}) = m - m^*. \tag{4.35}$$

To obtain the maximizing value of $\ln \mid B^{**'} B^{**} \mid$, we note

$$\mid (B_I, \ B_{II})' W (B_I B_{II}) \mid = \mid B_I, \ B_{II} \mid^2 \mid W \mid. \tag{4.36}$$

However,

$$(B_I, \ B_{II})' W (B_I, \ B_{II}) = \begin{bmatrix} B_I' W B_I & B_I' W B_{II} \\ B_{II}' W B_I & B_{II}' W B_{II} \end{bmatrix}, \tag{4.37}$$

and from Eqs. (4.29) and (4.33), we find

$$B_I' W B_{II} = 0, \quad B_{II}' W B_{II} = I_{m-m^*}. \tag{4.38}$$

Finally, from Eqs. (4.36), (4.37), and (4.38), we conclude

$$\ln \mid B^{**'} B^{**} \mid = \ln \mid B_I' W B_I \mid - \ln \mid W \mid. \tag{4.39}$$

Inserting the maximizing values of Eqs. (4.35) and (4.39) into Eq. (4.21), we obtain the "concentrated" likelihood function

$$L(\alpha_0, \Sigma_{11}; \ Y, \ X) \ = \ c^* - \frac{T}{2} \ln \mid \Sigma_{11} \mid + \frac{T}{2} \ln \mid B_I' W B_I \mid$$

$$- \frac{T}{2} \text{tr}(\Sigma_{11}^{-1} \alpha_0' M \alpha_0), \tag{4.40}$$

where $c^* = -(mT/2)[\ln(2\pi) + 1] + \frac{T}{2} m * - \frac{T}{2} \ln W$.

This essentially accomplishes the task we set out to accomplish initially. The parameters in which we had no interest, viz. Σ_{12}, Σ_{22}, A_0, have been eliminated, and now we are dealing, solely, with α_0 and Σ_{11}. Next, as in FIML, we make use of all *a priori* restrictions [3] on α_0, and maximize Eq. (4.40) with respect to the unknown parameters of α_0 and Σ_{11}. As in the case of FIML, it is not easy to give an explicit representation for the LIML estimator of α_0. However, the same remarks concerning algorithms for obtaining FIML estimators apply here as well.

---

[3] There may well be *a priori* restrictions on Σ_{11}, and such restrictions, of course, must be used. Typically, however, we do not assert that we know more about Σ_{11} beyond the fact that it is positive definite.

4.2   The Single Equation LIML Estimator

Here we examine in considerable detail the nature of the LIML estimator
when the subsystem of interest consists of a single equation, say the first.
In terms of the (standard) notation of the earlier discussion, we are dealing
with

$$
m* = 1, \quad \alpha_0 = \begin{bmatrix} \beta_{.1}^{\circ} \\ 0 \\ -\gamma_{.1} \\ 0 \end{bmatrix}, \quad B_I = \begin{bmatrix} \beta_{.1}^{\circ} \\ 0 \end{bmatrix}, \quad C_I = \begin{bmatrix} -\gamma_{.1} \\ 0 \end{bmatrix}, \quad \Sigma_{11} = \sigma_{11}.
$$

$$(4.41)$$

If we attempt to maximize Eq. (4.40), without imposing the standard normalization, we shall not find it possible to estimate, by LIML techniques,
all the elements of $\beta_{.1}^{\circ}$. In the end, there will remain one degree of ar-
bitrariness; this may be removed by imposing a normalization convention
on $\beta_{.1}^{\circ}$. In 2SLS, we did so, *ab initio*, by the condition $b_{11}^{*} = 1$. In LIML
estimation, we are more flexible. Instead of elaborating at this point, we
shall wait until the matter arises naturally in the discussion.

Let us return to the development of our argument, and partition M
conformably with α_0, as shown in Eq. (4.41). Thus,

$$
M = \begin{bmatrix} M_{11} & M_{12} & M_{13} & M_{14} \\ M_{21} & M_{22} & M_{23} & M_{24} \\ M_{31} & M_{32} & M_{33} & M_{34} \\ M_{41} & M_{42} & M_{43} & M_{44} \end{bmatrix}.
$$

$$(4.42)$$

From the discussion above, note that M_{11} is $(m_1 + 1) \times (m_1 + 1)$. Furthermore, partition W conformably with $(\beta_{.1}^{\circ'}, 0)'$, to obtain

$$
W = \begin{bmatrix} W_{11} & W_{12} \\ W_{21} & W_{22} \end{bmatrix}.
$$

$$(4.43)$$

In this notation, we have

$$
\alpha_0' M \alpha_0 = \beta_{.1}^{\circ'} M_{11} \beta_{.1}^{\circ} - 2\gamma_{.1}' M_{31} \beta_{.1}^{\circ} + \gamma_{.1}' M_{33} \gamma_{.1}
$$

$$
B_I' W B_I = \beta_{.1}^{\circ'} W_{11} \beta_{.1}^{\circ}.
$$

$$(4.44)$$

Thus, the concentrated LF, in the **special case** of the **first structural
equation**, may be written as

$$
L(\beta_{.1}^{\circ}, \gamma_{.1}, \sigma_{11}; Y, X) = c_0 - \frac{T}{2}\ln\sigma_{11} + \frac{T}{2}\ln(\beta_{.1}^{\circ'}W_{11}\beta_{.1}^{\circ}) \qquad (4.45)
$$

$$
- \frac{T}{2}\frac{1}{\sigma_{11}}\begin{pmatrix} \beta_{.1}^{\circ} \\ -\gamma_{.1} \end{pmatrix}'\begin{bmatrix} M_{11} & M_{13} \\ M_{31} & M_{33} \end{bmatrix}\begin{pmatrix} \beta_{.1}^{\circ} \\ -\gamma_{.1} \end{pmatrix},
$$

where,

$$c_0 = -\frac{mT}{2}[\ln(2\pi) + 1] + \frac{T}{2}(1 - \ln |W|). \qquad (4.46)$$

This is now to be maximized with respect to $\beta^\circ_{\cdot 1}$, $\gamma_{\cdot 1}$, and σ_{11}. We follow a stepwise maximization procedure. Maximizing, first with respect to $\gamma_{\cdot 1}$, and writing the result in column form, we obtain

$$\left(\frac{\partial L}{\partial \gamma_{\cdot 1}}\right)' = -\frac{T}{2}\frac{1}{\sigma_{11}}(-2M_{31}\beta^\circ_{\cdot 1} + 2M_{33}\gamma_{\cdot 1}) = 0, \qquad (4.47)$$

which implies

$$\gamma_{\cdot 1} = M_{33}^{-1}M_{31}\beta^\circ_{\cdot 1}. \qquad (4.48)$$

It is apparent that, for given $\beta^\circ_{\cdot 1}$ and σ_{11}, $\gamma_{\cdot 1}$ of Eq. (4.48) **globally** maximizes Eq. (4.45). Inserting Eq. (4.48) into Eq. (4.45) and maximizing with respect to σ_{11}, we find

$$\frac{\partial L}{\partial \sigma_{11}} = -\frac{T}{2}\frac{1}{\sigma_{11}} + \frac{T}{2}\frac{1}{\sigma_{11}^2}\beta^{\circ'}_{\cdot 1}(M_{11} - M_{13}M_{33}^{-1}M_{31})\beta^\circ_{\cdot 1} = 0, \qquad (4.49)$$

which implies

$$\hat{\sigma}_{11} = \beta^{\circ'}_{\cdot 1}(M_{11} - M_{13}M_{33}^{-1}M_{31})\beta^\circ_{\cdot 1}. \qquad (4.50)$$

Since, given $\beta^\circ_{\cdot 1}$, the (concentrated) LF is **concave**, the estimator in Eq. (4.50) corresponds to a **global maximum**. Now inserting Eqs. (4.50) and (4.48) into Eq. (4.45), we have

$$L(\beta^0_{\cdot 1}; Y, X) = c_0 - \frac{T}{2} - \frac{T}{2}\ln\left(\frac{\beta^{\circ'}_{\cdot 1}W^*_{11}\beta^{\circ'}_{\cdot 1}}{\beta^{\circ'}_{\cdot 1}W_{11}\beta^\circ_{\cdot 1}}\right), \qquad (4.51)$$

where,

$$W^*_{11} = M_{11} - M_{13}M_{33}^{-1}M_{31}. \qquad (4.52)$$

To maximize Eq. (4.51), it is simpler to use an alternative to the straightforward differentiation process. We first note that maximizing Eq. (4.51) is equivalent to **minimizing**

$$h(\beta^\circ_{\cdot 1}) = \frac{\beta^{\circ'}_{\cdot 1}W^*_{11}\beta^\circ_{\cdot 1}}{\beta^{\circ'}_{\cdot 1}W_{11}\beta^\circ_{\cdot 1}}. \qquad (4.53)$$

Remark 1. This is a convenient time to examine how normalization requirements intrude in LIML, and how they are handled. In Eq. (4.51) we have the concentrated LF, which is now to be maximized in order to obtain the estimator for $\beta^\circ_{\cdot 1}$, say $\hat{\beta}^\circ_{\cdot 1}$; inserting the latter in Eqs. (4.48) and (4.50), yields the estimators for σ_{11} and $\gamma_{\cdot 1}$, respectively, and thus completes the LIML estimation process. The difficulty with Eq. (4.51) (or (4.53) for that matter) is that the concentrated LF, as exhibited therein, is **homogeneous of degree zero** in the unknown parameter. Thus, the maximizing value of $\beta_{\cdot 1}^{\circ}$, if it exists, will not be unique. Indeed, if $\tilde{\beta}_{\cdot 1}^{\circ}$ is such a value, $c\tilde{\beta}_{\cdot 1}^{\circ}$, where c is any scalar, will be a maximizing value as well. We may eliminate this indeterminacy by imposing a **normalization requirement**. Thus, LIML does not escape the need to impose a normalizing convention, but it affords us greater flexibility in dealing with normalizations. While in 2SLS and 3SLS we were required *ab initio* to set, in the first equation, the first element of $\beta_{\cdot 1}^{\circ}$ **equal to unity**, in the present context this type of normalization **is not an integral part of the estimation procedure**; in fact, any other type of normalization will do as well. We may, for example, require that $\beta_{\cdot 1}^{\circ'} W_{11} \beta_{\cdot 1}^{\circ} = 1$. We shall not pursue such issues at this stage, preferring to continue our argument to its conclusion, without **first** imposing a normalization convention.

This is also a convenient time for showing that the stepwise maximization procedure, employed above, is fully equivalent to a "simultaneous" maximization approach. Thus, simultaneously maximizing we obtain, writing the results in column form,

$$\left(\frac{\partial L}{\partial \gamma_{\cdot 1}}\right)' = -\frac{T}{2}\frac{1}{\sigma_{11}}(-2M_{31}\beta_{\cdot 1}^{\circ} + 2M_{33}\gamma_{\cdot 1}) = 0$$

$$\frac{\partial L}{\partial \sigma_{11}} = -\frac{T}{2}\frac{1}{\sigma_{11}} + \frac{T}{2}\frac{1}{\sigma_{11}^2}(\beta_{\cdot 1}^{\circ'} M_{11}\beta_{\cdot 1}^{\circ} - 2\beta_{\cdot 1}^{\circ'} M_{13}\gamma_{\cdot 1} + \gamma_{\cdot 1}' M_{33}\gamma_{\cdot 1}) = 0$$

$$\left(\frac{\partial L}{\partial \beta_{\cdot 1}^{\circ}}\right)' = \frac{T}{2}\frac{2W_{11}\beta_{\cdot 1}^{\circ}}{\beta_{\cdot 1}^{\circ'} W_{11}\beta_{\cdot 1}^{\circ}} - \frac{T}{2}\frac{1}{\sigma_{11}}(2M_{11}\beta_{\cdot 1}^{\circ} - 2M_{13}\gamma_{\cdot 1}) = 0. \qquad (4.54)$$

From the first and second equations, we easily obtain Eqs. (4.48) and (4.50). Substituting these values in the third equation above, yields

$$\frac{1}{\sigma_{11}}(\lambda W_{11} - W_{11}^*)\beta_{\cdot 1}^{\circ} = 0, \text{ or } (\lambda W_{11} - W_{11}^*)\beta_{\cdot 1}^{\circ} = 0, \ \lambda = \frac{\sigma_{11}}{\beta_{\cdot 1}^{\circ'} W_{11}\beta_{\cdot 1}^{\circ}}.$$

Since $\sigma_{11} > 0$, the preceding implies that the LIML estimator of $\beta_{\cdot 1}^{\circ}$ is simply one of the characteristic vectors of W_{11}^* in the metric of W_{11}.[4] As we shall see momentarily, this is exactly the conclusion we should arrive at, when we proceed to minimize the expression in Eq. (4.53), which will complete the demonstration that the step-wise and simultaneous maximization of the LF are equivalent procedures.

Now, let us proceed with the formal aspects of minimizing Eq. (4.53). Since W_{11} and W_{11}^* [5] are both positive definite matrices, we can simul-

---

[4] For a definition of this term see Dhrymes (1984), p. 73.

[5] Note that W_{11} is the second moment matrix of residuals from the regression of

$$Y_1^{\circ} = (y_{\cdot 1}, y_{\cdot 2}, \ldots, y_{\cdot m_1+1})$$

taneously decompose them by

$$W_{11} = F'F, \qquad W_{11}^* = F'\Lambda F, \qquad (4.55)$$

where F is a nonsingular matrix, and Λ is the (diagonal) matrix of the characteristic roots of W_{11}^* in the metric of W_{11}, i.e. its diagonal elements are the roots of

$$|\lambda W_{11} - W_{11}^*| = 0. \qquad (4.56)$$

Thus, the ratio in Eq. (4.53) may be written, because of Eq. (4.55), as

$$h(\beta_{\cdot 1}^{\circ}) = \frac{\beta_{\cdot 1}^{\circ\prime} F'\Lambda F \beta_{\cdot 1}^{\circ}}{\beta_{\cdot 1}^{\circ\prime} F'F \beta_{\cdot 1}^{\circ}} = \frac{\zeta'\Lambda\zeta}{\zeta'\zeta}, \qquad (4.57)$$

where

$$\zeta = F\beta_{\cdot 1}^{\circ}. \qquad (4.58)$$

Therefore,

$$h(\beta_{\cdot 1}^{\circ}) = \sum_{i=1}^{m_1+1} \lambda_i \frac{\zeta_i^2}{\sum_{j=1}^{m+1} \zeta_j^2}. \qquad (4.59)$$

The coefficients of λ_i are positive, and $\lambda_i \geq 0$; thus, we conclude

$$\min_i \lambda_i \leq h(\beta_{\cdot 1}^{\circ}) \leq \max_i \lambda_i. \qquad (4.60)$$

Since we wish to find the **global minimum** of the expression in Eq. (4.53), we must choose the estimator of $\beta_{\cdot 1}^{\circ}$, say $\tilde{\beta}_{\cdot 1}^{\circ}$, by the condition,

$$\hat{\lambda} = \min_i \lambda_i, \qquad (4.61)$$

which means that $\tilde{\beta}_{\cdot 1}^{\circ}$ is chosen to be the characteristic vector corresponding to the smallest characteristic root of W_{11}^* in the metric of W_{11}^*. To emphasize this aspect, note that such a characteristic root and vector obey

$$W_{11}^* \hat{\beta}_{\cdot 1}^{\circ} = \hat{\lambda} W_{11} \hat{\beta}_{\cdot 1}^{\circ}. \qquad (4.62)$$

Premultiplying by $\hat{\beta}_{\cdot 1}^{\circ\prime}$, we obtain

$$\hat{\lambda} = \frac{\hat{\beta}_{\cdot 1}^{\circ\prime} W_{11}^* \hat{\beta}_{\cdot 1}^{\circ}}{\hat{\beta}_{\cdot 1}^{\circ\prime} W_{11} \hat{\beta}_{\cdot 1}^{\circ}}, \qquad (4.63)$$

---

on X, and W_{11}^* is the second moment matrix of residuals from the regression of Y_1° on X_1. We stress that X is the matrix of observations on all the predetermined variables of the entire system, while X_1 is the matrix of observations on the predetermined variables actually appearing in, or more precisely not known to be absent from, the first structural equation.

which, indeed, attains the *maximum maximorum* of the LF. Thus, in contrast to the FIML procedure we followed in Chapter 3, which only guarantees a **local maximum**, in the LIML procedure we find the ML estimators by locating the **global maximum** of the LF.

Substituting in Eqs. (4.48) and (4.50), we obtain the LIML estimators of $\gamma_{.1}$ and σ_{11} as well. Consequently, the LIML procedure with respect to the first structural equation is complete, except for the normalization condition. Since characteristic vectors are unique only up to scalar multiplication we may, at this stage, remove this last ambiguity by imposing **any normalization scheme we choose**. In this fashion, LIML is shown to be more flexible about normalization conventions than is 2SLS.

We have therefore proved the important

Theorem 1. Consider the GLSEM as in Theorem 10, of Ch. 3. The concentrated likelihood function, for LIML purposes, relative to the first m^* structural equations is given by

$$ L(\alpha_0, \Sigma_{11}; Y, X) \;=\; c^* - \frac{T}{2}\ln\mid \Sigma_{11}\mid + \frac{T}{2}\ln\mid B_I'WB_I\mid $$

$$ - \frac{T}{2}\mathrm{tr}\Sigma_{11}^{-1}\alpha_0'M\alpha_0, \tag{4.64} $$

where $c^* = -(mT/2)[\ln(2\pi) + 1] + (T/2)m^* - (T/2)\ln\mid W\mid$, α_0 consists of the first m^* columns of A^*, B_I consists of the first m^* columns of B^* and Σ_{11} is a submatrix of Σ consisting of the latter's first m^* rows and columns. Moreover, the LIML estimator of the parameters of the **first structural equation** is given by

$$ \hat{\gamma}_{.1} = M_{33}^{-1}M_{31}\hat{\beta}_{.1}^{\circ}, \quad \hat{\sigma}_{11} = \hat{\beta}_{.1}^{\circ\prime}W_{11}^*\hat{\beta}_{.1}^{\circ}, \tag{4.65} $$

where $\hat{\beta}_{.1}^{\circ}$ is the characteristic vector corresponding to the smallest characteristic root of $\mid \lambda W_{11} - W_{11}^*\mid = 0$. Such estimators are uniquely determined, once a normalization condition is imposed on $\beta_{.1}^{\circ}$.

4.3   Consistency of the LIML Estimator

In determining the asymptotic properties of the LIML estimator, and its relation to other estimators it is important, first, to establish its consistency. We proceed to that objective by a series of lemmata.

Lemma 1. Under the standard assumptions for the GLSEM of Theorem 1, and assuming the first equation of the system to be identified,

$$ \bar{W}_{11} = \plim_{T\to\infty} W_{11} = \Omega_{11}^{\circ}, \quad \bar{W}_{11}^* = \plim_{T\to\infty} W_{11}^* = \Omega_{11}^{\circ} + \Pi_{21}^{\circ\prime}M_{44}^*\Pi_{21}^{\circ}, \tag{4.66} $$

where Ω_{11}° is $(m_1 + 1) \times (m_1 + 1)$ defined by the partition

$$\Omega = \begin{bmatrix} \Omega_{11}^{\circ} & \Omega_{12} \\ \Omega_{21}^{\circ} & \Omega_{22} \end{bmatrix}, \tag{4.67}$$

i.e. it is the covariance matrix of the reduced form errors corresponding to the dependent variables appearing in the first equation, $X = (X_1, \ X_1^*)$ and

$$\bar{M}_{44}^* = \plim_{T \to \infty} \frac{1}{T} X_1^{*'} [I - X_1 (X_1' X_1)^{-1} X_1'] X_1^*. \tag{4.68}$$

Proof: By definition

$$W_{11} = \frac{1}{T} Y_1^{\circ'} N Y_1^{\circ}, \quad \text{and} \quad W_{11}^* = \frac{1}{T} Y_1^{\circ'} N_1 Y_1^{\circ}, \tag{4.69}$$

where

$$Y_1^{\circ} = X \Pi_1^{\circ} + V_1^{\circ}, \quad \Pi_1^{\circ} = \begin{bmatrix} \Pi_{11}^{\circ} \\ \Pi_{21}^{\circ} \end{bmatrix}, \quad \Pi_1^{\circ} = (\pi_{\cdot 1}, \ \Pi_1), \quad V_1^{\circ} = (v_{\cdot 1}, \ V_1)$$

$$N = I - X(X'X)^{-1} X', \quad N_1 = I - X_1 (X_1' X_1)^{-1} X_1'. \tag{4.70}$$

Making use of Eq. (4.70) we can rewrite Eqs. (4.69) as

$$W_{11}^* = \frac{1}{T} [V_1^{\circ'} N_1 V_1^{\circ} + \Pi_1^{\circ'} X' N_1 X \Pi_1^{\circ} + \Pi_1^{\circ'} X' N_1 V_1^{\circ} + V_1^{\circ'} N_1 X \Pi_1^{\circ}]$$

$$W_{11} = \frac{1}{T} V_1^{\circ'} N V_1^{\circ}. \tag{4.71}$$

Under the standard assumptions, we have that

$$\plim_{T \to \infty} \frac{1}{T} X' X = M_{xx} = \begin{bmatrix} \bar{M}_{33} & \bar{M}_{34} \\ \bar{M}_{43} & \bar{M}_{44} \end{bmatrix} \tag{4.72}$$

is a positive definite matrix. Hence,

$$\bar{M}_{44}^* = \bar{M}_{44} - \bar{M}_{43} \bar{M}_{33}^{-1} \bar{M}_{34},$$

which shows that $\bar{M}_{44}^*$ is a well defined (nonsingular) positive definite matrix. Moreover, $\plim_{T \to \infty} (X'U/T) = 0$, and consequently,

$$\plim_{T \to \infty} W_{11} = \plim_{T \to \infty} \frac{1}{T} V_1^{\circ'} V_1^{\circ} = \Omega_{11}^{\circ}, \quad \plim_{T \to \infty} \frac{1}{T} X' N_1 X = \begin{bmatrix} 0 & 0 \\ 0 & M_{44}^* \end{bmatrix},$$

$$\plim_{T \to \infty} W_{11}^* = \plim_{T \to \infty} \frac{1}{T} V_1^{\circ'} V_1^{\circ} + \plim_{T \to \infty} \frac{1}{T} \Pi_1^{\circ'} X' N_1 X \Pi_1^{\circ}. \tag{4.73}$$

q.e.d.

Remark 2. It is worth pointing out that, in the right member of

$$\plim_{T \to \infty} W_{11}^* = \Omega_{11}^\circ + \Pi_{21}^{\circ'} M_{44}^* \Pi_{21}^\circ, \tag{4.74}$$

the first matrix, Ω_{11}°, is nonsingular, while the second matrix is of rank m_1. This is so, since identifiability for the first equation implies that $\operatorname{rank}(\Pi_{21}^\circ) = m_1$.

Lemma 2. Let $\{\lambda_i : i = 1, 2, \ldots, m_1 + 1\}$ be the characteristic roots of $\bar{W}_{11}^{*'}$ in the metric of $\bar{W}_{11}$. Then $\lambda_i \geq 1$ for all i, and moreover,

$$\min_i \lambda_i = 1. \tag{4.75}$$

Proof: Both $\bar{W}_{11}$ and $\bar{W}_{11}^*$ are positive definite matrices. Thus, the roots of

$$\mid \lambda \bar{W}_{11} - \bar{W}_{11}^* \mid = 0 \tag{4.76}$$

are all positive. Rewriting, in view of Lemma 1, we find

$$\mid (\lambda - 1)\Omega_{11}^\circ - \Pi_{21}^{\circ'} \bar{M}_{44}^* \Pi_{21}^\circ \mid = 0. \tag{4.77}$$

Since $\Pi_{21}^{\circ'} \bar{M}_{44}^* \Pi_{21}^\circ$ is a positive semidefinite matrix (of order $m_1 + 1$ and rank m_1) we conclude that if λ_i is a solution to Eq. (4.76), $(\lambda_i - 1)$ is a solution to Eq. (4.77) and moreover, $\lambda_i \geq 1$. But obviously $\lambda = 1$ satisfies Eq. (4.77). Thus, $\min_i \lambda_i = 1$.

q.e.d.

Remark 3. The fact that $\operatorname{rank}(\Pi_{21}^{\circ'} M_{44}^* \Pi_{21}^\circ) = m_1$, ensures that $\lambda = 1$ is **not a multiple root** of $\mid \lambda \bar{W}_{11} - \bar{W}_{11}^* \mid = 0$. On the other hand, the reader should note that if $\lambda = 1$ **is a multiple root, of multiplicity** $s \geq 1$, the matrix Π_{21}° **would have rank** $m_1 + 1 - s$.

We may now prove

Lemma 3. The LIML estimators of $\beta_{\cdot 1}^\circ$, $\gamma_{\cdot 1}$ are consistent.

Proof: We first observe that if $\hat{\lambda}$ is the smallest characteristic root of $\mid \lambda W_{11} - W_{11}^* \mid = 0$, the LIML estimator of $\beta_{\cdot 1}^\circ$, say $\hat{\beta}_{\cdot 1}^\circ$, is obtained, subject to appropriate normalization, as the solution of

$$(\hat{\lambda} W_{11} - W_{11}^*)\hat{\beta}_{\cdot 1}^\circ = 0, \tag{4.78}$$

and as such it is a continuous function of the elements of W_{11} and W_{11}^*, as is also $\hat{\lambda}$. By Propositions 28 and 40, Chapter 4 of Dhrymes (1989), the limit, $\bar{\lambda} = \plim_{T \to \infty} \hat{\lambda}$, $\bar{\beta}_{\cdot 1}^\circ = \plim_{T \to \infty} \hat{\beta}_{\cdot 1}^\circ$, exists and, from the previous lemma (which shows $\bar{\lambda} = 1$), $\bar{\beta}_{\cdot 1}^\circ$ may be found from the solution of $(\bar{W}_{11} - \bar{W}_{11}^*)\bar{\beta}_{\cdot 1}^{\circ} = 0$. Using the result of Lemma 1, this is equivalent to the solution of

$$\Pi_{21}^{\circ'} M_{44}^* \Pi_{21}^{\circ} \bar{\beta}_{\cdot 1}^{\circ} = 0. \tag{4.79}$$

Since M_{44}^* is positive definite, Eq. (4.79) implies that $\Pi_{21}^{\circ} \bar{\beta}_{\cdot 1}^{\circ} = 0$. But the first equation is identified; hence, $\mathrm{rank}(\Pi_{21}^{\circ}) = m_1$, and all vectors p satisfying $\Pi_{21}^{\circ} p = 0$, are of the form

$$p = c\beta_{\cdot 1}^{\circ}, \tag{4.80}$$

where $\beta_{\cdot 1}^{\circ}$ is the true parameter vector. Consequently, $\bar{\beta}_{\cdot 1}^{\circ} = c\beta_{\cdot 1}^{\circ}$, and, if a common normalization scheme is imposed on both $\beta_{\cdot 1}^{\circ}$ and $\bar{\beta}_{\cdot 1}^{\circ}$, we conclude $c = 1$, which shows that

$$\hat{\beta}_{\cdot 1}^{\circ} \xrightarrow{P} \beta_{\cdot 1}^{\circ}. \tag{4.81}$$

From the representation, $\hat{\gamma}_{\cdot 1} = M_{33}^{-1} M_{31} \hat{\beta}_{\cdot 1}^{\circ}$, we obtain

$$\hat{\gamma}_{\cdot 1} \xrightarrow{P} \gamma_{\cdot 1} = \bar{M}_{33}^{-1} \bar{M}_{31} \beta_{\cdot 1}^{\circ}. \tag{4.82}$$

Combining Eqs. (4.81) and (4.82), we conclude

$$\operatorname*{plim}_{T \to \infty} \hat{\delta}_{\cdot 1}^{\circ} = \operatorname*{plim}_{T \to \infty} \begin{bmatrix} \hat{\beta}_{\cdot 1}^{\circ} \\ -\hat{\gamma}_{\cdot 1} \end{bmatrix} = \delta_{\cdot 1}^{\circ}. \tag{4.83}$$

q.e.d.

Remark 4. The consistency of $\hat{\sigma}_{11}$, in Eq. (4.50), as an estimator of σ_{11} is easily established under two interesting types of normalization. For example, under the standard normalization $\beta_{\cdot 1}^{\circ} = (1, -\beta_{\cdot 1}')'$, Eq. (4.50) assumes the form

$$\hat{\sigma}_{11} = \frac{1}{T} \hat{u}_{\cdot 1}' \hat{u}_{\cdot 1}, \quad \hat{u}_{\cdot 1} = y_{\cdot 1} - Y_1 \hat{\beta}_{\cdot 1} - X_1 \hat{\gamma}_{\cdot 1}.$$

The consistency of this quantity was established when we examined 2SLS estimation. Another useful normalization is

$$\beta_{\cdot 1}^{\circ'} \Omega_{11}^{\circ} \beta_{\cdot 1}^{\circ} = 1. \tag{4.84}$$

Under this normalization, imposed also on the corresponding estimates, we obtain $\hat{\lambda} = \hat{\sigma}_{11}$ and, by Lemma 2,

$$1 = \operatorname*{plim}_{T \to \infty} \hat{\lambda} = \operatorname*{plim}_{T \to \infty} \hat{\sigma}_{11}. \tag{4.85}$$

Lest this conclusion create undue concern, we note that

$$\operatorname*{plim}_{T \to \infty} \hat{\beta}_{\cdot 1}^{\circ'} W_{11} \hat{\beta}_{\cdot 1}^{\circ} = \beta_{\cdot 1}^{\circ'} \Omega_{11}^{\circ} \beta_{\cdot 1}^{\circ} = e_{\cdot 1}' \Sigma e_{\cdot 1} = \sigma_{11},$$

where $e_{\cdot 1}$ is an m-element column vector, all of whose elements are zero except the first, which is unity. The normalization in Eq. (4.84) implies then that $\sigma_{11} = 1$, and, again, the estimator of σ_{11} is consistent.

4.4   An Interesting Interpretation of LIML

The LIML estimator may be interpreted as minimizing the quotient of two "residual" variances. Thus, even if the structural error distribution is not specified to be normal, or is not specified at all, we can still proceed in essentially the same manner. The distribution free method that may be inspired by LIML estimation, is the **least variance ratio method** (LVR), which may be motivated as follows. Consider again the first structural equation

$$Y_1^\circ \beta_{.1}^\circ = X_1 \gamma_{.1} + u_{.1}, \tag{4.86}$$

and the reduced form corresponding to Y_1°. Thus,

$$Y_1^\circ = X\Pi_1^\circ + V_1^\circ = X_1\Pi_{11}^\circ + X_1^*\Pi_{21}^\circ + V_1^\circ, \tag{4.87}$$

using the partition of Π_1° given in Eq. (4.70). Postmultiply Eq. (4.87) by $\beta_{.1}^\circ$, to obtain

$$Y_1^\circ \beta_{.1}^\circ = X_1\Pi_{11}^\circ \beta_{.1}^\circ + X_1^* \Pi_{21}^\circ \beta_{.1}^\circ + V_1^\circ \beta_{.1}^\circ. \tag{4.88}$$

Comparing with Eq. (4.87), we see that we must have

$$\Pi_{11}^\circ \beta_{.1}^\circ = \gamma_{.1}, \quad \Pi_{21}^\circ \beta_{.1}^\circ = 0, \quad V_1^\circ \beta_{.1}^\circ = u_{.1}. \tag{4.89}$$

Equations (4.88) and (4.89) imply that, **for the true parameter** $\beta_{.1}^\circ$, $Y_1^\circ \beta_{.1}^\circ$ **does not depend on** X_1^*. Now, for an arbitrary vector say s, if we regress $Y_1^\circ s$ on X, we obtain the vector of residuals $\hat{V}_1^\circ s$, and if we regress $Y_1^\circ s$ on X_1, we obtain the vector of residuals $\tilde{V}_1^\circ s$. In either case, Eqs. (4.88) and (4.89) suggest that these residuals may be used to obtain two estimators of σ_{11}, viz.

$$\hat{\sigma}_{11} = \frac{1}{T} s' \hat{V}_1^{\circ'} \hat{V}_1^\circ s, \quad \tilde{\sigma}_{11} = \frac{1}{T} s' \tilde{V}_1^{\circ'} \tilde{V}_1^\circ s.$$

The first estimator ignores the restrictions placed on the parameters of Eq. (4.88) by Eq. (4.89), while the second estimator observes these restrictions. We further note

$$\tilde{V}_1^{\circ'} \tilde{V}_1^\circ - \hat{V}_1^{\circ'} \hat{V}_1^\circ \geq 0,$$

and consequently that

$$\frac{\tilde{\sigma}_{11}}{\hat{\sigma}_{11}} = \frac{s' \tilde{V}_1^{\circ'} \tilde{V}_1^\circ s}{s' \hat{V}_1^{\circ'} \hat{V}_1^\circ s} \geq 1. \tag{4.90}$$

In the test of the hypothesis: $Y_1^\circ s$ does not depend on X_1^*, and the quantity

$$\frac{\tilde{\sigma}_{11}}{\hat{\sigma}_{11}} - 1$$

is proportional to the F-statistic used to test that hypothesis. Since, in in this context, **we know that for the true parameter vector** $\beta^{\circ}_{\cdot 1}$, $Y^{\circ}_1 \beta^{\circ}_{\cdot 1}$ **does not depend on** X^*_1, a reasonable way for estimating $\beta^{\circ}_{\cdot 1}$, i.e. for determining s, is by the condition that the quantity in the middle member of Eq. (4.90) is minimized.

Remark 5. This is the motivation and the rationale for the LVR estimator. **Note that nowhere did we use the fact that the structural errors are normally distributed**. Note also that this procedure does not, directly, offer a way of estimating $\gamma_{\cdot 1}$, or σ_{11}. Of course we can mimic the LIML procedure and put

$$\tilde{\gamma}_{\cdot 1} = M^{-1}_{33} M_{31} \tilde{\beta}^{\circ}_{\cdot 1}, \quad \tilde{\sigma}_{11} = \frac{1}{T}(Y^{\circ}_1 \tilde{\beta}^{\circ}_{\cdot 1} - X_1 \tilde{\gamma}_{\cdot 1})'(Y^{\circ}_1 \tilde{\beta}^{\circ}_{\cdot 1} - X_1 \tilde{\gamma}_{\cdot 1}),$$

where $\tilde{\beta}^{\circ}_{\cdot 1}$ is a suitably normalized vector that minimizes the ratio in Eq. (4.90). It can easily be verified that the LVR estimator is completely equivalent to the LIML estimator. Hence, whatever properties are proved for the latter, will also hold for the former provided that the system's structural errors obey a certain set of minimal restrictions.

4.5   Indirect Least Squares (ILS)

In developing the theory of LIML and LVR estimation we notice that these procedures rely, implicitly, on estimates of the reduced form. In addition, when we examined the identification problem, in Chapter 3, we saw that one characterization of identifiability is intimately related to the question of whether structural parameters can be recovered from reduced form parameters. The method of ILS is a procedure that seeks to obtain estimators of the structural parameters from estimates of reduced form parameters. Specifically, it poses the question: if an estimate of the reduced form is given, can we obtain estimates of the structural parameters? Can we do so uniquely? What properties can be ascribed to this procedure, as an estimator of the structural form?

For definiteness, let us begin with the first equation. We are given $\hat{\Pi} = (X'X)^{-1}X'Y$ and we are asked if it is possible to estimate the parameters $\beta^{\circ}_{\cdot 1}$, $\gamma_{\cdot 1}$ of the first structural equation and, if so, what are the properties of the estimators thus obtained? From equation (3.19), in Chapter 3, we see that the structural and reduced form parameters obey

$$\begin{bmatrix} \Pi^{\circ}_{11} & \Pi_{12} \\ \Pi^{\circ}_{21} & \Pi_{22} \end{bmatrix} \begin{bmatrix} \beta^{\circ}_{\cdot 1} & B^*_{12} \\ 0 & B^*_{22} \end{bmatrix} = \begin{bmatrix} \gamma_{\cdot 1} & C_{12} \\ 0 & C_{22} \end{bmatrix}. \tag{4.91}$$

The equations involving the structural parameters of the first equation are

$\Pi_{11}^{\circ}\beta_{\cdot 1}^{\circ} = \gamma_{\cdot 1}$, and $\Pi_{21}^{\circ}\beta_{\cdot 1}^{\circ} = 0$ or, more compactly,

$$\Pi_1^{\circ}\beta_{\cdot 1}^{\circ} = (\gamma_{\cdot 1}^{'}, 0)^{'}, \quad \text{where } \Pi_1^{\circ} = (\Pi_{11}^{\circ'}, \Pi_{21}^{\circ'})^{'}. \tag{4.92}$$

For estimation purposes, it is natural to write the analog of Eq. (4.92) as

$$\hat{\Pi}_1^{\circ}\beta_{\cdot 1}^{\circ} = (\gamma_{\cdot 1}^{'}, 0)^{'}, \tag{4.93}$$

and, subject to a suitable normalization, seek estimators of the structural parameters, say $\tilde{\beta}_{\cdot 1}^{\circ}$, and $\tilde{\gamma}_{\cdot 1}$, by solving the system in Eq. (4.93). It is clear that the system is recursive, and that the key to the problem is the solution of $\hat{\Pi}_{21}^{\circ}\beta_{\cdot 1}^{\circ} = 0$, for the estimator $\tilde{\beta}_{\cdot 1}^{\circ}$. If the first equation is identified, we know that $\text{rank}(\Pi_{21}^{\circ}) = m_1$; the dimension of the matrix is $(G - G_1) \times (m_1 + 1)$, with $G - G_1 \geq m_1$ so that, at first glance, it is not clear how our objective is to be accomplished. Thus, while the identification condition regarding the rank of Π_{21}° is useful, it is not totally determinative in the present context. Let us examine the matter in some detail. Using the results from Proposition 32, Dhrymes (1984), we obtain,

$$\hat{\Pi}_{21}^{\circ} = \Pi_{21}^{\circ} + \left(X_1^{*'}N_1X_1^{*}\right)^{-1} X^{*'}N_1V_1^{\circ}. \tag{4.94}$$

If $\beta_{\cdot 1}^{\circ}$ is the true parameter vector, the identification (rank) condition implies that (the only nonnull) vectors, p , satisfying $\Pi_{21}^{\circ}p = 0$ are vectors of the form $p = c\beta_{\cdot 1}^{\circ}$, with $c \neq 0$. The issue with ILS estimation, however, is whether there are any nonnull vectors p such that

$$\hat{\Pi}_{21}^{\circ}p = 0. \tag{4.95}$$

In view of Eq. (4.94) we may rewrite Eq. (4.95) as

$$\Pi_{21}^{\circ}p + \left(X_1^{*'}N_1X_1^{*}\right)^{-1} X^{*'}N_1V_1^{\circ}p = 0. \tag{4.96}$$

The representation in Eq. (4.96) shows that, except for the special case of just identification, we cannot confidently assert the existence of a nonnull solution of Eq. (4.95). What is the problem here and why does this not arise with respect to Eq. (4.92)? The answer is rather simple, indeed. In Eq. (4.92), we know **by assumption** that we are dealing with a set of equations which is **consistent, in the sense of Ch. 3, Dhrymes (1984)**; this ensures that there exists a unique vector, viz. the true parameter vector $\beta_{\cdot 1}^{\circ}$, that satisfies **all** of the equations of that set. We **do not have a similar assurance**, however, in the case of the system in Eq. (4.95). Indeed, typically, we would not expect to find a **single** vector that satisfies **all** equations therein. Recall that there are $G - G_1 \geq m_1$ equations in that set; after normalization is imposed there are only m_1 free elements in the vector p . Unless it is a consistent set of equations, there is no single vector that can satisfy all these equations. At first, therefore, it might appear that no ILS estimators exist, except in the case of just identification. However, there are certain variations of the approach above, which we may wish to explore. Thus, after normalization, we could find a **nonsingular** submatrix of order m_1 and, **ignoring the remaining** $G - G_1 - m_1$ equations in Eq. (4.95), obtain a solution. If the equation is identified, we are assured that there is at least one, but there may well be as many as $(G - G_1)!/m_1!(G - G_1 - m_1)!$ such matrices. Hence, with this approach, there is at least one, and perhaps many more ILS estimators for the parameters of the first equation. Evidently, we need not discuss underidentified equations, since it is meaningless to ask for estimators of structural parameters in such a context. Consequently, in the ensuing discussion we shall deal with a system all of whose equations are identified; we shall also conduct our discussion for the general case of the ith equation, using the selection matrix apparatus developed in Chapter 1.

The relation between reduced form and structural parameters, in the ith equation, is given by $\Pi b_{\cdot i}^* = c_{\cdot i}$. Since

$$Y_i^\circ = Y L_{1i}^\circ, \quad X_i = X L_{2i}, \quad X_i^* = X L_{2i}^*, \quad b_{\cdot i}^* = L_{1i}^\circ \beta_{\cdot 1}^\circ, \quad c_{\cdot i} = L_{2i} \gamma_{\cdot i}, \quad (4.97)$$

it is clear that, under the standard normalization, we can rewrite Eq. (4.92) as

$$\Pi L_{1i}^\circ \beta_{\cdot i}^\circ = L_{2i} \gamma_{\cdot i}, \quad \text{or} \quad \Pi_i \beta_{\cdot i} + L_{2i} \gamma_{\cdot i} = \pi_{\cdot i}, \quad i = 1, 2, \ldots, m. \quad (4.98)$$

We may render the representation more compact, and actually simplify the discussion, if we use the S-notation of earlier chapters; thus, rewrite Eq. (4.98) as

$$S_i \delta_{\cdot i} = \pi_{\cdot i}, \quad \text{where} \quad S_i = (\Pi_i, \ L_{2i}), \quad \Pi_i = \Pi L_{1i}, \quad (4.99)$$

and recall from Chapter 3, that for an identified equation S_i is of full column rank.

Thus, if we are dealing with the true parameters of the model, there exists a unique (the true parameter) vector $\delta_{\cdot i}$, that satisfies the equation above. Indeed, this is so by construction! The difficulty with ILS is that we are not operating with the system in Eq. (4.99). Instead, we replace Eq. (4.99) by

$$\hat{S}_i \tilde{\delta}_{\cdot i} = \hat{\pi}_{\cdot i}, \quad (4.100)$$

in which the quantities Π_i and $\pi_{\cdot i}$ of Eq. (4.99) have been replaced by their OLS estimators, $\hat{\Pi}_i$, $\hat{\pi}_{\cdot i}$ and we seek an estimator, i.e. a vector, say $\tilde{\delta}_{\cdot i}$, satisfying Eq. (4.100). It is this quantity that is traditionally called the ILS estimator. If the equation in question is **just identified**, evidently $\hat{S}_i$ is a nonsingular matrix; hence, there exists a unique solution, viz.

$$\tilde{\delta}_{\cdot i} = \hat{S}_i^{-1} \hat{\pi}_{\cdot i}, \quad (4.101)$$

which is defined to be the (unique) ILS estimator of $\delta_{\cdot i}$. It is easily verified that the estimator in Eq. (4.101) also represents the 2SLS estimator of a just identified equation. Thus, **in the case of just identification, 2SLS and ILS estimators coincide**.

What if the equation in question is overidentified? Well, in such a case the $G \times (m_i + G_i)$ matrix, S_i, has the property

$$G > G_i + m_i, \quad \text{rank}(S_i) = G_i + m_i.$$

For Eq. (4.100) to have a solution, it must be a consistent system of equations, in the sense of Ch. 3 of Dhrymes (1984). More specifically, $\hat{\pi}_{\cdot i}$ must lie in the column space of $\hat{S}_i$. Defining $S_i^\circ = (\Pi_i^\circ, \; L_{2i})$, we see that the requirement above implies the existence of a nonnull vector, c, such that $\hat{S}_i^\circ c = 0$, or alternatively,

$$[(X'X)^{-1}X'Y_i^\circ, \; L_{2i}]c = 0. \tag{4.102}$$

We shall now show that, in general, this is satisfied only with $c = 0$. Let $c = (c_{\cdot 1}', \; c_{\cdot 2}')'$, and rewrite the condition above as

$$(X'X)^{-1}X'V_i^\circ c_{\cdot 1} = -(\Pi_i^\circ c_{\cdot 1} + L_{2i}c_{\cdot 2}). \tag{4.103}$$

But the right member of the equation above is a fixed constant; hence, the left member must also be a fixed constant; this, however, is not possible since $v_{t\cdot}$ has a nondegenerate distribution and the matrix multiplying V_i° is of rank $G(\geq m_i + 1)$. On the other hand, for the choice

$$c_{\cdot 1} = \beta_{\cdot i}^\circ, \qquad c_{\cdot 2} = -\gamma_{\cdot i},$$

i.e. for the true parameter vectors, the condition above reads

$$(X'X)^{-1}X'u_{\cdot i} = -(\Pi_i^\circ \beta_{\cdot i}^\circ + L_{2i}\gamma_{\cdot i}) = 0.$$

Clearly, this equation is not satisfied for any finite sample size; however, as (the sample size) $T \to \infty$ we have

$$\left(\frac{X'X}{T}\right)^{-1} \frac{X'u_{\cdot i}}{T} \overset{\text{P}}{\to} 0,$$

by the standard properties of the GLSEM. What the preceding discussion shows is that, for an overidentified equation, Eq. (4.100) is not a consistent system of equations, for finite T. In particular, this means that no vector $\delta_{\cdot i}$ exists that satisfies all equations of Eq. (4.100). Thus, strictly speaking in terms of the traditional definition, ILS estimators for the parameters of an overidentified equation do not exist, in the sense of vectors $\hat{\delta}_{\cdot i}$ that satisfy **all** equations of Eq. (4.100). The fact that, asymptotically, these equations admit of a unique solution means that we could eliminate the "excess" $G - G_i - m_i$ equations in Eq. (4.100) and solve the resulting abbreviated system. The estimates thus obtained are, evidently, consistent. But the choice of equations to be eliminated is arbitrary, and this procedure has nothing to recommend it in empirical applications. This is particularly so, since with small samples we have no criteria by which to rank the prospective candidates. We are thus led to

Definition 1. In the context of the GLSEM, consider the estimator of the reduced form $\hat{\Pi} = (X'X)^{-1}X'Y$. The ILS estimator of the structural parameters of the ith equation is defined to be the solution of the problem

$$\min_{\delta_{\cdot i}}(\hat{\pi}_{\cdot i} - \hat{S}_i \delta_{\cdot i})'(\hat{\pi}_{\cdot i} - \hat{S}_i \delta_{\cdot i}), \quad \hat{S}_i = (\hat{\Pi}_i, L_{2i}),$$

and is given by

$$\tilde{\delta}_{\cdot i} = (\hat{S}_i)_g \hat{\pi}_{\cdot i}, \tag{4.104}$$

where $(\hat{S}_i)_g$ is the g-inverse of $\hat{S}_i$.[6]

Remark 6. Because, for an identified equation, $\hat{S}_i$ is of full rank we can write explicitly,

$$(\hat{S}_i)_g = (\hat{S}_i'\hat{S}_i)^{-1}\hat{S}_i', \quad \tilde{\delta}_{\cdot i} = (\hat{S}_i'\hat{S}_i)^{-1}\hat{S}_i'\hat{\pi}_{\cdot i} \tag{4.105}$$

When $\hat{S}_i$ is nonsingular

$$(\hat{S}_i)_g = \hat{S}_i^{-1},$$

and when the equation in question is just identified, the definition of the ILS estimator in terms of Eq. (4.104) corresponds, exactly, to the usual definition. The advantage of the definition in Eq. (4.104), is that it provides a formal definition for the ILS estimator which is always appropriate, provided (all) the equations of the GLSEM are identified.

It is easy to establish the consistency of the estimators defined in Eq. (4.104). To do so we note that since

$$\plim_{T\to\infty} \hat{S}_i = S_i, \quad S_i = (\Pi_i, L_{2i}), \quad \plim_{T\to\infty} \hat{\pi}_{\cdot i} = \pi_{\cdot i}, \; i = 1, 2, 3, \ldots, m,$$

the probability limit of the estimators in Eq. (4.104) is well defined.[7] Thus,

$$\plim_{T\to\infty} \tilde{\delta}_{\cdot i} = \bar{\delta}_{\cdot i} = (S_i'S_i)^{-1}S_i'\pi_i \tag{4.106}$$

Now, the true parameter vector, $\delta_{\cdot i}$ satisfies Eq. (4.99); hence, substituting above we find

$$\bar{\delta}_{\cdot i} = (S_i'S_i)^{-1}S_i'S_i\delta_{\cdot i}, \quad i = 1, 2, \ldots, m, \tag{4.107}$$

---

[6] For a definition of the g-inverse and related topics see Ch. 3 of Dhrymes (1984).

[7] It is interesting that the ILS can be derived in a Bayesian context as well. See Zellner (1978), Zellner et al. (1988).

which concludes the consistency argument.

To establish the limiting distribution of such estimators, we observe that, using Eqs. (4.105) and (4.106), we find

$$\sqrt{T}(\tilde{\delta}_{.i} - \delta_{.i}) = \sqrt{T}\left[(\hat{S}_i'\hat{S}_i)^{-1}\hat{S}_i' - (S_i'S_i)^{-1}S_i'\right]\pi_{.i}$$

$$+ (\hat{S}_i'\hat{S}_i)^{-1}\hat{S}_i'\left(\frac{X'X}{T}\right)^{-1}\frac{X'v_{.i}}{\sqrt{T}}. \qquad (4.108)$$

Consider the matrix in brackets, in the right member of Eq. (4.109). Adding and subtracting $(\hat{S}_i'\hat{S}_i)^{-1}S_i'$, we find

$$(\hat{S}_i'\hat{S}_i)^{-1}\hat{S}_i' - (S_i'S_i)^{-1}S_i' = (\hat{S}_i'\hat{S}_i)^{-1}[(\hat{S}_i - S_i)' - \{\hat{S}_i'(\hat{S}_i - S_i)$$

$$+ (\hat{S}_i - S_i)'S_i\}(S_i'S_i)^{-1}S_i']. \qquad (4.109)$$

Consequently,

$$\phi_i = \sqrt{T}\left[(\hat{S}_i'\hat{S}_i)^{-1}\hat{S}_i' - (S_i'S_i)^{-1}S_i'\right]\pi_{.i} = (\hat{S}_i'\hat{S}_i)^{-1}\sqrt{T}(\hat{S}_i - S_i)'\pi_{.i}$$

$$- (\hat{S}_i'\hat{S}_i)^{-1}\hat{S}_i'\sqrt{T}(\hat{S}_i - S_i)\delta_{.i} - (\hat{S}_i'\hat{S}_i)^{-1}\sqrt{T}(\hat{S}_i - S_i)'S_i\delta_{.i}$$

$$= -(\hat{S}_i'\hat{S}_i)^{-1}\hat{S}_i'\sqrt{T}(\hat{\Pi}_i - \Pi_i)\beta_{.i}. \qquad (4.110)$$

Thus, Eq. (4.108) can be rewritten as

$$\sqrt{T}(\tilde{\delta}_{.i} - \delta_{.i}) = (\hat{S}_i'\hat{S}_i)^{-1}\hat{S}_i'\left(\frac{X'X}{T}\right)^{-1}\frac{X'V_i^{\circ}}{\sqrt{T}}\beta_{.i}^{\circ}$$

$$= (\hat{S}_i'\hat{S}_i)^{-1}\hat{S}_i'\left(\frac{X'X}{T}\right)^{-1}\frac{X'V}{\sqrt{T}}b_{.i}^*, \qquad (4.111)$$

where, evidently, $b_{.i}^*$ is the ith column of B^*, subject to the standard normalization. Hence, the ILS estimator for the system as a whole obeys,

$$\sqrt{T}(\tilde{\delta} - \delta) = (\hat{S}'\hat{S})^{-1}\hat{S}'\left[I \otimes \left(\frac{X'X}{T}\right)^{-1}\right]\left(I \otimes \frac{X'V}{\sqrt{T}}\right)\text{vec}(B^*). \qquad (4.112)$$

But,

$$\left(I \otimes \frac{X'V}{\sqrt{T}}\right)\text{vec}(B^*) = \frac{1}{\sqrt{T}}\text{vec}(X'VB^*) \qquad (4.113)$$

$$= \frac{1}{\sqrt{T}}\text{vec}(X'U) = \frac{1}{\sqrt{T}}\sum_{t=1}^{T}(I \otimes x_{t.}')u_{t.}',$$

and Eq. (4.113) can be written, in the more convenient form,

$$\sqrt{T}\left(\tilde{\delta} - \delta\right) = (\hat{S}'\hat{S})^{-1}\hat{S}'\left[I \otimes \left(\frac{X'X}{T}\right)^{-1}\right]\frac{1}{\sqrt{T}}\sum_{t=1}^{T}(I \otimes x'_{t\cdot})u'_{t\cdot}.$$

But this represents a variant of the standard limiting distribution problem we have encountered in all simultaneous equations contexts, and which was dealt with adequately in Ch. 2. Consequently, we conclude

$$\sqrt{T}(\tilde{\delta} - \delta) \sim N(0, \ C_{ILS}), \tag{4.114}$$

where

$$C_{ILS} = (S'S)^{-1}S'(\Sigma \otimes M_{xx}^{-1})S(S'S)^{-1}. \tag{4.115}$$

We have therefore proved

Theorem 2. Consider the standard GLSEM

$$y_{t\cdot}B^* = X_{t\cdot}C + u_{t\cdot}, \ t = 1, 2, 3, \ldots, T,$$

as in Theorem 1. Let $\hat{\Pi} = (X'X)^{-1}X'Y$ be the OLS estimator of the reduced form, and let $\tilde{\delta}_{\cdot i}$ be the indirect least squares (ILS) estimator for the parameters of the ith structural equation, according to Definition 1. Then,

i. the ILS estimator for the parameters of the ith structural equation can be interpreted as minimizing

$$\psi_i = (\hat{\pi}_{\cdot i} - \hat{S}_i\delta_{\cdot i})'(\hat{\pi}_{\cdot i} - \hat{S}_i\delta_{\cdot i}), \ i = 1, 2, 3, \ldots, m;$$

ii. the ILS estimator is consistent;

iii. if, by $\tilde{\delta}$ we denote the ILS estimator for the entire system, then

$$\sqrt{T}(\tilde{\delta} - \delta)_{ILS} \sim N(0, \ C_{ILS}), \ \ C_{ILS} = (S'S)^{'-1}S'(\Sigma \otimes M_{xx}^{-1})S(S'S)^{-1}$$

and $S = \text{diag}(S_1, \ S_2, \ldots, S_m)$.

Corollary 1. If the ith equation is just identified then 2SLS and ILS estimators are asymptotically equivalent.

Proof: The ith diagonal block of the covariance matrix in iii above is

$$\sigma_{ii}(S'_iS_i)^{-1}S'_iM_{xx}^{-1}S_i(S'_iS_i)^{-1} = \sigma_{ii}(S'_iM_{xx}S_i)^{-1},$$

which coincides with the corresponding block of the covariance matrix of the systemwide 2SLS estimator.

Corollary 2. If the ith equation is just identified then ILS and 2SLS estimators are numerically identical.

Proof: The ILS estimator is given, in this case, by

$$\tilde{\delta}_{\cdot i} = (\hat{S}_i'\hat{S}_i)^{-1}\hat{S}_i'(X'X)^{-1}X'y_{\cdot i} = \hat{S}_i^{-1}(X'X)^{-1}X'y_{\cdot i},$$

which is exactly the 2SLS estimator.

4.6   Relation of LIML to Other Estimators

The basic step in obtaining the LIML estimator is the determination of a vector, $\hat{\beta}_{\cdot i}^{\circ}$, satisfying $(\hat{\lambda}W_{11} - W_{11}^*)\hat{\beta}_{\cdot 1}^{\circ} = 0$. It is interesting that the ILS estimator is, also, intimately related to the matrix $W_{11}^* - W_{11}$. Retracing the steps in the proof of Lemma 1, it is easy to show that

$$T[W_{11}^* - W_{11}] = \hat{\Pi}_{21}^{\circ'}X_1^{'*}N_1X_1^*\hat{\Pi}_{21}^{\circ} \tag{4.116}$$

where, we remind the reader, $N_1 = I - X_1(X_1'X_1)^{-1}X_1'$. Theorem 2 implies that, in the case of **just identification**, there exists a vector, viz. the ILS estimator $\tilde{\beta}_{\cdot 1}^{\circ}$, which is unique, subject to normalization, such that $\hat{\Pi}_{21}^{\circ}\tilde{\beta}_{\cdot 1}^{\circ} = 0$. Thus, in the **just identified** case, the ILS estimator satisfies

$$(W_{11}^* - W_{11})\tilde{\beta}_{\cdot 1}^{\circ} = 0, \tag{4.117}$$

which shows that $\tilde{\beta}_{\cdot 1}^{\circ}$ is the characteristic vector corresponding to the unit characteristic root of W_{11}^* in the metric of W_{11}. Since such roots are bounded below by unity, we have therefore proved

Lemma 4. In the case of just identification, the smallest root, $\hat{\lambda}$, of $|\lambda W_{11} - W_{11}^*| = 0$, obeys $\hat{\lambda} = 1$.

We may, also, prove

Lemma 5. In the case of just identification, LIML and ILS estimators coincide.

Proof: By Lemma 4, in the case of just identification $\hat{\lambda} = 1$. Consequently, the LIML estimator obeys

$$(W_{11} - W_{11}^*)\hat{\beta}_{\cdot 1}^{\circ} = 0. \tag{4.118}$$

A comparison with Eq. (4.117) shows that ILS and LIML estimators coincide.

q.e.d.

It is interesting that we can further show that LIML is a member of the k-class of estimators. To show this, it is more convenient to introduce the following notation (for the ith equation):

$$TW_{11}^* = Y_i^{\circ\prime} N_i Y_i^{\circ} = \begin{bmatrix} y_{\cdot i}' N_1 y_{\cdot i} & y_{\cdot i}' N_i Y_i \\ Y_{\cdot i}' N_1 y_{\cdot i} & Y_i' N_i Y_i \end{bmatrix}, \quad N_i = I - X_i (X_i' X_i)^{-1} X_i'$$

$$TW_{11} = Y_i^{\circ\prime} N Y_i^{\circ} = \begin{bmatrix} y_{\cdot i}' N y_{\cdot i} & y_{\cdot i}' N Y_i \\ Y_{\cdot i}' N y_{\cdot i} & Y_{\cdot i}' N Y_i \end{bmatrix}, \quad N = I - X(X'X)^{-1} X'.$$

Thus, we can write the equations defining the LIML estimator as

$$y_{\cdot 1}'(\hat{\lambda} N - N_1) Y_1 \hat{\beta}_{\cdot 1} = y_{\cdot 1}'(\hat{\lambda} N - N_1) y_{\cdot 1}$$

$$Y_{\cdot 1}'(\hat{\lambda} N - N_1) Y_1 \hat{\beta}_{\cdot 1} = Y_{\cdot 1}'(\hat{\lambda} N - N_1) y_{\cdot 1}$$

$$X_1' Y_1 \hat{\beta}_{\cdot 1} + X_1' X_1 \hat{\gamma}_{\cdot 1} = X_1' y_{\cdot 1}. \tag{4.119}$$

In Eq. (4.119) we have imposed the standard normalization, i.e. we have now put $\hat{\beta}_{\cdot 1}^{\circ} = (1, -\hat{\beta}_{\cdot 1}')'$. Subject to the normalization above, the vector $\hat{\beta}_{\cdot 1}$ is uniquely determined by the LIML procedure. It is also clear that, in the second set of Eq. (4.119), the matrix $Y_1'(\lambda N - N_1) Y_1$ is nonsingular; moreover, in view of Eq. (4.118), the first equation of Eq. (4.119) is redundant, i.e. the vector $\hat{\beta}_{\cdot 1}$ obtained from the second set satisfies the first equation as well. Thus, we need only deal with the last two sets of equations. Premultiply the last set in Eq. (4.119) by $Y_1' X_1 (X_1' X_1)^{-1}$ and subtract from the second set to obtain the equivalent system,

$$Y_{\cdot 1}'(I - \hat{\lambda} N) Y_1 \hat{\beta}_{\cdot 1} + Y_1' X_1 \hat{\gamma}_{\cdot 1} = Y_1'(I - \hat{\lambda} N) y_{\cdot 1}$$

$$X_1' Y_1 \hat{\beta}_{\cdot 1} \qquad\quad + X_1' X_1 \hat{\gamma}_{\cdot 1} = X' y_1.$$

We observe, however, that $Y_1' N Y_1 = \hat{V}_1' \hat{V}_1$, where $\hat{V}_1$ is the matrix of residuals in the regression of Y_1 on X. Thus, we can rewrite the system above as

$$\begin{bmatrix} Y_1' Y_1 - \hat{\lambda} \hat{V}_1' \hat{V}_1 & Y_1' X_1 \\ X_1' Y_1 & X_1' X_1 \end{bmatrix} \begin{pmatrix} \hat{\beta}_{\cdot 1} \\ \hat{\gamma}_{\cdot 1} \end{pmatrix} = \begin{bmatrix} Y_1' - \hat{\lambda} \hat{V}_1' \\ X_1' \end{bmatrix} y_{\cdot 1}. \tag{4.120}$$

A comparison of Eq. (4.120) to Eq. (2.115) of Ch. 2 shows that, under the standard normalization, the LIML is a k-class estimator with $k = \hat{\lambda}$.

The preceding discussion may be summarized in

Theorem 3. Consider the model of Theorem 1, and suppose the first equation of the system is identified. Let $\hat{\lambda}$ be the smallest root of

$$| \lambda W_{11} - W_{11}^* | = 0.$$

Then, the following statements are true:

   i. if the first (i^{th}) equation is just identified, $\hat{\lambda} = 1$;

   ii. if the first (i^{th}) equation is just identified, ILS and LIML estimators of its parameters are identical;

   iii. LIML is a k -class estimator with $k = \hat{\lambda}$.

4.7   Limiting Distribution of LIML Estimators

From Eq. (4.120), we easily find that

$$
\begin{bmatrix} \hat{\beta}_{\cdot i} \\ \hat{\gamma}_{\cdot i} \end{bmatrix} - \begin{bmatrix} \beta_{\cdot i} \\ \gamma_{\cdot i} \end{bmatrix} = \begin{bmatrix} Y_i'Y_i - \hat{\lambda}\hat{V}_i'\hat{V}_i & Y_i'X_i \\ X_i'Y_i & X_i'X_i \end{bmatrix}^{-1} \begin{bmatrix} \hat{\Pi}_i'X' \\ X_i' \end{bmatrix} u_{\cdot i} \tag{4.121}
$$

$$
+ (1 - \hat{\lambda}) \begin{bmatrix} Y_i'Y_i - \hat{\lambda}\hat{V}_i'\hat{V}_i & Y_i'X_i \\ X_i' & X_i'X_i \end{bmatrix}^{-1} \begin{bmatrix} \hat{V}_i' \\ 0 \end{bmatrix} u_{\cdot i}.
$$

The first term in the right member of Eq. (4.121) behaves, asymptotically, exactly as the 2SLS estimator since

$$
\frac{1}{T} \begin{bmatrix} Y_i'Y_i - \hat{\lambda}\hat{V}_i'\hat{V}_i & Y_i'X_i \\ X_i'Y_i & X_i'X_i \end{bmatrix} \overset{P}{\to} C_{2SLS}^{-1}, \tag{4.122}
$$

and Eq. (4.122) is valid, in view of the fact that $\text{plim}_{T \to \infty} \hat{\lambda} = 1$. Thus, asymptotically,

$$
\sqrt{T} \left(\begin{bmatrix} \hat{\beta}_{\cdot i} \\ \hat{\gamma}_{\cdot i} \end{bmatrix} - \begin{bmatrix} \beta_{\cdot i} \\ \gamma_{\cdot i} \end{bmatrix} \right)_{LIML} \sim \sqrt{T} \left(\begin{bmatrix} \hat{\beta}_{\cdot i} \\ \hat{\gamma}_{\cdot i} \end{bmatrix} - \begin{bmatrix} \beta_{\cdot i} \\ \gamma_{\cdot i} \end{bmatrix} \right)_{2SLS}
$$

$$
+ \sqrt{T}(1 - \hat{\lambda})C_{2SLS}\frac{1}{T} \begin{bmatrix} V_i'u_{\cdot i} \\ 0 \end{bmatrix}. \tag{4.123}
$$

Notice, further, that $(1/T)\hat{V}_i'u_{\cdot i} \overset{P}{\to} D_i'\sigma_{\cdot i}$, which is a vector with finite elements, D_i being an appropriate submatrix of B^{*-1} , and $\sigma_{\cdot i}$ the ith column of Σ . Moreover, as we shall show in the appendix of this chapter, $\sqrt{T}(1 - \hat{\lambda}) \overset{P}{\to} 0$. Hence, we conclude from Eq. (4.123), that

$$
\sqrt{T} \left(\begin{bmatrix} \hat{\beta}_{\cdot i} \\ \hat{\gamma}_{\cdot i} \end{bmatrix} - \begin{bmatrix} \beta_{\cdot i} \\ \gamma_{\cdot i} \end{bmatrix} \right)_{LIML} \sim \sqrt{T} \left(\begin{bmatrix} \hat{\beta}_{\cdot i} \\ \hat{\gamma}_{\cdot i} \end{bmatrix} - \begin{bmatrix} \beta_{\cdot i} \\ \gamma_{\cdot i} \end{bmatrix} \right)_{2SLS} \sim N(0, \sigma_{11}C_{2SLS}),
$$

which shows that, subject to the standard normalization, LIML and 2SLS estimators have the same limiting distribution. It is clear, of course, that the covariance matrix of the limiting distribution can be consistently estimated and, thus, tests of significance can be carried out with respect to elements of $\beta_{\cdot i}^{\circ}$ and $\gamma_{\cdot i}$.

4.8   Classic Identifiability Tests

The limiting distribution, above, does not afford us a means for testing the validity of the exclusion restrictions that ensured identifiability in the first place. However, it is possible to construct such a test without undue additional computations.

Let us see how this may be motivated. We ask the basic question: if an equation is identified (by the standard exclusion restrictions), what connection, if any, exists between the rank condition for identification and the exclusion restrictions? In other words, what do the prior restrictions on the **structural parameters**, contained in the matrices B^*, C, imply for the reduced form matrix Π? To set forth the issue fully, with respect to the ith equation, we require a more careful notation. We begin with the obvious fact that for the ith equation we have, $\Pi b^*_{\cdot i} = c_{\cdot i}$; moreover, using the selection and exclusion matrices, as developed in Chapters 1, 2, and 3, yields $\beta^\circ_{\cdot i} = L^{\circ'}_{1i} b^*_{\cdot i}$, $\beta^*_{\cdot i} = L^{*'}_{1i} b^*_{\cdot i}$, $\gamma_{\cdot i} = L^{'}_{2i} c_{\cdot i}$, $\gamma^*_{\cdot i} = L^{*'}_{2i} c_{\cdot i}$ and enables us to write the relation above as

$$\Pi(L^\circ_{1i}, L^*_{1i}) \begin{bmatrix} \beta_{\cdot i} \\ \beta^*_{\cdot i} \end{bmatrix} = (L_{2i}, L^*_{2i}) \begin{bmatrix} \gamma_{\cdot i} \\ \gamma^*_{\cdot i} \end{bmatrix}.$$

The exclusion restrictions in the ith equation imply, $\beta^*_{\cdot i} = 0$ and $\gamma^*_{\cdot i} = 0$. Premultipying by $(L_{2i}, L^*_{2i})'$, we obtain

$$\begin{bmatrix} \Pi^\circ_{1i} & \Pi_{12} \\ \Pi^\circ_{2i} & \Pi_{22} \end{bmatrix} \begin{bmatrix} \beta^\circ_{\cdot i} \\ \beta^*_{\cdot i} \end{bmatrix} = \begin{bmatrix} \gamma_{\cdot i} \\ \gamma^*_{\cdot i} \end{bmatrix}. \qquad (4.124)$$

It is relatively easy to show, in the context above, that if the ith equation is identified, there are certain relations between the rank condition and the prior restrictions. In pariticular, we have

Lemma 6. Suppose the ith equation is identified; then the following statements are true:

    i. if, in Eq. (4.124), $\beta^*_{\cdot i} = 0$, **the condition**

$$\text{rank}(\Pi^\circ_{2i}) = m_i, \text{ is equivalent to } \gamma^*_{\cdot i} = 0; \qquad (4.125)$$

    ii. if, in Eq. (4.124) $\gamma^*_{\cdot i} = 0$, **the condition**

$$\text{rank}(\Pi^\circ_{2i}) = m_i, \text{ is equivalent to } \beta^*_{\cdot i} = 0. \qquad (4.126)$$

Proof: To prove i, (sufficiency), suppose the rank condition holds and

$$\Pi^\circ_{21} \beta^\circ_{\cdot i} = \gamma^*_{\cdot i}, \qquad \gamma^*_{\cdot i} \neq 0. \qquad (4.127)$$

In view of Eqs. (4.125) and (4.127), there exists a vector,[8] $p \neq c_1 \beta^\circ_{\cdot i}$, such that $\Pi^\circ_{2i} p = 0$. But this implies that if there exists a vector $\beta^\circ_{\cdot i}$ satisfying Eq. (4.127), the vector $p + \beta^\circ_{\cdot i} \neq c\beta^\circ_{\cdot i}, c$ arbitrary, also satisfies Eq. (4.127), which shows that the first equation is not identified. This is a contradiction.

(Necessity) Suppose $\gamma^*_{\cdot i} = 0$; since the ith equation is identified, all admissible structures have to satisfy the condition $\Pi^\circ_{2i} p = 0$, with a vector of the form $p = c\beta^\circ_{\cdot i}$, where $c \neq 0$ and $\beta^\circ_{\cdot i}$ is (part of an) admissible (structure). This means that the nullity of Π°_{2i} is unity, or equivalently, that its rank is m_i, which completes the proof of i.

To prove ii (necessity), we note that if $\beta^*_{\cdot i} = 0$, the rank condition is established by the argument given in the proof of i above, and will not be repeated. As for for the sufficiency part, suppose the rank condition holds but $\beta^*_{\cdot i} \neq 0$. We show that this entails a contradiction. In view of the rank condition, there exists a vector $p \neq 0$, such that $\Pi^0_{2i} p = 0$. The two pairs of vectors

$$\bar{b}^*_{\cdot i} = b^*_{\cdot i} + \begin{bmatrix} p \\ 0 \end{bmatrix}, \quad b^*_{\cdot i} = \begin{bmatrix} \beta^\circ_{\cdot i} \\ \beta^*_{\cdot i} \end{bmatrix},$$

$$\bar{c}_{\cdot i} = c_{\cdot i} + \begin{bmatrix} \Pi^\circ_{1i} p \\ 0 \end{bmatrix},$$

are seen to be admissible (i.e. to satisfy all prior restrictions) and to satisfy Eq. (4.124). On the other hand,

$$\bar{b}^*_{\cdot i} \neq k b^*_{\cdot i}, \quad \bar{c}_{\cdot i} \neq k c_{\cdot i}, \quad k \neq 0,$$

which implies that the first equation is not identified; this is a contradiction, unless $\beta^*_{\cdot i} = 0$.

q.e.d.

Remark 7. The tests proposed in this literature, initially, were not motivated by the hypothesis structure(s) of Lemma 6. Rather such (and subsequent) procedures are variants, or reinterpretations, of the basic test first given in Anderson and Rubin (AR) (1949), (1950), and alluded to in Chapter 2. The test in question is motivated by Lemma 2, and simply tests the null hypothesis that the limit of $\hat{\lambda}$ is unity; it relies on the limiting distribution of the statistic $T(\hat{\lambda} - 1)$, which we shall derive in the appendix to this chapter. The implicit alternative is that the limit is greater than unity, since by construction $\hat{\lambda} \geq 1$. This was termed at the time the "identification test", and the statistic above the "identification test statistic".

The difficulty with this test is that it is useful only when it rejects; Lemma 2 states that, for an **identified equation**, the smallest characterisitic root

---

[8] The reader should ask himself: how do we know that $p \neq c_i \beta^\circ_{\cdot i}$? Hint: Is $\beta^\circ_{\cdot i}$ in the column null space of Π°_{2i}?

of the limit of W_{11}^* in the metric of the limit of W_{11} **is unity**, i.e. that the (probability) limit of $\hat{\lambda}$ is unity. It **does not state that if this entity is unity, the equation in question is identified!** Thus, the appropriate hypothesis structure underlying the test statistic $T(\hat{\lambda} - 1)$, is given by $H_0 : \text{rank}(\Pi_{2i}^\circ) \leq m_i$, as against the alternative $H_1 : \text{rank}(\Pi_{2i}^\circ) = m_i + 1$. It is clear that a conclusion that $\text{rank}(\Pi_{2i}^\circ) = m_i + 1$, **means that the reduced form cannot admit of the restrictions placed on it by the prior (exclusion) restrictions on the structural parameters**, for if it did the matrix B^* would be **singular**, and one of the basic assumptions of the GLSEM **would be violated**. Acceptance, on the other hand does not tell us very much. It certainly does not tell us whether the equation in question is identified or underidentified, since **we do not know** that the limit of the smallest characteristic root being unity implies identification. In fact this is not true; consider, for example the case where the smallest root is a multiple root. This would preclude identification, although the test above could very well indicate acceptance.

Note further that this test can be carried out before a single structural parameter has been estimated; its virtue, **in this specific context**, lies in the implication that if the alternative, $\text{rank}(\Pi_{2i}^\circ) = m_i + 1$ is **accepted** we should terminate all efforts to estimate the contemplated GLSEM and think very seriously about revising it. Acceptance of the null, however, is not as momentous.

The connection between the smallest characteristic root $\hat{\lambda}$ and the prior restrictions was also explored as a possible vehicle for testing the validity of prior restrictions, beyond the framework of Lemma 6. To see how this may be accomplished let us examine how such tests may be implemented in the context of Lemma 6.

Remark 8. It is interesting that, after the structural parameters have been estimated, a LR test can be based on the test statistic involving the smallest characteristic root $\hat{\lambda}$. We begin by interpreting the test in question as implementing the first of the two alternatives given in Lemma 6. Thus, from the expression in Eq. (4.45), we see that if we maximize the concentrated likelihood function under H_0, of part i of Lemma 6, we find

$$\max_{H_0} L(b_{\cdot i}^*, c_{\cdot i}, \sigma_{11}; Y, X) = \left(c_0 - \frac{T}{2}\right) - \frac{T}{2}\ln\hat{\lambda},$$

where c_0 is as defined in Eq. (4.46). Maximizing under H_1, we easily verify that an estimator for $\beta_{\cdot i}^\circ$ does not exist, in the sense that, having concentrated the LF with respect to $c_{\cdot i}$ and σ_{11}, we shall conclude that, $W_{11}^* = W_{11}$ and thus, the concentrated form of the LF becomes

$$L(b_{\cdot i}^*, c_{\cdot i}, \sigma_{11}; Y, X) = \left(c_0 - \frac{T}{2}\right) + \frac{T}{2}\ln\left(\beta_{\cdot i}^{\circ'} W_{11}\beta_{\cdot i}^\circ\right) - \frac{T}{2}\ln\left(\beta_{\cdot i}^{\circ'} W_{11}\beta_{\cdot i}^\circ\right).$$

It is clear that the concentrated LF above **cannot be further maximized** with respect to $\beta_{\cdot i}^{\circ}$. Indeed, for all admissible values of the vector $\beta_{\cdot i}^{\circ}$, the value of the LF remains $c_0 - (T/2)$. Consequently, we may put, **by convention only**,

$$\max_{H_1} L(b_{\cdot i}^*, \ c_{\cdot i}, \sigma_{11} : Y, X) = c_0 - \frac{T}{2},$$

and determine the LR to be

$$\psi = \frac{\max_{H_0} L^*}{\max_{H_1} L^*} = \hat{\lambda}^{-(T/2)},$$

where L^* is the likelihood function whose log, L, is being referred to as the LF. Thus,

$$\psi^{-(2/T)} - 1 = (\hat{\lambda} - 1). \tag{4.128}$$

Clearly, $\hat{\lambda} - 1$ is a one-to-one transformation of the likelihood ratio and is, thus, a likelihood ratio test statistic. From the appendix to this chapter we know that, asymptotically,

$$T(\hat{\lambda} - 1) \sim \chi^2_{G-G_i-m_i}.$$

The hypothesis

$$\gamma_{\cdot i}^* = 0 \quad \text{or} \quad \text{rank}(\Pi_{2i}^{\circ}) = m_i$$

is accepted if

$$T(\hat{\lambda} - 1) \leq \chi^2(\alpha),$$

where $\chi^2(\alpha)$ is a number such that

$$\Pr\{T(\hat{\lambda} - 1) \leq \chi^2(\alpha) \mid H_0\} = 1 - \alpha,$$

and is, otherwise, rejected. The upper bound $\chi^2(\alpha)$ is determined by the level of significance, α, and the distribution $\chi^2_{G-G_i-m_i}$. The problem with the conclusions above is that they are derived by convention, in the case where **a unique maximing value for the equation's parameters does not exist**.

Remark 9. The discussion Remark 8 has pointed out certain ambiguities in the interpretation of the classic identification test(s) of Lemma 6, as a LR test, and of $T(\hat{\lambda} - 1)$ as a LRT statistic. This is the fact that, under H_1, and after concentration by partial maximization with respect to $c_{\cdot i}$ and σ_{ii}, the "concentrated likelihood function" **no longer contains** $\beta_{\cdot i}^{\circ}$. Thus, the value to be assigned to the latter's estimator remains completely arbitrary. We should also note that the same will be true, *mutatis mutandis*, if we choose to implement the second alternative noted in Lemma 6. The same will also be true if the alternative is specified to be $\gamma_{\cdot i}^* \neq 0$, $\beta_{\cdot i}^* \neq 0$. Indeed, any alternative that specifies an underidentified regime will result in precisely the same test statistic, if the convention applied in Remark

8 holds. In fact, it has been claimed in the literature, see Liu and Breen (1969), Fisher and Kadane (1972), Kadane (1974), Kadane and Anderson (1977), that the classic identification test deals with the last variant, viz. $H_0 : \beta^*_{\cdot i} = 0, \ \gamma^*_{\cdot i} = 0$, as against the alternative $H_1 : \beta^*_{\cdot i} \neq 0, \ \gamma^*_{\cdot i} \neq 0$.

The argument adduced is exactly the same we had used above to generate the interpretation that the classic identification test has as its null $H_0 : \beta^*_{\cdot i} = 0, \ \gamma^*_{\cdot i} = 0$, and as its alternative $H_1 : \beta^*_{\cdot i} = 0, \ \gamma^*_{\cdot i} \neq 0$. In this framework, partially maximizing with respect to σ_{ii} and $c_{\cdot i}$ we obtain the concentrated LF, under H_1, $L(b^*_{\cdot i}) = c_0 - (T/2) - (T/2)\ln(b^{*'}_{\cdot i} W b_{\cdot i}) + (T/2)\ln(b^{*'}_{\cdot i} W b^*_{\cdot i})$. Again a unique maximizing value for the parameters of the problem does not exist; however, **by convention we may assign**

$$\max_{H_1} L(b^*_{\cdot i}, c_{\cdot i}, \sigma_{11}; Y, X) = c_0 - \frac{T}{2}$$

and under that particular alternative, we obtain a likelihood ratio test statistic which is equivalent to that of the classic test, viz. $\psi = \hat{\lambda}^{-(T/2)}$. As we have shown above, less comprehensive (narrower) alternatives produce exactly the same likelihood ratio test statistic. Thus, we have a plethora of interpretations produced by convention when, in fact, estimators under the various alternatives do not exist!

The problem alluded to above, has a perfectly simple solution; we begin by observing that in the classic identification test, as initially put forth by AR, the test is carried out solely on reduced form parameters and, in principle, before any structural parameters have been estimated. Thus, it is reasonable in that context to think of it as an "identification" test, in a negative sense. However, **once structural parameters have been estimated, it is fruitless to question the identifiability of the equation in question**. For example, in 2SLS if an equation is not identified, we could not take the invertibility of $\tilde{S}'_i X' X \tilde{S}_i$ for granted. On the other hand, if identifiability holds then with probability one we would expect this matrix to be invetible. Hence, the existence of structural estimates, more or less *ipso facto*, guarantees identification. The next question is: is there a *bona fide* proper test, for which $T(\hat{\lambda} - 1)$ is the LRT statistic? The answer is yes, and the hypothesis structure of this test is:

$H_0 : \beta^*_{\cdot i} = 0, \ \gamma^*_{\cdot i} = 0$,

as against the alternative

$H_1 :$ the equation in question is just identified.

With this alternative, we have proper estimators under H_1, the estimator $\hat{\lambda}$ is uniquely determined, and the estimators of the structural parameters are uniquely defined as well. The preceding discussion may be summarized in

Theorem 4. Consider the GLSEM, under the standard conditions; the limiting distribution of the LIML estimator of the structural parameters of the ith equation, subject to the standard normalization, is given by

$$\sqrt{T}\left(\begin{bmatrix}\hat{\beta}_{\cdot i}\\\hat{\gamma}_{\cdot i}\end{bmatrix}-\begin{bmatrix}\beta_{\cdot i}\\\gamma_{\cdot i}\end{bmatrix}\right)_{LIML} \sim N(0,\ \sigma_{11}C_{2SLS}),$$

where

$$C_{2SLS}^{-1} = \plim_{T\to\infty}\frac{1}{T}\begin{bmatrix}Y_i'Y_i - \hat{\lambda}V_i'V_i & Y_i'X_i\\X_i'Y_i & X_i'X_i\end{bmatrix}$$

and thus the LIML estimator is asymptotically equivalent to the 2SLS estimator.

Moreover, prior to the estimation of structural parameters, the test of the hypothesis

$$H_0 : \mathrm{rank}(\Pi_{2i}^\circ) \le m_i$$

as against the alternative

$$H_1 : \mathrm{rank}(\Pi_{2i}^\circ) = m_i + 1,$$

can be based on the test statistic

$$T(\hat{\lambda} - 1) \sim \chi^2_{G-G_i-m_i},$$

and in case of rejection, may be interpeted as ruling out the existence of the contemplated GLSEM.

After structural parameters have been estimated, $T(\hat{\lambda} - 1)$ may also be interpreted as a LRT statistic in the test of the hypothesis $H_0 : \beta_{\cdot i}^* = 0$, $\gamma_{\cdot i}^* = 0$, as against the alternative $H_1 :$ the ith equation is just identified.

Consistent estimators for σ_{ii}, C_{2SLS} are available in the obvious way, i.e.

$$\hat{\sigma}_{ii} = \frac{1}{T}(y_{\cdot i} - Y_i\hat{\beta}_{\cdot i} - X_i\hat{\gamma}_{\cdot i})'(y_{\cdot i} - Y_i\hat{\beta}_{\cdot i} - X_i\hat{\gamma}_{\cdot i});$$

$$C_{2SLS}^{-1} = \frac{1}{T}\begin{bmatrix}Y_i' - \hat{\lambda}\hat{V}_i'\hat{V}_i & Y'X_i\\X_i' & X_i'X_i\end{bmatrix}, \quad \hat{V}_i = NY_i,$$

and tests of significance on elements of $\beta_{\cdot i}, \gamma_{\cdot i}$ can be carried out using the normal, or chi square tests implied by asymptotic distribution theory.

Corollary 3. If we are prepared, in degenerate problems, to assign by convention the value $\max_{H_1} L = c_0 - (T/2)$ when under H_1 any admissible vector, $b_{\cdot i}^*$, yields this value for the LF, the following tests are equivalent, in the sense that they have the same LRT statistic, viz. $T(\hat{\lambda} - 1)$:

i. $H_0 : \beta_{\cdot i}^* = 0$, $\gamma_{\cdot i}^* = 0$, as against the alternative $H_1 :$ the ith equation is just identified;

   ii. $H_0 : \beta^*_{\cdot i} = 0,\ \gamma^*_{\cdot i} = 0$, as against the alternative $H_1 : \beta^*_{\cdot i} = 0,\ \gamma^*_{\cdot i} \neq 0$;

  iii. $H_0 : \beta^*_{\cdot i} = 0,\ \gamma^*_{\cdot i} = 0$, as against the alternative $H_1 : \beta^*_{\cdot i} \neq 0,\ \gamma^*_{\cdot i} = 0$;

  iv. $H_0 : \beta^*_{\cdot i} = 0,\ \gamma^*_{\cdot i} = 0$, as against the alternative $H_1 : \beta^*_{\cdot i} \neq 0,\ \gamma^*_{\cdot i} \neq 0$,
      i.e. the ith equation is (clearly) **underidentified**.

Remark 10. Notice that parts i and iv of Corollary 3 are contradictory, which argues against the use of the convention.

Remark 11. In connection with the corollary, it should be stressed that a **just identified system** does not convey any more information than the reduced form, since it represents a mere **reparametrization**. We can make this quite transparent with the following argument. First, for a single equation we obtain, after imposing a normalization convention,

$$\Pi = (\Pi, I_G)A, \quad A = (B', C')',$$

the ith equation of which is

$$\pi_{\cdot i} = (\Pi, I_G)L_i \delta_{\cdot i}, \quad i = 1, 2, \ldots, m.$$

Premultiplying by $(L_{i2}, L^*_{i2})'$, we obtain

$$L'_{i2}\pi_{\cdot i} = L'_{i2}\Pi L_{i1}\beta_{\cdot i} + \gamma_{\cdot i}, \quad L^{*'}_{i2}\pi_{\cdot i} = L^{*'}_{i2}\Pi L_{i1}\beta_{\cdot i}.$$

In the just identified case $L^{*'}_{i2}\Pi L_{i1}$ is a $G^*_i \times m_i$ **nonsingular** matrix; solving uniquely for $\beta_{\cdot i}$, in the second equation above, we may substitute in the first to obtain a unique $\gamma_{\cdot i}$. Thus, for a given specification of what $L_{i1}, L^{*'}_{i2}$ are, we obtain a **unique** $\delta_{\cdot i}$, provided the matrix in question is nonsingular. However, this need **not be the only specification of** $L_{i1}, L^{*'}_{i2}$ for which we obtain a nonsingular submatrix of Π of order $G - G_i = m_i$. If other such submatrices exist we obtain an equally admissible vector, say $\bar{\delta}_{\cdot i}$. This implies the existence of **two** observationally equivalent structures yielding the same reduced form, if the only requirement is that the equation in question be **just identified**. The argument for the system as a whole may be put in similar form. Again, given normalization, the parameters in the ith structural equation are obtained as the solution of the equations

$$\pi_{\cdot i} = (\Pi, I_G)L_i \delta_{\cdot i}, \quad i = 1, 2, \ldots, m.$$

Just identification requires that the $G \times G + m$ matrix (Π, I_G) be of rank G. There are at most $(G + m)!/G!m!$ (square) submatrices of order G. To the extent that **more than** m such submatrices are **nonsingular** we shall have several observationally equivalent structures compatible with a given reduced form. This shows that the determination of structure from a given reduced form, through **just identification** restrictions only, may well be arbitrary. This is of particular relevance in emprical work involving the so called structural VAR model, examined briefly in Chapter 2, in which structural parameters are obtained by imposing just identification restrictions on the (estimated) covariance matrix of reduced form errors.

Questions and Problems

1. Verify Eqs. (4.73) and (4.74).

2. Give a formal argument supporting Remark 3.

3. Explain why $\tilde{V}_1^{o'}\tilde{V}_1^o - \hat{V}_1^{o'}\hat{V}_1^o \geq 0$, in the discussion following Eq. (4.89).

4. Verify Eq. (4.94).

5. If in Eq. (4.95), $\hat{\Pi}_{21}^o$ is $(G - G_1) \times (m_1 + 1)$, $G - G_1 \geq m_1$ explain why, in general, the null vector is the only solution.

6. Verify that, in Eq. (4.99), the rank condition for identification implies that the matrix, S_i, is of full rank.

7. Verify Eq. (4.110).
   Hint: $(S_i'S_i)^{-1}S_i'\pi_{\cdot i} = \delta_{\cdot i}$, and $S_i\delta_{\cdot i} = \pi_{\cdot i}$.

8. Verify the representation of Eq. (4.108) as in Eq. (4.111).
   Hint: $v_{\cdot i} - V_i\beta_{\cdot i} = V_i^o\beta_{\cdot i}^o = Vb_{\cdot i}^*$.

9. Show that

$$X(X'X)^{-1}X' - X_i(X_i'X_i)^{-1}X_i' = N_1X_1^*\left(X_1^{*'}N_1X_1^*\right)^{-1}X_1^{*'}N_1,$$

where $X = (X_i, X_1^*)$, $N_1 = I - X_i(X_i'X_i)^{-1}X_i'$.

10. In the discussion of Remark 9, verify that, under the alternatives $\gamma_{\cdot i}^* = 0$, $\beta_{\cdot i}^* \neq 0$, we obtain the same likelihood ratio as in the preceding discussion.

11. Verify that

$$Q \xrightarrow{P} -(\Pi_{21}'M_{44}^*\Pi_{21})^{-1}, \quad \sqrt{T}b \xrightarrow{d} -\Pi_{21}'\frac{X_1^{*'}N_1u_{\cdot 1}}{\sqrt{T}}, \quad \frac{X_1^{*'}N_1V_1}{T} \xrightarrow{P} 0.$$

   Hint: $X_1^{*'}N_1V_i/T$ converges to zero and $Y_i'N_1V_i/T$ converges to a finite quantity.

Appendix to Chapter 4

Limiting Distribution of $T(\hat{\lambda} - 1)$

In the preceding chapter we had occasion to consider the limiting behavior of $\sqrt{T}(\hat{\lambda}-1)$, as well as that of $T(\hat{\lambda}-1)$; we shall now prove the properties asserted to hold in the course of the earlier discussion.

Recalling from Eq. (4.124) that $T[W_{11}^* - W_{11}] = \hat{\Pi}_{2i}^{\circ'} X_i^{*'} N_i X_i^* \hat{\Pi}_{2i}^{\circ}$, we see immediately that $\operatorname{plim}_{T \to \infty} \hat{\beta}_{\cdot i}^{\circ'} W_{11} \hat{\beta}_{\cdot i}^{\circ} = \sigma_{11}$, and moreover,

$$(\hat{\lambda} - 1) = \frac{1}{T} \frac{\hat{\beta}_{\cdot i}^{\circ'} \hat{\Pi}_{2i}^{\circ'} M_{44}^* \hat{\Pi}_{2i}^{\circ} \hat{\beta}_{\cdot i}^{\circ}}{\hat{\beta}_{\cdot i}^{\circ'} W_{11} \hat{\beta}_{\cdot i}^{\circ}}, \quad \operatorname{plim}_{T \to \infty} \frac{X_i^{*'} N_i X_i^*}{T} = \bar{M}_{44}^* > 0. \tag{4.A.1}$$

Consequently, we see that, asymptotically,

$$T(\hat{\lambda} - 1) \sim (\sqrt{T} \hat{\Pi}_{2i} \hat{\beta}_{\cdot i}^{\circ})' \left(\frac{\bar{M}_{44}^*}{\sigma_{11}} \right) (\sqrt{T} \hat{\Pi}_{2i}^{\circ} \hat{\beta}_{\cdot i}^{\circ}).$$

We shall now establish the limiting properties of $\sqrt{T}(\hat{\lambda} - 1)$ and $T(\hat{\lambda} - 1)$. It is intuitively obvious that such properties are intimately related to the limiting distribution of $\sqrt{T}(\hat{\Pi}_{2i} \hat{\beta}_{\cdot i}^{\circ})$.

Now, the relations in Eq. (4.A.1) are valid for **any normalization**; in particular, they are valid for $\hat{\beta}_{\cdot i}^{\circ} = (1, -\hat{\beta}_{\cdot i}')'$, which is the standard normalization we shall empoy throught this appendix.

Lemma A1. The representation,

$$\hat{\Pi}_{2i}^{\circ} = \Pi_{2i}^{\circ} + \left(\frac{X_i^{*'} N_i X_i^{*}}{T} \right)^{-1} \frac{X_i^{*'} N_i V_i^{\circ}}{T},$$

is valid, where $V_i^{\circ} = (v_{\cdot i}, \; V_i)$, i.e. it is the matrix of reduced form errors corresponding to Y_i°.

Proof: See the discussion preceding Eq. (4.94), in the chapter.

Lemma A2. Subject to the standard normalization, the LIML estimator of $\beta_{\cdot i}^{\circ}$ is given by $\hat{\beta}_{\cdot i}^{\circ} = (1, \; -\hat{\beta}_{\cdot i}')'$, where $\hat{\beta}_{\cdot i} = \beta_{\cdot i} + Qb$,

$$Q = \left((\hat{\lambda} - 1) \frac{Y_i' N Y_i}{T} - \hat{\Pi}_{2i}' \frac{X_i^{*'} N_i X_i^{*}}{T} \hat{\Pi}_{2i} \right)^{-1}$$

$$b = (\hat{\lambda} - 1) \frac{Y_i' N u_{\cdot i}}{T} - \hat{\Pi}_{2i}' \frac{X_i^{*'} N_i u_{\cdot i}}{T}, \tag{4.A.2}$$

and $\hat{\Pi}_{2i}$ is obtained from $\hat{\Pi}_{2i}^{\circ}$ by eliminating the latter's first column.

Proof: Given the standard normalization we find, from the second set of Eq. (4.119), $\hat{\beta}_{\cdot i} = \beta_{\cdot i} + [Y_i'(\hat{\lambda} N - N_i) Y_i]^{-1} Y_i'(\hat{\lambda} N - N_i) u_{\cdot i}$. Using the partitioned inverse results in Ch. 2 of Dhrymes (1984), we obtain $\hat{\lambda} N - N_i = (\hat{\lambda} - 1) N - (N_i - N) = (\hat{\lambda} - 1) N - N_i X_i^{*} (X_i^{*'} N_i X_i^{*})^{-1} X_i^{*'} N_i$. Thus, we may write

$$Y_i'(\hat{\lambda} N - N_i) Y_i = (\hat{\lambda} - 1) Y_i' N Y_i - \hat{\Pi}_{2i}' (X_i^{*'} N_i X_i^{*}) \hat{\Pi}_{2i},$$

and note that $Y_i'(\hat{\lambda} N - N_i) u_{\cdot i} = (\hat{\lambda} - 1)' Y_i' N u_{\cdot i} - \hat{\Pi}_{2i}' X_i^{*'} N_i u_{\cdot i}$. Consequently,

$$\hat{\beta}_{\cdot i} = \beta_{\cdot i} + \left((\hat{\lambda} - 1) \frac{Y_i' N Y_i}{T} - \hat{\Pi}_{2i}' \frac{X_i^{*'} N_i X_i^{*}}{T} \hat{\Pi}_{2i}' \right)^{-1}$$

$$\times \left((\hat{\lambda} - 1) \frac{Y_i' N u_{\cdot i}}{T} - \hat{\Pi}_{2i}' \frac{X_i^{*'} N_i u_{\cdot i}}{T} \right). \tag{4.A.3}$$

q.e.d.

Corollary A1. The limiting distribution of $\sqrt{T} Q b$ is given by

$$\sqrt{T} Q b \sim -\Psi \left[\sqrt{T} (\hat{\lambda} - 1) D_i' \sigma_{\cdot i} - \Pi_{2i}' \zeta_T \right], \quad \zeta_T = \frac{X_i^{*'} N_i u_{\cdot i}}{\sqrt{T}}.$$

Proof: The preceding discussion implies $Q \xrightarrow{P} -\Psi = -(\Pi'_{2i}\bar{M}^*_{44}\Pi_{2i})^{-1}$; moreover,

$$\sqrt{T}b \sim \sqrt{T}(\hat{\lambda} - 1)\frac{V'_i N u_{\cdot i}}{T} - \hat{\Pi}_{2i}\zeta_T \xrightarrow{d} D'_i \sigma_{\cdot i} \sqrt{T}(\hat{\lambda} - 1) - \Pi_{2i}\zeta_T,$$

and asymptotically, $\zeta_T \sim N(0, \sigma_{ii}\bar{M}^*_{44})$.

q.e.d.

Lemma A3. $\sqrt{T}(\hat{\lambda} - 1) \xrightarrow{d} 0$.

Proof: From the representation above we have

$$\sqrt{T}(\hat{\lambda} - 1) = \frac{\hat{\beta}^{\circ\prime}_{\cdot i}\hat{\Pi}^{\circ\prime}_{2i}M^*_{44}\sqrt{T}(\hat{\Pi}^\circ_{2i}\hat{\beta}^\circ_{\cdot i})}{\hat{\beta}^{\circ\prime}W_{11}\hat{\beta}^\circ_{\cdot i}} \sim J_0\sqrt{T}(\hat{\Pi}^\circ_{2i}\hat{\beta}^\circ_{\cdot i}), \quad J_0 = \frac{\hat{\beta}^{\circ\prime}_{\cdot i}\hat{\Pi}^{\circ\prime}_{2i}\bar{M}^*_{44}}{\sigma_{11}}.$$

From Lemma A2 and Corollary A1, $\hat{\Pi}^\circ_{2i}\hat{\beta}^\circ_{\cdot i} = \Pi^\circ_{2i}\beta^\circ_{\cdot i} + M^{*-1}_{44}(\zeta_T/\sqrt{T}) - [\Pi_{2i} + M^{*-1}_{44}(X^{*\prime}N_i V_i/T)]Qb$. On the assumption that the equation in question is identified, we have $\Pi_{2i}\beta^\circ_{\cdot i} = 0$ and consequently,

$$\sqrt{T}(\hat{\Pi}^\circ_{2i}\hat{\beta}^\circ_{\cdot i}) \sim J_1\zeta_T + J_2\sqrt{T}(\hat{\lambda} - 1), \quad J_1 = \bar{M}^{*-1}_{44} - \Pi_{2i}\Psi\Pi_{2i}, \quad J_2 = \Pi_{2i}\Psi D'_i\sigma_{\cdot i}.$$

Combining the results above we find

$$(1 - J_0 J_2)\sqrt{T}(\hat{\lambda} - 1) \sim J_0 J_1 \zeta_T. \tag{4.A.4}$$

Since $J_0 J_1 \xrightarrow{P} 0$ and ζ_T has a well defined limiting distribution, we conclude that the right member of Eq. (4.A.4) converges in distribution to the degenerate random variable zero; moreover, since $(1 - J_0 J_2) \xrightarrow{P} 1$, we conclude $\sqrt{(\hat{\lambda} - 1)} \xrightarrow{d} 0$.

q.e.d.

Corollary A2. The entity $\sqrt{T}(\hat{\lambda} - 1)$ converges in probability to zero.

Proof: This follows from the fact that convergence in distribution to a constant (degenerate random variable) implies convergence in probability to that constant. See Proposition 40, Ch. 4 of Dhrymes (1989).

q.e.d.

Lemma A4. $\sqrt{T}(\hat{\Pi}^\circ_{2i}\hat{\beta}^\circ_{\cdot i}) \xrightarrow{d} N[0, \sigma_{ii}(\bar{M}^{*-1}_{44} - \Pi_{2i}\Psi\Pi'_{2i})]$; the covariance matrix $\sigma_{ii}(\bar{M}^{*-1}_{44} - \Pi_{2i}\Psi\Pi'_{2i})$ is singular with rank $G - G_i - m_i$.

Proof: Combining the results of Lemmata A1 and A2, we find

$$\hat{\Pi}^\circ_{2i}\hat{\beta}^\circ_{\cdot i} = \Pi^\circ_{2i}\beta^\circ_{\cdot i} + M^{*-1}_{44}\frac{X^{*'}_i N u_{\cdot i}}{T} - \left(\Pi_{2i} + \tilde{M}^{*-1}_{44}\frac{X^{*'}_i N_i V_i}{T}\right)Qb.$$

Since

$$Q \xrightarrow{\text{P}} -\Psi, \quad \sqrt{T}b \xrightarrow{\text{d}} -\Pi'_{2i}\frac{X^{*'}_i N_i u_{\cdot i}}{\sqrt{T}}, \quad \frac{X^{*'}_i N_i V_i}{T} \xrightarrow{\text{P}} 0,$$

and by the condition for admissibility and identification $\Pi^\circ_{2i}\beta^\circ_{\cdot i} = 0$, we may write

$$\sqrt{T}(\hat{\Pi}^\circ_{2i}\hat{\beta}^\circ_{\cdot i}) \sim \left(\bar{M}^{*-1}_{44} - \Pi_{2i}\Psi\Pi'_{2i}\right)\zeta_T,$$

and the conclusion of the Lemma follows immediately. It only remains to show that the covariance matrix is singular. Consider the characteristic equation

$$|\lambda\bar{M}^{*-1}_{44} - \Pi_{2i}\Psi\Pi'_{2i}| = 0.$$

The roots of this equation are exactly those of

$$|\lambda I - \Pi_{2i}\Psi\Pi'_{2i}\bar{M}^*_{44}| = 0,$$

and the **nonzero** roots of the latter are exactly those of

$$|\mu I - \Psi\Pi'_{2i}\bar{M}^*_{44}\Pi_{2i}| = 0;$$

the latter, however, has m_i **unit roots**. By Proposition 63 in Dhrymes (1984), there exists a nonsingular matrix P such that

$$M^{*-1}_{44} = P'P, \quad \Pi_{2i}\Psi\Pi'_{2i} = P'\Lambda P,$$

where Λ is the diagonal matrix containing the characteristic roots of $\Pi_{2i}\Psi\Pi'_{2i}$ in the metric of M^{*-1}_{44}. The covariance matrix, therefore is given by

$$\bar{M}^{*-1}_{44} - \Pi_{2i}\Psi\Pi'_{2i} = P'(I_{G-G_i} - \Lambda)P = P'\begin{bmatrix} 0 & 0 \\ 0 & I_{G-G_i-m_i} \end{bmatrix}P$$

which is evidently a positive semidefinite (singular) matrix of rank $G - G_i - m_i$.

q.e.d.

An almost immediate consequence of the preceding Lemma is

Theorem A1. Asymptotically, $T(\hat{\lambda} - 1) \sim \chi^2_{G-G_i-m_i}$.

Proof: From Eq. (4.A.1) and Lemma A4, we have the representation

$$T(\hat{\lambda} - 1) \sim \left[\frac{P'^{-1}}{\sqrt{\sigma}_{ii}} \sqrt{T}(\hat{\Pi}^{\circ}_{2i}\hat{\beta}_{\cdot i})\right]' \left[\frac{P'^{-1}}{\sqrt{\sigma}_{ii}} \sqrt{T}(\hat{\Pi}^{\circ'}_{2i}\hat{\beta}_{\cdot i})\right]. \qquad (4.A.5)$$

Since $\bar{M}^*_{44} = P^{-1}P'^{-1}$, Lemma A4 implies

$$\frac{P'^{-1}}{\sqrt{\sigma}_{ii}} \sqrt{T}(\hat{\Pi}^{\circ}_{2i}\hat{\beta}^{\circ}_{\cdot i}) \sim N(0, \ I_*), \ \ I_* = I_{G-G_i} - \Lambda \ = \ \mathrm{diag}(0, \ I_{G-G_i-m_i}).$$

Consequently, from Eq. (4.A.5) we conclude

$$T(\hat{\lambda} - 1) \sim \chi^2_{G-G_i-m_i},$$

since it is the sum of squares of $G-G_i-m_i$ mutually idenpendent $N(0, \ 1)$ variables.

q.e.d.

5

Nonlinear ML Methods

5.1 Motivation

In studying the GLSEM we took the structural model as the **primitive** concept, and dealt with it as such. However, from a formal point of view, we can also look upon it as a particular case of a system of regressions, sometimes termed seemingly unrelated regressions (SUR), which is **nonlinear** in some basic set of underlying parameters. A little reflection will also convince the reader that (GLSEM) models which are **nonlinear in the parameters only** are, also, a special case of such systems.

We should further point out that when dealing with asymptotic properties of the ML estimator, in the context of the GLSEM, we had relied on results obtained when studying 2SLS and 3SLS estimators. Thus, consistency and asymptotic normality for the ML estimators were established by showing that the difference between these estimators and 2SLS or 3SLS converged to zero, in the appropriate mode. This enabled us to conclude that, in the standard case, ML estimators were consistent and shared the same asymptotic distribution with 2SLS and 3SLS estimators. In order to prepare ourselves for dealing with intrinsically nonlinear problems, it behooves us to study the properties of ML estimators in a more general context. Thus, in what follows we shall examine the system

$$y_{t\cdot} = g(x_{t\cdot}, \phi) + u_{t\cdot},$$

where g is, at least, a measurable function, and usually continuously (twice) differentiable in ϕ and $x_{t\cdot}$. We shall also consider the case where the basic vector ϕ satisfies a number of restrictions, say $r(\phi) = 0$. An example of this is the GLSEM

$$y_t.B^* = x_t.C + u_t.. \tag{5.1}$$

In this case $g = x_t.CB^{*-1}$, $\phi = a^* = \text{vec}(A^*)$, $A^* = (B^{*\prime}, -C^\prime)^\prime$, and the restrictions $r(\phi) = 0$, represent the identification and normalization restrictions. If the vector $u_t.$ is i.i.d., normal with mean zero and covariance matrix Σ, we may write the LF as

$$L(\theta) = -\frac{Tm}{2}\ln(2\pi) - \frac{T}{2}\ln|\Omega| - \frac{T}{2}\operatorname{tr}\Omega^{-1}S(\Pi), \tag{5.2}$$

where

$$S(\Pi) = \frac{1}{T}(Y - X\Pi)^\prime(Y - X\Pi), \quad \Pi = CD, \quad \Omega = D^\prime\Sigma D, \quad D = B^{*-1}.$$

This is, indeed, the LF of a set of GLM, except that its parameters, Π, Ω, are a nonlinear function of the smaller parameter set $\theta = (a^\prime, \sigma^\prime)^\prime$, where $\sigma = \text{vec}(\Sigma)$.[1] Thus, imposing the standard normalization, the FIML estimator may also be formulated as

$$\max_\theta \frac{1}{T}L(\theta), \quad \text{subject to } L^{*\prime}a = 0,$$

where $\theta = (a^\prime, \sigma^\prime)^\prime$, $a = \text{vec}(A)$, $B^* = I - B$, $A = (B^\prime, C^\prime)^\prime$. This formulation is precisely analogous to the Lagrange multiplier formulation we had given for two and three stage least squares, in Chapter 1. Notice that here as well we have imposed the **normalization convention** directly.

5.2   A Mathematical Digression

The topics to be discussed in Sections 5.2 through 5.7 are of a more basic nature and apply to a more general inferential context than the specific issues of nonlinear single equation and simultaneous equations topics we shall deal with in Chapters 5 and 6. The reader may thus justifiably ask why such topics are introduced at this juncture. The answer is that they are introduced now, and in the main text rather than in an appendix, because they represent very basic and powerful tools for dealing with the econometric issues under discussion. Their mastery will greatly facilitate the solution

---

[1] Strictly speaking, σ, as defined above, contains redundant parameters due to the fact that Σ is **symmetric**. The proper definition would have σ contain **only** the distinct elements of Σ. However, in the range of applications we have in mind, no harm is done by defining σ in the manner in which we had defined it above, which has the additional merit of simplifying considerably a number of operations.

and understanding of the standard estimation and identification problems encountered in the nonlinear systems alluded to above. In particular, the topics to be discussed are Fisher information, which is related to aspects of the limiting distribution of ML estimators; the multivariate Cramer-Rao inequality which sets bounds on the covariance matrix of ML and other estimators; Kullback information, which is of fundamental importance in understanding the limiting behavior of ML and other estimators, and in aiding the formulation of identification conditions in complex estimation problems; and the martingale properties of likelihood and log likelihood functions, which facilitate the discussion of convergence of (normalized) likelihood functions through the various theorems pertaining to martingale convergence. Such topics are introduced at this juncture since there is no convenient single reference that treats these subjects at the level and detail required for our discussion. In order that such issues may be discussed adequately, we need to reintroduce the formal apparatus of Chapter 2. To give the reader an appreciation of the difficulties one may encounter in nonlinear contexts, and to provide further motivation, consider a nonlinear model with (log) likelihood function $L_T(\theta)$. The function is highly nonlinear in θ, which is specified to lie in some admissible space Θ. An explicit solution for its (ML) estimator is not available. We are therefore left to infer the properties of such estimator, if it exists, solely from the implicit definition of the ML estimator, viz.

$$L_T(\hat{\theta}_T) = \sup_{\theta \in \Theta} L_T(\theta).$$

In more cases than not, the previous training of the reader is likely to be insufficient to tackle such problems successfully.

The specific technical issues involved in the proof of the results adduced in Sections 5.2 to 5.7 are not of primary significance to the econometrics student or professional. They are included so that the reader may gain a fuller understanding of the process of reasoning involved, to remove the mystification that surrounds many aspects of asymptotics, and expose the manner in which the assumptions made produce the results one uses in the solution of econometric problems. The reader who has little interest in these issues may simply assimilate the statement of the various Propositions as well as various pertinent Remarks. This knowledge would be sufficient preparation for following the presentation in subsequent sections, as well as the discussions in Chapter 6.

In order to deal with the issues raised above, it is more convenient to employ again the formal apparatus first introduced in Chapter 2. Thus, consider the probability space $(\Omega, \mathcal{A}, \mathcal{P})$, where Ω is the sample space, $\mathcal{A}$ is the σ-algebra of subsets of Ω and $\mathcal{P}$ is a probability measure. If $X_{(n)}$ represents a class of random variables we wish to study, for example a certain sequence of random variables (r.v.),

$X_i : \Omega \to R$, $i = 1, 2, \ldots, n$

then $X_{(n)}$ induces a σ-subalgebra, say $\mathcal{G}_n \subset \mathcal{A}$. In this context,

$X_{(n)} : \Omega^n \to R^n$.

In the preceding, $\Omega^n = \Omega \times \Omega \times \cdots \times \Omega$, $R^n = R \times R \times \cdots \times R$, where each Cartesian product is taken n times. Let us denote by $\mathcal{G}_n = \sigma(X_1, X_2, \ldots, X_n)$ the σ-algebra induced by the sequence $X_{(n)} = (X_1, X_2, \ldots, X_n)$, and by $\mathcal{G}_0 = (\emptyset, \Omega)$ the trivial σ-algebra (corresponding to "constants"). In this fashion we have the (nested) sequence of subalgebras [2] $\mathcal{G}_0 \subset \mathcal{G}_1 \subset \cdots \subset \mathcal{G}_n \subset \cdots \subset \mathcal{A}$. In the literature, this sequence of σ-algebras is termed a **stochastic basis**; it is also, occasionally, called a **filtration**, and $X_{(n)}$ is said to be **adapted to the filtration**.

When dealing with estimation issues, as in the sections below, we generally face a situation in which the distributional characteristics of the random variable(s) under discussion are indexed by some parameter, say, $\theta \in \Theta \subseteq R^k$. In order to examine estimation issues we need to expand the framework in which we operate, although we shall not attempt to become excessively rigorous. In estimation problems, we begin with a class of admissible parameters, denoted just above by $\Theta \subseteq R^k$, which contains, in its interior, the "true" parameter point, say θ^0, or, equivalently, an open neighborhood thereof, say $N(\theta^0; \delta)$, for $\delta > 0$. The object of the estimation problem is to devise a procedure, such that when a sample is available we can unambiguously arrive at an estimate of the unknown parameter θ^0. Thus, we consider potentially many probabilistic configurations for the data, and the object is to chose the appropriate configuration, given the sample evidence. We note that in an estimation framework, we tend to refer to sequences of r.v. as **samples**, and to sequences of i.i.d. r.v. as **random samples**; moreover, only one value of θ, the "true" value θ^0, is relevant. [3] Since it is not known, and the whole object of the exercise is to estimate it, it makes sense to write the **admissible** probability measure(s) as $\mathcal{P}_\theta, \theta \in \Theta$, and the restriction of such measures on the sequence of nested σ-algebras, $(\mathcal{G}_n)$, induced by this family of random variables, as $\{\mathcal{P}_{n\theta} : \theta \in \Theta\}$. If we have a sample of size n, say $X_{(n)} = \{X_j : j = 1, 2, \ldots, n\}$, the (smallest) probability space on which this family of r.v. may be analyzed is denoted

---

[2] For a more detailed discussion of such issues the reader is referred to Dhrymes (1989) Ch. 5, or Chow and Teicher (1988), second edition, Ch. 1. These same two volumes could also serve as references for any mathematical terms encountered in this section with which the reader may be unfamiliar.

[3] In previous chapters we did not carefully distinguish between the "true" value of the parameter vector, and other possible values it might be assigned, because the context did not lend itself to confusion; in this and the next chapter we shall be far more careful to designate the "true" value of the parameter vector by a zero subscript, or superscript.

by $(\Omega, \mathcal{G}_n, \mathcal{P}_{n\theta})$, where $\mathcal{G}_n = \sigma(X_1, X_2, \ldots, X_n)$, i.e. it is the smallest σ-algebra induced by the sequence $X_{(n)}$, above. [4] This leads to

Definition 1. Consider the measurable space $(\Omega, \mathcal{A})$, together with the family of probability measures, $\mathcal{P}_\theta$, for $\theta \in \Theta \subseteq R^k$. The triplet $(\Omega, \mathcal{A}, \mathcal{P}_\theta)$, for $\theta \in \Theta$, as above, is said to be an econometric (or statistical) model. The model (or the family of measures) is said to be **dominated** if there exists a σ-finite measure, say μ, defined on $\mathcal{A}$, such that $\mathcal{P}_\theta$ is, for every $\theta \in \Theta$, absolutely continuous with respect to it (μ). This means that there exists, for each $\theta \in \Theta$, a $\mathcal{A}$-measurable (nonnegative) function, say h_θ, such that, for any $A \in \mathcal{A}$,

$$\mathcal{P}_\theta(A) = \int_A h_\theta \, d\mu,$$

and $\mathcal{P}_\theta(A) = 0$, if and only if $\mu(A) = 0$.

Remark 1. The measure μ is said to be a **dominant measure** relative to the family of probability measures, $\mathcal{P}_\theta$, $\theta \in \Theta \subseteq R^k$.

Definition 2. In the context of Definition 1, let $\{\theta_n : n \geq 1, \theta_n \in \Theta\}$ be any sequence in Θ. The collection,

$$\mathcal{P}_* = \left\{ \mathcal{P}_a : \mathcal{P}_a = \sum_{i=1}^{\infty} a_i \mathcal{P}_{\theta_i}, \ a_i \geq 0, \ \sum_{i=1}^{\infty} a_i = 1 \right\},$$

is said to be the **convex hull** of Θ.

The concepts introduced in Definitions 1 and 2 lead to the important

Proposition 1. In the context of Definitions 1 and 2, consider the econometric model $(\Omega, \mathcal{A}, \mathcal{P}_\theta)$, for $\theta \in \Theta \subseteq R^k$. There exists a probability measure, say $\mathcal{P} \in \mathcal{P}_*$, which is dominant with respect to the family of probability measures $\mathcal{P}_\theta$, $\theta \in \Theta$, i.e. there exist measurable functions, h_θ, such that for every $\theta \in \Theta$ and set $A \in \mathcal{A}$

$$\mathcal{P}_\theta(A) = \int_A h_\theta \, d\mathcal{P}, \tag{5.3}$$

---

[4] The relationship between this framework and the more familiar one involving cumulative distribution functions (cdf) and densities is as follows: the sequence $X_{(n)}$ induces the probability measure P_n on (R^n, $\mathcal{B}(R^n)$), through the relation $P_n(B) = \mathcal{P}_n(A)$, where for any $B \in \mathcal{B}(R^n)$, $A = X_{(n)}^{-1}(B) \in \mathcal{G}_n$. Using the special sets $B \in \mathcal{B}(R^n)$, such that $B = (-\infty, x_1] \times (-\infty, x_2] \times \cdots \times (-\infty, x_n]$, we define the cdf by the operation $F_n(x) = P_n(B)$, where $x = (x_1, x_2, \ldots, x_n)'$. If F_n is differentiable, its density function is given by f_n. In estimation we are interested in the parameters $\theta \in \Theta \subseteq R^k$, characterizing such density functions. Thus, we denote the density by $f_n(\cdot; \theta)$ and the family of distribution functions, by $P_{n\theta}$.

i.e. h_θ is a density for $\mathcal{P}_\theta$ and the latter is absolutely continuous relative to $\mathcal{P}$.

Proof: See Dacunha-Castelle, D. and M. Duflo (1986) vol. I.

Remark 2. The import of Proposition 1 is to detach the parameter from the operational probability measure so as to enable us to deal effectively with estimation and convergence of estimators.

5.3 Aspects of Likelihood Functions

We remind the reader that if $X = \{X_j : j = 1, 2 \ldots, n\}$ is a sample from a population characterized by the family of probability measures $\mathcal{P}_\theta$, such that $\theta \in \Theta \subseteq R^k$, and if the random variables possess density functions, the likelihood function, $L^*(X; \theta)$, [5] is simply the joint density of the observations in the sample. What, in part, defines Θ as the set of **admissible parameters** is the fact that for every $\theta \in \Theta$, $L^*(X; \theta)$ is a proper density function. Now, if we view L^* as a function from $\Omega \to R$ then it is a r.v., and we may denote its expectation by

$$\int_\Omega L^* \, d\mathcal{P}_\theta = E_\theta[L^*(X; \theta)] = g(\theta).$$

If we view L^* as a **composition**, i.e. first as a function

$$X : \Omega \to R^n,$$

and, thereafter, as a function from R^n into R then we observe that, for any $B \in \mathcal{B}(R^n)$, [6]

$$P_\theta(B) = \int_B L^*(\xi; \theta) \, d\xi.$$

The relation above is a Lebesgue integral, with ordinary Lebesgue measure. This gives an example of the result in Proposition 1; specifically, it shows that ordinary Lebesgue measure is dominant relative to the family of measures P_θ, which are defined on $(R^n, \mathcal{B}(R^n))$. Since the integral above, also, gives the probability that the sample observations $\{X_j : j =$

---

[5] To be more precise we should write $L_n^*(X; \theta)$, or at least $L^*(X_{(n)}; \theta)$, thus indicating the size of the sample, or the "length" of the sequence $X_{(n)}$. For reasons of notational simplicity, however, we shall follow this practice **only** when the context requires it for clarity.

[6] Note that the connection between $\mathcal{P}_{n\theta}$ and $P_{n\theta}$ is as follows: let $A = \{\omega : X(\omega) \in B\}$, then $\mathcal{P}_{n\theta}(A) = P_{n\theta}(B)$.

$1, 2, \ldots, n\}$ will assume values in the set B, it follows, therefore, that

$$\int_{R^n} L^*(\xi; \theta) \, d\xi = 1,$$

which is independent of θ. Thus, it is important to realize that

$$1 = \mathcal{P}_{n\theta}(\Omega) = \int_{\Omega} d\mathcal{P}_{n\theta} = \int_{R^n} L_n^*(\xi; \theta) \, d\xi \neq \int_{\Omega} L_n^*[X(\omega); \theta] \, d\mathcal{P}_{n\theta} = g(\theta).$$

5.3.1 An Interesting Inequality

It is interesting that if we take the expectations

$$E_{\theta^0}[L(\theta^0)] = \int_{\Omega} \ln L^*(\theta^0; \omega) \, d\mathcal{P}_{\theta^0}, \quad E_{\theta^0}[L(\theta; \omega)] = \int_{\Omega} \ln L^*(\theta; \omega) \, d\mathcal{P}_{\theta^0},$$

we would find

$$E_{\theta^0}[\ln L^*(\theta)] \leq E_{\theta^0}[\ln L^*(\theta^0)]. \tag{5.4}$$

To see this, consider the ratio $L^*(\theta)/L^*(\theta^0)$, where θ^0 is the "true" parameter point, and note that since the logarithm is a concave function, we have by Jensen's inequality, see Proposition 14 Ch. 2 of Dhrymes (1989),

$$0 = \ln E_{\theta^0} \left(\frac{L^*(\theta)}{L^*(\theta^0)} \right) \geq E_{\theta^0} \left(\ln \frac{L^*(\theta)}{L^*(\theta^0)} \right),$$

which is exactly Eq. (5.4) above.

5.4   Fisher Information

Consider the context above, i.e the sequence of r.v. $X_{(n)} = \{X_j : j = 1, 2, \ldots, n, \}$ defined on the probability space $(\Omega, \mathcal{G}_n, \mathcal{P}_{n\theta})$, where $\theta \in \Theta \subseteq R^k$.

Definition 3. Let X be a r.v. defined on the probability space above and having the density function $f(\cdot; \theta)$. The **Fisher information content** (FIC) [7] of, or the Fisher information contained in, the r.v. is given by

$$I(\theta) = \text{Cov}(\Phi), \quad \Phi = \frac{\partial \ln f(\cdot; \theta)}{\partial \theta}.$$

If θ is a vector of k elements, i.e. if the density function contains k parameters, I is a $k \times k$ **matrix**. If $k = 1$, I is a **scalar**.

---

[7] This concept is named after the English statistician Sir Ronald A. Fisher, who first suggested it. See, for example, R. A. Fisher (1934), or (1944), pp. 307ff.

Definition 4. (Generalization) Let $X_{(n)} = \{X_j : j = 1, 2, \ldots, n\}$ be a sequence of r.v. defined on the probability space of Definition 3. The FIC of the sample is given by

$$I_n(\theta) = \text{Cov}(\Phi_n), \quad \Phi_n = \frac{\partial \ln f_n(\cdot\,;\theta)}{\partial \theta},$$

where $f_n(\cdot\,;\theta)$ is the joint density of the sample. The **matrix** $I_n(\theta)$ is also referred to as the (Fisher) information matrix.

Remark 3. In the special case of **random samples** we find

$$f_n(\cdot\,;\theta) = \prod_{j=1}^{n} f(\cdot\,;\theta), \quad \Phi_n = \sum_{j=1}^{n} \frac{\partial \ln f(\cdot\,;\theta)}{\partial \theta}, \quad I_n(\theta) = nI(\theta).$$

Example 1. Consider the reduced form of the GLSEM

$$y_{t\cdot} = x_{t\cdot}\Pi + v_{t\cdot},$$

and suppose that $v_{t\cdot} \sim N(0, \Omega)$. The (log of the) density of $y_{t\cdot}$ is given by

$$\ln f(\theta) = -\frac{m}{2}\ln(2\pi) - \frac{1}{2}\ln|\Omega| - \frac{1}{2}[y_{t\cdot}' - (I \otimes x_{t\cdot})\pi]'\Omega^{-1}[y_{t\cdot}' - (I \otimes x_{t\cdot})\pi],$$

where $\pi = \text{vec}(\Pi)$, $\omega = \text{vec}(\Omega)$ and $\theta = (\pi', \omega')'$.

Differentiating, we find

$$\frac{\partial \ln f}{\partial \pi} = [y_{t\cdot}' - (I \otimes x_{t\cdot})\pi]'\Omega^{-1}(I \otimes x_{t\cdot}) = v_{t\cdot}\Omega^{-1}(I \otimes x_{t\cdot}) = v_{t\cdot}(\Omega^{-1} \otimes x_{t\cdot}).$$

Moreover,

$$\frac{\partial \ln f}{\partial \text{vec}(\Omega)} = -\frac{1}{2}\text{vec}(\Omega^{-1})' + \frac{1}{2}\text{vec}(v_{t\cdot}'v_{t\cdot})(\Omega^{-1} \otimes \Omega^{-1}).$$

Thus, the entity termed Φ, above, is given by

$$\Phi' = \begin{pmatrix} (\Omega^{-1} \otimes x_{t\cdot}')v_{t\cdot}' \\ \vdots \\ (1/2)(\Omega^{-1} \otimes \Omega^{-})[(v_{t\cdot}' \otimes v_{t\cdot}') - \omega] \end{pmatrix},$$

and we conclude that

$$E_\theta(\Phi'\Phi) = E_\theta \begin{bmatrix} \Phi_{11} & \Phi_{12} \\ \Phi_{21} & \Phi_{22} \end{bmatrix}$$

where

$$\Phi_{11} = (\Omega^{-1} \otimes x'_{t\cdot})v'_{t\cdot}v_{t\cdot}(\Omega^{-1} \otimes x_{t\cdot})$$

$$\Phi_{12} = (\Omega^{-1} \otimes x'_{t\cdot})v'_{t\cdot}(v_{t\cdot} \otimes v_{t\cdot} - \omega')\Omega^*$$

$$\Phi_{21} = \Phi'_{12}, \quad \Omega^* = (\Omega^{-1} \otimes \Omega^{-1})$$

$$\Phi_{22} = \frac{1}{4}\Omega^*[v'_{t\cdot}v_{t\cdot} \otimes v'_{t\cdot}v_{t\cdot} - (v'_{t\cdot} \otimes v'_{t\cdot})\omega' - \omega(v_{t\cdot} \otimes v_{t\cdot}) + \omega\omega']\Omega^*.$$

Since the odd moments of zero mean normals are null, we obtain $E_\theta(\Phi_{12}) = 0$. To evaluate $E_\theta(\Phi_{22})$, observe that the expectation of the last three terms in brackets yields $-\omega\omega'$ while, for the first term (in brackets), the expectation of the (r, q) element of the (i, j) block yields,

$$E_\theta(v_{ti}v_{tj}v_{tr}v_{tq}) = \omega_{ij}\omega_{rq} + \omega_{ir}\omega_{jq} + \omega_{iq}\omega_{jr}.$$

Consequently, the expectation of the (r, q) element of the (i, j) block of the bracketed term in the representation of Φ_{22} is

$$\omega_{ij}\omega_{rq} + \omega_{ir}\omega_{jq} + \omega_{iq}\omega_{jr} - \omega_{ir}\omega_{jq} = \omega_{ij}\omega_{rq} + \omega_{iq}\omega_{jr},$$

which means that the expectation of the entire term in brackets may be written as

$$[\omega_{ij}\Omega + \omega_{\cdot j}\omega'_{\cdot i}] = \Omega \otimes \Omega + \begin{bmatrix} \Omega \otimes \omega'_{\cdot 1} \\ \Omega \otimes \omega'_{\cdot 2} \\ \Omega \otimes \omega'_{\cdot 3} \\ \vdots \\ \Omega \otimes \omega'_{\cdot m} \end{bmatrix}.$$

It follows, immediately, that

$$E_\theta \left(\frac{\partial \ln f}{\partial \text{vec}(\Omega)}\right)' \left(\frac{\partial \ln f}{\partial \text{vec}(\Omega)}\right) = \frac{1}{4}(\Omega^{-1} \otimes \Omega^{-1}) + \Psi,$$

where

$$\Psi = \frac{1}{4}(\Omega^{-1} \otimes \Omega^{-1}) \begin{bmatrix} \Omega \otimes \omega'_{\cdot 1} \\ \Omega \otimes \omega'_{\cdot 2} \\ \Omega \otimes \omega'_{\cdot 3} \\ \vdots \\ \Omega \otimes \omega'_{\cdot m} \end{bmatrix} (\Omega^{-1} \otimes \Omega^{-1}).$$

The matrix in square brackets, in the right member, above, is not in a form convenient for further simplification. We observe, however, that it is a component of the **covariance matrix** of $\text{vec}(S) = (v'_t.v_t.)$. From Lemma 9, of Chapter 3, we have the relationship

$$\text{vec}(A) = I_{m,n}\text{vec}(A'),$$

where A is $m \times n$ and $I_{m,n}$ is a permutation matrix of order mn. It follows that $I'_{m,n} = I_{n,m} = I_{m,n}^{-1}$. If A is **symmetric** then it is, of course, square say $m \times m$, and moreover $I_{m,m} = I'_{m,m} = I_{m,m}^{-1}$, so that

$$\text{vec}(A) = I_{m,m}\text{vec}(A).$$

We, therefore, conclude that

$$I'_{m,m}\begin{bmatrix} \Omega \otimes \omega'_{.1} \\ \Omega \otimes \omega'_{.2} \\ \Omega \otimes \omega_{.3} \\ \vdots \\ \Omega \otimes \omega'_{.m} \end{bmatrix} = \begin{bmatrix} \Omega \otimes \omega'_{.1} \\ \Omega \otimes \omega'_{.2} \\ \Omega \otimes \omega_{.3} \\ \vdots \\ \Omega \otimes \omega'_{.m} \end{bmatrix}.$$

An intuitive way to see this is to note that the matrix in brackets above is part of the **covariance matrix** of $\text{vec}(S)$; the operation $I_{m,m}\text{vec}(S)$ leaves the diagonal elements of $S = v'_t.v_t.$ unchanged, but replaces s_{ij} by s_{ji}. For example, the second element of $\text{vec}(S)$, s_{21}, is replaced by the $(m+1)^{st}$ element, s_{12}; similarly with s_{31} and s_{13} and so on. By the symmetry of S, this is a set of pairs of identical elements. When we apply $I_{m,m}$ to the matrix above we effect a similar replacement of the rows of the components of the covariance matrix. Thus, for example, the second row, which contains the **covariances** of s_{21} with respect to the elements of $\text{vec}(S)$ is replaced by the row that contains the **covariances** of s_{12} relative to the elements of $\text{vec}(S)$. Since, however, $s_{21} = s_{12}$ the two rows are identical! Hence, the original matrix is not altered by this substitution. Similarly, we may establish that

$$\begin{bmatrix} \Omega \otimes \omega'_{.1} \\ \Omega \otimes \omega'_{.2} \\ \Omega \otimes \omega_{.3} \\ \vdots \\ \Omega \otimes \omega'_{.m} \end{bmatrix} = I_{m,m}(\Omega \otimes \Omega), \quad (\Omega \otimes \Omega)I_{m,m} = \Omega \otimes \Omega,$$

$$4\Psi = (\Omega^{-1} \otimes \Omega^{-1})I_{m,m}(\Omega \otimes \Omega)(\Omega^{-1} \otimes \Omega^{-1}) = \Omega^{-1} \otimes \Omega^{-1},$$

whence we conclude that

$$E_\theta(\Phi'\Phi) = \begin{bmatrix} \Omega^{-1} \otimes x'_t.x_t. & 0 \\ 0 & (1/2)\left(\Omega^{-1} \otimes \Omega^{-1}\right) \end{bmatrix}$$

is the FIC of a single observation on the reduced form of the GLSEM.

For a random sample of size T the FIC, or the Fisher information matrix, is given by

$$I_T(\theta) = \begin{bmatrix} \Omega^{-1} \otimes X'X & 0 \\ 0 & (T/2)(\Omega^{-1} \otimes \Omega^{-1}) \end{bmatrix}.$$

5.4.1 Alternative Representation of the Information Matrix

If X is a r.v. with density function $f(\cdot; \theta)$ then

$$E_\theta \left(\frac{\partial \ln f(\cdot; \theta)}{\partial \theta} \right) = 0.$$

This is so since, under certain regularity conditions, the left member above can also be written as

$$\int_R \frac{\partial f(\xi; \theta)/\partial \theta}{f(\xi; \theta)} f(\xi; \theta) \, d\xi = \frac{\partial}{\partial \theta} \int_{-\infty}^{\infty} f(\xi; \theta) \, d\xi = 0,$$

since f is, for every $\theta \in \Theta$, a **density function** and thus, its integral over R is unity! Moreover, the FIC defined in the previous section is given by [8]

$$I(\theta) = \text{Cov}(\Phi), \quad \Phi = \frac{\partial \ln f(\cdot; \theta)}{\partial \theta}.$$

It follows, therefore, that we have the simplification

$$I(\theta) = E_\theta(\Phi' \Phi).$$

Noting that

$$\frac{\partial^2}{\partial \theta \, \partial \theta} \ln f(\cdot; \theta) = \frac{\partial}{\partial \theta} \Phi = \frac{f \left(\partial^2 f/\partial \theta \, \partial \theta \right) - (\partial f/\partial \theta)' (\partial f/\partial \theta)}{f^2},$$

we find

$$-E_\theta \left(\frac{\partial^2}{\partial \theta \, \partial \theta} \ln f(\cdot; \theta) \right) = \int_{R^n} \left(\frac{1}{f} \frac{\partial f}{\partial \theta} \right)' \left(\frac{\partial f}{\partial \theta} \right) d\xi = E_\theta(\Phi' \Phi).$$

Thus, we conclude that

$$I(\theta) = -E_\theta \left(\frac{\partial^2}{\partial \theta \, \partial \theta} \ln f(\cdot; \theta) \right).$$

---

[8] Note that $I(\theta)$ is a $k \times k$ matrix, owing to the fact that θ is a k-dimensional parameter vector.

In the case of the sample $\{X_j : j = 1, 2, \ldots, n\}$, the same relations prevail, except that now the density, f, is replaced by the likelihood function, L^*, or L_n^* and the Fisher information is given by [9]

$$I(\theta) = -E_\theta \left(\frac{\partial^2}{\partial\theta\,\partial\theta} \ln L^*(\cdot\,;\theta) \right) = E_\theta \left(\frac{\partial\ln L^*}{\partial\theta} \right)' \left(\frac{\partial\ln L^*}{\partial\theta} \right).$$

Example 4. Consider, again, the problem examined in the first section, viz. the model

$$y_{t\cdot} = g_{t\cdot}(\phi) + u_{t\cdot}, \quad t = 1, 2, \ldots, T, \tag{5.5}$$

where $y_{t\cdot}$ is an m-element vector; similarly $g_{t\cdot}$, is a vector valued function that may contain some "exogenous" variables, in addition to the parameters ϕ. Utilizing this framework for the problem considered in the first section, we may write the likelihood function, for a sequence of observations $\{y_{t\cdot} : t = 1, 2, \ldots, T\}$, say,

$$L^*(\theta) = \prod_{t=1}^{T} f_t(y_{t\cdot}; \theta), \tag{5.6}$$

and note that it is simply the joint density function of (all) the observations, $y_{t\cdot}$, $t = 1, 2, \ldots, T$. The density of individual observations is given by $f_t(y_{t\cdot}; \theta)$, which for simplicity of notation we shall denote by $f_t(\theta)$. We further observe that

$$\int_{R^{Tm}} L^*(\theta)\,dy = 1, \quad \frac{\partial}{\partial\theta}\int_{R^{Tm}} L^*(\theta)\,dy = \int_{R^{Tm}} \frac{\partial}{\partial\theta} L^*(\theta)\,dy = 0, \tag{5.7}$$

and that the Fisher information contained in the sample is given by

$$I_T(\theta) = E_\theta(\Phi_T'\Phi_T), \tag{5.8}$$

where

$$\Phi_T = \frac{\partial\ln L^*}{\partial\theta} = \sum_{t=1}^{T} \frac{\partial\ln f_t(\theta)}{\partial\theta}.$$

5.5   The Cramer-Rao Bounds

It is interesting that the preceding discussion enables us to assign to any estimator of the parameter vector θ a "floor", i.e. a lower bound, below

---

[9] The notation

$$E_\theta \left(\frac{\partial\ln L^*}{\partial\theta} \right)' \left(\frac{\partial\ln L^*}{\partial\theta} \right)$$

is not in error. It is a consequence of the convention that vectors of partial derivatives (gradients) are written as row vectors.

which its covariance matrix cannot fall. This provides a way in which "efficiency" can be defined unambiguously. Thus, we may define an estimator to be efficient if, within a certain class, it attains this lower bound. Of course, we cannot ensure that such estimators will always exist; an additional disadvantage is that, in order to define efficiency, it is necessary to specify precisely the underlying density. Thus, this definition would not be applicable to distribution free estimators, i.e. to estimators which do not rely for their derivation on the underlying density function.

Proposition 2 (Cramer-Rao Inequality). Let

$$X = \{X_j : j = 1, 2, \ldots, n\}$$

be a sequence of r.v. defined on the probability space $(\Omega, \mathcal{A}, \mathcal{P}_\theta)$, as above. Let [10] $L_n(X; \theta)$, $\theta \in \Theta \subseteq R^k$, be the LF of the observations (sequence), and $T_n = h(X)$ be an estimator of the parameter vector θ, such that

$$E_\theta(T_n) = \int_{R^n} T_n(\xi) L_n^*(\xi; \theta) \, d\xi = m(\theta).$$

The covariance matrix of the estimator obeys

$$\mathrm{Cov}(T_n) \geq M(\theta)[I_n(\theta)]^{-1} M(\theta)', \quad M(\theta) = \frac{\partial m(\theta)}{\partial \theta}.$$

Proof: Define the vector of partial derivatives (the gradient or "score")

$$\frac{\partial L_n}{\partial \theta} = \frac{1}{L_n^*} \frac{\partial L_n^*}{\partial \theta} = \Phi_n,$$

and recall that $E_\theta(\Phi_n) = 0$; consequently, that

$$\mathrm{Cov}(T_n, \Phi_n) = E_\theta\{[T_n - m(\theta)]\Phi_n\} = E_\theta(T_n \Phi_n),$$

and moreover,

$$E_\theta(T_n \Phi_n) = \int_{R^n} T_n(\xi) \frac{\partial L_n^*(\xi; \theta)}{\partial \theta} \, d\xi$$

$$= \frac{\partial}{\partial \theta} \int_{R^n} T_n(\xi) L_n^*(\xi; \theta) \, d\xi = \frac{\partial m(\theta)}{\partial \theta} = M(\theta),$$

where $M(\theta)$ is a $k \times k$ matrix of the partial derivatives of the mean of the estimator, T_n. Now, for **arbitrary vectors**, $\alpha, \beta \in R^k$, define

$$\tau_n = \alpha' T_n, \quad \phi_n = \Phi_n \beta,$$

---

[10] We remind the reader that, generically, we denote the **likelihood function** by L^*, or L_n^*, and the **log likelihood** function (LF) by L, i.e. we have the relation $L = \ln L^*$.

and note the **scalar relations,**

$$\mathrm{Cov}(\tau_n, \phi_n) = \alpha' M(\theta)\beta.$$

From the Cauchy inequality we find

$$\left(\alpha' M(\theta)\beta\right)^2 = \left(E_\theta\{\alpha'[T_n - m(\theta)]\phi_n\}\right)^2 \leq \alpha' \mathrm{Cov}(T_n)\alpha\, \beta' \mathrm{Cov}(\Phi_n)\beta.$$

For the special case

$$\beta = [I_n(\theta)]^{-1} M(\theta)' \alpha,$$

and arbitrary $\alpha \in R^k$, the inequality above may be rendered as

$$\alpha' \mathrm{Cov}(T_n)\alpha \geq \alpha' M(\theta)[I_n(\theta)]^{-1} M(\theta)' \alpha.$$

Since α is arbitrary, we conclude that

$$\mathrm{Cov}(T_n) \geq M(\theta)[I_n(\theta)]^{-1} M(\theta)',$$

in the sense that the difference of the two matrices is positive semidefinite.

q.e.d.

Remark 4. When T_n is an unbiased estimator of θ, i.e. when $E_\theta(T_n) = \theta$, the relation above reduces to

$$\mathrm{Cov}(T_n) \geq [I_n(\theta)]^{-1} = \left\{-E_\theta\left[\frac{\partial^2 \ln L_n(\xi;\theta)}{\partial\theta\,\partial\theta}\right]\right\}^{-1},$$

which is the celebrated Cramer-Rao inequality.

Remark 5. We would be remiss if we did not note the trivially obvious fact that for the Cramer-Rao inequality to be valid we need to assert that, at least in some neighborhood of the "true" parameter point θ^0, the FIC, or the Fisher information matrix $I_n(\theta)$ is nonsingular. Indeed, in complex nonlinear models, where the distribution of ML estimators may not be determinable for small samples, it is an **identification condition** to assert that in an ϵ-neighborhood of the "true" parameter point θ^0 the appropriate limit of the information matrix is **nonsingular.**

We should also point out that in many of the models examined herein, it is not possible to determine small sample distributions. Thus, defining efficiency in terms of the Cramer-Rao inequality may not always be possible. It is shown, however, that, in large samples, and under certain conditions, ML estimators are efficient within the class of consistent uniformly asymptotically normal (CUAN) estimators; and, it is further shown, that under certain circumstances the covariance matrix of their limiting distribution is simply the inverse of the appropriate information matrix. For such topics the reader is referred to Rao (1973).

5.6   Martingale Properties of Likelihood Functions

Consider the sequence of r.v. $X_{(n)}$, defined on the probability space (Ω, $\mathcal{A}$, $\mathcal{P}$) and the econometric model (Ω, $\mathcal{A}$, $\mathcal{P}_\theta$), $\theta \in \Theta \subset R^k$. Define further the stochastic basis (sequence of σ-subalgebras) $\mathcal{G}_0 \subset \mathcal{G}_1 \subset \cdots \subset \mathcal{G}_n \subset \cdots \subset \mathcal{A}$, and suppose that the econometric model is dominated by a measure μ such that for every set $A \in \mathcal{G}_n$

$$\mathcal{P}_{n\theta}(A) = \int_A L^*(\theta; X_{(n)}) \, d\mu, \tag{5.9}$$

where $L^*(\theta; X_{(n)})$ is the likelihood function of the sample, i.e. the joint density of the sequence $X_{(n)}$. For notational convenience we shall also denote this likelihood function by $L_n^*(\theta)$. By Proposition 1, this measure μ can be taken to be a probability; an expectation with respect to μ will be denoted by E. To show that the stochastic sequence

$$\{(L_n^*(\theta), \mathcal{G}_n) : n \geq 1\}$$

is a martingale, we must demonstrate that

$$E \mid L_n^*(\theta) \mid < \infty, \quad E[L_n^*(\theta) \mid \mathcal{G}_{n-1}] = L_{n-1}^*(\theta). \tag{5.10}$$

The first condition evidently holds since L_n^* is a density; as for the second, we note that by definition, see Dhrymes (1989), Definition 14, Chapter 2, the conditional expectation $E[L_n^*(\theta) \mid \mathcal{G}_{n-1}]$ must be $\mathcal{G}_{n-1}$- measurable and, for every set $A \in \mathcal{G}_{n-1}$, it must satisfy

$$\int_A E[L_n^*(\theta) \mid \mathcal{G}_{n-1}] \, d\mu = \int_A L_n^*(\theta) \, d\mu. \tag{5.11}$$

If we choose $\mathcal{G}_n = \sigma(X_{(n)})$, the function L_{n-1}^* is $\mathcal{G}_{n-1}$-measurable; moreover, for any $A \in \mathcal{G}_{n-1}$ (note also that $A \in \mathcal{G}_n$ as well), we obtain

$$\int_A L_n^*(\theta, \omega) \, d\mu = \mathcal{P}_{n\theta}(A) = \mathcal{P}_{(n-1)\theta}(A) = \int_A L_{n-1}^*(\theta, \omega) \, d\mu. \tag{5.12}$$

We conclude, therefore, that

$$E[L_n^*(\theta) \mid \mathcal{G}_{n-1}] = L_{n-1}^*(\theta),$$

and consequently that the stochastic sequence

$$\{[L_n^*(\theta), \mathcal{G}_n] : n \geq 1\}$$

is, for every $\theta \in \Theta$, a martingale.

It is interesting that the LF is also a martingale. To show that, write the likelihood function as

$$L_n^*(\theta) = L^*(\theta; X_{(n)}) = \frac{L^*(\theta; X_{(n)})}{L^*(\theta; X_{(n-1)})} \frac{L^*(\theta; X_{(n-1)})}{L^*(\theta; X_{(n-2)})} \cdots \frac{L^*(\theta; X_{(1)})}{L^*(\theta; X_{(0)})}, \tag{5.13}$$

it being understood that $L_0^* \equiv 1$. The LF, L_n, is given by

$$L_n(\theta) = \sum_{i=1}^{n} [L_i(\theta) - L_{i-1}(\theta)], \qquad (5.14)$$

where for notational convenience we represent $L_n(\theta; X_{(n)})$ by $L_n(\theta)$. Its derivative (gradient) is given by

$$\frac{\partial L_n(\theta)}{\partial \theta} = \sum_{i=1}^{n} k_i(\theta), \quad k_i(\theta) = \frac{\partial}{\partial \theta} [L_i(\theta) - L_{i-1}(\theta)]. \qquad (5.15)$$

We note that $k_i(\theta)$ is $\mathcal{G}_i$-measurable, $E_\theta \mid k_i(\theta) \mid < \infty$, $E_\theta[k_i(\theta) \mid \mathcal{G}_{i-1}] = 0$. This implies [11] that

$$E_\theta \left[\frac{\partial L_n(\theta)}{\partial \theta} \;\middle|\; \mathcal{G}_{n-1} \right] = \frac{\partial L_{n-1}(\theta)}{\partial \theta},$$

and thus, the sequence

$$\left\{ \left[\frac{\partial L_n(\theta)}{\partial \theta}, \mathcal{G}_n \right] : n \geq 1 \right\}$$

is a martingale.

The significance of the discussion of this section is that stochastic sequences which are martingales, such as the likelihood function and the derivative of the LF studied in this section, converge a.c. under a variety of circumstances. For details see Dhrymes (1989), Ch. 5. This plays an important role in the demonstration of certain properties of ML estimators.

Remark 6. Note that in the preceding discussion of the LF, in connection with its martingale properties, nothing has been assumed regarding the extent to which the observations in the sample are or are not independent, or uncorrelated. Thus, such results hold quite generally and derive from the properties of density functions, and/or conditional density functions, and not from the independence, or lack thereof, of the elements within the sample.

---

[11] It should, perhaps, be pointed out that the reason for $E_\theta[k_i(\theta) \mid \mathcal{G}_{i-1}] = 0$ becomes quite transparent if we note that

$$k_i(\theta) = \frac{\partial}{\partial \theta} \left(\ln \frac{L_i^*}{L_{i-1}^*} \right) = \frac{\partial}{\partial \theta} \ln f_\theta(X_i \mid X_{(i-1)}),$$

where $f_\theta(X_i \mid X_{(i-1)})$ is the conditional density of the ith observation, given the sequence $X_{(i-1)}$. As we had noted above, however, the expectation of the derivative of the log of the density is null.

5.7   Kullback Information

Often the situation arises that we wish to measure the "distance" between two measures, or the similarity or dissimilarity of two probability measures. In this context, Kullback information plays an important role, as it does in the case of ML estimation. We begin the discussion with the case of two discrete probabilities.

Definition 5. Let Ω be a countable (discrete) set and let $\mathcal{A}$ be the set of all subsets of Ω; let P and Q be two probabilities defined on $\mathcal{A}$, such that $P(\omega_i) = 0$ whenever $Q(\omega_i) = 0$, together with the conventions that $0 \ln 0 = 0$, and $0/0 = 0$. The **Kullback information** [12] of P on Q is given by

$$K(P,Q) \;=\; \sum_{i=1}^{\infty} P(\omega_i) \ln \left(\frac{P(\omega_i)}{Q(\omega_i)} \right).$$

Definition 6 (Generalization). Let P and Q be probability measures defined on the measurable space $(\Omega, \mathcal{A})$, and suppose that Q is absolutely continuous with respect to P. Suppose further that P and Q are dominated by a measure μ, in the sense that there exists a measure μ, and integrable functions f and g, such that for every set $A \in \mathcal{A}$

$$P(A) = \int_A f \, d\mu, \quad Q(A) = \int_A g \, d\mu.$$

The Kullback information of P on Q is defined by

$$K(P,Q) \;=\; \int_\Omega f \ln \left(\frac{f}{g} \right) d\mu.$$

Remark 7. The term "Kullback information of P on Q" is somewhat infelicitous; from the point of view of its relevance in the discussion of ML estimators, it would be more appropriate if it were termed the "Kullback information of Q on P". It is, further, important to recognize that the Kullback information (which is a **scalar**) is nonnegative and **it is zero only if $P = Q$, a.c.** To see this, rewrite the integrand of Definition 6 as

$$K(P,Q) \;=\; \int_\Omega \left[\frac{f}{g} \ln \left(\frac{f}{g} \right) + 1 - \frac{f}{g} \right] g \, d\mu,$$

and note that the integrand in square brackets is an expression of the form $x \ln x + (1 - x)$, with $x = (f/g)$. Moreover, it may be verified that

---

[12] This concept is named after the American statistician S. Kullback see, for example, S. Kullback (1968).

$k(x) = x \ln x + 1 - x \geq 0$, for $x \geq 0$, and it is zero if and only if $x = 1$, i.e. if $f = g$, a.c. (relative to Q and hence P as well).

Example 2. Consider the econometric model (Ω, $\mathcal{A}$, $\mathcal{P}_\theta$), for $\theta \in \Theta \subset R^k$ and let θ^0 be the true parameter point, such that $N(\theta^0; \epsilon) \subset \Theta$, i.e. θ^0 is an interior point of Θ. Let $X_{(n)}$ be a sample, and $\mathcal{P}_{n\theta}$ the associated measure on the σ-algebra $\mathcal{G}_n$ induced by $X_{(n)}$. Suppose, further, that there is a dominant measure, say μ such that $\mathcal{P}_{n\theta} = L_n^*(\theta)\mu$, where L_n^* is the likelihood function of the sample. The Kullback information (KI) of $\mathcal{P}_{n\theta^0}$ on $\mathcal{P}_{n\theta}$ is given by

$$K(\mathcal{P}_{n\theta^0}, \mathcal{P}_{n\theta}) = \int_\Omega L_n^*(\theta^0, \omega) \ln \left(\frac{L_n^*(\theta^0, \omega)}{L_n^*(\theta, \omega)} \right) d\mu(\omega)$$

$$= E_{\theta^0}[L_n(\theta^0)] - E_{\theta^0}[L_n(\theta)],$$

where $L_n = \ln L_n^*$. By the inequality in Eq. (5.4) the KI above is non-negative. Another implication of the KI representation above is that the ML estimator of θ^0 minimizes, with respect to θ, the function whose expectation is the Kullback information of $\mathcal{P}_{n\theta^0}$ on $\mathcal{P}_{n\theta}$.

Example 3. Suppose, in Example 2 above, we shift our focus from the probability space (Ω, $\mathcal{A}$, $\mathcal{P}$) to the associated probability space (R^n, $\mathcal{B}(R^n)$, P), and consider the sequence $X_{(n)}$ together with the associated probability distributions $\mathcal{P}_{n\theta}$, corresponding to an econometric model whose true parameter is θ^0, as above. Suppose, further, that this model is dominated by ordinary Lebesgue measure, so that we can write, for any set $B \in \mathcal{B}(R^n)$

$$\mathcal{P}_{n\theta}(B) = \int_B f_\theta(\xi) \, d\xi.$$

The Kullback information of $\mathcal{P}_{n\theta^0}$ on $\mathcal{P}_{n\theta}$ is

$$K(\mathcal{P}_{n\theta^0}, \mathcal{P}_{n\theta}) = \int_{R^n} \ln \left(\frac{f_{\theta^0}(\xi)}{f_\theta(\xi)} \right) f_{\theta^0}(\xi) \, d\xi.$$

If we are dealing with **jointly normal** r.v. with mean vector μ and covariance matrix Σ, the Kullback information becomes

$$K(\mathcal{P}_{n\theta^0}, \mathcal{P}_{n\theta}) = -\frac{1}{2}\ln | \Sigma_0 | + \frac{1}{2}\ln | \Sigma | - \frac{1}{2} \left[\int_{R^n} (q_0 - q)\phi(\xi; \mu_0, \Sigma_0) \, d\xi \right],$$

where $q_0 = (\xi - \mu_0)' \Sigma_0^{-1}(\xi - \mu_0)$, $q = (\xi - \mu)' \Sigma^{-1}(\xi - \mu)$, and $\phi(\cdot; \mu_0, \Sigma_0)$ is the multivariate normal with mean vector μ_0 and covariance matrix Σ_0. Carrying out the integration, we find

$$K(\mathcal{P}_{n\theta^0}, \mathcal{P}_{n\theta}) = -\frac{1}{2}\ln \left(| \Sigma^{-1}\Sigma_0 | + m \right) + \frac{1}{2}\text{tr}\Sigma^{-1} \left[\Sigma_0 + (\mu - \mu_0)(\mu - \mu_0)' \right].$$

Partially maximizing with respect to Σ and inserting the result above, we find the "concentrated" KI,

$$K(P_{n\theta^0}, P_{n\theta}) = \frac{1}{2}\ln\left(\frac{|\Sigma_0 + (\mu - \mu_0)(\mu - \mu_0)'|}{|\Sigma_0|}\right),$$

which is, evidently, nonnegative and assumes its global minimum at $\mu = \mu_0$, which also implies $\Sigma = \Sigma_0$.

5.8 Convergence a.c. of ML Estimators

In this section we shall deal with the issue of **stong consistency of the ML estimator**, first in the case of a sample of independent random variables (elements) and thereafter in a more general context; secondly, we shall examine the validity of the expansion of the first order conditions defining the ML estimator, in order that we may obtain its limiting distribution. We begin with

Definition 7. Consider the probability space $(\Omega, \mathcal{A}, \mathcal{P})$ and the econometric model $(\Omega, \mathcal{A}, \mathcal{P}_\theta)$, $\theta \in \Theta \subset R^k$, with the "true" parameter, θ^0, being an **interior** point of Θ. A **contrast function** of this model, relative to θ^0, is a function

$$K : \Theta \times \Theta \longrightarrow R,$$

say $K(\theta^0, \theta)$, having a strict minimum at the point $\theta = \theta^0$, in the sense that $K(\theta^0, \theta^0) < K(\theta^0, \theta)$, for all $\theta \in \Theta$, $\theta \neq \theta^0$.

Definition 8. In the context of Definition 7, consider the (nested) sequence of subalgebras [13]

$$\mathcal{G}_0 \subset \mathcal{G}_1 \subset \mathcal{G}_2 \subset \cdots \subset \mathcal{G}_n \subset \cdots \subset \mathcal{A}.$$

A **contrast**, relative to θ^0 and K, is a function [14]

$$H : \mathcal{N} \times \Theta \times \Omega \longrightarrow R,$$

independent of θ^0, such that

---

[13] Basically, the motivation for the sequence of subalgebras is to provide the minimal probability space on which to describe certain sequences of r.v. Thus, for example, if we take $\mathcal{G}_0 = \{\emptyset, \Omega\}$, the trivial σ-algebra used to describe "constants", and $\mathcal{G}_n = \sigma(X_1, X_2, \ldots, X_n)$, we will have produced the sequence referred to in the text, which is quite suitable for studying the samples $\{X_{(n)} : n \geq 1\}$.

[14] In the description of the function, $\mathcal{N}$ represents the integers, i.e. $\mathcal{N} = \{0, 1, 2, \ldots\}$.

i. for every $\theta \in \Theta$, $H_n(\theta, \omega)$ is $\mathcal{G}_n$-measurable, i.e. it is a random variable;

ii. $H_n(\theta, \cdot)$ converges to the contrast function $K(\theta^0, \theta)$, at least in probability. [15]

A **minimum contrast estimator** (MC) associated with H is a function,

$$\hat{\theta} : \mathcal{N} \times \Omega \longrightarrow \Theta,$$

such that

$$H_n(\hat{\theta}_n) = \inf_{\theta \in \Theta} H_n(\theta).$$

The definition above makes possible the following important

Proposition 3. In the context of Definition 7, suppose, further,

i. $\Theta \subset R^k$ is closed and bounded (compact);

ii. $K(\theta^0, \theta)$, and $H_n(\theta, \omega)$ are continuous in θ;

iii. letting

$$c_n(\delta) = \sup_{|\theta_1 - \theta_2| \leq \delta} | H_n(\theta_1) - H_n(\theta_2) |,$$

there exist sequences $\{\epsilon_k : \epsilon_k > 0, k \geq 1\}$, and $\{\delta_k : \delta_k > 0, k \geq 1\}$, both (monotonically) tending to zero with k, such that the sets $F_n = \{\omega : c_n(\delta_n) > \epsilon_n\}$ obey $\mathcal{P}(F_n) \leq 2\epsilon_n$, and hence $\lim_{n \to \infty} \mathcal{P}(F_n) = 0$.

Then, every minimum contrast estimator is consistent.

Proof: Since $K(\theta^0, \theta)$ is continuous and $K(\theta^0, \theta^0) = 0$, there exists $\epsilon > 0$, such that

$$K(\theta^0, \theta) > 2\epsilon, \quad \text{for } \theta \in \bar{B}, \tag{5.16}$$

where

$$B = \{\theta : | \theta - \theta^0 | < \epsilon\}. \tag{5.17}$$

Since B is open, $\Theta^* = \Theta \cap \bar{B}$ is compact; consequently, there exists a countable set D, that is everywhere dense in Θ^*, say

$$D = \{\theta_i : i \geq 1\}.$$

Moreover, for $\epsilon_k < \epsilon$, there exists a finite open cover of Θ^*, say

$$\Theta^* \subset \bigcup_{i=1}^{N} A_i, \quad \text{with } A_i = \{\theta : | \theta - \theta_i | < \epsilon_k\}. \tag{5.18}$$

---

[15] When a statement like this is made, or when an expectation is taken, we shall always mean that the operations entailed are performed in accordance with the probability measure $\mathcal{P}_{\theta^0}$.

Next, note that we can write

$$H_n(\theta) = H_n(\theta_i) - [H_n(\theta_i) - H_n(\theta)].$$

Consequently, for sufficiently large n, we obtain

$$H_n(\theta) \geq H_n(\theta_i) - |H_n(\theta_i) - H_n(\theta)|$$

$$\inf_{\theta \in \Theta^*} H_n(\theta) \geq \inf_{1 \leq i \leq N} H_n(\theta_i) - \sup_{\theta_i \in D} \sup_{|\theta_i - \theta| < \delta_n} |H_n(\theta_i) - H_n(\theta)|$$

$$\geq \inf_{1 \leq i \leq N} H_n(\theta_i) - c_n(\delta_n), \tag{5.19}$$

where $\delta_n < \delta_k$. If $\hat{\theta}_n$ is the MC estimator, i.e. if $H_n(\hat{\theta}_n) = \inf_{\theta \in \Theta} H_n(\theta)$, we must show that its probability limit is θ^0. It is clear that $\hat{\theta}_n \in \bar{B}$ if and only if $\inf_{\theta \in \Theta^*} H_n(\theta) < H_n(\theta^0)$. This is so since, by the continuity of $H_n(\theta)$, if the condition above holds, there exists a neighborhood of θ^0, say $N(\theta^0; \epsilon) = \{\theta : |\theta - \theta^0| < \epsilon\}$, such that

$$\inf_{\theta \in \Theta^*} H_n(\theta) < H_n(\bar{\theta}), \quad \text{for } \bar{\theta} \in N(\theta^0; \epsilon),$$

and it is this type of neighborhood that constitutes the set B. Define now the sets

$$B_n = \{\omega : \hat{\theta}_n \in \Theta^*\}, \quad C_n = \{\omega : \inf_{\theta \in \Theta^*} [H_n(\theta) - H_n(\theta^0)] < 0\}$$

$$D_n = \{\omega : \inf_{1 \leq i \leq N} [H_n(\theta_i) - H_n(\theta^0)] - c_n(\delta_n) < 0\}, \tag{5.20}$$

and note that

$$B_n \subset C_n \subset D_n.$$

Define the sets

$$E_n = \{\omega : \inf_{1 \leq i \leq N} [H_n(\theta_i) - H_n(\theta^0)] < \epsilon_n\}, \quad F_n = \{\omega : c_n(\delta_n) > \epsilon_n\},$$

$$\tag{5.21}$$

and note that for $c_n(\delta_n) \leq \epsilon_n$

$$D_n \cap \bar{F}_n = \{\omega : \inf_{1 \leq i \leq N} [H_n(\theta_i) - H_n(\theta^0)] < c_n(\delta_n), \text{ and } c_n(\delta_n) \leq \epsilon_n\} \subseteq E_n.$$

$$\tag{5.22}$$

Since

$$D_n = (D_n \cap \bar{F}_n) \cup (D_n \cap F_n) \subset (E_n \cup F_n), \tag{5.23}$$

it follows that

$$\mathcal{P}(B_n) \leq \mathcal{P}(E_n \cup F_n) \leq \mathcal{P}(E_n) + \mathcal{P}(F_n). \tag{5.24}$$

By part iii of the premises of the proposition, $\mathcal{P}(F_n) \longrightarrow 0$, and, by Definitions 7 and 8

$$\inf_{1 \leq i \leq N} [H_n(\theta_i) - H_n(\theta^0)] \xrightarrow{P} \inf_{1 \leq i \leq N} K(\theta^0, \theta_i) - K(\theta^0, \theta^0) \geq 2\epsilon,$$

whence we conclude

$$\lim_{n \to \infty} \mathcal{P}_{\theta^0}(E_n) = 0, \text{ and hence } \lim_{n \to \infty} \mathcal{P}_{\theta^0}(B_n) = 0.$$

But this means that $\lim_{n \to \infty} \mathcal{P}_{\theta^0}(\bar{B}_n) = 1$, so that $\hat{\theta}_n$ is consistent for θ^0.

q.e.d.

Corollary 1. In the context of Proposition 3, suppose that

$$H_n(\theta) - H_n(\theta^0) \xrightarrow{\text{a.c.}} K(\theta^0, \theta)$$

uniformly for $\theta \in \Theta$. Then the MC estimator converges to θ^0 with probability one, i.e. it is **strongly consistent** for θ^0.

Proof: Proceed as in the proof of Proposition 3, and define the sets B, Θ^*, B_n, C_n, as defined therein. If the convergence

$$H_n(\theta) - H_n(\theta^0) \xrightarrow{\text{a.c.}} K(\theta^0, \theta),$$

is **uniform in** θ then

$$\inf_{\theta \in \Theta^*} [H_n(\theta) - H_n(\theta^0)] \xrightarrow{\text{a.c.}} \inf_{\theta \in \Theta^*} K(\theta^0, \theta) \geq 2\epsilon > 0. \qquad (5.25)$$

Consequently,

$$\limsup_{n \to \infty} C_n = C^*, \text{ obeys } \mathcal{P}(C^*) = 0. \qquad (5.26)$$

Since, by construction, $B_n \subset C_n$, we have that

$$B^* = \overline{\lim_{n \to \infty}} B_n \subseteq \overline{\lim_{n \to \infty}} C_n = C^*; \qquad (5.27)$$

hence, in view of Eq. (5.26) we conclude that $\mathcal{P}(B^*) = 0$. But this means that the ML estimator,

$$\inf_{\theta \in \Theta} H_n^*(\theta) = H_n^*(\hat{\theta}_n),$$

obeys $\hat{\theta}_n \in B$ with probability one, or that it converges a.c. to the true parameter θ^0.

q.e.d.

Remark 8. The Corollary actually shows that the event "$\hat{\theta}_n$ assumes a value in Θ^* infinitely often, (i.o.)" has probability zero; thus, the sequence (or any of its convergent subsequences) **cannot converge inside the set** $\Theta^* = \Theta \cap \bar{B}$, since the limit superior has probability zero! Therefore, to the extent that there is convergence, it must be in the set B. Since

$$\bar{B}_* = \liminf_{n\to\infty} \bar{B}_n = \limsup_{n\to\infty} B_n = B^*, \tag{5.28}$$

and since $\bar{B}_n = \{\omega : \hat{\theta}_n \in B\}$, it follows that

$$\mathcal{P}(\liminf_{n\to\infty} \bar{B}_n) = 1 - \mathcal{P}(B^*) = 1, \tag{5.29}$$

which is the standard (equivalent) form of the definition of strong consistency, stating as it does, that the event "$\hat{\theta}_n$ assumes a value in B", i.e. in a hypersphere of "radius" ϵ and "center" θ^0, occurs in all but a **finite number of samples**, i.e. it occurs for all but a finite number of index values, n.

5.8.1 Independent Observations

There are two ways of dealing with the issues presented by ML estimators; first, one can show that they are simply MC estimators, and as such they obey Proposition 3; another is to strengthen the premises of that proposition, still retaining their relevance for the type of problems dealt with in econometrics, in order to show strong consistency. We shall do both.

Proposition 4. In the context of Proposition 3, take $\Omega = R^m$, $\mathcal{A} = \mathcal{B}(R^m)$, $\mathcal{P}_\theta = P_\theta$, $\theta \in \Theta \subset R^k$ and suppose that the family of probability distributions (measures) P_θ is dominated by the (probability) measure μ.[16] Suppose, further, that

  i. the sequence $\{X_{(n)} : n \geq 1\}$ is i.i.d.;

  ii. Θ is closed and bounded (compact);

  iii. $P_{\theta_1} \neq P_{\theta_2}$ if $\theta_1 \neq \theta_2$;

  iv. the density, say $f_\theta(x)$, is, for each $x \in R^m$, continuous in θ and, for each $\theta \in \Theta$, $\mathcal{B}(R^m)$-measurable;

---

[16] We remind the reader that this means that for every θ there exists a density function, say f_θ, such that for every set $B \in \mathcal{B}(R^m)$,

$$P_\theta(B) = \int_B f_\theta \, d\mu.$$

v. there exists a P_{θ^0} -integrable function h, such that $|\sup_{\theta \in \Theta} \ln f_\theta|$
$\leq h$;

then, the ML estimator is an MC estimator, and thus consistent for θ^0.

Proof: The likelihood function of the sample (sequence $X_{(n)}$) is given by

$$L_n^*(\theta) = \prod_{i=1}^n f_\theta(X_i). \tag{5.30}$$

Define

$$H_n(\theta) = -\frac{1}{n} \sum_{i=1}^n \ln f_\theta(X_i) = -\frac{1}{n} \ln L_n^*(\theta) = -\frac{1}{n} L_n(\theta). \tag{5.31}$$

We note that

$$H_n^*(\theta) = H_n(\theta) - H_n(\theta^0) = \frac{1}{n} \sum_{i=1}^n \ln \left(\frac{f_{\theta^0}(X_i)}{f_\theta(X_i)} \right); \tag{5.32}$$

by premise i of the proposition, $\ln[f_{\theta^0}(X_i)/f_\theta(X_i)]$, $i \geq 1$, is a sequence of i.i.d. random variables with finite mean; moreover, H_n^* satisfies the conditions of Proposition 23, see Dhrymes (1989). [17] Consequently,

$$H_n(\theta) - H_n(\theta^0) \overset{\text{a.c.}}{\to} E_{\theta^0} \left[\ln \left(\frac{f_{\theta^0}(X_1)}{f_\theta(X_1)} \right) \right] = K(\theta^0, \theta). \tag{5.33}$$

We note that the Kullback information is a contrast function. Since by construction H_n is, for each ω, continuous in θ and, for each θ, $\mathcal{G}_n$-measurable, we need only establish that there exist two sequences $\{\delta_n : \delta_n \geq 0, \ n \geq 1\}$ and $\{\epsilon_n : \epsilon_n \geq 0, \ n \geq 1\}$, both tending to zero monotonically, such that the entity

$$c_n(\delta) = \sup_{|\theta_1 - \theta_2| \leq \delta} |H_n(\theta_1) - H_n(\theta_2)|$$

obeys

$$\lim_{n \to \infty} \mathcal{P}(F_n) = 0, \quad \text{where } F_n = \{\omega : \sup_{|\theta_1 - \theta_2| \leq \delta_n} |H_n(\theta_1) - H_n(\theta_2)| \geq \epsilon_n\}. \tag{5.34}$$

Since

$$H_n(\theta_1) - H_n(\theta_2) = [H_n(\theta_1) - H_n(\theta^0)] - [H_n(\theta_2) - H_n(\theta^0)], \tag{5.35}$$

---

[17] The relevant result reads: [Proposition 23 (Kolmogorov)]. Let $X_n : n \geq 1$ be a sequence of i.i.d. r.v. defined on the probability space $(\Omega, \mathcal{A}, \mathcal{P})$; let $E(X_1) = \mu$ and suppose $E|X_1| < \infty$. Defining $S_n = \sum_{i=1}^n X_i$ we have $(S_n/n) \overset{\text{a.c.}}{\to} \mu$.

it follows that

$$H_n(\theta_1) - H_n(\theta_2) \overset{\text{a.c.}}{\rightarrow} [K(\theta^0, \theta_1) - K(\theta^0, \theta_2)]. \qquad (5.36)$$

By the uniform continuity of the Kullback information and part v of the premises, the assertions made in Eq. (5.34) are justified.

Finally, we note that since the ML estimator minimizes $H_n^*(\theta)$, it satisfies all the conditions of Proposition 3; thus, it is a MC estimator and, consequently, it is consistent for θ^0.

q.e.d.

Example 7. Consider the GLSEM, $Y = YB + XC + U$ and, assuming normalization has been imposed, its associated reduced form

$$Y = X\Pi + V, \quad \Pi = CD, \quad V = UD, \quad D = (I - B)^{-1}. \qquad (5.37)$$

Alternatively, the reader may think of $D = B^{*-1}$, $B^* = I - B$, prior to normalization. In the contrast framework of the discussion above, let L_T be the LF, **divided by** T, put $H_T^* = L_T(\theta^0) - L_T(\theta)$ and note that

$$-L_T(\theta) = \frac{m}{2}\ln(2\pi) + \frac{1}{2}\ln|\Omega| + \frac{1}{2}\text{tr}\Omega^{-1}S(\Pi), \qquad (5.38)$$

where $S(\Pi)$ is as defined in Eq. (5.2). [18] From the discussion of Chapter 2, we easily conclude that

$$S(\Pi) \overset{\text{a.c.}}{\rightarrow} \Omega_0 + (\Pi - \Pi_0)' M_{xx}(\Pi - \Pi_0), \qquad (5.39)$$

uniformly in Π and Ω. Moreover, $S(\Pi_0)$ converges to Ω_0. Thus,

$$H_T^*(\theta^0, \theta) \overset{\text{a.c.}}{\rightarrow} -\frac{m}{2} - \frac{1}{2}\ln|\Omega^{-1}\Omega_0| + \frac{1}{2}\text{tr}\Omega^{-1}\Omega_0 \qquad (5.40)$$

$$+ \frac{1}{2}\text{tr}\Omega^{-1}(\Pi - \Pi_0)' M_{xx}(\Pi - \Pi_0) = K(\theta^0, \theta),$$

where a zero subscript indicates a "true" parameter, $\theta = (\pi', \omega^{*'})'$, where $\pi = \text{vec}(\Pi)$, $\omega^* = \text{vec}(\Omega)$ and Ω is the covariance matrix of reduced form errors. Minimizing Eq. (5.40), partially with respect to Ω, and inserting the result therein we obtain the "concentrated" KI

$$K(\theta^0, \theta) = \frac{1}{2}\ln\left(\frac{|\Omega_0 + (\Pi - \Pi_0)' M_{xx}(\Pi - \Pi_0)|}{|\Omega_0|}\right). \qquad (5.41)$$

---

[18] Note the unfortunate notational duplication; here Ω is the covariance matrix of the reduced form errors in the GLSEM. In a probability space context, however, Ω is the sample space. It is to avoid further confusion that, below, we define $\omega^* = \text{vec}(\Omega)$.

Eq. (5.41) has a unique global minimum with respect to Π, at $\Pi = \Pi_0$, which further implies $\Omega = \Omega_0$, and thus demonstrates the strong consistency of the OLS estimators for Ω and Π.

Example 8. Consider the GLSEM of Example 5, prior to normalization, i.e. consider the model $YB^* = XC + U$. Define the contrast H_T^* as above, to obtain

$$H_T^*(\theta) = -\frac{1}{2}\ln|\Sigma_0| + \frac{1}{2}\ln|B_0^{*'}B_0^*| + \frac{1}{2}\ln|\Sigma^{-1}| + \frac{1}{2}\ln|B^{*-1}B^{*'-1}|$$

$$-\frac{1}{2}\mathrm{tr}\Sigma_0^{-1}A_0^{*'}\tilde{M}_{zz}A_0^* + \frac{1}{2}\mathrm{tr}\Sigma^{-1}A^{*'}\tilde{M}_{zz}A^* \tag{5.42}$$

$$\tilde{M}_{zz} = \frac{1}{T}\begin{bmatrix} Y'Y & Y'X \\ X'Y & X'X \end{bmatrix}, \quad A^* = \begin{bmatrix} B^* \\ -C \end{bmatrix}. \tag{5.43}$$

As we had shown in Chapter 2, under a variety of circumstances,

$$\tilde{M}_{zz} \overset{\text{a.c.}}{\to} \begin{bmatrix} \Omega_0 & 0 \\ 0 & 0 \end{bmatrix} + (\Pi_0, I)' M_{xx}(\Pi_0, I) = M_{zz}. \tag{5.44}$$

Moreover, by the compactness of the parameter space Θ, the stability of the model, and the other assumptions regarding the exogenous variables of the model made in Chapter 2, it is clear that $H_T^*(\theta) \overset{\text{a.c.}}{\to} K(\theta^0, \theta)$, uniformly in Θ. To determine what the Kullback information is, for the GLSEM under consideration, we note that

$$A^{*'}\tilde{M}_{zz}A^* \overset{\text{a.c}}{\to} \Sigma_0 + (A^* - A_0^*)' \begin{bmatrix} \Omega_0 & 0 \\ 0 & 0 \end{bmatrix}(A^* - A_0^*)$$

$$+(A^* - A_0^*)'(\Pi_0, I)' M_{xx}(\Pi_0, I)(A^* - A_0^*)$$

$$+\Sigma_0(B_0^{*-1}B^* - I) + (B^{*'}B_0^{*'-1} - I)\Sigma_0,$$

and

$$A_0^{*'}\tilde{M}_{zz}A_0^* \overset{\text{a.c}}{\to} \Sigma_0. \tag{5.45}$$

Consequently,

$$\inf_{\theta\in\Theta} H_T^*(\theta) = L_T(\theta^0) - \sup_{\theta\in\Theta} L_T(\theta) \overset{\text{a.c.}}{\to} \inf_{\theta\in\Theta} K(\theta^0, \theta). \tag{5.46}$$

But,

$$K(\theta^0, \theta) = -\frac{1}{2}m - \frac{1}{2}\ln|\Sigma_0| + \frac{1}{2}\ln|B_0^{*'}B_0^*| + \frac{1}{2}\ln|\Sigma| - \frac{1}{2}\ln|B^{*'}B^*|$$

$$+\frac{1}{2}\mathrm{tr}\Sigma^{-1}(A^* - A_0^*)'P_0^*(A^* - A_0^*)$$

$$+\frac{1}{2}\mathrm{tr}\Sigma^{-1}(B^{*'}B_0^{*'-1})\Sigma_0(B_0^{*-1}B^*),$$

$$P_0^* = (\Pi_0, \ I)' M_{xx}(\Pi_0, \ I). \tag{5.47}$$

Noting that $\Omega_0 = B_0^{*'-1}\Sigma_0 B_0^{*-1}$ and, therefore, that $B_0^{*'}\Omega_0 B_0^* = \Sigma_0$, we can rewrite the Kullback information of Eq. (5.47) as

$$K(\theta^0, \theta) = -\frac{1}{2}m - \frac{1}{2}\ln|\Sigma^{-1}| - \frac{1}{2}\ln|\Omega_0| + \frac{1}{2}\ln|B^{*'}B^*| + \frac{1}{2}\mathrm{tr}\Sigma^{-1}J^*$$

$$J^* = B^{*'}\Omega_0 B^* + (A^* - A_0^*)'P_0^*(A^* - A_0^*). \tag{5.48}$$

The expression above may be (partially) minimized with respect to Σ^{-1}, yielding the first order conditions,

$$\frac{\partial K}{\partial \mathrm{vec}(\Sigma^{-1})} = -\frac{1}{2}\mathrm{vec}(\Sigma)' + \frac{1}{2}\mathrm{vec}(J^*)' = 0,$$

whence we obtain

$$\Sigma = J^*.$$

Noting that

$$\frac{1}{2}\ln|\Sigma| - \frac{1}{2}\ln|B^{*'}B^*| = \frac{1}{2}\ln|B^{*'-1}\Sigma B^{*-1}|,$$

and inserting the minimizer in Eq. (5.48), we obtain the "concentrated" Kullback information expression,

$$K^*(\theta^0, \theta) = \frac{1}{2}\ln\left(\frac{|\Omega_0 + B^{*'-1}(A^* - A_0^*)'P_0^*(A^* - A_0^*)B^{*-1}|}{|\Omega_0|}\right). \tag{5.49}$$

Remark 9. Since the expression in the large round bracket is equal to or greater than unity, it is **globally** minimized when we take $A^* = A_0^*$; when we do so the fraction becomes unity, in which case the Kullback information becomes null. Referring back to the partial minimization with respect to Σ, we see that when the choice $A^* = A_0^*$ is made, the expression therein implies $\Sigma = \Sigma_0$. However, in contrast to the situation in Example 7 where the global minimizer is clearly unique, due to the fact that M_{xx} and Ω are both positive definite, in the present case it is not entirely clear that $A^* = A_0^*$ is the only way in which $K^*(\theta^0, \theta)$ may be rendered null. This is so since the matrix P_0^* is of dimension $G + m$, but of rank G!

Hence, its null space is of dimension m and thus contains m linearly independent vectors, say the columns of the matrix H_0. If J is an arbitrary $m \times m$ **nonsingular matrix** consider the choice $A^* = A_0^* + H_0 J$, which implies $P_0^*(A^* - A_0^*) = P_0^* H_0 J = 0$. Consequently, the Kullback information of Eq. (5.49) does not satisfy the condition $K^*(\theta^0, \theta^{(1)}) = K^*(\theta^0, \theta^{(2)})$ **implies** $\theta^{(1)} = \theta^{(2)}$, unless further restrictions are imposed on the parameters. Indeed, in Chapter 3, we had devoted considerable time elucidating the nature of the identification conditions implied by the seemingly simple requirement on the Kullback information, just noted. The manner in which this was resolved, in Chapter 3, was to impose a sufficient number of (valid) a priori restrictions and a normalization convention; if such restrictions were required of $A^* - A_0^*$, in order to render it admissible, the **intersection of the null space of** P_0^* and **the class of admissible structures** (of the form $A^* - A_0^*$) would have the **null matrix as its only member**. Evidently, this would establish identification!

Alternative Derivation of the Identification Conditions for the GLSEM

The preceding discussion affords us a singularly felicitous opportunity to re-establish the identification conditions for the GLSEM, in a Kullback information context. In Remark 9 we have established that in order to have identification, any matrix A^* for which the (concentrated) Kullback information attains its minimum, must have the property that $A^* = A_0^*$, where A_0^* is the "true" parameter matrix. This means that a necessary and sufficient condition for identification is that $\Psi = (A^* - A_0^*)' P_0^* (A^* - A_0^*) = 0$, for every admissible matrix A^*. Noting that, subject to normalization, $A^* - A_0^* = A_0 - A$, where now $A = (B', C')'$, $B^* = I - B$, and A_0 is the true parameter matrix, we may rewrite Ψ in terms of A and A_0; moreover, since we are dealing with a positive semidefinite matrix, the condition $\Psi = 0$ is equivalent to

$$\mathrm{tr}(\Psi) = \sum_{i=1}^{m}(a_{\cdot i}^0 - a_{\cdot i})' P_0^*(a_{\cdot i}^0 - a_{\cdot i}).$$

Reintroducing the selection matrices L_i and $L = \mathrm{diag}(L_1, L_2, \ldots, L_m)$ of the preceding chapters we note that

$$a_{\cdot i}^0 - a_{\cdot i} = L_i(\delta_{\cdot i}^0 - \delta_{\cdot i}), \quad \mathrm{tr}\Psi = (\delta^0 - \delta)L'(I_m \otimes P_0^*)L(\delta^0 - \delta).$$

In this framework a necessary and sufficient condition for identification of the parameters of the system is that $L'(I_m \otimes P_0^*)L$ be a **positive definite matrix**. The ith diagonal block of that matrix, however, is of the form

$$L_i'(\Pi, I)' M_{xx}(\Pi, I)L_i = S_i' M_{xx} S_i,$$

which is thus required to be nonsingular, i.e. it is required that

$$\mathrm{rank}(S_i) = m_i + G_i, \quad \text{for every } i = 1, 2, 3, \ldots, m. \tag{5.50}$$

If we refer back to Chapters 2 and 3, we will verify that these were precisely the conditions for the identification of the ith structural equation.

Thus, we have derived the necessary and sufficient conditions for the identification of the equations of a GLSEM, solely in terms of the identification requirements placed on Kullback information!

5.8.2 *Generalizations*

In the preceding sections we have, strictly speaking, shown the strong consistency of the ML estimator only in the case of sequences of independent random variables (elements). The reader, however, should not conclude that such convergence occurs **only** in these circumstances. In fact, as Proposition 3 and Corollary 1 imply, the strong consistency of the ML estimator can be shown in a much wider variety of circumstances.

Moreover, in obtaining the limiting distribution of estimators in a non-linear ("messy") context, we typically employ a mean value theorem; the validity of this device has never been justified. In this section we shall address this last issue and provide the highlights for the strong consistency and limiting distribution of the ML estimator in the context of a more general class of stochastic sequences.

If we represent the likelihood function of a sequence $X_{(n)}$ as in Eq. (5.13), we note that the representation therein is compatible with the cases of i.i.d., independent, nonidentically distributed r.v., or dependent random variables. In our discussion we shall assume a certain set of conditions to which we shall have frequent reference. Thus, it is convenient to introduce

Definition 9. Let $(\Omega, \mathcal{A}, \mathcal{P}_\theta)$ be an econometric model and suppose $X_{(n)} = \{X_j : j = 1, 2, \ldots, n\}$ is a set of observations (sample) on that model; suppose, further, that the likelihood function of the observations is given by $L_n^*(\theta)$ of Eq. (5.13), and that the family of measures $\mathcal{P}_\theta$, $\theta \in \Theta$ is dominated by ordinary Lebesgue measure. We shall say that the likelihood function is **regular** if the following conditions hold:

i. L_i^* is the likelihood function, or the joint density of the elements, of the sequence $X_{(i)}$, $i \geq 1$;

ii. the likelihood function is (at least) twice continuously differentiable (although the continuity of the second derivatives can be relaxed);

iii. the operations below are valid,

$$h_i(\theta) = \frac{\partial}{\partial \theta} \int_{R^m} L_i^*(\theta; \xi) \, d\xi$$

$$= \int_{R^m} \frac{\partial}{\partial \theta} L_i^*(\theta; \xi) \, d\xi,$$

$$\frac{\partial^2}{\partial\theta\partial\theta}\int_{R^m}L_i^*(\theta;\xi)\,d\xi \;=\; \frac{\partial}{\partial\theta}h_i(\theta) \;=\; \int_{R^m}\frac{\partial^2}{\partial\theta\partial\theta}L_i^*(\theta;\xi)\,d\xi, \quad i\geq 1,$$

$$E_\theta\left(\frac{\partial}{\partial\theta}\ln L_i^*(\theta)\right) \;=\; 0, \quad i\geq 1,$$

$$-E_\theta\left(\frac{\partial^2\ln L_i^*(\theta)}{\partial\theta\partial\theta}\right) \;=\; E_\theta\left(\frac{\partial\ln L_i^*(\theta)}{\partial\theta}\right)'\left(\frac{\partial\ln L_i^*(\theta)}{\partial\theta}\right)$$

$$= \; I_i(\theta)$$

and the matrix in the rightmost member of the last equation is **invertible** at θ^0.

The invertibility of $I_n(\theta)$ at $\theta = \theta^0$ will suffice if the Hessian of the log likelihood function, i.e. the matrix of its second derivatives, is continuous, which is the reason for the condition in ii. If not, we must require that the matrix in question be invertible in some open neighborhood of θ^0.

We recall that the stochastic sequence $\{[(\partial L_n/\partial\theta), \mathcal{G}_n], \; n \geq 1\}$ is **a martingale**. Define, as in Eq. (5.15),

$$k_i(\theta) \;=\; \frac{\partial}{\partial\theta}[L_i(\theta) - L_{i-1}(\theta)], \quad v_i(\theta) \;=\; \frac{\partial}{\partial\theta}k_i(\theta)$$

$$\frac{\partial}{\partial\theta}L_n(\theta) \;=\; \sum_{i=1}^{n}k_i(\theta)$$

$$I_n^*(\theta) \;=\; \sum_{i=1}^{n}E\left(k_i(\theta)'k_i(\theta)\mid\mathcal{G}_{i-1}\right), \tag{5.51}$$

and note that (by the discussion in footnote 11 and Section 5.6)

$$E\left(k_i(\theta)'k_i(\theta)\mid\mathcal{G}_{i-1}\right) \;=\; -E\left[v_i(\theta)\mid\mathcal{G}_{i-1}\right]. \tag{5.52}$$

In examining the strong consistency of the ML estimator, in this more general context, we shall first provide a simple sufficient condition within the conceptual framework of Propositions 3 and 4; thereafter, we shall examine the same issue in the context of the usual expansion of the first order conditions of the ML problem. In this discussion it is assumed that the admissible parameter space is **compact**, i.e. $\Theta \subset R^k$, Θ compact. It is convenient to begin with the **scalar** parameter case, i.e. where $\Theta \in R^k$, with $k = 1$. Thus, the quantity $I_n^*(\theta)$, defined above, is simply a scalar and may be thought of as the sum of the conditional information content of the sample $X_{(i)}$, conditional on $\mathcal{G}_{i-1}$, or equivalently, given the subsequence $X_{(i-1)}$. The conditions required for stong consistency are, first

$$I_n^*(\theta) \overset{\text{a.c.}}{\to} \infty, \tag{5.53}$$

and, second,

$$\mathcal{P}(D_*) \geq 1 - q(\delta), \quad D_* = \liminf_{n \to \infty} D_n, \tag{5.54}$$

where

$$D_n = \{\omega : \sup_{\theta \in \Theta^*} [I_n^*(\theta^0)]^{-1}[L_n(\theta) - L_n(\theta^0)] < - c(\delta)\}.$$

In the preceding δ is the radius of a neighborhood about the true parameter point θ^0 in which $I_n^*(\theta)$ is positive, i.e. the neighborhood is defined in the context of the analogue of Eq. (5.17), viz.

$$B = \{\theta : |\theta - \theta^0| < \delta\}. \tag{5.55}$$

In the context above $c(\delta)$, $q(\delta)$ are positive, monotone sequences that tend to zero with δ . As in the discussion surrounding Propositions 3 and 4, define the reduced space,

$$\Theta^* = \Theta \cap \bar{B}, \tag{5.56}$$

i.e. the admissible space excluding a δ -neighborhood about the true parameter point θ^0 .[19] Now, it is not difficult to show that the conditions in Eqs. (5.53) and (5.54) almost immediately imply that the ML estimator converges strongly to the true parameter point, θ^0 .

Proposition 5. Consider the (regular) econometric model of Definition 9, subject to the conditions in Eqs. (5.53) and (5.54). The ML estimator of the parameter θ , say $\hat{\theta}_n$, converges with probability one to θ^0 .

Proof: Using the approach in the proof of Proposition 4, define

$$U(\theta) = [I_n^*(\theta^0)]^{-1}[L_n(\theta) - L_n(\theta^0)],$$

modify the definition of H_n^* , of Eq. (5.32) so that it now reads

$$H_n^*(\theta) = [I_n^*(\theta^0)]^{-1}[L_n(\theta^0) - L_n(\theta)], \tag{5.57}$$

and note that

$$U(\theta) = -H_n^*(\theta). \tag{5.58}$$

Consequently,

$$\sup_{\theta \in \Theta^*} U(\theta) = \sup_{\theta \in \Theta^*} -H_n^*(\theta) = - \inf_{\theta \in \Theta^*} H_n^*(\theta), \tag{5.59}$$

---

[19] Note that **the complement of** Θ^* **in** Θ **is simply the set** B .

and we see that we can also render the set D_n as

$$D_n = \{\omega : \inf_{\theta \in \Theta^*} H_n^*(\theta) > c(\delta)\}. \tag{5.60}$$

Define the sets

$$A_n = \{\omega : \hat{\theta}_n \in B\}, \quad n \geq 1, \tag{5.61}$$

where $H_n^*(\hat{\theta}_n) = \inf_{\theta \in \Theta} H_n^*(\theta)$. We first show that $D_n \subset A_n$. Suppose $\omega \in D_n$; then $\inf_{\theta \in \Theta^*} H_n^*(\theta) > c(\delta)$. But this means that $H_n^*(\hat{\theta}_n) = \inf_{\theta \in \Theta} H_n^*(\theta) \leq \inf_{\theta \in \Theta^*} H_n^*(\theta)$, which in turn implies that $\hat{\theta}_n \notin \Theta^*$ or, alternatively, $\hat{\theta}_n \in B$; hence $\omega \in A_n$. Since the ML estimator is a MC estimator, to show the strong consistency of the ML estimator it will suffice to show that $\mathcal{P}(A_*) = 1$, where $A_* = \liminf_{n \to \infty} A_n$ or, equivalently, that the probability of the event " $\hat{\theta}_n \in B$ for all but a finite number of values of the index n " is one. Evidently, if $\mathcal{P}(A_*) = 1$ then $\mathcal{P}(A^*) = 1$, where $A^* = \limsup_{n \to \infty} A_n$, owing to the fact that $\mathcal{P}(A^*) \geq \mathcal{P}(A_*)$. Since, by the structure of the argument this conclusion will hold for all $\delta > 0$, we will conclude that $\hat{\theta}_n \overset{\text{a.c.}}{\to} \theta^0$. Now, by definition

$$A_* = \lim_{n \to \infty} C_n, \quad C_n = \bigcap_{k=n}^{\infty} A_k,$$

and

$$\mathcal{P}(A_*) = \lim_{n \to \infty} \mathcal{P}(C_n). \tag{5.62}$$

Next, note that in view of the fact that $D_n \subset A_n$, for all $n \geq 1$, it follows that

$$1 - q(\delta) \leq \mathcal{P}(D_*) \leq \mathcal{P}(A_*). \tag{5.63}$$

q.e.d.

Remark 9. The key feature of proofs of strong consistency is to isolate a neighborhood about the true parameter point and to show that the estimator in question, which is a random variable (element) taking values in the admissible parameter space Θ, cannot take values in Θ^*, except perhaps for a finite number of the index values, i.e. $\hat{\theta}_n \in \Theta^*$, for at most a finite number of n. Hence, for nearly all n we have $\hat{\theta}_n \in B$, i.e. the estimator lies in a δ-neighborhood of the true parameter point θ^0; since $\delta > 0$ is arbitrary, save only for the requirement that $B \subset \Theta$, it follows that $\hat{\theta}_n \overset{\text{a.c.}}{\to} \theta^0$.

The preceding discussion, which closely parallels that of Hall and Heyde (1980) Ch. 6, [20] also indicates that the assumptions of Proposition 5 come

---

[20] In Hall and Heyde (1980), the assumption in Eq. (5.54) is rendered as $\underline{\lim}_{n \to \infty} \mathcal{P}(D_n) \geq 1 - q(h)$. This assumption, by an entirely similar argument, yields convergence in probability.

very close to assuming what is desired to prove. On the other hand, they may also be viewed as a set of conditions which, if satisfied by the LF, **easily lead** to the strong consistency of the ML estimator.

Remark 10. The modification of the proof in the case of arbitrary k, i.e. for **a vector of parameters**, is rather straightforward. Actually, the manner in which the proof is carried out only requires us, in the case of arbitrary k, to replace the **scalar** I_n^* by a **matrix**. The argument may be faciliated by returning to the device employed in Chapter 2, viz. by considering arbitrary linear combinations. Since $\theta \in R^k$ we consider the scalar $(\partial L_n / \partial \theta) \lambda$, and instead of the **matrix** $I_n^*(\theta)$ we consider the **scalar** $\lambda' I_n^*(\theta) \lambda$, for **arbitrary vector** $\lambda \in R^k$. Putting

$$I_n^\circ(\theta) = \lambda' I_n^*(\theta) \lambda, \tag{5.64}$$

the condition in Eq. (5.53) is replaced by

$$I_n^\circ(\theta) \overset{\text{a.c.}}{\to} \infty, \quad \text{for arbitrary } \lambda \in R^k, \tag{5.65}$$

and the entities U and H_n^* are redefined as

$$U(\theta) = [I_n^\circ(\theta^0)]^{-1}[L_n(\theta) - L_n(\theta^0)], \quad H_n^*(\theta) = -U(\theta); \tag{5.66}$$

otherwise, the argument remains exactly the same as above.

The demonstration of the strong consistency of the ML estimator in the alternative approach, is based on the expansion of the first order conditions

$$0 = \frac{\partial}{\partial \theta} L_n(\hat{\theta}_n) = \frac{\partial L_n}{\partial \theta}(\theta^0) + (\hat{\theta}_n - \theta^0)' J_n(\theta^*), \tag{5.67}$$

where θ^* is an intermediate point between $\hat{\theta}_n$ and θ^0, i.e.

$$|\theta^* - \theta^0| < |\hat{\theta}_n - \theta^0|, \quad \text{and} \quad J_n(\theta^*) = \sum_{i=1}^{n} v_i(\theta^*).$$

Proposition 6. Consider the regular econometric model of Definition 9, together with the conditions [21]

---

[21] The meaning of the notation $o(x_n)$, $n \geq 1$, $x_n > 0$, in the expression below is that the entity in question grows more slowly than x_n, i.e.

$$\frac{o(x_n)}{x_n} \overset{\text{a.c.}}{\to} 0, \quad \text{as } n \to \infty.$$

i. $I_n^*(\theta^0) \overset{\text{a.c.}}{\to} \infty$, in the sense that for **any** nonnull $\lambda \in R^k$,
$I_n^\circ(\theta^0) = \lambda' I_n^*(\theta^0)\lambda \overset{\text{a.c.}}{\to} \infty$;

ii. $J_n(\theta^*) \overset{\text{a.c.}}{\sim} I_n^*(\theta^0) + o(\| I_n^*(\theta^0) \|)$, as $n \to \infty$.

Then, the ML estimator of θ, say $\hat{\theta}_n$, converges with probability one to θ^0.

Proof: Since Θ is compact and θ^0 is an interior point of the admissible parameter space, the ML estimator $\hat{\theta}_n$ has the property that

$$\frac{\partial L_n}{\partial \theta}(\hat{\theta}_n) = 0. \tag{5.68}$$

Using the mean value theorem of calculus we obtain the representation in Eq. (5.67). Adding and subtracting $(\hat{\theta}_n - \theta^0)' I_n^*(\theta^0)$, we may rewrite that equation as

$$0 = \sum_{i=1}^{n} k_i(\theta^0) - (\hat{\theta}_n - \theta^0)' I_n^*(\theta^0) + (\hat{\theta}_n - \theta^0)' [I_n^*(\theta^0) + J_n(\theta^*)]. \tag{5.69}$$

We further note that

$$\frac{\partial L_n}{\partial \theta} \quad \text{and} \quad I_n^*(\theta) + J_n(\theta)$$

are both martingales. That the first is a martingale was established above; to show that the second is a martingale we need to establish, for $M_n(\theta) = I_n^*(\theta) + J_n(\theta)$ that it is integrable, which by definition it is, and moreover that

$$E_\theta(M_n(\theta) \mid \mathcal{G}_{n-1}) = M_{n-1}(\theta). \tag{5.70}$$

By definition, and using Eqs. (5.51) and (5.52),

$$E(M_n(\theta) \mid \mathcal{G}_{n-1}) = E_\theta \left([I_n^*(\theta) + J_n(\theta)] \mid \mathcal{G}_{n-1} \right)$$

$$= \sum_{i=1}^{n} E \left\{ [v_i(\theta) - E(v_i(\theta)|\mathcal{G}_{i-1})] \mid \mathcal{G}_{n-1} \right\}$$

$$= I_{n-1}^*(\theta) + J_{n-1}(\theta) = M_{n-1}(\theta),$$

which shows $M_n(\theta)$ to be a martingale. Premultiplying both sides of Eq. (5.69) by $[I_n^*(\theta^0)]^{-1}$, we find

$$\hat{\theta}_n - \theta^0 = [I_n^*(\theta^0)]^{-1} \frac{\partial L_n}{\partial \theta}(\theta^0) + \{I + [I_n^*(\theta^0)]^{-1} J_n(\theta^*)\}(\hat{\theta}_n - \theta^0). \tag{5.71}$$

We develop the argument first in the case $k = 1$, i.e. for scalar parameter. Since

$$\frac{\partial L_n}{\partial \theta}(\theta^0) = \sum_{i=1}^{n} k_i(\theta^0),$$

is a square integrable martingale, i.e. its second moments are finite and its (sample) conditional quadratic variation is given by $CV_n = I_n^*(\theta^0)$, such that $CV_n \overset{\text{a.c.}}{\to} \infty$, it follows from Proposition 14, Ch. 5 of Dhrymes (1989) that $[I_n^*(\theta^0)]^{-1} \sum_{i=1}^n k_i(\theta^0) \overset{\text{a.c.}}{\to} 0$. By condition ii of the proposition

$$\frac{J_n(\theta^*)}{I_n^*(\theta^0)} \overset{\text{a.c.}}{\to} -1. \tag{5.72}$$

Consequently, $\hat{\theta}_n \overset{\text{a.c.}}{\to} \theta^0$, thus establishing the strong consistency of the ML estimator.

For $k > 1$, consider the linear combination

$$\phi_n = \frac{\partial L_n}{\partial \theta} \lambda, \quad \text{for arbitrary } \lambda \in R^k.$$

It is easily shown that $\{(\phi_n, \mathcal{G}_n) : n \geq 1\}$ is a square integrable martingale with conditional quadratic variation $I_n^\circ(\theta) = \lambda' I_n^*(\theta)\lambda \overset{\text{a.c.}}{\to} \infty$. Consequently,

$$\frac{\phi_n}{\lambda' I_n^* \lambda} \overset{\text{a.c.}}{\to} 0. \tag{5.73}$$

Letting $r_{\max}(n)$ be the largest characteristic root of I_n^*, and noting that for arbitrary $\lambda \in R^k$, $\lambda' I_n^*(\theta)\lambda \leq r_{\max}(n) \lambda'\lambda$, we have that condition ii of the proposition implies

$$\| I_n^*(\theta) \| = r_{\max}(n) \overset{\text{a.c.}}{\to} \infty. \tag{5.74}$$

Consequently,

$$\left\| [I_n^*(\theta)]^{-1} \left(\frac{\partial L_n}{\partial \theta}\right)' \right\| \leq \frac{|(\partial L_n/\partial \theta)|}{\| I_n^*(\theta) \|} \overset{\text{a.c.}}{\to} 0, \tag{5.75}$$

so that the first term of the right member of Eq. (5.70) converges a.c. (in norm) to zero. By condition ii of the proposition

$$[I_n^*(\theta^0)]^{-1}[I_n^*(\theta^0) + J_n(\theta^*)] \overset{\text{a.c.}}{\to} (I - I) = 0.$$

Since the term $(\hat{\theta}_n - \theta^0) \in \Theta$, for all n, it is uniformly bounded. Consequently $(\hat{\theta}_n - \theta^0) \overset{\text{a.c.}}{\to} 0$.

$$\text{q.e.d.}$$

Remark 11. Note that no explicit assumption has been made regarding the nature of the likelihood function; thus, the results obtained would remain valid in a wide variety of contexts, so long as the conditions imposed in Propositions 4, 5 and/or 6 are satisfied. This is true of a number of stationary processes; for example, they remain valid for the general linear process, $X_i = \sum_{s=0}^{\infty} a_s \epsilon_{i-s}$, $\sum_{s=1}^{\infty} |a_s| < \infty$, the ϵ's being i.i.d., zero mean, finite variance random variables or elements.

In the typical econometric context, where second moments are assumed to exist, and where it may be shown that

$$\frac{I_n^*(\theta)}{n} \stackrel{\text{a.c.}}{\to} I(\theta), \tag{5.76}$$

we have

Corollary 2. In the context of Proposition 6, suppose Eq. (5.67) holds; then the limiting distribution of the ML estimator may be derived from

$$\sqrt{n}(\hat{\theta} - \theta^0) \sim -\left[\frac{1}{n}\sum_{i=1}^{n} v_i(\theta^0)\right]^{-1} \frac{1}{\sqrt{n}}\left[\sum_{i=1}^{n} k_i(\theta^0)\right], \tag{5.77}$$

or from the computationally more convenient form

$$\sqrt{n}(\hat{\theta} - \theta^0) \sim -\left[\frac{1}{n}\sum_{i=1}^{n} v_i(\theta^*)\right]^{-1} \frac{1}{\sqrt{n}}\left[\sum_{i=1}^{n} k_i(\theta^0)\right]. \tag{5.78}$$

Proof: We consider the standard form of the limiting distribution of the ML estimator to be that derived from

$$\sqrt{n}(\hat{\theta}_n - \theta^0) \sim \left[\frac{I_n^*(\theta^0)}{n}\right]^{-1} \frac{1}{\sqrt{n}} \frac{\partial L_n}{\partial \theta}(\theta^0). \tag{5.79}$$

We note that Eq. (5.78) may also be rendered as

$$\sqrt{n}(\hat{\theta}_n - \theta^0) \sim \{[I_n^*(\theta^0)]^{-1} J_n(\theta^*)\}^{-1} \left[\frac{I_n^*(\theta^0)}{n}\right]^{-1} \frac{1}{\sqrt{n}} \frac{\partial L_n}{\partial \theta}(\theta^0). \tag{5.80}$$

The quantity in the first set of curly brackets above converges a.c. to $-I$, by condition ii of Proposition 6; hence the corollary is proved relative to Eq. (5.78). Similarly, Eq. (5.77) may be rewritten as

$$\sqrt{n}(\hat{\theta}_n - \theta^0) \sim \{[I_n^*(\theta^0)]^{-1} J_n(\theta^0)\}^{-1} \left[\frac{I_n^*(\theta^0)}{n}\right]^{-1} \frac{1}{\sqrt{n}} \frac{\partial L_n}{\partial \theta}(\theta^0). \tag{5.81}$$

Again the entity in the first set of curly brackets above converges a.c., to $-I$, thus concluding the proof of the corollary, since we have already (a) justified the expansion of the first order conditions and (b) shown that the limiting distribution of the ML estimator may be obtained from the convenient representation in Eq. (5.78).

q.e.d.

An examination of broad conditions under which the limiting distribution of the ML estimator may be obtained lies outside the purview of this volume. The interested reader may consult Hall and Heyde (1980).

5.9   The General Nonlinear Model (GNLM)

5.9.1   Consistency

In this section we shall derive the ML estimator for the general nonlinear model

$$y_{t\cdot} = g(\phi; x_{t\cdot}) + u_{t\cdot}, \tag{5.82}$$

where $\{u_{t\cdot} : t \geq 1\}$ is a sequence of i.i.d. random vectors obeying

$$u_{t\cdot}^{'} \sim N(0, \Sigma_0). \tag{5.83}$$

Similarly, g is (an m-element) vector valued function. For ease of exposition we shall employ the notation $g_{t\cdot}(\phi)$ for $g(x_{t\cdot}, \phi)$. The LF is given by [22]

$$L_T(\theta) = -\frac{m}{2}\ln(2\pi) - \frac{1}{2}\ln|\Sigma| - \frac{1}{2}\mathrm{tr}\Sigma^{-1}S(\phi) = \frac{1}{T}\sum_{t=1}^{T} f_t(\theta), \tag{5.84}$$

where [23]

$$f_t(\theta) = -\frac{m}{2}\ln(2\pi) - \frac{1}{2}\ln|\Sigma| - \frac{1}{2}\mathrm{tr}\Sigma^{-1}[y_{t\cdot} - g_{t\cdot}(\phi)]^{'}[y_{t\cdot} - g_{t\cdot}(\phi)],$$

$$S(\phi) = \frac{1}{T}[Y - G(\phi)]^{'}[Y - G(\phi)] \tag{5.85}$$

$$G(\phi) = \begin{pmatrix} g_{1\cdot}(\phi) \\ g_{2\cdot}(\phi) \\ \vdots \\ g_{T\cdot}(\phi) \end{pmatrix}, \quad \theta = \begin{pmatrix} \phi \\ \sigma \end{pmatrix}, \quad \sigma = \mathrm{vec}(\Sigma).$$

We observe that $\{f_t : t \geq 1\}$ is a sequence of (scalar) square integrable, [24] independent (but not identically) distributed r.v. with mean

$$\bar{f}_t = -\frac{1}{2}\ln|\Sigma| - \frac{1}{2}\mathrm{tr}\Sigma^{-1}\Sigma_0 - \frac{1}{2}\mathrm{tr}\Sigma^{-1}g_{t\cdot}^{*'}g_{t\cdot}^{*}, \tag{5.86}$$

---

[22] For simplicity, in the remainder of this chapter we shall denote by L_T the LF **after division by** T; in terms of the notation in the earlier part of the chapter, the relation is $L_T = (1/T)\ln L^*$, where L^* denotes the likelihood function, i.e. the joint density of the T observations.

[23] In subsequent discussion we shall define f_t, **without the term** $-(m/2)\ln(2\pi)$, since the latter is a constant and does not really matter in the context of our discussion.

[24] Random variables whose second moment is finite are said to be **square integrable**.

where $g_{t\cdot}^* = g_{t\cdot}(\phi) - g_{t\cdot}(\phi^0)$. In order to invoke the properties of ML estimators, alluded to in Propositions 3 and 4, we need to examine whether the LF above converges either in probability or with probability one. To this end, consider the variance of the terms f_t. We find,

$$f_t - \bar{f}_t = -\frac{1}{2}\mathrm{tr}\Sigma^{-1}(u_{t\cdot}'.u_{t\cdot} - \Sigma_0) + \frac{1}{2}\mathrm{tr}\Sigma^{-1}(u_{t\cdot}'.g_{t\cdot}^*) + \frac{1}{2}\mathrm{tr}\Sigma^{-1}(g_{t\cdot}^{*'}u_{t\cdot}),$$

which may further be simplified to

$$f_t - \bar{f}_t = -\frac{1}{2}\left(u_{t\cdot}.\Sigma^{-1}u_{t\cdot}' - \mathrm{tr}\Sigma^{-1}\Sigma_0\right) + u_{t\cdot}.\Sigma^{-1}g_{t\cdot}^{*'}. \tag{5.87}$$

Since, in the case of the zero mean normal distribution odd moments vanish, to obtain the variance of the term above we need only consider

$$(f_t - \bar{f}_t)^2 \sim P_1^2 + P_2^2, \quad P_1^2 = \frac{1}{4}\left(u_{t\cdot}.\Sigma^{-1}u_{t\cdot}' - \mathrm{tr}\Sigma^{-1}\Sigma_0\right), \quad P_2^2 = (u_{t\cdot}.\Sigma^{-1}g_{t\cdot}^{*'})^2.$$

Taking expectations, we find

$$4E_{\theta^0}P_1^2 = \sum_{i,s,k,j}\sigma^{ij}\sigma^{ks}E_{\theta^0}u_{tj}u_{tk}u_{ts}u_{ti} - \left(\mathrm{tr}\Sigma^{-1}\Sigma_0\right)^2$$

$$= 2\mathrm{tr}\Sigma^{-1}\Sigma_0\Sigma^{-1}\Sigma_0, \tag{5.88}$$

$$E_{\theta^0}P_2^2 = \mathrm{tr}\Sigma^{-1}g_{t\cdot}^{*'}g_{t\cdot}^*.\Sigma^{-1}E_{\theta^0}u_{t\cdot}.u_{t\cdot}' = \mathrm{tr}\Sigma^{-1}\Sigma_0\Sigma^{-1}g_{t\cdot}^{*'}g_{t\cdot}^*,$$

so that

$$\mathrm{Var}(f_t) = \frac{1}{2}\left[\mathrm{tr}(\Sigma^{-1}\Sigma_0\Sigma^{-1}\Sigma_0)\right] + \mathrm{tr}(\Sigma^{-1}\Sigma_0\Sigma^{-1}g_{t\cdot}^{*'}g_{t\cdot}^*), \tag{5.89}$$

and, consequently, that

$$\mathrm{Var}(L_T) = \frac{1}{2T}\mathrm{tr}\Sigma^{-1}\Sigma_0\Sigma^{-1}\Sigma_0 + \frac{1}{T}\mathrm{tr}\Sigma^{-1}\Sigma_0\Sigma^{-1}\frac{G^{*'}G^*}{T}, \tag{5.90}$$

where $G^* = G(\phi) - G(\phi^0)$. Under the relatively mild condition that, for every $\theta \in \Theta$,

$$\frac{G'G}{T} \longrightarrow M_{gg}(\theta) \geq 0, \tag{5.91}$$

where the latter is a well defined matrix with finite elements, $\mathrm{Var}(L_T) \to 0$ and it follows that

$$H_T^* = L_T(\theta^0) - L_T(\theta) \overset{\mathrm{L}^2}{\to} K(\theta^0, \theta), \tag{5.92}$$

uniformly in θ, where $\overset{\mathrm{L}^2}{\to}$ denotes convergence in quadratic mean. Under the somewhat stronger condition that [25]

$$\mathrm{Var}(f_t) \leq k\,t^\alpha, \quad \alpha \in [0, \frac{1}{2}), \tag{5.93}$$

---

[25] This condition is invoked only so as to justify the use of Proposition 26; as we shall see below it can be relaxed; in fact, we only need $\alpha \in [0, 1)$.

it follows, by Proposition 26, Dhrymes (1989) p. 193, that

$$H_T^* \overset{\text{a.c.}}{\longrightarrow} K(\theta^0, \theta), \tag{5.94}$$

uniformly in θ.[26] It follows therefore from Corollary 1, that the ML estimator of θ converges with probability one to θ^0. The preceding discussion can be summarized in

Proposition 7. Consider the (vector) GNLM

$$y_{t\cdot} = g(x_{t\cdot}) + u_{t\cdot}, \quad t = 1, 2, 3, \ldots, T,$$

where $\{u_{t\cdot} : t \geq 1\}$ is a sequence of i.i.d. $N(0, \Sigma_0)$ random vectors, defined on the probability space $(\Omega, \mathcal{A}, \mathcal{P})$. Suppose, further, that

   i. g is a **vector valued** twice continuously differentiable function in θ and $x_{t\cdot}$;

   ii. the admissible parameter space, $\Theta \subset R^k$, is closed and bounded (compact); moreover, the "true" parameter θ^0 is **an interior point**, i.e. for some $\epsilon > 0$, the neighborhood $N(\theta^0; \epsilon)$ is totally contained in Θ;

   iii. the sequence $\{x'_{t\cdot} : t \geq 1\}$ lies in a set $\Xi \subset R^n$, such that Eq. (5.91) is satisfied a.e., in Θ and Ξ; in particular, this means that for all $\theta \in \Theta$ and $x_{t\cdot\cdot} \in \Xi$,

$$| g(x_{t\cdot}; \phi) |^2 < kt^\alpha, \quad \alpha \in [0, 1);$$

   iiia. or, alternatively, the sequence $\{x'_{t\cdot} : t \geq 1\}$ lies in a closed and bounded (compact) set $\mathcal{X} \subset R^n$.[27]

Then, the ML estimator of $\theta = (\phi', \sigma')'$, where $\sigma = \text{vec}(\Sigma)$ is a MC estimator and, moreover, it is strongly consistent for θ^0.

---

[26] Note that under the conditions (a) g is continuous in θ and $x_{t\cdot}$, (b) the sequence $\{x_{t\cdot} : t \geq 1\}$ is bounded, we conclude that $\text{Var}(f_t) < k$, **uniformly in** θ and the x-sequence, i.e. k does not depend on either θ or the x-sequence. In this case, Kolmogorov's criterion, Proposition 22, Dhrymes (1989) p. 186, gives a.c. convergence. Note that in the statement of that proposition there is a misprint; the premise should read

$$\sum_{n=1}^\infty \frac{\text{Var}(X_n)}{b_n^2} < \infty, \quad \textbf{not} \quad \sum_{n=1}^\infty \frac{\text{Var}(X_n)}{b_n} < \infty.$$

[27] Since the function g is continuous on the compact set $\Theta \times \mathcal{X}$, it is bounded. Thus, uniformly on that set, $| g | < K$, for some $K < \infty$.

Proof: We present here an outline of the proof, since the details were provided in the discussion above. Recalling $L_T = \ln(L^*)^{(1/T)}$, we obtain

$$H_T^*(\theta) = L_T(\theta^0) - L_T(\theta) = \ln\left(\frac{L^*(\theta^0)}{L^*(\theta)}\right)^{(1/T)}, \tag{5.95}$$

$$= \frac{1}{T}\sum_{t=1}^{T}\ln\left(\frac{f_t^*(\theta^0)}{f_t^*(\theta)}\right), \quad \text{where}$$

$$\ln f_t^* = f_t = -\frac{1}{2}\ln|\Sigma| - \frac{1}{2}\text{tr}\Sigma^{-1}[y_{t\cdot} - g_{t\cdot}(\phi)]'[y_{t\cdot} - g_{t\cdot}(\phi)].$$

If H_T^* converges, it evidently converges to the Kullback information of θ^0 on θ, [28] which is given by

$$\lim_{T\to\infty}\frac{1}{T}E_{\theta^0}\left(\frac{\ln f_t^*(\theta^0)}{\ln f_t^*(\theta)}\right) = K(\theta^0, \theta). \tag{5.96}$$

To examine issues of convergence, we first note that we can write

$$H_T^* = -\left[\frac{1}{2}\ln|\Sigma_0| + \frac{1}{2}\text{tr}\Sigma_0^{-1}S(\phi^0)\right] + \left[\frac{1}{2}\ln|\Sigma| + \frac{1}{2}\text{tr}\Sigma^{-1}S(\phi)\right]$$

$$TS(\phi) = [Y - G(\phi)]'[Y - G(\phi)] = [U - G^*(\phi, \phi^0)]'[U - G^*(\phi, \phi^0)]$$

$$G^*(\phi, \phi^0) = G(\phi) - G(\phi^0). \tag{5.97}$$

By Proposition 23, Ch. 3, Dhrymes (1989), $S(\phi^0) \overset{\text{a.c.}}{\to} \Sigma_0$, and this convergence is clearly uniform on Θ and Ξ. Thus, we need only be concerned about the second term, in large square brackets, of the first equation of Eq. (5.97). Noting that

$$S(\phi) = \frac{1}{T}\sum_{t=1}^{T}f_t(\phi), \quad g_{t\cdot}^*(\phi, \phi^0) = g_{t\cdot}(\phi) - g_{t\cdot}(\phi^0),$$

$$f_t = -\frac{1}{2}\ln|\Sigma| - \frac{1}{2}\text{tr}\Sigma^{-1}[u_{t\cdot}'u_{t\cdot} + g_{t\cdot}^{*\prime}g_{t\cdot}^* - u_{t\cdot}'g_{t\cdot}^* - g_{t\cdot}^{*\prime}u_{t\cdot}],$$

we find

$$\bar{f}_t = E_{\theta^0}[f_t(\theta)] = -\frac{1}{2}\ln|\Sigma| - \frac{1}{2}\text{tr}\Sigma^{-1}[\Sigma_0 + g_{t\cdot}^{*\prime}g_{t\cdot}^*]$$

---

[28] It is this peculiarity of the terminology that was commented upon in Remark 7.

$$\frac{1}{T}\sum_{t=1}^{T}E_{\theta^0}[f_t(\theta)] = -\frac{1}{2}\ln|\Sigma| - \frac{1}{2}\text{tr}\Sigma^{-1}\Sigma_0 - \frac{1}{2}\text{tr}\Sigma^{-1}\left(\frac{G^{*'}G^*}{T}\right).$$

Next, consider

$$f_t - \bar{f}_t = -\frac{1}{2}\ln\Sigma^{-1}[(u'_{t.}u_{t.} - \Sigma_0) - u'_{t.}g^*_{t.} - g^{*'}_{t.}u_{t.}].$$

From the earlier discussion, we find

$$\text{Var}(f_t) = \frac{1}{2}\text{tr}\Sigma^*\Sigma_0 + \text{tr}\Sigma^* g^{*'}_{t.}g^*_{t.}, \tag{5.98}$$

where $\Sigma^* = \Sigma^{-1}\Sigma_0\Sigma^{-1}$. Noting that by iii of the premises,

$$\frac{\text{Var}(f_t)}{t^2} < \frac{1}{2}\left(\frac{k_*}{t^{2-\alpha}}\right), \quad \alpha \in [0, 1), \tag{5.99}$$

for some constant $k_* < \infty$, we conclude that uniformly in Θ and Ξ,

$$\sum_{t=1}^{\infty}\frac{\text{Var}(f_t)}{t^2} < \infty.$$

If we follow iiia of the premises, $\text{Var}(f_t) < k_{**}$, also uniformly in Θ and $\mathcal{X}$. Thus, in either case the series above converges and by the Kolmogorov criterion, Proposition 22 Ch. 3 of Dhrymes (1989) we have convergence a.c., uniformly in the relevant admissible spaces. Thus H^*_T converges a.c. uniformly and by Corollary 1 the ML estimator $\hat{\theta}_T$ is **strongly consistent**.

q.e.d.

5.9.2 Identification

The discussion above also establishes the identifcation conditions for the GNLM. We note that in Proposition 7,

$$K(\theta^0, \theta) = -\frac{m}{2} - \frac{1}{2}\ln|\Sigma_0| + \frac{1}{2}\ln|\Sigma| + \text{tr}\Sigma^{-1}(\Sigma_0 + M_{g^*g^*})$$

where $M_{g^*g^*}$ is the limit of $G^{*'}G^*/T$, and $G^* = G(\phi) - G(\phi^0)$. Partially maximizing with respect to Σ, we find

$$\Sigma = \Sigma_0 + M_{g^*g^*},$$

and inserting in the expression for K we find the "concentrated Kullback information"

$$K(\theta^0, \theta) = \frac{1}{2}\ln\left(\frac{|\Sigma_0 + M_{g^*g^*}|}{|\Sigma_0|}\right).$$

which is globally minimized if and only if $M_{g^*g^*} = 0$. Imposing the usual identification condition that $K(\theta^0, \theta^1) = K(\theta^0, \theta^2)$ implies $\theta^1 = \theta^2$, and noting that $G^* = G(\phi) - G(\phi^0)$, it is clear that $M_{g^*g^*} = 0$ only if $\phi = \phi^0$. This establishes the identification and strong consistency of the ML estimator of θ^0.

5.9.3 Asymptotic Normality

We begin the discussion of the limiting distribution of the ML estimator with the case where $m = 1$, i.e. with the case of a single GNLM. In this context, g is **a scalar valued** function (of ϕ), and $y_{t.}$, $u_{t.}$ are **scalar r.v.** [29] Otherwise, the notation remains the same as above. Since our problem is rather simple, a number of the expressions derived above are simplified a great deal. Thus,

$$TL_T(\theta) = \sum_{t=1}^{T} f_t(\theta) = \sum_{t=1}^{T} \left[-\frac{1}{2} \ln(2\pi) - \frac{1}{2} \ln \sigma^2 - \frac{1}{2\sigma^2} (y_t - g_t)^2 \right]$$

$$I_T(\theta) = \sum_{t=1}^{T} \left(\frac{\partial f_t}{\partial \theta} \right)' \left(\frac{\partial f_t}{\partial \theta} \right), \quad J_T(\theta) = \sum_{t=1}^{T} \frac{\partial^2 f_t}{\partial \theta \partial \theta}. \tag{5.100}$$

It is clear from the definitions above, that $E_\theta[I_T(\theta)] = -E_\theta[J_T(\theta)]$, and that both involve summations of independent random elements (matrices), whose means are the same. If, in addition, the function g **has continuous second derivatives** and the $x_{t.}$-sequence lies in Ξ, then the (scalar) covariances

$$\mathrm{Cov}\left(\frac{\partial f_t}{\partial \theta_i}, \frac{\partial f_t}{\partial \theta_j} \right), \quad \mathrm{Cov}\left(\frac{\partial^2 f_t}{\partial \theta_i \partial \theta_j}, \frac{\partial^2 f_t}{\partial \theta_r \partial \theta_s} \right)$$

are **uniformly bounded**. Thus, by the Kolmogorov criterion, $[I_T(\theta)/T]$ and $[J_T(\theta)/T]$ both converge a.c., to their (common) limit

$$-\lim_{T \to \infty} E_{\theta^0} \left(\frac{\partial^2 L_T}{\partial \theta \partial \theta} \right) = \lim_{T \to \infty} T E_{\theta^0} \left(\frac{\partial L_T}{\partial \theta} \right)' \left(\frac{\partial L_T}{\partial \theta} \right).$$

The preceding discussion verifies the condition

$$[I_T(\theta)]^{-1} J_T(\theta) \overset{\text{a.c.}}{\to} -I,$$

---

[29] This terminology is somewhat redundant, since a random variable is, by definition, a scalar; one refers to more complicated entities such as vectors, matrices etc., as **random elements**.

uniformly in θ. [30] The remaining minor conditions, referred to in the earlier discussion, are that for sequences $\{\theta_T : \theta_T \in \Theta, \ T \geq 1\}$, converging to θ^0,

i. $[E_{\theta^0} I_T(\theta^0)]^{-1} E_{\theta_T} I_T(\theta_T) \to I$;

ii. $[I_T(\theta^0)]^{-1} I_T(\theta_T) \overset{\text{a.c.}}{\to} I$

iii. $[I_T(\theta^0)]^{-1} J_T(\theta_T) \sim [I_T(\theta^0)]^{-1} J_T(\theta^0) \overset{\text{a.c.}}{\to} -I$.

The conditions invoked or verified above, justify the following expansion,

$$T\frac{\partial L_T}{\partial \theta}(\hat{\theta}_T) = 0 = T\frac{\partial L_T}{\partial \theta}(\theta^0) - (\hat{\theta}_T - \theta^0)' J_T(\theta_T^*), \qquad (5.101)$$

where

$$| \theta_T^* - \theta^0 | < | \hat{\theta}_T - \theta^0 |,$$

and $\hat{\theta}_T$ is the ML estimator of $\theta^0 = (\phi^{0'}, \sigma_0^2)'$. It follows, therefore, that

$$\sqrt{T}(\hat{\theta}_T - \theta^0) = -\left[\frac{J_T(\theta_T^*)}{T}\right]^{-1} \sqrt{T}\frac{\partial L_T}{\partial \theta}(\theta^0). \qquad (5.102)$$

Since

$$\sqrt{T}\frac{\partial L_T}{\partial \theta}(\theta^0) = \frac{1}{\sqrt{T}} \sum_{t=1}^{T} \frac{\partial f_t}{\partial \theta}(\theta^0)$$

is a sequence of independent nonidentically distributed random vectors, with mean zero and covariance matrix

$$\frac{1}{\sigma_0^4} C_T^* = \frac{1}{T\sigma_0^4} \sum_{t=1}^{T} E_{\theta^0} \begin{bmatrix} u_t^2 \left(\frac{\partial g_t}{\partial \theta}(\phi^0)\right)' \left(\frac{\partial g_t}{\partial \theta}(\phi^0)\right) & u_t \left(\frac{\partial g_t}{\partial \theta}(\phi^0)\right)' \\ u_t \left(\frac{\partial g_t}{\partial \theta}(\phi^0)\right) & (1/4)\left(\frac{u_t^2}{\sigma_0^2} - 1\right)^2 \end{bmatrix}$$

---

[30] To make this argument clear, at the cost of belaboring the issue, put

$$I_t^*(\theta) = \left(\frac{\partial f_t}{\partial \theta}\right)' \left(\frac{\partial f_t}{\partial \theta}\right)$$

and note that $\| \text{Cov}(\text{vec}[I_t^*(\theta)]) \| < k_1$, for some constant $k_1 < \infty$. Similarly, defining

$$J_t^*(\theta) = \left(\frac{\partial^2 f_t}{\partial \theta \partial \theta}\right),$$

we also determine that $\| \text{Cov}(\text{vec}[J_t^*(\theta)]) \| < k_2$ for some $k_2 < \infty$. Hence, since the series $\sum_{t=1}^{\infty}(1/t^2) < \infty$, the Kolmogorov criterion applies and we have convergence a.c., uniformly in θ , as claimed. Note, further that this result is not confined to normal u_t -sequences; it is applicable to all sequences that have the properties claimed, except for normality, **provided they have finite fourth moments.**

$$= \frac{1}{\sigma_0^2} \begin{bmatrix} C_T & 0 \\ 0 & (1/2\sigma_0^2) \end{bmatrix}, \quad C_T = \frac{1}{T} \sum_{t=1}^{T} \left(\frac{\partial g_t}{\partial \theta}(\phi^0) \right)' \left(\frac{\partial g_t}{\partial \theta}(\phi^0) \right)$$

it follows that

$$\sqrt{T} \frac{\partial L_T}{\partial \theta}(\theta^0) \xrightarrow{d} N\left(0, \frac{1}{\sigma_0^2} C^* \right), \tag{5.103}$$

where

$$C^* = \lim_{T \to \infty} \frac{1}{T} C_T^* = \begin{bmatrix} C & 0 \\ 0 & (1/2\sigma_0^2) \end{bmatrix} \tag{5.104}$$

$$C = \lim_{T \to \infty} C_T. \tag{5.105}$$

Putting, for notational simplicity,

$$I(\theta^0) = -\lim_{T \to \infty} E_{\theta^0}\left(\frac{\partial^2 L_T}{\partial \theta \partial \theta}(\theta^0) \right) = \lim_{T \to \infty} T E_{\theta^0}\left(\frac{\partial L_T}{\partial \theta}(\theta^0) \right)' \left(\frac{\partial L_T}{\partial \theta}(\theta^0) \right)$$

$$= \frac{1}{\sigma_0^2} C^*, \tag{5.106}$$

we conclude, from Corollary 6, Ch. 4, Dhrymes (1989), that

$$\sqrt{T}(\hat{\theta}_T - \theta^0) \xrightarrow{d} N(0, [I(\theta^0)]^{-1}).$$

We now turn to the GNLM

$$y_t. = g_t.(\phi) + u_t., \quad t = 1, 2, \ldots, T,$$

where $g_t.$ is the (m-element) vector valued function, $g(x_t.; \phi)$, $x_t.$ being a n-element vector of **exogenous** variables. It is assumed that

i. the $x_t.$-sequence lies in a subset $\Xi \subset R^n$ such that Eq. (5.90) is satisfied;

$$| g(x_t.; \phi) |^2 \le k_1 t^\alpha, \quad \text{with } \alpha \in [0, 1),$$

and the first two derivatives of g obey similar restrictions, i.e.

$$\lim_{T \to \infty} \frac{1}{T} \sum_{t=1}^{T} \left\| \left(\frac{\partial g_t.}{\partial \phi} \right)' \left(\frac{\partial g_t.}{\partial \phi} \right) \right\| = m_1 < \infty, \tag{5.107}$$

for some constant m_1 which, incidentally, implies

$$\left\| \frac{\partial g_t.}{\partial \phi} \right\|^2 \le k_2 t^\alpha, \quad \alpha \in [0, 1), \tag{5.108}$$

where

$$\frac{\partial g_{t\cdot}}{\partial \phi} = \begin{bmatrix} \frac{\partial g_{t1}}{\partial \phi_1} & \frac{\partial g_{t1}}{\partial \phi_2} & \cdots & \frac{\partial g_{t1}}{\partial \phi_n} \\ \frac{\partial g_{t2}}{\partial \phi_1} & \frac{\partial g_{t2}}{\partial \phi_2} & \cdots & \frac{\partial g_{t2}}{\partial \phi_n} \\ \vdots & \vdots & & \vdots \\ \frac{\partial g_{tm}}{\partial \phi_1} & \frac{\partial g_{tm}}{\partial \phi_2} & \cdots & \frac{\partial g_{tm}}{\partial \phi_n} \end{bmatrix}, \tag{5.109}$$

and

$$\lim_{T \to \infty} \frac{1}{T} \sum_{t=1}^{T} \left\| \frac{\partial}{\partial \phi} \left[\mathrm{vec} \left(\frac{\partial g_{t\cdot}}{\partial \phi} \right) \right] \right\| = m_2 < \infty; \tag{5.110}$$

ia. alternatively, that the $x_{t\cdot}$-sequence lies in the closed and bounded (compact) set $\mathcal{X} \subset R^n$ and g is continuous, and has continuous second order derivatives;[31]

ii. the ("true") parameter θ^0 is an interior point of the closed and bounded (compact) admissible parameter set $\Theta \subset R^k$, where $\theta = (\phi', \sigma')'$, and $\sigma = \mathrm{vec}(\Sigma)$.

Writing, as before,

$$TL_T(\theta) = \sum_{t=1}^{T} f_t(\theta) \tag{5.111}$$

$$f_t = -\frac{m}{2}\ln(2\pi) - \frac{1}{2}\ln|\Sigma| - \frac{1}{2}\mathrm{tr}\Sigma^{-1}(y_{t\cdot} - g_{t\cdot})'(y_{t\cdot} - g_{t\cdot}),$$

we find, evaluating at θ^0

$$\left(\frac{\partial f_t}{\partial \phi}(\phi^0) \right)' = \left(\frac{\partial g_{t\cdot}}{\partial \phi}(\theta^0) \right)' \Sigma_0^{-1} u_{t\cdot}'. \tag{5.112}$$

$$\left(\frac{\partial f_t}{\partial \sigma}(\theta^0) \right)' = \frac{1}{2}(\Sigma_0^{-1} \otimes \Sigma_0^{-1})(u_{t\cdot}' \otimes u_{t\cdot}' - \sigma_0)$$

$$\left(\frac{\partial f_t}{\partial \theta}(\theta^0) \right)' = \begin{bmatrix} \left(\frac{\partial g_{t\cdot}}{\partial \phi}(\phi^0) \right)' \Sigma_0^{-1} u_{t\cdot}' \\ \frac{1}{2}(\Sigma_0^{-1} \otimes \Sigma_0^{-1})(u_{t\cdot}' \otimes u_{t\cdot}' - \sigma_0) \end{bmatrix} = w_{\cdot t\cdot}^*.$$

It is easily verified that

$$\sqrt{T}\left[\frac{\partial L_T}{\partial \theta}(\theta^0) \right]' = \frac{1}{\sqrt{T}} \sum_{t=1}^{T} w_{\cdot t\cdot}^*, \tag{5.113}$$

---

[31] These conditions imply the conditions in i.

represents the (normalized) partial sum of the sequence of independent random vectors $\{w^*_{.t}\}$, which have mean **zero**; since

$$w^*_{.t} = \left(\frac{\partial f_t}{\partial \theta} \right)'$$

we may, by the results of the previous section, find its covariance matrix through the relation

$$\text{Cov}(w^*_{.t}) = -E_{\theta^0} \left(\frac{\partial^2 f_t}{\partial \theta \partial \theta} \right). \tag{5.114}$$

Now,

$$\frac{\partial^2 f_t}{\partial \theta \partial \theta}(\theta^0) = - \begin{bmatrix} \tilde{I}_{11} & \tilde{I}_{12} \\ \tilde{I}_{21} & \tilde{I}_{22} \end{bmatrix},$$

where

$$\tilde{I}_{11} = \left(\frac{\partial g_{t.}}{\partial \phi} \right)' \Sigma^{-1} \left(\frac{\partial g_{t.}}{\partial \phi} \right) - (u'_{t.} \Sigma^{-1} \otimes I) \frac{\partial \text{vec} \left(\frac{\partial g_{t.}}{\partial \phi} \right)'}{\partial \phi}$$

$$\tilde{I}_{12} = \left[u_{t.} \otimes \left(\frac{\partial g_{t.}}{\partial \phi} \right)' \right] (\Sigma^{-1} \otimes \Sigma^{-1}) = \tilde{I}'_{21} \tag{5.115}$$

$$\tilde{I}_{22} = I \otimes (\Sigma^{-1} u'_{t.} u_{t.})(\Sigma^{-1} \otimes \Sigma^{-1}) - \frac{1}{2}(\Sigma^{-1} \otimes \Sigma^{-1}),$$

and it is easily verified that

$$E_\theta \left(\frac{\partial^2 f_t}{\partial \theta \partial \theta} \right) = - \begin{bmatrix} \left(\frac{\partial g_t}{\partial \phi} \right)' \Sigma^{-1} \left(\frac{\partial g_t}{\partial \phi} \right) & 0 \\ 0 & \frac{1}{2}(\Sigma^{-1} \otimes \Sigma^{-1}) \end{bmatrix}. \tag{5.116}$$

If conditions iii or iiia of Proposition 7 hold, and if the g has continuous second derivatives, it follows from the Kolmogorov criterion, cited above, that

$$\frac{\partial^2 L_T}{\partial \theta \partial \theta} \overset{\text{a.c.}}{\to} \lim_{T \to \infty} \frac{1}{T} \sum_{t=1}^T E_\theta \left(\frac{\partial^2 f_t}{\partial \theta \partial \theta} \right) = -C^*$$

$$C^* = \begin{bmatrix} C & 0 \\ 0 & \frac{1}{2}(\Sigma^{-1} \otimes \Sigma^{-1}) \end{bmatrix}, \tag{5.117}$$

uniformly in θ and the x_t-sequence. Since we can easily demonstrate that the sequence in Eq. (5.113) satisfies the Lindeberg criterion, it follows immediately that

$$\frac{1}{\sqrt{T}} \sum_{t=1}^T w^*_{.t} \overset{\text{d}}{\to} N(0, C^*). \tag{5.118}$$

Consequently, from Eq. (5.80), we conclude

$$\sqrt{T}(\hat{\theta}_T - \theta^0) \sim N(0, C^{*-1}), \quad C^{*-1} = \begin{bmatrix} C^{-1} & 0 \\ 0 & 2(\Sigma \otimes \Sigma) \end{bmatrix},$$

$$C = \lim_{T \to \infty} \frac{1}{T} \sum_{t=1}^{T} \left(\frac{\partial g_{t\cdot}}{\partial \phi} \right)' \Sigma^{-1} \left(\frac{\partial g_{t\cdot}}{\partial \phi} \right). \tag{5.119}$$

The discussion above may be summarized in

Proposition 8. Consider the (vector) general nonlinear model (GNLM)

$$y_{t\cdot} = g(x_{t\cdot}) + u_{t\cdot}, \quad t = 1, 2, 3, \ldots, T,$$

where $\{u_{t\cdot} : t \geq 1\}$ is a sequence of i.i.d. $N(0, \Sigma_0)$ random vectors, defined on the probability space $(\Omega, \mathcal{A}, \mathcal{P})$. Suppose, further, that

  i. g is a **vector valued continuous function** in ϕ and $x_{t\cdot}$, and has continuous second order derivatives;

  ii. the admissible parameter space, $\Theta \subset R^k$, is closed and bounded (compact); moreover, the "true" parameter θ^0 is **an interior point**, i.e. for some $\epsilon > 0$, the neighborhood $N(\theta^0; \epsilon)$ is totally contained in Θ;

  iii. the sequence $\{x'_{t\cdot} : t \geq 1\}$ lies in a set $\Xi \subset R^n$, such that for all $\theta \in \Theta$ and $x_{t\cdot} \in \Xi$,

$$\mid g(x_{t\cdot}; \phi) \mid^2 < kt^{\alpha}, \quad \alpha \in [0, 1),$$

  for some constant $k < \infty$;

  iiia. or, alternatively, the sequence $\{x'_{t\cdot} : t \geq 1\}$ lies in a closed and bounded (compact) set $\mathcal{X} \subset R^n$.[32]

Then, the ML estimator of $\theta = (\phi', \sigma')'$, where $\sigma = \text{vec}(\Sigma)$, obeys

$$\sqrt{T}(\hat{\theta}_T - \theta^0) \sim N(0, C^{*-1}).$$

An immediate consequence is

Corollary 3. The ML estimator of the "structural" parameter vector ϕ is, asymptotically, independent of the ML estimator of the covariance parameter vector σ.

Proof: In the limiting distribution of Proposition 8, the covariance matrix C^{*-1} is **block diagonal**.

---

[32] Since the function g is continuous on the compact set $\Theta \times \mathcal{X}$, it is bounded. Thus, uniformly on that set , $\mid g \mid < K$, for some $K < \infty$.

5.10   The GNLM with Restrictions

In dealing with restrictions on the parameter space we are really not follow-ing any procedures that are substantially different from those employed in the previous section; the reader should recall that we had earlier specified the admissible parameter space to be given by $\Theta \subset R^k$. This immme-diately implies that the admissible space is "restricted" since we do not specify $\Theta = R^k$. The difference in this section is that the restrictions are explicitly stated, so that more structure is imparted on the problem. Basi-cally, we begin as before by specifying that the admissible space is some, perhaps very large, **compact subset of** R^k; let this subset be denoted by Θ, as in previous discussion. When we impose restrictions, say of the form $r(\theta) = 0$, we deal with the **restricted admissible space**

$$\Theta^* = \{\theta : \theta \in \Theta \text{ and } r(\theta) = 0\}, \tag{5.120}$$

where r is an s-element, vector valued, twice continuously differentiable function. The effect of the restrictions is to reduce the dimension of the admissible parameter space. For example, in the case of linear restrictions, where the consequences are seen most clearly, a restriction of the form $A\theta = a$, where A is $s \times k$, of rank s, means that the restricted admissible space lies in a $(k - s)$-dimensional subspace of R^k. Of course, we continue to maintain that θ^0, the true parameter vector, is **an interior point of** Θ^*. We further note that the set

$$\mathcal{R} = \{\theta : r(\theta) = 0\} \tag{5.121}$$

is closed, in the sense that if $\{\theta_n : n \geq 1\}$ is a sequence in $\mathcal{R}$, with limit θ_* then $\theta_* \in \mathcal{R}$. Since the admissible parameter space obeys

$$\Theta^* = \Theta \cap \mathcal{R}, \tag{5.122}$$

it follows that Θ^* is also compact; evidently, we still maintain that $\theta^0 \in \Theta^*$, and that it is an interior point of Θ^* as well. The estimation problem is to find the ML estimator within this restricted space, i.e. through the operation $\sup_{\theta \in \Theta^*} L_T(\theta)$. Define the Lagrangian

$$S_T(\theta) = L_t(\theta) + \lambda' r(\theta), \tag{5.123}$$

where λ is a vector of Lagrange multipliers, and derive the first order conditions as

$$\frac{\partial S_T}{\partial \theta} = \frac{\partial L_T(\theta)}{\partial \theta} + \lambda' \frac{\partial r(\theta)}{\partial \theta}$$

$$r(\theta) = 0. \tag{5.124}$$

A solution to this system of equations will yield the restricted ML estimator, $\tilde{\theta}_T$, satisfying the condition

$$\sup_{\theta \in \Theta^*} L_T(\theta) = L_T(\tilde{\theta}_T). \tag{5.125}$$

Since Θ^* is compact, and the other relevant conditions hold, it follows by the discussion in previous sections that $\tilde{\theta}_T$ is strongly consistent, i.e. $\tilde{\theta}_T \overset{\text{a.c.}}{\to} \theta^0$. To determine its limiting distribution we have recourse to the devise of expanding the first order conditions, using the mean value theorem of calculus, thus obtaining

$$\begin{bmatrix} \frac{\partial^2 L_T}{\partial \theta \partial \theta}(\theta_*) & R(\tilde{\theta}_T)' \\ R(\theta_{**}) & 0 \end{bmatrix} \begin{pmatrix} \tilde{\theta}_T - \theta^0 \\ \tilde{\lambda}_T \end{pmatrix} = \begin{pmatrix} \frac{\partial L_T}{\partial \theta}(\theta^0) \\ r(\theta_0) \end{pmatrix}, \tag{5.126}$$

where θ_* and θ_{**} are intermediate points between $\tilde{\theta}_T$ and θ^0 . Under the hypothesis that the restrictions are **valid**, $r(\theta^0) = 0$, and the limiting distribution is given by [33]

$$\sqrt{T} \begin{pmatrix} \tilde{\theta}_T - \theta^0 \\ \tilde{\lambda}_T \end{pmatrix} \sim -\begin{bmatrix} A_{11} & A_{12} \\ A_{21} & 0 \end{bmatrix}^{-1} \begin{pmatrix} \sqrt{T}\frac{\partial L_T}{\partial \theta}(\theta^0) \\ 0 \end{pmatrix}$$

$$= -\begin{bmatrix} B_{11} & B_{12} \\ B_{21} & B_{22} \end{bmatrix} \begin{pmatrix} \sqrt{T}\frac{\partial L_T}{\partial \theta}(\theta^0) \\ 0 \end{pmatrix}. \tag{5.127}$$

Since L_T is defined **after division by T**, we have that, **in this discussion** as well as in the previous section,

$$\sqrt{T}\frac{\partial L_T}{\partial \theta}(\theta^0) = \frac{1}{\sqrt{T}} \sum_{t=1}^{T} w_{\cdot t}^*,$$

where $w_{\cdot t}^*$ is as defined in the last equation of Eq. (5.112), and

$$A_{11} = \lim_{T \to \infty} E_{\theta_0} \left(\frac{\partial L_T}{\partial \theta \partial \theta}(\theta^0) \right) = -C^*, \quad [\text{of Eq. (5.117)}]$$

$$A_{12} = R(\theta^0)' = \frac{\partial r}{\partial \theta}(\theta^0), \quad A_{21} = A_{12}'$$

$$B_{11} = A_{11}^{-1} - A_{11}^{-1} R'(RA_{11}^{-1}R')^{-1}RA_{11}^{-1}, \quad B_{21} = B_{12}'$$

$$B_{12} = A_{11}^{-1} R'(RA_{11}^{-1}R')^{-1}, \quad B_{22} = (RA_{11}^{-1}R')^{-1}.$$

---

[33] See Dhrymes (1989), Corollary 6, p. 243.

From Eq. (5.118) we see that

$$\frac{1}{\sqrt{T}} \sum_{t=1}^{T} w_{\cdot t}^* \overset{d}{\to} N(0, C^*).$$

It follows therefore, on the assumption that $r(\theta^0) = 0$ is **a valid set of restrictions**, that

$$\sqrt{T} \left(\frac{\tilde{\theta}_T - \theta^0}{\tilde{\lambda}_T} \right) \sim N(0, \Psi), \quad \Psi = \begin{bmatrix} B_{11} C^* B_{11} & B_{11} C^* B_{12} \\ B_{21} C^* B_{11} & B_{21} C^* B_{12} \end{bmatrix}. \quad (5.128)$$

Moreover,

$$B_{11} C^* B_{11} = C^{*-1} - C^{*-1} R' (R C^{*-1} R')^{-1} R C^{*-1} \quad (5.129)$$

$$B_{11} C^* B_{12} = (B_{21} C^* B_{11})' = 0, \quad B_{21} C^* B_{12} = (R C^{*-1} R')^{-1}.$$

Consider now the special case where there are **no cross parameter restrictions**, i.e.

$$r(\theta) = \begin{bmatrix} r_1(\phi) \\ r_2(\sigma) \end{bmatrix} = 0. \quad (5.130)$$

In this context

$$R(\theta) = \frac{\partial r(\theta)}{\partial \theta} = \begin{bmatrix} \frac{\partial r_1(\phi)}{\partial \phi} & 0 \\ 0 & \frac{\partial r_2(\sigma)}{\partial \sigma} \end{bmatrix} = \begin{bmatrix} R_1 & 0 \\ 0 & R_2 \end{bmatrix}, \quad (5.131)$$

and the covariance matrix of the limiting distribution becomes

$$\Psi = \begin{bmatrix} \Psi_{11} & 0 & 0 & 0 \\ 0 & \Psi_{22} & 0 & 0 \\ 0 & 0 & \Psi_{33} & 0 \\ 0 & 0 & 0 & \Psi_{44} \end{bmatrix}, \quad (5.132)$$

where

$$\Psi_{11} = C^{-1} - C^{-1} R_1' (R_1 C^{-1} R_1')^{-1} R_1 C^{-1}$$

$$\Psi_{22} = 2\{\Sigma \otimes \Sigma - (\Sigma \otimes \Sigma) R_2' [R_2(\Sigma \otimes \Sigma) R_2']^{-1} R_2(\Sigma \otimes \Sigma)\}$$

$$\Psi_{33} = (R_1 C^{-1} R_1')^{-1}, \quad \Psi_{44} = \frac{1}{2}[R_2(\Sigma \otimes \Sigma) R_2']^{-1}. \quad (5.133)$$

The preceding discussion has established

Proposition 9. In the context of Proposition 8 suppose, in addition, that the parameters of the model obey the restrictions $r(\theta)$, where r is an

s-element vector, continuously [34] differentiable and such that $R(\theta^0) = (\partial r/\partial \theta)(\theta^0)$ is nonsingular. Then, the following statements are true:

i. The restricted ML (RML) estimator obeys,

$$\sup_{\theta \in \Theta} S_T(\theta) = \sup_{\theta \in \Theta}[L_T(\theta) + \lambda' r(\theta)]$$

$$= L_T(\tilde{\theta}_T) + \lambda' r(\tilde{\theta}_T) = \sup_{\theta \in \Theta^*} L_T(\theta);$$

ii. the RML estimator is strongly consistent and its limiting distribution is given by

$$\sqrt{T}(\tilde{\theta}_T - \theta^0) \sim N(0, B_{11}C^*B_{11}),$$

where $B_{11}C^*B_{11}$ is as defined in Eq. (5.129);

iii. the RML estimators of ϕ and σ are asymptotically **mutually independent**;

iv. the Lagrange multiplier λ and the RML estimator of θ are asymptotically **mutually independent**;

v. in the special case where

$$r(\theta) = \begin{bmatrix} r_1(\phi) \\ r_2(\sigma) \end{bmatrix},$$

in addition to iv, the Lagrange multiplier corresponding to restrictions on ϕ is asymptotically **independent** of the Lagrange multiplier corresponding to restrictions on σ.

Remark 12. The reader has no doubt already noted the similarity between **linear** and **nonlinear** least squares procedures, whether restricted or unrestricted. Although the means by which we arrive at the results are rather different, the results themselves are remarkably similar. Thus, looking at the covariance matrix of the limiting distribution of the ML estimator of θ, as exhibited for example in Eq. (5.119), we see that it is *mutatis mutandis* identical with that of the **feasible Aitken estimator**. To produce maximal correspondence between this result and the system of GLM $y_t = x_t.B + u_t.$ we may write the covariance matrix C^{-1} of Eq. (5.119) as

$$C^{-1} = \left[\lim_{T \to \infty} \frac{1}{T} \left(\frac{\partial g}{\partial \phi} \right)' (\Sigma^{-1} \otimes I_T) \left(\frac{\partial g}{\partial \phi} \right) \right]^{-1},$$

$$g = \text{vec}(G), \quad g = (g_t.), \quad t = 1, 2, \ldots, T.$$

---

[34] Continuity of its first derivatives is the most convenient simple requirement; continuity of second derivatives could simplify somewhat a rigorous proof in making it simpler to use a residual in a certain Taylor series expansion.

If all (T) observations on the ith equation of the set of GLM above is written out we have $y_{.i} = X_i\beta_{.i} + u_{.i}$, where $\beta_{.i}$ contains the elements of the ith column of B, not known a priori to be null. Putting $X_* = \mathrm{diag}(X_1, X_2, X_3, \ldots, X_m)$ we have that the covariance matrix of the limiting distribution of the feasible Aitken estimator is given by

$$\left[\lim_{T\to\infty} \left(\frac{1}{T} X'_*(\Sigma^{-1} \otimes I_T)X_* \right) \right]^{-1}.$$

Comparing this with the representtion of C^{-1} we see that identifying X_* with $\frac{\partial g}{\partial\phi}$ gives a complete correspondence between the two representations. Moreover, a look at the expression for Ψ_{11}, in the special case of item v, shows the equivalence between the covariance matrices of the limiting distribution of the restricted and unrestricted estimators. This becomes obvious if, in addition to the identifications above, we identify R_1 with the matrix of restrictions in the linear case.

5.11   Tests of Restrictions

5.11.1   Generalities

As we pointed out when testing the prior restrictions in the GLSEM, there are basically three approaches. First, we can treat the restrictions as testable hypotheses; this means estimating the parameters of the GNLM without imposing the restrictions and then testing whether the **unrestricted** parameter estimates **conform to the restrictions**. This is the conformity test (CT), which is actually the most common test; note that when estimating **any model** a test of "significance" for a given parameter estimate is simply a conformity test; the "restriction" is that the parameter in question is **null**; we estimate without imposing the restriction in question, and then test whether the estimate conforms to the restriction.

Second, we can ask whether the restrictions are supported by the evidence, or information, contained in the sample through the likelihood ratio test (LRT). This essentially involves the ratio of $L_T^*(\tilde{\theta}_T)$ to $L_T^*(\hat{\theta}_T)$, i.e. the ratio of the supremum of the likelihood function over the **restricted** space, to the supremum of the likelihood function over the **unrestricted** space. This number is always equal to or less than unity; if it is close to unity, this means that the imposition of the restrictions does not materially affect the location of the estimator, within the admissible (unrestricted) space; thus, we would tend to accept the restrictions as true. If it is appreciably less than unity then we would tend to conclude that the restrictions are not valid.

A third test, which is closely related to the LRT is the Lagrange multiplier test (LMT). In this procedure we impose the restrictions by the method of Lagrange multipliers, even if it is possible and easy to impose the restrictions by substitution. We may then interpret the magnitude of the estimated Lagrange multipliers as the "shadow price", or the implicit cost of their (the restrictions') imposition. Note that the ratio of the LRT just is another measure of the cost of the imposition of these restrictions. Thus, if the "shadow price" is small, we would tend to conclude that the restrictions are correct, while if large, we would tend to reject the validity of the restrictions.

5.11.2 The Conformity Test

If we take the null hypothesis to be

$$H_0 : r(\theta^0) = 0,$$

and the alternative

$$H_1 : r(\theta^0) \text{ unrestricted}$$

then the extent of the nonconformity is given by the left member of

$$r(\hat{\theta}_T) - r(\theta^0) = \frac{\partial r}{\partial \theta}(\theta_\circ)(\hat{\theta}_T - \theta^0) = R(\theta_*)(\hat{\theta}_T - \theta^0), \qquad (5.134)$$

where, by the mean value theorem of calculus, $|\theta_* - \theta^0)| < |\hat{\theta}_T - \theta^0|$, and $R(\theta_*) = (\partial r/\partial \theta)(\theta_*)$. It follows therefore that, under H_0, its limiting distribution is given by

$$\sqrt{T}[r(\hat{\theta}_T) - r(\theta^0)] \sim N[0, R(\theta^0)C^{*-1}R'(\theta^0)].$$

Consequently, the CT test statistic is given by

$$\zeta_{CT} = T r(\hat{\theta}_T)'(\hat{R}\hat{C}^{*-1}\hat{R}')^{-1}r(\hat{\theta}_T), \qquad (5.135)$$

where the matrices $\hat{R}$, $\hat{C}^{*-1}$ are being evaluated at the **unrestriced** ML estimator $\hat{\theta}_T$. Note, further, that in "estimating" $\hat{C}^{*-1}$ we have number of options. One, for example, is to take the expression in Eq. (5.119) and substitute therein the unrestricted ML estimator, wherever the parameter θ occurs. Another is to estimate it by

$$\hat{C}^* = -\frac{\partial^2 L_T}{\partial \theta \partial \theta}(\hat{\theta}_T),$$

which is, by and large, the most common practice.

An alternative approach is to give a representation based on the difference between the restricted and unrestricted ML estimators. To this effect, and again using the mean value theorem of calculus, write

$$r(\hat{\theta}_T) = r(\tilde{\theta}_T) + \bar{R}(\hat{\theta}_T - \tilde{\theta}_T), \qquad (5.136)$$

where $\bar{R} = R(\theta^*)$, and $|\,\theta^* - \tilde{\theta}_T\,| < |\,\hat{\theta}_T - \tilde{\theta}_T\,|$. Noting that in the representation in Eq. (5.136) $r(\hat{\theta}_T) = 0$, we can alternatively write the CT statistic as

$$\zeta_{CT} = T\,(\hat{\theta}_T - \tilde{\theta}_T)'\,\bar{R}'\,(\hat{R}\hat{C}^{*-1}\bar{R}')^{-1}\bar{R}(\hat{\theta}_T - \tilde{\theta}_T). \qquad (5.137)$$

In Eq. (5.137) we may evaluate both $\bar{R}$ and $\hat{R}$, at the same point, say $\hat{\theta}_T$ since under both the null (of no restrictions), as well as the alternative $\hat{\theta}_T$ converges to θ^0. Evidently, this second alternative is not as attractive since it involves the additional computation of the restricted estimator.

5.11.3   The Likelihood Ratio Test

Put

$$z = \frac{\sup_{\theta \in \Theta^*} L_T^*(\theta)}{\sup_{\theta \in \Theta} L_T^*(\theta)}.$$

Upon taking logarithms,

$$\ln z = L_T(\tilde{\theta}_T) - L_T(\hat{\theta}_T).$$

The form above is not particularly useful in that its limiting distribution is not easily derivable as it stands. On the other hand, consider the following Taylor series expansion about $\hat{\theta}_T$,

$$L_T(\tilde{\theta}_T) = L_T(\hat{\theta}_T) + \frac{\partial L_T}{\partial \theta}(\hat{\theta}_T)(\tilde{\theta}_T - \hat{\theta}_T) + \frac{1}{2}(\tilde{\theta}_T - \hat{\theta}_T)'\,\frac{\partial^2 L_T}{\partial \theta \partial \theta}(\theta_*)\,(\tilde{\theta}_T - \hat{\theta}_T),$$

where

$$|\,\theta_* - \theta^0)\,| < |\,\hat{\theta}_T - \theta^0\,|.$$

Noting that the linear term above is null, and substituting

$$\underline{C}^* = -\frac{\partial^2 L_T}{\partial \theta \partial \theta}(\theta_*),$$

we derive, after some further manipulation, the LRT statistic

$$\zeta_{LRT} = 2T[L_T(\hat{\theta}_T) - L_T(\tilde{\theta}_T)] = T(\hat{\theta}_T - \tilde{\theta}_T)'\underline{C}^*(\hat{\theta}_T - \tilde{\theta}_T). \qquad (5.138)$$

Since, evidently, $\underline{C}^*$ is not known, we may substitute for it the Hessian evaluated at $\hat{\theta}_T$, so that operationally we have as the LRT statistic

$$\zeta_{LRT} = -T(\hat{\theta}_T - \tilde{\theta}_T)'\left(\frac{\partial^2 L_T}{\partial \theta \partial \theta}(\hat{\theta}_T)\right)(\hat{\theta}_T - \tilde{\theta}_T)$$

5.11.4 The Lagrange Multiplier Test

From the limiting distribution of the Lagrangian it is natural to define the LMT statistic as

$$\zeta_{LMT} = T\tilde{\lambda}' \tilde{R}\tilde{C}^{*-1}\tilde{R}'\tilde{\lambda}, \tag{5.139}$$

where $\tilde{R} = R(\tilde{\theta}_T)$, $\tilde{C}^* = \frac{\partial^2 L_T}{\partial\theta\partial\theta}(\tilde{\theta}_T)$. We note that the restricted estimator satisfies the first order conditions

$$\left(\frac{\partial L_T}{\partial\theta}(\tilde{\theta}_T)\right)' = -\tilde{R}'\tilde{\lambda},$$

and by the mean value theorem we can write

$$\frac{\partial L_T}{\partial\theta}(\tilde{\theta}_T) = \frac{\partial L_T}{\partial\theta}(\hat{\theta}_T) + (\tilde{\theta}_T - \hat{\theta}_T)'\frac{\partial^2 L_T}{\partial\theta\partial\theta}(\theta^*),$$

where $|\theta^* - \hat{\theta}_T| < |\tilde{\theta}_T - \hat{\theta}_T|$. Consequently,

$$\bar{C}^*(\hat{\theta}_T - \tilde{\theta}_T) = \tilde{R}'\tilde{\lambda}, \tag{5.140}$$

and we may render the LMT statistic as

$$\zeta_{LMT} = T(\hat{\theta}_T - \tilde{\theta}_T)'\bar{C}^*\tilde{C}^{*-1}\bar{C}^*(\hat{\theta}_T - \tilde{\theta}_T), \tag{5.141}$$

where $\bar{C}^* = \frac{\partial^2 L_T}{\partial\theta\partial\theta}(\theta^*)$.

5.11.5 Equivalence of the Three Tests

In this section we shall show that the three tests statistics defined above have **the same limiting distribution**. In the case of the LRT and LMT statistics this is quite evident in view of the fact that

$$\underline{C}^* \overset{a.c.}{\to} C^*, \quad \bar{C}^* \overset{a.c.}{\to} C^*, \quad \tilde{C}^* \overset{a.c.}{\to} C^*.$$

To demonstrate the same for the CT statistic, as well as to establish the nature of the limiting distribution, we need to obtain a more convenient expression for $(\hat{\theta}_T - \tilde{\theta}_T)$. From the discussion surrounding Proposition 8, we obtain that

$$\sqrt{T}(\hat{\theta}_T - \theta^0) \sim C^{*-1}\xi_T, \quad \xi_T = \sqrt{T}\left(\frac{\partial L_T}{\partial\theta}(\theta^0)\right)',$$

while from Eq. (5.127) we find

$$\sqrt{T}(\tilde{\theta}_T - \theta^0) \sim -B_{11}\xi_T.$$

Combining the two, and bearing in mind the definition of the B_{ij}, we conclude

$$\sqrt{T}(\hat{\theta}_T - \tilde{\theta}_T) \sim P'F(P\xi_T), \tag{5.142}$$

where

$$P'P = C^{*-1}, \quad F = PR'(RC^{*-1}R')^{-1}RP'. \tag{5.143}$$

We note that F is a symmetric, idempotent matrix of rank

$$\text{rank}(F) = \text{tr}(PR'(RC^{*-1}R')^{-1}RP') = \text{tr}I_s = s, \tag{5.144}$$

where, we remind the reader s is the number of restrictions. Moreover, $\hat{R} \overset{a.c.}{\to} R$, $\bar{R} \overset{a.c.}{\to} R$, $\tilde{R} \overset{a.c.}{\to} R$. Substituting from Eq. (5.142), in the relevant definitions, we find

$$\zeta_{CT} \sim T(P\xi_T)'F(P\xi_T), \quad \zeta_{LRT} \sim T(P\xi_T)'F(P\xi_T),$$

$$\zeta_{LMT} \sim T(P\xi_T)'F(P\xi_T).$$

Since, evidently, $P\xi_T \sim N(0, I)$, it follows that all three statistics have the same limiting distribution, viz.

$$\zeta_{CT} \sim \chi_s, \quad \zeta_{LRT} \sim \chi_s, \quad \zeta_{LMT} \sim \chi_s. \tag{5.145}$$

Questions and Problems

1. In Definition 4, show tthat $E_\theta(\Phi_n) = 0$, so that $I_n(\theta) = \text{Cov}(\Phi_n) = E_\theta\left(\frac{\partial f_n}{\partial \theta}\right)'\left(\frac{\partial f_n}{\partial \theta}\right)$.

2. In Example 1, obtain the expectations $E_\theta(\Phi_{11})$, $E_\theta(\Phi_{12})$, justifying your results.

   Hint: For zero mean normal (or, more generally, symmetric) distributions, **all odd moments are null**.

3. In Example 1, obtain the expectation $E_\theta(\Phi_{22})$, justifying your results.

   Hint: Using the moment generating, or characteristic, function of the multivariate normal show that the (r, s) element of the typical (i, j) block of $E_\theta(v'_{t.}v_{t.} \otimes v'_{t.}v_{t.})$ yields $\sigma_{ij}\sigma_{rs} + \sigma_{ir}\sigma_{js} + \sigma_{is}\sigma_{jr}$, for $r, s = 1, 2, \ldots, m$.

4. In the discussion near the end of section 5.4, consider the 3×3 matrix Ω. Verify that

$$\begin{bmatrix} \Omega \otimes \omega'_{.1} \\ \Omega \otimes \omega'_{.2} \\ \Omega \otimes \omega'_{.3} \end{bmatrix} = I_{3,3}(\Omega \otimes \Omega),$$

where

$$I_{3,3} = \begin{bmatrix} e_{.1}e'_{.1} & e_{.2}e'_{.1} & e_{.3}e'_{.1} \\ e_{.1}e'_{.2} & e_{.2}e'_{.2} & e_{.3}e'_{.2} \\ e_{.1}e_{.3} & e_{.2}e_{.3} & e_{.3}e_{.3} \end{bmatrix},$$

and $e_{\cdot i}$ is a three element column vector, all of whose elements are zero save the ith, which is unity.

5. Verify, in the discussion before Example 2, that

$$- E_\theta \left(\frac{\partial^2 \ln f(\cdot; \theta)}{\partial \theta \partial \theta} \right) = E_\theta (\Phi' \Phi).$$

6. In Example 6, verify the representation of the KI, $K(P_{n\theta^0}, P_{n\theta})$; in addition, show that its absolute minimum is zero and occurs at $\mu = \mu_0$, $\Sigma = \Sigma_0$.

7. In the proof of Proposition 3,

   i. explain why $H_n(\theta) \geq H_n(\theta_i) - |H_n(\theta_i) - H_n(\theta)|$;

   ii. verify that $B_n \subset C_n \subset D_n$;

   iii. verify Eqs. (5.23) and (5.24).

8. In the proof of Corollary 1, justify the transition from Eq. (5.25) to Eq. (5.27).

9. Show that

   i. $A_0^{*'} \tilde{M}_{zz} A_0^* \overset{\text{a.c.}}{\to} A_0^{*'} \bar{M}_{zz} A_0^* = \Sigma_0$;

   ii.

$$A^{*'} \tilde{M}_{zz} A^* \overset{\text{a.c.}}{\to} A^{*'} \bar{M}_{zz} A^* = [\Sigma_0 + \Sigma_0 B_0^{*-1} (B^* - B_0^*)$$

$$+ (B^* - B_0^*)' B_0^{*'-1} \Sigma_0 + (B^* - B_0^*)' \Omega_0 (B^* - B_0^*)$$

$$+ (A^* - A_0^*)' P_0^* (A^* - A_0^*)],$$

where $\Omega_0 = B_0^{*'-1} \Sigma_0 B_0^{*-1}$, and $P_0^* = (\Pi_0, I)' M_{xx}(\Pi_0, I)$.
Hint: Use $ZA^* = ZA_0^* + Z(A^* - A_0^*) = U + Z(A^* - A_0^*)$.

10. In Question 10, show that $A^{*'} \bar{M}_{zz} A^*$ can be simplified to $B^{*'} \Omega_0 B^* + (A^* - A_0^*)' P_0^* (A^* - A_0^*)$.

11. In Eq. (5.45), show that

$$\tilde{M}_{zz} \overset{\text{a.c.}}{\to} \begin{bmatrix} \Omega_0 & 0 \\ 0 & 0 \end{bmatrix} + (\Pi_0, I)' M_{xx}(\Pi_0, I).$$

Hint: Use $Y = X\Pi_0 + V$.

6
Topics in NLSE Theory

In this chapter we shall examine somewhat briefly topics in the theory of nonlinear simultaneous equations (NLSE), including NLML (nonlinear maximum likelihood), NL2SLS, NL3SLS, the so called generalized method of moments (GMM), as well as issues related to "causality", and the consequences of misspecification.

6.1   Nonlinear ML

It is difficult, perhaps even unwise, to present a general theory of nonlinear simultaneous equations (NLSE), since nonlinearity is a far broader class of functional forms than is linearity. In the latter case a general theory is quite feasible, and, indeed, has been discussed extensively in the preceding chapters. Nonlinearities, however, come in a great variety of forms, and any attempt to deal with the issues they raise in very general terms is apt to give rather obtuse results. In specific cases, the problems presented by nonlinearities are hardly more difficult than those encountered in linear models. For example, in the general linear model (GLM) with first order autoregressive errors, the nonlinearity occasioned by reducing the model, so that we deal with an error process of i.i.d. random variables, at the cost of introducing lags, is hardly more burdensome or more difficult to comprehend than is the simple GLM.

In the context of simultaneous equations theory, the most general (nonlinear) model we can consider is of the form

$$G^*(Y, X, U; \theta, \sigma) = 0, \quad G^* = (g^*_{ti}), t = 1, 2, \ldots, T, \ i = 1, 2, \ldots, m, \quad (6.1)$$

where Y, X have their usual meanings, i.e. they are the $T \times m$ and $T \times G$ matrices, respectively, of observations on the jointly dependent and predetermined variables of the system and so on. Of course, not much can be said about the model in Eq. (6.1); we shall deal instead with the simplified model

$$y_{t\cdot} = g_{t\cdot}(y_{t\cdot}, x_{t\cdot}; \theta) + u_{t\cdot}, \quad g_{t\cdot} = (g_{t1}, g_{t2}, \ldots, g_{tm}), \quad t = 1, 2, \ldots, T, \quad (6.2)$$

which has found extensive empirical applications. The model of Eq. (6.2), which may be termed the general nonlinear simultaneous equations model (GNLSEM) with additive errors, will be our general reference point, subject to the usual assumptions regarding the exogenous component, $p_{t\cdot}$, of the predetermined vector $x_{t\cdot} = (y_{t-1\cdot}, y_{t-2\cdot}, \ldots, y_{t-k\cdot}, p_{t\cdot})$. We shall maintain, for most discussions, the standard i.i.d. assumption, with mean zero and covariance matrix $\Sigma > 0$, but will allow the probability structure of the error vector, $u_{t\cdot}$, to be more complicated when we take up the discussion of the GMM.

The obvious minimand, in the absence of any distributional assumption, is

$$S^*(\theta, \sigma; Y, X) = \frac{1}{2} \sum_{t=1}^{T} (y_{t\cdot} - g_{t\cdot}(\theta))' \Sigma^{-1} (y_{t\cdot} - g_{t\cdot}(\theta))$$

$$= \frac{1}{2}(y - g)' (\Sigma^{-1} \otimes I_T)(y - g), \quad (6.3)$$

where for notational simplicity we use $g_{t\cdot}(\theta)$ instead of $g_{t\cdot}(y_{t\cdot}, x_{t\cdot}; \theta)$. The minimand of Eq. (6.3), however, has the disadvantage of yielding **inconsistent estimators** for the unknown parameters θ and $\sigma = \text{vec}(\Sigma)$, as is also the case in the standard 2SLS and 3SLS context.

If the distribution of the error process is jointly normal, the slightly modified, (through division by T) LF (log likelihood function) is given by (with $\phi = (\theta', \sigma')'$)

$$L_T(\phi; Y, X) = -\frac{m}{2}\ln(2\pi) - \frac{1}{2}\ln|\Sigma| + \frac{1}{2T}\ln|B'(\theta)B(\theta)| - \frac{1}{2}\text{tr}\Sigma^{-1}S(\theta), \quad (6.4)$$

where

$$B(\theta) = \prod_{t=1}^{T} \left(\frac{\partial u'_{t\cdot}}{\partial y_{t\cdot}} \right) = \prod_{t=1}^{T} \left(I - \frac{\partial g'_{t\cdot}}{\partial y_{t\cdot}} \right) = \prod_{t=1}^{T} B^*_t,$$

$$S(\theta) = \frac{1}{T}(Y - G)'(Y - G). \quad (6.5)$$

The LF of Eq. (6.4) is, *mutatis mutandis*, almost identical to that of the standard GLSEM problem; to see this, note that in the latter B_t^* becomes the constant matrix B^*, which, subject to the normalization convention, yields $B^* = I - B$, the diagonal elements of B being null. However, in the context of our discussion, since $B_t^* = I - (\partial g_t'./\partial u_t.)$, the diagonal elements of $B_t^* - I$ are not necessarily null.

The ML estimator of the underlying parameters of the GNLSEM (general nonlinear simultaneous equations model) may be obtained by straightforward maximization, as in Chapter 5, assuming that we have identification.

6.1.1 *Identification*

What are the identification requirements in the GNLSEM? In the literature there have been several attempts to devise a set of identification conditions parallel to those that have been established for the GLSEM. This effort has been somewhat misdirected, in that the issue of identification in a nonlinear context has certain aspects not found in linear models. In the GLSEM the dominant intuition, for understanding the identification issue, is that no equation in the model should be expressible in terms of linear combinations of other equations. This, in effect, prevents the parameter configuration of a given model from being confused with that of another, when both satisfy, in the normal case at least, the same likelihood function. Hence, the characterization of identification as the case in which all observationally equivalent structures are connected by trivial transformations.

In the nonlinear case, however, in addition to the requirement that no equation be expressible as a linear combination of others, there is the problem of **multiple solutions**. This problem has two aspects; first, we would like to maintain that given the predetermined variables we are able to determine unambiguously the conditional mean, or some such "average" measure, of the jointly dependent variables, [1] which would argue for two requirements induced by the inverse function theorem; first, that the dependent variables be expressible, at least piece wise, in terms of the predetermined variables and the errors; and, second, that the solutions so obtained be economically admissible. For example, an equation that reads $y^2 + a = u$, is inadmissible if $a > 0$ and $E(u) = 0$. These issues do not relate, strictly speaking, to identification but illustrate the additional complexities arising when dealing with the GNLSEM. Moreover, if parameter estimators are obtained by minimizing or maximizing a certain objective function, the resulting estimates are found by solving a system of nonlinear equations. However, nonlinear equations, typically, have multiple solutions. If $\kappa_T(Y, X; \phi)$ is the objective function to be minimized, we must require

---

[1] This is the analog of the requirement that the matrix B^* be **nonsingular** in the standard GLSEM.

that the estimator, say $\hat{\phi}$, satisfy the condition $\kappa_T(\hat{\phi}) = \inf_{\phi \in \Phi} \kappa_T(\phi)$, and not merely find a root (solution) of $(\partial \kappa_T(\theta)/\partial \theta) = 0$.
   If

$$\kappa_T(\phi) \xrightarrow{\text{a.c. or P}} K(\phi^0, \phi),$$

and K is a contrast function, the following argument produces the identification condition. First, it is shown that [2]

$$\kappa_T(\hat{\phi}) \xrightarrow{\text{a.c. or P}} \inf_{\phi \in \Phi} K(\phi, \phi^0),$$

where Φ is the admissible parameter set and K is a contrast function. Since the function (K) assumes its global minimum at the point $\phi = \phi^0$, the condition for identification must be that for no other point (other than ϕ^0) does the function assume its global minimum. This is formalized by stating the **identification requirement** as:

$$\text{If } K(\phi^0, \phi^{(1)}) = K(\phi^0, \phi^{(2)}) \text{ then } \phi^{(1)} = \phi^{(2)}. \tag{6.6}$$

We recall that this is what we did in Chapter 5, when we discussed nonlinear models, but not in a simultaneous equations context.

Almost invariably, the standard identification requirement given in the literature, for the normal case and *mutatis mutandis* for other cases as well, is that the matrix

$$I(\phi) = -\lim_{T \to \infty} E\left(\frac{\partial^2 L_T}{\partial \phi \partial \phi}(\phi^0)\right), \quad \phi = \begin{pmatrix} \theta \\ \sigma \end{pmatrix} \tag{6.7}$$

be **nonsingular at the true parameter point**, ϕ^0. Because of continuity, at ϕ^0, we are assured that the matrix is nonsingular in a neighborhood $N(\phi^0; \epsilon)$. While this condition is useful in obtaining a solution by calculus means, it has two disadvantages; it forces on us the artificial distinction between **local** and **global** identification, noted in Chapter 3, and it misleads by allowing the practitioner to think that any solution for which the Hessian of the objective function is nonsingular (negative definite in the standard normal ML case) yields the desired (ML) estimator. If the true parameter point, ϕ^0 is an interior point of the admissible parameter space, Φ, as we have implied above, the ML estimator may be found by solving the gradient of the LF set to zero. We must take pains, however, to take the solution that corresponds to the largest value of the LF, i.e. we must choose the *maximum maximorum*. A third minor disadvantage is that this condition is relatively more difficult to verify in practice than the alternative we have given, in terms of Kullback information.

---

[2] In this connection see the discussion in Chapter 5, regarding MC estimators.

6.1.2 Consistency of the ML Estimator

The consistency, or strong consistency, of the resulting estimators is obtained, if we show that the ML estimator is a MC estimator, by verifying, for the function $H_T = L_T(\phi^0) - L_T(\phi)$, where $L_T(\phi)$ is as defined in Eq. (6.4), the conditions stated in Propositions 3, 4 and/or Corollary 1 of Chapter 5. Specifically, we need to verify certain continuity conditions; that

$$H_T \overset{\text{a.c.}}{\to} K(\phi, \phi^0);$$

that K is a contrast function and it obeys the identification condition

$$\text{if} \quad K(\phi^1, \phi^0) = K(\phi^2, \phi^0) \text{ then } \phi^1 = \phi^2.$$

This identification condition is quite general, and it can be applied in any context in which one can verify that K is a contrast function, i.e. that it is nonnegative and assumes its global minimum (zero) at the true parameter point. Knowing the distribution of the errors is not essential, if one is prepared to prove, *de novo*, that the function K has such properties.

If the distribution is specified, so that L_T is a proper LF, K is the **Kullback information** of ϕ^0 on ϕ and, as such, it would automatically satisfy the requirements above except, possibly, for the identification condition. Evidently, whether this can be shown or not depends on the type of model considered, but in most regular cases this result would hold.

It is an interesting facet of this approach to the identification problem, that identification and (strong) consistency of the parameter estimators are established by the same argument.

Because the entire topic of the ML estimation of general NLSE is rather opaque, it is best if all theoretical developments be followed immediately by illustrations using simple models. In this discussion we shall make extensive use of a simple model, first employed in a paper by P.C.B. Phillips.

Example 1. Consider the simple GNLSEM, Phillips (1982), [3]

$$u_{t1} = \quad \ln y_{t1} \qquad + a_1$$

$$u_{t2} = b_1 y_{t1} \quad + y_{t2} \tag{6.8}$$

This set of equations employs a nonlinearity in the variables commonly found in econometric models.

---

[3] Note that this model is at once more general and more restrictive than the GNLSEM with additive error terms we examined above; for one, the error term in the first equation is multiplicative, when we express all left hand sides linearly, as was the case in the earlier expositions; for another, it is lacking in exogenous and lagged dependent variables with the exception of the fictitious variable which is unity for all observations, and corresponds to the constant term in the first equation. This aspect, however, is not a significant restriction of its generality in that we may easily introduce such variables.

In terms of the earlier discussion, note that this model easily yields an explicit reduced form, which is not always possible in NLSE. Thus, we obtain,

$$y_{t\cdot}' = \begin{pmatrix} e^{-a_1}e^{u_{t1}} \\ -b_1 e^{-a_1}e^{u_{t1}} + u_{t2} \end{pmatrix}. \qquad (6.9)$$

Even if we assume that the error process is one of i.i.d. random variables with

$$u_{t\cdot}' \sim N(0, \Sigma), \quad \Sigma > 0,$$

the distribution of the vector $y_{t\cdot}$ is much more complex since, from Eq. (6.9), it is seen to be a mixture of normal and lognormal random variables. It is relatively straightforward to show that

$$E(y_{t\cdot})' = \begin{pmatrix} e^{-a_1}e^{(1/2)\sigma_{11}} \\ -b_1 e^{-a_1}e^{(1/2)\sigma_{11}} \end{pmatrix}, \quad E(u_{t2}y_{t1}) = e^{-a_1}\sigma_{12}e^{(1/2)\sigma_{11}},$$

$$E(u_{t1}y_{t1}) = e^{-a_1}\sigma_{11}e^{(1/2)\sigma_{11}}, \quad E(u_{t2}y_{t2}) = \sigma_{22} - b_1 e^{-a_1}\sigma_{12}e^{(1/2)\sigma_{11}}.$$

$$E(u_{t1}y_{t2}) = \sigma_{12} - b_1 e^{-a_1}\sigma_{11}e^{(1/2)\sigma_{11}}, \quad E(y_{t1}^2) = e^{-2a_1}e^{2\sigma_{11}}.$$

$$E(y_{t2}^2) = \sigma_{22} - 2b_1 e^{-a_1}\sigma_{12}e^{(1/2)\sigma_{11}} + b_1^2 e^{-2a_1}e^{2\sigma_{11}}. \qquad (6.10)$$

Remark 1. The relations above disclose one of the most complicating features of the general NLSE model. In **linear models**, we need only assume that the (structural) error process is one of (independent) random variables with mean zero and finite variances, obeying a Lindeberg condition. This is, ordinarily, sufficient to allow for the development of asymptotic theory for estimators of structural parameters obtained in that context. In the case of the general NLSE model, however, such assumptions are totally insufficient. Note that in the example above, even if we assume that $\{u_{t\cdot}' : t \geq 1\}$ is a sequence of i.i.d. random variables with mean zero and covariance matrix $\Sigma > 0$, the moments of the dependent variables may not exist since the model, as stated above, **requires** for the definition of the moments of the $y's$ and the $u's$, the existence of the moment generating function (mgf) of u_{t1}. But existence of its mgf requires that u_{t1} possess moments of all orders and not merely up to second order!

The likelihood function, in terms of the error process, is given by

$$L^*(\phi; Y) = (2\pi)^{-T}|\Sigma|^{-(T/2)}e^{-(1/2)\sum_{t=1}^{T} u_{t\cdot}\Sigma^{-1}u_{t\cdot}'}.$$

Treating Eq. (6.9) as a transformation from u to y, we note that the Jacobian of this transformation over the sample, i.e. the square root of the determinant of the matrix $B(\theta)'B(\theta)$ of Eq. (6.4), is

$$J(y) = \left(\prod_{t=1}^{T} \frac{1}{y_{t1}^2}\right)^{(1/2)}.$$

Consequently, the LF (log likelihood function) in terms of the observables (divided by T) becomes

$$L_T(\phi; y) = -\ln(2\pi) - \frac{1}{2}\ln|\Sigma| - \frac{1}{T}\sum_{t=1}^{T}\ln y_{t1} - \frac{1}{2}\mathrm{tr}\Sigma^{-1}S(\theta), \qquad (6.11)$$

where

$$S(\theta) = \frac{1}{T}Z'Z, \quad Z = (z_{t\cdot}), \quad z_{t\cdot} = (a_1 + \ln y_{t1}, \ b_1 y_{t1} + y_{t2}) \ (6.12)$$

$$\theta = (a_1, b_1)', \quad \phi = (\theta', \sigma')', \quad \sigma = \mathrm{vec}(\Sigma).$$

We note that, for each $\omega \in \Omega$, the LF is a continuous function of the parameter ϕ, and is uniformly continuous if compactness of the parameter space is assumed. Needless to say, if $(\Omega, \mathcal{A}, \mathcal{P})$ is the probability space on which the error process $u_{t\cdot}$ is defined, the LF is $\mathcal{A}$-measurable, as well, for every admissible ϕ. Finally, define the function

$$H_T(\phi) = L_T(\phi^0; y) - L_T(\phi; y), \qquad (6.13)$$

and observe that the ML estimator minimizes the function above. Hence, by the discussion of Chapter 5, it is a MC estimator. [4] Moreover, since

$$H_T(\phi) = \frac{1}{2}\ln|\Sigma_0| - \frac{1}{2}\ln|\Sigma| + \frac{1}{2}\mathrm{tr}\Sigma_0^{-1}S(\theta^0) - \frac{1}{2}\mathrm{tr}\Sigma^{-1}S(\theta), \qquad (6.14)$$

we conclude that

$$H_T(\phi) \overset{\mathrm{a.c.}}{\to} \frac{1}{2}\ln|\Sigma_0| - \frac{1}{2}\ln|\Sigma| + \frac{1}{2}\mathrm{tr}\Sigma_0^{-1}\bar{S}(\theta^0) - \frac{1}{2}\mathrm{tr}\Sigma^{-1}\bar{S}(\theta), \qquad (6.15)$$

where $\bar{S}(\theta), \bar{S}(\theta^0)$ are, respectively, the a.c. limits of $S(\theta)$ and $S(\theta^0)$. Precisely,

$$\bar{S}(\theta^0) = \Sigma_0, \quad \bar{S}(\theta) = \Sigma_0 + C_1 + C_2,$$

where

$$C_1 = \alpha \begin{bmatrix} 0 & \sigma_{11}^0 e^{(1/2)\sigma_{11}^0} & e^{(1/2)\sigma_{11}^0} \\ \sigma_{11}^0 e^{(1/2)\sigma_{11}^0} & 2\sigma_{12}^0 \end{bmatrix},$$

$$C_2 = \begin{bmatrix} \beta^2 & \alpha\beta e^{(1/2)\sigma_{11}^0} \\ \alpha\beta e^{(1/2)\sigma_{11}^0} & \alpha^2 e^{2\sigma_{11}^0} \end{bmatrix}, \qquad (6.16)$$

---

[4] If the distribution of the error process is normal, as claimed, the function $H_T(\phi)$ converges, at least in probability, to the Kullback information (of ϕ^0 on ϕ) which is a **contrast function**, i.e. it is a nonnegative function which assumes its global minimum, viz. zero, at $\phi = \phi^0$; if the assertion is erroneous, as in the case of the so called pseudo-ML estimators, we can no longer claim that $K(\phi^0, \phi)$ is the Kullback information; thus, the claim that it is a contrast function has to be established by a direct argument.

and

$$\alpha = (b_1 - b_1^0)e^{-a_1}, \quad \beta = (a_1 - a_1^0), \tag{6.17}$$

and where a zero subscript or superscript indicates the true parameter point. The preceding result is easily established, if we write the vector $z_{t\cdot}$ of Eq. (6.12) as

$$z_{t\cdot} = [a_1^0 + \ln y_{t1} + (a_1 - a_1^0), \quad b_1^0 y_{t1} + y_{t2} + (b_1 - b_1^0)y_{t1}] = u_{t\cdot} + v_{t\cdot},$$

where $v_{t\cdot} = [a_1 - a_1^0, \quad (b_1 - b_1^0)y_{t1}]$. In this context

$$\Sigma_0 \;=\; \text{a.c. limit of} \;\; \frac{\sum_{t=1}^{T} u'_{t\cdot} u_{t\cdot}}{T}$$

$$C_1 \;=\; \text{a.c. limit of} \;\; \frac{\sum_{t=1}^{T} (u'_{t\cdot} v_{t\cdot} + v'_{t\cdot} u_{t\cdot})}{T}$$

$$C_2 \;=\; \text{a.c. limit of} \;\; \frac{\sum_{t=1}^{T} v'_{t\cdot} v_{t\cdot}}{T}.$$

Thus, the Kullback information in this context is

$$K(\phi, \phi^0) = \frac{1}{2}\ln|\Sigma_0| - \frac{1}{2}\ln|\Sigma| + \frac{1}{2}\text{tr}\Sigma_0^{-1}\Sigma_0 - \frac{1}{2}\text{tr}[\Sigma^{-1}(\Sigma_0 + C_1 + C_2)]. \tag{6.18}$$

When the normality assertion is correct, we are assured that [5] $K(\theta, \theta^0) \geq 0$; when not, but other suitable conditions hold, H_T will also converge to a function like K; in such a case, however, its nonnegativity cannot be assured and must be separately established. Just to see what this entails we shall verify the nonnegativity of K. To do so, first minimize K with respect to $\sigma = \text{vec}(\Sigma)$, thus obtaining

$$\frac{\partial K}{\partial \text{vec}(\Sigma^{-1})} = \frac{1}{2}\left[-\text{vec}(\Sigma)' + \text{vec}(\Sigma_0 + C_1 + C_2)'\right] = 0, \tag{6.19}$$

which implies $\Sigma = \Sigma_0 + C_1 + C_2$; inserting this minimizer in Eq. (6.18) we find the "concentrated" Kullback information,

$$K^*(\theta, \theta^0) = \frac{1}{2}\left(\ln\frac{|\Sigma_0 + C_1 + C_2|}{|\Sigma_0|}\right). \tag{6.20}$$

---

[5] This is evident from Proposition 14 (Jensen's inequality), Dhrymes (1989), i.e.

$$\ln E_{\phi^0}\left(\frac{L^*(\phi)}{L^*(\phi^0)}\right) \geq E_{\phi^0}\ln\left(\frac{L^*(\phi)}{L^*(\phi^0)}\right),$$

in view of the fact that H_T converges to the **the limit of its expectation**.

A necessary and sufficient (nas) condition for the nonnegativity of the function is that

$$|\Sigma_0 + C_1 + C_2| \geq |\Sigma_0|. \tag{6.21}$$

To find the conditions under which this is so, consider the characteristic roots of the matrix in the left member of Eq. (6.21) in the metric of the matrix in the right member, i.e. the roots of

$$0 = |\lambda \Sigma_0 - (\Sigma_0 + C_1 + C_2)| = |\mu I - A|, \tag{6.22}$$

where

$$\Sigma_0 = TT', \quad T = (\sigma_{11}^0)^{-(1/2)} \begin{bmatrix} \sigma_{11}^0 & 0 \\ \sigma_{12}^0 & \delta \end{bmatrix}, \quad \delta^2 = |\Sigma_0|$$

$$T^{-1} = (\sigma_{11}^0)^{(1/2)} \begin{bmatrix} (\sigma_{11}^0)^{-1} & 0 \\ -(\sigma_{12}^0/\delta\sigma_{11}^0) & (1/\delta) \end{bmatrix}$$

$$A = T^{-1}(C_1 + C_2)T'^{-1}, \quad \mu = \lambda - 1.$$

By Proposition 63, Dhrymes (1984), there exists a nonsingular matrix, P such that [6]

$$\Sigma_0 = P'P, \quad \Sigma_0 + C_1 + C_2 = P'\Lambda P, \quad \Lambda = \text{diag}(1 + \mu_1, 1 + \mu_2, \ldots, 1 + \mu_n). \tag{6.23}$$

Thus, the nas condition of Eq. (6.21) becomes

$$\frac{|\Sigma_0 + C_1 + C_2|}{|\Sigma_0|} = \prod_{i=1}^{n}(1 + \mu_i) \geq 1. \tag{6.24}$$

Now, if the matrix $C_1 + C_2$ is positive semidefinite, $\mu_i \geq 0$ for all i, and the condition is automatically satisfied. If not, however, some of the μ_i may be negative. Without loss of generality let the last $n - k$ be negative, and the first k being nonnegative; to gain some insight into the nas condition of Eq. (6.24), we may render it as

$$\prod_{i=1}^{k}(1 + \mu_i) \geq \frac{1}{\prod_{i=1}^{n-k}(1 + \mu_{k+i})}, \tag{6.25}$$

which indicates that the magnitude of the negative roots cannot be "too close" to one. To verify the nas condition, in the present case, we need to compute the matrix A, which is found to be

$$A = T^{-1}(C_1 + C_2)T'^{-1} = \begin{bmatrix} (\beta^2/\sigma_{11}^0) & \gamma \\ \gamma & \zeta \end{bmatrix}, \tag{6.26}$$

---

[6] Even though the case we consider involves only a 2×2 matrix we give the result for the general case.

where

$$\gamma = \frac{\alpha(\sigma_{11}^0 + \beta)e^{(1/2)\sigma_{11}^0} - \beta^2(\sigma_{12}^0/\sigma_{11}^0)}{\delta}$$

$$\zeta = \left(\frac{\sigma_{11}^0}{\delta^2}\right)\left[\left(\alpha e^{(1/2)\sigma_{11}^0} - \beta\frac{\sigma_{12}^0}{\sigma_{11}^0}\right)^2 + \alpha^2 e^{\sigma_{11}^0}(e^{\sigma_{11}^0} - 1)\right],$$

so that for $\alpha \neq 0$, $\beta \neq 0$, the diagonal elements of A are positive, provided $\sigma_{11}^0 > 0$. The characteristic roots of A are simply the solutions to the equation

$$\mu^2 - \left(\zeta + \frac{\beta^2}{\sigma_{11}^0}\right)\mu + |A| = 0. \tag{6.27}$$

We may easily solve the equation, and actually attempt to verify the condition of Eq. (6.25) directly, but this would be a far more cumbersome task than is necessary. It is far simpler to work with the condition of Eq. (6.24), which implies that the nas condition is [7]

$$0 \leq (\mu_1 + \mu_2 + \mu_1\mu_2) = \left(\zeta + \frac{\beta^2}{\sigma_{11}^0}\right) + |A| = \psi. \tag{6.28}$$

A relatively simple calculation will show that

$$\psi = \frac{1}{\delta^2}\left\{\frac{\beta^2\delta^2}{\sigma_{11}^0} + \sigma_{11}^0\left[\alpha(1-\beta)e^{(1/2)\sigma_{11}^0} - \beta\left(\frac{\sigma_{12}^0}{\sigma_{11}^0}\right)\right]^2\right\}$$

$$+ \frac{1}{\delta^2}\left\{\alpha^2 e^{\sigma_{11}^0}(\sigma_{11}^0 + \beta^2)(e^{\sigma_{11}^0} - 1 - \sigma_{11}^0)\right\} \geq 0, \tag{6.29}$$

so that K has, indeed, the properties we claim for it. Thus, the ML estimator of θ converges, at least in probability, to the true parameter θ^0. This is so since ψ is null if and only if $a_1 = a_1^0$ and $b_1 = b_1^0$, implying $C_1 = 0$, $C_2 = 0$, and thus $\Sigma = \Sigma_0$. Moreover, the ML estimator of θ can be shown to be strongly consistent, as well, since it may be verified that the convergence a.c. of H_T to K is uniform in θ, if the admissible parameter space is compact and the condition regarding the dominance of the LF by an integrable function holds.

The question often arises as to what are the consequences of removing the normality assumption from the ML procedure employed in Example 1. More precisely, we continue using the "LF" function of Eq. (6.11), even though the error process, $u_{t\cdot}$, is no longer assumed to be normal. We note that we still maintain the i.i.d. assumption, as well as the assumption that

---

[7] The nas condition for the general case is evident; it is that the sum of the coefficients of the characteristic equation in question is **nonnegative**.

$\Sigma_0 > 0$; moreover, if the admissible parameter space is compact and that "LF" is dominated by an integrable function, all developments in Example 1 remain valid, up to Eq. (6.20). What will be different now is the definition of the matrices C_i, $i = 1, 2$, as well as the matrix A and everything related to them. We examine this case in Example 2, below.

Example 2. We consider again the model in Eq. (6.8) and the "LF" in Eq. (6.11), but we no longer assume that the error process is normal; we only assume that the process is one of i.i.d. random vectors with mean zero and (true) covariance matrix $\Sigma_0 > 0$. Equation (6.9) is still valid but the expressions in Eq. (6.10) are no longer valid. For the sake of modest generality, we treat the case of an n-element vector u; the moment generating function (mgf) of the error process is given by

$$M(t_1, t_2, \ldots, t_n) = E(e^{t' u}). \tag{6.30}$$

For our problem $n = 2$, and the expressions of Eq. (6.10) become

$$M(1,0) = E(e^{u_1}), \quad M_1(1,0) = E(u_1 e^{u_1}), \quad M_2(1,0) = E(u_2 e^{u_1}),$$

$$M_{11}(1,0) = E(u_1^2 e^{u_1}), \quad M(2,0) = E(e^{2u_1}), \tag{6.31}$$

where

$$M_i(t_1, t_2, \ldots, t_n) = \frac{\partial M}{\partial t_i}, \quad M_{ij}(t_1, t_2, \ldots, t_n) = \frac{\partial^2 M}{\partial t_i \partial t_j}, \quad i, j = 1, 2, \ldots, n. \tag{6.32}$$

Evidently, the expressions required for our problem, i.e. $E(u_1 y_1)$, $E(y_1^2)$, $E(u_2 y_1)$ and $E(\bar{y}_1)$ can all be obtained from Eq. (6.31), once the mgf is given.

Proceeding entirely in the same fashion as in Example 1, we find

$$C_1 = \alpha \begin{bmatrix} 0 & M_1(1,0) \\ M_1(1,0) & 2M_2(1,0) \end{bmatrix} \tag{6.33}$$

$$C_2 = \begin{bmatrix} \beta^2 & \alpha\beta M(1,0) \\ \alpha\beta M(1,0) & \alpha^2 M(2,0) \end{bmatrix}$$

$$C_1 + C_2 = \begin{bmatrix} \beta^2 & \alpha[M_1(1,0) + \beta M(1,0)] \\ \alpha[M_1(1,0) + \beta M(1,0)] & \alpha^2 M(2,0) + 2\alpha M_2(1,0) \end{bmatrix}.$$

Put

$$\eta = \alpha M_1(1,0) + \alpha\beta M(1,0) = \alpha[M_1(1,0) + \beta M(1,0)]$$

$$\lambda = \alpha^2 M(2,0) + 2\alpha M_2(1,0) = \alpha[\alpha M(2,0) + 2M_2(1,0)].$$

In this notation,

$$C_1 + C_2 = \begin{bmatrix} \beta^2 & \eta \\ \eta & \lambda \end{bmatrix} \tag{6.34}$$

and

$$A = T^{-1}(C_1 + C_2)T'^{-1}$$

$$= \sigma_{11}^0 \begin{bmatrix} (1/\sigma_{11}^0) & 0 \\ -(\sigma_{12}^0/\sigma_{11}^0\delta) & (1/\delta) \end{bmatrix} \begin{bmatrix} \beta^2 & \eta \\ \eta & \lambda \end{bmatrix} \begin{bmatrix} (1/\sigma_{11}^0) & -(\sigma_{12}^0/\sigma_{11}^0\delta) \\ 0 & (1/\delta) \end{bmatrix}$$

$$= \begin{bmatrix} (\beta^2/\sigma_{11}^0) & \gamma \\ \gamma & \zeta \end{bmatrix}, \tag{6.35}$$

where

$$\zeta = \frac{\sigma_{11}^0}{\delta^2}\left[\phi - 2\eta\left(\frac{\sigma_{12}^0}{\sigma_{11}^0}\right) + \beta^2\left(\frac{\sigma_{12}^0}{\sigma_{11}^0}\right)^2\right], \quad \gamma = \frac{1}{\delta}\left[\eta - \beta^2\left(\frac{\sigma_{12}^0}{\sigma_{11}^0}\right)\right]. \tag{6.36}$$

An easy calculation shows

$$|A| = \left(\frac{\beta^2}{\sigma_{11}^0}\right)\zeta - \gamma^2 = \frac{1}{\delta^2}\left[\beta^2\alpha^2 M(2,0) + \beta^2 2\alpha M_2(1,0) - \eta^2\right]. \tag{6.37}$$

The nas condition for identification is that $\psi \geq 0$, where ψ is obtainable as the sum of the trace, and the determinant of the matrix A; thus,

$$\psi = \frac{\beta^2}{\sigma_{11}^0} + \zeta + |A| = -\frac{1}{\delta^2}\left[\eta^2 + 2\sigma_{12}^0\eta - \sigma_{11}^0\beta^2\left(\frac{\sigma_{12}^0}{\sigma_{11}^0}\right)^2\right] \tag{6.38}$$

$$+ \frac{1}{\delta^2}\left\{\left(\frac{\beta^2\delta^2}{\sigma_{11}^0}\right) + (\sigma_{11}^0 + \beta^2)[\alpha^2 M(2,0) + 2\alpha M_2(1,0)]\right\}.$$

If the condition $\psi \geq 0$ is satisfied, we can be assured of certain facts:

i. $|\Sigma_0 + C_1 + C_2| \geq |\Sigma_0|$; which shows that K is indeed nonnegative;

ii. the global minimum of the function occurs when $\psi = 0$; but this implies the condition $\mu_i = 0$, $i = 1, 2$;

iii. in turn, ii implies that the global minimum is attained if and only if $A = 0$, since the latter is a symmetric matrix; or, equivalently, that the global minimum is attained if and only if $C_1 + C_2 = 0$;

iv. by the structure of the matrix A, the condition in iii can hold if and only if $\alpha = 0$ and $\beta = 0$, so that $a_1 = a_1^0$, $b_1 = b_1^0$ and $\Sigma = \Sigma_0$; or, equivalently, condition ii can hold if and only if $\phi = \phi^0$.

Consequently, if the distribution specified for u obeys the nas condition for identification, the "quasi-ML" estimator of ϕ will be strongly consistent, provided that K is a contrast function, i.e. that it is nonnegative and assumes its global minimum, viz. zero, at the true parameter point ϕ^0, and certain other conditions hold.

Remark 2. The preceding result is a restricted one, only to the extent that the Jacobian term (in the LF) does not contain any unknown parameters. In a more general context the function K would be of the form

$$K(\phi, \phi^0) = \ln \left(\frac{|\bar{B}'^{-1}(\theta)\bar{S}(\theta)\bar{B}^{-1}(\theta)|}{|\bar{B}'^{-1}(\theta^0)\Sigma_0\bar{B}^{-1}(\theta^0)|} \right),$$

where

$$\frac{1}{T}\ln|B'^{-1}(\theta)S(\theta)B^{-1}(\theta)| \overset{\text{P or a.c.}}{\longrightarrow} \ln|\bar{B}'^{-1}(\theta)\bar{S}(\theta)\bar{B}^{-1}(\theta)|.$$

A development of the argument in this context would lead to qualitatively similar results; thus, the numerator matrix would be expressible as the denominator matrix plus a component, equivalent to the matrices C_i of the previous discussion. A matrix similar to A will result, and identification will be defined precisely as before. In this framework, (strong) consistency would follow, provided one can show that the matrix A is the null matrix if and only if $\theta = \theta^0$.

Example 2 demonstrates that there is an entire class of GNLSEM for which the "quasi-ML" estimator may be consistent or strongly consistent.[8] To show that the class of models for which the "quasi-ML" estimator of the parameters of the GNLSEM is (strongly) consistent is not vacuous, we consider the case where the error process is a mixture of multivariate normals.

---

[8] In the case of the **GLSEM** if the ML estimator is consistent and asymptotically normal, the "quasi-ML" estimator has the same properties; one easily establishes this fact by noting:

i. the identification condition **does not depend on the normality assumption**;

ii. a consistency or strong consistency proof may be based on the asymptotic equivalence of the ML and 3SLS estimators; evidently, the proof for the latter does not depend on the normality assumption;

iii. the limiting distribution is obtained from the expansion of the derivative $(\partial L_T/\partial\theta)$, using the mean value theorem, which does not depend on the normality assumption, and a central limit theorem applied to $\sqrt{T}(\partial L_T/\partial\theta)(\theta^0)$ which, similarly, does not depend on the normality assumption.

Example 3. Consider the GNLSEM and the "LF" as in the preceding examples, but suppose that the error process is a mixture of multivariate normals with mixing distribution G, as follows:

$$u \sim N(0, \omega\Omega_0), \quad \Omega_0 = (\omega_{ij}^0), \tag{6.39}$$

where Ω_0 is a fixed positive definite matrix and $\omega > 0$ is a scalar. The notion here is that ω is a random variable generated by the mixing distribution G. This is akin to the Bayesian case, in which one might argue that, conditional on ω, the vector u has the distribution in Eq. (6.39) but that, unconditionally, it has the density function

$$f(u) = \int_0^\infty (2\pi\omega)^{-(n/2)} |\Omega_0|^{-(1/2)} e^{-(1/2\omega)u' \Omega_0^{-1} u} \, dG(\omega). \tag{6.40}$$

The mgf of u is easily obtained as

$$M(t) = E(e^{t' u})$$
$$= \int_0^\infty \left(\int_{R^n} (2\pi)^{-(n/2)} |\omega\Omega_0|^{-(1/2)} e^{t' u} e^{-(1/2)u' (\omega\Omega_0)^{-1} u} \, du \right) dG(\omega)$$
$$= \int_0^\infty e^{\xi^* \omega} dG(\omega), \quad \xi^* = \frac{1}{2} t' \Omega_0 t. \tag{6.41}$$

The relationship between the second moments of u and the elements of the matrix Ω_0 is easily obtained, if we note that

$$\sigma_{ij}^0 = E(u_i u_j) = \frac{\partial^2 M}{\partial t_i \partial t_j}(0,0) = \omega_{ij}^0 \int_0^\infty \omega dG(\omega) = \mu \omega_{ij}^0, \tag{6.42}$$

where μ is simply **the mean of the distribution** function G.

Special Case: $G(\omega) = 1 - e^{-\lambda\omega}$.

The distribution above is, evidently, differentiable and its derivative is given by

$$g(\omega) = \lambda e^{-\lambda\omega}, \tag{6.43}$$

which is recognized as the exponential distribution [9] with parameter $\lambda > 0$. Since here

$$E(\omega) = \int_0^\infty (\lambda\omega) e^{-\lambda\omega} d\omega = (1/\lambda), \tag{6.44}$$

---

[9] The exponential distribution is a member of the family of gamma distributions, of which the chi-squared is also a member, well known to econometricians.

it follows from Eq. (6.42) that

$$\omega_{ij}^0 = \lambda\sigma_{ij}^0. \tag{6.45}$$

Using Eq. (6.45), and noting that $\xi^* = \lambda\xi$, we obtain the mgf as

$$M(t) = \int_0^\infty \lambda e^{-\lambda(1-\xi)\omega}\, d\omega = [1/(1-\xi)]. \tag{6.46}$$

We note that (using also Eq. (6.45))

$$\xi(1,0) = \frac{\sigma_{11}^0}{2}, \quad \xi(2,0) = 2\sigma_{11}^0, \quad \frac{\partial\xi}{\partial t_1}(1,0) = \sigma_{11}^0, \quad \frac{\partial\xi}{\partial t_2}(1,0) = \sigma_{12}^0.$$

Therefore, [10]

$$M(2,0) = [1/(1-2\sigma_{11}^0)], \quad M(1,0) = (1/s), \quad s = 1 - (\sigma_{11}^0/2)$$

$$M_1(1,0) = (\sigma_{11}^0/s^2), \quad M_2(1,0) = (\sigma_{12}^0/s^2). \tag{6.47}$$

With the current distributional assumption the entities of Eq. (6.38) become

$$\eta = \left(\frac{\alpha}{s^2}\right)[\sigma_{11}^0 + \beta s], \quad \gamma = \left(\frac{1}{\delta}\right)\left[\eta - \beta^2\left(\frac{\sigma_{12}^0}{\sigma_{11}^0}\right)\right] \tag{6.48}$$

$$\zeta = \left(\frac{\sigma_{11}^0}{\delta^2}\right)\left[\phi - 2\eta\left(\frac{\sigma_{12}^0}{\sigma_{11}^0}\right) + \beta^2\left(\frac{\sigma_{12}^0}{\sigma_{11}^0}\right)^2\right], \quad \lambda = \frac{\alpha^2}{1-2\sigma_{11}^0} + \frac{2\alpha\sigma_{12}^0}{s^2},$$

whence it follows that

$$\psi = \frac{\beta^2}{\sigma_{11}^0} + \zeta + |A| = \left(\frac{1}{\delta^2}\right)\left\{\sigma_{11}^0\left[\left(\frac{\alpha}{s}\right)\left(1-\frac{\beta}{s}\right) - \beta\frac{\sigma_{12}^0}{\sigma_{11}^0}\right]^2\right\} \tag{6.49}$$

$$= + \left(\frac{1}{\delta^2}\right)\left\{\frac{\beta^2\delta^2}{\sigma_{11}^0} + (\sigma_{11}^0 + \beta^2)\left[\frac{\alpha^2}{1-2\sigma_{11}^0} - \frac{\alpha^2}{s^2} - \frac{\alpha^2\sigma_{11}^0}{s^4}\right]\right\}.$$

---

[10] It might appear, from the expression for $M(2,0)$, that we have a significant restriction on the second moment matrix of the error process, since the expression for $M(2,0)$ **requires that** $\sigma_{11}^0 < (1/2)$. Actually, this is not so much a restriction on the GNLSEM as it is a restriction on the mixture of normals, which we have specified as the distribution of the error process. The condition results "because" we require the existence of the moment $E(y_1^2)$. If, in addition, we should require the existence of $E(y_1^k)$, i.e. if we require $E(e^{ku_1})$ to exist, we should obtain the condition $\sigma_{11}^0 < (2/k^2)$. This in no way restricts the GNLSEM, but tells us that mixtures of normals may have stringently restricted covariance parameters, depending on the order of moments of the underlying random variables whose existence we wish to assert.

It is evident, from the last member above, that $\psi \geq 0$, and that $\psi = 0$ if and only if $\alpha = 0$ and $\beta = 0$ or, equivalently if and only if $a_1 = a_1^0$ and $b_1 = b_1^0$ and consequently, that $\Sigma = \Sigma_0$. In turn, this means that the function

$$K(\theta, \phi^0) = \frac{1}{2}\ln\left(\frac{|\Sigma_0 + C_1 + C_2|}{|\Sigma_0|}\right)$$

is nonnegative and assumes its global minimum, viz. zero, at the point $\theta = \theta^0$, and $\sigma = \sigma_0$ ($\phi = \phi^0$), i.e. it is a contrast function.

6.1.3 Limiting Distribution of ML Estimators

Consider again the model of Eq. (6.2) and assume

i. the sequence $\{u'_t : t = 1, 2, \ldots\}$ is one of i.i.d. random vectors with the distribution $N(0, \Sigma)$ and $\Sigma > 0$;

ii. the admissible parameter space, Φ, is compact, and the true parameter point, ϕ^0, is an **interior** point;

iii. the Hessian of the LF converges, at least in probability, i.e.

$$-\frac{\partial^2 L_T}{\partial\phi\partial\phi} \xrightarrow{\text{P or a.c.}} -\lim_{T\to\infty} E_{\phi^0}\left(\frac{\partial^2 L_T}{\partial\phi\partial\phi}(\phi^0)\right) = I(\phi^0);$$

iv. the gradient of the LF obeys a central limit theorem (CLT), i.e.

$$\sqrt{T}\left(\frac{\partial L_T}{\partial\phi}(\phi^0)\right) \xrightarrow{\text{d}} N(0, \Psi_\phi);$$

v. the LF satisfies the identification condition of the previous section, and the conditions stated in Propositions 3 and 4 of Chapter 5.

If these conditions are satisfied, it is easy to obtain the limiting distribution of the ML estimator. Precisely, expanding the gradient of $L_T(\phi)$ we find

$$\left(\frac{\partial L_T}{\partial\phi}(\hat{\phi})\right)' = \left(\frac{\partial L_T}{\partial\phi}(\phi^0)\right)' + \frac{\partial^2 L_T}{\partial\phi\partial\phi}(\phi^*)(\hat{\phi} - \phi^0), \qquad (6.50)$$

where $|\phi^* - \phi^0| \leq |\hat{\phi} - \phi^0|$. We may rewrite Eq. (6.50) as

$$\sqrt{T}(\hat{\phi} - \phi^0) = -\left(\frac{\partial^2 L_T}{\partial\phi\partial\phi}(\phi^*)\right)^{-1}\sqrt{T}\left(\frac{\partial L_T}{\partial\phi}(\phi^0)\right)'. \qquad (6.51)$$

In view of the relation of ϕ^* to $\hat{\phi}$ and the fact that the latter converges, at least in probability to ϕ^0, it follows that if the five conditions listed above hold, we have that

$$\sqrt{T}(\hat{\phi} - \phi^0) \xrightarrow{\text{d}} N(0, C_{ML}), \quad C_{ML} = [I(\phi^0)]^{-1}\Psi_\phi[I(\phi^0)]^{-1}.$$

While the conditions above offer a very general set of necessary and sufficient conditions for obtaining the limiting distribution of (at least) a consistent ML estimator of the parameters of the GNLSEM, they are not, of course, sufficiently precise so that, by merely inspecting the functions $g_{t.}$, we should be able to determine whether the model in question yields consistent and asymptotically normal estimators. On the other hand given any specific model we can investigate, in the manner noted in this chapter, whether it does, indeed, yield such estimators. The outstanding research problem in this literature is to obtain a characterization of the class of functions, $g_{t.}$, which admit of at least consistent and asymptotically normal estimators for their parameters.

We examine below whether the models considered in the preceding examples yield asymptotically normal estimators.

Example 4. Consider again the model of Eq. (6.8) and, for the sake of simplicity, let us confine our attention to the parameters a_1, b_1. The reader may assume that the LF has been partially maximized with respect to Σ so that the **concentrated** LF becomes

$$L_T(\theta; y) = -[\ln(2\pi) + 1] - \frac{1}{2}\ln|S(\theta)| - \frac{1}{T}\sum_{t=1}^{T}\ln y_{t1}, \qquad (6.52)$$

and thus depends **only on** θ. We note, from Dhrymes (1984), Proposition 103,

$$\frac{\partial L_T}{\partial \theta} = -(1/2)\frac{\partial \ln|S(\theta)|}{\partial |S(\theta)|}\frac{\partial |S(\theta)|}{\partial \text{vec}(S(\theta))}\frac{\partial \text{vec}(S(\theta))}{\partial \theta}$$

$$= -(1/2)\text{vec}\{[S(\theta)]^{-1}\}'\frac{\partial \text{vec}[S(\theta)]}{\partial \theta}.$$

It easily follows that

$$\left(\frac{\partial L_T}{\partial \theta}(\theta^0)\right)' = -\frac{1}{|S(\theta^0)|}\left(\frac{1}{T}\right)\sum_{t=1}^{T}\begin{bmatrix} s_{22} & -s_{21} \\ -s_{12}y_{t1} & s_{11}y_{t1} \end{bmatrix}u'_{t.}.$$

By Proposition 11, Corollary 6 of Ch. 3, in Dhrymes (1989),

$$\sqrt{T}\left(\frac{\partial L_T}{\partial \theta}(\theta^0)\right)' \sim -\frac{1}{\sqrt{T}|\Sigma_0|}\sum_{t=1}^{T}\begin{bmatrix} \sigma_{22}^0 & -\sigma_{21}^0 \\ -\sigma_{12}^0 y_{t1} & \sigma_{11}^0 y_{t1} \end{bmatrix}u'_{t.}.$$

The right member of the equation above is seen to be the sum of i.i.d. random vectors, with mean

$$E_{\theta^0}\left(\begin{bmatrix} \sigma_{22}^0 & -\sigma_{21}^0 \\ -\sigma_{12}^0 y_{t1} & \sigma_{22}^0 y_{t1} \end{bmatrix}u'_{t.}\right) = \begin{pmatrix} 0 \\ \sigma_{11}^0 M_2(1,0) - \sigma_{12}^0 M_1(1,0) \end{pmatrix}. \qquad (6.53)$$

Thus, a necessary condition for asymptotic normality is that

$$\sigma_{11}^0 M_2(1,0) - \sigma_{12}^0 M_1(1,0) = 0. \tag{6.54}$$

Note that this is a condition on the distribution of the error process, not a condition on the structural parameters of the model. If the condition above is satisfied, it is simple to show that

$$\sqrt{T}\left(\frac{\partial L_T}{\partial \theta}(\theta^0)\right)' \sim N(0, \Psi_\theta), \quad \Psi_\theta = \frac{1}{|\Sigma_0|^2}\begin{bmatrix} \sigma_{22}^0|\Sigma_0| & \gamma \\ \gamma & \delta \end{bmatrix}$$

$$\gamma = \sigma_{11}^0 e^{-a_1^0}[\sigma_{22}^0 M_{12}(1,0) - \sigma_{12}^0 M_{22}(1,0)] \tag{6.55}$$

$$+\sigma_{12}^0 e^{-a_1^0}[\sigma_{12}^0 M_{12}(1,0) - \sigma_{22}^0 M_{11}(1,0)]$$

$$\delta = \sigma_{11}^0 e^{-2a_1^0}[\sigma_{11}^0 M_{22}(2,0) - \sigma_{12}^0 M_{12}(2,0)]$$

$$+\sigma_{12}^0 e^{-2a_1^0}[\sigma_{12}^0 M_{11}(2,0) - \sigma_{11}^0 M_{12}(2,0)].$$

Since

$$\left(\frac{\partial L_T}{\partial \theta}(\theta^0)\right)' = -\frac{1}{|S(\theta^0)|}\left(\frac{\partial |S(\theta)|}{\partial \theta}\right) \xrightarrow{P} 0, \tag{6.56}$$

it follows that

$$-\frac{\partial^2 L_T}{\partial \theta \partial \theta} \sim \frac{1}{2|S(\theta)|}\frac{\partial^2 |S(\theta)|}{\partial \theta \partial \theta} \xrightarrow{P} I(\theta^0) \tag{6.57}$$

$$= \frac{1}{|\Sigma_0|}\begin{bmatrix} \sigma_{22}^0 & -\sigma_{12}^0 e^{-a_1^0} M(1,0) \\ -\sigma_{12}^0 e^{-a_1^0} M(1,0)] & e^{-2a_1^0}[\sigma_{11}^0 M(2,0) - M_1^2(1,0)] \end{bmatrix}.$$

From Eqs. (6.55) and (6.57), we conclude that

$$\sqrt{T}(\hat{\theta} - \theta^0) \sim N(0, C_\theta), \quad C_\theta = [I(\theta^0)]^{-1}\Psi_{\theta^0}[I(\theta^0)]^{-1}. \tag{6.58}$$

Case of Normal Errors

When the error process obeys $u \sim N(0, \Sigma_0)$, the necessary condition of Eq. (6.54) becomes

$$\sigma_{11}^0 M_2(1,0) - \sigma_{12}^0 M_1(1,0) = (\sigma_{11}^0 \sigma_{12}^0 - \sigma_{11}^0 \sigma_{12}^0)e^{(1/2)\sigma_{11}^0} = 0,$$

so that the ML estimator, of the parameters in this model, has a normal limiting distribution centered about the true parameter vector. Noting that

σ_0^{ij} is the i,j element of Σ_0^{-1}, the covariance matrix of that distribution is given by C_θ, which may be easily obtained as

$$I(\theta^0) = \frac{1}{|\Sigma_0|} \begin{bmatrix} 1 & 0 \\ 0 & \eta \end{bmatrix} \begin{bmatrix} \sigma_{22}^0 & -\sigma_{12}^0 \\ -\sigma_{21}^0 & \sigma_{11}^0(e^{\sigma_{11}^0} - \sigma_{11}^0) \end{bmatrix} \begin{bmatrix} 1 & 0 \\ 0 & \eta \end{bmatrix}$$

$$= \begin{bmatrix} 1 & 0 \\ 0 & \eta \end{bmatrix} \begin{bmatrix} \sigma_0^{11} & \sigma_0^{12} \\ \sigma_0^{21} & \sigma_0^{22}(e^{\sigma_{11}^0} - \sigma_{11}^0) \end{bmatrix} \begin{bmatrix} 1 & 0 \\ 0 & \eta \end{bmatrix}$$

$$\eta = e^{-a_1^0} e^{(1/2)\sigma_{11}^0}$$

$$\Psi_{\theta^0} = \begin{bmatrix} 1 & 0 \\ 0 & \eta \end{bmatrix} \begin{bmatrix} \sigma_0^{11} & \sigma_0^{12} \\ \sigma_0^{21} & \sigma_0^{22} e^{\sigma_{11}^0} \end{bmatrix} \begin{bmatrix} 1 & 0 \\ 0 & \eta \end{bmatrix}$$

$$= I(\theta^0) + \sigma_0^{22} \sigma_{11}^0 \begin{bmatrix} 1 & 0 \\ 0 & \eta \end{bmatrix} \begin{bmatrix} 1 & 0 \\ 0 & 1 \end{bmatrix} \begin{bmatrix} 1 & 0 \\ 0 & \eta \end{bmatrix}$$

$$C_{\theta^0} = [I(\theta^0)]^{-1} + \sigma_0^{22} \sigma_{11}^0 \begin{bmatrix} 1 & 0 \\ 0 & (1/\eta) \end{bmatrix} \epsilon\epsilon' \begin{bmatrix} 1 & 0 \\ 0 & (1/\eta) \end{bmatrix} \tag{6.59}$$

$$\epsilon \quad \text{is the second column of } \begin{bmatrix} \sigma_0^{11} & \sigma_0^{12} \\ \sigma_0^{21} & \sigma_0^{22}(e^{\sigma_{11}^0} - \sigma_{11}^0) \end{bmatrix}^{-1}.$$

Thus, we conclude that $\sqrt{T}(\hat{\theta} - \theta^0) \sim N(0, C_{\theta^0})$, with C_{θ^0} as defined in Eq. (6.59).

Case of Mixture of Normals

As before, we deal with the special case where the mixing distribution is exponential, with parameter λ. To examine whether this "quasi-ML" estimator has limiting distribution which is normal, and to determine what the latter's parameters are, we recall that the mgf is given by $(1/(1-\xi))$, with $\xi = (1/2)t'\Sigma_0 t$.

$$M(1,0) = \frac{1}{s}, \quad M(2,0) = \frac{1}{1 - 2\sigma_{11}^0}, \quad s = \left(1 - \frac{\sigma_{11}^0}{2}\right),$$

$$M_2(1,0) = \frac{\sigma_{12}^0}{s^2}, \quad M_1(1,0) = \frac{\sigma_{11}^0}{s^2}, \quad M_{11}(1,0) = \frac{\sigma_{11}^0}{s^2} + \frac{2(\sigma_{11}^0)^2}{s^3},$$

$$M_{22}(1,0) = \frac{\sigma_{22}^0}{s^2} + \frac{2(\sigma_{12}^0)^2}{s^3}, \quad M_{12}(1,0) = \frac{\sigma_{12}^0}{s^2} + \frac{2\sigma_{11}^0 \sigma_{12}^0}{s^3},$$

$$M_{11}(2,0) = \frac{\sigma_{11}^0}{(1 - 2\sigma_{11}^0)^2} + \frac{8(\sigma_{11}^0)^2}{(1 - 2\sigma_{11}^0)^3}, \tag{6.60}$$

$$M_{12}(2,0) = \frac{\sigma_{12}^0}{(1 - 2\sigma_{11}^0)^2} + \frac{8\sigma_{11}^0 \sigma_{12}^0}{(1 - 2\sigma_{11}^0)^3}$$

$$M_{22}(2,0) = \frac{\sigma_{22}^0}{(1 - 2\sigma_{11}^0)^2} + \frac{8(\sigma_{12}^0)^2}{(1 - 2\sigma_{11}^0)^3}.$$

Thus, the nas condition for asymptotic normality in Eq. (6.54) becomes, in this case,

$$\sigma_{11}^0 M_2(1,0) - \sigma_{12}^0 M_1(1,0) = \frac{\sigma_{11}^0 \sigma_{12}^0}{s^2} - \frac{\sigma_{11}^0 \sigma_{12}^0}{s^2} = 0,$$

and it is seen that even in this substantially misspecified model the limiting distribution is normal with mean zero. To find out the covariance parameters, we need to determine the expressions for the matrices Ψ_{θ^0} and $I(\theta^0)$, of Eqs. (6.55) and (6.57), respectively. Using the mgf of Eq. (6.46) we easily determine that

$$\gamma = -\frac{e^{-a_1^0}\sigma_{12}^0}{s^2}|\Sigma_0|, \quad \delta = \frac{e^{-2a_1^0}\sigma_{11}^0}{(1 - 2\sigma_{11}^0)^2}|\Sigma_0|, \tag{6.61}$$

so that for this special case, the matrices Ψ_{θ^0}, $I(\theta^0)$ of Eqs. (6.55) and (6.57), respectively, become

$$\Psi_{\theta^0} = \begin{bmatrix} \sigma_0^{11} & (\sigma_0^{12}/s^2)e^{-a_1^0} \\ (\sigma_0^{21}/s^2)e^{-a_1^0} & [\sigma_0^{22}/(1 - 2\sigma_{11}^0)^2]e^{-2a_1^0} \end{bmatrix}, \tag{6.62}$$

and

$$I(\theta^0) = \begin{bmatrix} \sigma_0^{11} & (\sigma_0^{12}e^{-a_1^0}/s) \\ (\sigma_0^{21}e^{-a_1^0}/s) & \sigma_0^{22}e^{-2a_1^0}\left(\frac{1}{1-2\sigma_{11}^0} - \frac{\sigma_{11}^0}{s^4}\right) \end{bmatrix}. \tag{6.63}$$

As is evident from the expressions above, $I(\theta^0) \neq \Psi_{\theta^0}$. To make their similarities and differences more apparent we may rewrite them as

$$\Psi_{\theta^0} = A_1 \begin{bmatrix} \sigma_0^{11} & \sigma_0^{12} \\ \sigma_0^{21} & \sigma_0^{22}\zeta_1 \end{bmatrix} A_1$$

$$I_{\theta^0} = A_2 \begin{bmatrix} \sigma_0^{11} & \sigma_0^{12} \\ \sigma_0^{21} & \sigma_0^{22}\zeta_2 \end{bmatrix} A_2$$

$$A_1 = \begin{bmatrix} 1 & 0 \\ 0 & (e^{-a_1^0}/s^2) \end{bmatrix}, \quad A_2 = \begin{bmatrix} 1 & 0 \\ 0 & (e^{-a_1^0}/s) \end{bmatrix}$$

$$\zeta_1 = \frac{s^4}{(1 - 2\sigma_{11}^0)^2}, \quad \zeta_2 = \frac{s^2}{1 - 2\sigma_{11}^0} - \frac{\sigma_{11}^0}{1 - 2\sigma_{11}^0}. \tag{6.64}$$

Thus, there is no further simplification, and the limiting distribution is given by Eq. (6.58) with $I(\theta^0)$ and Ψ_{θ^0} as in Eq. (6.64).

The result above creates a certain degree of surprise since one "usually" expects in ML problems that the analogs of $I(\theta^0)$ and $\Psi(\theta^0)$ would be equal!

Example 5. In this example we explore the possibility that the phenomenon noted above is due to not knowing the covariance matrix, and if we did the "normal" expectation will hold. The case where Σ_0 is not known was examined earlier, now we examine the case where it is known. Thus, we are dealing with the entities

$$\sqrt{T}\frac{\partial L_T}{\partial \theta}(\theta^0) = -\frac{1}{2}\mathrm{vec}(\Sigma_0^{-1})'\frac{\partial \mathrm{vec}(S)}{\partial \theta}(\theta^0) \tag{6.65}$$

$$= -\frac{1}{\sqrt{T}}\sum_{t=1}^{T}\begin{pmatrix} \sigma_0^{11}u_{t1}+\sigma_0^{12}u_{t2} \\ \sigma_0^{21}u_{t1}y_{t1}+\sigma_0^{22}u_{t2}y_{t1} \end{pmatrix}$$

$$\frac{\partial^2 L_T}{\partial\theta\partial\theta}(\theta^0) = -\frac{1}{2}[\mathrm{vec}(\Sigma_0^{-1})'\otimes I_2]\begin{pmatrix} \frac{\partial^2\mathrm{vec}(S)}{\partial\theta\partial a_1} \\ \frac{\partial^2\mathrm{vec}(S)}{\partial\theta\partial b_1} \end{pmatrix} - \begin{bmatrix} \sigma_0^{11} & \sigma_0^{12}\bar{y}_1 \\ \sigma_0^{21}\bar{y}_1 & \sigma_0^{22}s_{y_1 y_1} \end{bmatrix}.$$

The limiting distribution of the first term is exactly the same as in the previous example; the probability limit of the second expression above, however, obeys

$$\frac{\partial^2 L_T}{\partial\theta\partial\theta}(\theta^0) \xrightarrow{\mathrm{P\ or\ a.c.}} -\begin{bmatrix} \sigma_0^{11} & \sigma_0^{12}e^{-a_1^0}M(1,0) \\ \sigma_0^{21}e^{-a_1^0}M(1,0) & \sigma_0^{22}e^{-2a_1^0}M(2,0) \end{bmatrix} = -I(\theta^0). \tag{6.66}$$

In the case of normal errors, an easy calculation shows that

$$\sqrt{T}(\hat{\theta}-\theta^0) \sim N(0,[I(\theta^0)]^{-1}), \tag{6.67}$$

as one would "normally" expect. Comparing with the next to the last expression in Eq. (6.59), we see that the second term therein is the "price" we pay for not knowing Σ_0. We see, therefore, that in NLSE there is a difference in the limiting distribution of the estimators of the structural parameters depending on whether we do or do not know Σ_0. In the context of the GLM, or the GNLM, however, there is no such difference.

In the case where the errors are a mixture of multivariate normals, the matrix Ψ_{θ^0} remains the same as in Eq. (6.62), but the matrix $I(\theta^0)$, of Eq. (6.63), now becomes

$$I(\theta^0) = \begin{bmatrix} \sigma_0^{11} & (\sigma_0^{12}e^{-a_1^0}/s) \\ (\sigma_0^{21}e^{-a_1^0}/s) & \sigma_0^{22}e^{-2a_1^0}\left(\frac{1}{1-2\sigma_{11}^0}\right) \end{bmatrix}. \tag{6.68}$$

The relationship between the two matrices, Ψ_{θ^0} and $I(\theta^0)$, remains as in Eq. (6.64), except that now we define

$$\zeta_2 = \frac{s^2}{1 - 2\sigma_{11}^0}. \qquad (6.69)$$

Again the covariance matrix of the limiting distribution of the estimator of θ is "smaller" in the case where Σ_0 is known, relative to the case where it is not, in the sense that their difference is at least positive semi-definite. This is in accord with the general intuition that if more valid information is used in estimation, the "efficiency" of the resulting estimators is improved! Still one can think of other contexts in which knowing the covariance matrix parameters does not improve the efficiency of the estimators of other parameters in the model.

6.1.4 Relation of Structural and Covariance Parameter (ML) Estimators

In the discussion of Example 4 we notice, from Eqs. (6.58) and (6.59), that the covariance matrix of the limiting distribution of the estimator of θ is not $[I(\theta^0)]^{-1}$, as one might have expected through intuition carried over from the GLM, and the GNLM. On the other hand, when the covariance matrix is known the familiar result reappears. This raises the question of whether the intuition we carry from such models is based on an incomplete understanding of the conceptual framework, which is sufficiently correct for the GLM and GNLM, but is not appropriate in the context of NLSE. The objective of this section, is to draw attention to certain fundamental aspects of ML theory, similarities and differences between ML and distribution free procedures, as well as between ML estimators in the context of NLSE and other models.

Remark 3. Even though, in Eq. (6.59), we employ the notation $I(\theta^0)$, [11] which suggests the **Fisher information** matrix, we should be careful to point out that, in the discussion leading to Eq. (6.59), $I(\theta^0)$, **denotes neither the information matrix, nor its inverse**. The reader may perhaps be perplexed as to why the matrix $I(\theta^0)$ **is not the information matrix**. Indeed, in a great deal of the literature of econometrics this would appear to be the case.

To illuminate the issues raised in Remark 3, we begin with basic ML theory. It is well established therein that if $L_T(\phi)$ is the (log) likelihood function, the Fisher information matrix, as well as the inverse of the covariance

---

[11] This is often the case with authors who use derivations based on the **concentrated LF**.

matrix of the limiting distribution of the ML estimator of ϕ, is given by

$$I(\phi^0) = -\lim_{T\to\infty} E_{\phi^0}\left(\frac{\partial^2 L_T}{\partial\phi\partial\phi}(\phi^0)\right), \text{ or}$$

$$= \lim_{T\to\infty} E_{\phi^0}\left[\left(\frac{\partial L_T}{\partial\phi}(\phi^0)\right)'\left(\frac{\partial L_T}{\partial\phi}(\phi^0)\right)\right], \text{ or}$$

$$= -\operatorname*{plim}_{T\to\infty}\left(\frac{\partial^2 L_T}{\partial\phi\partial\phi}(\phi^0)\right).$$

We may think of this matrix as a block matrix with blocks I_{ij}, $i, j = 1, 2$, such that (using only the third version above)

$$I_{11}(\phi^0) = -\operatorname*{plim}_{T\to\infty}\left(\frac{\partial^2 L_T}{\partial\theta\partial\theta}(\phi^0)\right), \quad I_{12}(\phi^0) = -\operatorname*{plim}_{T\to\infty}\left(\frac{\partial^2 L_T}{\partial\theta\partial\sigma}(\phi^0)\right)$$

$$I_{22}(\phi^0) = -\operatorname*{plim}_{T\to\infty}\left(\frac{\partial^2 L_T}{\partial\sigma\partial\sigma}(\phi^0)\right), \quad I_{21}(\phi^0) = I_{12}'(\phi^0).$$

The limiting distribution of the ML estimator, say $\hat{\phi}_T$, of ϕ is obtained from the relation

$$\sqrt{T}(\hat{\phi} - \phi^0) = -\left(\frac{\partial^2 L_T}{\partial\phi\partial\phi}(\phi^*)\right)^{-1}\sqrt{T}\frac{\partial L_T}{\partial\phi}(\phi^0),$$

$|\phi^* - \phi^0| \le |\hat{\phi} - \phi^0|$. In the preceding, as in all discussion in this chapter, we take θ to correspond to the **structural parameters**, and σ to correspond to the **covariance parameters**. Now, if we are interested in the structural parameters **alone**, we can obtain their marginal distribution from the joint distribution of the ML estimator above. It is an elementary property of normal distributions that the marginal distribution in question is **also normal**, more precisely

$$\sqrt{T}(\hat{\theta} - \theta^0) \sim N(0, [I_{11} - I_{12}I_{22}^{-1}I_{21}]^{-1}).$$

Next, note that we may obtain an estimate of the structural parameters, either by solving for the entire set of parameters and confining our attention to the subset of interest, which is, implicitly, what we did above, **or we can concentrate the LF** by first maximizing with respect to Σ, inserting the maximizing value in the LF, and maximizing the concentrated LF with respect to θ. It is intuitively clear that the two approaches yield the same result. Thus, whatever method is employed, the ML estimator of θ would have the same limiting distribution, which was easily obtained above from the limiting distribution of $\hat{\phi}_T$.

On the other hand if one considers the GLM either with i.i.d. errors, or autocorrelated errors, or the GNLM, it would appear that the covariance matrix of the limiting distribution of the structural parameters is the equivalent of $I_{11}^{-1}(\theta^0)$, and this is true whether the variance or covariance parameters are known a priori or are estimated. For example, in the GLM $y = X\beta + u$, under normality and the standard assumptions we have, asymptotically,

$$\sqrt{T}(\hat{\beta} - \beta_0) \sim N(0, [I_{11}(\phi^0)]^{-1}),$$

where $\phi = (\beta', \sigma^2)'$ and

$$I_{11}(\phi^0) = -\plim_{T\to\infty} \left(\frac{\partial^2 L_T}{\partial\theta\partial\theta}(\phi^0) \right) = \frac{1}{\sigma_0^2} M_{xx}$$

$$I_{12}(\phi^0) = -\plim_{T\to\infty} \left(\frac{\partial^2 L_T}{\partial\theta\partial\sigma^2}(\phi^0) \right) = \plim_{T\to\infty} \left(\frac{1}{T\sigma^4} \right) u'X = 0,$$

$$I_{22}(\phi^0) = -\plim_{T\to\infty} \left(\frac{\partial^2 L_T}{\partial\sigma^2\partial\sigma^2}(\phi^0) \right) = \frac{1}{2\sigma^4}, \quad I_{21}(\phi^0) = I_{12}'(\phi^0).$$

For a system of GLM, [12] say, $Y = XB + U$, with covariance matrix Σ_0, where restrictions may be imposed on B, so that not all variables appear in all equations, say $\operatorname{vec}(B) = L^*\beta$ for an appropriate selection matrix, L^*, we similarly obtain

$$I_{11}(\phi^0) = -\plim_{T\to\infty} \left(\frac{\partial^2 L_T}{\partial\beta\partial\beta}(\phi^0) \right) = L^{*'}[\Sigma_0^{-1} \otimes M_{xx}]L^*$$

$$I_{12}(\phi^0) = -\plim_{T\to\infty} \left(\frac{\partial^2 L_T}{\partial\beta\partial\sigma}(\phi^0) \right) = \plim_{T\to\infty} L^{*'} \left[I \otimes \left(\frac{X'U}{T} \right) \right]$$

$$\times (\Sigma_0^{-1} \otimes \Sigma_0^{-1}) = 0,$$

$$I_{22}(\phi^0) = -\plim_{T\to\infty} \left(\frac{\partial^2 L_T}{\partial\sigma\partial\sigma}(\phi^0) \right) = \frac{1}{2}(\Sigma_0^{-1} \otimes \Sigma_0^{-1}), \quad I_{21}(\phi^0) = I_{12}'(\phi^0).$$

In the relations above, convergence may be a.c., depending on the underlying assumptions. In any event, $I_{12}(\phi^0) = 0$, and this remains true whether Σ_0 is known a priori, or is concurrently estimated. As for the GNLM, we note from the discussion of Chapter 5 (Sections 5.9 and 5.10), that again whether the covariance matrix Σ_0 is known or not, has no effect on the limiting distribution of the structural parameters.

---

[12] This is the so called seemingly unrelated regressions (SUR) model.

Let us now take up the issue of the GLSEM and examine whether knowing the covariance matrix Σ_0 has any effect on the limiting distribution of $\sqrt{T}(\hat{\delta} - \delta_0)_{FIML}$; a casual reading of the discussion in Chapter 4 might suggest that the answer is negative, since the limiting distribution $\sqrt{T}(\hat{\delta} - \delta_0)_{FIML}$ is the same as that of $\sqrt{T}(\hat{\delta} - \delta_0)_{3SLS}$. In fact, this is not generally true, and the limiting distribution of the ML estimator of the structural parameters does depend on what is known about Σ_0. This aspect was the subject of a paper in the early sixties, Rothenberg and Leenders (1964), who basically investigated the consequences of knowing that Σ is diagonal. Their findings were presented as an isolated result and it is fair to say that over the years it has not received the attention it deserved. Here we shall examine how knowledge of Σ_0 affects the properties of the ML estimator of the structural parameter vector, δ. We may write the LF, in the notation of Chapter 3, as

$$L_T(\delta, \sigma) = -\frac{m}{2}\ln(2\pi) + \frac{1}{2}\ln|B^{*'}WB^*| - \frac{1}{2}\ln|\Sigma| - \frac{1}{2}\mathrm{tr}\Sigma^{-1}A'MA,$$

$$P = B^{*'}WB^*, \quad W = \frac{1}{T}(Y'NY), \quad N = I - X(X'X)^{-1}X'. \ (6.70)$$

Recalling that

$$\frac{\partial \mathrm{vec}(A)}{\partial \delta} = -L, \quad \frac{\partial \mathrm{vec}(B^*)}{\partial \delta} = -(I \otimes I^*)L, \quad I^* = (I_m, 0_{m \times G}),$$

we obtain,

$$\left(\frac{\partial L_T}{\partial \delta}\right)' = -L'(I \otimes I^{*'})\mathrm{vec}(WB^*P^{-1}) + L'\mathrm{vec}(MA\Sigma^{-1})$$

$$\left(\frac{\partial L_T}{\partial \sigma}\right)' = \frac{1}{2}\left(\mathrm{vec}(\Sigma^{-1}A'MA\Sigma^{-1}) - \mathrm{vec}(A'MA)\right).$$

We also establish that

$$\hat{I}_{11} = -\frac{\partial^2 L_T}{\partial \delta \partial \delta} = -L'(P^{-1} \otimes I^{*'}WI^*)L + L'(\Sigma^{-1} \otimes M)L$$

$$+ 2L'(P^{-1} \otimes I^{*'}WB^*P^{-1}B^{*'}WI^*)L$$

$$\hat{I}_{12} = -\frac{\partial^2 L_T}{\partial \delta \partial \sigma} = L'(I \otimes MA)(\Sigma^{-1} \otimes \Sigma^{-1}), \quad \hat{I}_{21} = (\hat{I}_{12})'$$

$$\hat{I}_{22} = -\frac{\partial^2 L_T}{\partial \sigma \partial \sigma} = -\frac{1}{2}\left[I - 2(I \otimes \Sigma^{-1}A'MA)\right](\Sigma^{-1} \otimes \Sigma^{-1}).$$

It is apparent that

$$\hat{I}_{11}(\phi^0) \xrightarrow{\text{P or a.c.}} L'\left[(\Sigma_0^{-1} \otimes (\Pi_0, I)'M_{xx}(\Pi_0, I)\right]L + 2L'\left[\Sigma_0^{-1} \otimes \Omega_0^*\right]L,$$

$$\hat{I}_{12}(\phi^0) \overset{\text{P or a.c.}}{\longrightarrow} L'(\Sigma^{-1} \otimes I^{*'}B^{*'-1}), \quad \hat{I}_{21} \overset{\text{a.c. or P}}{\longrightarrow} (\Sigma^{-1} \otimes B^{*-1}I^{*})L$$

$$\hat{I}_{22}(\phi^0) \overset{\text{P or a.c.}}{\longrightarrow} \frac{1}{2}(\Sigma^{-1} \otimes \Sigma^{-1}), \quad \Omega_0^{*} = I^{*'}\Omega_0 I^{*}.$$

We shall denote the limits of the entities on the left of the relations above by $I_{ij}(\phi^0)$. Since by normality fourth order moments exist (in fact all higher even moments are finite and all odd moments are null), applying one of the standard CLT we find

$$C_{11} = L'[\Sigma^{-1} \otimes (\Pi_0, I)' M_{xx}(\Pi_0, I)]L + 2L'(\Sigma^{-1} \otimes \Omega_0^{*})L$$

$$C_{12} = L'(\Sigma^{-1} \otimes I^{*'}B^{*'-1}), \quad C_{21} = C_{12}'$$

$$C_{22} = \frac{1}{2}(\Sigma^{-1} \otimes \Sigma^{-1}), \quad C = \begin{bmatrix} C_{11} & C_{12} \\ C_{21} & C_{22} \end{bmatrix}$$

$$\sqrt{T}\left(\frac{\partial L_T}{\partial \phi}(\phi^0)\right) \overset{\text{d}}{\to} N(0, C),$$

and consequently

$$\sqrt{T}(\hat{\phi} - \phi^0) \overset{\text{d}}{\to} N(0, C^{-1}).$$

A crucial difference in this result as compared to that in the GLM, SUR, or the GNLM is that the block element $C_{12} = I_{12}(\phi^0)$ is not null.

From standard normal theory we find that the marginal distribution of the ML estimator of δ is given by

$$\sqrt{T}(\hat{\delta} - \delta_0) \overset{\text{d}}{\to} N(0, C^{*-1}),$$

where

$$C^{*-1} = (C_{11} - C_{12}C_{22}^{-1}C_{21})^{-1} = \{L'[\Sigma^{-1} \otimes (\Pi, I)' M_{xx}(\Pi, I)]L\}^{-1},$$

in view of the fact that $-C_{12}C_{22}^{-1}C_{21} = -2L'(\Sigma^{-1} \otimes \Omega_0^{*})L$.

Now, what would happen if the covariance matrix were known? First, we would not need to estimate it; thus, we would have no need for the derivatives

$$\frac{\partial L_T}{\partial \sigma}, \quad \frac{\partial^2 L_T}{\partial \delta \partial \sigma}, \quad \frac{\partial^2 L_T}{\partial \sigma \partial \sigma}.$$

Second, the derivative $\partial L_T/\partial \delta$, and the entity $I_{11}(\phi^0)$ will remain the same as before. Consequently,

$$\sqrt{T}\left(\frac{\partial L_T}{\partial \delta}(\phi^0)\right)' \overset{\text{d}}{\to} N(0, C_{11})$$

$$\sqrt{T}(\hat{\delta} - \delta_0)_{ML} \overset{\text{d}}{\to} N(0, C_{11}^{-1}),$$

since, from the results above $I_{11}(\phi^0) = C_{11}$. Comparing the two covariance matrices, it is easily established that

$$C_{11} - C^* \geq 0, \quad \text{and hence that } C^{*-1} - C_{11}^{-1} \geq 0,$$

showing that the efficiency of the ML estimator of δ is improved if the covariance matrix Σ_0 is known. One may prove a similar result if there are valid restrictions on Σ_0 and are imposed in the estimation process. The same, however, cannot be said, in either case, for the 3SLS estimator. We may remind the reader that the latter depends only on a prior consistent estimator of Σ_0, and no matter what is the nature of its elements, the consistent estimator will converge to Σ_0; thus, imposing any restrictions on the consistent estimator can at best have a small sample, not an asymptotic, effect.

Remark 4. The preceding discussion has settled the formalities as to why, in the context of ML estimation, knowing something about the covariance matrix may improve the efficiency of other (structural) parameter estimators. However, it has not given us any intuitive principle by which we can judge as to when an improvement will or will not occur. This intuitive principle is easily supplied by the observation that in the (multivariate) normal the mean, μ, and the covariance matrix, Σ, are independent parameters and their respective estimators are mutually independent as well. Thus, in models where there is a **rigid separation between mean and covariance parameters** no improvement will occur if we know (all or something of) the covariance matrix; in models where some parameters are both mean **and** covariance parameters we would expect improvement. All the results that occasioned some "concern" can be "explained" by this principle, without having to calculate $I_{12}(\phi^0)$ which is often cumbersome to obtain. Thus, in the GLM σ^2 and β are distinctly covariance and mean parameters respectively. In the SUR model Σ and β are distinctly covariance and mean parameters as well. Similarly, in the discussion of the GNLM in Section 5.9, it is clear that what we termed there ϕ and Σ are distinctively mean and covariance parameters respectively. But what about the GLSEM? It would appear that there too, Σ and δ are distinctly covariance and mean parameters! Unfortunately, this is a false perception since the probability characteristics of the GLSEM **are uniquely** determined by its likelihood function, and the latter is uniquely determined by the reduced form parameters, $\Pi = CB^{*-1}$ and $\Omega = B^{*-1}\Sigma B^{*-1}$. Since the parameters of intestest to us are B^*, C, Σ, we see that one of them, B^*, is **both a mean and covariance parameter**. Thus, mean and covariance parameters are mixed up and what we know about Σ may well affect how we perceive B^*.

The preceding also shows that ML is a far more "sophisticated" estimator than is 3SLS; this should be borne in mind when dealing with the GNLSEM with additive errors, in which mean and variance parameters are "mixed up", as in the case of the GLSEM. Before the reader dismisses 3SLS, we ought to point out that the ML estimator is vulnerable, since its "sophistication" depends on the **truth** of the assertion that the structural errors are jointly normal; 3SLS, on the other hand, does not depend on such specific distributional assumptions.

6.1.5 *Estimators in Structurally Misspecified Models*

In this section we consider the true model to be

$$a_1^0 + a_2^0 x_t + \ln y_{t1} = u_{t1}, \quad b_1^0 y_{t1} + y_{t2} = u_{t2}, \tag{6.71}$$

where, for clarity, we have added the superscript, 0, in order to distinguish the true model from the one we specify for estimation; the latter is the one we employed in the previous examples.

It is clear that the resulting "quasi"-ML or, more appropriately, pseudo-ML estimators would be **inconsistent**. The objective here is to determine, if possible, the inconsistency involved, and the limiting distribution of the properly centered pseudo-ML estimators. It is also evident that even though we deal with a specific small model, the procedure we shall develop is of general applicability.

All steps taken in the arguments of Examples 1, 2 and 3 remain valid up to the point of arguing about the consistency and limiting distribution of the resulting estimators. Since our "working" model is given by Eq. (6.8), rather than Eq. (6.71), the "LF" is given by Eq. (6.11), and the function to be minimized is given by Eq. (6.13). To determine the inconsistency involved we have two options: First, we can find the (a.c.) limit of the function H_T, as in Eq. (6.14), and then obtain the values of a_1 and b_1 that correspond to the **global minimum** of that function. This, however, is a most cumbersome approach since we do not necessarily know, in the face of misspecification, that the function K, employed extensively in the examples above, is necessarily a contrast function (in fact it is not), or that it is nonnegative and, most cumbersome of all, finding its global minimum is inordinately difficult.

Second, we may proceed to Eq. (6.50) and see how misspecification intrudes in the derivation of the limiting distribution of the pseudo-estimators. If we follow this approach, the use of the function H_T is completely superfluous; thus, we revert to the "LF". Partially maximizing with respect to Σ, we find

$$\Sigma = S(\theta), \quad L_T(\theta) = -[\ln(2\pi) + 1] - \frac{1}{2}\ln|S(\theta)| - \frac{1}{T}\sum_{t=1}^{T} \ln y_{t1},$$

where L_T is the concentrated "LF". Differentiating with respect to $\theta =$

$(a_1, b_1)'$, yields

$$\left(\frac{\partial L_T}{\partial \theta}\right)' = -\frac{1}{2|S(\theta)|}\left(\begin{array}{c} s_{22}(a_1 + \overline{\ln y_1}) - s_{21}(b_1\bar{y}_1 + \bar{y}_2) \\ s_{11}(b_1 s_{y_1 y_1} + s_{y_1 y_2}) - s_{12}(a_1\bar{y}_1 + s_{y_1 \ln y_1}) \end{array}\right);$$

the equations above are to be solved, to obtain the pseudo-ML estimator, say $\hat{\theta}$; the equations in question are nonlinear in the unknown parameters, and the solution can be obtained only by iteration. If we now proceed as in Eq. (6.50) we have a problem; the mean value theorem we had applied therein "works" because the ML estimator is consistent. Thus, we have the assurance that when we evaluate the Hessian of the LF at a point, say θ^* , **intermediate** between $\hat{\theta}$ and θ^0 , the Hessian so evaluated converges, at least in probability, to the (negative of the inverse of the) Fisher information matrix, evaluated at the true parameter point. Since here we are dealing with an **inconsistent estimator**, the same approach will not lead to the solution we seek. In misspecified models, the analog of expanding the gradient of the LF about the true parameter point in correctly specified models, is to expand about the **probability limit of the pseudo-ML estimator**. Thus, let $\bar{\theta}^* = \theta^0 + \bar{\theta}$ be this probability limit, and consider the expansion [13]

$$\frac{\partial L_T}{\partial \theta}(\hat{\theta}) = \frac{\partial L_T}{\partial \theta}(\bar{\theta}^*) + \frac{\partial^2 L_T}{\partial \theta \partial \theta}(\theta^{**})(\hat{\theta} - \theta^0 - \bar{\theta}), \tag{6.72}$$

where $|\theta^{**} - \bar{\theta}^*| \leq |\hat{\theta} - \bar{\theta}^*|$. It is clear that the Hessian in Eq. (6.72) converges, at least in probability, to the limit of the expectation of the Hessian evaluated at $\bar{\theta}^*$, which is a well defined entity. Moreover, rewriting Eq. (6.67), we have

$$\sqrt{T}(\hat{\theta} - \theta^0 - \bar{\theta}) = -\left(\frac{\partial^2 L_T}{\partial \theta \partial \theta}(\theta^{**})\right)^{-1}\sqrt{T}\frac{\partial L_T}{\partial \theta}(\bar{\theta}^*). \tag{6.73}$$

The equation above displays the nature of the problem in misspecified models as being essentially similar to that in correctly specified models. The major difference is simply the point at which the mean value theorem expansion takes place. If

$$L_T(\theta) \overset{\text{a.c.}}{\to} \bar{L}^*(\theta),$$

uniformly in θ , it follows – see the discussion in Chapter 5 relating to MC estimators – that

$$\sup_{\theta \in \Theta} L_T(\theta) \overset{\text{a.c.}}{\to} \sup_{\theta \in \Theta} \bar{L}^*(\theta).$$

---

[13] When we use the notation θ^0 , in this context, we mean the restriction of the true parameter point to those parameters that actually appear in the model, and we exclude those that correspond to omitted variables.

Since we operate on the assertion that the global maximum can be found by differentiation, by assuming that θ^0 is an interior point of Θ,[14] it follows that

$$\frac{\partial \bar{L}^*}{\partial \theta}(\bar{\theta}^*) = 0, \quad \text{and moreover} \quad \frac{\partial L_T^*}{\partial \theta}(\bar{\theta}^*) \overset{\text{a.c.}}{\to} 0. \tag{6.74}$$

It remains now to find the probability limit of the Hessian, evaluated at $\bar{\theta}^*$ and the limiting distribution of the vector in the right member of Eq. (6.73). We note, however, that the exact derivation of the limit of the Hessian is unnecessary, since the latter can be consistently estimated, as simply the Hessian evaluated at the pseudo-ML estimate! Next, we deal with the limiting distribution of the vector, where

$$\sqrt{T}\left(\frac{\partial L_T}{\partial \theta}(\bar{\theta}^*)\right)' \sim -\frac{\sqrt{T}}{|\bar{S}(\bar{\theta}^*)|}\frac{1}{T}\sum_{t=1}^{T}\left[\begin{pmatrix} \bar{s}_{22} & -\bar{s}_{21} \\ -\bar{s}_{12}y_{t1} & \bar{s}_{11}y_{t1} \end{pmatrix}\begin{pmatrix} \bar{a}_1^* + \ln y_{t1} \\ \bar{b}_1^* y_{t1} + y_{t2} \end{pmatrix}\right]$$

$$\sim -S_1\frac{\sqrt{T}}{T}\sum_{t=1}^{T}\zeta_{t\cdot}', \tag{6.75}$$

where

$$S_1 = \frac{1}{|\bar{S}(\bar{\theta}^*)|}\begin{pmatrix} \bar{s}_{22} & -\bar{s}_{21} & 0 & 0 \\ 0 & 0 & -\bar{s}_{12} & \bar{s}_{11} \end{pmatrix} = \begin{pmatrix} \bar{s}^{11} & \bar{s}^{12} & 0 & 0 \\ 0 & 0 & \bar{s}^{21} & \bar{s}^{22} \end{pmatrix}$$

$$\zeta_{t\cdot}' = \begin{pmatrix} \bar{a}_1^* + \ln y_{t1} \\ \bar{b}_1^* y_{t1} + y_{t2} \\ \bar{a}_1^* y_{t1} + y_{t1}\ln y_{t1} \\ \bar{b}_1^* y_{t1}^2 + y_{t1}y_{t2} \end{pmatrix}, \quad \bar{\theta}^* = (\bar{a}_1^*, \bar{b}_1^*)',$$

$$S(\bar{\theta}^*) \overset{\text{a.c.}}{\to} \bar{S}(\bar{\theta}^*), \quad \overline{\ln y}_1 = \frac{1}{T}\sum_{t=1}^{T}\ln y_{t1}, \quad \bar{y}_i = \frac{1}{T}\sum_{t=1}^{T}y_{ti},$$

$$s_{y_i \ln y_1} = \frac{1}{T}\sum_{t=1}^{T}y_{ti}\ln y_{t1}, \quad s_{y_i y_j} = \frac{1}{T}\sum_{t=1}^{T}y_{ti}y_{tj}, \quad i = 1, 2,$$

and $\bar{s}_{ij}$ is the i, j element of $\bar{S}(\bar{\theta}^*)$. By construction, the right member of Eq. (6.75) represents the (asymptotic equivalent of the) gradient of the pseudo LF as proportional to a linear transformation of $(1/\sqrt{T})\sum_{t=1}^{T}\zeta_{t\cdot}'$, the latter being a sequence of independent random vectors, which on the surface do not appear to have mean zero. On the other hand, from Eq.

---

[14] Actually, to this we must add uniqueness of the global maximum.

(6.74), we find that

$$0 = \frac{\partial \bar{L}^*}{\partial \theta}(\bar{\theta}^*) = -S_1 \lim_{T \to \infty} \frac{1}{T} \sum_{t=1}^{T} E(\zeta'_{t\cdot}). \tag{6.76}$$

Since the series of Eq. (6.76) converges, it follows that the tail vanishes. [15] Consequently, we may write the second representation of Eq. (6.75) as

$$\sqrt{T}\frac{\partial L_T}{\partial \theta}(\bar{\theta}^*) \sim -\frac{1}{T} \sum_{t=1}^{T} \left(\zeta'_{t\cdot} - E(\zeta'_{t\cdot}) \right) = \sqrt{T}S_1 \frac{1}{T} \sum_{t=1}^{T} \xi'_{t\cdot},$$

$$\xi'_{t\cdot} = \zeta'_{t\cdot} - E(\zeta'_{t\cdot}), \tag{6.77}$$

$$\xi'_{t\cdot} = \begin{bmatrix} u_{t1} \\ u_{t2} + (\bar{b}_1^* - b_1^0)e^{-a_1^0}\nu_{0t}[e^{u_{t1}} - M(1,0)] \\ [(\bar{a}_1^* - a_1^0)\nu_{0t} - a_2^0\nu_{1t}]e^{-a_1^0}[e^{u_{t1}} - M(1,0)] \\ (\bar{b}_1^* - b_1^0)e^{-2a_1^0}\nu_{2t}[e^{2u_{t1}} - M(2,0)] \end{bmatrix}$$

$$+ \begin{bmatrix} 0 \\ 0 \\ e^{-a_1^0}\nu_{0t}[u_{t1}e^{u_{t1}} - M_1(1,0)] \\ e^{-a_1^0}\nu_{0t}[u_{t2}e^{u_{t1}} - M_2(1,0)] \end{bmatrix}$$

$$\nu_{0t} = e^{-a_2^0 x_t}, \qquad \nu_{1t} = x_t e^{-a_2^0 x_t}, \qquad \nu_{2t} = e^{-2a_2^0 x_t}$$

$$\nu_{3t} = x_t e^{-2a_2^0 x_t}, \qquad \nu_{4t} = x_t^2 e^{-2a_2^0 x_t}, \qquad \nu_{5t} = e^{-3a_2^0 x_t},$$

$$\nu_{6t} = x_t^2 e^{-3a_2^0 x_t}, \qquad \nu_{kt} = e^{-(k-3)a_2^0 x_t} \quad k \geq 7. \tag{6.78}$$

It may be verified that the $\xi_{t\cdot}$, $t \geq 1$ are a sequence of independent random vectors with mean zero and a finite covariance matrix, Ξ_t; moreover, they obey the Lindeberg condition, provided

$$\lim_{T \to \infty} \frac{1}{T} \sum_{t=1}^{T} \nu_{kt} = \nu_k, \tag{6.79}$$

are finite entities, for as many k as the problem requires. [16] With this

---

[15] Note, in addition, that not only

$$\frac{\partial L_T}{\partial \theta}(\hat{\theta}) = 0, \quad \text{but also} \quad T\frac{\partial L_T}{\partial \theta}(\hat{\theta}) = 0,$$

i.e. it is not division by T that renders the entity small.
[16] In this problem we require that, at least, $k = 7$.

proviso, we conclude that

$$\sqrt{T}(\hat{\theta} - \theta^0 - \bar{\theta}) \sim N(0, \Psi), \quad \Psi = \begin{bmatrix} \psi_{11} & \psi_{12} \\ \psi_{21} & \psi_{22} \end{bmatrix} \tag{6.80}$$

$$\psi_{11} = (\bar{s}^{11}, \bar{s}^{12})\Xi_{(1)}(\bar{s}^{11}, \bar{s}^{12})',$$

$$\psi_{12} = (\bar{s}^{11}, \bar{s}^{12})\Xi_{(2)}(\bar{s}^{21}, \bar{s}^{22})'(= \psi_{21})$$

$$\psi_{22} = (\bar{s}^{21}, \bar{s}^{22})\Xi_{(3)}(\bar{s}^{21}, \bar{s}^{22})' \tag{6.81}$$

$$\Xi = \begin{bmatrix} \Xi_{(1)} & \Xi_{(2)} \\ \Xi'_{(2)} & \Xi_{(3)} \end{bmatrix} = \lim_{T\to\infty} \sum_{t=1}^{T} \mathrm{Cov}(\xi'_{t\cdot}) = \lim_{T\to\infty} \sum_{t=1}^{T} \Xi_t.$$

Consequently,

$$\sqrt{T}(\hat{\theta} - \bar{\theta}^*) \sim N[0, I^{*-1}(\bar{\theta}^*)\Psi_{\bar{\theta}^*}I^{*-1}(\bar{\theta}^*)], \quad I^*(\bar{\theta}^*) = \operatorname*{plim}_{T\to\infty} \frac{\partial^2 L_T}{\partial\theta\partial\theta}(\bar{\theta}^*).$$

Remark 5. The practical significance of the result above is rather limited; on the other hand, it allows us to gain an insight into the consequences of misspecification in the GNLSEM. With a number of assumptions, regarding the magnitude of the ν's and the coefficients of omitted variables, we might even produce an approximation to the proper covariance matrix of estimators in misspecified models. This may be of some help in assessing the sensitivity to misspecification of test of significance results.

6.2   Nonlinear 2SLS

In this section we consider the application of 2SLS techniques to nonlinear models. It is always rather difficult to extend methods developed for linear models to a nonlinear context. It is also the case that least squares is an approach that "mimics" ML procedures, when the distribution of the errors is jointly normal. Similarly, in a nonlinear context, it may be thought that if we know the LF we can determine the function to the minimized in the context of NLLS. This was, indeed, the approach we followed, implicitly, when we dealt with the GNLM. In the simultaneous equations context, however, the problem is far more complex, and the transition from ML to least squares-like procedures is not so straightforward. How one makes this transition depends on how one views the fundamental nature of 2SLS and 3SLS. Precisely, is their fundamental nature that suggested first by Theil (1953) and exposited in the first chapter, or is it what we have called, also in Chapter 1, the **canonical structural form**, and first introduced into the literature by Dhrymes (1969), (1970). If we take the first point of view, the appropriate generalization in the context of the GNLSEM is to estimate the reduced form, thus obtaining the entities $\hat{y}_{t\cdot}$, and thereafter to substitute these for the variables $y_{t\cdot}$, whenever they appear as "explanatory" variables. The procedure is then completed by performing **nonlinear least squares**, or linear least squares, as the occasion requires. This is the approach taken by Goldfeld and Quandt (1965), (1972), Kalejian (1971), and several other authors. Unfortunately, this approach has not yielded very fruitful results. If we take the second point of view we note, at the risk of being rather repetitive, that the GNLSEM is given by [17]

$$y_{t\cdot} = g_{t\cdot}(y_{t\cdot}, x_{t\cdot}; \theta) + u_{t\cdot}, \quad g_{t\cdot} = (g_{t1}, g_{t2}, \ldots, g_{tm}), \quad t = 1, 2, \ldots, T,$$

which was first introduced in Eq. (6.2), it being understood that $\{u'_{t\cdot} : t \geq 1\}$ is a sequence of i.i.d. random vectors with mean zero and covariance matrix $\Sigma > 0$. The observations on the entire system may be represented as

$$Y = G(\theta) + U, \quad Y = (y_{t\cdot}),$$

$$G(\theta) = [g_{t\cdot}(\theta)], \quad U = (u_{t\cdot}), \quad t = 1, 2, \ldots, T, \text{ while}$$

$$y_{\cdot i} = g_{\cdot i}(Y, X; \theta) + u_{\cdot i}, \quad i = 1, 2, \ldots, m, \tag{6.82}$$

represents the (T) observations on the ith equation of the system; needless to say, not all dependent variables (columns of Y), and not all predetermined variables (columns of X), nor all elements of the unknown vector of parameters, θ, need appear in all equations. For clarity of exposition, when the occasion arises we shall denote those that are not excluded through prior restrictions by Y_i, X_i, and $\theta_{\cdot i}$, respectively.

The method of nonlinear 2SLS that appears most commonly in the literature is a derivative of that given in Dhrymes (1969), as cited above. To achieve maximal correspondence with the discussion in Chapter 1, let the vector of unknown parameters in the ith equation, $\theta_{\cdot i}$, have $k_i = m_i + G_i$ elements, and let W_i be (at least) a $T \times k_i$ (of rank k_i) matrix of "instruments". The term "instruments" is perhaps inappropriate here in that we are not about to obtain the usual IV estimator; all that is meant by this term, for the moment, is that $(\sum_{t=1}^{T} w_{t\cdot}^{(i)'} u_{ti}/T)$ converges to zero, at least in probability, and $\sqrt{T}$ times that entity admits of a CLT.

---

[17] Actually, as pointed out at the beginning of the chapter, this model is not really a **general model**; it is best termed the GNLSEM **with additive errors**. In particular, the examples we considered in the previous section are not special cases of this model, in that the error term in the first equation of these examples is **multiplicative**. However, nearly all literature on nonlinear 2SLS and 3SLS refers to the GNLSEM with additive errors.

The model of Eq. (6.82) will be our reference point, subject to the usual assumptions regarding the exogenous component, $p_t.$, of the predetermined vector $x_t. = (y_{t-1.}, y_{t-2.}, \ldots, y_{t-k.}, p_t.)$. The motivation for the canonical structural form approach is to make the simultaneous equations model conform to the requirements of the GLM as closely as possible, at least asymptotically. Following this approach, in the current context, let R_i be a nonsingular (square) matrix of dimension (at least) k_i , such that

$$W_i' W_i = R_i R_i' \tag{6.83}$$

and consider the transformation

$$y_{.i}^* = h_{.i} + r_{.i}, \quad y_{.i}^* = R_i^{-1} W_i' y_{.i}, \quad i = 1, 2, \ldots, m,$$
$$h_{.i} = R_i^{-1} W_i' g_{.i}(Y_i, X_i; \theta_{.i}), \quad r_{.i} = R_i^{-1} W_i' u_{.i}. \tag{6.84}$$

The NL2SLS estimator of the unknown parameter $\theta_{.i}$, introduced in the literature by Amemiya (1974), is simply the (nonlinear) least squares estimator of that parameter, in the context of the model as exhibited in Eq. (6.84). More specifically minimizing, with respect to $\theta_{.i}$, the function

$$S_{Ti}(\theta) = \frac{1}{2T} (y_{.i}^* - h_{.i})' (y_{.i}^* - h_{.i}) = \frac{1}{2T} (y_{.i} - g_{.i})' W_i (W_i' W_i)^{-1} W_i' (y_{.i} - g_{.i}),$$

we obtain the NL2SLS estimator, say $\hat{\theta}_{.i}$ as

$$S_{Ti}(\hat{\theta}) = \inf_{\theta_{.i} \in \Theta} S_{Ti}(\theta_{.i}). \tag{6.85}$$

Thus, in principle, all of the results in Chapter 5 are applicable, *mutatis mutandis*, to the context of this discussion.

6.2.1 Identification and Consistency of NL2SLS

It would be futile to attempt to characterize identification here in the same manner as is done for the GLSEM; although it is a **necessary** condition that none of the equations of the GNLSEM be equivalent to a linear combination of other structural equations, it is clearly not a sufficient one. By far, the most essential character of identification in this context is that the limit of S_{Ti} , whether in probability, a.c., or in quadratic mean be a **contrast function**, i.e. be nonnegative and assume its global minimum (i.e. zero) if and only if $\theta_{.i} = \theta_{.i}^0$.

Let us now formalize this discussion; first, suppose

$$S_{Ti}(\theta) = \frac{1}{2T} \left[\frac{(y_{.i} - g_{.i})' W_i}{T} \left(\frac{W_i' W_i}{T} \right)^{-1} \frac{W_i' (y_{.i} - g_{.i})}{T} \right] \overset{\text{a.c. or P}}{\to} K_i(\theta_{.i}, \theta_{.i}^0).$$

For the limit above to be well defined, we require of the matrix W_i

(A.1) $\text{rank}(W_i) = k_i, \quad (W_i'W_i/T) \overset{\text{a.c.}}{\to} M_{ii} > 0$,

in an appropriate mode.[18] Second, if the convergence above is taken as given, how do we define identification for the ith equation? Assuming, in addition to (A.1),

(A.2) $S_{Ti}(\theta) \overset{\text{a.c. or P}}{\longrightarrow} K_i(\theta_{\cdot i}, \theta_{\cdot i}^0)$, uniformly in Θ;

(A.3) $K_i(\theta_{\cdot i}, \theta_{\cdot i}^0) \geq 0$, and $K_i(\theta_{\cdot i}^{(1)}, \theta_{\cdot i}^0) = K_i(\theta_{\cdot i}^{(2)}, \theta_{\cdot i}^0)$,
    if and only if $\theta_{\cdot i}^{(1)} = \theta_{\cdot i}^{(2)}$.

we see that the (P or a.c.) limit of S_{Ti} is a **contrast function**; thus, if the conditions above hold, the NL2SLS estimator is a **minimum contrast estimator**. By Propositions 3, 4, and Corollary 1 of Chapter 5, we may conclude, therefore, that this estimator converges **a.c. or P** to the true parameter vector, according as S_{Ti} converges to K_i a.c. or P. Finally, we come to the ultimate question: what must be true about the structural error process, i.e. the vector sequence $u_{\cdot i}$, and the vector sequence $g_{\cdot i}$ for the consistency and identification results above to hold? From the definition of the function K_i we see that we require the existence of the limits of

$$(W_i'u_{\cdot i}/T), \quad (W_i'g_{\cdot i}/T), \tag{6.86}$$

in one mode of convergence or another. We require, therefore the assumptions

(A.4) $(W_i'g_{\cdot i}/T) \overset{\text{a.c. or P}}{\longrightarrow} f_{\cdot i}(\theta_{\cdot i}, \theta_{\cdot i}^0)$ uniformly for $\theta \in \Theta$;

(A.5) $(W_i'u_{\cdot i}/T) \overset{\text{P or a.c.}}{\longrightarrow} 0$, as well as the technical assumption

(A.6) the admissible parameter space Θ is compact, and the true parameter point, $\theta_{\cdot i}^0$, is an **interior point** of Θ.

Note that in the context of this discussion (A.1) and (A.4) imply (A.2). As a matter of research strategy, as well as exposition, it is best if assumptions such as (A.2) are avoided, in that they refer to synthetic entities; it is preferable to confine assumptions to more primary entities such as those in (A.1) and (A.4). In any event, utilizing (A.1) through (A.6) and assuming the mode of convergence is a.c.,[19] we have that

$$S_{Ti}(\theta_{\cdot i}) \overset{\text{a.c.}}{\to} K_i(\theta_{\cdot i}, \theta_{\cdot i}^0) = [f_{\cdot i}^*(\theta_{\cdot i}, \theta_{\cdot i}^0)]' M_{ii}^{-1} f_{\cdot i}^*(\theta_{\cdot i}^0, \theta_{\cdot i}^0), \tag{6.87}$$

---

[18] For example, if we view the elements of W_i as nonrandom and $\{W_i : T \geq k_i\}$ as a matrix sequence in some space, say $\mathcal{X}$, convergence as an ordinary limit (OL) is appropriate ; if its elements are random, but (asymptotically) independent of the structural error process, convergence either in probability or a.c. is appropriate.

[19] Although this may appear unduly strong to the reader, we note that by Kolmogorov's zero-one law, a sequence of **independent** variables either **converges a.c.**, or **does not converge** at all.

uniformly for $\theta_{\cdot i} \in \Theta$, where

$$f_{\cdot i}^*(\theta_{\cdot i}, \theta_{\cdot i}^0) = f_{\cdot i}(\theta_{\cdot i}, \theta_{\cdot i}^0) - f_{\cdot i}(\theta_{\cdot i}^0, \theta_{\cdot i}^0).$$

Evidently $K_i \geq 0$, and the parameters of the ith equation are identified if and only if

$$f_{\cdot i}^*(\theta_{\cdot i}^{(1)}, \theta_{\cdot i}^0) = f_{\cdot i}^*(\theta_{\cdot i}^{(2)}, \theta_{\cdot i}^0), \quad \text{implies} \quad \theta_{\cdot i}^{(1)} = \theta_{\cdot i}^{(2)}.$$

Moreover,

$$S_{Ti}(\hat{\theta}) = \inf_{\theta_{\cdot i} \in \Theta} S_{Ti}(\theta) \overset{\text{a.c.}}{\to} \inf_{\theta_{\cdot i} \in \Theta} K_i(\theta_{\cdot i}, \theta_{\cdot i}^0) = K_i(\bar{\theta}_{\cdot i}, \theta_{\cdot i}^0) = 0,$$

and the strong consistency of the NL2SLS estimator follows from the identification condition.

In the preceding discussion we have proved

Theorem 1. Consider the GNLSEM of Eq. (6.82) under assumptions (A.1) through (A.6) of this section; then, the following statements are true:

   i. the parameter vector in the ith equation, is identified;

   ii. the NL2SLS estimator of that structural parameter vector, $\hat{\theta}_{\cdot i}$, obeys
$\hat{\theta}_{\cdot i} \overset{\text{a.c.}}{\to} \theta_{\cdot i}^0$.

Remark 6. In the preceding it is assumed (implicitly) that, if dynamic, the GNLSEM is stable, and that the exogenous variables of the model are "well-behaved". All that is meant to be conveyed by these provisos is that nothing in the exogenous variables, and/or the dynamic aspects of the model, invalidates any of the six basic assumptions made above. We do not propose, however, to examine these issues. Notice, further, the complete equivalence between the assumptions here and in the GLSEM. Assumption (A.1) has an exact counterpart in the GLSEM, as does (A.3). In the GLSEM, (A.4) corresponds to the statement that $(W_i' Z_i / T)$ converges, where Z_i is the matrix of observations on the (right hand) explanatory variables; or, equivalently, to the statement that $(W_i' Z_i \delta_{\cdot i} / T)$ converges **uniformly for** $\delta_{\cdot i}$ in the admissible parameter space! Similarly, (A.5) and (A.6) have exact counterparts in the GLSEM. Thus, the conceptual differences of solving the estimation problem in the context of the GLSEM and the GNLSEM with linear error terms are rather miniscule.

Remark 7. Although the estimator above is known as "NL2SLS", it is not clear what the "two stages" are. It is actually better described as limited information nonlinear simultaneous equations (LINLSE) instrumental variables (IV) estimator, based on an ill-specified model. [20] In the linear

---

[20] It is regrettable that the term "limited information" has become somewhat

case, the stages in question are quite apparent, at least in the conceptual framework, if not in the computational procedure. In point of fact, the estimator above is just one within a class of estimators determined by the choice of the "instrument" matrix W_i.

6.2.2 Asymptotic Normality of NL2SLS

Given the development in the preceding section, the NL2SLS estimator may be found as the solution to

$$\frac{\partial S_{Ti}}{\partial \theta_{.i}} = 0,$$

provided that, of all possible solutions, we choose the one corresponding to the *minimum minimorum*, i.e. the **absolute minimum**. Since in the preceding discussion we had established its consistency, to find its limiting distribution we need only expand the gradient (first order conditions) by the mean value theorem, about the true parameter point, $\theta_{.i}^0$. Doing so we find

$$\left(\frac{\partial S_{Ti}}{\partial \theta_{.i}}(\hat{\theta}_{.i})\right)' = \left(\frac{\partial S_{Ti}}{\partial \theta_{.i}}(\theta_{.i}^0)\right)' + \left(\frac{\partial^2 S_{Ti}}{\partial \theta_{.i}\partial \theta_{.i}}(\theta_{.i}^*)\right)(\hat{\theta}_{.i} - \theta_{.i}^0),$$

where $|\theta_{.i}^* - \theta_{.i}^0| \leq \hat{\theta}_{.i} - \theta_{.i}^0|$. It follows, therefore, that the limiting distribution of the estimator may be found from

$$\sqrt{T}(\hat{\theta}_{.i} - \theta_{.i}) = -\tilde{H}_i^{-1}(\theta^*)\tilde{F}_i'(\theta^0)\tilde{M}_{ii}^{-1}\frac{1}{\sqrt{T}}\sum_{t=1}^{T} w_{t.}^{(i)'} u_{ti}, \qquad (6.88)$$

where $w_{t.}^{(i)}$ is the tth row of W_i, and

$$\left(\frac{\partial S_{Ti}}{\partial \theta_{.i}}(\theta_{.i}^0)\right)' = -\frac{1}{T}\left(\frac{\partial g_{.i}}{\partial \theta_{.i}}(\theta^0)\right)' W_i \left(\frac{W_i' W_i}{T}\right)^{-1}\frac{1}{T}\sum_{t=1}^{T} w_{t.}^{(i)'} u_{ti}$$

---

nebulous in recent literature. The basic concept originally embodied in the term, was that in estimating the ith equation of a model, we ignored *a priori* restrictions placed on the remainder of the system; we did not necessarily ignore (sample) information conveyed by it in the form of the exogenous and lagged dependent variables contained therein. For example, in the "first stage" of 2SLS, in the context of the GLSEM, we estimate the reduced form using the predetermined variables appearing in all equations of the system and not merely those appearing in the given equation. In Amemiya (1975) "limited information" is intended to mean that one may leave the remainder of the system ill-specified, even to the extent of ignoring it, and merely write an *ad hoc* description of the "reduced form" of some of the dependent variables of the system.

$$\tilde{F}_i(\theta_{\cdot i}) = \frac{1}{T}W_i' \left(\frac{\partial g_{\cdot i}}{\partial \theta_{\cdot i}}\right)(\theta_{\cdot i}), \quad \tilde{M}_{ii} = \frac{W_i' W_i}{T},$$

$$\tilde{H}_i = \frac{\partial^2 S_{Ti}}{\partial \theta_{\cdot i}\partial \theta_{\cdot i}} = \frac{1}{T}\left[\left(\frac{\partial g_{\cdot i}}{\partial \theta_{\cdot i}}\right)' W_i\right]\left(\frac{W_i' W_i}{T}\right)^{-1}\left[\frac{1}{T}W_i'\frac{\partial g_{\cdot i}}{\partial \theta_{\cdot i}}\right]$$

$$-\frac{1}{T}(I_{k_i} \otimes q_{i\cdot})\frac{\partial}{\partial \theta_{\cdot i}}\left[\text{vec}\left(\frac{\partial g_{\cdot i}}{\partial \theta_{\cdot i}}\right)\right];$$

$$q_{i\cdot} = (y_{\cdot i} - g_{\cdot i})' W_i (W_i' W_i)^{-1} W_i'. \tag{6.89}$$

Noting that if

$$\tilde{F}_i(\theta_{\cdot i}^0) \overset{\text{a.c. or P}}{\longrightarrow} F_i(\theta^0), \quad \tilde{M}_{ii} \overset{\text{a.c. or P}}{\longrightarrow} M_{ii}, \tag{6.90}$$

$$\tilde{H}_i(\theta_{\cdot i}^*) \overset{\text{a.c. or P}}{\longrightarrow} H_i(\theta^0) = F_i(\theta^0)' M_{ii}^{-1} F_i(\theta^0), \quad \text{provided}$$

$$\gamma_j = \frac{1}{T}W_i'\frac{\partial^2 g_{\cdot i}}{\partial \theta_{\cdot i}\partial \theta_{ji}} \overset{\text{a.c. or P}}{\longrightarrow} 0, \quad j = 1, 2, \ldots k_i,$$

the estimator in the left member of Eq. (6.88) behaves, asymptotically, as

$$\sqrt{T}(\hat{\theta}_{\cdot i} - \theta_{\cdot i}) \sim H_i^{-1}(\theta^0) F_i'(\theta^0) M_{ii}^{-1} \frac{1}{\sqrt{T}}\sum_{t=1}^{T} w_{t\cdot}^{(i)'} u_{ti}. \tag{6.91}$$

Evidently, in order to ensure the existence of the limiting distribution we need the following conditions:

(A.7) the matrix $F_i(\theta_{\cdot i})$ is well defined (and of full column rank) for $\theta_{\cdot i}^0 \in \Theta$;

(A.8) the matrix of instruments W_i is (minimally) such that M_{ii} is nonsingular and the sequence $(W_i' u_{\cdot i}/\sqrt{T})$ admits of a **central limit theorem**;

(A.9) $\gamma_j \overset{\text{a.c. or P}}{\longrightarrow} 0, \quad j = 1, 2, 3, \ldots, m$.

(A.10) the matrix $H_i(\theta_{\cdot i}^0)$ is **nonsingular**, i.e. the matrix $H_i(\theta_{\cdot i})$ is nonsingular at the true parameter point $\theta_{\cdot i}^0$.

Notice that (A.7) through (A.9) imply (A.10) and hence that $H_i(\theta_{\cdot i}^0)$ is **nonsingular**. Moreover, by the continuity of its elements, it is nonsingular in some neighborhood about $\theta_{\cdot i}^0$. In addition, (A.9) ensures that the sequence

$$\zeta_T^* = \frac{1}{\sqrt{T}}\sum_{t=1}^{T}\zeta_t, \quad \zeta_t = (w_{t\cdot}^{(i)'}\lambda)u_{ti},$$

for arbitrary conformable vector λ, minimally satisfies a Lindeberg condition; or satisfies some other condition that implies the Lindeberg condition, such as for example a Liapounov CLT condition. Since

$$H_i = F_i' M_{ii}^{-1} F_i,$$

we conclude from Eq. (6.91) that

$$\sqrt{T}(\hat{\theta}_{\cdot i} - \theta_{\cdot i}^0) \sim N(0, \sigma_{ii}[H_i(\theta_{\cdot i}^0)]^{-1}). \tag{6.92}$$

We have therefore proved

Theorem 2. Under the conditions of Theorem 1, augmented by assumptions (A.7), (A.8) and (A.9), the NL2SLS estimator obeys

$$\sqrt{T}(\hat{\theta}_{\cdot i} - \theta_{\cdot i}^0) \sim N(0, \sigma_{ii}[H_i(\theta_{\cdot i}^0)]^{-1}),$$

where

$$\frac{1}{T} W_i' \left(\frac{\partial g_{\cdot i}}{\partial \theta_{\cdot i}}(\theta^0) \right) \overset{\text{a.c.}}{\to} F_i, \quad \frac{W_i' W_i}{T} \overset{\text{a.c.}}{\to} M_{ii}, \quad H_i = F_i' M_{ii}^{-1} F_i.$$

6.2.3   Choice of an Optimal NL2SLS Estimator

As pointed out earlier, the NL2SLS estimator, above, is really a **class of estimators** defined by the choices one makes regarding the "instrument" matrix W_i. If we specify this class, it may become possible to choose an "optimal" estimator. As a matter of notation, put

$$Z_i = \frac{\partial g_{\cdot i}}{\partial \theta_{\cdot i}}(\theta_{\cdot i})$$

and note that the nature of Z_i is known, except for the unknown parameter vector $\theta_{\cdot i}$; when we evaluate at the **true parameter vector**, $\theta_{\cdot i}^0$, we write Z_i^0; when we evaluate at a **consistent estimator**, say $\tilde{\theta}_{\cdot i}$, we write $\tilde{Z}_i$. If we add an additional assumption

$$(A.10) \qquad (W_i' \bar{Z}_i^0 / T) \overset{\text{OL}}{\to} F_i(\theta_{\cdot i}^0),$$

(convergence as an ordinary limit), where $\bar{Z}_i^0 = E(Z_i^0)$, i.e. it is the **expected value** of Z_i^0, it follows that, putting

$$W_i = \bar{Z}_i^0, \tag{6.93}$$

the limiting distribution of the resulting NL2SLS estimator has a covariance matrix obeying

$$[C_{NL2SLS}(\bar{Z}_i^0)]^{-1} = \lim_{T \to \infty} \frac{\bar{Z}_i^{0'} \bar{Z}_i^0}{T}.$$

If a instrument matrix W_i is used, we have

$$[C_{NL2SLS}(W_i)]^{-1} = \lim_{T \to \infty} \frac{1}{T} \bar{Z}_i^{0'} \left[W_i (W_i' W_i)^{-1} W_i' \right] \bar{Z}_i^0,$$

and it is evident that

$$C_{NL2SLS}(W_i) - C_{NL2SLS}(\bar{Z}_i^0) \geq 0.$$

Thus, the absolute bound on the covariance matrix of the limiting distribution of the NL2SLS within this general class is given by $C_{NL2SLS}(\bar{Z}_i^0)$. [21] Since this choice is generally not available to us, let us be a bit more realistic, and define the class of admissible instruments by

$$\mathcal{C}_i = \{W_i : W_i = X\tilde{A}\},$$

where $\tilde{A}$ may be a stochastic matrix such that $(\tilde{Z}_i' X \tilde{A}/T)$ converges to a well defined (nonstochastic) matrix, and X is the matrix of predetermined variables of the system, and if that is not possible, an appropriate submatrix thereof.

Remark 8. We recall, from Chapter 2, that in the context of the GLSEM, 2SLS is the optimal IV estimator, when the class of admissible instruments (in the proper sense of that term) is given by $\mathcal{C}_i$. Within the class $\mathcal{C}_i$ it is simple to show that, in the current context, the optimal estimator is that given by the choice $\tilde{A} = (X'X)^{-1} X' \tilde{Z}_i^0$.

Corollary 1. Under the conditions of Theorem 2, consider the class of admissible instruments $\mathcal{C}_i = \{W_i : W_i = X\tilde{A}\}$, such that

$$\frac{W_i' Z_i^0}{T} = \frac{\tilde{A}' X' Z_i^0}{T} \overset{P \text{ or a.c.}}{\longrightarrow} F_i, \qquad \tilde{A} \overset{P \text{ or a.c.}}{\longrightarrow} A$$

where A, F_i are well defined nonstochastic matrices, and X is the matrix of observations on the predetermined variables of the GNLSEM. The minimum variance NL2SLS estimator within the class $\mathcal{C}_i$ corresponds to the choice $\tilde{A} = P = (X'X)^{-1} X' \tilde{Z}_i$.

Proof: The covariance matrices of the limiting distribution, with the choice of **general** $\tilde{A}$ and the choice P, are given, respectively, by

$$C_{NL2SLS}(\tilde{A}) = \plim_{T \to \infty} \left[\frac{\tilde{Z}_i' X \tilde{A}}{T} \left(\frac{\tilde{A}' X' X \tilde{A}}{T} \right)^{-1} \frac{\tilde{A}' X' \tilde{Z}_i}{T} \right]^{-1},$$

---

[21] Amemiya (1975) notes that the optimal choice, within the class of **nonstochastic** instruments, is given by of $W_i = \bar{Z}_i^0$. The resulting estimator, of course, is not **feasible**. One might wonder whether using in its place $\tilde{Z}_i$, i.e. substituting for $\theta_{\cdot i}^0$ a consistent estimator, say, $\tilde{\theta}_{\cdot i}$ will yield the same results. The answer is not very transparent, since it would depend on whether or not, and to what extent, this substitution will complicate the derivation of the limiting distribution.

$$C_{NL2SLS}(P) = \plim_{T\to\infty} \left[\frac{\tilde{Z}_i'X}{T}\left(\frac{X'X}{T}\right)^{-1}\frac{X'\tilde{Z}_i}{T}\right]^{-1},$$

and an argument similar to that in Section 3 of Chapter 2, will show that $C_{NL2SLS}(\tilde{A}) - C_{NL2SLS}(P) \geq 0$.

q.e.d.

Remark 9. This shows, *mutatis mutandis*, the complete analogy between 2SLS in the GLSEM, and the estimator that has come to be known as the NL2SLS estimator in the context of the GNLSEM. When we confine our attention to the class of instruments that lie in the space spanned by the columns of the predetermined variables (i.e. the columns of the matrix X) we obtain the result that the optimal set is simply the projection of $Z_i^0 = (\partial g_{\cdot i}/\partial \theta_{\cdot i})$ on that space, just as in the case of the GLSEM it is shown that 2SLS is an optimal IV estimator, when the instruments are confined to the projection of the right hand jointly dependent and predetermined variables on the space spanned by the columns of X. Thus, basically, this rendition of NL2SLS (and NL3SLS for that matter) does not pose any novelty in the derivation of the limiting distribution, relative to the discussion of this topic in Chapter 2. In the literature, however, the class of admissible instruments is not precisely stated.

6.3   Nonlinear 3SLS

In this discussion, we have reference again to the model of Eq. (6.82); putting $y = \text{vec}(Y)$, $g(\theta) = \text{vec}[G(\theta)]$, $u = \text{vec}(U)$ and noting that $\text{Cov}(u) = \Sigma \otimes I_T$, we have to deal with the GNLSEM

$$y = g(\theta) + u. \tag{6.94}$$

The literature on this subject has two distinct bifurcations; one, given in Jorgenson and Laffont (1974), hereafter JL, is a precise analogue of Dhrymes (1969), which was discussed extensively in Chapter 2. Specifically, it is as follows: given an "instruments" matrix, W_0, let RR' be a nonsingular decomposition of $W_0'W_0$ and consider the transformation

$$(I \otimes R^{-1}W_0')y = (I \otimes R^{-1}W_0')g + (I \otimes R^{-1}W_0')u. \tag{6.95}$$

In the GLSEM this is what we have called the **canonical structural form**, and in that case $W_0 = X$, while here we leave W_0 unspecified for the moment. We note that the covariance matrix of the error process in Eq. (6.94) is $\Sigma \otimes I_q$, where $q = \text{rank}(W_0)$, and sufficient assumptions are made to ensure that

$$\frac{g(\theta)^{'}(I_m \otimes W_0)}{T} \left[I_m \otimes \left(\frac{W_0^{'}W_0}{T} \right)^{-1} \right] \frac{(I_m \otimes W_0)^{'} u}{T}$$

converges, in probability or a.c., to zero. This is exactly the objective of the transformation leading to the **canonical structural form**. Just as 3SLS is the (feasible) Aitken estimator of the structural parameters of the GLSEM in canonical form, so in the context of the GNLSEM the feasible, [22] (nonlinear) Aitken estimator in the model above is the NL3SLS estimator proposed by JL. [23] More precisely, the latter estimator is obtained by minimizing

$$S_{T3}^{JL} = \frac{1}{2T}(y - g)^{'}(\tilde{\Sigma}^{-1} \otimes W_0(W_0^{'}W_0)^{-1}W_0)(y - g). \tag{6.96}$$

The other suggestion, made by Amemiya (1977), desires to have different "instruments" for different equations. If we make a similar transformation as above, but allow different instruments for different equations, we have the "instrument" matrix $W = \text{diag}(W_1, W_2, \ldots, W_m)$, and the transformation

$$W^{'}y = W^{'}g + W^{'}u, \tag{6.97}$$

yields an error process with covariance matrix $W^{'}(\Sigma \otimes I_T)W$, which does not involve directly the **inverse of the original structural error covariance matrix**. Perhaps for this reason, Amemiya (1977), suggests the transformation

$$W^{'}(\Sigma^{-1} \otimes I_T)y = W^{'}(\Sigma^{-1} \otimes I_T)g + W^{'}(\Sigma^{-1} \otimes I_T)u.$$

The covariance matrix of the transformed model is $(W^{'}\Phi^{-1}W)$, and Amemiya's suggestion, in this context, represents the NL3SLS estimator as the feasible (nonlinear) Aitken estimator, with a prior consistent estimator of Σ, i.e. it is obtained by minimizing [24]

$$S_{T3}^{A} = \frac{1}{2T}(y - g)^{'}\tilde{\Phi}^{-1}W(W^{'}\tilde{\Phi}^{-1}W)^{-1}W^{'}\tilde{\Phi}^{-1}(y - g), \quad \tilde{\Phi} = \tilde{\Sigma} \otimes I_T,$$

---

[22] Feasible, here as in the GLSEM, means using a prior consistent estimator for the unknown covariance matrix Σ.

[23] Actually JL suggest that, with $W_0 = X$, perhaps not all predetermined variables should be employed, most likely because of concern with degrees of freedom problems.

[24] Several authors when dealing with all the equations of the GNLSEM, tend to write the equations as $g_{t\cdot} = u_{t\cdot}$, i.e. they dispense with the normalization we had imposed. Note that since little is being said about what variables appear in what equations, little generality is gained or lost by choosing one of the two approaches. On the other hand one has to be cautious at the computational stage.

with respect to the parameter θ, which is the stacked vector of the (distinct) parameters appearing in each of the m equations of the system.

Remark 10. One may conjecture that exactly the same, or at least asymptotically equivalent, estimators may be obtained through the feasible Aitken estimator of the model as transformed in Eq. (6.97), i.e. by minimizing

$$S_{T3} = \frac{1}{2T}(y - g)' \tilde{D}(y - g), \quad \tilde{D} = W(W'\tilde{\Phi}W)^{-1}W'. \tag{6.98}$$

The reason for this conjecture is as follows: denote by

$$\tilde{A} = \tilde{\Phi}^{-1}W(W'\tilde{\Phi}^{-1}W)^{-1}W'\tilde{\Phi}^{-1}, \quad \tilde{D} = W(W'\tilde{\Phi}W)^{-1}W', \tag{6.99}$$

the matrices, respectively, of the quadratic forms in S_{T3}^A and S_{T3}; further, note that the characteristic roots of A and D, both in the metric of Φ^{-1} (and both defined in terms of Φ rather than $\tilde{\Phi}$) are given by the (same) matrix $\Lambda = \text{diag}(I_q, 0)$, where $q = \text{rank}(W)$; thus, with P and Q suitable nonsingular matrices, we have the decompositions

$$\Phi^{-1} = Q'Q, \quad A = Q'\Lambda Q, \quad \Phi^{-1} = P'P, \quad D = P'\Lambda P.$$

The relations above imply that there exists an orthogonal matrix S, such that $P = SQ$, and hence that

$$A = P'S\Lambda S'P = P'S_q S_q'P, \quad D = P'\Lambda P = P_q'P_q, \tag{6.100}$$

where P_q, S_q are the columns of P, S, respectively, corresponding to the nonzero (unit) roots in Λ. Thus, we may restate these minimands, alternatively, as

$$
\begin{aligned}
S_{T3}^A &= \frac{1}{2T}(y-g)'P'S\Lambda S'P(y-g) = \frac{1}{2T}(y-g)'P'S_q S_q'P(y-g) \\
S_{T3} &= \frac{1}{2T}(y-g)'P'\Lambda P(y-g) = \frac{1}{2T}(y-g)'P_q'P_q(y-g), \tag{6.101}
\end{aligned}
$$

and we see that the two minimands differ only by the arbitrary orthogonal matrix S.

Note further that the NL3SLS proposed by JL is **a special case of the two procedures discussed in this Remark**. To see that, take $W = (I \otimes W_0)$ and note that under these conditions (common instruments W_0 for all equations) we have

$$A = D = \Sigma^{-1} \otimes W_0(W_0'W_0)^{-1}W_0'.$$

6.3.1 Identification and Consistency of NL3SLS

The discussion here will be relatively brief since the argument is, *mutatis mutandis*, identical to that given for NL2SLS. For simplicity we shall deal with the estimator obtained through the operation

$$\inf_{\theta \in \Theta} S_{T3} = \inf_{\theta \in \Theta} \frac{1}{2T}(y - g)' D(y - g),$$

where D is a suitable matrix and may be chosen to be D, as defined in Eq. (6.99); we denote by $\hat{\theta}_T$ the estimator of the parameter vector in the entire system, and below list the appropriate form of the assumptions stated earlier

(A.1)$'$ $\mathrm{rank}(W) = q,$ $(W'\Phi W/T) \overset{\text{a.c.}}{\longrightarrow} M_{ww} > 0$;

(A.2)$'$ $S_{T3}(\theta) \overset{\text{a.c. or P}}{\longrightarrow} K_{(}\theta,\theta^0)$, **uniformly in** Θ;

(A.3)$'$ $K(\theta,\theta^0) \geq 0$, and $K(\theta^{(1)},\theta^0) = K(\theta^{(2)},\theta^0)$, if and only if $\theta^{(1)} = \theta^{(2)}$;

(A.4)$'$ $(W'g/T) \overset{\text{P or a.c.}}{\longrightarrow} f(\theta,\theta^0)$, and $f(\theta,\theta^0)$ is well defined;

(A.5)$'$ $(W'u/T) \overset{\text{P or a.c.}}{\longrightarrow} 0$, as well as the technical assumption

(A.6)$'$ the admissible parameter space Θ is compact, and the true parameter point, θ^0, is an **interior point** of Θ.

In view of the earlier discussion, in connection with the NL2SLS estimator, we have

Theorem 3. Consider the GNLSEM of Eq. (6.82) under assumptions (A.1)$'$ through (A.6)$'$ of this section; moreover, assume that convergence therein is a.c., and uniform for $\theta \in \Theta$; then

   i. the parameter vector in the entire system, θ, is identified;

   ii. the NL3SLS estimator of that structural parameter vector $\hat{\theta}$, obeys

$$\hat{\theta} \overset{\text{a.c.}}{\longrightarrow} \theta^0.$$

Proof: Evident from the preceding discussion.

6.3.2   Asymptotic Normality of NL3SLS

As before, the NL3SLS estimator may be found as the solution to

$$\frac{\partial S_{T3}}{\partial \theta} = 0,$$

provided that of all possible solutions we choose the one corresponding to the *minimum minimorum*, i.e. the **absolute minimum**. Let that estimator be denoted by $\hat{\theta}_T$; in order to derive its limiting distribution we need only expand the gradient (first order conditions) by the mean value theorem, about the true parameter point, θ^0 . Doing so we find

$$\left(\frac{\partial S_{T3}}{\partial \theta}(\hat{\theta})\right)' = \left(\frac{\partial S_{T3}}{\partial \theta}(\theta^0)\right)' + \left(\frac{\partial^2 S_{T3}}{\partial \theta \partial \theta}(\theta^*)\right)(\hat{\theta} - \theta^0),$$

where $|\theta^* - \theta^0| \le \hat{\theta} - \theta^0|$. It follows, therefore, that the limiting distribution of the estimator may be found from

$$\sqrt{T}(\hat{\theta} - \theta) \sim H^{-1} F' M_{ww}^{-1} \frac{1}{\sqrt{T}} \sum_{t=1}^{T} S_t' u_t', \qquad (6.102)$$

where

$$S_t' = \begin{bmatrix} w_{t\cdot}^{(1)'} & 0 & 0 & 0 & 0 \\ 0 & w_{t\cdot}^{(2)'} & 0 & 0 & 0 \\ 0 & 0 & w_{t\cdot}^{(3)'} & 0 & 0 \\ \vdots & \vdots & \vdots & \vdots & \vdots \\ 0 & 0 & 0 & 0 & w_{t\cdot}^{(m)'} \end{bmatrix},$$

$w_{t\cdot}^i$ is the tth row of W_i , and

$$H(\theta^0) = \text{limit P or a.c. of } \left(\frac{\partial^2 S_{T3}}{\partial \theta \partial \theta}(\theta^*)\right),$$

$$F(\theta^0) = \text{limit P or a.c. of } \frac{1}{T} W' \frac{\partial g}{\partial \theta}(\theta^0) \textbf{ and OL of } \frac{1}{T} W' E \left[\frac{\partial g}{\partial \theta}(\theta^0)\right],$$

$$M_{ww} = \text{limit a.c. or P or OL of } \frac{1}{T} W' \Phi W,$$

$$H(\theta^0) = F(\theta^0)' M_{ww}^{-1} F(\theta^0). \qquad (6.103)$$

Evidently, in order to ensure the existence of the limiting distribution we need the following additional conditions:

(A.7)$'$ the matrix $F(\theta^0)$ is **of full column rank**, and M_{ww} is **nonsingular**;

(A.8)$'$ the matrix of instruments W is (minimally) such that the sequence $(W' u/\sqrt{T})$ admits of a **central limit theorem**.

(A.9)$'$ $(Du \otimes I)[\partial \text{vec}(\partial g/\partial \theta)/\partial \theta] \overset{\text{P or a.c.}}{\longrightarrow} 0$.

(A.10)$'$ the matrix $H(\theta^0)$ is **nonsingular at the true parameter point** θ^0 and thus, by the continuity of its elements, it is nonsingular in an open neighborhood about θ^0.

We may summarize our discussion in

Theorem 4. Under the conditions of Theorem 1, augmented by assumptions (A.7)$'$ through (A.10)$'$, the NL3SLS estimator obeys

$$\sqrt{T}(\hat{\theta} - \theta^0) \sim N(0, [H(\theta^0)]^{-1}),$$

where

$$\frac{1}{T}W'\left(\frac{\partial g}{\partial \theta}(\theta^0)\right) \xrightarrow{\text{a.c.}} F, \quad \frac{W'\Phi W}{T} \xrightarrow{\text{a.c.}} M_{ww}, \quad H = F'M_{ww}^{-1}F.$$

6.3.3 Optimum NL3SLS and Computational Aspects

Consider the two NL3SLS estimators corresponding to S_{T3} and S_{T3}^A; first, it is clear from their respective limiting distributions that if, in the S_{T3}^A-based procedure we take as "instruments" W, while in the S_{T3}-based procedure we take as "instruments" $\Phi^{-1}W$ the two procedures yield **asymptotically equivalent** estimators. Moreover, if in the latter we take as "instruments" $\tilde{\Phi}^{-1}W$ the two procedures yield **numerically identical** estimators, provided the same algorithm is involved in obtaining them. Consequently, the two procedures have the same covariance bound, and this bound is given by

$$[C_{NL3SLS}(\Phi^{-1}\bar{Z}^0)]^{-1} = \lim_{T\to\infty} \frac{1}{T}\left(\bar{Z}^{0'}\Phi^{-1}\bar{Z}^0\right), \quad \bar{Z}^0 = E\left(\frac{\partial g}{\theta}(\theta^0)\right).$$

Thus, the two procedures are completely equivalent, and there is really no reason to ever employ the more complicated procedure involved in S_{T3}^A.

Let us now briefly consider the choice of "instruments"; it would seem reasonable that the elements of the matrix W **should** come from the exogenous and predetermined variables of the model; for if some of the elements of W do not appear in the model, how could one maintain the argument that they are relevant in providing information regarding the parameters of the model? This, effectively, restricts us to functions of the matrix X, realistically elements of its column space. In fact, we can prove

Corollary 2. Under the conditions of Theorem 4, consider the class of admissible "instrument" matrices

$$\mathcal{C} = \{W : W = (I_m \otimes X)(\Sigma^{-1} \otimes I_T)\tilde{A}\},$$

$$\tilde{A} = \text{diag}(\tilde{A}_1, \tilde{A}_2, \ldots, \tilde{A}_m), \quad \text{rank}(A) = k \le mG, \quad \text{such that}$$

$$\frac{W'Z^0}{T} = \frac{\tilde{A}'(\Sigma^{-1} \otimes I_T)(I_m \otimes X)'Z^0}{T} \xrightarrow{\text{P or a.c.}} F, \quad \tilde{A} \xrightarrow{\text{P or a.c.}} A,$$

where A, F are well defined nonstochastic matrices, and X is the matrix of observations on the predetermined variables of the GNLSEM, or a suitable subset thereof, if there are degrees of freedom problems. The minimum variance NL3SLS estimator within the class $\mathcal{C}$ corresponds to the choice

$$\tilde{A} = P = [I_m \otimes (X'X)^{-1}X']\tilde{Z},$$

so that the chosen "instrument" matrix is

$$\tilde{W} = (I_m \otimes X)(\tilde{\Sigma}^{-1} \otimes I_T)P = [\tilde{\Sigma}^{-1} \otimes X(X'X)^{-1}X']\tilde{Z},$$

where $\tilde{\Sigma}$ is a prior consistent estimator of Σ, and $\tilde{Z} = (\partial g/\partial\theta)$ is evaluated at $\tilde{\theta}$, a prior consistent estimator of θ^0.

Proof: The covariance matrices of the limiting distribution, with the choice of **general** $\tilde{A}$ and the choice P, are given, respectively, by

$$\tilde{\Psi} = \left(\frac{\tilde{A}'(\tilde{\Sigma}^{-1} \otimes X')\tilde{Z}}{T} \right),$$

$$C_{NL3SLS}(\tilde{A}) = \plim_{T\to\infty} \tilde{\Psi}' \left(\frac{\tilde{A}'(\tilde{\Sigma}^{-1} \otimes X'X)\tilde{A}}{T} \right)^{-1} \tilde{\Psi},$$

$$C_{NL3SLS}(P) = \plim_{T\to\infty} \left(\frac{\tilde{Z}'[\tilde{\Sigma}^{-1} \otimes X(X'X)^{-1}X']\tilde{Z}}{T} \right)^{-1},$$

and an argument similar to that given for Corollary 1, will show that $C_{NL3SLS}(\tilde{A}) - C_{NL3SLS}(P) \geq 0$.

$$\text{q.e.d.}$$

Remark 11. The optimal choice within the class $\mathcal{C}$, above, corresponds to the same choice one makes in showing that 3SLS is an optimal IV estimator in the context of the GLSEM; in the latter case it involves the projection of $Z = (Y, X)$, the totality of variables in the system, on the space spanned by the columns of X, the matrix of predetermined variables. In the present (NL3SLS) case it involves the projection of $\tilde{Z} = (\partial g/\partial\theta)(\tilde{\theta})$ on the column space of the matrix of the predetermined variables, X, as well. Operationally, this means that the NL3SLS is obtained in three steps:

i. obtain the NL2SLS estimators $\tilde{\theta}$ and $\tilde{\Sigma}$;

ii. evaluate $\tilde{Z}$ and regress the latter (by GLS) on X, thus obtaining the entity

$$\tilde{W} = (\tilde{\Sigma}^{-1} \otimes X(X'X)^{-1}X')\tilde{Z};$$

iii. form the minimand

$$S_{T3} = \frac{1}{2T}(y - g)'\tilde{W}(\tilde{W}'\tilde{\Phi}\tilde{W})^{-1}\tilde{W}'(y - g),$$

and obtain the estimator $\hat{\theta}_T$ that obeys $S_{T3}(\hat{\theta}_T) = \inf_{\theta \in \Theta} S_{T3}(\theta)$.

6.4 GMM

6.4.1 Reformulation of GMM as NL2SLS and NL3SLS

This method was introduced into the literature by Hansen (1982) as a novel estimation procedure for nonlinear models. As an estimation procedure, however, GMM is a rather minor modification of the methods examined in the previous two sections, in the context of nonlinear models with **additive structural errors**. Its framework differs from that employed in NL2SLS and NL3SLS in two respects: first, the set of "instruments" by which identification and estimation is carried out is left as a primitive in NL2SLS and NL3SLS; in practice, the class of admissible instruments is taken to be the space spanned by the predetermined variables of the model in question. In that context, given the standard i.i.d. assumption regarding the structural error terms, **all predetermined variables may serve as instruments**. In the GMM context, which was inspired by the "rational expectations" approach, "instruments" are defined **within the model** through assertions that some variables are uncorrelated with ("orthogonal" to) the structural errors; second, the errors are asserted to be strictly stationary [25] (as are the dependent variables and instruments); thus, the proof of consistency, and asymptotic normality is obtained under more general conditions, in GMM, than was the case in the earlier literature.

Abstracting from these motivational aspects, the GMM is nothing more than the GNLSEM with additive errors, treated in bascially the same manner as NL2SLS and NL3SLS. There is no difficulty, in the latter context, with a specification that the error process is stationary; what such an assertion would mean is that the class of instruments should be confined to some space spanned by the **exogenous variables** of the model, which are asserted to be independent or uncorrelated with the error process. Thus, the **major difference** between GMM and NL2SLS, NL3SLS is the **manner in which "instruments" are defined** or rationalized, or motivated in the two strands of this literature and nothing more.

We shall briefly outline the procedure as given in Hansen, and then recast the problem in the framework of the previous two sections. Without loss

---

[25] Hansen is not explicit as to what stationarity is being assigned, **strict stationarity** or **covariance stationarity**. One is left to infer the precise meaning from the context, see also the discussion below.

of generality, write the econometric model as [26]

$$y_{t\cdot} = g(y_{t\cdot}, x_{t\cdot}; \theta) + u_{t\cdot} = g_{t\cdot}(\theta) + u_{t\cdot}, \qquad t = 1, 2, \ldots, T,$$

$$z_{t\cdot} = h(y_{t\cdot}, x_{t\cdot}, \theta), \qquad t = 1, 2, \ldots, T. \tag{6.104}$$

Hansen's assumptions imply that the u- and z-processes are **jointly (strictly) stationary**. [27] The question now arises as to what we are to assume regarding the "predetermined" variables, $x_{t\cdot} = (\underline{y}_{-1}, p_{t\cdot})$, where $p_{t\cdot}$ is the vector of **exogenous variables** and $\underline{y}_{-1} = (y_{t-1\cdot}, y_{t-2\cdot}, \ldots, y_{t-k\cdot})$. Actually, far from adding generality and/or complicating the arguemnt **it is simpler to assume the exogenous variables to be (strictly) stationary** than to allow them to be arbitrary nonstochastic sequences. If we allow the latter, we destroy the (strict) stationarity property of the class of predetermined variables. [28] It is further assumed that [29]

$$E(u_{t\cdot} \otimes z_{t\cdot})' = 0, \quad \text{for all } t. \tag{6.105}$$

Thereafter the problem is defined as a minimum chi-squared problem with

---

[26] In Hansen, the model is written as $u_{t\cdot} = F(x_{t\cdot}; \theta)$ and $z_{t\cdot} = G(x_{t\cdot}; \theta)$. In Hansen's notation $x_{t\cdot}$ stands for $(y_{t\cdot}, x_{t\cdot})$ in our notation, the distinction between predetermined and jointly dependent variables being muted. It is assumed that $\{x_{t\cdot} : t \geq 1\}$ is a **(strictly) stationary process**, a term to be defined below. Note that this implies that $u_{t\cdot}$ and $z_{t\cdot}$ are **jointly** strictly stationary processes.

[27] A stochastic sequence $\{X_n : n \geq 1\}$ defined on the probability space $(\Omega, \mathcal{A}, \mathcal{P})$ is said to be strictly stationary, if for every k, $\mathcal{P}(A_{(1)}) = \mathcal{P}(A_{(k+1)})$, where $A_{(1)} = \{\omega : (X_1, X_2, \ldots) \in B\}$ and $A_{(k+1)} = \{\omega : (X_{k+1}, X_{k+2}, \ldots) \in B\}$, for any $B \in \mathcal{B}(R^\infty)$. It is also said to be **ergodic** if and only if every **invariant set** relative to it has $\mathcal{P}$-measure either zero or one. For greater detail on these and related issues, see Dhrymes (1989) Ch. 5, pp. 338ff, especially pp. 357ff. Ergodicity, however, is not generally familiar to econometricians, and we will refrain from using it unless the context makes it is absolutely necessary.

Hansen actually does not specify the probability characteristics of the u- and z-processes; it is merely stated that $\{x_n : n \geq 1\}$ is a **stationary process**; since the author defines $u_n = F(x_n; \theta)$, $z_n = G(x_n; \theta)$, for suitably measurable functions, and subsequent arguments imply that the z- and u-processes are jointly stationary, one has to conclude that the stationarity in question must be **strict stationarity** since **a measurable transformation of a weakly stationary process** is not necessarily weakly stationary.

[28] Incidentally this is the "reason" why it is not only convenient, which it certainly is, but almost imperative that the "instruments" be asserted to be (strictly) stationary. In this fashion, **all variables** in the model are stationary, thus simplifying matters considerably. On the other hand, in the context of **rational expectations** models, the underlying theory implies that certain variables are uncorrelated (orthogonal in the appropriate Hilbert space context) with certain other variables.

[29] These are the "orthogonality" conditions which define the "instruments" of the model.

weighting matrix $J_T' J_T$, i.e. one obtains an estimator of θ , say $\hat{\theta}_T$ by the operation

$$\inf_{\theta \in \Theta} S_T(Y, X; \theta) = S_T(\hat{\theta}_T), \tag{6.106}$$

where

$$S_T = \frac{1}{2}|h_T|^2, \qquad h_T = J_T \frac{1}{T} \sum_{t=1}^{T} (u_{t\cdot} \otimes z_{t\cdot})'. \tag{6.107}$$

It is further assumed that $J_T \overset{\text{a.c.}}{\to} J$, where J is an appropriate nonstochastic matrix. This is a formulation which is, *mutatis mutandis*, identical to that given in Dhrymes (1969), Amemiya (1974), Jorgenson and Laffont (1974) and others, which may be seen as follows: put

$$\Gamma_T = \sum_{t=1}^{T} (u_{t\cdot} \otimes z_{t\cdot})' = \frac{1}{T} \sum_{t=1}^{T} \text{vec}(z_{t\cdot}' u_{t\cdot}) \tag{6.108}$$

$$= \frac{1}{T}\text{vec}(Z'U) = \frac{1}{T}(I \otimes Z')(y - g), \quad \text{and note that}$$

$$S_T = \frac{1}{2T^2}(y - g)'(I \otimes Z)W_T(I \otimes Z')(y - g), \quad W_T = J_T' J_T,$$

where [30]

$$Z = (z_{t\cdot}), \quad Y = (y_{t\cdot}), \quad G(\theta) = (g_{t\cdot}(\theta)), \quad X = (x_{t\cdot}), \quad U = (u_{t\cdot}),$$

$$y = \text{vec}(Y), \quad u = \text{vec}(U), \quad g = \text{vec}[G(\theta)]. \tag{6.109}$$

It is evident that, apart from the scalar term T^{-2} , the objective function of GMM is the one considered, e.g., in Eq. (6.98) above, with

$$\tilde{D} = (I \otimes Z)W_T(I \otimes Z')!$$

Since, for every T , the matrix W_T has the nonsingular decomposition $W_T = P_T' P_T$ we may proceed as follows: Consider the system $y = g + u$ and transform on the left by $P_T(I \otimes Z')$ to obtain

$$P_T(I \otimes Z')(y - g) = P_T(I \otimes Z')u; \tag{6.110}$$

the method of GMM consists of **applying nonlinear least squares** to the system in Eq. (6.110); but this is **exactly the nonlinear 2SLS or 3SLS framework**. The difference is, as we had noted earlier, that in the latter "instruments" is left as a primitive context, while in the former "instruments" is something that is defined by the rational expectations framework.

---

[30] The objective function S_T has been divided by two for notational convenience only.

Thus, the formal or estimation aspects of the GMM are neither more nor less general than what we had studied in the preceding two sections, and the particularly complex manner in which its formulation is stated in Hansen (1982) is a definite barrier to a clear understanding of what it entails.

6.4.2 Identification and Consistency

Having reformulated the GMM problem as the problem encountered in NL2SLS and NL3SLS, we shall employ the framework of the last section in dealing with estimation and limiting distribution issues. First, we reconcile a few superficial discrepancies. We note that the objective function for NL3SLS, given in iii of Remark 11, is

$$S_{T3} = \frac{1}{2T}(y - g)'\tilde{W}(\tilde{W}'\tilde{\Phi}\tilde{W})^{-1}\tilde{W}'(y - g),$$

while the objective function of the reformulated GMM problem is given by

$$S_T = \frac{1}{T^2}(y - g)'(I \otimes Z)W_T(I \otimes Z')(y - g), \quad W_T = J_T'J_T;$$

the apparent discrepancy is resolved by noting that in S_T, it is assumed that $W_T \overset{a.c.}{\to} \bar{W}$, the latter being a nonstochastic posititive definite matrix; to give S_{T3} a structure comparable to that of S_T, we need to divide by T, i.e. to rewrite it as

$$S_{T3} = \frac{1}{2T^2}(y - g)'\tilde{W}\left(\frac{\tilde{W}'\tilde{\Phi}\tilde{W}}{T}\right)^{-1}\tilde{W}'(y - g).$$

It is then evident that the entities S_{T3} and S_T are **identical**, if we make the association

$$\left(\frac{\tilde{W}'\tilde{\Phi}\tilde{W}}{T}\right)^{-1} = W_T, \quad \tilde{W} = (I \otimes Z).$$

If we were to specify a particular parametric covariance structure, the GMM will become either NL2SLS or NL3SLS, depending on the choice of the weighting matrix, and there is nothing further to discuss; thus, we shall examine the probabilistic properties of the "GMM" estimators, on the assertion that the error and "instruments" (the u- and z-processes, respectively,) are, as in Hansen, **jointly (strictly) stationary**. The assumptions under which we shall operate are the following:

(B.1) the admissible parameter space $\Theta \subset R^k$ is compact, and contains an open neighborhood of the true parameter point θ^0;

(B.2) $p_t.$, $u_t.$, $z_t.$ are, respectively, s-, m- and q-element (zero mean) jointly strictly stationary, square integrable sequences defined on the probability space $(\Omega, \mathcal{A}, \mathcal{P})$;

(B.3) for all t, $E(z'_{t\cdot} u_{t\cdot}) = 0$ and [31]

$$\frac{Z'G(\theta)}{T} \overset{a.c.}{\to} M_{zg}(\theta), \quad \text{uniformly for } \theta \in \Theta;$$

(B.4) $W_T \overset{a.c.}{\to} \bar{W}$.

Given the conditions above, it is simple to deduce that

$$S_T(\theta) \overset{a.c.}{\to} f(\theta, \theta^0)' \bar{W} f(\theta, \theta^0) = K(\theta, \theta^0), \tag{6.111}$$

$$f(\theta, \theta^0) = \text{a.c. limit of } \frac{1}{T}(I \otimes Z')[u + g(\theta^0) - g(\theta)]$$

$$= m_{zg}(\theta^0) - m_{zg}(\theta), \quad m_{zg} = \text{vec}(M_{zg}).$$

To the assumptions above, we now add the **identification condition**

(B.5) If $K(\theta^1, \theta^0) = K(\theta^2, \theta^0)$ then $\theta^1 = \theta^2$.

It may be verified that for all $\theta \in \Theta$, $\theta \neq \theta^0$, $K(\theta, \theta^0) > 0$ and that $K(\theta^0, \theta^0) = 0$. Thus, K is a constrast function and, by the discussion of Chapter 5, we conclude that $\hat{\theta}_T \overset{a.c.}{\to} \theta^0$.

6.4.3 Asymptotic Normality

To find the limiting distribution of the estimator developed above, we note that it obeys

$$\frac{\partial S_T}{\partial \theta}(\hat{\theta}_T) = 0;$$

and that it converges a.c. to the true parameter vector θ^0. In addition, we recall that, in this context, the instruments $z_{t\cdot}$ are defined **within the**

---

[31] This condition, for example, will be satisfied if

$$\begin{pmatrix} p'_{t\cdot} \\ u'_{t\cdot} \\ z'_{t\cdot} \end{pmatrix} = \begin{bmatrix} A_1(L) & 0 & 0 \\ 0 & A_2(L) & 0 \\ 0 & 0 & A_3(L) \end{bmatrix} \begin{pmatrix} \epsilon'_{t1\cdot} \\ \epsilon'_{t2\cdot} \\ \epsilon'_{t3\cdot} \end{pmatrix},$$

such that $\epsilon_{t\cdot} = (\epsilon_{t1\cdot}, \epsilon_{t2\cdot}, \epsilon_{t3\cdot})$ is an i.i.d. sequence with mean zero and covariance matrix Σ. In the representation above, L is the lag operator, $A_i(L) = \sum_{j=0}^{\infty} a_{ij} L^j$, and $\sum_{j=0}^{\infty} ||a_{ij}|| < \infty$, for all $\theta \in \Theta$, i.e. the lag coefficient matrices, which may be functions of θ, are dominated by sequences, say a_{ij}^*, obeying $\sum_{j=0}^{\infty} ||a_{ij}^*|| < \infty$, where the norm of the matrix a_{ij} is taken to be the (square root of the) largest characteristic root, or (alternatively) the trace of $a_{ij}^* a_{ij}^{*\prime}$. This will suffice for all realistic applications in econometrics, and at the same time will eliminate the need for conditions that are meaningless to the average practitioner such as ergodicity and k^{th} moment continuity.

model, and we note from Eq. (6.104) that we have $z_{t\cdot} = h_{t\cdot}(\theta^0)$ where for notational convenience we suppress the fact that the instruments may (and typically do) depend on the current endogenous and predetermined variables of the system. Expanding the first order conditions about θ^0 we have by the mean value theorem,

$$0 = \left(\frac{\partial S_T}{\partial \theta}(\hat{\theta}_T)\right)' = \left(\frac{\partial S_T}{\partial \theta}(\theta^0)\right)' + \frac{\partial^2 S_T}{\partial \theta \partial \theta}(\theta^*)(\hat{\theta}_T - \theta^0).$$

We observe that

$$\left(\frac{\partial S_T}{\partial \theta}(\theta^0)\right)' = -\tilde{Q}'W_T\left[\frac{1}{T}\sum_{t=1}^{T}(u_{t\cdot}' \otimes z_{t\cdot}')\right]; \qquad (6.112)$$

$$\frac{\partial^2 S_T}{\partial \theta \partial \theta}(\theta^0) = \tilde{Q}'W_T\tilde{Q} + V_T;$$

$$\tilde{Q} = \frac{1}{T}\left((I_m \otimes Z')\frac{\partial g}{\partial \theta}(\theta^0) + (I_q \otimes U')\frac{\partial z}{\partial \theta}(\theta^0)\right)$$

$$= \frac{1}{T}\sum_{t=1}^{T}\left((I_m \otimes z_{t\cdot}')\frac{\partial g_{t\cdot}'}{\partial \theta}(\theta^0) + (I_q \otimes u_{t\cdot}')\frac{\partial z_{t\cdot}'}{\partial \theta}(\theta^0)\right);$$

$$V_T \stackrel{\text{P or a.c.}}{\longrightarrow} 0, \quad V_T = \frac{1}{T}\left[(y-g)'(I \otimes Z)W_T \otimes I\right]\left(\frac{\partial \text{vec}(\tilde{Q})}{\partial \theta}\right).$$

Thus, in addition to (B.3) we require the assumption

(B.6) $\quad \frac{1}{T}\left((I_m \otimes Z')\frac{\partial \text{vec}(G)}{\partial \theta} + (I_r \otimes U')\frac{\text{vec}(Z)}{\partial \theta}\right)(\theta^0) \stackrel{\text{a.c. or P}}{\longrightarrow} Q(\theta^0),$

$\quad \text{rank}(Q) = k,$

in which case, we conclude immediately that

$$\frac{\partial^2 S_T}{\partial \theta \partial \theta}(\theta^*) \stackrel{\text{a.c. or P}}{\longrightarrow} Q'\bar{W}Q.$$

To complete our discussion, we require the limiting distribution of

$$\xi_{(T)} = \frac{1}{\sqrt{T}}\sum_{t=1}^{T}\xi_{t\cdot}', \quad \xi_{t\cdot}' = (u_{t\cdot}' \otimes z_{t\cdot}').$$

We note that the process $\{\xi_{t\cdot}' : t \geq 1\}$ is **also** strictly stationary;[32] moreover, if the joint distribution of $(u_{t\cdot}, z_{t\cdot})'$ possesses **fourth order moments,** the distribution of $\xi_{t\cdot}$ will possess **second order moments,** so

---

[32] Let $(\Omega, \mathcal{A}, \mathcal{P})$ be the probability space on which the u- and z-processes are defined. To prove this statement it will suffice to show that for arbitrary

that ξ is a **covariance stationary process**. By the Wold decomposition theorem, see Brockwell and Davis (1987, p. 180) **every covariance stationary process** and, in particular ξ, has the decomposition

$$\xi'_{t\cdot} = \sum_{t=0}^{\infty} A_j \epsilon'_{t-j\cdot} + \zeta'_{t\cdot}, \quad A_0 = I, \quad \{\epsilon'_{t\cdot} : t \geq 1\} \text{ is i.i.d. } (0, \Sigma)$$

$$\sum_{j=-\infty}^{\infty} \|A_j\| < \infty, \quad E(\epsilon'_s \zeta_r) = 0, \text{ for all } s, r, \quad \Sigma > 0, \tag{6.113}$$

where $\|A_j\|$ indicates the norm of the matrix A_j.[33] In lieu of appealing to Hannan (1973) and the references given therein, we may assume (minimally) that the purely deterministic component, $\zeta_{t\cdot}$, obeys $\zeta_{t\cdot} = 0$, so that

$$\xi_{(T)} = \frac{1}{\sqrt{T}} \sum_{t=1}^{T} \xi'_{t\cdot} \sim \sum_{j=0}^{\infty} A_j \left(\frac{1}{\sqrt{T}} \sum_{t=1}^{T} \epsilon'_{t-j\cdot} \right).$$

---

s, r, n, the joint distributions of $\xi_{(s)} = \{\xi_{s+i\cdot} : i = 1, 2, \ldots, n\}$ and $\xi_{(r)} = \{\xi_{r+i\cdot} : i = 1, 2, \ldots, n\}$, are identical. Let $B_n \in \mathcal{B}(R^n)$, and $B_{\infty,nr}$, $B_{\infty,ns}$, be the cylinder sets with cylindrical base B_n, in the $r+1, \ldots, r+n$, and $s+1, s+2, \ldots, s+n$ space coordinates, respectively. Putting $w_{t\cdot} = (u_{t\cdot}, z_{t\cdot})$, we note that $\xi_{t\cdot} = f(w_{t\cdot})$, where f is a Borel function. Let $\xi^*_{(s)} = (\cdot, \cdot, \cdot, \xi_{(s)}, \cdots)$, $\xi^*_{(r)} = (\cdot, \cdot, \cdot, \xi_{(r)}, \cdots)$ (similarly for $w^*_{(s)}$, $w^*_{(r)}$) and note that

$$A_{ns} = \xi_{(s)}^{-1}(B_n) = w_{(s)}^{-1} \circ f^{-1}(B_n) = w_{(s)}^{-1}(C_n), \ C_n = f^{-1}(B_n),$$

$$A_{nr} = \xi_{(r)}^{-1}(B_n) = w_{(r)}^{-1} \circ f^{-1}(B_n) = w_{(r)}^{-1}(C_n).$$

Since w is **strictly stationary**, we conclude that $\mathcal{P}(A_{ns}) = \mathcal{P}(A_{nr})$. Noting that

$$A_{\infty,ns} = \xi_{(s)}^{*-1}(B_{\infty,ns}) = w_{(s)}^{*-1} \circ f^{-1}(B_{\infty,ns}) = w_{(s)}^{*-1}(C_{\infty,ns}),$$

$$A_{\infty,nr} = \xi_{(r)}^{*-1}(B_{\infty,nr}) = w_{(r)}^{*-1} \circ f^{-1}(B_{\infty,nr}) = w_{(r)}^{-1}(C_{\infty,nr}),$$

$$C_{\infty,ns} = f^{-1}(B_{\infty,ns});$$

we conclude, again by the stationarity of w, that $\mathcal{P}(w^*_{(s)} \in B_{\infty,nr}) = \mathcal{P}(A_{\infty,nr})$, $\mathcal{P}(w^*_{(r)} \in B_{\infty,ns}) = \mathcal{P}(A_{\infty,ns})$ and, consequently, that $\mathcal{P}(A_{\infty,nr}) = \mathcal{P}(A_{\infty,ns})$, which shows that ξ is a strictly stationary process.

[33] If, in the Wold decomposition $\zeta_{t\cdot} = 0$, the process is said to be **purely non-deterministic**, while if the decomposition consists **only of** $\zeta_{t\cdot}$, i.e. the first term is zero, **it is said to be purely deterministic**.

To examine the limiting distribution of the entity in the right member above, choose N sufficiently large and consider

$$\rho_N = \sum_{j=0}^{\infty} A_j \epsilon_{Tj} - \sum_{j=0}^{N} A_j \epsilon_{Tj}, \quad \epsilon_{Tj} = \frac{1}{\sqrt{T}} \sum_{t=1}^{T} \epsilon'_{t-j}. \tag{6.114}$$

For each j, ϵ_{Tj} obeys a **Lindeberg condition**, and thus, $\epsilon_{Tj} \overset{\text{d}}{\to} N(0, \Sigma_0)$. By the condition in Eq. (6.113), $\rho_N \overset{\text{q.m.}}{\to} 0$ (absolutely), and hence in probability as well. Since for fixed N,

$$\sum_{j=0}^{N} A_j \epsilon_{Tj} \overset{\text{d}}{\to} N(0, C_N \Sigma_0 C_N),$$

we conclude that, letting $N \longrightarrow \infty$,

$$\xi_{(T)} \overset{\text{d}}{\to} N(0, K), \quad K = C \Sigma C', \quad C = \sum_{j=0}^{\infty} A_j, \tag{6.115}$$

$$\sqrt{T}(\hat{\theta}_T - \theta^0) \overset{\text{d}}{\to} N(0, \Psi), \quad \Psi = (Q' \bar{W} Q)^{-1} Q' \bar{W} K \bar{W} Q (Q' \bar{W} Q)^{-1}.$$

It is clear that the limiting distribution depends on the choice of the weight matrix $\bar{W}$; applying the same reasoning as we employed in discussing the NL2SLS and NL3SLS, we easily see that

$$\Psi \geq (Q' K^{-1} Q)^{-1},$$

so that the lower bound of the covariance matrix of the limiting distribution above is given by $\Psi = (Q' K^{-1} Q)^{-1}$, provided K is invertible. In this framework, however, we are not at liberty to choose instruments at will, since the instruments are specified within the model. But, what is almost equivalent, we are free to choose the weighting matrix. If the matrix K is **nonsingular** the "optimal" weighting matrix is given by $\bar{W} = K^{-1}$, which attains the lowest bound, i.e.

$$(Q' K^{-1} Q)^{-1} Q' K^{-1} K K^{-1} Q (Q' K^{-1} Q)^{-1} = (Q' K^{-1} Q)^{-1}. \tag{6.116}$$

If K is singular we use, in lieu of K^{-1}, the generalized inverse K_g. We further note that since

$$C \Sigma C' = \sum_{\tau=-\infty}^{\infty} K(\tau), \quad K(\tau) = E(\xi'_{t+\tau} \cdot \xi_{t \cdot}), \tag{6.117}$$

in the case of nonsingular K, the feasible **optimal** GMM estimator is obtained by the operation

$$\min_{\theta \in \Theta} S_T = \frac{1}{T^2} (y - g)' (I \otimes Z) \left[\sum_{\tau=-T}^{T} \left(1 - \frac{|\tau|}{T} \right) \hat{K}(\tau) \right]^{-1} (I \otimes Z')(y - g),$$

(provided the inverse above exists), where

$$\hat{K}(\tau) = \frac{1}{T} \sum_{t=1}^{T} \xi'_{t+\tau} . \xi_t.$$

it being understood that for a negative index, or for an index exceeding T, the contribution of the (corresponding) term is null. We may summarize the results of the preceding discussion in

Theorem 5. Consider the GNLSEM with additive error terms of Eq. (6.104), together with assumptions (B.1) through (B.6) and the simplifying assertion that the process $\xi'_{t.}$ is, in effect, a **purely nondeterministic, strictly stationary process.** The following statements are true:

i. The estimator obtained by the operation $\inf_{\theta \in \Theta} S_T = S_T(\hat{\theta}_T)$, obeys $\hat{\theta}_T \overset{\text{a.c.}}{\to} \theta^0$;

ii. the limiting distribution of the estimator in i is given by

$$\sqrt{T}(\hat{\theta}_T - \theta^0) \sim N(0, \Psi), \quad \Psi = (Q'\bar{W}Q)^{-1}Q'\bar{W}K\bar{W}Q(Q'\bar{W}Q)^{-1},$$

$$K = \lim_{T \to \infty} \sum_{\tau=-T}^{T} \left(1 - \frac{|\tau|}{T}\right)K(\tau), \quad K(\tau) = E(\xi'_{t+\tau} . \xi_t.);$$

iii. if K is nonsingular, the lowest bound for the covariance matrix of the limiting distribution, which is $(Q'K^{-1}Q)^{-1}$, is attained by the choice $\bar{W} = K^{-1}$.

Remark 12. Note that if we estimate K by

$$\hat{K}_T = \sum_{\tau=-T}^{T} \left(1 - \frac{|\tau|}{T}\right)\hat{K}(\tau), \quad \hat{K}(\tau) = \frac{1}{T}\sum_{t=1}^{T}\xi'_{t+\tau} . \xi_t.,$$

and, subject to that, carry out the procedure above we shall obtain the analogue of the **feasible Aitken estimator**, or the analogue of NL3SLS in a simpler context.

6.4.4   Tests of Restrictions

We may think of the condition $E(\xi'_{t.}) = 0$ for all t, as the analog of the identifying restrictions in the context of the GLSEM. Although in the "GMM" context these restrictions play a different role, nonetheless they serve to define "instruments", and hence to identify the underlying structural parameters. Just as we found ways to test the prior restrictions in the GLSEM, tests of the "orthogonality conditions" may be devised in this context as well. In fact, such tests are available rather directly. Noting that $\hat{\xi}_{t\cdot} = f(\hat{w}_{t\cdot}) = f[y_{t\cdot} - g_{t\cdot}(\hat{\theta}_T), \hat{z}_{t\cdot}]$, and

$$y_{t\cdot}' - g_{t\cdot}'(\hat{\theta}_T) = u_{t\cdot}' - \frac{\partial g_{t\cdot}'}{\partial \theta}(\theta^*)(\hat{\theta}_T - \theta^0), \quad |\theta^* - \theta^0| \le |\hat{\theta}_T - \theta^0|;$$

$$\hat{z}_{t\cdot}' = z_{t\cdot}' + \frac{\partial z_{t\cdot}'}{\partial \theta}(\theta^*)(\hat{\theta}_T - \theta^0), \tag{6.118}$$

$$\frac{\partial f}{\partial \theta}(\theta^*) = -(I_m \otimes z_{t\cdot}'(\theta^*))\frac{\partial g_{t\cdot}'}{\partial \theta}(\theta^*) + (u_{t\cdot}' \otimes I_q)\frac{\partial z_{t\cdot}'}{\partial \theta}(\theta^*),$$

$$\hat{\xi}_{t\cdot}' = \xi_{t\cdot}' + \frac{\partial f}{\partial \theta}(\theta^*)(\hat{\theta}_T - \theta^0), \tag{6.119}$$

we obtain,

$$\hat{\xi}_{(T)} = \frac{1}{\sqrt{T}}\sum_{t=1}^T \hat{\xi}_{t\cdot} = \xi_{(T)} - \frac{\partial f}{\partial \theta}(\theta^*)\left(\frac{\partial^2 S_T}{\partial \theta \partial \theta}\right)^{-1}\left(\sqrt{T}\frac{\partial S_T}{\partial \theta}(\theta^0)\right)$$

$$\sim P^*\xi_{(T)}, \quad P^* = I - \tilde{Q}(\tilde{Q}'W_T\tilde{Q})^{-1}\tilde{Q}'W_T. \tag{6.120}$$

It follows immediately from Theorem 5, that under the null, i.e. that all uncorrelatedness (orthogonality) conditions hold,

$$\hat{\xi}_{(T)} \xrightarrow{d} N(0, \Phi), \quad \Phi = \plim_{T\to\infty} P^*KP^{*'}. \tag{6.121}$$

We next note that Φ is **singular**. This is so since we may write

$$\Phi = P\bar{W}K\bar{W}P', \quad P = \bar{W}^{-1} - Q(Q'\bar{W}Q)^{-1}Q';$$

By (B.6) Q is $mq \times k$ of rank k, and the condition $mq \ge k$ **is necessary** for the invertibility of the Hessian of the function to be minimized. To determine the rank of P note that the characterisitc roots of $Q(Q'\bar{W}Q)^{-1}Q'$, in the metric of $\bar{W}^{-1}$ are $mq - k$ zeros and k unities. Hence by Proposition 63, Dhrymes (1984), there exists a nonsingular matrix, say H, such that

$$P = H'H - H'\begin{bmatrix} I_k & 0 \\ 0 & 0 \end{bmatrix}H = H'\begin{bmatrix} 0 & 0 \\ 0 & I_{mq-k} \end{bmatrix}H,$$

whence it follows that $\text{rank}(\Phi) = mq - k$.

We can carry out tests on all or part of the "orthogonality conditions", as in the previous discussions of identifiability or specification tests; in view of the singularity of Φ, such tests can only have the following unambiguous meaning; let F_s, of dimension $mq \times s$, be a selection matrix that chooses $s \le mq - k$ "orthogonality" conditions to be tested. The test statistic for the null $E(\xi_{t\cdot}) = 0$, for all t, as against the alternative that $E(F_s'\xi_{t\cdot}') \neq 0$, is given by

$$\hat{\xi}_{(T)}F_s(F_s'\Phi F_s)^{-1}F_s'\hat{\xi}_{(T)} \sim \chi_s^2.$$

Remark 13. Notice that we require at least k orthogonality conditions as a **maintained hypothesis**. From a mathematical point of view it does not make any difference which k of the conditions have been selected as maintained. Thus, the expression

$$\hat{\xi}_{(T)}\Phi_g\hat{\xi}_{(T)}' \sim \chi^2_{mq-k},$$

provides a test statistic for an unambiguous test of the **null that all orthogonality conditions** are vaild as asserted, as against the **alternative that only** k of them are valid, i.e. the alternative is that we have "just identification". Notice, further, that this is an aspect of tests of prior restrictions in SE models that was discussed at length in Chapter 2, as well as in Chapter 4. In the context of 2SLS and 3SLS estimation of parameters in the GLSEM, the issue arises in connection with tests of **prior zero restrictions**, while in the context of "GMM" estimation of parameters in the GNLSEM with additive errors, the issue arises in connection with tests of the "orthogonality" conditions. This further affirms the conceptual unity of the GLSEM, NL2SLS, NL3SLS and GMM approaches to the simultaneous equations problem.

We may summarize the preceding discussion in

Corollary 3. Consider the GNLSEM with additive errors of Theorem 5. Tests of the orthogonality conditions may be based on the limiting distribution of

$$\hat{\xi}_{(T)} = \frac{1}{\sqrt{T}}\sum_{t=1}^{T}(\hat{u}_{t\cdot} \otimes \hat{z}_{t\cdot}),$$

which, under the null, is $N(0, \Phi)$, with

$$\Phi = P\bar{W}K\bar{W}P', \quad P = \bar{W}^{-1} - Q(Q'\bar{W}Q)^{-1}Q', \quad \text{rank}(\Phi) = k.$$

6.5 Causality and Related Issues

6.5.1 Introduction

When we studied the GLSEM we imposed prior restrictions that served to identify the parameters of the model, and we classified variables as **jointly dependent, lagged dependent, and exogenous**. We also observed that in order that parameters be estimated consistently the model needed to contain variables that, in varying degrees of stringency, were unrelated to the structural error process. In the previous chapters we also introduced various tests that addressed the validity of the prior restrictions, but we never questioned the fact that some of the variables contained in the GLSEM were in some sense unrelated to the error process. This section deals with such topics.

A veritable literature has developed around the issues of "causality", "strict exogeneity", "weak exogeneity" and "predeterminateness". It is quite outside the objectives of this volume to provide a thorough analysis of the issues involved; we shall only touch the highlights, and the reader interested in greater detail may consult the excellent review paper by Geweke (1984).

6.5.2 Basic Concepts

In the standard (benchmark) model,

$$y_{t\cdot}B^* = x_{t\cdot}C + u_{t\cdot}, \quad t = 1, 2, \ldots, T,$$

the errors are i.i.d. and thus, it is simple to conclude that

$$E(y_{t-j}'.u_{t\cdot}) = 0,$$

even when the system is dynamic, provided we have stability. Consequently, it was natural in the early development of econometrics to define the class of predetermined variables, say $x_{s\cdot}$, to consist of the **lagged dependent** and **exogenous** variables. Such variables have the property that they are at least **uncorrelated** and, under the i.i.d. assumption, **independent** of the error terms $u_{t\cdot}$, for $s < t$. As we pointed out in Chapter 1, however, this is not a satisfactory classification scheme, if the specification of the error process is allowed wider scope. In particular, the class of "lagged endogenous" and "exogenous variables" would be of little interest if we changed the probabilistic specification of the error process to, say, strict or even weak stationarity! We are thus led to

Definition 1. Let $z_{t\cdot} = (y_{t\cdot}, x_{t\cdot})$ be the set of variables contained in the GLSEM (or GNLSEM with additive errors); an element therein, say z_{tj}, is said to be **predetermined at time** t **with respect to the** i^{th} **equation**, if the sequence $\{z_{sj} : s < t\}$ is independent of the structural error u_{ti}; it is said to be **predetermined at time** t **with respect to the system**, if the sequence $\{z_{sj} : s < t\}$ is independent of the structural error vector $u_{t\cdot}$. A variable is said to be predetermined with respect to the ith equation, or the system, if it is predetermined at time t, **for all** t, respectively, for the ith equation, or the system.

Remark 14. Notice that by Definition 1, both the class of lagged dependent and exogenous variables, as well as y_{tq}, $q < i$ are predetermined at time t, for all t, with respect to the ith equation, if the GLSEM is **simply recursive**.

Definition 2. A variable z_{tj} is said to be **strictly exogenous** relative to the system above, if and only if the sequences

$$\{z_{tj} : t = 0, \pm 1, \pm 2, \ldots\}, \quad \text{and} \quad \{u_{t.}' : t = 0, \pm 1, \pm 2, \ldots\},$$

are mutually independent, in the sense that their joint distribution is the product of their respective marginal distributions.

Remark 15. In the first four chapters of this volume, we usually wrote $x_{t.} = (y_{t-1.}, y_{t-2.}, \ldots, y_{t-k.}, p_{t.})$, and we termed the vector $p_{t.}$ the vector of **exogenous variables**. In the terminology of this section this means that the elements of $p_{t.}$ are **strictly exogenous** relative to the system above.

Another interesting concept, introduced into the literature by Engle, Hendry and Richard (1983), is that of "weak exogeneity". Unlike the two other concepts above which are completely determined by the model and the nature of the variables' probabilistic properties, weak exogeneity depends, in addition, on the investigator's objectives or "loss function". Specifically, we have

Definition 3. In the context of the GLSEM (or the GNLSEM with additive errors), a set of variables, say $z_{t.}^{(r)}$ which is a subvector of $z_{t.}$, $t = 1, 2, \ldots, T$, is said to be **weakly exogenous** if and only if there is a one to one **reparameterization**, say $\phi = H(\theta)$, θ being the parameter set of the model, such that $\phi = (\phi_1', \phi_2')'$, and the likelihood function can be decomposed as

$$L(\phi; Z) = L_1(\phi_1; Z^{(*)}|Z^{(r)})L_2(\phi_2; Z^{(r)}),$$

where $Z^{(r)} = (z_{t.}^{(r)})$, $Z^{(*)}$ is the complement of $Z^{(r)}$ in $Z = (z_{t.})$, ϕ_1 is the parameter set of interest to the investigator, and ϕ_2 is a set of nuisance parameters.

Remark 16. In slightly more familiar terms, the reader may think of $Z^{(*)}$ as Y and of $Z^{(r)}$ as X. The decomposition then would read

$$L(\phi; Z) = L_1(\phi_1; Y|X)L_2(\phi_2; X).$$

Of course, there is nothing remarkable about writing the joint distribution of the jointly dependent (Y), and "predetermined" variables (X) as the product of the conditional distribution of the former, given the latter, and the marginal distribution of the latter. The real restriction here is that **the parameters of interest appear only in L_1, while the parameters in L_2 are of no direct interest**.

There are two aspects to the underlying issues: first, what are the (abstract) logical requirements for defining entities which can serve as "instruments" for the consistent estimation of parameters of the model. The second, and equally important, aspect is: even if we settle on the appropriate set of properties to be possessed by instruments, how can we be assured that our assertion of such properties with respect to certain variables is valid? It is at this stage that the notion of "causality" becomes relevant.

The term "causality" is grossly inappropriate for what it seeks to describe in econometrics. As usual, the origins of the term lie in other disciplines, in which perhaps it is more suited to the circumstances it seeks to describe. [34] The basic notion is this: if in some sense x "causes" y then we should be better able to "explain" y with x rather than without it. A slightly more formal definition, introduced into the econometrics literature by Granger (1963), (1968), is given below.

Definition 4. Consider the set of variables $z_{t\cdot} = (y_{t\cdot}, x_{t\cdot}, q_{t\cdot})$ and adopt the notation, say $Y_{t-1} = \{y_{t-s\cdot} : s \geq 1\}$, etc. Suppose we consider the class of best linear one step ahead predictors of the variables in y and/or the variables in x, and suppose further that the only "relevant" information for that purpose is contained in $Z_{t-1} = (Y_{t-1}, X_{t-1}, Q_{t-1})$. Let $P_{(Z)}$, $P_{(Y,Q)}$, $P_{(X,Q)}$ be projection operators into the space spanned by Z_{t-1}, (Y_{t-1}, Q_{t-1}) and (X_{t-1}, Q_{t-1}), respectively. Then, x is said to cause y if and only if

$$E\left|y_{t\cdot}' - P_Z(y_{t\cdot}')\right|^2 \leq E\left|y_{t\cdot}' - P_{Y,Q}(y_{t\cdot}')\right|^2.$$

If the condition above does not hold then we say that x does not "cause" y. The definition is perfectly symmetrical, i.e. the meaning of y "causes" x is obtained by simply interchanging the roles of x and y above.

Remark 17. The connection between this concept and estimation in the context of the GLSEM, or the GNLSEM with additive errors is this: if $y_{t-s\cdot}$, for some s, "causes" $x_{t\cdot}$, this would most certainly mean that $x_{t\cdot}$ **cannot be an exogenous variable** since this finding would violate the condition that the joint distribution of the exogenous variables be **independent** of the (joint distribution of the) error process, $u_{t\cdot}$. If, on the other hand, y **does not cause** x, we have no evidence that $x_{t\cdot}$ is cor-

---

[34] The term "causal", meaning that something can be represented in terms of something else either wholly or in part, occurs in the literature of time series. For example, Brockwell and Davis (1987), p. 83, second edition (1992), define an ARMA(m,n), (i.e. an autoregressive moving average process,) say $x_{t\cdot}$, to be "causal", or a "causal function" of $\{\epsilon_{t\cdot}\}$, if

$$\sum_{j=0}^{m} A_j x_{t-j\cdot}' = \sum_{i=0}^{n} B_i \epsilon_{t-i\cdot}, \quad \text{is representable as} \quad x_{t\cdot}' = \sum_{s=0}^{\infty} C_s \epsilon_{t-s\cdot}',$$

with $\sum_{s=0}^{\infty} \|C_s\| < \infty$.

related with $u_t.$. More concisely, if y "causes" x then the elements in X_{t-1} cannot be predetermined at time t, or exogenous. Consequently, the GLSEM is not correctly specified. If y does not "cause" x then the elements of X_{t-1} could be predetermined at time t, or exogenous. Note, however, that this does not argue for the correctness of the specification of the GLSEM, since the same result would hold for any model containing the same list of variables.

We now turn to the implementation of such procedures. To this end, suppose that the $z_t.$ can be characterized as a (strictly nondeterministic) **covariance stationary process**, and suppose further that the matrix of spectral densities, [35]

$$f_{zz}(\lambda) = \begin{bmatrix} f_{yy}(\lambda) & f_{yx}(\lambda) \\ f_{xy}(\lambda) & f_{xx}(\lambda) \end{bmatrix}$$

is continuous almost everywhere on $[-\pi, \pi)$ and is strictly bounded away from zero. The assumptions made are sufficient to ensure that if we begin with the relatively innocuous statement

$$z'_{t.} = \sum_{s=0}^{\infty} A_s \epsilon'_{t-s.}, \tag{6.122}$$

where the ϵ-process is one if i.i.d., zero mean and positive definite covariance matrix random vectors, we can obtain the representations

$$x'_{t.} = \sum_{j=1}^{\infty} B_{1j} x'_{t-j.} + \eta'_{t1.}, \quad \text{or, alternatively,} \tag{6.123}$$

$$x'_{t.} = \sum_{j=1}^{\infty} C_{1j} x'_{t-j.} + \sum_{j=1}^{\infty} C_{2j} y'_{t-j.} + \eta'_{t2.} \tag{6.124}$$

In this context one says that y "causes" x if $C_{2j} \neq 0$, for at least one index j. In practice this is implemented by running a "regression" of $x_t.$ on its own lags (how many?) and on the lags of $y_t.$ (how many?) Then one

---

[35] Unfortunately, in the treatment of this topic we cannot be as complete as we sought to be in earlier discussions, due to the nature of the mathematics involved. Suffice it to say, however, that the reader may think of the matrix of spectral densities as the Fourier transform of the autocovariance (matrix) function of the z-process as defined earlier, i.e. $K(\tau) = E(z'_{t+\tau.} z_{t.})$, and

$$f_{zz}(\lambda) = \frac{1}{2\pi} \sum_{\tau=-\infty}^{\infty} K(\tau) e^{-i\tau\lambda}, \quad \lambda \in [-\pi, \pi).$$

carries out an F, or an asymptotic chi-squared, test on the collection of co-efficients of $y_{t-1.}, y_{t-2.}, \ldots$; if the hypothesis that they are null is rejected, one concludes that y "causes" x; thus, $x_{t-1.}$ and higher order lags cannot serve as predetermined or exogenous variables. If the hypothesis is accepted, one concludes that y does not "cause" x and thus $x_{t-1.}$ and higher order lags can serve as predetermined or exogenous variables. There are certain elaborations of causality, in terms of "instantaneous causality", as well as in terms of bilateral representations of the y-process. The former involves the addition of the term $C_{20}y_t.$ in the representation of Eq. (6.124), while the latter involves substituting, therein, the term $\sum_{j=-\infty}^{\infty} C'_{2j}y_{t-j}.$ for the expression involving the lags of y.

Remark 18. While the framework we presented above appears, conceptually, to be rather elegant it leaves nearly as many unanswered queries, as the assertions of *a priori* restrictions, and exogenous variables in the context of the standard GLSEM. For example, given the rather limited time series data economists possess, one cannot accommodate too many variables; thus, a model involving three (3) jointly dependent (y) and five (5) variables (x) asserted to be exogenous, entails five equations of the type in Eq. (6.124) if we wish to test whether y "causes" x. Even if only two lags of each variable are employed, each equation would contain 16 variables; if we used three (3) lags, each equation would contain 24 variables and so on. The many possibilities available are bound to create conflicts and contractictions in empirical results, and their intepretation. Moreover, if we obtain the finding that y "does not cause" x when the former contains, say, m-elements, we have no assurance, in implementations with real world data, that augmenting y with an additional variable would necessarily yield the same conclusion, for the original m y's.

Questions and Problems

1. Consider the function $H_T(\phi)$ of Eq. (6.14);

    i. show that it is

        1. continuous in ϕ, for any $w \in \Omega$;

        2. $\mathcal{A}$-measurable, for each $\phi \in \Phi$, where (Ω, $\mathcal{A}$, $\mathcal{P}$) is the probability space over which the error process ($u_t.$) is defined;

    ii. in responding to part i, how did you handle the exogenous variables, i.e. the elements of the x-sequence?

2. Derive the a.c. limit of $H_T(\cdot)$ in Eq. (6.14), and explain your argument step by step.

3. Verify the relationships in Eq. (6.42).

4. Verify the claims of Eqs. (6.66) and (6.67).

5. Verify that the sequence $\{\xi'_{t\cdot} : t \geq 1\}$ of Eq. (6.77) is one of zero mean independent variables and obtain the covariance matrix $\Xi = \mathrm{Cov}(\xi'_{t\cdot}\xi_{t\cdot})$.

6. In the discussion of Section 1.4 verify that, in dealing with the GLSEM,

$$\left(\frac{\partial L_T}{\partial \delta}\right)' = -L'(I \otimes I^{*'})\mathrm{vec}(WB^*P^{-1}) + L'\mathrm{vec}(MA\Sigma^{-1})$$

$$\left(\frac{\partial L_T}{\partial \sigma}\right)' = \frac{1}{2}\left(\mathrm{vec}(\Sigma^{-1}A'MA\Sigma^{-1}) - \mathrm{vec}(A'MA)\right).$$

$$\frac{\partial^2 L_T}{\partial \delta \partial \delta} = L'(P^{-1} \otimes I^{*'}WI^*)L + L'(\Sigma^{-1} \otimes M)L$$

$$+ 2L'(P^{-1} \otimes I^{*'}WB^*P^{-1}B^{*'}WI^*)L$$

$$\frac{\partial^2 L_T}{\partial \delta \partial \sigma} = -L'(I \otimes MA)(\Sigma^{-1} \otimes \Sigma^{-1}),$$

$$\frac{\partial^2 L_T}{\partial \sigma \partial \sigma} = \frac{1}{2}\left[I - 2(I \otimes \Sigma^{-1}A'MA)\right](\Sigma^{-1} \otimes \Sigma^{-1}).$$

7. In Eq. (6.84) obtain the conditions under which $(1/T)h'_{\cdot i}r_{\cdot i} \to 0$, at least in probability.

8. Obtain the conditions under which $(\tilde{Z}'_i W_i/T)$ converges to a well defined matrix, at least in probability, where Z_i is as defined just above Eq. (6.93).

9. If the system in Eq. (6.94) is transformed by $R^{-1}W'(\tilde{\Sigma}^{-(1/2)} \otimes I_T)$, where $\tilde{\Sigma}$ is a prior consistent estimator of Σ, show that the NL3SLS is simply the NLLS estimator of θ in that context.

10. Show that the matrices A and D of Eq. (6.99), as modified by the surrounding discussion, have the same characteristic roots in the metric of Φ^{-1}, i.e.
$$|\lambda\Phi^{-1} - A| = 0, \quad \text{and} \quad |\mu\Phi^{-1} - D| = 0,$$
have the same roots.

11. Complete the proof of Corollary 2 by showing that $C_{NL3SLS}(\tilde{A}) - C_{NL3SLS}(P) \geq 0$.
    Hint: Let V, M_{xx}, A denote, respectively, the appropriate limits of $[(I \otimes X')\tilde{Z}]/T$, $X'X/T$, $\tilde{A}$; consider, then, the characterisitc roots of $\Phi^{-1}A[A'(\Sigma^{-1} \otimes M_{xx})A]^{-1}A'\Phi^{-1}$ in the metric of $\Sigma^{-1} \otimes M_{xx}^{-1}$.

12. Find the covariance bounds of the limiting distribution of the two estimators that minimize, respectively, S_{T3}^A and S_T ; verify that they are the same.

13. In the discussion of GMM show that

$$(Q'\bar{W}Q)^{-1}Q'\bar{W}K\bar{W}Q(Q'\bar{W}Q)^{-1} \geq (Q'K^{-1}Q)^{-1}.$$

Bibliography

Amemiya, T. (1974), "The Nonlinear Two-Stage Least-Squares Estimator", *Journal of Econometrics*, vol. 2, pp. 105-110.

Amemiya, T. (1975), "The Nonlinear Limited Information Maximum Likelihood Estimator and the Modified Nonlinear 2SLS Estimator", *Journal of Econometrics*, vol. 3, pp. 375-86.

Amemiya, T. (1977), "The Maximum Likelihood and the Nonlinear Three-Stage Least-Squares Estimator in the General Nonlinear Simultneous Equations Model", *Econometrica*, vol. 45, pp. 955-968.

Anderson, T. W. (ed.) (1955), *Selected Papers in Statistics and Probability by Abraham Wald*, New York: McGraw Hill.

Anderson T. W. and H. Rubin (1949), "Estimation of the Parameters of a Single Equation in a Complete System of Stochastic Equations", *Annals of Mathematical Statistics*, vol. 20, pp. 570-582.

Anderson T. W. and H. Rubin (1950), "The Asymptotic Properties of Estimates of Parameters in a Complete System of Stochastic Equations", *Annals of Mathematical Statistics*, vol. 21, pp. 570-582.

Anderson, T.W. and N. Kunitomo (1992), "Tests of Overidentification and Predeterminateness in Simultaneous Equation Models", *Journal of Econometrics*, vol. 54, pp. 49-78.

Basmann, R. L. (1957), "A Generalized Classical Method of Linear Estimation of Coefficients in a Structural Equation", *Econometrica*, vol. 25, pp. 77-83.

Basmann, R. L. (1960), "On Finite Sample Distributions of Generalized Classical Linear Identifiability Test Statistics", *Journal of the American Statistical Association*, vol. 55, pp. 650-659.

Basmann, R. L. (1961), "A Note on the Exact Finite Sample Frequency Functions of Generalized Classical Linear Estimators in Two Leading Overidentified Cases", *Journal of the American Statistical Association*, vol. 56, pp. 619-633.

Basmann, R. L. (1962), "On the Application of the Identifiability Test Statistic in Predictive Testing of Explanatory Economic Models", *Indian Economic Journal* (Econometric Annual), vol. 12, pp. 387-403.

Basmann, R. L. (1974), "Exact Finite Sample Distributions and Test Statistics", in Intrilligator, M. D. and D. A. Kendrick (eds.) *Frontiers of Quantitative Economics*, vol. II, Amsterdam: North Holland.

Bernanke, B. (1988), "Alternative Explanations of the Money, Income Correlation", *Carnegie-Rochester Conference Series on Public Policy*, vol. 28, pp. 49-99.

Blanchard, O. J. and M. Watson (1986), "Are Business Cycles All Alike?", in R. J. Gordon (ed.), *The American Business Cycle*, Chicago: University of Chicago Press.

Blanchard, O. J., and D. Quah (1989), "Dynamic Effects of Aggregate Demand and Supply Disturbances", *American Economic Review*, vol. 79, pp. 655-673.

Brockwell, P. J., and R. A. Davis (1992), second edition, *Time Series: Theory and Methods*, New York: Springer-Verlag.

Byron, R. P. (1972), "Limited Information Using the Newton Solution", *Australian Economic Papers*, vol. 11, pp. 112-118.

Byron, R. P. (1974), "Testing Structural Specification Using the Unrestricted Reduced Form", *Econometrica*, vol. 42, pp. 869-883.

Chamberlain, G. (1982), "The General Equivalence of Granger and Sims Causality", *Econometrica*, vol. 50, pp. 569-582.

Chow, Y. S. and H. Teicher (1988), *Probability Theory* (second edition), New York: Springer-Verlag.

Christ, C. (1983), "Founding of the Econometric Society and *Econometrica*", *Econometrica*, vol. 51, pp. 3-6.

Christ, C. (1985), "Early Progress in Estimating Quantitative Economic Relationships in America", *American Economic Review* (special issue), vol. 75, pp. 39-52.

Dacunha-Castelle, D. and M. Duflo (1986), *Probability and Statistics*, vols. I and II, New York: Springer-Verlag.

Dhrymes, P. J. (1969), "Alternative Asymptotic Tests of Significance and

Related Aspects of 2SLS and 3SLS Estimated Parameters", *The Review of Economic Studies*, vol. 36, pp. 213-236.

Dhrymes, P. J. (1970), *Econometrics: Statistical Foundations and Applications*, New York: Harper & Row.

Dhrymes, P. J. (1974), *Econometrics: Statistical Foundations and Applications*, A Study Edition, New York: Springer-Verlag.

Dhrymes, P. J. (1973), "Restricted and Unrestricted Reduced Forms: Asymptotic Distributions and Relative Efficiencies", *Econometrica*, vol. 41, pp. 119-134.

Dhrymes, P. J. (1978), *Introductory Econometrics*, New York: Springer-Verlag.

Dhrymes, P. J. (1984), *Mathematics for Econometrics* (2nd edition), New York: Springer-Verlag.

Dhrymes, P. J. (1989), *Topics in Advanced Econometrics: Probability Foundations*, New York: Springer-Verlag.

Engle, R. F. (1984), "Wald, Likelihood Ratio and Lagrange Multiplier Tests in Econometrics", Ch. 13 in Griliches, Z. and M. D. Intrilligator (eds.) (1984).

Engle, R. F., D. F. Hendry and J. F. Richard (1983), "Exogeneity", *Econometrica*, vol. 51, pp. 277-304.

Fisher, F. M. (1961), "On the Cost of Approximate Specification in Simultaneous Equation Estimation", *Econometrica*, vol. 29, pp. 139-170.

Fisher, F. M. (1966), *The Identification Problem in Econometrics*, New York: McGraw-Hill.

Fisher, F. M. and J. B. Kadane (1972), "The Covariance Matrix of the Limited Information Estimator and the Identification Test: Comment", *Econometrica*, vol. 40, pp. 901-904.

Fisher, R. A. (1934), "The Amount of Information Supplied by Records of Families as a Linkage in the Population Sampled", *Annals of Eugenics*, vol. 6, pp. 71-76.

Fisher, R. A. (1944), *Statistical Methods for Research Workers*, 8th edition, New York: Stechert.

Fisher, R. A. (1950),*Statistical Methods for Research Workers*, 11th edition, Edinburgh: Oliver and Boyd.

Frisch, R. (1933), "Propagation Problems and Impulse Problems In Dynamic Economics" in *Economic Essays in Honor of Gustav Cassel*, London: George Allen and Unwin.

Frisch, R. (1934), *Statistical Confluence Analysis by Means of Complete Regression Systems*, Oslo: Universitetets Okonomiske Institutt.

Geweke, J. (1982), "Measurement of Linear Dependence and Feedback Between Time Series", *Journal of the American Statistical Association*, vol. 77, pp. 304-324.

Geweke, J. (1984), "Inference and Causality in Economic Time Series Models", Ch. 19, in Griliches, Z. and M. D. Intrilligator (eds.), (1984).

Girshick, M. A. and T. Haavelmo (1953), "Statistical Analysis of the Demand for Food: Examples of Simultaneous Estimation of Structural Equations", in Hood W. C. and T. C. Koopmans (eds.), (1953), pp. 92-111.

Goldfeld, S. M. and R. E. Quandt (1968), "Nonlinear Simultaneous Equations: Estimation and Prediction", *International Economic Review*, vol. 9, pp. 113-136.

Goldfeld, S. M. and R. E. Quandt (1972), *Nonlinear Methods in Econometrics*, Amsterdam: North Holland.

Granger, C. W. J. (1963), "Economic Processes Involving Feedback, *Information and Control*, vol. 6, pp. 28-48.

Granger, C. W. J. (1969), "Investigating Causal Relations by Econometric Models and Cross-Spectral Methods", *Econometrica*, vol. 37, pp.424-438.

Granger, C. W. J. and P. Newbold (1977), *Forecasting Economic Time Series*, New York: Academic Press.

Granger, C. W. J. and A. A. Weiss (1983), "Time Series Analysis of Error Correcting Models", pp. 255-278 in *Studies in Econometrics, Times Series and Multivariate Statistics*, New York: Academic Press.

Griliches, Z. and M. D. Intrilligator (1983), *Handbook of Econometrics*, vol. I (1983), vol. II (1984), vol. III (1986), Amsterdam: North Holland.

Haavelmo, T. (1943), "The Statistical Implications of a System of Simultaneous Equations," *Econometrica*, vol. 11, pp. 1-12.

Haavelmo, T. (1944), "The Probability Approach in Econometrics", *Econometrica*, vol. 12, supplement.

Hall, P. and C. C. Heyde (1980), *Martingale Limit Theory and Its Applications*, New York: Academic Press.

Hannan, E. J. (1970), *Multiple Time Series*, New York: Wiley.

Hannan, E. J. (1973), "Central Limit Theorems for Time Series Regression", *Zeitschrift fur Wahrscheinlichkeitstheorie und verwandte Gebiete*, vol. 26, pp. 157-170.

Hansen, L. P. (1982), "Large Sample Properties of the Generalized Method of Moments Estimators", *Econometrica*, vol. 50, pp. 1029-1054.

Hausman, J. A. (1978), "Specification Tests in Econometrics", *Econometrica*, vol. 46, pp. 1251-1271.

Hausman, J. A. (1983), "Simultaneous Equation Models", Ch. 7 in Griliches, Z. and M. D. Intrilligator (eds.), (1983).

Hausman, J. A. and W. E. Taylor (1981), "Panel Data and Unobservable Individual Effects", *Econometrica*, vol. 49, pp. 1377-1398.

Henderson, H. V. and S. R. Searle (1981), "The Vec-Permutation Matrix, the Vec Operator and Kronecker Products: A Review", *Linear and Multilinear Algebra*, vol. 9, pp. 271-288.

Holly, A. (1982), "A Remark on Hausman's Specification Test," *Econometrica*, vol. 50, pp. 749-759.

Hood, W. C. and T. C. Koopmans (eds.) (1953), *Studies in Econometric Method*, Cowles Foundation Monograph No. 14, New York: Wiley.

Hsiao, C. (1983), "Identification", Ch. 4 in Griliches, Z. and M. D. Intrilligator (eds.), (1983).

Hsiao, C. (1985), *The Analysis of Panel Data*, Cambridge: Cambridge University Press.

Hwang, H. (1980), "A Comparison of Tests of Overidentifying Restrictions", *Econometrica*, vol. 48, pp. 1821-1825.

Johnson N. L., and S. Kotz (1970), *Continuous Univariate Distributions-2*, Boston: Houghton Mifflin.

Jorgenson, D. W., and J. Laffont (1974), "Efficient Estimation of Nonlinear Simultaneous Equations with Additive Disturbances", *Annals of Economic and Social Measurement*, vol. 3, pp. 615-640.

Kadane, J. B. (1974), "Testing a Subset of the Overidentifying Restrictions", *Econometrica*, 42, pp. 853-868.

Kadane, J. B. and T.W. Anderson (1977), "A Comment on the Test of Overidentifying Restrictions", *Econometrica*, vol. 45, pp. 1027-1032.

Kalejian, H. H. (1971), "Two-Stage Least Squares and Econometric Systems Linear in Parameters but Nonlinear in the Endogenous Variables", *Journal of the American Statistical Association*, vol. 66, pp. 373-374.

Khazzoom, J. D. (1976), "An Indirect Least Squares Estimator for Overidentified Equations", *Econometrica*, vol. 44, pp. 741-750.

Klein, L. R. (1950), *Economic Fluctuations in the United States, 1921-1941*, New York: Wiley.

Klein, L. R. (1955), "On the Interpretation of Theil's Method of Estimating Economic Relationships", *Metroeconomica*, vol 7, pp. 147-153.

Klein, L. R. and H. Barger (1954), "A Quarterly Model of the U.S. Economy", *Journal of the American Statistical Association*, vol. 49, pp. 413-437.

Klein, L. R. and A. S. Goldberger (1955), *An Econometric Model of the United States, 1929-1952*, Amsterdam: North Holland.

Koopmans, T. C. (ed.) (1950), *Statistical Inference in Dynamic Economic Models*, Monograph 10, Cowles Commission for Research in Economics, New York: Wiley.

Koopmans, T. C. and W. C. Hood (1953), "The Estimation of Simultaneous Linear Economic Relationships", Ch. 6 in Hood W. C. and T. C. Koopmans (eds.), (1953).

Kullback, S. (1968), *Information Theory and Statistics*, New York: Dover.

Liu, T. C. (1960), "Underidentification, Structural Estimation and Forecasting", *Econometrica*, vol. 28, pp. 855-865.

Liu, T. C. and W. J. Breen (1969), "The Covariance Matrix of the Limited Information Estimator and the Identification Test", *Econometrica*, vol. 37, pp. 222-227.

Liu, T. C. and W. J. Breen (1972), "The Covariance Matrix of the Limited Information Estimator and the Identification Test: A Reply", *Econometrica*, vol. 40, pp. 905-906.

Mann, H. B. and A. Wald (1943), "On the Statistical Treatment of Linear Stochastic Difference Equations", *Econometrica*, vol. 11, pp. 173-220.

Nagar, A. L. (1962), "Double k-class Estimators of Parameters in Simultaneous Equations and Their Small Sample Properties", *International Economic Review*, vol. 3, pp. 168-188.

Newey, W. K. (1985), "Maximum Likelihood Specification Testing and Conditional Moment Tests", *Econometrica*, vol. 53, pp. 1047-1070.

Rao, C. R. (1950), "Methods of Scoring Linkage Data Giving Simultaneous Segregation of Three Factors", *Heredity*, vol. 4, pp. 37-59.

Rao, C. R. (1972), second edition, *Linear Statistical Inference and Its Applications*, New York: Wiley.

Ravenkar, N. and P. Mallela (1972), "The Power of an F-test in the Context of a Structural Equation", *Econometrica*, vol. 40, pp. 913-916.

Rothenberg, T . J. and C. T. Leenders (1964), "Efficient Estimation of Simultaneous Systems", *Econometrica*, vol. 32, pp. 57-76.

Sargan, J. D. (1964), "Three-Stage Least-Squares and Full Maximum Likelihood Estimates", *Econometrica*, vol. 32, pp. 77-81.

Scheffe, H. (1959), *The Analysis of Variance*, New York: Wiley.

Scheffe, H. (1977), "A Note on a Formulation of the S-method of Multiple Comparison", *Journal of the American Statistical Association*, vol. 72, pp. 143-146.

Sims, C. A. (1972), "Money, Income and Causality", *American Economic Review*, vol. 62, pp. 540-552.

Sims, C. A. (1980), "Macroeconomics and Reality", *Econometrica*, vol. 48, pp. 1-48.

Szroeter, J. (1983), "Generalized Wald Methods for Testing Nonlinear Implicit and Overidentifying Restrictions", *Econometrica*, vol. 51, pp. 335-353.

Theil, H. (1953), "Estimation and Simultaneous Correlation in Complete Equation Systems", mimeograph, The Hague: Central Plan Bureau.

Theil, H. (1958), *Economic Forecasts and Policy*, Amsterdam: North Holland.

Theil, H. and A. Zellner (1962), "Three Stage Least Squares: Simultaneous Estimation of Simultaneous Equations", *Econometrica*, vol. vol. 30, pp. 54-74.

Tinbergen, J. (1939), *Statistical Testing of Business Cycle Theories, vol. II: Business Cycles in the USA, 1919-1932*, Geneva: League of Nations.

Wald, A. (1950), "Note on the Identification of Economic Relations", Ch. 3 in Koopmans, T. C. (ed.) (1950), pp. 238-244; also reprinted in Anderson, T. W. (ed.) (1955), *Selected Papers in Statistics and Probability by Abraham Wald*, New York: McGraw-Hill.

Wegge, L. (1978), "Constrained Indirect Least Squares Estimators", *Econometrica*, vol. 46, pp. 435-450.

White, H. (1982), "Maximum Likelihood Estimation of Misspecified Models", *Econometrica*, vol. 50, pp. 1-26.

White, H. (1983), "Corrigendum", *Econometrica*, vol. 51, p. 513.

Zellner, A. (1978), " Estimation of Functions of Population Means and Regression Coefficients Including Structural Coefficients", *Journal of Econometrics*, vol. 8, pp. 127-158.

Zellner A., L. Bauwens and H. K. Van Dijk (1988), "Bayesian Specification Analysis and Estimation of Simultaneous Equation Models Using Monte Carlo Methods", *Journal of Econometrics*, vol. 38, pp. 39-72.

Index